ALSO BY William J. Mann

Edge of Midnight: The Life of John Schlesinger

Behind the Screen: How Gays and Lesbians Shaped Hollywood

Wisecracker: The Life and Times of William Haines

KATE

KATE

THE WOMAN WHO WAS HEPBURN

William J. Mann

Henry Holt and Company
New York

Henry Holt and Company, LLC
Publishers since 1866
175 Fifth Avenue
New York, New York 10010
www.henryholt.com

Henry Holt® and ® are registered trademarks of Henry Holt and Company, LLC.

Distributed in Canada by H. B. Fenn and Company Ltd.

Library of Congress Cataloging-in-Publication Data

Mann, William J.
    Kate : the woman who was Hepburn / William J. Mann.—1st ed.
        p.   cm.
    Includes index.
    ISBN-13: 978-0-8050-7625-7
    ISBN-10: 0-8050-7625-5
    1. Hepburn, Katharine, 1907–2003.   2. Motion picture actors and actresses—United
States—Biography.   I. Title.

PN2287.H45M27 2006
791.4302'8092—dc22
[B]   2006043367

Henry Holt books are available for special promotions and premiums.
For details contact: Director, Special Markets.

First Edition 2006

Designed by Meryl Sussman Levavi

Printed in the United States of America

10 9 8 7 6 5 4 3 2 1

For Timothy Huber

"That public creature is something I invented.

It's not me. Not at all."

—Katharine Hepburn

CONTENTS

CATCH HER IF YOU CAN

In the first light of dawn, wearing wrinkled khakis and a floppy hat, Katharine Hepburn charged up the hill from her bungalow. Without knocking, she rushed into the mansion of her friend and favored director George Cukor and began invading his kitchen cabinets. Alerted by pans crashing, Cukor's assistant Charles Williamson hurried in to discover what he took at first to be a bag lady: a small, sixtyish woman, arms loaded with flour, unsweetened chocolate, and sugar. For a moment they regarded each other silently.

"I'm baking brownies," Hepburn finally said, staring him down—Tracy Lord, Tess Harding, Eleanor of Aquitaine, all defying him to scold. But Williamson expressed only surprise that she was there at all. No one, not even Cukor, had known she was in town.

"Go ahead," she said, shaking her finger, a smile crossing her face. "Try to figure me out. You'll never get it right. No one ever does."

"She liked to keep people guessing," said Williamson, remembering that day in the early 1970s as Hepburn scampered back down the hill, skirting Cukor's famous pool and his elaborate terraced gardens. With its imposing ivy-covered walls, the Cukor estate, high in the Hollywood hills, offered the impregnability of a medieval castle. "Out in the world, Hepburn was one thing," said Williamson, "but at George's, she was quite another. And she liked people wondering which one was real."

Whether baking brownies at six in the morning or cooking up publicity for a movie, Katharine Hepburn always knew how to walk a fine line between reality and image. Though she'd insist hype and hoopla had no place in her world, she was an expert at the game she was playing. "Katharine Hepburn, public, private," she mused, her eyes twinkling on cue in *All About Me*, the 1993 documentary based on her life. "Can you tell which is which? Sometimes I wonder myself." She seemed to be daring us to find out, throwing down the gauntlet, wondering if anyone was ever really going to give her a chase.

For all her vaunted aversion to the trappings of movie stardom, Hepburn reveled in the sport of celebrity. "I used to duck the press all the time, just for fun," she said in 1992. "I think it was sort of a game." Indeed, "the more insulting the press was," she admitted elsewhere, "the more it stimulated me." As early as 1933, one reporter observed that Hepburn's "whole attitude expressed one thing: 'Try to find out anything about me.'" For more than sixty years, that challenge never changed. "Catch me if you can," she once called out to a gang of newshounds—just the sort of competition that fired her spirit.

As I write these words in 2006, nearly four years after her death, the Hepburn legend remains largely as she left it, as sacrosanct as Lady Liberty and perhaps as durable. It has seemed enough to just stand back and admire, and certainly there is much that is admirable about Katharine Hepburn. She was an exemplar of achievement, an American cultural icon. Her very name conjures up indomitability, independence, Yankee common sense, Emersonian self-reliance. Of all Hollywood's female legends, only Marilyn Monroe trumps her in terms of worldwide recognition. Yet Monroe's name invokes Victim; Hepburn's, by contrast, stands for Survivor. Maverick. Champion.

Her passing on June 29, 2003, at the age of ninety-six, proved an unexpected media sensation. A year later, the auction of her personal effects at Sotheby's generated a whole new cycle of publicity, with eleven thousand of the Hepburn faithful passing through in five days. As the myth was merchandised, however, the more interesting woman behind it risked being lost to history— without us even knowing it was happening. That's because, for decades, we had taken the myth at face value. The depth of our admiration had convinced us that we knew the real Kate, that public and private were one and the same.

"She starred in seven jillion movies," the critic Mary McNamara wrote, "won all those Oscars, but in the end, Katharine Hepburn was loved for her *self*, for being who she was."

Who she was. The public really thought it knew. And therein lay her secret. The historian Daniel Boorstin has written that the "most important question of our lives" is "what we believe to be real." Indeed, Hepburn's herculean endurance depended upon our faith that she was 100 percent authentic. We understood that other great stars might live behind a manufactured public image. But Hepburn—*Kate*—was seen as thoroughly real. Her defiantly iconoclastic persona was predicated on the belief that *there was no image*, that she was beyond all that claptrap.

But how much of it was really true?

"She was very shrewd, very aware of everything when it came to her career and her image," said her friend the screenwriter James Prideaux. "There wasn't much that Kate *wasn't* aware of. But then she was apt to turn around and declare she didn't care *what* her public image was." Only "half of the time," Prideaux said, would he take her at her word.

"So I've had control," Hepburn admitted late in life, sitting in an old black leather swivel chair in her New York house, her tennis-shoed feet up on a hassock. "And anyone who has control is a fool if they don't make the best of it."

Most accounts of Hepburn's life—books and articles—have been written by friends, fans, or journalists who took the trip up the steep, narrow stairs of her town house in New York's Turtle Bay or drove out to her summer home in Fenwick, Connecticut. All her biographers, accurately or not, have implied some kind of "cooperation" from the star. After she died, it was the impression of some that A. Scott Berg, her most recent chronicler, was putting the final polish on the legend as Hepburn wanted it told. Yet Berg, admitting his lack of objectivity upfront, acknowledged in the introduction to *Kate Remembered* (published immediately upon her death and offering a warm, witty, loving account of their friendship) that the four-time Oscar winner merited a more thorough, full-scale biography.

As a reporter and cultural historian, I have attempted to supply the book Berg describes. I am a great admirer of Hepburn's, but I was not a friend nor would I consider myself a fan. Unlike other biographers, I do not begin my account with an in-person meeting with the star. Instead of the living legend, I start with the relics she left behind.

On the day of her estate sale at Sotheby's, I watched and listened as the bidding grew frenzied. Auctioneers' voices ratcheted higher; phones rang nonstop; Internet bidding nearly shut down the servers. Some of the items being sold were exquisite. The diamond and sapphire jardiniere brooch from Howard Hughes was estimated at $15,000, while the true value of other artifacts was priceless: the purchase agreement for *The Philadelphia Story*, telegrams between Hepburn and Hughes, the star's first contract with RKO. But many of the other lots on the block bordered on the absurd: rolled-up newspaper that she used as hair curlers; a NO TRESPASSING sign; her (unsigned) Bloomingdale's credit card. "Look at Lot 647," Scott Berg groaned to the press. "Her tennis shorts! That is crossing the line."

The faithful didn't agree. "I'd love to bid on her wedding dress," a New Yorker gushed. "Can you imagine owning Katharine Hepburn's wedding dress?"

It was, to look at it, nothing special: crushed velvet, cream colored, with gold embroidery around the neck and a diamond pattern on the chest. Hepburn had worn it in 1928, when she married Ludlow Ogden Smith, always a shadowy figure in previous accounts of her life. Looking at the wedding dress, I couldn't help but wonder about this young man named Smith and his bride. The starting bid was $2,500, but the gown ended up selling for more than *ten times* that amount.

Overall, $5.9 million was taken in. Sotheby's would register more new clients with this auction than any other. What was most surprising was the degree of devotion to someone so long out of the limelight. "You would think," observed one of Hepburn's friends as we passed the faithful clutching photographs from *Bringing Up Baby* and *Adam's Rib*, "she had been Princess Diana."

Give or take Liz Taylor, Katharine Hepburn was the only great star of Hollywood's golden age to live into the twenty-first century. While she survived, no truly authentic biography could be written. Few intimates would consent to interviews; those who did were guided by the outlines of the myth she helped create. For as long as she lived, her legend, with its wonderful tales of grit and ambition and luck and love—as well as its omissions, obfuscations, and outright inventions—was scrupulously maintained.

But it's time to take a second look at the legend. Katharine Hepburn was a critical figure of the twentieth century, significant enough to truly understand and fully appreciate. Many of her friends, family, and associates, previously committed to silence, have come around to believing that a deeper portrait of Hepburn is both valuable and fitting. Here, in these pages, for the first time, they tell their stories.

In addition, previously unavailable letters and private papers have been uncovered, allowing me to consider the private Hepburn in a new light. A vast amount of new reporting, new sources, and new ideas has gone into my attempt to bring to life a woman whose truth lived behind the artifice of her seeming naturalness.

That is key. "Kate," the figure the world thought it knew so well, was in fact a construct hewn by the publicists, the media, and most especially by Katharine Houghton Hepburn herself. In real life, she never thought of herself as "Kate," but as "Kathy" or "Kath," the name she'd been called as a girl. "Kate" was for the public. Her public self was a "creature," she said, "this terrible character, Kate Hepburn, whom I've invented." To a Bryn Mawr class in the 1980s, she admitted, "I'm very different from the one everyone seems to know. She's a legend . . . I really don't know her. I'm sort of like the man who cleans the furnace. I just keep her going."

Alongside her doppelgänger, the real woman lived uneasily. "She couldn't live up to the image, even though she was the one who created it," observed her nephew Kuy Hepburn. "She had a whole industry behind her, selling her. There was x amount of it that was her, and x amount that was created."

For such a creature, conventional biographies hold limited value. Accordingly, you will not find here detailed plot synopses of films, descriptions of how scenes were shot, or comparisons of the directing styles of Howard Hawks and George Stevens. All that's been done. (The films are all here, however, considered for the ways they shaped and propelled the legend.) Neither should you expect a strict, linear chronology to progress through these pages, nor anecdotes retold merely for form's sake. No one needs another biography that tells, yet again, how Spencer Tracy—or Joe Mankiewicz—or *somebody*—promised to cut Hepburn down to size. I don't want to rehash the familiar.

Rather, I think it's time to move the camera in for a more intimate look at a woman who beautifully sustained her singular grace notes for nearly seventy years. Possessed of an unshakable faith in herself, her morality, and her worldview, she was venerated by a public starved for heroes. In 1971, her friend and frequent screenwriter Garson Kanin credited Hepburn's endurance to the fact that "people know (magically, intuitively) that she stands for something"—even if they had no clear idea just what that something was.

We forget that she wasn't always so beloved. If anyone had predicted in 1939 that Katharine Hepburn would one day be named by the American Film Institute as the greatest movie star of all time, the laughter would have echoed through the heartland. In the 1930s, Hepburn had alienated much of the public with her eccentric approach to gender, sexuality, and stardom. She dressed in old clothes, wore no makeup, and drove around in a truck. After a first halfhearted attempt, she refused subsequent efforts by studio publicists to link her romantically with men. Instead, she spent her time with Laura Harding, a Philadelphia heiress with whom she shared a house. Even worse, she spoke out about politics, something never done by actors of the era, throwing her support to—of all candidates—the socialist Upton Sinclair. All of this brought reams of bad press. By the end of the decade, Hepburn was one of the most unpopular actresses in America.

What's fascinating is that this figure, once reviled, could morph into such a heroine. After all, she was never "one of us." Born into the upper class (less "upper" than was suggested), she had decidedly patrician tastes ("I'm a bit of a crêpe suzette"), was left of center politically, and defied cherished norms such as marriage and a woman's place in society. Despite the insistence of her rapturous fans, she was never as beautiful as Greta Garbo or Grace Kelly. Nor was there the sex appeal of Ava Gardner or Lana Turner. She didn't make headlines like Liz Taylor, didn't bare her soul like Judy Garland. As an actress, she didn't have the power or range of Bette Davis.

Yet she survived them all—not only in years but in the public imagination. She became "ingrained into the culture" in a way none of the others managed. "The Great Kate," the columnist Liz Smith wrote after Hepburn's death, "was one star whose effect outstripped even her acting career. Her influence for free-thinking, independence, woman's rights, common sense will reverberate for ages. We all owe her an all-American debt!"

The figure once called a snob, rumored to be a lesbian, and suspected of communism became a symbol of true-blue, red-blooded Americana. The *New York Times* claimed in 1991 that Hepburn had a "face for Mount Rushmore." At Hepburn's death, the writer Maureen Dowd linked her with Ronald Reagan as a symbol of the American character: "They emanated a sense that they were royalty, even as they displayed a frontier ethic."

The creation of this mythic Hepburn can be used as a mirror on how public identity is constructed and maintained—"image craft," as it has come to be called. Decades before Hollywood publicists built reputations on their mastery of image craft, Hepburn had extraordinary success with it all on her own. Within a couple of years after being labeled box-office poison, she had engineered a triumphant comeback in *The Philadelphia Story*—and from then on, she remained in firm control of her career and public image. Nearly everything that would be written about her after that point would contain elements of hagiography. Even when reviews for a film or play were not exactly glowing, most critics found a way to remark on her admirable "real-life" qualities. The columnist Anna Quindlen articulated the position Hepburn had come to occupy in the culture by the 1980s, when she called the actress not only "woman of the year" but "woman of a lifetime."

I don't necessarily disagree. But hagiography has never been useful as a genre. In truth, the real woman was every bit as fascinating as the legend. Far more sophisticated than Kate made herself out to be—more worldy, more honest—the real Hepburn utilized a shrewd understanding of the shifting zeitgeist to keep herself on top. Generations of willing journalists provided able assistance, but the Hepburn legend was chiefly maintained by none other than the lady herself. And so pervasive does this image of her remain that, during interviews, I'd occasionally have to stop some of Kate's closest intimates and ask if they weren't merely rattling the legend. They'd often stop, think, and admit, red-faced, they were.

Indeed, some of these people were witnesses to that legend actually taking shape. Michael Pearman, a friend of George Cukor's and a canny observer of the celebrities of his day, took me back in time to a night in December 1935. Across the high-gloss parquetry floors of Cukor's oval sitting room, Hepburn was anxiously pacing back and forth, telling the director they needed to find some way to "cook it up." They'd all just come from the disastrous premiere of their infamous flop *Sylvia Scarlett*, in which Kate spent most of the time masquerading as a boy. Pearman remembered how determined she was to find a way out of the fiasco.

"Oh, George," she said—pronouncing his name "Jo-udge"—"we've got to cook it up for ourselves, really cook it up."

"What she was saying," Pearman said, remembering her pacing like a lioness, her red hair flying, "was that they had an image problem and they had to fix it. They had to make it up to the public somehow."

Ever alert to such problems, Hepburn always knew how to "cook it up." When the public grew too suspicious of the sexual subversion of her early pictures, she came back in the guise of the brittle Tracy Lord for an official upbraiding in *The Philadelphia Story*. That much has been pointed out before. But this sort of reinvention became a recurring pattern. No one ever seemed to notice, because Hepburn's modus operandi was hidden in plain sight, protected by the perception that she was free of spin, that she had no ulterior motives, that stardom to her was a bore—"a bo-ah!"

Yet look closely and the various wanderings of her career take on new meaning. *The African Queen* becomes not just a chance great script but a deliberate stab at rehabilitation by Hepburn, Humphrey Bogart, and John Huston, all of whom had been painted Red by Communist witch-hunters just a year before. Hepburn the Traitor was supplanted by Hepburn the Patriot, who sails down a muddy river enduring hardships for the glory of her country.

From iconic films like this, the public took images and melded them with ones from "real life." We saw Kate shoveling snow off the roof of her house in New York, swimming in Long Island Sound in January, chopping firewood at the age of seventy-five. All this kept up the fiction that the "reel life" and the "real life" Hepburn were one and the same. Indeed, shortly before her death, a small book called *Katharine Hepburn Once Said* offered "great lines to live by," mixing quotes from interviews with lines from her films, as if all were equally hers.

This conflation of public and private personae guaranteed that Hepburn was enshrined like no other female movie star. While her contemporaries faded into obscurity, Kate made the *Dictionary of Cultural Literacy*. In 1996 she was named one of the one hundred most influential women *of all time*, up there with Eleanor Roosevelt, Marie Curie, Joan of Arc, and (I do not jest) the Virgin Mary. In a Reuters poll in 1999, Hepburn was named the "greatest" film actress of the twentieth century, paired, fittingly, with that other all-American, John Wayne.

"Cook it up" she certainly had.

Such durability, however, demands considerable flexibility. It's striking just how many reinventions of Kate there were. In the 1930s, she was the pants-wearing tomboy. In the 1940s, she became the career woman tamed by the love of a man (usually Spencer Tracy). In the 1950s, after being savagely attacked by the anti-Communist smear campaign, she became the upstanding (but lonesome) spinster. By the 1960s and 1970s, gracefully sidestepping the grotesqueries of Joan Crawford, Bette Davis, and Tallulah Bankhead, she was rewarded with her final role: the wise grandmother, doling out sage advice to the public.

The press—usually cast as her adversaries—were in fact eager accomplices in her mythmaking. After a rough start, Kate learned how to tango with the fourth estate. She might be photographed running from reporters, covering her face, but such coverage always seemed to spike just when she needed it most, when a love affair with Leland Hayward might distract from declining box office, or an airplane flight with Howard Hughes might help promote a picture. Perhaps the most fascinating of Hepburn's relationships to chart— and all of them are uniquely compelling—was the one she had with the press.

In fact, for all her talk about privacy, by the 1980s she was inviting practically any reporter who knocked on her door inside to chat. Yet no matter how often she appeared in magazines, television specials, and publicity for her memoirs, the fiction that Hepburn was "notoriously private" retained currency, dutifully reiterated in nearly every profile. To many in the media, the idea had become a joke, but it was reported nonetheless; the legend was just too entrenched to go away. In truth, Hepburn was merchandising her myth long before Sotheby's ever put her hair curlers on the block.

Yet her story remained incomplete. Isolde needed her Tristram.

In 1986, almost eighty, her eye on history, Hepburn agreed to speak at a testimonial for her longtime costar and reputed paramour Spencer Tracy. "I've decided to tell the world Spence and I were lovers," she told her astonished confidant, the costume designer Noel Taylor. On several sheets of lined yellow paper, she'd written a letter to the deceased Tracy in her famous scrawl, her letters as angular as she was, her words separated by impatient dashes. (Garson Kanin once said he was giving her a box of commas, semicolons, and periods for Christmas.) "Dear Spence," Hepburn wrote. "Is it a nice long rest you're having? You know, I never believed you when you said you just couldn't get to sleep. That night when—oh, I don't know, you felt so disturbed. And I said, Well, go on in—go to bed. And I'll lie on the floor and I'll talk you to sleep. I'll just talk and talk and you'll be so bored, you're bound to drift off."

So much left unsaid in that letter, yet so very much more implied. When she finished reading, she asked Taylor what he thought. Remembering the moment, Hepburn's old friend laughed. "What do you say to Katharine Hepburn?" he asked. "You just say, 'It's wonderful, Kate. Wonderful.'"

Another friend, James Prideaux, was also treated to a recitation of the letter. Prideaux found himself shedding a tear even as he doubted the veracity of her words. "Never underestimate Kate's sense of drama," he said. "She knew what to play up or play down, and it was time to play Tracy up."

Though Hepburn had at first been outraged by Kanin's 1971 memoir *Tracy and Hepburn*—which had filled the world in on all the supposedly true details of her star-crossed love affair with Spence—she would ultimately use it as a blueprint for her own mythmaking. Before her appearance at the testimonial, her only mention of Tracy had been as costar and friend. The public had respected her taste and silence, but had embraced the romantic myth as spun by Kanin and others. By agreeing to speak at the Tracy testimonial (which ended with Hepburn reading her letter to Spence in a filmed tribute), she seemed finally prepared to give the public what it wanted: her verification that the stories were true.

To her legend's tough self-reliance she could now add another, more human, trait. She had loved and lost. Hepburn the Indomitable now wanted us to believe that, around Tracy, she'd been just another woman who had suffered the heartaches of romance. How we loved learning that this old lioness in winter hadn't been some stiff-collared cold fish.

In many ways, Kanin's book had been a publicity godsend. As the screenwriter who helped shape the Tracy-Hepburn team, who put the wisecracking dialogue into their mouths for three classic films, Kanin had convinced the public that "Spence" and "Kate" talked the same, lived the same, *were* the same in real life as we saw them in the movies. With Kanin as her bible, Hepburn moved through the last two decades of her life burnishing the legend.

Once again, she succeeded, brilliantly. At the Sotheby's auction, a three-inch bronze sculpture of Tracy's head, made by Hepburn herself, brought about the fiercest bidding war, selling for a whopping $316,000. (Toulouse-Lautrecs had gone for considerably less.) No mere piece of amateur sculpture, the bust of Tracy was in fact a talisman of one of the great love stories of the twentieth century. "Hollywood's longest-running extramarital affair," wrote Frank Rich of the *New York Times*, "somehow transcended its provenance in tabloid gossip to become the stuff of legendary romantic Americana."

Hepburn's promulgation of the Romance of Spence and Kate broke the ice that had always surrounded her, and turned their relationship into a love fable for the ages. But there was an unintended result, too. One more image was layered onto our perception of Hepburn. Her supposed indulgence of Tracy's alcoholism—a conclusion that couldn't be avoided as more stories emerged—led some columnists to question if Kate the Great had actually been Kate the Great Enabler.

Yet by making Tracy so central to her story, Hepburn had created this dilemma for herself. The image of a victimized Katharine Hepburn, wounded by Tracy's alcoholism and womanizing, threatened the integrity of the rest of her story. How could she still be strong and independent if she was taking all this abuse? The solution she found was simple. In her memoir and especially in the film *All About Me*, her eyes misty and her chin quivering, she assured us that it had never been a sacrifice to bend her will to Tracy's, to put up with his faults. When you're in love, that's what you do. That's how she cooked it up, anyway.

Even writing those words, I'm resistant to the cynicism they project. Surely love does have a place in Hepburn's narrative, and I don't doubt for a second that she really did love Tracy. But I do question just how physical, and how constant, that love was. Challenged on the authenticity of his portrait, Kanin later snapped, "I never said they *made* love, did I?" He didn't need to. The public filled in the blanks, and Hepburn didn't seem to mind.

In truth, she only started speaking out about Tracy after most of those who'd known them together in their prime were dead: Cukor, Ruth Gordon, Chester Erskine, Joe Mankiewicz (who had urged one Tracy biographer, "Don't let Kate take the ball!"), Irene Selznick (who, after watching Hepburn's onstage tribute to Tracy in 1986, whispered, "What has happened to Sister Kate?"), and, of course, Tracy's wife, Louise. Only Kanin was still alive, and he'd already said all he intended to say. Early on in my research, one of Tracy's old friends said to me, "If Spencer had lived longer than he did, and could see what his relationship with Hepburn was made into, he wouldn't have recognized it."

Indeed, as I have documented in these pages, Hepburn and Tracy never lived together. The "twenty-six years together" Hepburn often referred to were mostly spent apart, separated by thousands of miles. For large segments of that time, they did not view themselves as a couple, and neither— as letters document—did their close friends. No matter the stories she told of "our house," Hepburn did not make her home with Tracy but rather within a community of women. Laura Harding, Emily Perkins, Constance Collier, Eve March, Frances Rich, Phyllis Wilbourn, and finally Cynthia Mc-Fadden were the ones to provide anchor, solace, and family.

Here is another of the minefields I have attempted to navigate. The women with whom Hepburn associated were never conventionally married wives and mothers. Many were, in fact, lesbian. Given the fact that Hepburn's sexuality has been speculated about from the beginning, any biographer who does not thoroughly consider the question is not doing his or her job. Indeed, the impression of lesbianism that has always swirled around Hepburn is encouraged by the fact that the men who populated her inner circle were nearly all homosexual, from the 1930s to the 1990s. Striking, too, is the fact that, except for Leland Hayward, all of the men with whom Hepburn was seriously romantically linked left behind rumors of sexual ambiguity themselves.

For many of the people I spoke with, the question of Hepburn's sexuality was the elephant in the room that they tripped over, time and time again, picking themselves up and dusting themselves off without ever admitting that they'd fallen. By avoiding the subject or becoming anxious, they made the issue far more central than it needed to be, though some, including Hepburn's brother Bob, received the question with thoughtful equanimity.

Sexuality, of course, needs to be understood in context with the times. In decades past, especially in Hepburn's worldly circles, sexuality was far more fluid than it is in today's more rigidly defined, politically charged atmosphere. In such a context, contemporary terminology is meaningless. There will be no labeling in this book. Rather, I attempt to understand Hepburn's sexuality the way I attempt to understand everything else about her, as part of the larger narrative of her life and legend.

Yet it's also time to take off the blinders. That Hepburn loved other women, that she made her life with women, is a defining aspect of her story. It is, in fact, one of the most important things one needs to understand about her. To ignore such a reality, either through a determined act of will or through unconscious cultural myopia, is to squash complexity and smooth over contradictions—not to mention fail to grasp the truth of both Kate *and* Katharine Hepburn.

Taking her at her own word is far more useful than attempting to pin her with a modern-day label. "When you come right down to it," she said, "I haven't lived life as a woman at all. I've lived life as a man." She said this, or variants thereof, numerous times. Significantly, she saw herself as "the *man* who cleaned the furnace," not the "woman," not the "person." The automatic reaction is to agree: yes, she did live as a man. The sort of fame and power that, in her day, came much more commonly to men than to women made it possible for her to make her own choices and do as she pleased. Yet there's possibly more meaning in her words. Katharine Hepburn, who shaved her head and renamed herself "Jimmy" at the age of ten, lived life as a man—a heterosexual man—not just in terms of a man's privilege but in the way a man sees, perceives, and interacts with his world. She often spoke of herself as distinct from other women, as a completely different sort of creature.

Seeing her from this vantage point explains so much: why, in the 1970s, such dissonance existed between Hepburn and the women's movement, the groundwork for which her mother had so diligently laid six decades earlier. Why was Katharine the Younger so lukewarm in her support? Why did she make statements insisting a woman could never really have both a family and a career? "Don't do them both," she warned women on Dick Cavett's show in 1973, "because you just get split in half . . . You *cannot* have it all." Her words baffled and annoyed many feminists. In fact, the view she was articulating was the perspective of a *man*—which is, fundamentally, how she saw herself. Never simply a "liberated" woman who'd lived by her own rules, Hepburn was a figure quite apart from the norm. "I'm a missing link," she admitted to Cavett. "I don't belong anywhere." Considered from this vantage point, her relationships with women might also be better understood.

"Biography," wrote Garson Kanin in *Tracy and Hepburn*, "is a field that requires delicate expertise. How does one go about finding the needle of truth in the haystack of facts?" So delicate did Kanin find the task that he didn't even bother to try, giving himself the same out Scott Berg took thirty years later, admitting to being "biased" and therefore incapable of writing a "comprehensive biography" of Hepburn. Raising the flag of *Rashomon*, Kanin even suggested that the pursuit of truth, at least as far as Hepburn was concerned, was an impossibly confounding task. There might, he suggested, exist many equally valid versions of her story.

In her later years, Hepburn tried to narrow it down to just one, lending her imprimatur to two memoirs, three biographical documentaries, and all those interviews. She was "smart and romantic enough," the film historian and critic David Thomson said, "to do her own stone tablets." But in private (and fortunately tape-recorded) conversations, she admitted she was much too "secretive" (in her peculiar pronunciation, she placed the accent on the second syllable) to ever really tell the truth. "The interesting things which have happened to me, which have made me go down this path . . . or take this turn," she said, "I would never tell anybody what those were. I really would never tell anybody."

So she gave them a legend instead. To Dick Cavett she admitted she tended to "embroider" the accounts she told of her life. Even as early as 1939, the mythology surrounding her was plain. The *New York Times* observed that the stories about Hepburn had grown to "proportions that would make didactic Aesop turn over in his Delphic grave." It's why, in writing this book, if I could not find a primary source for a story, I did not use it, no matter how many times it had been written before.

In fact, I was able to trace back many stories to a handful of seminal pieces that distilled the legend in the public mind over the course of six decades. In all of these articles, Hepburn had a hand. For example: Every account of her life has drawn extensively on a five-part piece by Lupton Wilkinson that ran in late 1941 in the *Saturday Evening Post*. A little digging, however, revealed that Hepburn steered the writer in the execution of the final product. To use Wilkinson as bedrock, therefore, as so many Hepburn biographers have done, becomes problematic. Wilkinson's true usefulness is not in his "facts" but in understanding the way he, and others like him, helped shape Hepburn's legend.

Making the funhouse effect even funnier, it wasn't just Hepburn's chroniclers who recycled the legend. The star could be found doing it herself. Though she claimed never to read anything written about her, close friends said she always made sure to find out what was being said. Sometimes the inventions of others found their way into her own "memories." Consider the nonsense tale of Hepburn insisting that Ludlow Ogden Smith change his name to Ogden Ludlow so she wouldn't be confused with the singer Kate Smith. It originated in the gossip columns of the 1930s. But sixty years later, enough writers had repeated it that Hepburn actually told the anecdote herself in the documentary *All About Me*—as if it were true and she was divulging it for the first time.

Indeed, by the time of her death, a hodgepodge of anecdotes and myths had emerged that passed for absolute truth. They were retold in her obituaries, acted out onstage, showcased even on the Hollywood screen, making the circle complete. Cate Blanchett was widely hailed for her portrayal of Hepburn in the film *The Aviator* for nailing Kate "just right"—but what she really captured so flawlessly was the legend. Not without reason did I ask myself at the outset of this project if it was even still possible, this late in the game, to find my way back through the maze to where it all began.

The announcement that Hepburn's papers had been given to the Margaret Herrick Library at the Academy of Motion Picture Arts and Sciences offered some hope, but the continued delays in making them available eventually led me to proceed without them. It's possible the papers will be opened by the time this sees print, in which case they will be incorporated into a second edition. However, I believe that this book can stand on its own, secured by the ample new research I have conducted and the contributions of many of Hepburn's intimates. What the Hepburn papers contain is unknown; there may be some wonderfully revelatory material, and there may not. To wait for the papers meant in some ways waiting on Hepburn, as her estate was still determining the timetable. After seventy years, I thought it was finally time to tell the story outside the star's control.

And, as tricky as the maze has been, I think I found my way, re-creating Hepburn's world as a tool for understanding her. I didn't so much need to re-create movie sets and proscenium arches, the realm of previous biographies, but rather the private, inner circle of Hepburn's life and work. Famous friends and costars like Cary Grant and Lauren Bacall, I quickly discovered, did not unlock her secrets. To penetrate such an elaborately veiled life, I had to identify the people who truly mattered to her, and find in their less carefully cloaked lives glimpses of Hepburn's own truths. In this regard, the stories of Alice Palache, Phelps Putnam, Jack Clarke, Ludlow Ogden Smith, Laura Harding, Suzanne Steell, Eve March, Jane Loring, Frances Rich, Constance Collier, Irene Selznick, Nancy Hamilton, David Eichler, Robert Helpmann, Michael Benthall, and many others, as revealed through letters, wills, and the memories of their friends and families, tell us much more about Hepburn than any of her more famous associates could—with the notable exception of George Cukor, whose lifelong friendship and mentorship are at the heart of this book.

Many have lamented that so many of Hepburn's supporting cast is dead. It's as if, determined to make sure no one spoke out of turn, Hepburn waited until most of her friends were gone before passing away herself. A few, like Fran Rich and Noel Taylor, held on, and I am enormously grateful for their insights. I am also fortunate that, in research for previous projects, I spoke with many who had some connection to Hepburn. Some had worked with her; others, like Max Showalter, were personal friends. While at the time their mentions of Hepburn seemed just a footnote to my studies, their recollections proved invaluable when I turned to telling her life story. So many have since died; their stories came just in time.

There may be a segment of the public, Kate's loyal following, who will believe I am attempting to tear down the legend. That is certainly not my intent. Much of what we've believed about Hepburn is, in fact, true. She was independent, generous, frank, loyal, committed to excellence. She could also be terribly narcissistic and obsessed with fame—but she was also the little girl yearning for her father's affection, the idealistic child still hurt by being shunned for her family's radical politics. No aspect of her personality is less than fascinating. She lived according to the dictates of her times but also as she chose, creating a private world and a public life in an environment where almost no one manages either.

Indeed, understanding the fullness and complexity of Hepburn's story should not detract from what she has meant to people's lives. Rather, it should do just the opposite. "We are all interested in watching a skillful feat of magic," Boorstin observed. "We are still more interested in looking behind the scenes and seeing precisely how it was made to seem that the lady was sawed in half."

If this book helps us understand Hepburn better, to comprehend the place she has come to occupy in the American mind—indeed, in the world's—it will do so not by tearing down and discarding the images of her we have come to treasure, but by gathering and reassembling them into a new, more variegated, and, I hope, even more beautiful re-creation. In this meeting and melding of perspectives from the past and the present, a more satisfying and relevant understanding of Katharine Hepburn might be found for these times.

I'm left recalling a story told to me by James Prideaux. He and Hepburn were leaving a theater when he spied a group of photographers. Assuming Kate would want to duck them, Prideaux gestured toward a rear exit. But Hepburn, despite being in her eighties and no longer so spry, winked at him. Rubbing her hands together, she announced, "Let's go!"

In that moment Prideaux saw not an old lady but a young girl. After all these years, she was still the daredevil. Out into the waiting photographers she charged, elbowing them aside with lots of commands to "Move it, buster!" Prideaux laughed. "She was giving them her very best impression of Katharine Hepburn, and she was loving every minute of it."

Catch me if you can, she always seemed to be saying. I don't think she would have minded one more round of the chase. Perhaps she might have even relished it. One final story: As a young reporter for a now-defunct magazine in Hepburn's hometown of Hartford, I was assigned to write an article about her early years. She declined an interview, but I pushed on, discovering in the old Hartford city directories her true birth date, May 12, 1907, two years and several months earlier than the date she'd always claimed. At this point, her memoir—which would finally admit the true date—had not yet been published. So it was with some awkwardness that I wrote my story. When the article appeared, I sent her a copy, along with a note hoping she didn't mind my revelation. Back came a typewritten note with just one line of response. "Dear William Mann," she wrote. "Good sleuthing."

My hope is she would see this book the same way.

KATE

A SEA CHANGE

F rom the window of her New York town house, Kath Hepburn, the new queen of Hollywood, looked up and down the quiet, early morning street. It seemed that she was actually going to be spared the reporters who usually lurked beyond the iron railing in front of her brownstone. Her getaway would be fast and clean.

At twenty-six, red-haired, freckle-faced Kath was the star she'd always dreamed of becoming. It was the morning of March 17, 1934. Her agent, Leland Hayward, had just called to announce that she'd won the Academy Award for *Morning Glory*. But the news would not alter Kath's travel plans— nor her mood. She and her friend Suzanne were getting out of town—as far away from show business as they could.

Later, as the two women snaked through the Fifth Avenue traffic, Kath couldn't have missed the crowds gathering for the annual St. Patrick's Day parade—a temporary break from the grim tidings of hard times. Of course, Kath herself had never suffered many of the hardships faced by those less fortunate during the Depression. Her chief concern during the previous years had been, as ever, her career. Fired by Broadway managers, waiting in the wings for opportunities that never arose, Kath nevertheless had remained convinced that fame was her due.

She was right. Marching into Hollywood like a determined conqueror, she'd scored a smash in her very first picture, *A Bill of Divorcement.* The acclaim was of the sort she lived for, ever since she'd tottered out onto a makeshift stage as a twelve-year-old Beast to her best friend Ali Barbour's Beauty. From that moment on, Katharine Hepburn's dream had been to be famous. For something. For anything.

Now she was. And she was running away.

The problem was: Fame wasn't supposed to be like these past twenty months. It shouldn't be something to *escape.* It was supposed to be glamorous, exciting, exhilarating. Stardom to Kath was Leatrice Joy, beaming serenely from the screen of the State Theatre in Hartford, dazzling the wide-eyed girl. But Kath's fame had turned out to be much more complicated than that. The night before had brought her an Oscar, but the month before, the critics had been shouting for her head, sniggering at her ignoble Broadway flop in the play *The Lake.* To make matters worse, her new picture, *Spitfire,* was so abysmal that many were calling her a fraud. The rejections hurt. Kath didn't understand why her ambition hit people the wrong way; surely it was the kind of desire all Americans were raised to value.

But her failures had simply provided ammunition to those who had been waiting to shoot her down, and they were legion. From the start, Hepburn had been a troublesome star who'd wanted everything on her terms. Paying dues, Kath seemed to imply, was for lesser mortals. Her method for attracting publicity wasn't to show up at premieres with a handsome leading man on her arm, but rather to walk around town with a real live gibbon clinging to her neck. "The stormy petrel of the RKO studios," *Vanity Fair* called her, "subject for raging controversy on two continents." In 1934, people either loved Katharine Hepburn or despised her.

Burning up the wires from the West Coast in the days before the Oscars, Leland Hayward tried to tell her how she could fix things, what she needed to do and say to remain on top. Achieving fame had been the easy part, Kath realized; holding on to it was a whole other experience, one she couldn't have imagined when she first set her sights on Hollywood. As she listened to what Leland was suggesting, she balked. Was it any wonder she and Suzanne were heading for France? Was it any wonder she was just about ready to call it quits?

So determined she had been, so ambitious. And now she was considering turning her back on it all. Had her father been right? He'd called her a show-off that day six years ago when she'd announced she was becoming an actress. For such conceit he'd slapped her across the face. But nothing could deter her from following her dream.

"There she is!"

By the time Kath stepped out of the car onto the pier, the horns of the French liner *Paris* were wailing mournfully behind her. And, of course, the reporters had caught up to her. Had she really thought she'd eluded them? Bowler-hatted sharks from the tabloids surged forward, their boxy handheld cameras already positioned at their eyes.

"Miss Hepburn!"

"Miss Hepburn," Suzanne echoed, "has no comments."

"Not even a 'thank you' for the award?"

"Nothing," Suzanne told them.

Depressed and confused, Kath was oblivious to appearing ungrateful. All she wanted to do was get out of the city. Despite the warm day, she wore a wool hat, pulling it down almost to her eyes. Scampering around to the lower level of the pier, she lost herself among the gray coats and brown faces, making her way onto the ship via the third-class gangplank.

The thirty-five-thousand-ton *Paris* was less the floating Versailles of earlier French liners and more a modern objet d'art, with art nouveau staterooms and art deco fluting along its grand marble staircases. Launched in 1921, the largest vessel ever built in France, the *Paris* boasted private telephones in many cabins and in the anterooms first-class passengers used to receive visitors. Gone were the old-fashioned round portholes, replaced with square, velvet-curtained windows that looked out onto wooden decks polished to a high gloss. Marlene Dietrich's daughter Maria Riva, soon to board the ship herself, would remember it "sparkling like a bottle of French perfume."

Such heady fragrance, however, had no effect on Katharine Hepburn. Hurrying to her chintz-decorated stateroom, she left Suzanne to deal with the press.

"We will be abroad for four or five weeks," Suzanne announced as she walked down the hall, pursued by a phalanx of reporters.

"Where will you be going?"

"Paris, the Riviera."

"Why the secrecy? Why won't Miss Hepburn talk to us?"

Suzanne just slipped inside the stateroom, shutting the door quickly behind her. There was nothing more to say.

Huddled inside, sitting cross-legged on the bed, Kath would have been surprised had it ended there. Certainly she expected the reporters to once again bang upon the door, and they did. This was the price of fame. She'd learned that much in the past twenty months.

Impatiently, Suzanne opened the door once more. "I said that would be all!"

"And who are you?" a newsman demanded.

"My name is Suzanne Steell." She didn't spell her last name for them; in their reports, they'd quite naturally get it wrong, writing it as *Steel* or *Steele*, inadvertently setting up a mystery that would take more than seventy years to unravel. "I am an old friend of Miss Hepburn's, and she has nothing more to say." Then she firmly closed the door.

Even in her fugue, Kath may have smiled at the term *old friend,* so bold-faced was Suzanne's exaggeration. They'd known each other no more than three months, though it's possible they had met casually at some point earlier. Suzanne had attended New York's prestigious Spence School, and Kath's best friend, the heiress Laura Harding, counted many Spence graduates among her acquaintances. But the bond that connected Kath and Suzanne had been forged only recently. It had been Suzanne—and Suzanne alone, Kath felt—who'd stood by her as *The Lake* died a slow, painful, and very public death.

In the bleak days after the play's closing, Kath had taken refuge with Suzanne. Tall and full-figured, five years older than her movie-star friend, Suzanne possessed the kind of ingrained self-confidence Kath always admired. Suzanne suffered no fool gladly, from cabdrivers to theater critics. She issued orders with all the imperiousness of an opera diva—a style learned, in fact, at the elbow of Madame Maria Jeritza, her former mentor and the famed prima donna of the Metropolitan Opera. As she often did when in retreat, Kath simply folded herself into her friend's embrace and let her lead the way.

Outside their stateroom door, the reporters kept up their hammering, but time was short: the ship was scheduled to sail at noon. Eventually the shouting died down, the whistles blew, and the *Paris*, slow and steady, began its inexorable slide down the Hudson River.

It would be the last transatlantic voyage that the young woman called Kath ever took.

Of course, Katharine Hepburn—Kate—would make the journey many more times. But on this St. Patrick's Day in 1934 she was leaving in a sad, disappointed, and disoriented state. When she returned, she'd be a very different person.

As recalled by friends, and documented by references in her own letters, this trip marked the first major turning point in Hepburn's career. She had scaled the heights—only to discover the enormous, unexpected costs of all that she had so desired. Crestfallen and deeply hurt, she had wired George Cukor, her friend and director: "Don't expect me back. You'll have to find another Red"—a reference to her hair, not her political leanings.

Her friend Max Showalter called this period "the most difficult time of her whole career." That description echoed the sentiment of Worthington Miner, director of *The Lake*, who remembered Hepburn as "totally demoralized" by the experience. In fact, the play's failure and the brutish behavior of its producer, Jed Harris, would leave an impression on Kath that would remain the rest of her life.

"If there was a moment that her Hollywood career might have ended," reflected Showalter, "it was [at this point]. There was tremendous pressure on her, and she hadn't learned how to survive quite yet."

If Leland Hayward had thought the news of her win from the Academy of Motion Picture Arts and Sciences might lift her spirits, he was wrong. Kath's wounds from *The Lake* were still too raw, and the drubbing *Spitfire* was taking only made things worse. Back on the Coast, the *Los Angeles Times* critic Edwin Schallert seemed to be gunning for her. "Katharine Hepburn—ha, ha, ha!" Schallert wrote, gloating over the failure of *Spitfire*. "Whoever said she was a box office draw? In *Little Women*, yes—but then there were three other girls."

She had never taken criticism very well. As a youngster, she'd climb a tree to sulk after being scolded by her father. Much later, she'd pretend reviews didn't bother her. She'd joke, in fact, that the critics weren't hard *enough* on her. But inside she despised them, those beasts with their poison pens: she hated to be called less than great. That fact never changed, but in 1934 she hadn't yet learned the art of deflection. Her heart was still strapped to her shirtsleeve. She took things very personally.

"In this courier's opinion," Brooks Atkinson, influential critic of the *New York Times*, had written after the New York premiere of *The Lake*, "Miss Hepburn is not a full-fledged dramatic actress yet . . . [S]he has not yet developed the flexibility of first-rate acting and her voice is a rather strident instrument."

Of course, it was Dorothy Parker's smug little quip (that Hepburn "ran the gamut of emotions from A to B") that forever sealed the historical verdict against *The Lake*. In truth, not all the reviews were bad—some were quite approving—but Hepburn herself would fuel the legend of *The Lake*'s disaster, because that's how she saw it at the time: the world had turned against her. No matter that she had just won the Oscar. What counted was the way the story got spun, and the tale being told in the first few months of 1934 was that Hepburn had flopped on Broadway. One magazine headlined its story: HOW HAUGHTY HEPBURN WENT DOWN IN FLAMES. Wounded, she followed her instincts, which told her to run away, to go climb a tree.

"What Susan always told me," said the costume designer Miles White, using Suzanne Steell's real name, "was that she and Kate Hepburn were escaping from Hollywood by going to Europe. Hepburn thought her career was over. She was devastated."

In 1934, Katharine Hepburn was not yet the formidable personage of our cultural memory. She was just six years out of college, a slender girl of moderate privilege for whom success in films had come quickly and easily. This criticism, tough and mean-spirited as it was, was the first real test of her adult life, and she was running away. "I thought I was through," she remembered. "My career was over and all that was left for me to do was go back home a failure." That would never do, of course, not with the sting of her father's hand on her cheek still fresh in her memory.

Given the Academy Award, her despair may seem overwrought. Yet to understand Hepburn's crisis we must move beyond the professional. Not long before, the press had discovered a very personal secret about her: she had a *husband*. In 1928, just out of Bryn Mawr, she had married Ludlow Ogden Smith. As Kath had taken her first baby steps onto the stage, Luddy had been her rock—as in much the same way Suzanne would be, more briefly, later on. But the paths of husband and wife had diverged not long after, with Luddy settling into anonymity as an industrial engineer and Kath setting out to make her name.

When she first went to Hollywood, Katharine Hepburn never mentioned her husband. But the newshounds had a way of sniffing out the details of stars' lives. In a fan-magazine article late in 1933, the story of Kath's marriage had been spelled out. Every morning since, a parade of shouting, snapping reporters had trailed Luddy to his office on Vanderbilt Avenue. Even the compliant young man had found his breaking point. What might the press say about him? About them and their untraditional marriage?

Leland Hayward worried about that, too. Times were changing. The Hollywood of March 1934 was a very different place from what it was when Kath first stepped off the train in Pasadena in July 1932. In those twenty months, the Production Code—that draconian list of dos and don'ts concerning what

Americans could and could not see on the screen—had been forced down the throats of even Hollywood's most powerful producers. Bowing to the fear of boycotts threatened by conservative reformers (particularly unnerving, given the precarious economic times), Hollywood had reluctantly ceded its creative imprimatur to the censors. It wasn't just on-screen content that was affected; the stars suddenly found their personal lives under a microscope as well. Racy images so popular in the freewheeling 1920s—the rakish John Barrymore, the free-loving Clara Bow, the sexually ambiguous Marlene Dietrich—were suddenly out of style, replaced by upstanding heroes and sweet, ladylike girls next door.

Yet from her very first day in Hollywood, Katharine Hepburn had been known best for one thing: her pants. Today, Hepburn's trousers have become a beloved cultural icon, but in the early 1930s they were considered subversive. Independent women seemed to offer a threat to the millions of men out of work, men whose sense of mastery over their lives and families had been lost. Traditional gender roles took on a certain sacredness. By 1934, Katharine Hepburn (in pants) was not a comforting image for much of the population—not even to many women. Though some took inspiration from her defiant persona, many more, as frightened as their husbands, preferred to keep the apples secure in the cart.

Sailing out of New York Harbor in March 1934, Kath was beginning to grasp that, if she was to survive and prosper in this new Hollywood, she would have to change, rethink, reinvent. Academy Award or not, Katharine Hepburn—with her men's trousers, gibbon, and abandoned husband—was not going to sell tickets or attract media adoration. For the damage didn't end there. Even more troubling than the discovery of Luddy were the stories about Laura Harding, whom some in the press were labeling "Hepburn's other half." The Hollywood underground buzzed with rumors that the two women were more than just friends.

Considering Laura a liability, Leland urged Kath to send her away. Yet such an action seemed inconceivable. Laura—polished, sophisticated Laura—from an aristocratic Main Line Philadelphia family, had been with Kath every moment since her arrival on the West Coast. Laura had taken charge of her career, designing Kath's wardrobe, handling her press, even negotiating on Kath's behalf with producers, directors, and—much to his growing annoyance—Leland himself. Not a few reporters wondered just what hold this Miss Harding had over Miss Hepburn. Setting tongues wagging, Laura had once answered an RKO official's demand to know who she was by declaring curtly, "Miss Hepburn's husband." Gales of laughter had erupted over the comment when she and Kath returned to the house they shared in Franklin Canyon. But at the studio there were no guffaws.

"What kind of queer arrangement is this?" asked one newspaper caption, juxtaposing photos of Kath and Laura with images of "Hepburn's forgotten husband."

The arrival of Suzanne, Leland insisted, only made things worse. Usually her agent's word was gospel for Kath. She adored Leland. Few things were more enjoyable than sitting with her leg draped over the arm of a chair, listening to Leland brag of seducing Hollywood's most beautiful women. Handsome, rangy Leland Hayward, in his finely tailored flannel suits and diamond cuff links, was one of the shrewdest agents Hollywood ever produced. He knew everyone. Lying on the couch in his office, he'd prop three telephones on his chest, talking on all three at once. To keep his sanity, the phones never rang, just glowed with a soft red light to announce incoming calls.

Laura's presence in Kath's life, Leland argued, was bad enough, but at least Laura was an elegant and mannerly Philadelphia blueblood. Suzanne—or Susan, as she was born, the daughter of a scrappy New York journalist named Willis Steell—was something else entirely. At age nineteen, she'd been singing in the chorus of a Broadway play when she was spotted by Madame Maria Jeritza, the tempestuous Austrian opera singer known as much for her luxurious blond hair as for her voice. In January 1923, the diva announced she had chosen Susan Steell as her protégée, and for the next seven years, the rechristened Suzanne remained at Jeritza's side. In her early twenties, Steell was tall, lithe, and pretty—"statuesque, like a Gibson girl," according to Miles White. Jeritza, fourteen years Suzanne's senior, delighted in the younger woman's company and was seen with her in New York, Paris, and Vienna far more often than with her husband, Baron Leopold von Popper.

Inevitably, Jeritza's flamboyant reputation led to gossip. A 1930 Austrian novel featured a lead character based on the star, thinly disguised: a bisexually adventurous opera singer with a milquetoast titled husband. Another character, a young protégée, seemed modeled after Suzanne. Called *Riff-Raff*, the novel was based on "a lot of dirt about Jeritza," according to its author, Roderick Mueller-Guttenbrunn, and became an instant European best seller. Both Jeritza and Popper sued for defamation. Meanwhile, Suzanne Steell quietly sailed out of the tempest, returning to America on October 5 on the SS *Rochambeau*.

Not long afterward, Steell found herself a new friend, though this time it would be she who played the mentor. The official version, given by Hepburn herself, was that Steell strode into her dressing room during the run of *The*

Lake and offered to give her voice lessons. No doubt recalling Brooks Atkinson's crack about her voice being a "strident instrument," Kath agreed.

Many have lamented the "enigma" of Suzanne Steell, wondering just who this mysterious woman was who took Hepburn under her wing at this low point in her career. In truth, Steell was no mystery at all. She'd made a name for herself in France singing in Massenet's *Werther*. Since returning to New York, she had performed at the Town Hall with selections from Rameau and Ravel. The *New York Times* called Steell's voice "full and round," her diction "unusually good." Just prior to walking into Kath's dressing room, she had appeared in a much-publicized performance at the American Women's Association clubhouse on West Fifty-seventh Street, taking on all the roles in Molière's *School for Wives*. The *New York Sun*, reviewing an earlier run of the show, thought Steell moved "easily and pleasantly" between masculine and feminine gestures. Those who knew her insisted such was the case for Steell in her private life as well.

In the paranoid climate of post-Code Hollywood, stars could not afford being touched by scandal, however distant. Leland Hayward surely considered Hepburn's friendship with Suzanne Steell a disaster waiting to happen. Although *Riff-Raff* was never published in the United States, the publicity from it trailed Jeritza, and Leland did not want it attached to Kath. Laura Harding shared his concern. Her animosity toward Steell remained evident forty years later when she repeated secondhand horror stories about her to the author Charles Higham. While Kath allowed Suzanne to move in with her and cook all her meals, everyone else thought she needed to be dumped. Such talk could only have deepened Kath's depression as the *Paris* pulled out of the harbor. Luddy, Laura, now Suzanne. How much, Kath may have wondered as the ship sailed past the Statue of Liberty, was this career of hers going to cost?

Five decades later, speaking to a Bryn Mawr graduating class, Hepburn said, "Acting is a funny kind of a career to go into. You are presuming to say: 'I am a fascinating thing.' I think that by necessity [acting] is an unhealthy profession."

That was less Hepburn talking than an echo of her father, who never changed his opinion about Kath's ambition. One of Dr. Thomas Hepburn's favorite sayings was that unless she could be either the bride or the corpse—in other words, the star of the show—she wasn't interested in being seen.

How much did Kath reflect on her desire for fame and her father's opposition to it during her transatlantic crossing of March 1934? Only the barest details of her actions aboard ship have come down to us. Purchasing a last-minute ticket, a fan-magazine writer snuck on board, but the best the spy was able to do was peer under the aluminum lids of the trays Kath set outside her door. Later, *Movie Mirror* would report she had brioche for breakfast and cold cuts for lunch, and she left her stateroom only to slip furtively into the screening room, hunching down way in back, to catch the movies being shown on board.

If Laura Harding's later testimony is to be believed, Suzanne Steell quickly grew bored with Kath's reclusiveness and found her way to the glittery dining room, where she proceeded to drink too much and talk accordingly. Harding was biased in her recollections, of course, having felt supplanted by Suzanne. But Kath was certainly not in a sociable mood for much of the crossing.

How much did she decide before the ship docked at Le Havre? How much had she concluded about her career and ambition? We can't know for certain, but there's a tantalizing suggestion that she was digging in her heels, refusing to change her ways. On board the *Paris* was another actress, Jeanne Aubert, about Hepburn's age, vivacious and pretty, fresh from a highly publicized legal victory in which an American judge had declared her jewels her own property and not that of her former husband. Did Hepburn and Aubert meet on board? Usually photographed swathed in furs and pearls, Aubert was a fashion plate of Parisian styles. But when she stepped off the *Paris* at Le Havre, Aubert was wearing white duck trousers and a man's tie. Questioned by reporters, she insisted that pants were simply more comfortable to wear—the same thing Kath had been telling everybody for a year and a half.

With much less fanfare did Hepburn slink off the ship. If Suzanne had been eager to show her old haunts to her movie-star friend, she was quickly disappointed. Kath immediately changed the agenda. Instead of heading to the Riviera, where they'd planned to stop at Cannes (the scene of Kath's recent film-festival win as best actress for *Little Women*), Kath wanted to linger in Paris. She wanted to find Josephine Day Bennett, an old friend of her mother's then living in Saint-Germain.

Kath's decision to seek out Jo Bennett at this critical juncture gives us our best insight into what was going on in her mind at the time. It was an attempt to regain some balance after being thrown off stride. Faced with the first real turning point of her adult life, she looked not to the future but to the past, to a woman who had marched shoulder to shoulder with Kit Hepburn carrying placards demanding VOTES FOR WOMEN. Young Kathy had sometimes been there as well, trooping along at their sides, her tiny fist clenched around strings bobbing with helium balloons. Jo Bennett offered a link to the childhood that had so defined Kath's sense of herself. She had even been there that tragic day in 1921 when Kath's older brother Tom had died. If going home to Mother and Dad wasn't an option, Kath would seek out the next closest thing to them.

Jo Bennett was a colorful figure, part of Ernest Hemingway's Parisian circle. Married to the expatriate painter Richard Brooks, she was also the former lover of Harold Stearns, the model for the dissipated Harvey Stone in Hemingway's *The Sun Also Rises*. While Kath's precise conversation with Bennett that day in late March 1934 can only be guessed at, it seems to have offered her some much-needed clarity. Within a day, she had canceled any further plans and booked passage on the *Paris*'s return trip to New York on March 27.

"It would seem to me that what [Bennett] offered at that point was a touchstone," said Kath's brother Bob. "You see, we would often turn to our parents for advice, even as adults. [Kath] was perhaps the best one for doing that. There were certain core values that we were taught and that we always believed in. One of these was the virtue of persistence, of not giving up. I suspect that may be what [Bennett] reminded her about, perhaps not even in so many words, but simply through her connection to my parents and their values."

Hepburn herself would later say, "Dad may have thought acting was cheesy, but worse than being cheesy was being a quitter."

"What I understood," said Suzanne Steell's friend Miles White, "was that Kate Hepburn suddenly gave up her rash decision to run away and announced that she needed to go back home, that she had to give her career another chance."

This time, sailing westward, Kath proved anything but a recluse. It seems a good bet that Bennett knew Hemingway would be on the ship, returning from a safari in Africa, where he'd shot three lions, a buffalo, and twenty-seven other beasts. It's not difficult to believe that back in Los Angeles, hearing of this opportunity, Leland Hayward felt his publicist's heart beat just a little faster. What better way to herald Hepburn's return to the States than to pair her with America's most famous rugged individualist?

When Hemingway stepped off the gangplank in New York on April 3, a beaming Katharine Hepburn was at his side. No longer ducking the magnesium flares, she was facing them head-on—and in a fashionable French beret and a slash of bright red lipstick to boot. They made an odd-looking couple, Hepburn so lean and spare, Hemingway so broad and lumbering, as reporters corralled them against the wooden railing of the ship.

"Don't be a mug," Hemingway teased her, suggesting she cooperate.

"Of course," she declared, and suddenly she was ordering champagne all around. "I never meant to cause you any inconvenience," she purred as the steward poured each of the newsmen a glass of bubbly.

"Miss Hepburn," one reporter managed to ask, "why did you come back home?"

"I was homesick," she replied simply, as the cameras began to flash.

For what, she was asked. "I'm sure I don't know," she answered.

"Did you see trousers on any of the women in Paris?" another reporter asked. Kath smiled and shook her head no. "Then did you wear them your-self while you were there?"

"Only to bed," she said, to still more laughter.

How different her homecoming was. This way and that she posed for the cameras, smiling those red lips wide. She seemed in no hurry to get away.

It all seemed so impromptu, yet these things never happen quite so spon-taneously. Surely Leland Hayward had wired the press that they would find a very different Hepburn than the one they'd chased out to sea two weeks ear-lier. Surely he'd arranged for the champagne. But why, the reporters asked, had she left in so much secrecy before?

"I just needed a vacation and so I took it," she said, laughing at sugges-tions of "domestic troubles." "I can't explain why I do things. I just do them."

Sometime between March 17, when she sailed, and April 3, when she re-turned, Katharine Hepburn had made a decision that forever altered her life. She wouldn't run away. She'd give the press and the public what they wanted. The cheeky girl known as Kath, who had been brought up to believe she could have it all and have it her way, had to be quelled. Somewhere out there in the middle of the Atlantic the naïveté of Kath gave way to a new, more practical vision of herself. The price of fame, she realized, was not so high that she couldn't afford to pay. She had dreamed of being a star too long to sacrifice her hopes to the whims of a childish girl.

"I was a star before I knew how to be a star," she admitted many years later. "And then I thought, well, I've got to learn how to be a star."

If she had left New York with a woman around whom swirled whispers of deviancy and scandal, Hepburn returned now on the arm of a knight of un-questioned masculine reputation—the kind of man with whom she always enjoyed being publicly linked. During their mutual posturing in front of the cameras, Hemingway declared her "very nice" and Kath announced she liked him "immensely"—setting scribes to scribbling about a shipboard romance between actress and author (no matter that Mrs. Hemingway stood nearby).

On the Coast, Leland Hayward was jubilant. No doubt he'd instructed Kath carefully on her next pronouncement: she was fit and ready, she told the reporters, to go back to work. And the role she was most looking forward to playing? None other than Joan of Arc.

In that brief span of seventeen days, Katharine Hepburn had gone from haughty to heroic, sinner to saint. Suzanne Steell and all she represented had been left behind—though the woman herself would go on, inconveniently reminding people of her brief association with Hepburn as the years passed. Reverting to her real name of Susan, Steell became well known on Broadway as a mannish, cigar-chomping character. She played Mme. Dilly in *On the Town,* Mother Burnside in *Auntie Mame,* and General Matilda B. Cartwright in *Guys and Dolls.* A couple of times over the years she made attempts to contact her old pal Hepburn, but she was always rebuffed. An obese Susan Steell died of a heart attack in 1959.

Hepburn's fate, of course, was very different. In order to go on with her career after those troubled times in 1934, Kath knew she needed to cut her losses and chart a new path—a shrewd, practical assessment of the changes happening in Hollywood.

Two years previous, she might have made a different decision. She might have walked away from Hollywood, unwilling to tolerate such restrictions on her private life. But something had happened in the interim. Hepburn had had a taste of success, of extraordinary fame, and she had *liked* it. She hadn't expected to be a sensation in pictures. She'd assumed she'd go back to New York and continue in the theater. But RKO had wanted more films from her. Fan letters piled up at the studio. Crowds gathered around her plane when she landed in New York, even if she sometimes chose to bedevil them by touching down in New Jersey, just to give them the chase. In the midst of all of this ballyhoo, Kath discovered she *liked* being a movie star, liked it a great deal. Moviemaking itself might have become a "chore" in this new Hollywood, but it served a purpose. It kept her famous. Not yet was any sense of personal artistry a driving force in her life. That would come later. In 1934, Kath's motivation was all about the fame.

While she had been at sea, Edwin Schallert headlined her dilemma in his column: HEPBURN IN HOT SPOT. "Will Katharine Hepburn dare to return to Hollywood?" Schallert asked. "What effect will the flip-flop done by her play, 'The Lake,' have upon her picture career? Has the awarding of a prize by the Academy of Motion Picture Arts and Sciences saved her from a big, bad slump? What is *Spitfire,* the weakest she has made during her movie experience, going to do to her popularity?"

Katharine Hepburn was twenty-six years old. She was an Academy Award winner, a movie star of the top rank, but her image was inchoate and contradictory. Garson Kanin would observe that she had two smiles, one private and merry, the other "sudden, radiant, dazzling" and reserved for the public. Certainly it was this latter smile that she flashed that day on the deck of the *Paris*—perhaps the moment she learned how to conjure it. For within days of her return, she would file for divorce from Luddy. Within weeks, she'd banish Laura from L.A. to the East Coast. And soon word would be leaked to the press that Kath and Leland Hayward—handsome, savvy, shrewd Leland—were in love and planning to marry.

The time had come to create Kate.

SUCH A GOOD FAIRY-TALE TELLER

Fade in on the stately granite and brownstone of Hartford, Connecticut. If this were indeed a movie, a title card on the screen would announce: FIFTEEN YEARS EARLIER. From that sparkling afternoon on board the *Paris* in April 1934, we can trace a direct line forward in the creation of the icon called Kate. But that shouldn't imply there weren't occasional sightings of her earlier. Take the day in the fall of 1919, when the girls of the Oxford School staged a charity benefit at the Hartford Club. Dolled up as daisies, daffodils, and tulips, they performed the "Dance of the Flowers." Twelve-year-old Kathy Hepburn played a forget-me-not.

Of course, if she'd had her way, she wouldn't have been there at all; she would have much preferred to be outside climbing trees. But her parents were seated in the audience, her brothers Tom and Dick beside them. So Kathy smoothed out the crepe paper petals that radiated from her face and gave her brief time on stage her very best shot.

This may be when Kate, looking out through Kathy's eyes, first envisaged the possibilities of a performer's life. Startled by the applause following her little dance, she stood there, unable to move, just drinking it all up. Only with great reluctance did she finally allow a teacher to draw her back behind the curtain.

The forget-me-not remembered that applause. It would, in fact, shape the rest of her life. To her family, she would declare she wanted to be the most famous person "in the entire world." Whether done up in a flannel donkey's head for her turn as the Beast, as a scheming Bluebeard menacing his wives, or as a rambunctious Topsy in *Uncle Tom's Cabin* (Little Eva, she said, was too much of a "goody-goody" to interest her), Kathy learned early how to shape reality, create character, and earn approval. By her own account, her childhood was lived less in reality than in her imagination, where she spun fantasy versions of herself influenced by stories and myths. "Fairy tales," she admitted later on, "were a big piece of my life, and I was such a *good* fairy-tale teller."

Americans like to make fables of their movie icons' lives. Right from the beginning of her public life, Katharine Hepburn's origins were veiled in romance and fantasy. Even her birth is still sometimes a matter of confusion. Katharine Houghton Hepburn was born in Hartford, Connecticut, on May 12 (not November 8) in 1907 (not 1909) in a small apartment rented by her parents on South Hudson Street (not the more famous Hawthorn Street address where the family moved later). She was the second child and first daughter of Dr. Thomas Norval Hepburn, a surgeon at Hartford Hospital who specialized in the treatment of venereal disease, and Katharine Houghton Hepburn, an activist for women's suffrage and later for legalized birth control. He was called "Hep"; she was usually known as "Kit."

"I am totally, completely, the product of two *fascinating* individuals who happened to be my parents," Katharine Hepburn told us, bringing (as always) a larger-than-life quality to the description of her parents. Rare was the conversation, Garson Kanin said, that she didn't reference the wise words of Hep or Kit, and always with the reverence of a landmark Supreme Court decision. It was an analogy Hepburn wouldn't have found far from the mark. "I've had a pretty remarkable life," she said, "but compared to my mother and father, I'm dull."

Such was her brilliance in creating interest: if Katharine Hepburn was dull in comparison, how truly thrilling must have been her family! Certainly the romantic patina she overlaid onto her childhood—aided by the many chroniclers of her life—elevated Hep and Kit into exemplars of East Coast aristocracy, tinged with a lively, eccentric appeal. Peer through the kaleidoscope and you can see them: blue smoke coiling lazily from Hep's pipe as Kit, tall and patrician, serves tea to the esteemed guest seated at their table. It might be Mrs. Emmeline Pankhurst, the British suffragist, or Emma Gold-man, the political radical, or George Bernard Shaw, the genius playwright. At the sidelines is young Katharine, who in later years could carry on grandiosely when she described the family dinner table: "Every conceivable topic was dis-cussed," she said. "Venereal disease, feminism, Marxism, Darwinism. Our parents were bound to have a positive effect on us as they fought to free women and men from fear and helplessness, to protect the dignity of the hu-man being."

In these images of the Hepburn salon, Kit wears a flowing Chinese silk tea robe embroidered with birds and flowers ("Mother's Mandarin outfit," her daughter would call it). Indeed, Kit's legend was already well established by the time of her death, when her obituaries called her Hartford's own "Madame de Staël." Soaking up all this atmosphere, we were told, was the young Kathy Hep-burn, perpetually at her mother's elbow, her small hands gripping the var-nished wood of the old oak table. With brothers Tom and Dick, she chimed in with whatever questions popped into her mind. Part of the legend of the Hep-burn dinner table has always been this precociousness of the children. Encour-aged by freethinking parents, they'd ask anything: "What does gonorrhea look like?" "Will we have a Bolshevik revolution here, too?"

Always behind them in these romantic scenes was the fire roaring in the parlor. Over the mantel were the words inscribed there by the house's previ-ous owner, the writer Charles Dudley Warner: LISTEN TO THE SONG OF LIFE. Nearly every article written about Katharine Hepburn's origins would in-clude this motto, which seemed to perfectly embody the Hepburn family's worldview. It would also, presumptively, be treated as Katharine's own.

Although much of this picture is a result of Hollywood mythologizing, it's certainly true that the Hepburns marched to their own drummers. They did indeed frequently entertain artistic, intellectual acquaintances. Dr. Hep-burn, for example, was "completely crazy about [Shaw] way before anybody else in Hartford had even heard of him," said his daughter. But the urge to embellish proved irresistible. Here is the place in the legend where we tradi-tionally see Hep contacting Shaw after reading his foreword to *Damaged Goods,* Eugène Brieux's groundbreaking play about syphilis. We've been told that Hep, determined to break down the barriers that prevented free discus-sion of sexually transmitted diseases, arranged to have the play printed and distributed throughout the United States. The legend would have us believe that, after the publicity from *Damaged Goods* helped establish the American Social Hygiene Association, Hep turned down a "big job" with the organiza-tion, preferring to remain in his provincial practice.

But here are the facts: The American Social Hygiene Association emerged in late 1911 not as a result of *Damaged Goods* but instead from grand jury investigations into the prostitution trade in New York City. It owed its beginning less to Dr. Thomas Hepburn than to John D. Rockefeller Jr., who put up much of the original financing for the organization. Hep's involvement with the Brieux play (published with Shaw's foreword in May 1911) may well have helped sound the alarm. But because of the way many of the stories of the Hepburns have been at least slightly "heightened," many people today still credit Dr. Hepburn with founding the nation's first organization to combat venereal disease.

Here is the image that lingers of Thomas Norval Hepburn: redolent of sweet Kentucky burley tobacco, still in his tie and waistcoat, sipping tea with his wife and children on tree stumps in their backyard. Every day, even if he had to rush his last patient out of the office, Hep made it home for teatime. Afterward, he would teach the children how to turn somersaults on the lawn. "Show me how fast you can run," he'd challenge Kathy and her siblings. In seconds they'd be sprinting across the yard, their teacups discarded in the grass.

But he wasn't just being playful. "He was always pushing us to do better, because he wanted excellence," said his son Bob. "No. He *demanded* excellence."

"Can't you climb any higher than that?" Dr. Hepburn once challenged Kathy. Halfway to the top of their big hemlock tree, she kept going until she reached the highest branches. Later, a neighbor called, asking if the family knew that Kathy was perched so high in the tree. Of course they knew, Hep replied. "Just don't say anything," he said. "You see, she doesn't know it's dangerous."

Or so the legend goes.

How did Katharine Hepburn's beginnings become so romanticized? In many ways, she became a figure of American myth, not unlike Betsy Ross or Paul Bunyan. And as is the case with all myths, stories about her were told and retold through the years by different people for different reasons. Hepburn's "creation story" evolved as our needs and expectations changed along with the times.

American movie-star legends were once used by society, both consciously and unconsciously, to help inculcate certain kinds of behavior and values: heroism, perseverance, patriotism. But such stories took time and effort to develop. In July 1932, when Katharine Hepburn first went to Hollywood, her story wasn't yet the polished narrative we can find today in books and magazines. It was a very unfinished work. Early on, Hepburn's studio employers and their mythmakers didn't even acknowledge that her father was a doctor, much less a venereal disease specialist. Initially he was said to be a very wealthy, East Coast *capitalist*: New York banker A. Barton Hepburn. Katharine, early stories went, was "wealthy in her own right." Such stories allowed her to embody that romantic archetype of the downtrodden Depression, the "Park Avenue heiress." One fan magazine headlined its article HOLLYWOOD'S SIXTEEN MILLION DOLLAR CINDERELLA, promising to reveal how Hepburn had "won true fame despite the handicap of riches."

Though she'd imply differently later, such nonsense would not have been distributed without a least some level of consent from her. She may have felt, since she presumed her stint in Hollywood would be brief, that it didn't matter if some lowbrow fan magazine fictionalized her life. Or she may have realized—as she increasingly did later on—that such image making was necessary if she was to prosper and secure the kind of fame she so desired, while maintaining at least some vestige of privacy and independence.

It was not uncommon to manufacture a history for a new star. Talking pictures, and the more "realist" cinema they inaugurated, had been around for less than five years at the time of Hepburn's arrival in Los Angeles in 1932. Trappings of the more fanciful silent era could still be found. It wasn't so long before that Theda Bara—an anagram for Arab Death—had been invented out of whole cloth, obliterating the memory of the real Theodosia Goodman of Cincinnati. What was unusual in Hepburn's case was that the studio chose a very real, yet unrelated, family to masquerade as Kath's own. Alonzo Barton Hepburn, who died in 1925, had been well known in Manhattan as the president of Chase National Bank. His real daughter, Cordelia, was in the newspapers the same year as Kath's film debut, with press coverage of the birth of her son. Making it all even more surreal, A. Barton Hepburn *Junior* had gone on the stage about the same time as his "sister" Katharine and would ultimately have a career of his own on the stage and screen.

Just what these Hepburns thought of RKO's appropriation of their family is unknown, but it's possible that they collaborated, at least through their silence. Laura Harding's mother, Mrs. Horace Harding, was a friend of Mrs. A. Barton Hepburn's. Laura came from the same social world as the other Hepburns; she may have helped give her friend's bio an East Side spin. Rich bankers and their heiresses were far better copy for a Depression-era readership than a venereal disease specialist and radical feminist.

Back in Hartford, Dr. and Mrs. Hepburn went about their business with little awareness of their daughter's masquerade. They were never movie fans.

Kit Hepburn, even after her daughter became a star, would profess ignorance over the names of her fellow players. ("Cary Grant? Clark Gable? I can
never keep them straight.") Movies were lowbrow entertainment, the Hepburns believed, and—for all their work to help the downtrodden—there was
always a bit of noblesse oblige to the family, a bit of instinctive snobbery. Kit
might champion legalized birth control, but her efforts were targeted at perpetually pregnant immigrants, not women of her own class; Mrs. Hepburn,
after all, bore six children. In those first few months while their daughter
was becoming a star, Hep and Kit likely didn't mind that their names weren't
being spelled out in *Photoplay*.

Of course, the Hepburns were hardly the type to please Hollywood image makers either. RKO publicists had surely recoiled when they first learned
the reality of Kath's parents—the complete antithesis of the kind of conservative types Hollywood preferred. Indeed, the very livelihoods of Hep and
Kit—venereal disease and birth control—involved subjects classed as forbidden by the Production Code.

Accordingly, Kath's real parents were not maneuvered into the official version of her biography until nearly a year of her film career had passed. In
early 1933, when the screen star checked into Hartford Hospital for an undis-
closed illness, hospital leaks confirmed that she was under the care of her father. Soon after, in *Modern Screen*, came a description of Dr. Hepburn as a
"well-known surgeon"; Kath's mother, the magazine wrote, was a niece of
Alanson B. Houghton, the former U.S. ambassador to Germany and Britain.

This early version of Dr. and Mrs. Hepburn conjured up visions of a
kindly provincial caregiver and his supportive, blue-blooded wife. But after
Kath's stardom skyrocketed with *Morning Glory* and *Little Women,* the public's demand for more information grew. In late 1933, just as Kath took to the
Broadway stage in *The Lake,* RKO publicists decided to appease demands by
offering to the press the first version of what would later become the classic
Hepburn story.

This rather complicated marketing task was entrusted to Adela Rogers
St. Johns, a veteran Hearst journalist and (not incidentally) prolific screenwriter of the silent era. St. Johns's article, titled "The Private Life of Katharine
Hepburn," was published in January 1934 in *Liberty* magazine. To St. Johns
goes the credit for the basic outlines of the now-familiar Hepburn myth. All
the elements were set forth by her: the wise, nurturing parents; the raucous,
intellectually stimulating household; the devotion among the siblings. It was
truer than the earlier sketches of Hepburn history, but it definitely shored
up the trouble spots.

With St. Johns's article, we see the first glimmerings of the "myth of the family," which would become so important to Hepburn's image. In St. Johns's words, the Hepburns had taught Kath that the "creed of life is individualism"— an explanation for the iconoclasm, trousers, and gibbon. For the first time, readers also learned of Mrs. Hepburn's work as a suffragist. St. Johns linked the struggle for women's votes to "every American crusade from the Boston Tea Party." So sounded the first strains of patriotism in the Hepburn myth.

St. Johns's spin was eagerly anticipated by RKO, for the studio was building up its new star at a very precarious time. When the article appeared, Hollywood was in the midst of the battles over the Production Code, and here was RKO trying to promote an actress whose mother advocated for birth control—a direct challenge to the Code's leading proponent, the Roman Catholic Church. (As believers in eugenics, both Dr. and Mrs. Hepburn often found themselves at loggerheads with the church.) So St. Johns sidestepped Mrs. Hepburn's crusade and instead played up her six lively offspring. (In addition to Tom, Kath, and Dick, there was Bob, Marion, and Peggy, too.) Young Katharine, St. Johns assured us, had similar maternal instincts. "To watch her with her young sister Marion," St. Johns wrote, "is to realize her soul is as maternal as her mother's—that mother who bore six children to grow up in the fine old Connecticut home with its famous garden."

There it was: the image the studio wanted to overlay onto reality. And it worked. The *Liberty* article became the basis of all the stories to follow through the years, all purporting to tell the "real story" of Katharine Hepburn's past. From 1934 onward, every portrait of Dr. and Mrs. Hepburn presented them as saints. Eccentric, unorthodox, opinionated—but saints nonetheless. Rarely would an interview go by in which Katharine Hepburn would not pay homage to "Mother and Dad," describing them in ways that echoed the strains first heard in St. Johns's piece.

Another landmark article appeared in 1941, when Hepburn was riding the wave of her comeback with the film *The Philadelphia Story*. This one built upon the framework St. Johns had laid down seven years earlier. Here we have direct evidence of the myth being consciously, deliberately nudged along by the star herself: several letters document Hepburn's cooperation with the author in arranging for people to be interviewed. "This is to introduce Lupton Wilkinson, who is doing a story on me for *The Saturday Evening Post*," Hepburn wrote to Theresa Helburn of the Theater Guild. "Please tell him all the horrible things you know about me from the time we first met, as he is trying to do a truthful, and at the same time, amusing and not too objectionable tale."

Like Adela Rogers St. Johns, Wilkinson brought to the task certain quali-
fying credentials. Having been a movie publicist before turning to journalism, Wilkinson knew how to pen a story to please temperamental stars. He'd
written about Hepburn before, in fact, showing her to good advantage in the
Los Angeles Times. Spread out over five issues of the *Post* (from late 1941 to
early 1942), Wilkinson's subsequent elaboration of the legend would prove
even more influential than St. Johns's piece. Every single subsequent chronicler would draw upon Wilkinson, usually treating his words as gospel. Kit's
birth control could no longer be avoided, so Wilkinson deftly worked in the
fact that she had given birth to Dick while in the midst of her campaign.
"Opponents found it difficult," he wrote, "to charge with unfemininity
someone who might, at any moment, excuse herself to nurse her baby."

The legend of Katharine Hepburn's family took time to build, but after
Wilkinson's piece it was enshrined into American popular culture. Stories of
the family's raucous dinner-table conversations with their famous intellectual
or artistic guests quickly took their place among the liveliest elements of the
Hepburn mythos. The children in these stories all speak out of turn and ask
provocative questions; no subject is off-limits. Even as they grew into adults,
this image remained, of various Hepburns walking in and out of the house,
each possessed by his or her own mission and sense of self-importance. No
matter who was their guest, they debated the great issues of the day, interrupting each other, starting fights, making up, and starting all over again. Sex,
politics, art—such were the dinner-table conversations on which the Hepburns were raised. They *listened to the song of life*. From this brilliant chaos of
bohemian stimulation sprang the wondrous figure we know as Kate.

Or so we believe, thanks to the scene setting of Adela Rogers St. Johns
and Lupton Wilkinson. In Hollywood, first impressions, serving as the basis
for everything written throughout a star's trajectory, are repeated over and
over, eventually passing for truth.

But the truth was always there for anyone who wanted to see it. "It wasn't
all so rosy," said Bob Hepburn, "as people like to say."

NOBODY LIKES CRYBABIES

A Sunday in late summer, Keney Park, Hartford, 1909. Piling his family into his battered, doorless, open-air Maxwell roadster, license plate 3405, Dr. Thomas Hepburn drove to the thickly forested 695-acre park in the city's north end. It was a gorgeous day. Along a shady path, Kit pushed two-year-old Kathy in a stroller, while several steps behind her Hep walked hand in hand with four-year-old Tommy. Ladies carrying parasols nodded as the family walked past. Gentlemen paused long enough to share a good word with Hep.

But then, all at once, little Tommy Hepburn's face began to twitch. Hep stopped walking. Ahead of him, Kit became aware that her husband and son were no longer following her, and she turned, looking back. What she saw was Tommy's right cheek pushing involuntarily upward, forcing his eye to close in rapid blinks. Hep stood over him, glaring.

"Stop it, Tommy," he ordered. "Stop it now."

When the boy's face continued to twitch, Hep glanced around. Walking nearby, in their Sunday best, were important men: colleagues, businessmen, politicians, and potential patients. Tommy's tics were drawing attention.

Once more Hep told his son to stop, though he knew the boy was powerless to do so.

Some months earlier, little Tommy had been diagnosed with chorea, or Saint Vitus' dance. Dr. Hepburn understood quite well the etiology of the disease. At Johns Hopkins, he had studied under Dr. William Osler, one of the leading experts on Saint Vitus, who insisted that the disorder was exacerbated if the child perceived he was being watched or judged.

Still, as his son Bob would recall from the family lore, Dr. Thomas Hepburn refused to continue their walk and ordered them all back to the car. Hep had no patience for Tommy's "habits." A boy with these sorts of problems was not an effective advertisement for his father's curative skills. Hep actually feared that his son's disability could hurt his practice, which he was still struggling to build. By 1909 the twenty-nine-year-old doctor's reputation was not yet really secure. For all his iconoclasm, Thomas Hepburn knew he couldn't allow his bohemian reputation to scare off his straitlaced, puritan neighbors, many of whom stubbornly resisted being won over.

"Some people in Hartford thought the Hepburns were horrible," said Hep's youngest daughter, Peg. "I grew up knowing what it was like to not be spoken to." Her older sister Katharine knew it, too, recalling how one prominent lady refused to acknowledge Kit on the street. Little Kathy, looking up into the lady's cold, distant eyes, was hurt by such shunning. It was a memory that would color her personality all of her life.

In fact, few places would be less sympathetic to the maverick Hepburns than Hartford. When the young Tom Hepburn, a Virginia native who had just graduated from Johns Hopkins Medical School, decided to settle there, Hartford was a place of greenery and wealth, one of the richest small cities in America. Wide tree-lined boulevards radiated north, south, and west from the city's architecturally rich downtown, home to a preponderance of insurance companies that gave Hartford its reputation as the insurance capital of the world. Though stateliness, even stodginess, might have characterized downtown, out on the rolling hills of the Nook Farm neighborhood there was a pocket of liberalism: Harriet Beecher Stowe pioneered the education of girls and encouraged abolitionist thought, while next door Mark Twain wrote *The Adventures of Huckleberry Finn.*

Yet despite exposure to characters like Stowe and Twain, Hartford remained a fundamentally conservative Republican place. A distant cousin of Kit's, Fannie Houghton Bulkeley, the wife of a former governor of Connecticut, publicly repudiated Mrs. Hepburn's feminism in the *Hartford Courant.* "There were people who truly believed," said Bob Hepburn, "that what Mother was advocating was the destruction of the American home."

Early on, some well-placed ladies in Hartford society took Kit aside and warned her that her political involvement threatened her husband's practice. To Hep's credit, he did not ask his wife to cease and desist. Still, there were tensions; Hep was a pragmatic and practical man who had family responsibilities. "He was struggling, which I think hasn't been widely known," said Bob Hepburn. "So he would get angry."

The conventional belief has been that the Hepburns were very wealthy. It's true that Katharine Hepburn came from a privileged social world, especially on her mother's side, and later Dr. Hepburn made quite a good living for himself. But when his children were very young, Hep was "working very hard," his son pointed out, and "money wasn't easy." Sometimes in these lean years, the doctor would take out his frustrations on the people around him. Often, those people were his children.

That Dr. and Mrs. Hepburn were not the paragons of parenting they've always been portrayed as being isn't really surprising. Precious few people could live up to the rosy portraits painted by Hollywood publicists or the glowing testimonials Hepburn would give about her father and mother. Of course, not all of what she told us about her parents is myth. Certainly, the great gift that Hep and Kit bestowed upon their children was the sense of life's possibilities. They taught their family that out beyond Hartford was a great wide world, and they were entitled to take their places in it.

Yet behind the encouragement and the intellectual foundation, there was also something cold about Katharine Hepburn's childhood. "I think it's what defined everything else," said her good friend Noel Taylor. "Everything came back to that. Kate went through her life trying to please her father, and he was *very* hard to please."

Seventy years later, Katharine Hepburn would profess to be proud of Hep's reputation as a "spanking Dad." Jutting out her chin, she stared down an interviewer as if daring a challenge. "Were we spanked?" she crowed. "We were *beaten*." She seemed to imply that, given the fine results of her parents' methods, maybe *all* children should be so disciplined. Sure, she told Garson Kanin, she was "cuffed around a lot" as a girl, but she said this not with regret or anger, but with pride. The extent of her father's physical discipline was downplayed. After all, what parent *didn't* strike a child in those days? "Spare the rod" was seen as indulgent mollycoddling.

But not everyone thought Hep's treatment of his children was either normal or beneficial. Among these was Kathy's maternal aunt, the freethinking Edith Houghton Hooker. A suffragist and political activist like her sister Kit, Edith never fell under her brother-in-law's charismatic spell. One night, as several family members recalled, Edith was appalled to witness an ugly scene at the dinner table after Kathy, aged ten or so, spoke out of turn. Without warning, Hep reached over and slapped the little girl across the face, knocking the fork from her hands and the food from her mouth.

Such behavior was confusing: On the one hand, the children were encouraged to express their own opinions. But if they touched a nerve—and they never knew when that might happen—they were silenced, sometimes with force. Consider the time when Kathy, still quite young, spilled a glass of milk during a family dinner. As she herself told the story, she laughed instead of apologizing, which sent Hep into a rage. Grabbing his daughter's hand, he dragged her up the stairs. Everyone in the family, including the little girl's mother, sat silently with eyes downcast—except for brassy Edith, who stood up, outraged.

Seventy years later, the story became something else, a memory that Kate used in her memoir as an example of her father's capacity for fun and games. As Kate told it, her father was only pretending that day—to get meddlesome Edith's goat. Upstairs, he told Kathy to scream and carry on and make believe he was hurting her. Good little actress that she was, she flew into the part with gusto. Returning to the dinner table with a smug expression, Hep seemed oblivious to the daggers Edith was shooting at him with her eyes.

This was the kind of narrative kept in rotation during countless interviews throughout Katharine Hepburn's career. Her official accounts of her father's discipline were lighthearted tales that scoffed at more tolerant forms of parenting. But clearly, from all accounts, Hep was a strict arbiter of final authority, no matter the spin Lupton Wilkinson tried to bring. Wilkinson described the Hepburn household as a place where "the child is entitled to an explanation for all rulings," and insisted that Dr. Hepburn "spanked [his children] only when sweet reason failed." But Bob Hepburn, himself often on the receiving end, felt it failed more than occasionally.

"So many stories Kate tells of her childhood have her sitting at the tops of trees, refusing to come down," said her friend Max Showalter. "What drove her up there, did you ever wonder? Knowing her father's temper, it rather makes you think, doesn't it?"

Once more, Keney Park. The summer of 1910. This time it was Kathy trembling as she walked beside her father up a steep grassy hill. Hep was pushing a shiny new bicycle specially made for the little girl at the nearby Pope Manufacturing Company. Just three years old, Kathy was in the park that day to learn how to ride a bike. Not a tricycle, as some accounts have portrayed, but a regular two-wheeler, albeit a scaled-down version, as per Dr. Hepburn's specific instructions.

"Hop on," he told his daughter.

She hesitated.

"Hop on, Kathy," Hep repeated.

She looked up at him, this small, freckled, red-haired girl in her Buster Brown bowlcut. She shook her head no.

Hep didn't argue with her. He simply picked her up and placed her on the seat. Out flew her kicking legs, her hands clutching in terror at the air. "I was scared to death," she recalled. But her protests ceased when her father, whispering in her ear, threatened to give her a spanking.

"Now grip the handlebars," he instructed her.

Kathy began to cry.

"Nobody likes crybabies," Hep said. And with that, he pushed the bike down the hill.

Later, telling the story, Hepburn would defend her father. Sure, she might have been terrified, but Dad, as always, knew best. She went on to *love* bike riding, she insisted, pedaling all over Hartford.

True enough, but that was later. The training session described above occurred when she was *three*. That day, Kathy rode smack into an old man and fell crying to the ground, skinning both her knees. The next day Hep was once more holding that bike, beckoning Kathy to join him for yet another excursion to Keney Park. Yes, indeed, she learned to ride a bicycle at a young age, younger than most. But not before weeks went by, weeks of more abject terror and scraped legs. Still, "nobody likes crybabies" became one more motto for Hepburn's life, often repeated after she became a star.

It's not surprising that, in his early days as a physician, Hep should be driven by concerns over his reputation. Ever since he'd been a boy growing up in the backwoods of Virginia and Maryland, Tom Hepburn had been conscious of status, or the lack thereof. His mother, Nina Powell Hepburn, a loyal daughter of the Confederacy, had long remained bitter over the loss of the southern way of life. To her four sons and one daughter she lamented loudly the great mansions burned to the ground, the fine old families—hers included—whose fortunes and reputations had been destroyed. Her discontent even extended to her own husband, who Nina thought had walked away from his own heritage of landed gentility.

But Sewell Hepburn believed it was God himself who had compelled him to take to the back roads of the war-torn South as an itinerant Episcopal minister. Moving from village to village, rattling over rutted clay roads in horse-drawn wagons, young Tom Hepburn absorbed his mother's resentment. After all, as he would tell own his children many times, he believed the old family lore that they were direct descendants of James Hepburn, earl of Bothwell, erstwhile husband of Mary, Queen of Scots. Watching his father dig their wagon out of yet another ditch, Tom determined that muddy roads and ramshackle housing would have no place in his future.

In the words of his son-in-law Ellsworth Grant, Thomas Hepburn carried "a lifelong chip on his shoulder." To these Yankees, whom his mother had blamed for the destruction of her world, he always felt he had to prove himself. After he married and became a father, he grew frustrated and embarrassed by the cramped apartment he and his wife shared on South Hudson Street. About 1910, Hep found a dwelling far more fitting to the image he wanted to convey: the former Charles Dudley Warner house at 133 Hawthorn Street, just down the road from the gilded Twain and Stowe mansions. The redbrick Gothic, rented from the adjacent Arrow electric factory (thankfully obscured by trees), boasted three gables trimmed in delicate black Victorian filigree. From the pitched roof rose two old-fashioned chimneys, and thick green ivy crept over the walls. It was the perfect English country house for an aspiring American aristocrat, even one with reforming tendencies.

At first, the Hepburns had only one servant, a mulatto woman named Ida Wood, but that would soon change. Nannies, cooks, drivers—all were on Hep's list. Yet he understood that even more reflective of his status than his household would be his children. From them, he demanded achievement and perfection.

Tommy's problems did not fit the picture. Hep sometimes seemed convinced, deep down, that despite all the medical opinion to the contrary, his son was simply being weak. Kit—as well as Lizzie Byles, Bertha Bitner, and Fanny Ciarrier, the servants who eventually filled out the Hepburn household—only made things worse, fluttering around the boy and indulging his nervousness. After all, hadn't Hep himself risen up against the odds of a downtrodden childhood?

Sewell Hepburn had instilled into his son very high expectations for male children. "In this machine age of good roads and so many opportunities," Sewell wrote in his journal, "it is hard to realize what the boy of one hundred thirty years ago had to pass through. Yet that age produced men. . . . They blazed the way for us. We owe them a debt of gratitude we will never be able to repay."

Hep's own life had been what his father would have called "a triumph of the will." He expected a similar effort from Tommy. To coddle him was to make him weak. When the boy awoke with night terrors (a common experience among children with chorea), Hep often refused to allow his wife to go to him. Tommy's cries would echo through the house until, exhausted, the child fell back to sleep.

For all her commitment to the empowerment of women, it's startling to realize just how deferential Kit Hepburn was to her husband, who seems to have been an ambivalent sort of feminist. It's true that Dr. Hepburn enjoyed tweaking conservatives with his support for women's rights. After the *New York Times* ran an editorial opposed to expanding suffrage, Hep fired off a sarcastic response claiming that the paper had convinced him that his "chivalry," of which he had been "inclined to be proud," was "nothing more than a bribe given by man to woman to prevent her from refusing to 'recognize his manhood as a title to supremacy.'"

Such grandstanding aside, Hep retained a very traditional view of marriage. *Chivalrous* might indeed describe his support for his wife's causes: he sometimes appeared to be a man granting a lady a favor out of the beneficence of his superior position. For all his talk of equal rights, when Hep arrived home every night, he still expected to find Kit "behind the tea set." And unless she was off leading a march on Washington, Mrs. Hepburn made sure to oblige.

Kit seems to have tolerated her second-class position inside the household because her work outside, where things *really* mattered, offered escape. She'd remember pushing Tom and Kathy in a baby carriage and thinking, "I've got a B.A. and an M.A. degree, and here I am . . . a nursemaid to the rising generation." She decided she was meant to do more. Not long afterward, Kit would find herself standing at a podium in front of an audience at Hartford's Parsons Theater, insisting she would not be part of "a torpid womanhood, willing to sit back and wait" for change. Rather, she wanted to be part of the few who stood out as "different from the rest . . . people who understand where the race is going and why progress has to be helped by individual human beings."

Such commitment meant Kit was frequently away from home. Indeed, between the years 1910 and 1920—or from the time Kathy was three until she was thirteen—Kit was often gone for weeks at a time, a reality downplayed in most accounts of her daughter's childhood. But the journals of Florence Kitchelt, one of Kit's comrades-in-arms, reveals a schedule that was not uncommon: "It was Sunday in Washington, Monday in Baltimore, Tuesday in Germantown, Wednesday in Swarthmore, Thursday in Philadelphia and New York, Friday in Englewood and Sunday will be Orange."

"We knew Mother was off doing good work," said her son Bob. "That's why she had to be away from home as often as she was."

In truth, as much as she loved her children, Kit Hepburn, crusader, was bored by day-to-day child rearing. Though she might cherish her nightly visits to the children's bedsides, where she'd read to them or sing them to sleep, she was far more interested in her campaign to improve the lives of Hartford's prostitutes than she was in the daily grind of raising kids. Those details were better left to nannies and, significantly, to Hep. Her activism was Kit's way out—her lifeline—though she understood such freedom carried conditions. "My father was fine with my mother working outside the house," their daughter Peg Hepburn Perry observed, "though he told her in no uncertain terms, 'You must never make more money than I do.' He thought it would hurt his practice to have a wife more successful than he was."

Kit showed little resentment of her husband's authority. Rather, she spent her life, if the tales recorded by her friends, her sister, and her children are to be believed, deeply in love with him, a model of wifely devotion that her daughter Katharine always admired. When, as a lovestruck girl, Kit had first brought the young Tom Hepburn home to meet her family, the affluent, influential Houghtons had considered him beneath her. The brash young medical student, two years Kit's junior, seemed to offer little but good looks and driving ambition—the very qualities that had, in fact, won Kit's heart.

For his part, Hep found Kit's aristocratic features and broad shoulders equally irresistible, but it was her heritage that commanded his interest. The Houghtons were an old upstate New York family, the very sort of people Hep, as a son of the South, had both resented and envied all his life. To possess Kit was to possess everything he was not. Indeed, theirs would be a passionate union. Ardent kisses between mother and father were not unfamiliar to the Hepburn children, nor was the sight of their naked bodies. Hep would sit stark naked reading the Sunday paper while Kit sunbathed in the nude. Never did any of their offspring have to wonder where babies came from, not when the sounds from their parents' room were unabashedly explained as the joyous expressions of lovemaking.

Yet as much as she loved her husband, what really ensured the success of the Hepburn marriage was Kit's escape hatch, her ability—so rare for women of her generation—to get out of the house and find her own calling. And if Kit Hepburn routinely deferred to her husband at home, in the real world she charted her own course, even if it meant treading where few "proper ladies" had ever gone before.

On a raw, wet afternoon in April, her cloak drawn tightly around her, Kit Hepburn sloshed through the muddy banks of the Connecticut River, taking photographs of the decaying tenements that lined the city's east side. How her opinion of Hartford had changed. When she and Hep had first moved there, the city had seemed stately and manicured. But the more Kit investigated, the more she discovered. On this spring afternoon, after making her way inside one decrepit building, she spied a naked child fishing a dead rat out of a toilet. Lifting her heavy box camera to her eyes, she snapped a photograph, then hurried to the police department—which, as she later pointed out, was just a block away.

The police considered her a busybody, but Kit Hepburn was a woman on fire. In 1908, when Kathy was just a few months old, Mrs. Hepburn's advocacy for women's rights was kindled. Although much of Kit's crusading has been chronicled before, the implications of her work have been surprisingly overlooked. In many ways, Kit's activism was an outgrowth of her husband's battle against venereal disease. When Hartford's "white slave" traffic was exposed, Kit made cleaning up the city's east side her personal mission. The fact that the brothels stood in the shadow of the police station and on land owned by the Catholic Church infuriated her. How long had the powers-that-be allowed this to go on?

On the prostitution issue, Kit cut her political teeth. Almost a century later, her very personal outrage still rings out from the accounts she left behind. Disrupting rallies for Hartford City Council candidates, shouting at the top of her lungs, Kit Hepburn demanded to know if the gentlemen "would continue the public brothel in the midst of the poorer residential section and give public sanction to the dens of disease." The cigar-chewing politicians booed her roundly before hustling her out of the room.

Undeterred, Kit would traipse down to the east side, Jo Bennett at her side, her bulky box camera slung around her neck. Snapping dozens of photographs of the painted girls and skulking johns and the children trapped in their midst, Kit had them published in local newspapers. But the reaction of the good citizens of Hartford was not what she expected. "It was not the conditions that shocked them, strange to say," she told an audience two years later, "but the fact that we were determined to *speak* of these conditions."

Such opposition only made her more determined. Monitoring the 1911 trial of a government agent accused of taking a kickback from the prostitution trade, Kit found herself the only woman in the courtroom. For her, the real culprit was the prosecution witness Pasquale "Patsie" Fusco, a sly, sneering thirty-seven-year-old Italian immigrant believed to have transported more than a hundred girls over the New York border. Fusco's "resorts" had been raided several times, but it was not until the end of the trial that he was arrested himself, in large part due to the noise being made by Hartford women like Kit Hepburn and Jo Bennett.

While she was no doubt concerned about the "dens of disease," Kit's true motivation was the plight of the prostitutes themselves—girls barely out of their teens like "Birdie" Brannigan, whom Fusco kept at his house on Talcott Street, and Margaret Raynis, lured from a broken home on Long Island with the promise of making big money in Hartford. "There was always an unwed mother or two living in the attic of our house," Katharine Hepburn would remember for her friend James Prideaux. Kit would offer them shelter, and Hep would deliver their babies. This passion for women's lives united all of Kit's close friends, from Jo Bennett to college pal Bertha Rembaugh, a lawyer living in New York, who served as treasurer of the Women's Society for the Prevention of Crime.

Moving into suffrage work was the logical next step in Kit's concern for the welfare of women. As vice president of the Connecticut Woman Suffrage Association, she hoisted her skirts and climbed atop platforms to speak to sparsely attended assemblies around Hartford, such as the gathering arranged by the family's cook, Ida Wood, at her largely Negro church. Quivery at first, Kit's voice grew more confident with every oration. Accompanied by her sister Edith Hooker and Jo Bennett, Mrs. Hepburn soon began venturing farther afield. In September 1910, all three women were among the leading strategists at the National Woman Suffrage Association's planning meeting in New York. With the patronizing attitude that passed for objectivity in those days, the *Times* wrote that the women planned to "divide into districts and go after recruits, just like real politicians."

Kit Hepburn was as real a politician as ever lived. Just a small sample of old clippings reveals her range. Sidelined only by her successive pregnancies (and then only as long as she had to), she found herself riding the rails up and down the Eastern Seaboard. In January 1911, she addressed the Maryland State House. In December 1913 (by now president of the CWSA), she led a delegation to Washington to meet with President Woodrow Wilson. In October 1915, she debated suffrage with the prominent "Anti" Lucy Price at Carnegie Hall in New York. (In the audience, firmly on the "Pro" side and unaware of their quirky overlapping destinies, was Mrs. A. Barton Hepburn.) In November 1917, she opened the convention of the National Woman's Party in Philadelphia, standing beside delegates in the prison uniforms they'd worn while in jail for picketing the White House.

During these years, the intensity of the suffrage campaign had ratcheted up dramatically, with many activists being arrested, manhandled, and threatened. Jo Bennett, thrown into jail, found her hunger strike savagely subverted by authorities who force-fed her through a tube down her throat. Kit herself knew what it was like to be pelted with tomatoes, to have the vilest names hurled at her as she marched through the streets. She'd bring this intensity home with her, sharing the horrific details but rarely the emotions that came with them, preferring to keep these to herself in long, quiet meditations in her room.

Through it all, she became a savvy political strategist. Nowhere is this more evident than in her handling of the case of Bessie Wakefield, a Connecticut woman accused of murdering her husband in June 1913. Despite her obvious guilt, Wakefield, just twenty-four years old and the mother of three small children, commanded a strong base of public sympathy. In the popular press, "mother" trumped "murderess." When Wakefield's trial began in New Haven in late October, many were horrified to think "poor little Bessie," as the tabloids called her, might be put to death; but that was precisely the sentence handed down after she was found guilty on November 4. Large crowds gathered outside the governor's office in Hartford to chant for clemency; nearly twenty-five thousand letters and telegrams, delivered in bulging sacks the next day, demanded the same thing.

That behind such an outpouring was a persistent, prevailing sexism was not lost on Connecticut suffrage leaders. In the public mind, women deserved more sympathy than men because they were, after all, the weaker sex. Two decades earlier in neighboring Massachusetts, Lizzie Borden had been found not guilty of her parents' murders in large part because jurors simply could not conceive of a woman committing such horrible crimes. If suffrage leaders were to rally to Wakefield's side now, they would be undermining their own cause, appearing to espouse "special treatment" for women, a traditionally "Anti" position.

Indeed, immediately after the sentence, Jo Bennett told the press that, although she personally opposed capital punishment, "when a man and a woman are both found equally guilty of murder, no distinction should be made." Elizabeth Bacon of the Hartford Equal Rights Club agreed: "As long as the present law exists, both sexes should suffer equally."

But Kit's reading of the public pulse was very different. For two days she watched as Connecticut society women became politicized for the first time in their lives. They were banging out letters on their typewriters and trooping downtown to join the throngs calling for clemency. Kit was inspired to try another tack. Elbowing her way to the front of the crowd, she stepped up onto a soapbox and announced the Connecticut Woman Suffrage Association would lead the effort to prevent Wakefield from hanging. "It is my contention," Kit's voice rang out, "that no woman should pay the death penalty when women are barred from participation in the lawmaking functions. No woman should be hanged unless women concur, equally with men, in the legal operations whereby such a situation was brought about."

It was a brilliant strategy, capitalizing on public sentiment and harnessing it for the suffragists' side. From that point on, movement leaders stayed on message. A few days later, the prominent New York suffragist Alva Vanderbilt Belmont offered the same opinion as Kit: *Bessie Wakefield should not hang.* That Emmeline Pankhurst was staying with the Hepburns in Hartford around this time is significant: the Wakefield case, by now making headlines all across the country, was lassoed into service for the national suffrage movement. When, in fact, pressure from women's groups led to a second trial for "poor little Bessie"—in which she was given a life sentence instead of death—Kit's farsighted political instincts were validated. By her own account, the Wakefield case had done more to rally women to the side of the suffragists than anything else before.

Sitting at the table while her mother hashed out strategy with Pankhurst was six-year-old Kathy. She probably understood little more than the fact that a woman might hang, but she would clearly absorb her mother's canny instincts for gauging what the public wanted. The Wakefield case would be parlor talk in the Hepburn house for years. Surely Kathy came to see her mother's brilliance in the matter. Later, she'd play a lawyer defending a woman very similar to Bessie Wakefield in *Adam's Rib*, a part written especially for her by Garson Kanin. In the ways of shaping personal image and public sentiment, Kathy could have had no better teacher than Kit Houghton Hepburn.

Take a look at Kit now, frozen in time in old photographs, and see the truth of that statement. At a time when most suffragists were considered dried-up old prunes, Kit dazzled with her pastel-colored dresses and fashionable wide-brimmed hats. She was young, vibrant, and (not incidentally) extremely fertile, the mother of all those bright, attractive children. This was the face the suffrage movement liked to put forward. Sympathy for their position would not be won by stiff-backed, unsmiling old maids.

It's significant, too, that, unlike most of her peers, Kit was nearly always identified in the press as an adjunct of her husband: "Mrs. Thomas N. Hepburn." It was easier, after all, to sway men to the suffragists' side if the woman doing the swaying was properly deferential. But Kit's deference wasn't duplicitous; it was how she really lived. If by using her husband's name she could advance the cause, all the better; but she would never have *not* considered using Hep's name.

Consider this story. After passage of the Nineteenth Amendment in 1920, when Kit's long battle to secure a woman's right to vote was finally won, several Connecticut politicos asked her to run for the Senate. She was thrilled. But when she rushed into her husband's study to give him the news, Hep lifted one eyebrow over his newspaper and replied calmly, "Well, fine, Kit. When do we get our divorce?" Mrs. Hepburn declined the offer.

That, too, became a lesson for her daughter. Women might take their place at the table, but only after they'd set it for men.

JIMMY WAS HER NAME

On the screen, a jagged, overexposed home movie flickers into view. The title might have been *Kathy Hepburn Versus the Tree*. Kicking, scratching, fighting, she takes hold of the spindly bare branches, madly determined to climb to the top. Three times she attempts to encircle the trunk with her legs, swinging out wildly like a cat. Though she is wearing a skirt, she seems blithely unconcerned about exposing her underwear, making the exhibition all the more humorous for those gathered to watch. But it is a losing battle; the tree is simply too slender to support the teenage girl's weight. It bends over, twisting this way and that, frustrating any attempts to gain leverage. Even as she is flung upward like a rag doll, her feet dangling in the air, Kathy refuses to surrender her branch. Finally, nearly snapping from the effort, the tree delivers her back to the ground, and the grainy little clip fades to black.

Our earliest image of Katharine Hepburn is a rare melding of Kathy and Kate, a scrawny ten-year-old skinhead grinning impishly into the camera. "Jimmy was my name, if you want to know," she said, years later. Being a girl was "a torment," she insisted, so she dodged the experience altogether. She shaved her head, dressed in boy's clothes, and rechristened herself Jimmy. "I could stand on my hands," Hepburn said. "I could turn handsprings. I could do a flying somersault off Dad's shoulders." Seventy years later, Jimmy's bravado could still be heard through Kate's voice.

It's impossible not to love Jimmy, even if he was a bit of a show-off, especially in front of pretty girls. Under the sharp blue skies of the family's summer house at Fenwick, Connecticut, Jimmy would pose, flexing sinewy muscles for the camera. On the pier with Ali Barbour, Jimmy practiced his dives for a local contest. All Ali could manage was a "prayer dive," kneeling at the end of the pier and falling into the water. "Pathetic," Jimmy muttered, and prepared to show her how things were done—with a half-gainer.

Rubbing hands together, Jimmy took off on a running start down the old wooden pier. High over the water the child jumped, one leg extended with back arched and pointed toes, twisting that skinny little body down into a frontal dive into the water. "Brilliant!" Jimmy shouted, emerging from the waves yards away.

Jimmy was never modest. Jimmy was irrepressible. With Florence Miel, the pretty daughter of the Trinity Church pastor, he'd cut up in class and heckle the teacher. But these efforts to impress cost Jimmy a reprimand from Dr. and Mrs. Hepburn, along with the humiliating command to bring the teacher a geranium as penance. The potted plant sat on the teacher's desk for weeks, teaching Jimmy a lesson: "If you sin, you pay"—a bromide recalled later in Hollywood, Kate Hepburn would tell us, where geraniums were everywhere and sin abounded.

Jimmy's best friends, however, weren't dainty little girls but Fenwick's crusty old fishermen. Bill Ingham was "the first man I ever loved"—or so Garson Kanin had Kate aver. She was six years old, maybe seven, possibly eight; the chronicles differ on that fact and many others. Barbara Leaming, the author of a 1995 Hepburn biography, called the fisherman Frank: "Tall, erect, raw-boned [in] leather hipboots." Frank, or Bill, or somebody by the name of Ingham apparently saved the young Kathy Hepburn and her brother Tommy when they "did something stupid" in the waters of Long Island Sound. According to the stories usually told, Kathy repaid the Inghams by fervently rallying her fellow Fenwickians to their side when a group of wealthy landowners tried to displace the family's fish house on the jetty. "I'm going to change the world," Leaming actually has the six-year-old shouting as she runs along the beach in her campaign to save the Inghams.

Once more, a reality check. The story originates with Hepburn, who told it to Lupton Wilkinson for his *Saturday Evening Post* article. It was then picked up by nearly all of her biographers. First, Kanin turned it into an example of one of Hepburn's early crushes. Christopher Andersen magnified the tale's drama so it became a daring rescue at sea. Leaming took the narrative a step farther still, having Kathy emerge from it as a prepubescent crusader, already conscious of a manifest destiny to change the world.

Here are the facts: there was no Bill Ingham, at least not by the time Kathy Hepburn was old enough to swim. And Frank Ingham was a dairy farmer, not a fisherman. So much for the leather hipboots. Surely, however, under these layers of myth exists a nugget of truth: the Inghams, like many along the coast, regularly fished from the pier, and Jimmy no doubt found a place among them, watching the fisherfolk haul in their catches and fillet majestic bluefin tuna. Indeed, Katharine Hepburn's loyalty to the Inghams (who later went into the ice business) would be recalled by the old-timers of Fenwick: for years she wouldn't have a refrigerator, insisting on keeping her old icebox.

Fenwick was the most enduring backdrop in Hepburn's life. "Now it's summer and we go to Fenwick," Kate warbled in her memoir, *Me.* "Paradise," she called their summer retreat. "Heaven." In 1912, the Hepburns bought their three-story shingled summer cottage. The floorboards creaked, the windows rattled, and the place was often cold and damp. Up in the expansive, drafty attic the children made their bedrooms, and it was not for many years that electricity or indoor plumbing was installed. Until then, the family made do with cold ceramic chamberpots and a smelly outhouse out back. No matter the dinginess of the house, however, salty sea breezes blew in from the Sound from every window, and the front porch, where Kit so often nodded peacefully off to sleep, afforded unobstructed views of two weather-beaten lighthouses standing sentinel at the marshy mouth of the Connecticut River.

The seashore seemed to encourage Dr. Hepburn's competitive spirit. At Fenwick he bought Tommy a fourteen-foot-long "sneakbox" boat so he could compete in the races held at nearby South Cove. Hep became a man obsessed. His sons—first Tommy, then Dick and Bob—were put up against the sons of his Fenwick neighbors, all of whom hailed from Hartford's upper-crust, old-money families like the Barbours, Posts, and Brainards. These Brahmins stirred resentment within Hep. Waxing Tommy's sneakbox, he could be heard muttering that unlike his brother-in-law Don Hooker (who'd helped put up the cash for the Fenwick house), *he* still had to work for a living.

The races at South Cove were Hep's chance to even the score. In 1915, he determined that his son, his namesake, would defeat those other men's sons—or overturn his slippery sneakbox in the process. Standing on the pier as Tommy sliced through the water, Hep shouted so loudly that family members recalled his face turning red and the veins popping out in his neck. When Tommy came in second, his father pushed his way down the sun-washed pier and bawled him out in front of everyone. When Tommy won, however, Dr. Hepburn simply clapped the boy on the back. There was never any praise. "It would just go to his head," Hep argued. "That's how you spoil a child."

"A pompous egotist," Dick Hepburn would later call his father, but Tommy never grumbled. What the boy wanted most was to please his dad, and from the outside, it would appear he was extremely successful in that endeavor. So often did Tommy Hepburn win contests—sailing, running, diving, jumping—that officials had to limit the number of ribbons a boy could earn. Hep trained Tommy hard, from ice-cold baths first thing in the morning to sprints along the back path timed with a stopwatch. When Tommy entered the Kingswood School (a private boy's academy in West Hartford), he ran track, swam, golfed, played tennis, and joined the wrestling squad—and he won at all of them. But never a word from his father-coach about the string of ribbons and medals that accumulated over the boy's bed.

In many ways, Dr. Thomas Hepburn was no different from most upper-class, white, Anglo-Saxon, Protestant men of his generation. Too much praise was considered unseemly, possibly even damaging to the child's psyche. No doubt Hep loved his children; the warmhearted letters he wrote them throughout his life attest to that. And he wasn't always so serious or driven. A delightful home movie taken when Kathy was a teenager shows Hep performing a spirited jig around the Christmas tree, then grabbing Kit and waltzing robustly around the room. He had a sharp, engaging sense of humor. He was a terrific storyteller who could hold his children, and later his grandchildren, enthralled for hours.

But none of the Hepburn offspring could ever remember him saying that they'd made him proud. He demanded the moon and never seemed satisfied even when it was delivered. Once his daughter Marion asked him why that was. "I expect you to do well," he replied. "That's the norm." His inability to praise was something his children—with the exception of his oldest daughter—would remark on in their later years. "The really sad thing," Marion wrote, "is that he was a fantastically talented and gifted and charming man."

Kit, when she was around, did her best to compensate for her husband's aloofness. She'd gush over the children's accomplishments in athletics or at school. When she saw their downcast expressions when their father failed to do the same, Kit took them aside to gently explain, "Daddy just can't express that kind of thing."

But anger—he could express anger. "His was like the thunderous voice of God," remembered Bob Hepburn. When Dr. Thomas Hepburn was angry, the whole house knew it. As they entered their teens, what continued to motivate the Hepburn children's fierce desire to please was the plain and simple emotion of *fear*. Fear of their father's disapproval, of the sting of his hand. He was the ultimate authority in their lives, in effect their god, especially since, despite the quivering disapproval of Grandfather Sewell Hepburn, the children were raised without any religious faith. The Word began and ended with Hep.

Standing on the sidelines, Jimmy Hepburn stewed, unable to understand being left out of his brother's games. There Hep was, coaching Tommy to run faster, clocking him, shouting after him, keeping his full and undivided attention on his eldest son. But Jimmy was ignored.

It wasn't fair. Hadn't Jimmy already proven himself on the trapeze wire rigged across their gravel walkway? It was Jimmy, not Tommy, who'd learned to swing by the knees—and how Hep had cheered for his little daredevil then, his "Redtop." How Jimmy had beamed under Dr. Hepburn's approval. "I could outdive, outswim, outrun most of the boys around me, and that included my brothers," Katharine Hepburn would boast years later. To grab a moment in the spotlight away from Tommy was a terrific coup. "Look at me, look at me!" it seemed the young Kathy Hepburn was forever crying.

"Go ahead then," her father would say with some exasperation, turning to look over his shoulder at her. "Show me what you can do."

So Kathy flipped; she tumbled; she ran around the block. When someone dared suggest that, as a girl, she couldn't possibly be as tough as her brother, she hunched up her shoulders, bent her head forward, and ran smack into a tree like a battering ram. "You see how tough I am!" she crowed—a favorite story of hers for the rest of her life.

In many ways Katharine Hepburn spent her entire life crying, "Look at me!" As a girl, she relished being the center of attention at her birthday parties and was frustrated when her mother wouldn't let her win at all the games. Later, as a star, she took secret delight at making so many magazine covers. "Look at me!" one friend remembered her shouting, lifting up a magazine. She'd claim she didn't know where she got this need to "display" herself, pleading an essential shyness, which was indeed part of her makeup. But whereas she could be quiet and reserved in large groups, the need to show off and draw attention existed side by side with her shyness. It was there from the beginning, and it would always drive her.

Her sister Marion's son, Jack Grant, would write that the Hepburn siblings grew up in a "self-dramatizing" atmosphere. Competition was a way of life. "Each family member was expected to have a . . . purpose of great moment," Grant said, "and without exactly bragging, to show this off unreservedly. . . . All the children grew up with a sense of life as theatre."

Bob Hepburn agreed. "To get my father's attention wasn't easy," he said. "You had to be very, very good." And so Kathy was, competing against an idolized older brother who was also very, very good—not to mention four younger upstarts always nipping at her heels.

"She just didn't think of herself as a girl," said Bob—and in that simple observation lies the key to understanding the entirety of Katharine Hepburn's life. Boys—and boys' activities and achievements—were what Hep prized. Kathy held on to a certain maleness almost as a birthright. Boys were free, in the words of the historian Lillian Faderman, "to range widely through life and escape the overdetermined narrowness of a female's existence." Such overdetermination was precisely what the young Kathy Hepburn chafed against, and what imagining herself as Jimmy allowed her to escape.

Yet while his hair would grow out and his name would be abandoned, Jimmy never truly went away. In her heart, Kate remained Jimmy, as she admitted in the autobiographical screenplay she wrote toward the end of her life. Even after the outward manifestations of Jimmy disappeared, the young Kathy Hepburn kept his spirit alive—in dungarees, in chaps, in well-pressed white slacks. She played tennis. She rode horseback astride, instead of that silly, girly sidesaddle. Golf she had learned at the age of five, and by her teens she was competing in state championships.

Her tomboyishness would always have great appeal for the public, even if it would prove a bit troublesome to studio image makers in the 1930s. Many girls had, after all, rebelled against dress codes of ribbons and skirts and the prohibitions that kept them away from the games of boys. They understood the kind of early crushes that Hepburn admitted having on Miss Catherine Watson, her twenty-one-year-old gym teacher at the Oxford School, the girls' companion to Tommy's Kingswood. "Why—why Cathy Watson!" Hepburn declared. "[She had] a soft and gentle face, soft sandy hair—it was long and she did it in a knot and velvet ribbon she wore around her head. . . . I thought about her and watched her and waited for her and brought her presents. Just love it was—first crush."

"Kate was never a conventional girl," remembered Hepburn's friend Jean Poindexter, with whom she attended the Oxford School. "She was never interested in dresses or pretty things. She always wanted to play with the boys. I was like that, too, but I got over it. She never did."

The tomboy is a vital, defining element in the persona of Kate, lifted directly from her own life and layered onto her original Hollywood image with care and precision. Her most successful early film was *Little Women*, directed by her friend George Cukor, who knew Hepburn's boyish side quite well. Jo March, the quintessential tomboy of American literature, is Jimmy Hepburn, forever climbing down trellises and swinging from tree branches. "She *was* Jo," said her brother Bob, "she really was." When Jo is told that she will be a proper young lady by wearing her hair up, she retorts, "No, I'm not, and if turning up my hair makes me so, I'll wear it down till I'm a hundred."

In *Little Women*, delicate, dainty Joan Bennett stands in for delicate, dainty Ali Barbour or Florence Miel. When sister Meg asks Jo when she will stop her "childish, romping ways," Jo replies, "Not until I'm old and stiff and have to use a crutch." But even when she was old and stiff, Kate Hepburn was still riding a boy's bike.

There is a reason *Little Women* would be such a hit and other, frillier pictures—*The Little Minister, Quality Street, A Woman Rebels*—would be flops. It's because *Little Women* was real and the others were fakes. Katharine Hepburn was playing herself, and it showed.

Like Jo March, the young Kathy Hepburn was irrepressible—especially paired with Ali Barbour, the Beauty to her Beast. Ali, short for Alice, was a doe-eyed beauty whose father, Colonel Lucius Barbour, served as commander of the governor's foot guard. The Barbour family, like most of Hartford's elite, owned a house at Fenwick, not far from the Hepburns'. Cheered on by her friend (Ali "had nerve to burn," Hepburn would remember), Kathy concocted a game of sneaking into the empty summer homes. The girls snooped around, pulling open drawers, lolling about on the divans.

It was all good-natured fun—until Ali convinced Kathy to let Bob Post tag along. Bob Post, with his cowlick and crooked smile, hailed from one of Connecticut's oldest and wealthiest families. Ali had a crush on him, and so Kathy had tolerated his presence—until the boy persuaded them to vandalize one place with talcum powder. Caught and disgraced, Kath "no longer had any use for Bob Post."

But for many of the parents in the exclusive neighborhood, it was Kathy Hepburn they had no use for. Like her parents, she was a troublemaker. Once again Kathy had run into the wall of disapproval that kept the Hepburns shunned in some quarters. It left her unsure of herself, unless she could act out like Jimmy.

As Kathy entered her teens, her most frequent companion remained her brother Tommy. Far from resenting him for receiving the lion's share of their father's regard, Kathy *adored* him, precisely because he gave her what she so craved: attention. From her parents, she had to fight for it, but with her brother, there was never that problem. He doted on Kathy, and she, in turn, bolstered him through his difficult times. Despite the blue ribbons and good grades, Tommy was still nervous at school, easily distracted; there were often days, even weeks, when the boy was too anxious, too easily brought to tears, to attend classes. No one could ever quite pin down what his anxiety was. "Whatever it was," Kate would remember, "he simply could not cope."

Yet while his parents were at a loss as to the best way to respond, his adoring sister stepped in to offer simple support and acceptance. Kathy's caretaking inspired Tommy's devotion. "You're my best girl," Tommy always insisted.

One story, probably apocryphal, has at least the ring of emotional truth. In it, Kathy attends her first school dance and finds herself ignored by the children of Hartford's elite (shades of *Alice Adams*). But stalwart Tommy stands by her all night. (In one version, he even punches a boy who calls Kathy "goofy.") The anecdote crystallizes the nature of their relationship. She boosted him; he was devoted to her. Such symbiosis would imprint all of Katharine Hepburn's significant relationships with men.

Within the pressurized atmosphere of the Hepburn household, Kathy and Tommy had found their means of survival. Many were the times when Kit, coming home from a week of crusading, would marvel at the bond between her two eldest children. Where, she asked, did Tommy end and Kathy begin?

But one nagging difference remained between them: anatomy. For all her identification with her brother, Kathy was still different. He was a boy, after all, and boys could go places that girls could not. Their parents, teachers, sometimes even Tommy himself would tell Kathy she needed to wait behind. Sitting at the window of their house on Hawthorn Street, Kathy watched resentfully as Tommy trooped off with his Kingswood chum Jimmy Soby, their fishing poles or ice skates slung over their shoulders. How Kathy longed to join them in their adventures, like walking across the narrow rim of the roof of the Mark Twain house. In fact, her adoption of the name "Jimmy" may have been Kathy's way of "becoming" Jimmy Soby, the boy whose place she often found herself envying.

"There was something very different about her," said Jean Poindexter. "[It was] as if she just didn't consider herself one of us. She'd look at her girlfriends

as if she didn't understand them, as if they were speaking a different lan-
guage."

At times her temper seemed modeled after her father's, and she was
known to occasionally treat her friends as Dr. Hepburn did his children. "We
were playing golf at the Hartford Golf Club," Poindexter remembered. Both
girls were hotheaded, and their games often got "quite lively." But Kathy,
Poindexter insisted, always had the last word. After missing an easy putt, the
twelve-year-old Kathy cursed like a sailor and threw her putter in frustration, stalking off the grounds. "It just missed me," Poindexter recalled. "The
putter landed in the ground handle-first."

In 1917, before Kathy had even turned ten, the family left the fabled house
on Hawthorn Street. Hep was determined to move his family into a house
that he owned, and so he purchased an indifferent Victorian at 352 Laurel
Street a few blocks away. Clearing the books out of the study and the philo-
dendrons from the solarium, the family loaded up a truck and moved to
what Kit always referred to as "that unimaginative house." It was here that
Kathy spent the bulk of her youth.

But such a simple abode could have no place in the legend. It offered no
gables, no gingerbread molding, no motto engraved over the mantel exhorting them to listen to the song of life. Accordingly, Hawthorn Street, with its
romantic, historical traditions, would be forever enshrined as Kathy's childhood home.

"Have you seen the Mark Twain house, the Harriet Beecher Stowe
house?" Hepburn asked in the 1988 documentary *They Called Me Kathy*.
"The windows bathed in the sun. Cozy places to sit, full of ideas for living and
for enjoying. And although it's a generation before, it's the same atmosphere
that I was brought up in." Twain, Stowe, Hepburn. She seemed to like the association.

But for the four youngest children, their childhood home was that
"unimaginative" house on Laurel Street—providing one more distinction
between them and Tommy and Kathy. "It was Dad, Mother, Tom and me,"
Hepburn would say. "Then there were the rest of the children."

Within the Hepburn household, there would always be the sense of two
families. The four years between Kathy and Dick were enough of a chasm to
split the children into two distinct groups. Tommy and Kathy remembered
Hawthorn Street. They remembered their father before he became successful, when there weren't so many servants in the house. It gave them a special,
even favored position with their parents.

Kit Hepburn seems to have been conscious of this split and would do her best to try to bridge it. Years later, when Dick Hepburn wrote a play about Katharine's romance with Howard Hughes, his mother discreetly offered her son support and encouragement, even as Hep raged at the young man for trying to ruin his sister's life. Bob Hepburn recalled his mother with far more sympathy than he did his father, and his anecdotes about her suggest that Kit was a more frequent presence in the lives of her younger children than she was for Tommy and Kathy. Indeed, by the time Bob, Marion, and Peggy were in school, the vote for women had been won, and Kit's next cause, birth control, didn't really get going for several years.

In truth, the special relationship that Kathy enjoyed with her parents was heavily weighted toward her father. Nearly all of the personal anecdotes about her childhood involve Hep. Both she and Tommy were shaped far more by their father than they were by their mother. The bulk of their time was spent with Hep, playing his games and following his lead. Right from the start, Kathy was unmistakably her father's daughter. When she was born, her mother had held her up to the light to see the color of her hair. Convinced that she was a redtop, Kit pronounced Kathy then and there a Hepburn.

Katharine Hepburn would live in awe of both her parents, but it was her father whom she truly understood. She shared his desire to win, to triumph, to prove his worth. It wasn't just his anger on the golf course she modeled. From Hep she inherited the undeniable narcissism that propelled her life, the need to always come out on top, to be first, to be best. Her mother, meanwhile, so intense and dedicated, never athletic or competitive, seemed a creature apart from herself. Kit was an angel, a saint, a holy warrior whose good works Kathy could admire from afar but never fully comprehend.

Indeed, Kit's lifetime commitment to fighting for the welfare of other women was a cause her daughter could never truly join. Many are the childhood stories of Kathy romping through the fields with her father, but when Katharine Hepburn would remember her mother, she was usually in the background, or missing entirely. There are precious few anecdotes of Kit and Kathy alone. It would appear Kit never quite understood this bundle of contradictions she had brought into the world, and her daughter, though admiring, could never fully relate to Kit either. Indeed, like her father, Katharine Hepburn would prove to be intellectually but not emotionally committed to the idea of equality between the sexes. "That wasn't her battle," said one friend, a woman. "At least she didn't see it as such."

Ironically, what she took from her mother was not Kit's passion but her passivity. Growing up in the Hepburn household, Kathy came to believe that final authority always rested with the male. Absent a man—which is how she would, in fact, spend most of her life—a woman was fully capable of making her own decisions. She never doubted that. But when a man was involved, the natural order was to defer to him.

No matter that she was the daughter of a suffrage crusader, Katharine Hepburn would never feel empathy toward other women as being part of an oppressed group or shared movement. Like Hep, she considered the issue of women's rights not as a calling for herself but as something for other people, something for "girls"—and "girl" was never a defining aspect of Kathy's identity, not when she was competing with Tommy in relay races and diving contests, constantly waving her hands and shouting to her father, "Look at me! Look at me!" She didn't grow up to be her mother's kind of woman. Rather, Katharine Hepburn grew up to be her father's kind of man.

SOME PEOPLE ARE NEW YORK

S tepping off the train onto the platform at Grand Central Station in June 1919, twelve-year-old Kathy Hepburn was ready to go. She loved her visits to the city. The main concourse was still only a few years old at the time, and its shimmering blue-green ceiling, depicting the constellations of the nighttime sky, routinely took visitors' breaths away. But Kathy was already racing her brother Tom past the towering four-sided clock, eager to step outside onto the street, where the new Hotel Biltmore on Madison Avenue rose an imposing twenty stories.

The legend of Hepburn has always stressed the significance and influence of Hartford and Fenwick on our developing heroine. "Some people," Kate once declared, "are New York or London or—God help them—Los Angeles. I am Hartford." Plain, simple, unpretentious—that's what she was trying to get across. But in truth she was New York almost as much as she was Hartford. Ultimately, she'd live in Manhattan for more than seventy years, but her experience of the city dated back even earlier than that. She may have wanted us to think, especially as she grew older, that she was unaffected Hartford, but sophisticated New York was there, too, almost from the very beginning.

With an easy familiarity, she hustled through the crowds beside her mother and brother as they headed toward Times Square. There, the great Broadway theaters dazzled her: the neo-Georgian Belasco, the baroque Lyceum, the beaux arts Globe, the terra-cotta Plymouth, the venerable old Empire with its Pompeiian red and gold interior. On the marquees she might have glimpsed the names of Billie Burke, Fay Bainter, Alla Nazimova, or John Barrymore—all actors with whom she'd someday work. Occasionally Kit would take the children to see a show, but in truth, Mrs. Hepburn had little use for the theater and all that make-believe. Usually their destination in Times Square was far more utilitarian: the subway.

Lifting her long skirt, Kathy hurried down the subway stairs, often—she would specifically remember—crinkling up her nose at the smell of exhaust. She never did learn to abide that smell, but how she loved the rush of the underground train, the speed with which it could whisk her from one part of the city to another. She knew exactly how much a subway ticket cost—tokens and turnstiles were still a few years in the future—and she could name all the stops between Times Square and Christopher Street, where they invariably got off.

Climbing the steps back into the New York morning, Kathy would gaze around her at the colorful sights of Greenwich Village—three hours and a world away from Hartford. Then in its heyday as the capital of American bohemia, the Village wore its eccentricity as a badge of honor. "One should be surprised at nothing," an observer remarked at the time, for along those narrow, crooked streets south of Fourteenth walked artists, poets, political radicals, and the ubiquitous "short-haired women and long-haired men," to use a phrase of the day. The Village was a place, according to a contemporary report in the *New York Times*, where "men and women and eccentrics . . . conform not to the rules that harass Murray Hill or Park Avenue." A flyer advertising one of the Village's infamous balls, circa 1918, bore an illustration of several couples dancing, some same-sex: "Come all ye Revelers, when you like, with whom you like! Wear what you like! Unconventional? Oh, to be sure!"

Kit brought the children to the Village so that they could visit their two "aunts," college friends of Kit's, Bertha Rembaugh and Mary Towle. Both were lawyers, partners in life as well as in their groundbreaking practice. At Bryn Mawr, Towle had been Kit's best friend, and she continued to be a frequent visitor to the Hepburn household, despite the fact that Hep seems not to have liked her very much. Sitting opposite Towle at the table, he'd tease her with increasingly graphic "sex talk" until, trailed by gales of laughter, poor Auntie would excuse herself, blushing, from the room.

To Hep, there was something comical about these serious and easily ruf-fled aunts. But Kathy held a different view. She could not have helped but notice that, without benefit of husbands, Towle and Rembaugh had carved out impressive places for themselves in the big city and the world. In 1919, Aunt Bertha had been the first woman to run for a municipal court judge-ship in New York. Hers was a historic campaign that, although unsuccessful, won an endorsement from the *Times*. Much was made of Rembaugh's famil-iar presence at night court, where she defended prostitutes without pay. Small and slender in her man's suit and tie and slicked-back hair, Aunt Bertha cut a poised, dignified figure in court. But she was never happier than when she could pull on her drawstring pants and head out to sea in her cat-boat. Years on the water had left her skin brown and leathery and imbued her with a certain "tang," as one reporter called it, "like that of the salt spray she enjoys, thoroughly alive."

Opposite this imposing partner, Mary Towle held her own. She was tall and dithery, but her outward flutter belied a sharp, probing intelligence. In 1921, she would become the first woman named as an assistant U.S. attorney east of the Mississippi. When this historic appointment brought headlines, U.S. Attorney William Hayward, the man who'd appointed her, told re-porters that Mary Towle was "a real lawyer and a real person. . . . I expect her to do a regular lawyer's work." (Years later, Hayward's son Leland would be Katharine Hepburn's agent.)

Visiting her aunts' small, cozy eighteenth-century house on Waverly Place, Kathy found herself within a fellowship abuzz with political and artistic activity. At any given time, several like-minded women shared living quarters with Towle and Rembaugh. In one corner, Rachel Bernstein, a private-school teacher, might be playing the piano; her sister, the artist Eva Bernstein, might be painting flowers at an easel by the window. Rushing past them would be the lawyer Helen Barnes, waving a list of city voters pledged to support Rembaugh's run for the judgeship. At various times, the household consisted of other women as well, including two other teachers, Louise Morrison and Mary Blake, as well as Anna Lessing, a Czech-born Socialist hired as a maid. She took to educating her employers by standing beside the ancient redbrick fireplace and reading aloud passages from *Das Kapital*.

Petted and fussed over within this collective of unofficial, unmarried "aunts," Kathy got a glimpse of an alternative, woman-centered domestic world. In Hep's house, which was, after all, a man's house, Auntie Towle might find herself teased and rattled. But within her own sphere she was relaxed, assured, authoritative, and resolute. It's clear that Kit Hepburn wanted her children, of both sexes, exposed to this feminist style of life.

But the visits to Auntie Towle and Aunt Bertha weren't just social calls. As young as six years old, Kathy would hold tight to her mother's hand as they hurried through Sheridan Square to attend luncheon meetings of Heterodoxy, the radical feminist organization. In these years, Heterodoxy met at Polly's Restaurant on MacDougal Street, nestled among some of the most insurrectionist addresses in the city. On one side stood the rebellious Provincetown Playhouse; on the other, the militant Washington Square Book Shop. Above the restaurant gathered the literati of the Liberal Club, the place where Jack London, Upton Sinclair, Vachel Lindsay, Theodore Dreiser, and Sinclair Lewis gathered to thrash out society's ills. It was a block of poets, anarchists, and freethinkers. To move among them, H. L. Mencken said, was to prove that you had "pulled at least a handful of hair from the whiskers of Longfellow."

Kit's various recollections of Heterodoxy suggest that, although she was not an official member, she often found herself at meetings either as a guest or as an invited speaker. Others who spoke to the group were Margaret Sanger, Amy Lowell, and Emma Goldman. Kit, especially as the suffrage movement intensified, would have been much in demand. Such activity revitalized her. Indeed, the Village was the one travel destination for which she seems to have regularly included her children, perhaps hoping they might imbibe its spirit of freedom. To ground not only Kathy but also Tommy in feminist thinking was important to her. While men were not allowed at Heterodoxy meetings, young boys—their minds as yet "uncorrupted by a patriarchal system"—were sometimes allowed to attend with their mothers.

For her part, Kathy was less interested in all the highfalutin talk than she was in the table of sweets, pushing as many into her mouth and pockets as possible. A memory of this was indelibly imprinted upon the writer Nina Wilcox Putnam, a Heterodoxy member and occasional visitor to the Hepburn home. While twelve "grave intellectual ladies sat discussing matters of social revolution," Putnam recalled, the young Kathy "screamed at her play, snatched dainties from the women's plates, and acted as 'natural' as a young savage—all unreproved." But such leniency impressed rather than offended Putnam, who called Kit "clever" and applauded the "new mode of child-rearing." How else, Putnam and those like her believed, would young girls grow up to think for themselves?

Putnam was just one of the leaders of the Village's cultural flowering whom Kit befriended through Heterodoxy. There was also the founder of the Provincetown Playhouse, Susan Glaspell; the actress Margaret Wycherly (who, as an old woman, would play Katharine Hepburn's mother-in-law in *Keeper of the Flame*); and the famous, flamboyant Mabel Dodge, arts patron and *salonnarde*. Kit's closest friend in the group was perhaps Fola La Follette, the firebrand daughter of Senator Robert La Follette of Wisconsin.

It was here, in fact, under the amber light of Polly's Tiffany lamps, that Kit would meet so many of the famous names who provided the colorful revolving backdrop of the Hepburn legend: Emma Goldman, Fannie Hurst, Mary Margaret McBride. Every other Saturday, Heterodoxy brought together from thirty to fifty women to discuss the issues of the day. Among the assembled were communists, nudists, lesbian couples, and curious heterosexual married women. The writer Inez Haynes Irwin considered the women of Heterodoxy "at home with ideas. . . . All could talk; all could argue; all could listen." The labor organizer Elizabeth Gurley Flynn (known as the "Rebel Girl" of the Industrial Workers of the World) wrote that Heterodoxy offered "a glimpse of the woman of the future, big-spirited, intellectually alert, devoid of the old 'feminine.'"

Such sorority led to Kit's inexorable drift toward socialism during and after World War I. In 1919, her friend Rose Pastor Stokes had been imprisoned for political agitation under the sweeping provisions of the controversial Espionage Act. Kit's instinctive distrust of the government was fueled by the incident. All around her, close friends were signing on to the socialist cause. Jo Bennett was perhaps the most radical. She and her husband would soon dispose of their "worldly goods" and move to a simple log cabin among a colony of communists at Katonah, New York. (Ultimately Jo decided she'd had enough, abandoning her husband and moving to Paris.)

Watching all of this through impressionable eyes, Kathy saw, among other things, that fervent politics could arouse equally passionate reactions. Auntie Towle was forced to backtrack on some of her socialist activity after being caught in a melee that led to fisticuffs at Rector's Hotel in Times Square. Kathy's own parents, who never argued over child rearing or household rules, could really get heated over politics. Hep, having grown up poor, thought there was nothing wrong in working hard, making a lot of money, and keeping it; Kit, the daughter of affluence, came to believe in sharing the wealth. "She grew up with the attitude that money grows on bushes," said her son Bob. "But that changed for her when she got a look at the world."

During her time at Bryn Mawr, Kit had read and been inspired by social-ist writings. But it was really her connection to the women of Heterodoxy that moved her closer to strict Marxist thought. For many early feminists, socialism was the only political ideology to embody the tenets of the women's movement boldly and unambiguously. In the 1910s, many believed it was inevitable that within a decade, the United States would become a so-cialist republic. Kit was among them.

"Mother was thrilled when Lenin took over in Russia," Bob said. "She essentially became a communist"—though never an actual party member. No doubt that was a great relief to her daughter later on, when the times took a precarious political turn.

That Hep deplored his wife's socialist impulses became well known. Years later, in his book *Tracy and Hepburn*, Garson Kanin would portray the politi-cal sparring between Hep and Kit as an early incarnation of the Spence-and-Kate show. Kanin tells the probably apocryphal tale of factory workers who'd gotten into the habit of eating their lunches on the sidewalk outside the Hep-burn home. Casting Kit as the type of self-righteous crusader her daughter would make famous on-screen, Kanin has Mrs. Hepburn so fired up over the workers' plight that she grandly invites them to use the family lawn instead of the sidewalk. Of course, the rough-and-tumble laborers make a mess of things, and Hep—as surely as if played by Spencer Tracy—turns to his proud yet crestfallen wife and quips, "Well, my dear, now you've learned something about the difference of having principles and acting on them."

In April 1917, the United States entered World War I. The conflagration that was draining the lifeblood of Europe would have a far more beneficial im-pact on the life of Katharine Hepburn. "It was World War I that really made my father's practice," said her brother Bob. "His competition went off to war, and Dad got everyone coming to him."

Thirty-eight years old and exempt due to his large family, Hep saw his practice finally start to boom during the war years. But it wasn't just the hike in the family revenues that benefited his children. Their father's absorption in work meant that Kit could often slip into New York and cultivate her trea-sured kinships with the women of Greenwich Village. Kathy may not have felt any rousing need to join her mother's cause beyond helping blow up bal-loons for rallies—indeed, she preferred to spend her Saturdays with Tom jumping off the piers at the end of Christopher Street—but she was still ab-sorbing the examples of the independent, rule-defying women around her, especially her two aunts.

On the surface, Towle and Rembaugh might not seem as radical as some of their Heterodoxy friends. Operating within established political structures, they had to be cautious about any such associations. But Mabel Dodge's description of Heterodoxy members as "unorthodox women, women who did things and did them openly" could apply equally to Towle and Rembaugh. The quiet example of their lives was instruction enough. From her aunts, Kathy heard a message that reached all too few girls of her generation: that marriage did not have to be a woman's only option.

It was a way of life that would leave a lasting impact on Katharine Hepburn. In a fascinating, if tongue-in-cheek, examination of "marriage customs" among Heterodoxy members, the writer Florence Seabury identified three categories: the "monotonists," who, because of tradition, had married men and were now resigned to making the best of it; the "varietists," who practiced serial, though unmarried, monogamy; and the "resistants," who did not seriously mate with men at all.

For the most part, Hepburn would structure her own life as a "resistant," living among a community of women apart from men, an arrangement that seemed quite natural to her. "I always thought that marriage was sort of a funny institution," she'd say, despite the supposedly egalitarian marriage of her parents. In 1975, reflecting back on her life, she said, "I've always thought men and women are not too well suited to each other. It's inevitable that they should come together, but . . . how well suited are they to live together in the same house?"

When her mother explained the facts of life to her, leaving out (as the unsentimental Kit was wont to do) all the romantic trappings of love and marriage, Kathy was thrilled. "Oh, then I can have a baby without getting married," she said. Clearly alluding to her overbearing father, Kathy explained, "I don't want any man bossing my children."

Indeed, there was precedent for what young Kathy desired in the Village. Bertha Rembaugh adopted a daughter, Julia, not much older than Kathy herself. The unmarried Anna Lessing was raising her son in a household of women. When Margaret Sanger (later to be Kit's compatriot in her fight for legalized birth control) fled the country in 1914 to avoid arrest, it was to a lesbian couple in the Village (Helen Marot and Caroline Pratt) that she entrusted the raising of her children.

But the experience of women like Auntie Towle and her friends suggested that motherhood itself was not necessarily the ultimate fulfillment of womankind. "It's a splendid feeling," wrote Margaret Anderson, the publisher of the Village's avant-garde journal, the *Little Review* (one of the publications

Kit read faithfully). "I am no man's wife, no man's delightful mistress, and I will never, never, never be a mother. . . . I have always held myself quite definitely aloof from natural laws."

From an early age, Kathy would have understood that those "natural laws" were far more flexible in places like Greenwich Village than they were in Hartford. When Kit spoke to her daughter about sex, she also explained homosexuality with a surprisingly modern, nonjudgmental approach. "Mother was certainly exposed to [lesbianism] in her work," said Bob Hepburn. "I don't think she was shocked or offended by it." Certainly among her Heterodoxy friends she counted several overt lesbians. They included the suffragist Katharine Anthony and the educator Elisabeth Irwin, who were longtime partners, as were the child welfare advocate Dr. Sara Josephine Baker and the writer I. A. R. Wylie.

Indeed, by the time of the First World War, the Village had become a haven for women and men living in nontraditional sexual partnerships. There was no way Kathy could have missed expressions of gay life. Just steps from her aunts' house stood at least twenty tearooms and restaurants "catering to a temperamental element." The *New York Times* reported "bobbed-haired, bobbed-skirted girls" kissing "odd-looking spinsters of uncertain age" in between taking puffs of their cigarettes—right on the street for all to see.

The question looms for us, as it likely did, at some point, for Kathy: were Aunties Towle and Rembaugh lovers? Yes, they shared their homes, their lives, and their work, but were they lesbians? Before the war, Towle and Rembaugh shared a rental home at 107 Waverly Place; Rembaugh later moved to Grove Street and Towle to Charlton Street. At various points, both of them invited other women to share their living quarters. In 1920, Rembaugh and Towle bought property together (from the philanthropist William Sloane Coffin) on the south side of Charlton between Varick and MacDougal. The two women formed a legal trust and lived in adjoining houses.

It must be remembered that Towle and Rembaugh came from a generation known for "romantic friendships," in which women's feelings for each other, however passionate, were not viewed as sexual. In "protecting" themselves from men, the culture believed, these same-gendered couples had saved themselves from the "corruption" of sexuality. According to nineteenth-century sexologists, a woman's sexual desire was "in abeyance" until awakened by a man. Two women, then, couldn't possibly be sexual together, but rather constituted an expression of "ideal friendship," a concept dating back to Aristotle.

Of course, many of these women may not have been as asexual as presumed. What went on in the privacy of their bedrooms is unknowable, though from the evidence collected in those letters and journals that survive, many do seem to have remained chaste, permitting kisses and caresses with their companions (and suffering pangs of jealousy when one of them spent time with another). But the detailed truth in these cases was hardly likely to be committed with pen to paper, and surely for some women kissing and hugging led inevitably to other things that we would unambiguously describe today as "lesbian" activity.

Not until the 1890s was lesbianism discussed in the medical literature, and not until after World War I did the concept gain wide public understanding. By that time, Aunties Towle and Rembaugh could not have avoided at least asking themselves some questions about their essential natures—if they hadn't already done so long ago. What conclusions they might have reached can only be speculation. Certainly Kit Hepburn, for all her directness about sex, never implied to her children that their beloved aunts were sexually involved. But she gave their relationship the kind of respect and acknowledgment she gave heterosexual couples, and it's this lesson that is ultimately the more important in Kathy's social education.

Yet for all her exposure to women-loving women, for all her devotion to her aunts, Hepburn sometimes exhibited an ambivalent attitude toward homosexuality. Years later, sitting in a Parisian hotel room with Garson Kanin and Ruth Gordon, she would make the startlingly disingenuous comment that she didn't believe in the existence of homosexuality—at least not between men. Leaving aside for the moment the existence of George Cukor, Michael Benthall, Robert Helpmann, and most of her close male friends, Hepburn's early years in free-loving Greenwich Village would seem to give the lie to her statement. But, significantly, even in such an artful moment, calculated for whatever personal reasons, she could not deny that she accepted the reality of lesbians.

"Think about this carefully now," said one of Hepburn's good friends who, like many, retreated into anonymity whenever the subject turned to sex. "If she went through her life thinking like a man—and she said that herself many times—of course she'd feel uncomfortable by the idea of male homosexuals. Straight men always do. But women? Straight men don't usually have problems with lesbians."

Katharine Hepburn might occasionally play the prude, both on and off the screen, but in fact, from a young age, she was sophisticated about sex. When puberty came, she greeted it nonchalantly, all of it explained in detail by her mother well ahead of time. She was used to the sight of naked bodies:

her parents', her sisters', even her brothers'. Sex held no great mystery for her, nor, as yet, any great appeal. By her early teens, she was well on her way to physically becoming a woman, and she understood the ways of adults far better than most girls her age. Yet there remained a Peter Pan quality about her: wise, yes, but stubbornly resistant to the calls of society and biology. No matter what her body told her, Katharine Hepburn, by her own admission, remained Jimmy in her soul.

TAKING WHAT LIFE HAS TO OFFER

If Kit had been with them, they would have already been hustling toward Times Square and the subway. But on this day it was Auntie Towle who'd taken the train into the city with Kathy and Tom, and Auntie always preferred a less hectic means of travel. With a flick of her handkerchief, she hailed one of the city's red and green paneled cabs, and the three of them piled in for the ride downtown to the Village.

It was Tuesday, March 29, 1921. Kathy and Tom were on Easter break from school. After spending the holiday with the Hepburns in Hartford, Auntie had agreed to take the two eldest children back with her to New York. Tom had been showing signs of his old nervousness again, and his parents hoped the excursion might "divert" him. Kathy, now thirteen, was, as ever, eager to traipse along.

The story of that fateful trip has been told and retold many times, but much has been missed or gotten wrong. Kit did not go with the children to New York, despite newspaper accounts to the contrary, which were based on Hep's later testimony. Kathy, far from having "outgrown" Jimmy by this time, as some biographers have asserted, was not at all interested in buying pretty dresses during her stay. She changed from her travel clothes into a pair of dungarees the moment they entered Auntie's redbrick townhouse at 26 Charlton Street.

Tom was fifteen. His nervousness that spring has never been fully explained. Part of it was simply exhaustion from years of trying so hard to please his father as the best athlete and scholar. For the most part, he seemed to be bearing up remarkably well. The previous autumn he'd won his colors with the Kingswood School football team. During the previous few months he'd begun the intensive preparations to apply to Yale University, where (as Hep told the press) he hoped to study surgery and follow "in Father's footsteps."

But there was more going on than just the usual pressures. Tom had missed school several times recently due to anxiety. Crying and shaking, he'd been unable to get out of bed. Dr. Hepburn would later pin the duress on a messy relationship with a girl, explaining that Tom had been trying to "break off [an] affair," but the girl in question wasn't going away easily. In fact, both she and her mother, Hep reported, had been "pestering" the boy.

Much later, talking about her brother to Scott Berg, Katharine Hepburn would remember it the other way around, that "maybe a girl had rejected" Tom—but then added, volunteering the information, "Maybe a boy." That she would allow for this possibility is significant, as she knew Tom better than anyone else.

No matter what had set his nerves jangling, Tom did seem cheered by the hustle and bustle of the city, just as his parents had hoped. Immediately after arriving at Auntie Towle's that afternoon, the siblings rushed out, as Kathy would report, to "explore" the Village. For a couple of curious teenagers, one of them possibly in the midst of some sexual confusion, the bohemian neighborhood was a minefield. A quick jaunt down Charlton to MacDougal would have taken them past the shop of the "Chinese philosopher," who painted pictures of naked women on his wall. Heading under the elevated railroad that crossed West Third, they would have passed flyers for Susan Glaspell's social protest play *The Inheritors*. If they peered down an alleyway, they might have seen, as one writer observed, "the bizarre recreations of late-rising chorus ladies." Continuing on into the heart of the commercial district along Sixth Avenue and Sheridan Square, Kathy and Tom could not have missed places like the Red Mask and Trilby's, with their colorful posters of female impersonators. *Variety* joked that such places shouldn't be confused with Ireland, "even if the fairies may be seen there."

On every street corner something provocative awaited. The "Tramp Poet" walked about reciting soliloquies from Shakespeare. Romanian gypsies hawked their wares at batik shops. Breakfast in the Village could go on until four in the afternoon, with dozens of cafés, most below sidewalk level, enticing youth with fresh-baked pastries and the promise of scintillating conversation.

In fact, just two days before Kathy and Tom's arrival, Eleanor Hayden, a writer for the *Times,* had considered this very idea: the effect of the Village's notorious free speech on curious young visitors. "You may hear almost anything," she wrote, "and the more intent people are on proving their points the less regard they have for the seventeen-year-old youths and maidens who may be in their midst and getting their first heavy dose of exactly this sort of free discussion." Hayden noted the case of a runaway boy from a "respectable boarding school" who'd "heard and seen a good bit" in the Village before being "yanked back to his conventional atmosphere by astounded relatives."

This particular youth and maiden, however, were blissfully free of such adult interference. Usually Tom and Kathy were chaperoned by Kit, but on this visit, possibly for the first time, they drank up the sights and sounds of the Village on their own. It was the start of a week filled with thrills. On the morning of Friday, April 1, the neighborhood was held in thrall by a broad-daylight shoot-out at a jewelry store on Bleecker Street. The proprietor had just laid out his pearl necklaces in a showcase when he looked up to see four young men with pistols. Shots rang out, with one bullet hitting the jeweler in the arm and another leaving a furrow across his scalp. Snatching the pearls, the burglars ran off down Grove Street, right past Aunt Bertha's old house. As news of the crime spread rapidly through the Village, dozens of young people, out of school for the Easter break, gathered to watch the chase. Even if Tom and Kathy weren't among them—and knowing their personalities, it's hard to imagine they weren't—they would have heard about the dramatic finale when police cornered the crooks on Greenwich Avenue to cheers.

That night, Auntie Towle bundled her two young charges once more into a taxi and headed uptown to the Selwyn Theatre on Forty-second Street. They paid a quarter each for the 8:30 show of the new Fox picture, *A Connecticut Yankee in King Arthur's Court,* starring the dapper comedian Harry Myers. The film isn't so much adaptation as spoof: Myers plays a contemporary fellow who gets conked on the head while reading Twain's novel and dreams he's transported back to King Arthur's time. He then sets about remaking sixth-century England in the image of jazz-age Hollywood. Knights wear suits of armor equipped with Prohibition-style hip flasks and exchange their horses for motorcycles. (In Twain's novel, they rode bicycles.) Today the film has been largely forgotten, but in its day it was a huge hit. Two weeks before the Hepburns saw it, the *Times* had given it a rave review, commending Fox for sparing no cost in the grand tournament scene, where every available motorcyclist in L.A. was recruited for the spectacle of an army of bikers roaring down the road in full armor.

Not for any grand pageantry, however, has the film lingered in the Hepburn legend. Rather, it's been for the supposed impact it had on the sensitive, high-strung Tom Hepburn who sat wide-eyed in the audience. The film was a comedy, and much of it is lighthearted fluff. But there's one scene where Queen Morgan Le Fay (played by Rosemary Theby) takes Myers down into her dungeon, where we witness, in grotesque silhouette, the beating and impaling of slaves. This is the only scene in the film that could possibly have given Tom "the horrors," as Kathy would describe later.

In the days to come, she would in fact attach a great deal of significance to this film. Together with her father, she'd insist *A Connecticut Yankee* influenced Tom's actions during the next forty-eight hours; those chroniclers who came along later simply took them at their words. None, however, apparently bothered to see the film. It still exists, and while not all of its reels have survived, one can easily draw some conclusions. While the dungeon scene might well inspire "the horrors" even in children less sensitive than Tom, it's doubtful that it could have influenced the boy in the ways Kathy insisted. Tom's fate that weekend can hardly be explained away by the silly, far-fetched antics of a photoplay.

The next day, all seemed calm and happy. Their uncle Lloyd Hepburn, an insurance broker living in Washington Heights, arrived to take Tom and Kathy sightseeing. They toured the Battery and rode the elevator up the fifty-eight stories of the Woolworth Building. When they returned to Auntie Towle's that evening, the house was filled with people. Auntie's mother and sister, both named Sarah, were living with her at the time, and tonight they were joined by Aunt Bertha and a handful of others from their tight-knit group. Tom played his banjo for them as the fire crackled in the small living room. Applauding his musical talents, several of the women kidded the boy about being a "romantic."

Morning would come soon, and the siblings were set to return to Hartford on the 10:20 train. Tom had already bought the return-trip tickets. His suitcase was packed, his clothes laid out for the next day. Bidding good night to Auntie, the two teens headed upstairs to bed, Kathy to a second-floor guest room and Tom to the attic. Usually used as a storage space, the attic had been transformed into a bedroom, giving the boy some privacy.

Kathy awoke early the next morning. Tom, however, seemed to be sleeping in. With their train scheduled to depart in just over an hour, Auntie finally insisted that Tom be roused. Climbing the two flights of stairs, Kathy found the attic door locked. When her brother didn't respond to her pounding, Kathy broke the lock and forced her way in. It's curious that she didn't call Towle to do this; she was breaking her aunt's property, after all. It suggests that alarm bells were already going off in the young girl's head.

Stepping inside the darkened room, Kathy didn't notice anything except for Tom's empty bed. But as she ventured farther into the shadowy attic, she brushed against something in the dark. It was Tom, slumped over but apparently standing, with some kind of fabric tied around his neck. His body was cold and stiff. Kathy screamed.

Every account of what happened next differs widely. Based solely on the reports from the police and the medical examiner, the following is the most accurate reconstruction possible. Hearing Kathy scream, Mary Towle came running up the stairs. Tom was not (as biographers have claimed for years) dangling from the ceiling. According to the coroner's description, he did indeed appear to be standing; his feet were most certainly on the floor. But around his neck a muslin bedsheet had been braided into a noose. It trailed up and around a ceiling beam before being secured to a heavy metal bedspring leaning against the wall.

In that small attic with its sloped ceiling, it would have been impossible for the boy to hang. The beam was too low, and Tom too tall. Despite all the hundreds of accounts claiming otherwise, Tom Hepburn did not hang himself. He died from slow, deliberate strangulation.

Struggling to control a mounting hysteria, Auntie Towle untied the noose. The boy's body crumpled to the floor. Someone, possibly Kathy or Towle's mother or sister, ran next door to fetch Bertha Rembaugh. Later, Kathy would have blurred memories of running outside and banging on neighbors' doors for help, but it was Aunt Bertha who had the presence of mind to call the police. Two patrolmen responded but found little to do except summon a doctor from nearby St. Vincent's Hospital, who told them what they all surely already knew, that Tom was dead. The only things left to do now were to contact the coroner—and the boy's parents in Hartford.

Accompanied by Jo Bennett, Hep and Kit arrived by car that afternoon, probably between one and two o'clock. In the agonizing interim—four long hours of silence torn by occasional outbursts of grief from Auntie—Kathy sat alone in the parlor listening to the clock tick on the mantel. Tom's banjo was at her feet, his body upstairs.

Arriving about the same time as the Hepburns was the coroner, Dr. Thomas Gonzales. Tall and austere with dark, commanding eyes, Gonzales was not likely to have been a comforting presence. Colleagues would remember a stern demeanor obscuring an essentially compassionate nature. One of a new breed of city official, Gonzales had been appointed by Mayor John Purroy Mitchel as part of his reform of city government. Previously, the coroner's office had been a political plum, with a succession of saloonkeepers and real estate men holding the post. But Gonzales and his superior, Charles Norris, experts in the new science of forensics, took their work very seriously. Looking down at the lifeless Tom Hepburn, Gonzales was not pleased that the boy's body had been moved. Still, the circumstances of his death seemed quite clear. When the low ceiling had stymied the teenager's attempt to hang, Tom had bent his knees and thrown his weight forward, forcing the noose to tighten, choking himself to death.

Not so fast, objected Mary Towle. As the group turned to look at her, Auntie began ranting about a missing front-door key. She raised the possibility that someone might have come in during the night and murdered the boy. Dr. Hepburn, as any parent might, quickly latched on to the theory. After all, he had always been suspicious of the bohemian Village and leery of Towle's socialist friends. But Gonzales dismissed the idea out of hand, writing in his report that "the position of body, absence of sign of struggle, and fact that [the] stairs are squeaky . . . clearly indicates suicide."

The circumstances of Tom's death were bewildering—since it was abundantly clear that, had he wished it, he could have escaped death's grip quite easily. Since his feet never left the floor, all he would have had to do was stand upright and untie the noose. Instead, it was painfully obvious that he had pulled and pulled and pulled until he could no longer breathe.

Broken, Hep had to accept the verdict of suicide. Kit, Auntie Towle, Aunt Bertha, Jo Bennett all nodded their assent. A call was made to Hartford, where Hep's sister, Selina Hopkins, was watching the younger children. When a reporter called the house, Hopkins confirmed it was suicide, adding, "God only knows why he did it."

The only one who seemed unconvinced was Kathy, who kept talking about the film and telling police investigators that it had given Tom "the horrors." At first, no one seems to have given her much credence. Early newspaper reports acknowledged the theory that "a motion picture may have affected his mind," but then dismissed it, as police did, because *A Connecticut Yankee* was "a funny one."

Yet Kathy's intransigence on the matter is significant. Far from being, as some writers have suggested, the only one wise enough to accept from the start that Tom's death was suicide, it would appear she clung quite stubbornly to the belief that it was accidental. And why wouldn't she? Tom was her hero, after all. He was everything she wished she could be, and she knew him better than everyone else. He was just trying a stunt, she insisted. Somehow the movie had influenced him, but no one bothered to ask her how. Her tantrum could not have pleased her father, who was already trying to find a way to regain control over the situation. Once Gonzales had released Tom's body from the morgue, the family, along with Jo Bennett, accompanied it across the river to the crematorium in New Jersey. For all their grief, tears would not be part of it.

"I can remember standing with Dad on the bow of the ferry," Hepburn wrote in her memoir. "I looked across at Mother. . . . She was crying. My mother was crying. Oh dear. What can I do? I'd never seen my mother cry before. And I never saw her cry again. *Never*. She was stalwart." Neither did Dr. Hepburn cry. "He took," his daughter said, "what life had to offer."

That night, Hep stepped out onto Mary Towle's front steps to address the reporters gathered in the street, eager for news of this latest Village sensation. It was here, on that chilly evening in New York, as her proud, stoic father stepped forth with his prepared statement, that Katharine Hepburn's long dance of distrust with the press began. Peering out the window at the scene, she watched as these strangers, jostling for position and shouting out questions, intruded into a very painful, very private time.

"My son was normal in mind and body," Hep said, his voice thick but holding steady as the newsmen wrote down his every word. The only explanation was that Tom must have been "suddenly afflicted with adolescent insanity."

Inside, Kathy was furious. Hep would later say she "left me when I called it suicide." Refusing to speak to him or to stay in the place where Tom had died, Kathy spent Sunday night with her uncle Lloyd Hepburn at his house uptown.

The sun that rose the next morning into a bright blue, cloudless sky found Dr. Thomas Hepburn in a completely different frame of mind. Although he had consented to the suicide verdict, the newspaper headlines that confronted him in the harsh light of day seemed to change his mind. MYSTERY IN SUICIDE OF SURGEON'S SON, read the morning's *Times*. DR. HEPBURN'S

SON HANGS HIMSELF, blared the front page of the *Hartford Courant*. It was only then, on Monday morning, staring at the bold print that made Tom's death so indisputable, so real, that Hep seemed willing to indulge Kathy's theories.

"I am convinced that I have done the boy an injustice," read Dr. Hepburn's revised statement, sent out immediately to the New York papers and telephoned to Hartford. He had gone back upstairs, Hep explained, to inspect the room for clues. Tom's bed, he insisted, showed no signs of thrashing or turning, indicating the boy had enjoyed a peaceful night's rest. His clothes had been packed for the trip home. "Suicide was the farthest from his thoughts," Hep now believed. "He was in the best mental, nervous and physical condition that I have ever seen him. He had never been so gay as in the preceding ten days. . . . He always had the complete confidence of his parents, being allowed great freedom of action."

Tom's death, then, was "a deplorable accident." For good measure, Hep made use of Kathy's harping about *A Connecticut Yankee*. He now insisted that Tom had been trying to imitate a hanging scene from a motion picture, trying to work up a stunt as "a special treat for his little brothers when he came home."

Of course, those who had seen the film (Hep had not) must have scratched their heads trying to imagine what scene Tom was trying to imitate. The only scene in the picture that could possibly be called a hanging comes when the heroine (Pauline Starke) is discovered in the dungeon, secured by her neck in a cage with her chin resting on a bar, her toes barely touching the floor. The threat isn't that she'll hang, however, but that she'll be thrashed by a jailer wielding a spiked club. Nor did Hep's newfound enthusiasm for the film theory reconcile what Kathy had said earlier, that the scene had given Tom "the horrors." How had "the horrors" suddenly mutated into a "special treat" for Tom's brothers?

No one confronted Hep with such trivialities, however, least of all Kathy. What mattered to her, when she returned from Uncle Lloyd's, was that her father had had a change of heart. Eagerly helping him build his case, she rattled off various other stunts Tom had pulled in the past—even a fake hanging about a year before, or so they both agreed. By the time the afternoon *Hartford Times* was printed that day, the headline across the front page was very different: SON NOT SUICIDE SAYS DR. HEPBURN. In the subhead, it was averred that the "movie version of Mark Twain story" had caused a "miscarriage" of a make-believe hanging. And so Harry Myers's lighthearted film was forever stained with a perverse kind of immortality.

Later that morning, the four of them—Hep, Kit, Kathy, and Jo Bennett—set out for home. Arriving back on Laurel Street late Monday afternoon, there were no tears, just a simple explanation to the younger children that Tom was gone and not coming back. A few days later, Hep drove to the crematorium in Springfield, Massachusetts, where Tom's remains had been sent. With him he took his son Bob, who had observed his eighth birthday in a shell-shocked silence on the day his parents had come home from New York. Bob recalled his father was in a brooding, bitter mood on that drive to Springfield. Snapping at the undertaker that they needed no "fancy urn" for Tom's remains, Hep instead produced a candy box. No funeral was held for the bright, athletic boy who'd had so much life ahead of him. In fact, Tom Hepburn's name was barely mentioned by his family ever again.

More than sixty years later, stretched out in her rattan Casablanca chair with the white upholstered cushions, looking out onto the sharp blueness of Long Island Sound, Katharine Hepburn finally reconsidered what had happened that long-ago Sunday morning in New York. Scratching out her memoirs on a pad of yellow legal paper, her stream of consciousness punctuated by dashes, she gave the story one final twist.

Despite her efforts and those of her father to blot out the verdict of suicide, it had, over the years, seeped into the public consciousness. A handful of biographies had left the distinct impression that Tom's death had not been an accident. If Kate were to cling to the accidental theory now, she might be accused of living in denial. So instead, she took a different tack. Removing herself entirely from the machinations that went on after Tom's death, she stated it was her father, on his own, who came up with the theory of accidental death through "practicing hanging." Like the rest of the world, she now declared, she hadn't bought it. "I thought at first it wasn't possible that he was practicing hanging." But in truth she had been the one to *insist* on the idea, storming out on her father when he'd dared utter the word *suicide* to the press.

But despite the revision to her own history, the message that ultimately came through in her memoir was exactly the same as it had been in 1921. She would try, one more time, to suggest that her beloved brother hadn't deliberately removed himself from her life: "Now I wonder [about the death being suicide]," she wrote. "Deep in my heart—I wonder."

In private, however, according to Scott Berg, she had come to the same conclusion that Dr. Gonzales had all those years ago. She'd argue out various possible scenarios, always trying to find some small detail that everyone had overlooked. Yet always she returned reluctantly to what seemed undeniable truth: that Tom had taken his own life.

Certainly the facts seemed to support it, especially after the family, at long last, read the medical examiner's report. Katharine Houghton, the daughter of Kate's sister Marion, sent for a copy in 1995; the details of Tom's determined efforts to choke himself could not have been easy reading for his survivors. Then, of course, there was the family history of suicide to consider. By the time of Tom's death, suicides already haunted both sides of the boy's family: his mother's father and his father's brother. As if to underscore the point, two days after receiving the news of Tom's death, another of Hep's brothers closed himself in his garage with his car's motor running. His wife found him dead in the morning.

Still, deep in Kathy's heart, she wondered.

Hep's obduracy might be chalked up to a parent's grief—or to the determined efforts of a man concerned about his reputation as a physician and caregiver. Kathy's thoughts, however, must be given greater credence. She knew Tom better than anyone else did. She had been at his side those last five days.

One line of inquiry, in fact, was not pursued in the investigation. No one asked what Tom had done, whom he had met, or what he had seen in his explorations of the Village in the days before he died. Just what sorts of "free discussions," as Eleanor Hayden had called them in the *Times* that very week, might Tom have listened to? What thoughts was he ruminating on in his last hours? Was he depressed, or was he stimulated?

It's fair to ask these questions because Hepburn herself raised the possibility that Tom might have been going through some form of sexual confusion. She knew her brother was troubled—likely the reason she broke the door to Tom's room without calling first for her aunt. Did she fear his confusion and turmoil might lead him to do something drastic? We cannot know exactly what she was thinking, but whatever it was, it might offer the first clue as to why sex and sexuality would always prove so vexing for Katharine Hepburn. If sexual desire had played any part in her brother's death, perhaps her own desires would then become disturbing to her, producing conflicted, contradictory feelings.

In her seminal article about the Hepburns, Adela Rogers St. Johns would hardly touch the story of Tom's death, referring vaguely to the "tragic" death of an older brother. Details didn't start to emerge until 1941 with Lupton Wilkinson's five-parter on the Hepburns in the *Saturday Evening Post*. Skirting around the specifics, Wilkinson ruled that "the question of suicide or accident was wholly academic . . . her adored brother was dead."

But Wilkinson's article also gave us, for the first time, an odd tale about Dr. Hepburn's Maryland boyhood. According to Wilkinson, Hep had pulled tricks on naive Yankees by pretending to lynch a "Negro who could tighten the muscles of his neck so he could not be choked." For an anecdote in an article designed to bolster Hepburn's comeback in *The Philadelphia Story*, the story seemed a strange choice. But as far as Tom's death was concerned, it did support the idea of a prank. Although the anecdote appears in none of the contemporary accounts of Tom's death, some later accounts (like a scurrilous 1956 report in the scandal rag *Inside Story*) would detail elaborate scenes of the boy trying to re-create his father's stunt.

Indeed, by the time the book-length Hepburn biographies started coming out in the 1970s, the facts of that tragic day half a century earlier had become loose and haphazard. Garson Kanin wrote that Tom died on Easter Sunday instead of the following week; Charles Higham gave the year as 1920, the place as Boston, and, for the first time, linked Kathy's decision to become an actress to her desire to find illusion in the wake of Tom's death. In various magazine articles in the 1980s, Hepburn herself tried sharing a few new details with the writer Christopher Andersen; they were later included in two books about her. In Andersen's account of Tom's death scene, Kathy is depicted as holding her brother's stiff body up off the floor when she cannot untie the noose, in the desperate, heartbreaking hope that he might still be alive. A romantic image—but given the description of the body in the coroner's report, it was simply not possible.

In the psychoanalytic confessional Age of Oprah, Tom's death proved irresistible to Hepburn biographers. Andersen quoted Kate as saying she became "two people instead of one" after Tom's death, "a boy and a girl." Indeed, conventional wisdom came to hold that Katharine Hepburn's entire life, her every motivation and every decision, could be traced directly back to, and explained by, this early loss. The truth is, however, that the greatest impact of Tom's death came not from the tragedy itself but from the family's reaction to it—or, to be more precise, their *lack* of reaction. "When my brother disappeared," Kate told a reporter, still finding the reality of Tom's death too painful to actually articulate, "we were not encouraged to think about it more than we should. We were advised to get on with it." And with no faith, no belief in God to console them with promises of a reunion with Tom in heaven, their stoicism seemed the only practical response.

No tears, no mentions of loss. Taking what life had to offer. Grinning and bearing. These were the examples set by Dr. and Mrs. Hepburn. If Kit cried again after that harrowing first day on the ferry, her daughter speculated, "she cried alone." Tears were anathema in the Hepburn household. "That's why my father hated going to see Kate's movies," Bob Hepburn remembered. "He said they always made him cry, and he hated to cry."

To an old way of thinking, it was an admirable way to live. Crying and grieving were signs of weakness, and self-reflection was self-indulgent. "The conversation [in the Hepburn house] was never anything of a personal nature," said Peg Hepburn Perry. "There were no personal anythings in our family."

Part of Katharine Hepburn's legend has always been about forbearance: tears are for sissies. Indeed, the people of her inner circle would always be those who had the steel to grin and bear: Laura Harding, Phyllis Wilbourn, Irene Selznick, George Cukor. Nobody likes crybabies! But in one key way she departed from her upbringing. There would always be room in her life for a series of Toms, men who *couldn't* quite take what life had to offer, men who struggled, who drank, who fretted, who cried—and who seem to have lived with some of the same guilt and sexual confusion that plagued that bright-eyed Hepburn boy who never saw sixteen.

NEVER A MEMBER OF THE CLUB

Looking down onto the magnolia-shaded Bryn Mawr campus on a spring morning in 1926, Dean Helen Taft Manning could not have been happy. There was a letter she had to write, the kind she always tried to avoid. From her large oval windows ornamented with tracery, she had grown accustomed to seeing Kath Hepburn hurrying across the grassy Jacobean quadrangle in her usual uniform of blue skirt, untucked blouse, woolen socks, and scuffed tennis shoes. Unfailingly, the girl seemed dour and moody, traipsing after the better-dressed, more animated girls always two steps ahead of her.

Despite Kit Hepburn's status as a celebrated alumna, her daughter had failed to achieve the required degree of merit in her coursework. Dean Manning was obligated to write the Hepburns a letter recommending the eighteen-year-old's withdrawal. It was not an expulsion—not yet. But college guidelines demanded that any student who failed repeatedly to accomplish "superior work" in at least 60 of the required 120 hours per semester would not be permitted to graduate. Zeroing in on such underachievers, Dean Manning usually prevailed upon them to drop out on their own before being ordered to do so.

During her first two years of college, Kath Hepburn's progress was minimal. "I was stupid, just stupid," she remembered. Only by the skin of her teeth had she even gotten into the college, scoring a 62 on the physics entrance exam (60 was passing). But her problems went beyond her grades; she was having troubles with college life in general. She had made few friends, and Bryn Mawr's emphasis on privacy—most girls had their own rooms—fostered Kath's isolation. She rose at 4:00 a.m. to shower in the empty bathroom, then took breakfast in her room, as she did all her meals. Sometimes she'd use part of her seventy-five-dollar monthly allowance to eat off-campus. Other girls would spy her hunched over her plate reading a book, her red hair pulled back in an unruly ponytail. Once so aggressive in tennis, golf, and diving, she now shunned extracurricular athletics—partly because her poor grades meant sports were not allowed, but also because she preferred hiding out in her suite in Pembroke West.

Later on, some would say Bryn Mawr and Katharine Hepburn were perfectly matched: a feminist institution nurturing a feminist icon. But that wasn't the case in the beginning. It's true that the college, one of the famed Seven Sisters schools, located in the wooded hills nine miles west of Philadelphia, had been founded to provide women with opportunities long denied (including the first Ph.D. programs for women). Bryn Mawr's mission would remain unchanged through the years: to offer women rigorous intellectual training and the chance to undertake original research. The recently retired M. Carey Thomas, president of Bryn Mawr for twenty-eight years, had reshaped the intellectual landscape for American women. Indeed, her message had advanced far beyond academic progress: not only did Bryn Mawr encourage scholarship among women, but it taught them to lead independent lives. One would think this worldview might have fit Hepburn like a glove.

Yet Kath didn't enter college fired with any ideas of "proving herself" as a woman. Such was never part of her thinking. Still, as she wandered across the hilly acres that surrounded the campus, she may well have found some resonance in the words of Dean Thomas, who had famously rejected the long-held presumption of a separate women's culture. Along with her fight for equal opportunities, Carey Thomas had also struck a few blows against the very essentialism of gender, something Kath, without ever articulating a word, had struggled against ever since she first shaved her head. Thomas's vision, imprinted on the psyche of Bryn Mawr, was that the "life of the mind was neuter."

Although retired for two years by the time Kath arrived in September

1924, Carey Thomas remained a vital presence during Kath's time at Bryn Mawr. She continued to live in the Deanery with her companion, Mary Garrett, and served as a life trustee and director of the college. In 1925, she rallied students to support the equal rights amendment proposed by the National Women's Party. Her legacy was everywhere—from the schedule of courses to the layout of the dormitories. Thomas had been instrumental in the design of the campus, eliminating all encroachments of domesticity, which she viewed as detrimental to a woman's educational experience. Students had their own suites, each with a wood-burning fireplace. After the girls had left for classes, housekeepers would scurry into their rooms to make their beds and haul away their laundry. Nothing was to interfere with a student's ability to hunker down at one of the tall wooden desks in the ornate reading room of the library, named for Thomas and modeled after an Oxford dining hall, and study deep into the night.

Yet this is not the picture that emerges of Kath's first two years of college. After she became a movie star—but before her success had roused the college into reclaiming her—Hepburn was just a vague memory for Bryn Mawr faculty. Quizzed by a fan-magazine writer in 1934, the best they could recall was her untidiness, and how she had often been reprimanded for her appearance. Disheveled, moody, unmotivated—these are the traits of a college student who feels alien in a new environment. It is not an unfamiliar story. Like many before and after her, Kath's first two years of college life were marked by a deep depression. So blue was she that when she suffered an attack of appendicitis her sophomore year, she told her family she hoped she'd die—simply so she wouldn't have to go back to school.

To understand Kath's state of mind at Bryn Mawr, it is necessary to consider the years previous, the interim between Tom's death in April 1921 and her own departure from her parents' household in September 1924. After losing Tom, the Oxford School had seemed increasingly intolerable, the giggling of teenaged girls isolating Kath in her grief. "I knew something that the girls did not know," she said, in characteristic dramatic style: "tragedy." Hep eventually agreed that his daughter could withdraw from the school. For the next three years, she would take private lessons with a tutor.

In many ways, Kath's childhood was over. "I was like my father and mother's—I don't know what—the extra one, you know," she said, years later, describing how her parents treated her differently from her siblings. "But I wasn't a child." It was one more mark of difference that set Kath Hepburn apart from others and colored the whole of her life.

It's possible she might have withdrawn from school regardless of Tom's death. Jean Poindexter's insistence that Kath "just never fit in" predated the loss of Tom. As early as age fourteen, Hepburn was headstrong enough to maneuver herself out of any uncomfortable situation. Not for her other people's rules and regimens; private tutoring was "heaven," she'd remember, for suddenly she had time to ride her bike and play golf. Instead of taking notes in history class, she was out on the links at the Hartford Golf Club taking lessons from Jack Strait, whose string of victories in the Professional Golfers Association made him a far more attractive mentor than any teacher.

The fact that Hep agreed to this tutoring is significant. In the wake of Tom's death, a shift seems to have occurred in the father-daughter relationship. Striding beside her out onto the green, their caddies hauling their clubs behind them, Dr. Hepburn had time to observe the changes in his little Redtop. Her shoulders broadening, her golf swing hardening, the girl who had lived in Tom's shadow took her place as her father's favorite. With Kit channeling her own grief into renewed activism, Hep found himself more and more in the company of his eldest daughter, taking frequent long walks with her along the beach, talking about their golf swings and tennis serves.

In August 1923, sixteen-year-old Kath Hepburn, her face deeply tanned and freckled from the sun, her red hair cut short, and her white skirt sharply pleated, won the Connecticut women's golf championship. The final games were held not far from Fenwick, and Kath's win was greeted with great surprise and admiration by all the Hepburns' affluent neighbors. But if the family stories are true, no one beamed brighter than Hep. Tom might be gone, but Dr. Hepburn had discovered there might still be a champ in the family after all.

Kath would, in fact, do her best to fill up the void her brother had left. Sometime during the years before she left for Bryn Mawr, with the bemused complicity of her family, she assumed Tom's November birth date as her own. It also seems that she took on at least some of his ambitions. Not only would she be the new star athlete, but there was more: at some point, as talk turned to college, Kath decided she would be the doctor Hep wanted.

Finally she had what she'd so long craved: her father's undivided attention. It was a bond the younger children would always envy, creating another barrier that separated Kath from her siblings. Previous accounts have depicted Katharine Hepburn, movie star, routinely retreating to the embrace of her brothers and sisters in Connecticut, finding with them a sustenance that was lacking in an artificial Hollywood. But in fact, Kath's only peer among her siblings had been Tom. With Marion and Peg, eleven and thirteen years her junior, Kath was more an aunt than a sister. Her brother Bob was six years younger, "and in those six years," he said, "there was a world of different experience." Only Dick, four years younger than Kath, might have risen to take Tom's place. But with the dreamy, undisciplined Dick, Kath would always clash, right up to their last days at Fenwick.

After she became a star, there was even more distance from her siblings. Arriving home in Hartford, she'd drop an armful of gifts on the floor for the children and retreat to the study to talk on the phone to Leland Hayward or Laura Harding. "She would breeze in, breeze out," said her brother-in-law Ellsworth Grant. "She'd come in with a flurry and leave with a flurry."

That shouldn't imply that the siblings weren't, as the legend holds, loyal and loving. Of course they loved each other. But in conversation, despite much insight offered into the family dynamic, Hepburn's surviving brother and sister quickly revealed an obvious truth: they didn't really know her. They were too young to remember her as Kathy or, even more critically, as Jimmy. They called her "Katty," in fact, a corruption of Kate and Kathy, a result of Marion's youthful inability to make the *th* sound. What they knew of their sister was largely her generosity, how she helped Dick's children with college and encouraged Marion's daughter in an acting career. But they didn't know *her*.

To her brothers and sisters, especially in those critical years before she left for college, Kath was the entitled older sister—Dad's favorite—who got to stay home while they trooped off to school. Teachers came to Kath, not the other way around. Such experience imprinted her life with an expectation of service. For the first two years she had a succession of tutors lugging up the front steps of Laurel Street. But the teacher who most profoundly shaped her mind didn't arrive until the fall of 1923. He was a wise, finicky, eccentric Englishman named William O. Williams, whom everyone called "Wow."

Wow was forty-nine when he started tutoring Kath. The small, wizened bachelor was forever sniffling, coughing, or complaining of a bad back; whether his many ailments were real or psychosomatic, no one could say. When Kath first met him, he had only just been hired as a faculty tutor by the Kingswood School, and he took a decidedly dim view of American customs. Presenting himself daily at Laurel Street in starched collar and dickey, he insisted that he and Kath stop for tea in the middle of the day. From Wow, Kath would develop her lifelong Anglophilia; no doubt her tutor was the inspiration for her peculiarly British affectations, like calling trolleys "trams" and pronouncing *hurricane* as "hurra-cun."

From Wow, she also learned to prize eccentricity. With Handel as back-drop, Wow would regale Kath with stories of motorcycling across Europe. Despite seeming shy at first meeting, Kath's tutor could open up and pontif-icate on anything from ethics to history to cosmic rays in outer space. Kate's friends thought she could be similar. With her teacher she also shared a basic practicality. At all times Wow carried a small satchel containing a change of socks, a few ounces of tea, a little kettle and Sterno stove, and a Smith and Wesson revolver.

Although Wow was easily shocked by rambunctious American students, longtime Kingswood colleagues thought he secretly admired their lack of in-hibitions. Kath was his only female charge. But in her defiance of convention, including her preference for boys' clothes and her impatience with silly fem-inine prattle, Wow seems to have recognized something familiar. He, too, had taken his own singular path, recalled by one colleague as "strangely full of zeal and adventure." Without a wife and family, Wow had devoted his life to exploring the world and passing on his impressions. OMNES OMNIA DOCEBAT reads the plaque to his memory at the Kingswood School: "He taught every-body everything."

Kath certainly adored him. Free from competition from other students, she was her teacher's only focus, his singular objective. William O. Williams was the first, but hardly the last, cultured bachelor to focus his attention on her, offering direction and inspiration.

After three years of freedom from silly girl talk, it's no wonder that Kath found herself chafing against the regimented days at Bryn Mawr, where dozens of other girls competed for their professors' time. Kath Hepburn was just one of many, a position she never could abide for long. When Dean Man-ning's letter recommending her withdrawal arrived, Kath no doubt saw it as a blessing, perhaps imagining a gracious, well-timed retreat. After all, failure of a basic biology class had convinced her (and Hep) that medicine wasn't in her future. She would settle on a history/philosophy major but still found herself barely squeaking through.

Her intelligence was not the issue. Rather, it was her lack of self-confidence, a nagging little devil that had been whispering in her ear ever since she was a girl trying to live up to her father's expectations and to overcome the disapproval of Hartford's elite. Throughout her life, Katharine Hepburn would attempt to compensate for this insecurity either by overachieving—what Hep called "showing off"—or by withdrawing. This period was defi-nitely an example of the latter.

The discomfort Kath felt is critical to understand because it informs our grasp of the rest of her life. When she'd withdrawn from Oxford, she became the center of her tutors' universe—a not-so-different experience from what she had come to enjoy with her father. After so many years of making a fuss about it, she was finally being looked at and affirmed—a paradigm she'd strive to maintain her entire life.

No wonder Bryn Mawr was initially *agony* (her word). She was no longer the center of attention. She was also, practically speaking, burdened by a lack of study skills. After being indulged by tutors for three years, she had forgotten, in effect, how to go to school. And while she despised the very idea of attending classes, of adhering to other people's schedules, she loathed even more the nonsense conversations she was forced to endure in the dining hall, where silly little ninnies chattered on about boys, clothes, and engagement rings. "I was really not at home or at ease with a lot of strange girls," she'd remember. She had been forced into the world of ordinary young women. She might as well have been dropped down into the mountains of Mongolia.

She'd use a story (repeated endlessly by chroniclers) to explain away her antisocial impulse in those first two years. Not long after she first arrived on campus, she walked into the dining hall that connected her dorm, Pembroke West, with Pembroke East. As she told the story, she was carrying her tray, minding her own business, when she overheard an upperclassman remark, "Conscious beauty." She was so hurt that she withdrew completely.

Telling the story, Hepburn would insist the comment was directed at her, but she never explained why. It does seem curious. She herself admitted she was no beauty then. She had troublesome skin that often broke out in blotches and redness. The condition worsened as the years passed, demanding long hours in makeup chairs. She was also thin, without much of a bosom, and her hair was so fine and straight it sometimes was impossible to tame.

So where did "conscious beauty" come from? The story was first reported in the Hepburn-engineered *Saturday Evening Post* article by Lupton Wilkinson, in which the future star was said to be wearing a "flame-colored dress" at the time of the incident, suggesting it was her clothing and not her looks that prompted the snide comment. Later accounts, however, including her autobiography, would amend the remark to "*self*-conscious beauty" and revise the wardrobe to a more modest blue skirt with buttons down the front and an Icelandic blue and white sweater. These later versions also informed us that the unnamed speaker was a "New York sophisticate"—Hepburn's way of casting her tormenter as a snob, and herself, in her chunky wool sweater, as a down-to-earth innocent.

For publicists and press agents, however, the story served another, even more useful purpose: it told us that, even though she didn't quite realize it, Katharine Hepburn was beautiful from the start. *Born* beautiful, a diamond in the rough who offended jealous sophisticates. In one fell swoop, this story, which traditionally begins every account of Kath's time at Bryn Mawr, not only explained away her isolation and depression (who would *want* to socialize with such harpies?) but also spotlighted her latent star quality. It was meant to assure all who read it that by college Hepburn was already the glamorous star we know from Hollywood—Eva Lovelace, maybe, or a young Tracy Lord.

But she wasn't. Jimmy Hepburn had not yet transformed. She was lonely, awkward, and boyish. *Modern Screen* got this bit of Hepburn's history right: at Bryn Mawr, one of its writers reported, "Katharine was an ugly duckling . . . long and leggy and thin as a bean pole. She had innumerable freckles and her hair was too straight and too abundant and too unruly."

Never again would this be so baldly stated. The gangly teenager's depression those first two years was fueled by the fact that suddenly she felt both invisible and plain. "When I was a kid," she'd recall in a rare moment of vulnerability, "I always hoped someone would say, 'What beautiful eyes you have.' . . . No one ever said it to me."

Kath's deep-seated insecurities—about her appearance, her intellect, her charm—became overwhelming during her first two years at college. She'd later admit it was the "blond, blue-eyed girls" who got noticed on campus. By sitting alone in her room, Kath could avoid any chance of competing with them, whether for a professor's attention or for a seat in the dining hall. They didn't come banging on her door, either. "I was never a member of the club," she once said. "I never knew what the other girls were talking about."

And yet, just as she had since her days as a tyke diving off the Fenwick piers, Kath spent her early college life chasing after the pretty-girl crowd, including her best friend, Ali Barbour, enrolled in the same freshman class. Adjusting to college might have proven easier had she and Ali been given rooms in the same dormitory, but Ali was over in Merion Hall.

Still, what little social life Kath knew was provided by Ali and her debutante friends. They included Mary "Megs" Merrill, the daughter of Charles E. Merrill of textbook publishing fame, and Verona Layng, the granddaughter of a railroad founder, who was introduced to society at the Colony Club during her freshman year. Another member of the clique, Hope Yandell, would also be introduced at the Colony Club in 1925. Finally, there was Alita Davis, the niece of Dwight Davis (former governor-general of the Philippines). Alita topped them all by being presented at Buckingham Palace, ironically by Kath's grandaunt Mrs. Alanson B. Houghton.

Around these upper-class princesses there gathered a circle of handmaidens, of whom Kath was just one. Had it not been for Ali, it's doubtful she would have been allowed to tag along even as infrequently as she did. Kath, with no sense of fashion and no social connections, had nothing to recommend her. She didn't even possess what other handmaidens like Alice Palache had: gregarious natures and high grades.

If Kath was the archetype of the campus loner, sullen and withdrawn, Palache (as she was always known) was the gregarious overachiever, smart as a whip and involved in many extracurricular activities, from the glee club to the hockey team (of which she was the captain). "Everybody is so nice to you here that you don't feel like a freshman at all," Palache wrote to her father. "Everybody speaks to you whether they've met you or not. The campus itself is so lovely that it is a pleasure just to be here anyway." (This was written at the same time Kath was hiding out in her room.)

Palache was Ali Barbour's roommate in Merion Hall, where freshmen were sometimes placed two to a room. Her letters home reveal how devoted Palache was to her classmates. When Ali (or Alita or Hope) didn't stay on campus for weekends, Palache found herself "desolate." A plain girl, she lived for her friends' tales of *amour* with boys from other schools. "Ali Barbour has just returned from a weekend at Princeton and consequently is not yet coherent," Palache gushed to her mother in late 1924 or early 1925. "So I shall soon go to bed and hope at least for a somewhat organized account of her exploits tomorrow."

Palache kept tabs on everyone. She knew, for example, that Ali's Princeton beau had eloped with another girl even before Ali did. "She was somewhat worried," Palache wrote, "as he hadn't written her in two weeks, exactly the time he eloped." It was "altogether quite horrible," Palache said, to have to keep the truth from her friend.

No doubt Ali's heartbreak contributed to her withdrawal from college at the end of her freshman year. Alita Davis, Verona Layng, and Megs Merrill would also drop out, the latter two with rings on their fingers. And so when Dean Manning's letter arrived in Hartford in late May 1926, Kath surely regarded it with some measure of relief. Without Ali and the others, the campus would seem even lonelier, and she all the more bereft.

But Hep wouldn't hear of it. He refused Manning's recommendation, loathing the idea that any child of his might be a quitter. Lupton Wilkinson quoted Dr. Hepburn's letter back to the dean in the seminal *Saturday Evening*

Post article: "If I had a patient in hospitalization," Hep wrote, "and the patient grew worse, I should not discharge him, but try to work out a more efficacious treatment."

That treatment, as it turned out, came from an unexpected source. When she returned to campus in the fall of 1926, the nineteen-year-old Kath would find at least one friend remained. It would be through the spunky, devoted Alice Palache that Kath discovered not only the formula for succeeding at college but also the relationship dynamics that would define the rest of her life.

GETTING HER BALANCE

L adies and gentlemen, Katharine Hepburn."

Applause thundered across the quad as the legendary star, in black cap and gown, strode up to the podium to deliver a speech at the convocation of the Bryn Mawr class of 1985. Looking out at the assembly of girls seated where once she had tagged along after Ali and Alita in her disheveled clothes, Kate flashed one of her most luminous smiles.

"Bryn Mawr was my springboard into adult life," she told the graduates, in that tremulous voice most of them recognized chiefly from *On Golden Pond.* "Slowly you work your way to the end of the board. You begin to get your balance. You're getting set for the spring, the leap. . . . And you jump, with some hope of landing on your feet." Her head was quivering, fueling those nettlesome rumors of Parkinson's disease, but still, how impressive she seemed up there, looking out over the sea of young women. Her eyes twinkled. "I got my balance," she said after a pause.

Yes, she did, after all. But such an outcome was scarcely imaginable in the autumn of 1926, when Kath found herself once more in the hills of Pennsylvania, facing her toughest courseload yet: in addition to advanced trigonometry and theoretical biology, she had two first-year philosophy courses as part of her new major.

Later, she'd say that her desire to try out for college dramatics, forbidden under the merit law until her grades had improved, was her motivation to buckle down. But no contemporary evidence suggests acting was a career goal at this point. Kath's academic seriousness at the outset of her junior year was more likely a result of her father's admonition that she do better *or else*. After all, college wasn't cheap—tuition for 1926–27 was $400, plus a room rental of $275 and a boarding fee of $200, paid twice a year—and Hep never did like seeing money going to waste.

Her better grades can also be attributed to her deepening friendship with the industrious Alice Palache, for whom Kath replaced the much-lamented Ali Barbour. "[Kath] really is a wonderful girl," Palache wrote home. "She makes me feel quite gay, and when I'm not with her, I wish I were."

The two girls had much in common. They were both nineteen and had never had a beau to call their own. Like Kath, Alice Palache came from a comfortable upper-middle-class background. Her father was Charles Palache, a professor of mineralogy at Harvard; her mother, Helen Markham, a founder of the Buckingham School for Girls in Cambridge. Palache's dark features and unusual name—pronounced "pa-LAH-chee"—led some to presume she was Italian, but her father was descended from Sephardic Jews. Like the Hepburns, the Palaches stood a little apart from the community. But Dr. Palache, like Hep, had distinguished himself professionally as president of the Mineralogy Society of America. Meanwhile, his articulate wife, like Kit Hepburn, championed opportunities for women.

That some considered his three accomplished daughters (Alice, Mary, and Jeannette) a bit offbeat seems not to have disturbed Charles Palache. His granddaughter Jude Gregory would remember him teaching her to value eccentricity and difference in a single phrase borrowed from the poet Robert Owen: "All the world is queer save thee and me, and even thou art a little queer." Alice, in other words, seems to have grown up in an environment that prized original thinking every bit as highly as did the Hepburns.

Well, almost. One significant difference became obvious the first time Kath took Palache home to Hartford. "I never in my whole life saw my father naked, never," Palache said—but there was Hep, coming out of his bath, not bothering to cover up and talking a blue streak as he reached out to shake the blushing girl's hand. It was all Palache could do to keep her eyes on his face. And it didn't end with Dad. "We'd all sit around," Palache said, "boys and girls together, without many clothes on, and nobody paid much attention one way or another, which was brand new to me."

Although Kath now had a roommate—her socialite friend Hope Yandell—most of her time was spent with Palache in the Thomas library. One can walk up that curved teakwood stairwell today, emerging into the gargantuan reading room with its vaulted ceiling and hung with the fragrance of old books, to imagine Kath hunched over one of the tall partitioned desks, Palache standing beside her. Quizzing her friend in whispered tones, Palache would shake her head at incorrect answers and clap Kath on the back when she got it right. When Kath grew tired or frustrated, which was often, Palache would refuse to let her quit, holding her down by the shoulders if need be.

"She was plenty smart, but she was badly trained," Palache said of Kath. "She used to memorize practically everything, and it nearly got her down with philosophy because you really couldn't [employ memorization in philosophy]. I used to help her with it, although I didn't know much about philosophy."

For Palache, studying just came so much easier than it did for Kath. "I could hear her brains going around," Hepburn would remember, "and I'd die of jealousy."

Alice Palache was one of those girls who thrived on college life, effortlessly juggling everything. In her letters home, she was forever using the word *hectic* to describe her days. After classes, she'd sew costumes for the glee club, then race across campus to meet with President Marion Edwards Park as a student representative. In the winter there was hockey; in spring there was baseball, "the new fad on campus," for which Palache signed on as pitcher. "I am so swamped in things I have to do," she wrote to her mother. "I really get more and more appalled at what one has to accomplish in any given time in this place. I can't wait for a period of real leisure to arrive." Yet she wasn't really so appalled; her letters weren't complaints. Palache adored her time at Bryn Mawr, so much so that she never really left: in her postgraduate life, she'd sit on the college's board of directors.

For Kath, Palache's tutoring paid off. For the rest of her life, she'd insist that Bryn Mawr owed Palache two diplomas, one for herself and one for Kath. Indeed, by the end of the first semester of her junior year, Kath's marks showed such improvement that Palache encouraged her to try out for the spring production of A. A. Milne's *The Truth About Blayds*. Kath agreed, finally breaking out of her self-imposed exile. The once-withdrawn girl was now flinging off her clothes every chance she got, whether to splash naked in the cloister fountain after a long night of studying or to brave a blizzard bareass on the roof of her dorm. Watching her, the girls of Bryn Mawr must have wondered who this new student was, and where she had suddenly come from.

That the autumn of 1926 marked a turning point is underscored by the fact that, almost overnight, Hepburn went from being known as the sullen "Katharine" (or occasionally "Kay") to being hailed as "Kate." Although she'd still think of herself as "Kath," the name used by her parents, she allowed Palache to use the new nickname, and others followed suit.

There they sit, Kate Hepburn and friends, hunkered down in Palache's room in Merion Hall late at night, drinking cups of hot muggle—thick melted chocolate cut with steamed condensed milk. Palache always made sure to have it handy, knowing Kate's voracious cravings for all things chocolate. Sometimes they'd wash down chocolate-covered strawberries or peanuts with the muggle, their sugar buzzes spiraling ever higher, making them sillier by the minute. But their talk wasn't about boys or clothes the way it was among other girls. Instead, they traded stories of their own exploits, of sneaking into the village for ice cream or over to Haverford for a movie. Always they'd be seated in a circle, and Kate, more often than not, was smack dab in the middle.

The group's ever-ready chauffeur was Elizabeth "Lib" Rhett, of the South Carolina oil family. Her father, who made money in the tobacco business, provided Lib with a brand-new black and yellow Chrysler that she kept, against college regulations, garaged in the village. Late at night or on weekends, Lib and her friends would pile in for a joyride through the rolling hills beyond the campus. Quieter, but just as eager to join in on the fun, was Adele Merrill (no relation to Megs), whose father was the president of the Bank of New York.

These girls might have come from the same upper crust as Kath's previous friends, but this gang was different. They were pranksters. Rebels. Daredevils. Down the ivy-covered trellis they'd crawl, inching past other girls' windows. Over to Haverford they'd sneak to catch Gloria Swanson in *The Untamed Lady*. One hundred miles they'd drive into New York to see the latest Broadway sensation. In April 1926, they sat spellbound by Helen Hayes in *What Every Woman Knows*, which Palache pronounced "charming beyond belief."

She might have used the same phrase to describe any one of these cherished outings with her friends: the once studiously obedient girl had found herself embraced by a clique of rule breakers—and she loved it. Dubbing the four of them the Three Musketeers and D'Artagnan, she saw herself as D'Artagnan, always trying to keep up. Kath, not surprisingly, was Athos, the leader of the bunch.

How had Hepburn's transformation occurred? Blossoming under the worshipful gaze of Palache, Kath had discovered that to become this new person, this "Kate"—this popular girl with a loyal circle of friends—she needed to make herself *adorable.* It was the word she would always use to describe herself when trying to influence people. And by all accounts, she was the group's adored ringleader. Her word was the bugle call; it was Kath who planned their forays and instigated the joyrides in Lib's Chrysler. Off they'd go, whooping every time the car rounded a hill, their hands waving in the air, their laughter trailing them on the winding country roads.

"It was Kate Hepburn," recalled a relative of one of her college friends, "who'd see notices of particular shows in the newspaper and get them all to drive into New York. Whatever Kate said to do, they all did. They could never say no to her."

Certainly, that's not hard to imagine, for adorable she had indeed become, flashing that smile, fully conscious of the force of her personality. It was the ineffable quality of charisma: Jimmy, enticing Ali to follow him off the pier; Kathy, lording over her friends who always came back for more. "You couldn't help but love her, even if she got mad," Jean Poindexter observed about an earlier decade, but it held true all of her life.

"Kate could be terribly demanding, there's no doubt about that," said Noel Taylor, a good friend. "But there was just something so simple about her, so innocent in a way, that you *wanted* to do things for her. You never resented what she asked."

"Before you can be a friend of hers," Palache once explained, "you submerge yourself and your opinions in many respects." That was because Hepburn was "inclined to be self-contained . . . self-centered really," though Palache insisted that underneath she was "not cold at all." Another friend, the actor Jack Larson, mentioned "something soft . . . under her shell."

That softness was her vulnerability, her obvious need to be liked and noticed. It was the need of a *child*, really, a little girl waving her hands so that her father might look at her. It was her childlikeness that tempered her friends' response to her more imperious moods, keeping her safely cocooned within a band of supportive, protective devotees.

Yet her friends could never be merely sycophants. All her life Hepburn was wise to flatterers and yes-men, sniffing them out and refusing to tolerate their presences. Even as a young woman, her retinue had to be more than simply acquiescent. They had to be strong characters, fully engaged in their own lives. The cowering sort was simply never Miss Hepburn's cup of tea. Lib and Adele, with their elite backgrounds and moneyed connections, knew their own minds; even Palache, for all her devotion to "her Kate," was a strong, formidable campus leader.

Their high spirits, Palache said, led them into more "hijinks" than most of the girls on campus. "We really were very exclusive," Palache remembered. One who *was* allowed into their ranks was Alita Davis, who often came back to campus to visit and was surprised and delighted to discover that her formerly mousy friend Kath now shared her love of tennis.

Finally, Kath could blossom. And just in time, too. The 1920s were years of cultural provocation, a time when Victorian taboos were being rejected. "It is true," admitted Dean Manning, "that college girls smoke more cigarettes, wear less clothing and go on more late parties in automobiles than their predecessors in 1910." The new generation of students, she said, were much more frank, much more likely to criticize policies to their professors.

In the days since Kit Houghton graduated in 1900, Bryn Mawr had certainly changed. Kit's generation had worn a cap and gown to class; college girls now showed up to class in skirts that barely covered their knees. In Kit's day, students had adhered to rules that forbade them to mix with outsiders. Now Kath and her friends slipped easily and often into the village for asparagus with Hollandaise sauce at the King of Prussia Inn.

With the right to vote won and the war in Europe ended, modern college girls spent much of their time "drinking deeply of life" instead of fighting for the causes so dear to their mothers. In 1923, Kit herself had spoken out against this new kind of college girl, soon to be personified by her own daughter. "Young people today are either making love or learning how to earn their living," she declared in one speech. "It takes something highly emotional to stir [young women] to action." Rather ruefully, she added: "Like love."

Under the old order, Ali Barbour's mooning over her Princeton beau would never have been tolerated; she'd have been scolded for capitulating to male domination. But for Kath's peers, women like Mary Towle and Bertha Rembaugh were increasingly viewed as dried-up old maids. Not by Kath necessarily, who knew these women far better than most, but by the girls around her, with whom she shared a conviction that life was an adventure and that gender should not obstruct their enjoyment of anything that roused their fancy.

If there was any political agitation on the women's campuses, it was over cigarettes. Many older women considered the cause hardly comparable to the noble pursuit of suffrage. But the battle represented "part of the general breaking down of differences between the sexes," as one educator saw it. "The cigarette itself," wrote the *New York Times,* was "a torch of liberty." In November 1925, President Park bowed to the inevitable when she accepted a petition from students and designated one room in every dorm where smoking would be permitted.

Moralists were outraged. The industrialist Alonzo B. See, who'd once said he'd like to "burn all the women's colleges," declared Bryn Mawr "a smoking emporium." The *Los Angeles Times* editorialized: "Woman purloined the pants of man and he accepted the indignity. . . . But now having appropriated his bobbed head and his smoke, what has he left?"

The controversy was still hot two years later when, on a warmer-than-average day in October, Kath Hepburn lit up a cigarette in her dorm room and decided to take a puff. According to Hepburn's version of the story, a pack of perfumed cigarettes had been left mysteriously at her door. "Heavens— what is this?" she'd recall thinking. "Oh, a good smell—I think I'll try one." Finding the taste "weird," she insisted she put it out and threw the cigarettes away. But someone had seen her—she had left her door open into the hall— and later that day she was written up for smoking in her room. When she asked who reported her, she was told it was confidential.

Her version of the story made it seem as if she'd been set up: the cigarettes left there to entice her, and she'd taken only one puff, just one! Still, President Park suspended her for a week, from Sunday, October 23, to Friday evening, October 28. To Dr. Hepburn, Park wrote, "I am sorry that after living in a community for three years your daughter did not feel responsible herself in such matters and that the community had to take it in hand."

How that letter seems to have rankled Kath. More than sixty years later, she would quote it in her memoir, along with her version of the tale recounted above. But her account seems more than a bit disingenuous. (*"Heavens— what is this?"*) In truth, as evidenced by Palache's letters, Kath was a regular smoker by this time. But once again Hep fired off another sarcastic letter to Park, which Kate would also quote, in full, in her memoir. While ostensibly offering support for the idea "that she must obey the rules," Dr. Hepburn called such rules "irrational," deconstructing Park's application of them in a way that made the policy sound absurd. For good measure, he added that "Katharine rarely smokes."

While Hep's pontifications had no effect on changing Kath's suspension, they did impart a strong message to his daughter. It was the same message sent between the lines in his previous missive to his daughter's nemesis. Implied in both letters was the notion that rules were for other people. They didn't apply to Katharine Hepburn.

On a winter weekend night in early 1927, soon after the second semester of their junior year had begun, Kath, Palache, and several others scrambled into Lib Rhett's Chrysler and tore out of town. Heading north to New York on the old Route 1 through New Jersey, their goal was to see *The Captive*, then the most notorious production on Broadway.

"It was Hepburn's idea," recalled the relative of one of her friends. "It was the kind of thing they were always doing. My [relative] remembered going to see *The Captive* as quite the daring thing to do, and certainly they never told [any officials] at the college."

This particular anecdote, preserved and passed down by one of her crowd, was not among those told in Hepburn's memoir. Nor was it one of those spirited jaunts to New York that Palache so enjoyed writing home to her mother about. But from Palache's letters we do know that excursions to see Broadway shows were not uncommon among the friends, and contemporary newspaper accounts confirm the preponderance of college girls at nearly every performance of *The Captive*. One police officer estimated young girls made up 60 percent of the audience, "unescorted girls [in] twos and threes [sitting] together."

What made *The Captive* so appealing to these young playgoers was its "forbidden" theme of lesbianism; after all, anything forbidden always works as catnip on students. Taking their *Playbills* from the uniformed ushers at each door, Kath and her friends made their way to their seats amid a throng of people, for every performance of *The Captive* was packed. Looking up at the stage as the curtains opened on act one, Kath watched the unfolding story of Irene De Montcel, a woman torn between leading a "respectable" life and following the passionate call of another woman.

"Lesbian love walked out onto a New York stage for the first time last night," one critic wrote after the premiere of *The Captive*, the American title of Edouard Bourdet's French drama *La Prisonnière*. For five months, the play had been the talk of Broadway. Outraged moralists, led by the publishing magnate William Randolph Hearst, were trying to shut it down. Of course, the controversy only served to swell the crowds, especially among college-age women, which fueled the panic even more. "If all the ladies present were not weakened," the critic George Jean Nathan feared, "they were at least made curious."

Beyond its forbidden theme, there was another reason *The Captive* was so attractive to college girls. It gave a name to an experience many of them already knew firsthand. Returning to campus, Kath and her friends would certainly have recognized echoes of the play in their own lives. In fact, "crushes" had long been part of the women's college experience. In letters to her sisters, who had attended Bryn Mawr before her, Palache was frequently effusive about how "attractive" she found her fellow students. One, in particular, was Gertrude Macy, then a junior and later to be Broadway actress Katharine Cornell's companion. "She sits right in front of me," Palache wrote to her sister Mary. "Gert's hair does fascinate me." Apparently, Mary had also told her to be on the lookout for another girl, one Bette Whiting, for when Bette asked Palache to dance at a freshman party, the younger girl was overjoyed. There were others, too, that Palache kept her eye on: "Yes, I did ask to dance with Emily Glessner," she wrote to Mary, "but she was not on my card."

Girls dancing with girls, of course, was nothing remarkable on a campus devoid of boys. Yet the fact that such intimacy sometimes led to passionate feelings should also not be surprising. While it's true that, for most, same-sex crushes were just a passing phase, for others these feelings didn't end at graduation, as we understand much better today. Some girls found their college crushes only the beginning of a lifelong orientation toward other women. And this may have been the case for Alice Palache.

Her letters reveal nothing sexual—they were mostly written to her parents, after all—but they do make plain that her crush on Kath was heartfelt. Preparing to spend a weekend with the Hepburns in Hartford, Palache wrote to her mother asking for her "orange and lace evening dress." She wanted to look "special," she explained later, so that "Kate wouldn't be sorry she brought me home." Virtually every letter contains a mention of "my darling Kate": "Kate and I" did this; "Kate thinks" that. On Christmas gifts for her sisters, Palache signed Kate's name as well as her own. And while frequently commenting on the beaux of other girls, not once does Palache suggest that she herself might be interested in a boy. When a rumor went around that she was engaged to Charlie Caddock, a family friend who'd visited, Palache was "to no end amused." Toward the end of her junior year, she wrote that she had "no time for anything or anybody—except Kate, of course, always my Kate."

Some in her family, when questioned about their aunt, could not see Palache as anything other than traditionally heterosexual. Others took a more nuanced view. Her grandniece Cadigen Wiley recalled a definite gay presence among friends of the three Palache sisters. "And of the three," she mused, recalling the sisters, "Alice was the warm, loving, passionate one. So if any of them would have been in touch sensually that way, it would've been Alice."

Palache would, in fact, marry, but quite late in life. In her postcollege letters, however, she would continue on exactly as she had as a girl, never mentioning any beaux while frequently writing to her mother and sisters about impassioned friendships with other women. By the 1940s, she had grown close enough to one woman to spend the holidays with her and to want to bring her home so that Professor and Mrs. Palache might meet her. "I know you'd both like her," she wrote. And through all of this, whenever Kate Hepburn was in town, Palache would drop everything and everybody to see her.

How did Hepburn return Palache's feelings? After all, here was a girl who'd grown up with feminist and lesbian role models, who'd always instinctively identified with males, who'd just seen *The Captive* on Broadway. Given such a context, it's neither inconceivable nor even very radical to consider the possibility that sexual experimentation occurred—if not with Palache, then with someone else in her clique. "They were definitely the experimenting kind," agreed the relative of Kath's friend. "I always got the impression from my [relative] that they were very sexually free and adventurous."

Certainly college has always been a time for experimentation, and the spirit of the times was encouraging of it, perhaps even more so than today's. A study conducted during this period revealed that 50 percent of U.S. women college graduates acknowledged having had "intense emotional attachments" with other women, with 26 percent admitting "overt physical practices." Yet despite their rebellious natures and tomboy reputations, all of Kath's college pals would go on to marry and, except for Palache, have children—although Lib Rhett and Alita Davis took the time to become semiprofessional athletes first (Lib in badminton, Alita in tennis). Both women settled down at the relatively advanced age of twenty-eight.

For the girls of Bryn Mawr, there was another important example of women partnering with each other: the exalted memory of Carey Thomas, who had loved and lived with two women (in succession) right on campus. Gertrude Stein had even fictionalized the story of Thomas's loss of Mamie Gwinn to a male professor in her novel *The Making of Americans*, published in 1925 and well read on campus. Sophisticated readers, of which the girls of Bryn Mawr were a subset, knew exactly whom Stein was writing about. To dabble in a same-sex relationship was merely to emulate their esteemed founder, who we know was held in great reverence by both Kath and Palache.

To not fully consider the possibilities of same-sex experience, especially when the context of Kath's life and times seems to demand it, is to do a disservice to her story. She was, it seems, a young woman of sophistication and complexity. In this light, let us envision the night of April 8, 1927, when Katharine Hepburn, in tweed jacket and tie, strode out onto the Bryn Mawr stage as the young Oliver Blayds. Her hair, always short, had been shorn almost to the scalp by fingernail scissors (though she topped that with an ill-fitting man's wig). In many ways, Milne's play was a fitting vehicle for our heroine's dramatic debut: *The Truth About Blayds* tells the story of a family coping with a famous relative whose image is revealed to be a construct, a clever subterfuge of smoke and mirrors. As the namesake grandson, Kath seemed "a bit too conscious" of being onstage, the college reviewer thought, but she nonetheless "made an engaging boy, roguish and merry."

So roguish and merry did Kath feel after playing the part that she convinced Palache to join her, both of them dressed as men, on a jaunt into Philadelphia. Anyone who's seen *Sylvia Scarlett* knows Hepburn could pass quite credibly as a handsome young man, and while Palache would remember the whole episode as "silly business," the impulse that led to such a jaunt was a defining part of Kath's personality. Such gender play was relished; we see it again and again in her story (and even, daringly, in those early films). She likely indulged herself yet again when *Blayds* was performed at the Colony Club in New York later that spring as a benefit for the New York Alumnae Regional Scholarship. Kath's friend would tell her family an additional story of the pals all trooping into Greenwich Village after the show, Hepburn in her man's jacket and shorn head. Kath knew her way around the Village quite well, of course, and here several clubs openly welcomed women in men's clothing.

Bob Hepburn, at the time a smart, sharply observant teenager, was always particularly struck by the fast-talking athletic girls in tennis shorts and bobbed hair who trailed along behind Kath when she came home. Gradually, he began to question his sister's sexuality. "I always wondered," he said, "but never asked." Despite the Hepburns' openness about sex, there were certain boundaries, Bob said, he never crossed with Kath.

If Kath did experiment sexually at Bryn Mawr, she would hardly be the first or last college girl to do so. Yet even as she blossomed into a young woman, sex was not a major preoccupation in her life. "There was always a discomfort for her with the physical nature of sex," one close friend believed, a condition he said held true for her relationships with both men and women. "The sheer physicality of [sex], the skin-to-skin contact, was something . . . she always seemed uncomfortable with." With girls, at least, sexual experimentation need not progress much beyond kissing; and for

Kath, who not so long ago had seen herself as Jimmy, the experience may have seemed rather natural.

Certainly, she never spoke of marriage during this time. "We didn't think she'd ever [get married]," Bob Hepburn said. In this, Kath was closer to the model set by the older generation of educated women personified by Carey Thomas than to most girls her age, for whom marriage and family now defined their futures. For these girls, Dean Helen Taft Manning offered a new role model. The attractive daughter of President William Howard Taft had entered into a very public, very egalitarian marriage with Yale's Frederick Manning, who'd left his post and relocated to Bryn Mawr, teaching at nearby Swarthmore, when his wife was appointed dean in 1925.

Of this social shift, Kath was not unconscious. Visiting her aunt Edith Hooker in Baltimore sometime during her junior year, she was asked what it was that modern college girls most wanted. "They want to fall in love and get married," she quickly replied. In her own book on Hepburn, Barbara Leaming seemed to miss the irony in those words, presenting the anecdote as if it reflected Kath's own sincere feelings. But, in fact, she was *mocking* the trend; none of her close friends fit the mold of the female waiting for a ring. There is nothing to indicate that Kath, having grown up with Mary Towle, Bertha Rembaugh, and the women of Heterodoxy, had suddenly turned into a romantic. Everything, in fact, points to the opposite. "She wasn't boy crazy at all," Palache insisted. Kath's attitude, she said, was strictly "take 'em or leave 'em alone."

Her passion, as ever, remained athletics. Soon after junior year, Kath took part in another statewide golf championship, defeating the nearly ten-years-older Mrs. M. J. Lawlor 3–2 in the semifinal round in Bridgeport. The next day, for the title, she faced the well-known Georgianna Bishop, forty-nine years old and a steely-eyed veteran of hundreds of matches. This time, Hepburn's famous luck failed her. On June 3, Bishop trounced the cocky teenager 7–5. "Miss Hepburn's overeagerness appeared to be her undoing," one local sports reporter observed, "for she did not appear to have the remarkable control displayed by Miss Bishop."

That same overeagerness would contribute to various crises in the future. But Katharine Hepburn's eventual mastery of the art of control would, in the end, prove far more remarkable than anything Miss Georgianna Bishop displayed that day on the links.

Thirty thousand people crushed onto the piers on a bright, sunny morning in late June 1927. Some were debarking on summer vacations; most were bidding loved ones farewell. With a strong breeze blowing in off the Hudson, Kath and Palache, having been dropped at West Forty-fifth Street by Hep, pushed through the throng toward their waiting ship, each lugging a heavy canvas suitcase plastered with travel stickers. Off on an adventure, they were euphoric. Never would Palache forget the image of Kath running alongside her train as it arrived in Hartford from Boston, jubilantly waving a check for five hundred dollars from her father.

"It will be just the two of us," Palache wrote, "with no distractions, just Kate and I." It was their last summer vacation before graduation, and they'd spend it traveling through England and France. Kit had taken the same trip when she was Kath's age with Mary Towle, and Palache had been to Europe with her mother a few years before. The two sets of independent-minded parents had given their consent without any punctilios over chaperones. The girls traveled student third-class, and although neither Kath nor Palache ever mentioned the name of their ship, it was likely either the *Sierra Ventana* or, prophetically, the *Paris*, both of which steamed out of New York Harbor on June 25.

Yet if Palache had been looking forward to time alone with "her Kate," she was quickly delivered of that expectation. Something seems to have changed for Hepburn during that summer. For a girl whose attitude toward boys had been "take 'em or leave 'em," suddenly she was taking them far more often than not. Recovering from some initial seasickness (Palache played music to soothe her), Kath plunged headfirst into shipboard life. Most of the trip would be dominated by "the eternal talking of Kate," Palache said, and most of her jabbering would be directed at boys. While Palache might complain that the ladies' lounge was "generally full of men," Kath was invigorated by the presence of the opposite sex. With one young man in particular, a law student, Eugene O'Dunne, she formed a fast friendship. Palache, though she never grumbled, was often left behind.

O'Dunne, whom the girls called "Jim," had suffered from the same seasickness as Kath and had likewise been grateful for Palache's musical cure. The son of a prominent Baltimore judge, Jim was boyishly handsome, six feet tall, and given to the kind of bon mot and clever repartee that Hepburn would find attractive in men all her life. He'd just graduated in June with a B.A. from Johns Hopkins, Hep's alma mater, and had plans to start Harvard law the next year. Traveling with a friend, Louis Rawlins, also of Baltimore, who was sometimes paired with Palache, O'Dunne seemed just as interested in Kath as she was in him. When the ship docked at Plymouth, the two young people pledged to keep in touch, although, since Kath and Palache planned to "rough it," avoiding hotels, there was no way Jim could respond to any letters she sent.

In London, for seventy-five dollars, the girls bought a tiny open-air Morris Cowley car they dubbed "Little Lina," motoring out to Oxford and then on toward Wales. Sleeping in the car under the open sky or in haylofts discovered in barns, they were a bit ragged by the time they pulled over in a small Welsh village for provisions. As Kath waited with the car, a hay wagon rattled up alongside. Gazing down at Kath was the wagon's driver, a dark young man, "the handsomest creature" she'd ever seen. For a moment she indulged a fantasy of running off with him, until Palache came out of the store and the "spell was broken."

This sudden interest in the opposite sex came after three years of intense emotional (possibly even physical) attachments to other females. Was Kath worried about who she might turn out to be? Or was she simply sending Palache and the others a message, even unconsciously, that she would not be easily defined—that she was no Irene De Montcel, so unambiguously one thing and not the other?

There is another important consideration to explain Kath's sudden enthusiasm for the male species. On the cusp of turning twenty-one, she had discovered—for the first time—that men might find her attractive. They were responding to her as a young woman, not as a pal, and she seems to have found it exhilarating. By the time of her European adventure, her hair had grown long again, and her skin, as seen from her passport photo, was clear. She had also filled out, the striking bone structure that had made her such a good-looking boy now serving her well as a female. She hadn't become a beauty overnight. But it seemed that she was discovering her own particular appeal, and men were responding. For a girl who yearned to be the center of things, the regard of men was a fascinating plaything.

Still, the bond with Palache was only strengthened by the trip. Palache's letters brim over with affection for her friend. "She is a grand person to be with and to take about," Palache wrote home, "and we are having more fun together than I believed possible." From Wales the girls traveled north through Scotland, where they stayed with "friends of friends" in Montrose, enjoying hot baths and champagne. It was Kath's first taste of bubbly, Palache wrote, "and she didn't recognize it." Their only guide was a well-worn road map and "the advice of people along the way." To her mother, Palache mused, "We missed very little and enjoyed what we saw much more in light of [being] explorers and discoverers."

Palache drove 2,050 of the 2,100 miles and didn't complain. When they'd completed the circle back to London, planning to push on to Paris, they went hunting for a buyer for Little Lina. In *Me*, Kate would write that they sold the car "for more than [they'd] paid for it, which was certainly lucky." This supported the idea that Kate offstage was—like the Kate of the movies—able to talk anybody into anything. In Palache's oral history, she reported that they had simply broken even, selling the car back to the same dealer they'd bought it from on Great Portland Street. Neither story is true. To her mother, Palache wrote on July 26 that they'd sold Little Lina for "a little less than what [they] paid for it." Even in such trivial matters, legends had a way of flowering.

In Paris, the girls indulged themselves with a private bath at Cayre's Hotel, prompting Palache to declare they felt "luxurious." Their time in France was far more relaxing than their experience in Britain. Kath spent hours roaming through the Louvre. During the second week of August, she and Palache spent "two lovely days" at Versailles and Chantilly. On their last night in Paris, the girls took in the Folies Bergère, that legendary spectacle of extravagance, nudity, and song. Palache pronounced it "an appalling spectacle without too much beauty."

Meanwhile, Kath hadn't forgotten Eugene O'Dunne. Knowing he'd be returning on the *Leviathan* a week later than their own scheduled departure, she abruptly announced to Palache that they must change their plans so they could travel home with Jim. Barging up to the shipping office, Kath was told it would cost them fifteen dollars apiece to change their tickets. To offset the balance, Kath offered herself and Palache as cigarette girls, but the clerk declined. Their only choice was to travel steerage, and for that they needed vaccinations. The resulting shot caused Kath's leg to swell up, and she limped for the duration of the voyage home.

The *Leviathan* lived up to its name, with a 114-foot runway for mail-delivery biplanes on the top deck. The girls found themselves far below in a tiny cabin with no way into student third-class. Determined to find O'Dunne, Kath persuaded someone, a crewman presumably, to lift a door "all the way up" and let her sneak upstairs. She spent much of the return trip with Jim instead of Palache, who took her abandonment in stride. The crossing was marred only by fears of agitation among Italians in steerage upset over the executions of the anarchists Nicola Sacco and Bartolomeo Vanzetti in Massachusetts. At Southampton, armed guards boarded the ship for the protection of passengers.

Once the *Leviathan* docked at its pier on West Forty-fourth Street on September 5, Kath seems to have forgotten her fascination with Eugene O'Dunne. But men in general remained forefront in her mind. A month later, standing as bridesmaid for Ali Barbour at Hartford's South Church, Kath looked lovely—and quite feminine—on the arm of her escort. All of Ali's attendants wore "shades of the maple leaf, from pale to deep." Kath's gown was flame-colored, like leaves in autumn, the color perhaps chosen to match her hair.

Early the next morning, or one around this time, Kath stole into her brother Dick's room and planted a kiss on their sleeping houseguest, Robert McKnight, a Yale friend of Ali's new husband, Moreau Brown. McKnight would remember opening his eyes to the sight of Kath turning tail and running out. A handsome young man, McKnight had been a finance major at Yale, though the only figures he was really interested in were those he could sculpt. Rather than head to Wall Street, he planned to continue his studies at Yale Art School. Kath had met him the previous spring, when she'd accompanied Ali to a Yale dance.

Although no evidence supports it (Palache's letters, for example, usually so detailed, never mention him), Hepburn would later label McKnight one of her "beaux." In truth, there was simply no time for their friendship to turn into a romance. By October, Kath was back at school, and by the end of the year she was deep in the thrall of a new relationship. McKnight's true part in the legend seems to have been the opportunity to give a name to one of the men who the legend liked to tell us flocked around the young Hepburn. For his part, McKnight seems not to have minded the role. When Kate sent Lupton Wilkinson to speak to him, McKnight told him all about the kiss and suggested, on the strength of it, that he'd thought he and Hepburn might have been in love.

No matter the reality of her relationship with McKnight, Kath was emboldened by her newfound appeal to men and began her senior year feeling more rebellious than ever. Her suspension for smoking, leveled just days after Ali's wedding, bespoke a new position on campus. So did her part in a second school production, as Teresa in G. Martinez Sierra's *The Cradle Song*. No longer the roguish boy, "Katherine [sic] Hepburn was so extraordinarily lovely to look at," one enraptured fellow student opined, "that it was difficult to form any judgment on her acting."

Not so long before, romance had seemed an alien, even irrelevant concept. Now, as Teresa, Kath stood on stage quoting lyrical testaments to love: "Do you know how I would like to spend my life? . . . Sitting on the ground at his feet, looking up into his eyes, just listening to him talk. . . . He knows everything—everything that there is to know in the world, and he tells you such things! The things that you have known yourself, in your heart, and you couldn't find out how to say them. Even when he doesn't say anything . . . it is wonderful."

These were the sorts of words that would, in fact, come to define how Katharine Hepburn would think women should express their love for men. They were words that likely carried particular resonance for her as she uttered them during the run of the play—for by the time *The Cradle Song* premiered on December 17, Kath was deeply in love for the first time in her life.

FLYING UP ONTO A PINK CLOUD

Disrobing in front of the critic Edmund Wilson, the poet H. Phelps Putnam displayed, with a certain "conscious pride," long red gashes the length of his back. Wise to the ways of the world, Wilson presumed the gashes to be evidence of a sexually masochistic whipping. Later he surmised they might also have come from a woman with long nails and an overheated passion. But, whatever the source of the marks, what's most significant was the "conscious pride" with which the poet displayed them. He wore them like badges of honor.

"It is from the blood and not from the brain that Putnam attempts to rise," the writer Russell Davenport once observed of his friend. "One who does not feel his veins swell—with lust or wine or whatever—has no [chance] to understand."

From across the dining table at Dean Manning's house, Kath Hepburn locked eyes with this man, this lusty, moody, married, alcoholic poet thirteen years her senior. Right from the start there was something between them. He called her the Kid. She called him Phelpie. "I took one look at him," Hepburn would remember, "and I was stricken with whatever it is that strickens one at once and for no reason when one looks at a member of the opposite sex. I was fascinated."

Sometime probably during her sophomore year, Kath sat down for lunch at Clynnoc, Dean Manning's cozy Victorian residence with large windows overlooking the tennis courts. Across from her sat Putnam, a guest of Manning's husband. Put, as friends called him, was of medium height and slender. Deep-set dark eyes complemented a luxuriant mat of black hair on his chest and arms. His voice, long and drawn out with a Boston accent, was invariably hoarse, jagged from years of asthmatic wheezing. Though he was just a little past thirty, his hair had gone prematurely gray. He possessed a brooding, Brontëan beauty. In Kath's besotted opinion, Put's prominent brow made for "a very handsome head."

Equally struck was Put. "[A] rising flame / Of honor and dishonor and / A gong resounding overland," he wrote in a poem he'd later acknowledge was inspired by Kath.

Just what she was doing lunching with the dean is unknown; Kath certainly wasn't a pet of the administration. But Palache was, and it's a good bet that she was the conduit through which Kath came to Putnam's attention. Hailing from Jamaica Plain, a suburb of Boston across the river from Palache's hometown of Cambridge, Put was acquainted with Palache's sisters. Dragging Kath along with her to a gathering at the dean's, Palache likely made the first introduction. There was another connection on campus as well: Putnam had a sister, Frances, in Kath's class, though it does not appear that they knew each other well.

When that lunch occurred, however, is a bit murky. Hepburn said she met Putnam during the spring of her senior year. Despite that imprecise statement, Barbara Leaming offered enormous specificity in her biography of Hepburn. She placed the first meeting between the two during the May Day celebrations on campus and described Putnam as an aggressive suitor, inveigling a luncheon invitation at the dean's house after seeing Kath perform on stage. Yet there is absolutely no evidence for this. Dean Manning certainly did not make it a habit to facilitate meetings between students and her husband's friend, whose reputation as a philanderer was well known. The fact that Put had a sister in Kath's class would have made Manning even more wary of the potential for gossip.

Actually, from Putnam's own letters, we can deduce that he met Kath considerably earlier than her senior year. He would tell Russell Davenport that his poem "Marjory" was based on her, the name chosen because it contained the same number of syllables as "Katharine." That poem was written in 1926 and published the following year as part of Putnam's first collection, *Trinc*—all well before his supposed first meeting with Kath in spring 1928.

Fortunately, Put's voluminous correspondence allows us to chart his whereabouts with some degree of precision. In 1926, he was at Bryn Mawr in March and then again in December, retreating from an unhappy Boston marriage to a refuge offered by Fred Manning. In March, Kath would have been eighteen, a sophomore, still withdrawn and gawky, not yet the blossom of her junior year. It's possible this was the point at which they met, suggested by one of Put's poems, originally called "Girl's Curse" and published in *Trinc* as "Death Song of Childhood": "She came to me a stormy day, / It was beneath the wild March skies; / Sometimes she stumbled on her way / Because the tears were in her eyes."

Certainly, Kath was unhappy her sophomore year, though given her aversion to wallowing it was unlikely she shed many tears. But as a poet's metaphor for discontent, "the tears in her eyes" might well identify her. In fact, March 1926 was quite the stormy month in eastern Pennsylvania, the skies often wild with rain and wind. (March of 1927, by contrast, was an early harbinger of spring, with mostly clear skies and warm air.) In Put's poem, the unnamed girl bemoans a loss of innocence, brought on by "sinful" kisses. This also doesn't sound like Kath; if Put kissed her, she may have blushed, but she surely wouldn't have spent any time worrying about it. Still, the poem wasn't written from her perspective.

By December, Kath had started to come out of her shell; it was around this time that she jumped naked in the cloister fountain. She and Putnam may have met again at this point, and she may have been more receptive to his friendship.

Yet from her own account and from the letters of Palache, there's no evidence of an older brother of one of her classmates, a poet who made frequent visits to the dean's house, playing any part in her life. Kath was far more engaged with her girlfriends, heading into New York to see *The Captive* and other plays. It's quite possible, however, that Put had fixated on her, as a kind of image of the spirit of youth that he extolled in his poetry. Indeed, if Kath provided the inspiration for "Marjory," the poet would have had to fall under her spell by December 1926 at the very latest, for in January he sold his manuscript, including "Marjory," to the publisher George Doran.

After meeting her at Manning's, Putnam seems to have admired "the Kid" mostly from afar, as one might look back repeatedly on an exotic work of art. This spirited girl, rapidly transforming into a woman before his eyes, became Putnam's muse: "And when I wish to dream my whole / Spirit burns with an unknown name— / Marjory, Marjory." They likely saw each other again in Boston over the Christmas holidays, when Kath visited Palache, and possibly in Hartford on the occasional weekend during 1927. (We know Putnam was frequently there to visit his friend Farwell Knapp, whose house was not far from the Hepburns'.) Not until late that year, however, did Putnam return to Bryn Mawr. Only at that point, sometime in the late fall, was Put's infatuation at last reciprocated.

Was there a kiss? A walk on a chilly autumn night? Something happened to shift the dynamic between them, with Kath toppling headfirst into her first real love affair. "I flew up onto a pink cloud," she recalled, "sailing" blissfully through the waning days of her college career. Yet there was no sex; the poetry Put would write about her is infused with an unconsummated longing, and Hepburn herself always insisted she kept her virginity until the man who would be her husband took it away. Still, her memories of Putnam expose a rush of romantic feeling. For a girl who'd only recently begun paying attention to romantic feelings, it must have been a bewitching experience. Climbing down the trellis outside her window, she'd remember taking midnight strolls, mooning over "Phelpie." No one else in her life would ever elicit such romantic, love-struck memories.

He was certainly a romantic figure. People like Edmund Wilson and John Farrar—Putnam's editor at Doran and later a founder of Farrar Straus— compared Putnam to F. Scott Fitzgerald and Edna St. Vincent Millay, and expected a career to match. At the time Kath fell for him, Putnam's poetry collection *Trinc*—Rabelaisian for "drink"—had just been published and was the talk of literary circles. Attending a book-launch celebration in New York, Kath and Palache glimpsed the witty, sophisticated crowd that surrounded Phelpie. That he'd based key passages of his work on her—*her*, not Ali or Megs or Hope—could only have enchanted Kath all the more.

Yet for all his idealization of "the Kid," Phelps Putnam was never a monogamous man. Even as he escorted the college senior around the room—her polished, scrubbed face in stark contrast to the rouge and lipstick of his other women friends—Put was worried about a girl he had gotten pregnant who needed money for an abortion.

And if he might claim *love* set his relationship with Kath apart, even that wasn't an exclusive sort of amour. "I allowed an affair," Putnam wrote to his confidant Russell Cheney in January 1928, "which until then had been a grand poetic stimulus, to become something which may become a permanent positive or negative affect in my existence. At the same time I gradually grew into another affair which is creeping up and up on me because it is founded on . . . honesty, and that means a godawful lot to me." He was, he told Cheney, "in love" with three people at once: "x and y" and Ruth, his long-suffering, neglected wife.

The exact truth is unknown, but it seems likely Kath was the "grand poetic stimulus" who, by the close of 1927, had become for Putnam something else, something that might become "permanent." If so, such permanency posed a threat both to Ruth and to "y"—who could have been any number of other women, or as Kath no doubt eventually realized, other *men*. It was enough to leave Putnam "weeping a lot" and "going blah."

He had also been drinking heavily—like other men yet to appear in Kath's life.

On May 4, a warm, sunny Friday afternoon, some twenty thousand spectators, Hep and Kit among them, took their seats in the bleachers or stood on the lawn in anticipation of the annual Elizabethan celebration of May Day. All around them the magnolias were blossoming as if on cue. Trumpets sounded, followed by six young women dressed as courtiers marching through Pembroke Arch, carrying a litter holding a bejeweled Queen Elizabeth, played by the Bryn Mawr alumna Louise Fleischmann Maclay. Two snorting oxen appeared next, pulling a cart bearing the white maypole, followed by dancers, jesters, Robin Hood, Maid Marian, and Jack in the Green, the mystical chimney sweep of English tradition—all portrayed by Bryn Mawr students.

Then came the plays, enacted at various spots around campus. Kath had been cast in *The Woman in the Moone* by John Lyly. Inspired no doubt by her poet inamorato, who stood watching with eagle eyes from the audience, Kath threw herself into the part of Pandora, rushing to and fro across the lawn. Removing her sandals, she scampered barefoot across the grass in her flowing white translucent gown. Her hair became a wild, sensuous prop, billowing behind her as she ran. Her drama teacher, Samuel Arthur King, had encouraged her to play broadly, to go over the top, surely reckoning that bigger was better when spectators were so distant and dispersed. From the moment she shook her hair loose and kicked off her sandals, Hepburn's transformation was complete: from shy, awkward ugly duckling to star.

Later, Hep's only comment about her performance would be that everyone could see her dirty bare feet. But Kath would gush to anyone who listened that she had felt transformed. Eyewitnesses agreed. Gone was the memory of "the girl with the tight bun of reddish hair screwed up on the top of her head," said the author Hortense Flexner King, Bryn Mawr class of 1907 and a member of the audience. Instead, King saw a poised young barefoot nymph flitting across the lawn, a girl so far in character that she never once recoiled from "the sharpness of the grass in front of the grandstand."

In front of a grandstand, Kath Hepburn could put up with anything. The applause first heard nine years previous at the Hartford Club came washing back over her. Not for anyone else was the audience cheering, only for her: "I was just thinking about myself," she recalled with stark honesty. "I was the brilliant feature." Basking in the thunderous ovation, she knew this was what she wanted for the design of her life. She decided that the theater, and the applause it promised, was her destiny.

In the months leading up to May Day, Kath's sojourns into New York had taken on a new urgency. Her sights were now set on an acting career, and she wanted to absorb as much as she could. In February, Kath, Palache, and Lib Rhett took in all five hours of Eugene O'Neill's *Strange Interlude* with Lynn Fontanne at the John Golden Theater. There were numerous other plays as well, with Palache's letters often mentioning seeing "a play or two" with Kath.

Late in life, pressed about when and why she decided on acting, she'd claim ignorance: "I think it just happened. I honestly can't remember." But then, some candor: "I wanted to be famous. I wanted to be noticed." Elsewhere, more candor still: "I didn't really care in what."

For a girl who remained deeply insecure about her looks and her charm, performing offered a panacea. Makeup could disguise her bad skin. Costumes could fill out her figure and make her seem enticing. Her Pandora had proven how completely she could break free of the fears and withdrawal of her youth when let loose upon the stage. Kath's narcissism, her fierce desire for attention, was merely cover for years of low self-esteem. Not only was she still the little girl desperate for her father's attention, she was also in many ways still trying to prove her family's worth—and, by extension, her own—to all those people who had once shunned them in the street. "Being snubbed in our town gave me the goose one needs to get up and do something," she'd recall. And "do something" she certainly did.

Her self-absorption was only egged on by her friends, particularly two young men who flattered and cajoled her into accompanying them to a little house they shared in Easttown, in the woods of Chester County. There, in the privacy of their secluded bungalow, Jack Clarke and Luddy Smith persuaded her to take off her clothes for their camera. For a girl who'd grown up accustomed to naked bodies, her disrobing was nothing extraordinary, and she didn't need to worry that they'd make a pass at her: Jack, at least, was overtly homosexual. Besides, both men insisted their primary goal was to document her beauty—and to be called beautiful was still such a novelty that Kath agreed readily to pose any way they wanted. For years, she'd keep those photographs as fond mementos. When she misplaced them, she wondered: would they ever be discovered, and would the person who found them gaze upon the vibrant young girl and think she looked like Katharine Hepburn?

Although Luddy would play the greater role in her life, it was Jack with whom Kath originally had the stronger connection. Jack Clarke was one of those young men for whom the term *lost generation* seemed coined. Restless and reckless after serving in the world war, they were young people disillusioned with the American way of life. Jack never held a job. Tall and thin and "fascinating looking" (according to Kath), he was "a Philadelphia blade with lots of good social connections," his cousin Virginia Soule remembered. "He was dashing, delightful . . . [always] with a cravat around his neck."

From adventure to adventure Jack would jump, rich enough never to have to worry about the bills. He roamed through Europe; he invested in business; he bought and sold property on whims and dares. His father, John S. Clarke Sr., had founded Autocar, one of the country's first automobile manufacturing concerns, in 1898; within a few years the company was the area's largest employer. At a time when many such companies were going under, Autocar wisely specialized, concentrating on building trucks; by the mid-1920s, John Clarke and his brother Louis oversaw forty-five branches throughout the United States.

The Clarkes lived on Yarrow Street, adjacent to the Bryn Mawr campus, in a great old rambling house called Robindale. His wife having been committed to an asylum, Mr. Clarke enjoyed having company, frequently inviting students and their guests in for meals and lively parlor conversation. During their own college days, Palache's older sisters had also been guests of Mr. Clarke, a tradition Palache was pleased to continue. "Today we had a swell lunch at Mr. Clarke's," she wrote to her sister Jeannette in January 1927, "with everything from sherry to strawberries for dessert."

Jack Clarke's sisters, Louise and Agnes, twelve and fourteen years older than Kath, were frequently on hand as well. Society columns reported on their voyages to Europe and South America. Like Megs and Hope, the Clarke sisters were the kind of young women Kath always envied and admired and enjoyed being around, even if she never quite had the means to keep up. Louise and Agnes must have been fascinating for her in another way as well: well into their thirties, they had never married, and according to Kath they never planned to.

It was with the brash Jack, however, that Kath clicked immediately. Eight years her senior, Jack was the first homosexual man she would call friend, and it was from him that she formulated her particular list of unspoken imperatives to which every future gay friend had to adhere. Like Jack, they had to be masculine, or at least capable of putting on a good show; they had to be cultured and well connected; and most of all, they had to be discreet about sexual matters. What she liked about Jack was what she liked about all her homosexual male friends: there was no threat of sexual intimidation, and, without wives and children, all their attention could be directed at her.

Also like her later homosexual friends, Jack held out the promise of helping Kath in her career. He had excellent connections. Among his closest pals were Richard Aldrich, a wealthy socialite angling to become a Broadway producer (he'd go on to revolutionize American summer theater and marry Gertrude Lawrence); and Francis R. Hart, a young playwright and recent Harvard graduate working for Edwin Knopf, a producer for the Auditorium Players in Baltimore.

On Saturday, May 12, Kath's twenty-first birthday (though few knew it, thinking the day fell in November), Lib Rhett drove her to Baltimore to meet with Knopf, Jack having arranged for an introduction through Hart. But introductions went only so far. "I wanted no part of her," Knopf would remember. He didn't like her messy hair or shiny nose. Worst of all: "Excitement had blotched her skin under her freckles." Since Knopf recalled the scene for the seminal *Saturday Evening Post* article, in which Hepburn and her associates were busy laying down the spin, his account—wherein the awkward girl proves her mettle and wins a part—needs to be taken with a grain of salt. But the blotchy skin also suggests some veracity to his story: Hepburn often broke out when she was nervous.

Discouraged, Kath steeled herself to return and audition for Knopf's upcoming production of *The Czarina*. Auditions were set for the last weekend before graduation, so Lib, busy with last-minute details, couldn't be counted on to play chauffeur again. Knowing her father would balk if she asked him for train fare, Kath wired Robert McKnight for the money.

So it was that, while her friends savored their last weekend of college life, Kath arose early on Saturday, June 2, and boarded the train for Baltimore, embarking on the first leg of a career that would last some seventy years. Rattling across the tracks through the countryside, stopping in Philadelphia, then Wilmington, the train took several hours to reach its destination. If she'd been prone to introspection, Kath might have taken the time to reflect on her passage from college into the larger world, and to consider where the relationship with Putnam might be heading. But as she would prove time and time again, where her career was concerned, she could be acutely singular in her focus. *Concentration,* several friends said, was always one of Hepburn's most-used words, and a quality she much admired in others. No doubt that day on the train her mind concentrated on the audition and the audition only.

Her determination paid off. Hustling herself over to the grand old Auditorium Theatre on Howard Street, she landed a part in Knopf's play, even if it was just a bit, as a lady-in-waiting to the czarina, played by Mary Boland.

When, the next night, Kath sat in the recently dedicated Goodhart Memorial Hall on the Bryn Mawr campus for the traditional baccalaureate sermon, she must have been bored, even irked, by the impassioned address by Rabbi Stephen Wise of the Free Synagogue of New York, who exhorted modern youth not to forsake religion. "There is no easy way through Egypt to Canaan," the rabbi thundered. With the events of the previous day still uppermost in her mind, all Kath cared about was getting through Bryn Mawr to Baltimore.

On a rainy night in February 1928, Farwell Knapp, assistant tax commissioner for the state of Connecticut, was awakened by a loud pounding on the door of his house in West Hartford. Hurrying downstairs, he found his old friend from Yale, Phelps Putnam. The poet was drunk and spitting mad. He'd had an argument with his friend, the painter Russell Cheney, whose niece was Knapp's wife, and he had come from Cheney's farm across the river in South Manchester, hoping to take shelter with Knapp.

It had been a bad winter for Put, and the spring would only get worse. While Kath dreamed of a glorious career, Putnam was in a downward spiral. Soon after the New Year, he'd endured one of his periodic blowouts with his wife. As he was apt to do, Put took refuge among the male camaraderie he venerated in his poetry. To Kittery, Maine, he'd headed first, where Cheney had a cottage, the "Ditty Box." Afterward he'd tagged along back to the farm in South Manchester with Cheney and his companion, the Yale professor F. O. Matthiessen, whom everyone called "Matty." The problem was that when Put and Cheney got together, they tended to drink heavily and were soon at each other's throats. Their altercations usually ended with one or both passed out on the floor, leaving Matty to clean up the mess.

From Knapp's, Putnam, still obviously drunk, fired off a letter to Cheney: "When I come to you with a sick, empty, and confused soul . . . you go away. What the hell?" Clearly, Cheney had proven unable or unwilling to ameliorate the pain Putnam perpetually carried around with him. Suffering from heart palpitations, as well as asthma in the spring and fall, Put was never in good health. But it was his alcoholism that exacerbated everything else, including anguish over an increasingly complicated love life. Early in 1928, Putnam seems finally to have grasped this: "I have always considered it [drinking] to be a physical rather than a spiritual question," he wrote to Cheney. "I can drink too much for a feller with my diseases—that's a truth. But up to now, drinking has always seemed to contribute to my spirit rather than destroy it."

What drove Putnam to the bottle—to "the poetry of the liquid nightingale," a trait he believed he shared with his fellow poet Hart Crane? Put said drinking allowed him an escape from the pain of his asthma and headaches, but it went deeper than that. To understand Putnam is to understand the dynamics that would govern nearly all of Katharine Hepburn's romantic attachments with men.

Born in 1894, the son of an insurance executive, Howard Phelps Putnam early on rebelled against the petit bourgeois future presumed for him. Luckily, his "essentially unworldly" parents, according to his sister Frances, regarded a poet son "not as a curse but as a blessing." When he went off to Yale, Putnam first found his place in the world. Part of the Yale Renaissance generation, a period of time that produced graduates like Archibald MacLeish, Cole Porter, Monty Woolley, Philip Barry, Stephen Vincent Benét, Henry R. Luce, and Thornton Wilder, Putnam forged relationships within the intensely male college environment that would remain the most important of his life. Among his Skull and Bones comrades, there was Knapp, Charlie Walker, and Lawrence Tighe, later Yale's treasurer, but most of all there was Fred Manning, whom Putnam called his "bleak friend, my rare unswerving company." Put was best man at Manning's wedding and often seemed a third wheel in his friend's marriage. At the dean's house at Bryn Mawr, a room was always available for Putnam. Manning's daughters knew him as "Uncle Put," the moody, dreamy man with whom their father routinely disappeared as soon as school holidays began.

Putnam never really got over the trauma of graduation in 1916. His poetry is filled with epistles to his cherished friends, both his original classmates and those who came along later, younger Yale men with whom he bonded. Russell "Mitch" Davenport and Max Foster were immortalized in Putnam's poetry (and in a painting by Russell Cheney) as "Les Enfants Pendus," which the poet translated as "the hung-up children." The three of them are depicted in the poem as hanging by their necks from a tree, although they are not dead.

The most significant of Put's postcollege relationships, however, was with Cheney. During his senior year he'd seen Cheney, a Yale alumnus, on campus. He would remember thinking: "This is quite a feller. You'll see a lot of specimens around this place but nobody like Cheney . . . You could tell it by looking at him, that he was extraordinary."

Soon after graduation, his asthma particularly acute, Putnam sought relief in the dry climate of the American West, where he met up again with the tall, handsome painter, like him a sufferer of lung ailments. Cheney was thirty-five, Putnam twenty-two, exactly the same age difference that would separate Putnam from Kath. Through art and through drink, the two men connected; after several weeks of flirtation, both admitted feelings for each other. "I've seen so many people going along full of friendship but never finding it out because they would never say it," Putnam wrote to Cheney. "Now I can say you are my friend, Russell, and I love you." He hoped Cheney would know what he meant when he wrote those words, and how the painter had "found [Putnam's] heart."

"Your letter was so damned good to get," Cheney replied. "I suppose I did know—but just the same, a thing you want so much might color all the little things your instincts had built on. But now I know it didn't. You bet I 'get' you through what you say."

Soon afterward, they became lovers. When Putnam returned to the East, he barraged Cheney with a string of love letters. "One thing I know, one unhowled truth for us," Put declared. "I love you, and you me—It is enough! It is the point of flame round which the world of misty l'amour turns." He signed the missive, "Sad lines written by a fond swain."

Fond he may have been, but faithful he was not. For all his male bonding, Putnam remained obsessed with the conquest of women. "The female adventures that I loved [I would] conceal [from Cheney]," Putnam admitted years later. Indeed, his womanizing would become as much a part of his legend as his poetry; many of his unpublished poems, in fact, deal crudely with male-female sex. "Fucking Is Fun" he titled one poem: "[T]he best remembered art / Is a well prepared, . . . drawn out fuck." In "Sonnets to Some Sexual Organs," he wrote, "You lead us, master, sniffing to the hunt, / In quest forever of the perfect cunt."

For all that, he seemed not to like women very much. His friend Charlie Walker said Put "denigrated" women "as a species." Reading his letters does give testimony to a deep, fundamental misogyny: "That nifty little piece of arse I had out in Sioux City has gone and got it into her head that I knocked her up, the dizzy bitch," Put wrote to Mitch Davenport in 1928. "The joke she hadn't counted on is that she thinks I'm Frank Holcomb from San Fran. Just the same, that little whore gave me some good times."

A similar attitude pervades his poetry. David Bergman, a professor of English at Towson State University and the author of several books of literary criticism, concluded about Putnam's work: "He doesn't like women although he feels compelled to be with them. The reasons are unclear, since he doesn't find them physically attractive or emotionally supportive. What he nostalgically looks back toward is the homosocial world of college in which he could be with the boys."

The affair with Cheney ended around 1919. They remained close, however, even after Cheney entered into his twenty-year relationship with Matthiessen, with whom he found what few homosexuals of that era ever did: a lasting, fulfilling commitment. "As Put says," Cheney wrote to Matthiessen, "you have given me something he never could, no matter how close we were."

Putnam liked people to believe—indeed he himself may have believed—that the reason he hadn't been able to give Cheney what he wanted was because he wasn't homosexual. He insisted, without prejudice, that Cheney and Matty were different creatures than he: "The . . . 'Third Sex' school will hail you," Putnam wrote to Matty in 1928, "together with their master, Cheney, in that dim future which we, alas, shall not see."

Though he was clearly denying an essential aspect of himself, Putnam *was* different from Cheney and Matthiessen and the forthright way in which they lived their lives. In 1920, Putnam had married Ruth Peters. The couple fought often, living separately for long stretches. During these times, Putnam took refuge with Cheney or Fred Manning. Never did he hold a job for long. There was a brief stint as an editor at the *Atlantic Monthly*, but mostly Put paid his bills by writing freelance advertising copy.

All along, he kept up his pursuit of women, bragging about his exploits in letters to Davenport. Sometimes his accounts seem hollow, like the tall tales told by a blowhard drunk. Indeed, as the decade wore on, his alcoholism only got worse, leading one to suspect that his stories were exaggerations, and the drinking a convenient excuse: *I'm sorry, my dear, I'm simply too drunk to finish this tonight.*

Putnam wasn't alone in his sexual conflicts. Among his close friends, at least two, Mitch Davenport and Farwell Knapp, offer striking parallels to his own life: both were trapped in unhappy marriages and only truly content when in the company of men they loved. In Davenport's case, his letters and journals reveal homosexual experiences in college, as well as a lifelong sexual struggle that often left him depressed and bitter. In addition, a third member of their group, Charlie Walker (who'd also marry and have children), was arrested in 1916 on an apparent morals charge, which usually meant public homosexual activity.

In that pre-Stonewall world, the modern dichotomy of closeted versus "out" is neither accurate nor useful. Few homosexuals based their identities or sense of themselves on their sexual desire. Despite their feelings and even the occasional same-sex experience (often in college), these people married and had children; they wanted the social currency marriage offered. Putnam's friend Gerald Murphy, a (married) artist and socialite, had many affairs with men but observed, "Outside of a man and a woman, and children and a house and a garden, there's nothing much." Even some artists, usually more likely to flout social mores, saw the benefits of marriage; the homosexual poet Witter Bynner, another friend of Putnam's, proposed to Edna St. Vincent Millay, though he later reneged on his proposal.

Others, however, took a more radical route. While still not "out" in a modern sense—for such a construct did not yet exist—they acknowledged their homosexuality, first to themselves, then to a few select friends. Some, like Cheney and Matthiessen (and Mary Towle and Bertha Rembaugh), even managed to find lifelong companions. Yet far more common were people like Putnam and Davenport, who could never conceive of themselves as homosexual, despite their love for other men. Homosexuals were fairies, pansies, or "little boys"—a label Cheney once angrily derided as "filthy" when a friend used it to describe his largely gay circle of friends. (Interestingly, it was also a term Katharine Hepburn would later use herself to refer dismissively to George Cukor's gay friends.)

The fates of these men are telling. The number of suicides in Putnam's circle is striking: Farwell Knapp put a gun to his head; Parker Lloyd-Smith, boon companion of Mitch Davenport, leaped from the twenty-third floor of a building. Even Matthiessen, the most grounded of the whole group, plunged from the twelfth floor of a Boston hotel in 1950, depressed over Cheney's death and weary of being hounded for both his homosexuality and his political views.

Putnam, by the spring of 1928, seemed headed in that same direction himself, drinking himself to an early grave. Long-simmering internal conflicts, exacerbated by the pull of his various current relationships, exerted a heavy toll. Over and over again, it would be Cheney he would turn to for some amelioration of the pain, and despite his relationship with Matthiessen, Cheney did his best. He retained a soft spot for Putnam, often sending him money or providing refuge during crises. Of course, Put knew just how to tug

at the older man's heartstrings, signing his letters "your baby Byron" or gushing that hearing his voice was like "eating golden leaves." Matty, not a little
jealous, cautioned Cheney to beware of his former lover: "[D]earest, to keep
your friendship with Put you must learn to give yourself to him and hold
your detachment at the same time."

But when Cheney did detach from Putnam, as he appears to have done
that February of 1928, he often provoked drinking binges for the both of
them. After Putnam's head had cleared, he sent off an apology to Cheney for
starting the whole thing: "My trouble . . . is that I become childish when my
soul goes flat on me."

All of this flies in the face of what has been written before, depicting Putnam as enraptured and inspired and productive in his relationship with
Kath. That might have described him *before* she returned his affections,
when she was simply "a grand poetic stimulus." But now his soul was "flat."
Too many potential problems loomed: the "Kid" was graduating and would
expect more from him. Meanwhile, as always, there was Ruth, waiting back
at their house in Jamaica Plain. And clearly there were unresolved issues
with Cheney. "The doc says my heart is bad," Put wrote to Cheney, just days
before watching Kath's glorious turn as Pandora. "He doesn't know how bad
it is. If he did he'd cross himself and put a holy wafer on my forehead."

Part of his despair also came from the disappointing response to *Trinc*.
By early January, it had sold five hundred copies, not bad for poetry books
but well below Putnam's grandiose expectations. Most of the reviews agreed
that while Putnam had promise, this first effort fell short of the mark. "At
times an inspired amateur, but an amateur still," one critic concluded. The
New York Times thought he had "poetic power, if he knew how to handle it,"
but then added the damning adjective *sophomoric*. Angered by such comments, Putnam fired off defensive letters to Doran, prompting his editor,
John Farrar, to reply, "I am proud to have published your book, sorry only
that you have had so little pleasure in it."

The man Kath fell in love with in 1927 was a man of deep contradictions
and staggering insecurities. Despite having had a book published, of which
many poets only dreamed, he was not happy. Kath saw his torment; how
could she have not? "I always liked bad eggs," she'd admit, years later, "always, always . . . attracted to them." Troubled men—perhaps stirring memories of her father or her brother—were irresistible to her. Troubled men
who adored her, who needed her, who seemed to come back to life only under her touch. Men with secrets, with conflicts, whose very sexual ambiguity
attracted her just as hers attracted them. Between Kath and Putnam there

was passion, no question about that, but it wasn't sex that drove their passion. It was need. It was longing. It was fear.

Sitting beside his parents watching his sister graduate on the morning of June 7, 1928, Putnam probably said nothing, barely even raised an eyebrow, when Katharine Hepburn made her own way up to the podium to accept her diploma. Not yet was the world wise to their love. Yet he had done the one thing that could only complicate his life—and hers—even further. He had asked the Kid to live with him.

ECSTASY

A t the wheel of the car, Kath looked over at her father in the passenger seat, grim and silent after the words she had just spoken.

"I'm going to be an actress," she repeated. But still Dr. Hepburn said nothing.

Until now, everything had been going smoothly. After the graduation ceremonies, they'd waved a cheerful good-bye to Kath's college years and set off on the trek back to Hartford. Thirty miles outside Bryn Mawr, crossing through the village of Doylestown, Kath had finally worked up the nerve to break the news of her career decision. The mood in the car had abruptly changed.

"I already have a job," she continued, rushing to fill the silence. She glanced at her mother in back, who was suddenly on pins and needles, leaning forward. Kath proceeded to tell them about *The Czarina*, rehearsals for which were scheduled to start in four days.

Finally Hep could hold his temper no longer. "This is just you being a show-off!" he bellowed. A burst of invective ensued between father and daughter, with Kit's attempts to calm them proving pointless. By the time they reached New York, they had all fallen stubbornly silent, and remained that way for the rest of the ride home.

Home was, in fact, no longer there: Hep had finally built his castle, an impressive brick and slate mansion on Bloomfield Avenue in West Hartford, a residence befitting his status as senior surgeon at Hartford Hospital. The architect had incorporated many features similar to 133 Hawthorn—the gables, the trim—but the house Kath came home to that day in June 1928 was largely alien to her, as she'd visited only a few times before. Bloomfield Avenue would always be her father's house, never her own.

Indeed, Hep took a fierce pride in the house, patting himself on the back for purchasing stocks during the war, when most of his competition was off fighting, and then selling them for several times their original value in the economic boom of the 1920s—just *before* the stock market crash. Such good fortune seemed to suggest the gods smiled on him, even if his colleagues at the hospital had recently failed to elect him chief of surgery, a decision that deeply rankled and left him sensitive to all slights.

Yet, even at full force, Hep had lost some of his power to shock and awe his daughter. Now a young woman, Kath was not about to step back into the role she had played as a girl, meekly submitting to her father's will in exchange for his attention. One might actually consider those few days between graduation and the start of her career her true coming of age. While the battles raged, she held on determinedly. Her ambition clearly was a sore point for Hep. Despite the fact that he'd raised his children to strive for attention, Dr. Hepburn loathed people who sought publicity for selfish reasons, which is what he called Kath now. "I can still hear his shouts," Marion Hepburn recalled, years later, "his fine and fiery performance"—an exhibition she termed *medieval.*

Yet for all the angry words tossed about, to Hep's surprise, his stubborn eldest daughter was not backing down. Eye to eye with her, Dr. Hepburn called acting "a sordid lifestyle, one step from the streets." If Kath persisted with the idea, he threatened, he'd cut off her allowance.

"Then do it," she said, standing defiantly before him.

Hep could bear her insolence no more. He slapped her across the face.

Watching the scene, Kath's brothers and sisters recoiled. Never before had they seen anyone stand up to their father in that way. Kath simply turned around, walked upstairs, and began packing. One way or another, she would be in Baltimore on June 11.

Where Kit was in all of this is a mystery. That formidable lady, so persuasive and politically cunning on the world stage, seems to have once again retreated to the background on the domestic front. It seems to be where she was most comfortable on those occasions when her husband's temper took over. The Hepburn legend would imply that Kit gave her tacit approval to her daughter's choice, secretly working behind the scenes to soften Hep's opposition. Some of that may be true; Kit certainly believed women should make their own choices in life. "I think Mother was glad to see me do something rather than marry," Hepburn would say later. But Kit was also a bit of a snob, especially about popular culture, and would have had to feign any enthusiasm for her daughter's choice of career. After devoting her life to improving conditions for women, she may well have been dismayed watching Kath dance off to play a lady-in-waiting.

Later, on occasion, Hepburn would imply that she had indeed disappointed her mother. Once she stated quite plainly that Kit was "horrified," that she "thought acting was silly." The fact that Palache was soon working for the Birth Control Clinical Research Bureau, where Kit sat on the board, could only have made Kath's choice of careers stand out even more starkly in her mother's mind.

No matter her parents' opinions, Kath left the house as planned on June 9 and boarded the train for Baltimore. With her she took just one bag and a paltry amount of money she'd managed to save on her own. Hep never broke, never gave in even to wish her well.

In *Stage Door*, one of Katharine Hepburn's best movies of the 1930s, there's a scene between her character, Terry Randall, the patrician socialite who wants to be an actress, and her father, a proud, stubborn aristocrat who opposes her. Terry is calm and articulate in defending her ambition, to which her father draws an affectionate sigh and asks, "Will you come back home if you are a failure?"

"I don't have that kind of pride," she replies. "Would you have me?"

Her father smiles. "You're still my favorite daughter."

Originally written for the stage by Edna Ferber and George S. Kaufman, *Stage Door* offers a happy mirror image of reality. The above scene would be layered onto the legend as the years went by, standing in for what really happened between Kath and her father. Terry Randall is so much like Hepburn— arrogant, ambitious, not a little condescending, and quite charming on top of it all—that it was easy to believe.

Yet just how affronted Hep remained after Kath left for Baltimore is indicated by her choice of lodging. She may have hoped to stay with Edith Hooker, as her aunt had hosted her when she'd driven down with Lib Rhett in May for her first meeting with Knopf. Edith was no doubt sympathetic to her niece's ambition; she herself had briefly flirted with a stage career, study-ing with Richard Mansfield in Paris. But instead, Kath decamped at the Bryn Mawr Club. As much as she may have regretted it, Edith knew all too well the fury her brother-in-law would exhibit if she offered succor to his errant daughter at this time.

As always, this too would pass. Katharine Hepburn forgave her father, making sure that all future accounts of her rise presented their disagreement as an entertaining sort of squabble. Accordingly, we were told that in the mail there soon arrived ten dollars—not her allowance, for Hep had cut that off—but his winnings from a bridge game. It was Hep's way of saving face while still assuring his daughter she had his support.

But, in truth, the rift between father and daughter did not heal fully for years. Every inch her father's daughter, always as stubborn as he was, Kath now had even more motivation to be famous: to prove her father wrong. She had no choice but to succeed.

During the ensuing weeks in Baltimore with the Auditorium Players, Kath smelled for the first time the greasepaint of the theater. She heard the rattle of the curtain being hoisted up and down. She listened to the echo her voice made in the empty theater during rehearsals. She was a working ac-tress. The very idea of it filled her up, made her blood race. She was a girl transformed: Mary Boland, the star of the company, would recall they were "all awed and excited at the way [their] ugly duckling blossomed."

But the company was in trouble. Operating in the red, Knopf and his partner, William Farnsworth, greeted their new player with gloom and pes-simism. Soon after Kath's arrival, Knopf sailed to Paris to try to secure some foreign funding. His trip appears to have not been productive. Farnsworth told the press that the company lost money every week. So there were lots of hopes—and careers—riding on *The Czarina*.

But when the play opened on June 18—the first time Katharine Hepburn trod professionally across the boards—the house was only half full. *The Cza-rina* ended up bringing in just $4,259.50, about a third of the gross for *The Captive*, the company's biggest hit that year.

Still, Kath was relieved when Knopf signed her for their next show, the sex comedy *The Cradle Snatchers*, also starring Mary Boland. The bo-somy, dithery star took a liking to the young actress, giving her "all sorts of bits and pieces," Kath remembered. Again her part was small, but Kath was encouraged by the larger crowds and nine curtain calls. The following week she again essayed a bit part in Maxwell Anderson's *Saturday's Children*, which has never before been included in her stage credits, and then went into rehearsals for Samuel Shipman's *Crime*, starring Kenneth MacKenna.

But for Knopf and Farnsworth, the tide had not turned. On July 8, Farnsworth strode into the theater and handed each member of the company his personal check for one week's employment, announcing the Auditorium Players was folding immediately. "Baltimoreans want dirt and not art in the theater," a bitter Farnsworth sniffed to the press. Some, like MacKenna, were tapped for a New York production that Farnsworth and Knopf hoped to mount later that summer, but most had only that one week's check to get them through to their next job.

Later, Lupton Wilkinson would rewrite history to fit the demands of the Hepburn legend, portraying MacKenna telling Knopf prophetically that he thinks they'd be "smart" to keep Kath on. (Knopf responds, in a perfect narrative segue, "You too, eh?") But in truth, Kath was at a standstill. Going home was not an option, not if it meant facing her father's smug "I told you so." Unlike Terry Randall in *Stage Door*, she did indeed have that kind of pride. The only offer in front of her was the one from Phelpie to live with him in New York. So, downhearted, she started packing her bag.

Like a scene in a movie, pages of a calendar lift off and blow away. The first week of July turns into the second. The provincial streets of Baltimore fade out as the skyline of Manhattan superimposes itself on the screen. A veritable highway of barges and ships steams along the East River. Zoom in now on one particular building on the waterfront, a railroad tenement with a heavy black iron fire escape. Two figures are hunkered down in a corner. One of them is Katharine Hepburn. The other is H. Phelps Putnam.

She'd remember Mitch Davenport's flat on Beekman Place as "quiet" and "romantic." For hours she'd sit there, gazing out along the river and Roosevelt Island beyond, Putnam at her side, scribbling away in his cat-scratch penmanship (not unlike her own) in a spiral-bound journal.

Kath was in heaven, almost literally, in their little perch. Life was suddenly very good. Davenport, heading for Paris, had turned over his flat to Putnam, who was working on a new book of poems. Sitting at his feet, Kath watched Phelpie write and took a giddy satisfaction in playing his muse. "She was the unexplained, the end of love, / The one who occupies the dreamy self," Putnam wrote of her. The girl who'd hidden out in her dorm room could scarcely have imagined such a life. On top of all that, she'd heard from Knopf, who'd given her a bit part in the show they were planning, *The Big Pond*. After tryouts, it was headed for Broadway. Kath was on her way.

In her youthful innocence, this is what she imagined living with a man could be like. Inspiring. Romantic. But ultimately platonic. That's important to understand, for again, Hepburn's relationship with Phelps Putnam informs all of her future connections with men. Now that she was an adult, Kath's discomfort with "skin-to-skin" contact manifested itself quite specifically. Several friends insisted she had a lifelong aversion to the actual act of sexual intercourse. "That seemed to be the line she didn't like to cross," said one. "She could enjoy the affections of men up to that point, but loathed going any further." For a girl who'd always identified with males, it's not a surprising perspective; the consummation of the sexual act may have felt somehow unnatural to her. She seemed content with the kind of mutual platonic adoration she had with Putnam, perhaps supplemented by the occasional honorable kiss or caress.

Yet the lack of physical intimacy between them could be attributed as much to Putnam, who was still struggling with his own inner demons. They may have at least attempted some sexual intimacy. Consider Putnam's poem penned as therapy at Cheney's suggestion: "Up in your room, remember, / We had a racket / You took off your little skirt / And I, my jacket." But that's all they take off. Rather than his body, what the narrator bares is his "soul," which leaves him "unsteady" and "under fit for estasy" when away from his wife. As an explanation for Putnam's impotence, it was as good as any other.

Certainly no such compunction had stopped Putnam in the past, not if some woman in Sioux City was carrying his child. But things had changed. As his relationship with Kath intensified, Put gave his friends the impression that he was "deeper in hell than ever." What seems paradoxical is actually not. Kath's easy camaraderie, her lack of demand for sex, her unquestioning acceptance of his moods, brought Putnam's dissatisfaction with his marriage into stark relief. At the same time, he couldn't blame Ruth for wanting more from a husband; what woman wouldn't? Except the Kid, of course, who was, after all, a creature apart. Putnam's guilt only increased: Ruth, he said, was "more noble than most women."

That very nobility made things worse. When Put's friends invited Ruth to Cheney's house in Kittery, they sent back reports of her "high spirits"—though Knapp interpreted them as "a conscious determination to keep a stiff upper lip, to maintain her poise and self-reliance." In such a context, Put's downward spiral throughout 1928 isn't difficult to fathom. Driven by guilt over a marriage that should never have happened in the first place, he was now additionally humiliated by his failure to sexually perform with Kath.

Yet Kath danced through that summer in a bubble of optimism. Of course she knew that Phelpie was "vaguely married," but it didn't seem to faze her. Kath rationalized that whatever problems existed in the Putnam marriage predated her—so she could skip along blithely, free of any guilt. She wasn't trying to replace Ruth; indeed, if Put had feared that Kath would demand more now that she was out of college, he was wrong. She simply loved being in love, needing nothing more than that—certainly not sex. "I had no intention of living in sin with Phelpie," she wrote. "I just wanted living. Sin could wait. Living itself was a sort of ecstasy . . . I was on my own in a high state of excitement."

That glorious summer would leave a huge impression. "Phelps knew everyone," Hepburn remembered. She'd always be drawn to people with connections, who had a sense for what was "in." Of course, she already knew New York, but she had seen it as an outsider. Now Putnam took her to places like Tony's, the speakeasy made famous by the humorist Robert Benchley and his crowd, housed in the basement of a four-story brownstone on West Forty-ninth Street. There, in the smoky darkness, bathtub gin was served in ceramic mugs, often highly sugared to disguise the taste of alcohol in case any undercover feds were afoot. Over in a corner, the owner, Anthony Soma, could be spotted singing bel canto while standing on his head. In such an anything-goes atmosphere, people like Benchley and Edmund Wilson held court, pronouncing upon the latest theatrical or literary sensation. They liked to tease Kath: "I was their victim," she recalled for Dick Cavett. The impressionable young woman soaked it all up—and enjoyed her mugs of sweet vino blanc.

She'd probably arrived in New York sometime during the second week of July, around the same time Putnam showed up from Boston. Davenport didn't depart until August 3, however, so Kath, for a couple of weeks, had bunked in with her aunt Betty Hepburn, widow of her father's brother Charles, at her house on East Eightieth Street. This gave Kath time to get to know Davenport, who would become her closest friend among Putnam's crowd. Mitch's brooding intensity was quite appealing to her. Sitting with him on his fire escape, a low moon hanging over the river, Kath would listen sympathetically as Mitch shared his heartache over the breakup of his engagement (to another of Russell Cheney's nieces). Certainly, she was wise enough to understand the fundamental nature of Mitch's problems with women, just as she likely guessed the truth of her own paramour's conflicted sexuality. Yet it didn't matter; it was all part of the social whirl and giddy sense of experimentation that were part of these times. Hepburn and her circle of friends were people who lived with sexual ambiguity, who made room for it.

Meanwhile, she had a play to do. Rehearsing one day with Kenneth MacKenna, who'd trekked north to star in *The Big Pond*, Kath's voice (as she herself described) suddenly shot up into the top of her head. Dropping an arm around her pointy shoulder blades, MacKenna took her aside. "You need a voice coach," he told her. When she asked him who, he smiled and told her to leave it to him.

"Dear Frances," read MacKenna's note of introduction. "More customers! Miss Katherine [sic] Hepburn . . . really has talent and loads of personality and charm. Stands awfully and never sits in a chair if there's an inch of floor available."

"Frances" was Miss Frances Robinson-Duff, the doyenne of New York's acting coaches, a big, full-figured woman, fifty years old, with a lilting, musical voice. Kath found her "stout—big stomach, medium bosom, corseted." For Robinson-Duff, it was all about the diaphragm. In her top-floor studio on East Sixty-second Street, she kept a bronze statue of a musician with a woman swooning between his knees; across the woman's stomach the musician wielded a bow, as if to cut her in half—or play her like an instrument. Engraved below the figures on the statue's base was the phrase LIFE PLAYING ON THE DIAPHRAGM.

Looking over the skinny little thing who'd climbed the steep stairs to her studio, Robinson-Duff raised one eyebrow. Suddenly, she snatched Kath's hand and placed it under her heaving bosom. "Feel and listen," she instructed. "Experience first-hand the proper use of the diaphragm." Pursing her lips and sucking in a long, deep breath, Robinson-Duff then proceeded to dramatically blow out a candle. It was a moment Hepburn never forgot.

"It was somehow very embarrassing to me," she recalled. "Her bosom—her diaphragm—the top of that corset."

"Miss Robinson-Duff's Breathing Exercises" were typed up and mimeographed, handed out to all her clients (who included, at that time, the actresses Ina Claire and Ruth Chatterton). "Close one nostril," read the first exercise, "and inhale to the depth of the lungs, trying to pack the breath in well against the base in the back. Advance the corners of the lips and blow slowly out, moving the diaphragm muscle in and out rhythmically. When the diaphragm arrives out, open the jaw and relax the lips, close the jaw and again exhale renewing this 'in and out' movement of the diaphragm."

Kath bought into the process completely. "Producing air from the diaphragm rather than straining the throat" became a lifelong career goal for her, one she never fully mastered, she believed, given how often her voice would go hoarse in parts that were "fast and loud." But Robinson-Duff did teach her one trick: how to call "Hey!" straight from the diaphragm. That "Hey!" can be heard in *Little Women* and again almost sixty years later, sounding exactly the same, in *The Man Upstairs*. It was a sound she made often in her private life, too, that deep-throated, diaphragmatic "Heeey!" echoing up through her New York town house or across the beach at Fenwick.

Robinson-Duff didn't come cheap: tuition for the twenty-five-week schedule of classes ranged from $100 to $125 (private lessons were even more), and Kath, by her memory, had something less than $250 left to her name. So she wrote to her father, arguing that if she was going to pursue an acting career, she ought to do it right. Most likely the letter was sent while she was still at Betty Hepburn's house, for Hep wouldn't have approved of the cohabitation with Putnam. Though Dr. Hepburn paid for the voice lessons, it's clear that tension remained between them, something that caused Kath, and no doubt her parents as well, considerable heartache. "None of us liked the separate ways," she would remember of this period, suggesting their separation wasn't so easily mended by ten dollars won at a bridge game.

Portrait of the high point just before the fall: Kath kissing Putnam good-bye as she tears off for rehearsals, rushing up East Fifty-fourth Street toward the subway, feeling herself subsumed into the pulsing, sweltering rhythm of New York in midsummer. Just two months out of college, she was headed for a major Broadway premiere, and not just in a bit part anymore. One day during rehearsals for *The Big Pond*, she'd been in the right place at the right time, called up onstage to take over the major part of Barbara after Knopf, in a snit, had fired the actress, Lucile Nikolas, who'd been cast in the role. When one considers how long it took for Bette Davis or Margaret Sullavan to make it that far, toiling through years of drama schools, stock companies, and provincial theaters, Hepburn's easy leap to Broadway is even more remarkable. It was happening just as she'd imagined it would—or "should," as she recalled in her memoir. Such easy access would always be her expectation.

"Kate is really extraordinary and extremely good," gushed Palache after sitting in on the dress rehearsal at the National Theatre on Forty-first Street. "Everyone is thrilled with her." To the adoring Palache, her friend's life had suddenly become a fairy tale: a personal maid at the theater, a queenly salary of $125 a week, clothes supplied by Bergdorf-Goodman. With Lib Rhett at her side, Palache cheered herself hoarse at the August 11 tryout of the play in Great Neck, Long Island. The show, Palache reported, was "a howling success."

To Palache, "her Kate" could do no wrong. But to Knopf, she hadn't done a thing right. Playing alongside such seasoned veterans as MacKenna, Harlan Briggs, Reed Brown Jr., and Doris Rankin, Kath stood out like the clumsy amateur she still was. Years later, she'd remember her nerves that night. Making her entrance, she realized the elastic of her panties was loose. Fearful they'd fall off in the middle of the scene, she abruptly stepped out of them and handed them to a mortified stagehand. Once onstage, she talked, moved, did everything too fast. Still, the first applause stimulated her, as it always did: "Well, that's that," she thought. "I'm a star."

Not quite. While the part of Barbara was often just "a tool for the play . . . to feed the plot," at other times it required the actress to be "complex, creative, not wholly an ingénue." That was the assessment of Lucile Nikolas, who was brought back in after Knopf decided Kath was out. It was Frances Robinson-Duff who informed her the next morning that she'd been fired. In one of those quirky acts that frequently characterized her, Kath insisted on going to the theater and wishing Nikolas and the rest of the cast well. Ostensibly it was to show that she was a good sport, but it seems also somewhat of a shaming gesture, given how uncomfortable her presence made the cast.

A family gathering had been planned at Fenwick, probably at Kit's urging, to celebrate Kath's debut. Palache and Lib Rhett motored up the next day with another friend, the law student Graeme Smith, "all prepared to bring the good tidings of Kate's success." But then came a phone call from their fallen friend, informing them she'd lost the job "through inexperience." *But*, Kath quickly added, J. J. Shubert, one of the show's backers, had been incensed over her firing and demanded she be put back. When Knopf refused, Shubert had offered her a five-year contract "at almost any salary she wanted"—or so Palache reported. The problem was, Kath explained, that she considered Shubert a "bum," so had no choice but to turn him down. "Consequently," Palache wrote breathlessly to her mother, "she is very much in demand by four or five big producers. It all seems too good to be true!"

Here, at the very outset of her career, we see an astonishing example of the Hepburn spin already at work. Fired and disgraced, she still had Palache singing that everything was "too good to be true"—a message surely intended to be relayed, as it was, to Dr. and Mrs. Hepburn waiting at Fenwick.

Yet it's difficult to imagine Shubert making such a fuss over a supporting player; even less credible is the picture of Knopf disregarding a direct order from such an important backer, especially in the midst of a first, struggling Broadway season. But most absurd of all is Kath, an ambitious novice, turning down a very generous offer from a famous producer. What finally proves the account false is its timing: Palache wrote to her mother the day after Kath's performance in Great Neck, which simply doesn't allow enough time for offers to be made and refused.

In truth, no "big producers" were waiting in the wings. Stories of Arthur Hopkins leaping up out of the audience to grab "the heat of life" that Knopf had so foolishly fired are poppycock. The truth was that after being tossed out of *The Big Pond*, Kath had no prospects or plans, and slunk back to Phelpie's disheartened.

Could it have been that, faced with such a morose companion, Putnam withdrew? Sympathy never was his strong point. "Like a kid, I am so occupied with my own misery that I fail to see anyone else's misery," he'd written to Cheney just months earlier. Looking back, Hepburn would remember how accustomed Phelpie was to good food and drink—a problem, as he was always broke. Common sense suggested that her poet-lover was hoping her theatrical career would support him. When it became apparent this wasn't happening, Putnam started drinking more heavily. His tendency to be "cranky and idiosyncratic" only increased. The Kid's unhappiness seemed unbearable in the face of his own.

During the first week of September, Putnam left to attend birthday celebrations at Murray Bay, Quebec, for William Howard Taft, the former president, current chief justice, and father-in-law of Fred Manning. No Manning family gathering would be complete without "Uncle Put," but Hepburn would recall his departure as a break, implying that Putnam left because he feared commitment. This may well be true. She herself, however, remained in a "romantic daze, walking through the streets ten feet above the ground"— still, apparently, in love. But Putnam's departure allowed another man to reenter her life: that friend of Jack Clarke's who'd taken those nude photos of her. A man by the name of Ludlow Ogden Smith.

Once more, flash forward to Fenwick, Kate Hepburn in her rattan Casablanca chair, giving an interview that would be transcribed and woven into her memoirs, the way so much of *Me* was constructed. One can almost see her through the words she left behind, suddenly sitting forward, her finger wagging to make a point.

"Listen, let me tell you," she said about Luddy. "Yes, he was my beau but—and that's the biggest *but* you've ever heard: He was my friend!"

That September of 1928, she sure needed a friend. Out of work, the brief idyll with Putnam over, Kath dragged herself over to Park Avenue and hid out in the spare bedroom of Megs Merrill and her husband, Armitage Watkins. For kindness and sustenance, she once again turned to Jack Clarke, who hosted her at the flat he shared with his sisters in Murray Hill. Frequently, there was a fifth for dinner as well: Jack's close friend Luddy Smith.

Like Jack, Ludlow Ogden Smith was eight years older than Kath, born in February 1899 to a prominent Main Line family. His father, Lewis Lawrence Smith, was a lawyer; his mother, Gertrude Gouverneur Clemson Smith, one of Philadelphia's most formidable grandes dames. In the city, the Smiths lived in the fashionable Rittenhouse Square neighborhood, but they considered home to be their country estate, Sherraden, in rural Strafford, Chester County. Sitting across the table from each other at the Clarkes', Luddy and Kath would have quickly discovered much in common. Both had lost a beloved older brother. Luddy's grandfather, like Kath's, had been an Episcopalian minister. And, with a little urging from Jack, both began swapping childhood tales of carrying placards in suffrage parades. Gertrude Smith was famous in Philadelphia for driving her yellow automobile decorated with signs urging VOTES FOR WOMEN until passage of the amendment was secured.

Yet it was the disappointment each had caused their strict, demanding fathers that was likely the strongest bond between Kath and Luddy. Lewis Smith had expected his son to follow his footsteps into law. From his office in the Widener Building in downtown Philadelphia, Lewis had carved a name for himself as a powerful, persuasive criminal prosecutor. But, from an early age, Ludlow Ogden Smith had demonstrated he would not be easily set on any expected path.

It was not a question of intelligence; young Ludlow possessed a shrewd, inquisitive mind. Even by the age of five, he could take machinery apart and effortlessly reassemble it. Fascinated by trains, he'd spend hours staring at a locomotive, examining its components. One day, when his mother received a note from the school inquiring about several absences, the eight-year-old Ludlow's secret was revealed: he'd been ditching school to watch the Italian laborers build a nearby railroad. Later, Luddy built his own model railroad, laying down elaborate rails and switches of his own design across the expanse of the attic floor.

He was a sensitive, compassionate boy. Tucked away in her box of mementos Gertrude Smith kept an essay Luddy had written when he was thirteen, after chancing upon a four-year-old orphan selling newspapers on Chestnut Street. "I gave him a five-cent piece and my best wishes," Luddy wrote, clearly heartbroken. "It has always made me feel sorry for newsboys selling their papers and breathing the unhealthy air of the city."

Playing croquet on the rambling acres of Sherraden, young Ludlow lived a very different life from that newsboy, but the child's plight seemed to echo his own discontent. In the shadow of his older, more athletic brother Lewis, whom the family called "the Prince," Luddy struggled to carve out a life of his own. Lewis Gouverneur Smith possessed all of the traits his younger brother did not. He could run a mile in six minutes, pole-vault seven feet, broad-jump more than fifteen feet—and still jog back to his father barely out of breath. Luddy, by contrast, underperformed in nearly every athletic endeavor during the summer of 1916 at the Culver Military Academy in Indiana—though he achieved perfect scores in punctuality and neatness. Despairing of the boy's abilities, the troop commander assigned him to remedial gymnastics. It would be the only stark difference between Luddy and Kath, who was a top athlete and anything but neat.

In his uniform of blue shirt, black tie, gray riding breeches, and black puttees, Luddy spent his days at Culver rough-riding horses and lugging heavy army sabers and carbines. It was a regimen meant to train boys for eventual military service, and with the war raging in Europe, Luddy rued the path his father had set him upon. Only in protest had he boarded the train to Culver, and immediately upon arrival he'd written to complain of the rigid schedule of drills and lessons to his mother, who was far more indulgent of him than his father.

To Luddy's credit, he eventually proved himself at Culver, just as he'd eventually master nearly every task that was set before him throughout his life. "You wouldn't know your son now," he wrote proudly to his mother near the end of his time at Culver, "with . . . his straight shoulders and shortcut military talk." While the troop commander did recommend that Luddy get more involved in athletics, "for he is not nearly as active as he should be," he still praised the boy's proficiency at learning to ride. Luddy's chief disappointment was that he hadn't grown to the magic height of six feet, which his brother had already attained by his age. Luddy would stop just short at five feet eleven and a half inches.

That fall, at his father's insistence, he kept up the family tradition by enrolling at the University of Pennsylvania, from which his brother had graduated in 1914. Although Luddy was a member of the Phi Kappa Sigma fraternity and lived in the fraternity house, he tended (in another echo of

Kath's life) to shrink from sports or club activities while in college. His friends tended to be off-campus men, usually rich, idle, and older. "I have always associated with people older than myself," he'd recall, "and have even caught myself regarding people of my own age as much younger."

His parents expressed some worry over these friendships, though they didn't explain exactly why. An incident in the spring of 1917 may have raised their concerns further. While Lewis and Gertrude were away, police were called to Sherraden after Luddy reported he'd been shot in the arm. In a statement to police, the eighteen-year-old said he'd discovered a burglar in the pantry and had shot him with the Smith and Wesson .38 special his father had given him for his birthday. In the ensuing chaos, the burglar had fired as well, hitting Luddy's right arm and ripping through Gertrude's expensive landscape wallpaper. Although police expected the wounded burglar to turn up for treatment at some hospital, no culprit was ever caught.

From their letters, especially those of Lewis Smith, it's clear that Luddy's parents hoped military service might "straighten up" their second son. The United States had entered the war in April, and Luddy, being a member of the Students' Army Training Corps, left school to head for Charleston, North Carolina, and basic training. Once again, he was soon grousing to his mother. His brother Lewis was already chasing after German U-boats in the north Atlantic, and the reality that Luddy would soon be joining him was daunting. "It is hard to realize that the Navy is home for a long time now," Luddy wrote. But the call of duty inspired him: "We are doing it for real and definite purpose . . . transforming a mass of drones into a swarm of angry workers which will eventually sting the Prussian beast to death."

Such braggadocio aside, he remained the sensitive boy of his youth. After a night's carousing in Charleston with a pack of "lively" French sailors, Luddy wrote to his mother, "Underneath all the gaiety and lightheartedness . . . they [are] nothing more than a lot of grown-up lonely children, pathetically eager to be nice to everybody in their own way and asking nothing better than to have others be nice to them."

Luddy's goal was aviation; as ever, his interest was in machinery and how things worked. Fascinated by the naval airplanes, he signed up for the Flying Corps. "I was up in the air . . . in one of the big 'H' boats," he wrote home in late September. "It is a wonderful sensation to see the earth, or rather the water, sliding away from beneath you while your ears are deafened by a roar like that of a half-dozen unmuffled high-powered automobile engines." With basic training complete, he headed home to await his call to serve.

It never came. By November, the war was over. But all danger wasn't past. Three months later, in the waters off the Azores, Lieutenant Lewis G. Smith was washed overboard in an accident on board the destroyer *Yarnall*. Luddy was devastated. Once more like Kath, he determined that he'd live as much for his brother as for himself. Rejecting his father's call that he return to the study of law, Luddy impulsively signed on to a merchant ship. Lewis and Gertrude were horrified. For the crew of hardy seamen, the lanky twenty-year-old served as bugle boy, sounding reveille and taps, a fitting role for a lad who loved music and could already play a variety of instruments.

By May 1919, however, Luddy was back on dry land, ensconced in a New York bank job surely arranged by his father, earning eighty-five dollars a week. Growing bored with the work after just five months, Luddy suddenly announced he was quitting, and asked his father to please reinstate his allowance. For the next few months, he passed the time with other young playboys like Brandon Barringer of Haverford, knocking around tennis balls at the Mill Dam country club or fiddling with a Ouija board, the latest fascination of the idle rich. From his departed brother, Luddy delivered stirring messages of comfort to his bereaved mother.

Such mystical practices held far greater appeal for him than organized religion, which he strongly disdained, another trait he'd have in common with Kath. An Episcopalian minister entrusted by Gertrude to sway her son back to the church discovered Luddy had "some crude ideas that nobody ought to adopt a religion until he has a large experience of life." Luddy told the minister quite frankly that he disliked the Episcopalian Church and preferred the Quakers, but "was averse to the whole notion of joining any church." History's greatest thinkers, he insisted, weren't Christians but the ancient Greeks and Romans.

With Luddy burning to experience such Old World culture, it's perhaps not surprising that one of the messages from the Ouija board was to "take Ludlow abroad soon." Exasperated by his son's lack of ambition, Lewis Smith finally agreed that Luddy should be sent to school in Europe, and chose the University of Grenoble in France for an eight-month course of study in languages and literature.

In the indigo shadows of the magnificent Alps, Luddy blossomed, falling in with a clique of sophisticated European friends, eating dandelions and sardines at sidewalk cafés. Photos from the period reveal a strikingly handsome, confident-looking man with dark eyes and full lips. Skiing regularly, he took jaunts to London, Paris, and Rome. Most influential were the courses he took at Grenoble's electrical institute, finally allowing his mechanical mind some practical application. At the end of the eight months, he chose to stay on at Grenoble at least until the spring. His parents worried that he intended to become, like so many of his generation, a permanent expatriate. Ratcheting up the pressure, Lewis ordered his son to come home, get a job, and get married.

"Not for me," Luddy boldly proclaimed. "I prefer the life of single wickedness." Confessing to his parents that he'd never marry, he insisted that Sherraden would one day go to his younger brother Lawrence (called Sam) and his eventual wife, rather than himself. "As a matter of fact I don't think I shall ever fall in love," Luddy wrote, "for I have a great deal of trouble in learning to like people, even those that I know are charming, and outside of the few real friends that I have, I should prefer to walk by myself."

His rejection of marriage went deeper than that. Before sailing back to the States, Luddy sent home photos of himself posing with various young men against the backdrop of the Swiss Alps. Once back in Philadelphia, he met Jack Clarke through Brandon Barringer and was soon part of Jack's crowd of hard-drinking, late-night-partying Jay Gatsbys.

He had something else in common with Jack as well. Michael Pearman, a close friend of Cole Porter's and the companion of high-society ladies, would later meet Luddy at the Sutton Square house of Lillie Havemeyer, the sister of Mrs. William K. Vanderbilt. Havemeyer, a well-traveled gadabout in her fifties, preferred cultured young homosexual men as her escorts, and Luddy, Pearman said, "fit that bill quite well." Luddy was charming, connected, and discreet. "A quiet boy," Pearman said, "but very funny, too. The ladies all adored him."

Luddy's children from his second marriage would reject any suggestion that their father was anything other than 100 percent heterosexual. His son Lewis said he'd always understood Luddy and Jack Clarke were "rowdy womanizers." (Of course, Phelps Putnam was also known as a womanizer.) Yet by the age of thirty, Luddy had never been seriously linked to any woman. Most of his time was spent with Jack, whose family recalled things differently than Luddy's, explaining that Jack's homosexuality, while discreet, was never a secret. Much of the two men's time together was spent at their getaway cottage in the woods at Easttown, a few miles from Strafford. Of course, for a sophisticate of the Roaring Twenties, sexual experimentation—extramarital or same-sex—was nothing remarkable, simply part of the sexual license granted during provocative times. "Goodness may get you to heaven," Luddy quipped, "but it rather cramps good fun, innocent or not."

Yet the parental pressure he faced to conform to a more traditional lifestyle often proved overwhelming. Trading in his motorcycle for a Ford and settling into a job as an underwriter, Luddy did his best to accommodate his father, who nonetheless was forever chastising him for being lazy and careless. Such a lifetime of contention inevitably colored the relationship between father and son. "I should like to find some way to get close to him," Luddy would write, "but somehow I always feel as if I were talking to a person whose emotions are theories and whose thoughts and feelings are academic. He never seems moved by any passionate desire for anything."

Passion, on the other hand, was the driving force of Luddy's life, setting up an inevitable clash of wills. As a result, in early 1923, Luddy seems to have suffered some kind of breakdown, being taken to Pinehurst, North Carolina, by his mother to recuperate at the Holly Inn resort. The sun, rest, horseback riding, and swimming worked wonders. By March, Luddy's "wrecked health" was "rapidly picking up," and he assured his father he'd soon be well enough to "start work without trouble." Employment, however, remained sporadic. Returning to Philadelphia, Luddy worked briefly for the Indemnity Insurance Company of North America and then as a stockbroker.

This conflict with his father and the pressures Luddy felt to get married are critical to understand if we are to fully grasp his courtship of Kath. That's not to imply the courtship was inauthentic. Whatever Luddy's relationships with men were, they did not detract from the intensity of his devotion to Kath. (Indeed, his focus on her is not surprising. Even staunchly homosexual men of the era were still sometimes fired by notions of marriage and family, developing strong attachments to women they idealized and with whom they might fulfill the social obligation of marriage.) Luddy had chanced upon Kath—a girl with little interest in sex who was also driven by fierce ambition. For men like Luddy and Phelps Putnam, whose own lives often felt adrift, the combination held great appeal. If marriage was a prerequisite for social credentialing, a wife like Kath—so untraditional, so free-spirited, so physically undemanding—seemed the perfect fit.

"Was he in love with her?" A rhetorical question posed by Michael Pearman. Reflecting on what he knew of Luddy from the 1930s, he said, "I imagine he was. But it wasn't a physical love, and of course she knew that."

Yet it was physical enough for Kath to fold herself into Luddy's protective arms, stretched out on a couch—a pose immortalized in a sketch made by Jack Clarke's sister Agnes in 1928 and preserved among Hepburn's personal papers. Kath seems to have found a safe haven in Luddy's embrace. He was constantly touching her arm, offering her a seat, asking how she felt. Like Kath, he was a caretaker by nature; and just as, years ago, Kathy and Tom Hepburn had shored up the weak links in each other's natures, so now did Kath and

Luddy look out for each other. She gave him purpose; he gave her adulation. In response to her depression over being fired from *The Big Pond,* his impulse was to make things better. By showering her with attention, he did.

His Ford Model A screeching to a stop in front of Megs's building on Park Avenue, Luddy would hop out and rush around to open Kath's door so she could slide into the passenger seat. Off they'd fly, the wind in her hair, taking the shore road along the Connecticut coast toward Fenwick. During Kath's depression of late 1928, Luddy proved to be her shining knight to the rescue. And, as ever when someone doted, Kath ate it all up.

"They were perfect companions," said Michael Pearman. "If only they had left it at that."

THE END OF HER VIRTUE

In the sharp sea air, the cat-o'-nine tails swaying in the breeze, a family reunion was taking place at Fenwick, the first since Kath had stormed off for Baltimore. All were arranged around the oak dining table with its ancient white china, chipped from years of use, and silver grown dull from lack of polish. The unmistakable aroma of autumn on the beach hung over everything, moist old wood and a brine so strong one could taste it on the tongue.

In those last few days of fall 1928, the Hepburn clan was determined to grab one more junket on the waves. Outside, Dick was struggling to get Tommy's old sneakbox onto the water. Bob was holding one end while the girls, Marion and Peggy, stood knee-deep in the chilly water. Up on the porch Hep languorously smoked his pipe while Kit grilled Kath's guest, Ludlow Smith, on his politics. When she was finished, Mrs. Hepburn sat back in her chair with a satisfied smile. She and the young man both planned to cast their votes for Herbert Hoover in a few weeks' time.

Standing a bit apart was Kath. She was as pleased as her mother. Phelpie could never have managed such easy rapport with her parents. With his round pink cheeks and full red lips, Luddy exuded optimism, where Putnam's darkness in spirit, while fueling a certain romantic aura, often left his friends with a sense of foreboding. Luddy was also far more handsome, though Kath called him "odd-looking" with his long nose and eyes set far apart in his face. Still, she was drawn to him. And if it wasn't in the way she'd been drawn to Putnam, with whom she was unquestionably still in love, it was a more enduring kind of attraction, similar to how she'd been attracted to Jack Clarke, and would later be to Garson Kanin, Bobby Helpmann, and even Scott Berg. Luddy was her pal, her confidant, her rock.

He was probably also the reason her father had warmed toward her. Luddy's easygoing yet deferential manner had won Hep over. At the dinner table, the young man always made sure to turn to the patriarch after offering any opinion and ask, "But what do *you* think, sir?" Starting that fall, Luddy became a frequent presence in the Hepburn household. Kit often stole him away for what twelve-year-old Marion Hepburn called one of their "prolonged talks"—rambling political discussions of the kind Kit could never have with her quick-tempered husband. Not only did they agree on most topics, but Kit found Luddy also made her laugh—quite an experience for a woman who took herself and her causes *very* seriously.

Indeed, as Michael Pearman recalled, Luddy could be a very funny man. Years later, the two of them would entertain their society patronesses by trading bon mots back and forth like tennis balls. Luddy's sense of humor is evident in letters he wrote to his parents. When his mother had some teeth pulled, leaving her face black and blue, he quipped, "People will admire Father for his good aim and look down on you for your lack of ability to dodge." His simple trick of touching his tongue to his nose could reduce Kath to hysterics.

Luddy wasn't the only lift to her spirits that autumn. By the middle of September, Kath also had a job. Soon after Putnam's departure, she'd begun rehearsals for *Night Hostess,* a risqué cabaret comedy with a cast of "chumps, musicians, hostesses, croupiers, attendants, winners, losers and hoodlums"— not to mention a couple of guys in gorilla suits. After her humiliation at the hands of Knopf, the show was Kath's salvation, though she chose to work under a stage name, Katherine Burns, and years later would deny the whole experience to the *Playbill* columnist Louis Botto. "Why would I appear under the name Katherine Burns?" she huffed. "Anyway, I would never spell Katherine with an 'e.'"

Of course, there were many reasons she would choose to appear under the name Katherine Burns, with or without the *e*. Part of it was pride. After being tossed out of *The Big Pond*—a high-toned, drawing-room comedy—

The most important man in Katharine Hepburn's life: her father, Dr. Thomas Norval Hepburn (*The Alan Mason Chesney Medical Archives of the Johns Hopkins Medical Institutions*)

The impish Jimmy Hepburn—the most authentic face of Katharine Hepburn—with "Aunt" Mary Towle at Fenwick (*The Connecticut Historical Society*)

Kit Hepburn was an often distant Madonna around whom her children gathered in reverence. LEFT TO RIGHT: Kathy, Marion, Bob, Peggy (on lap), Tom (standing behind his mother), and Dick. A few months after this portrait was taken, Tom was dead. (*The Connecticut Historical Society*)

At Bryn Mawr, Kath Hepburn made an "engaging boy, roguish and merry" in the campus production of *The Truth About Blayds*. (Bettman/CORBIS)

College life was made palatable by the devoted Alice Palache, who became a friend for life. *(The Schlesinger Library, Radcliffe Institute, Harvard University)*

The poet H. Phelps Putnam—the first and perhaps the last headlong passion of Hepburn's life *(Yale Collection of American Literature, Beinecke Rare Book and Manuscript Library)*

On the rebound from Putnam, Kath married Ludlow Ogden Smith, seen here standing in front of his family's estate outside Philadelphia, around the time Hepburn met him. *(American Philosophical Society)*

The public Katharine Hepburn first emerged on Broadway in *The Warrior's Husband*—bounding out on stage with so much zest that many in the audience gasped out loud. *(Photofest)*

The awkward ugly duckling blossomed into a breathtaking swan—who, despite the legend, wasn't above posing for some glamour publicity in the beginning. *(Photofest)*

Arriving in Hollywood, Kath told a skeptical George Cukor she thought her New York designer outfit was very smart. "Well, I think it stinks," Cukor told her. "We can proceed from there." *(Photofest)*

For all the noise she'd make about privacy, the young Katharine Hepburn did everything she could to get the press to notice her—even wandering around town with a gibbon clinging to her neck. *(Academy of Motion Picture Arts and Sciences)*

For about six years, Kate and Laura Harding were inseparable. Here Laura shows a home movie she took to the cast and crew of *Christopher Strong*. Director Dorothy Arzner is in back, Hepburn far right. *(Courtesy Emily King)*

"If Kate had a great love other than herself, it was Laura Harding," said one friend. Laura (here on the set of *The Little Minister*) was the guiding force of Hepburn's early career. *(Billy Rose Theatre Collection, New York Public Library for the Performing Arts, Astor, Lennox and Tilden Foundation)*

Returning on the *Paris* in April 1934, Hepburn adopted a new ploy with the press. Later she'd admit to learning how to make herself "adorable." *(Photofest)*

Despite her reputed antipathy toward Hollywood, in her early years in the screen colony Hepburn had a ball. Here she takes in the rays by Cukor's famous pool with gadabout Anderson Lawler...
(*Photofest*)

... and here she attends a private screening with Douglas Fairbanks Jr. and Marlene Dietrich.
(*Bettmann/CORBIS*)

In the 1930s, there were several men in Kate's life. The high-flying Leland Hayward was the kind of man she wished she could have been—but she was never in love with him. *(Photofest)*

During the making of *Mary of Scotland*, Kate fell hard for director John Ford—though the romance was brief, and talk of marriage between them has been exaggerated. *(Photofest)*

There were also several women, like Nancy Hamilton (above) and Frances Rich (right), with whom Kate established much more enduring relationships. *(Billy Rose Theatre Collection, New York Public Library for the Performing Arts, Astor, Lennox and Tilden Foundation/Photofest)*

With Elissa Landi, Hepburn seemed to enjoy stirring up a bit of gossip by posing planeside in matching furs. *(Bettman/CORBIS)*

She was also being deliberately provocative with *Sylvia Scarlett*, which she and director George Cukor called their "little love child." The film about gender confusion nearly did both of them in with the public. Here, a portent of doom when Kate nearly drowned during one scene. *(Bettmann/CORBIS)*

After the hurricane of 1938 destroyed the Hepburn home at Fenwick, Kate spent days digging out family heirlooms from the sand. In her public life, it was also a period of salvaging and rebuilding her career. *(Connecticut Historical Society)*

Although *The Philadelphia Story* brought Kate back after being labeled "box-office poison," it was *Woman of the Year* that introduced the romance that served the legend best. Here George Stevens directs Kate falling in love with Spencer Tracy—which she was doing in real life as well. *(Academy of Motion Picture Arts and Sciences)*

Like Putnam and Ford, Spence was a married man—and despite all presumptions to the contrary, he never wanted anyone other than Louise Treadwell (here with their son, John) to be his wife. *(Bettman/CORBIS)*

Tracy's boon companion in the late 1930s was horseman and playboy Tim Durant. *(Bettman/CORBIS)*

As the Hepburn legend grew, it was guided by the sure hand of Garson Kanin, who as a young Hollywood upstart had first conceived the idea for *Woman of the Year*. Other than Kate herself, no one did more to shape the legend than Kanin. *(Photofest)*

By the early 1950s, Hepburn was firmly on the road to apotheosis—largely through her role in *The African Queen*, the film that rescued both her and Humphrey Bogart from the nightmare of the House Un-American Activities Committee. Here Kate confers with Bogie before setting out for Africa. *(Photofest)*

Separated from Spence in the 1950s, Kate found herself rejuvenated by her great (and platonic) friendship with Irene Selznick. Here they set the style in an open car during a visit with Noël Coward in Jamaica. *(Getty Images)*

Other close friends during this
period included the flamboyant
Bobby Helpmann, Kate's costar
in *The Millionairess*. *(Photofest)*

No one was more influential in shaping
Hepburn's personal and professional life in
the late 1940s and 1950s than the formidable
Constance Collier. Here Collier accompanies
Kate to Ethel Barrymore's birthday party.
LEFT TO RIGHT: Collier, Judy Garland,
Hepburn, Barrymore *(The Huntington Library)*

An ailing Spence eventually proved irresistible
to Kate's need to play caretaker. With *Guess
Who's Coming to Dinner*, their legend was
preserved in amber. *(Academy of Motion
Picture Arts and Sciences)*

Kate on the *Dinner* set. Niece Katharine Houghton and
costar Isabel Sanford listen raptly to her instructions.
(Academy of Motion Picture Arts and Sciences)

After Spencer's death, Hepburn's inner circle included Anthony Harvey and Bobby Helpmann, here sharing a laugh in her New York town house *(Lilly Library, Indiana University)*

There was also Noel Taylor, the costume designer on her final films. *(Courtesy Noel Taylor)*

But the light at the end of Hepburn's life was provided by Cynthia McFadden, whose high cheekbones led to stories—encouraged by both of them—that the younger woman was Kate's secret daughter. *(Lilly Library, Indiana University)*

A delightful moment between two old friends: Hepburn and Cukor caught on the set of *Love Among the Ruins*. Despite a brief rift in the late 1970s, the two remained devoted. *(Photofest)*

Yet most faithful of all was Phyllis Wilbourn, who remained at Kate's side for nearly forty years. "Phyllis and I are one," Kate told friends. *(Getty Images)*

In 1989, Hepburn opened Fenwick for Cynthia's wedding, where Cynthia shocked the party into silence when she delivered the first piece of wedding cake to "Aunt Kate's" face. *(Photograph © 1989 M. Petty Photography, LLC)*

Our last image of Kate from 1994: impish, chubby, and adored the world over *(Photofest)*

she surely considered playing a "hostess" (euphemism for "prostitute") in a lightweight cabaret a definite comedown. Meanwhile, the glowing reviews for Lucile Nikolas in *The Big Pond* only added salt to her wounds. Given all this, a stage name served a practical purpose: since Kath was actively seeking other work, she wouldn't appear already committed should a better offer come along.

At least the show would be opening in Minneapolis, far from Broadway. To Dick Cavett in 1973, Hepburn admitted her part in *Night Hostess,* playing what she called "a wicked fascinator." The garish makeup, she said, made her feel ludicrous: "I never did learn how to be *that kind* of a fascinator." She told Cavett she left the show in Minneapolis. ("I don't think it ever came to New York.") The show would rarely be included in her credits.

But the actress Barbara Willison would have an inconveniently sharp memory, at least as far as Hepburn was concerned. Willison remembered performing with Hepburn on Broadway around this time and sharing a room with her as well. "Katharine never wore a nightgown," Willison recalled, "but because she was sharing a room she went out specially and bought one." During rehearsals (for a play Willison didn't name), they'd wait their calls in the auditorium, Kath with her legs draped over the seats—"very unladylike in those days," Willison clucked.

Yet a close study of Willison's credits revealed she never appeared in any production with Katharine Hepburn; she did, however, play in *Night Hostess* with Katherine Burns. Both of them were in the cast on the night of September 12, 1928, when the show had its New York opening at the Martin Beck Theatre. It seems clear that Katherine Burns and Katharine Hepburn were one and the same. Census records and city directories for New York, New Jersey, and Connecticut revealed no Katherine Burnses who listed their occupation as actress. In no other play did Katherine Burns ever appear; no clippings were found for her in any collection of theater ephemera; no references were found in online searches of contemporary newspapers. It's as if she never existed. That's because she didn't.

In truth, *Night Hostess* had offered Kath a job when she needed it most. Her hiring seems to have come courtesy of the play's director, Winchell Smith, who hailed from Hartford and whose brother Oliver was a surgical colleague of Hep's. Apparently, Dr. Hepburn's pique at Kath's choice of career did not preclude him from helping his out-of-work daughter land a job. The play would give Katharine Hepburn her first chance to walk out onto a Broadway stage, but such an inauspicious debut, rouged and bewigged, would never do for the legend. Consequently, *Night Hostess* would be sidelined and obscured.

But Barbara Willison retained fond memories of her time with her fellow "hostess." Kath was always "full of verve," Willison said, reciting Shakespeare between rehearsals. "I always knew she was destined for big things."

Willison also remembered Luddy. As the three of them hurried down a cold New York street, Willison would recall Kath teasing her beau—her *friend*—that if only he'd buy her a fur coat, she'd marry him.

Soon there was a more auspicious role for Kath. A chill wind blew through the brownstone row of the Yale campus on the night of October 30. Bundled up in coats and mufflers, Yalies were heading toward downtown, where a play first presented on campus the previous February was being remounted at the Shubert Theatre, as a tryout for its Broadway opening in November. It was Arthur Hopkins's *These Days*, starring the well-regarded actors Helen Freeman and George MacQuarrie.

For audience member Phelps Putnam, however, the draw was the small part of Veronica Sims, played by Miss Katharine Hepburn. Standing before the old ivory and gold-leaf theater on College Street, his coat collar turned up high and his fedora angled low on his head, Putnam hoped to get in and out of the performance without being recognized. He wanted to keep any scuttlebutt from getting back to Ruth. But Kath knew he'd be out there. Meeting with her for an early dinner, Put had poured on the charm and promised her the moon. Unnerved by how close she'd gotten to Ludlow Smith, he told her that he wanted to put their relationship back on track.

Kath seems to have received this news with equanimity. She was likely still infatuated with Putnam. But she was also on the verge of making it, she believed, and despite her reconnection with Phelpie, she kept her focus on the show. To be hired by Hopkins had been a dream come true for her, and the advance notices for *These Days* gave every indication it would be an enormous Broadway hit.

How quickly things always seemed to change for Kath. Giving her notice to Winchell Smith, she'd been only too happy to skip out of *Night Hostess*. Of course, she'd later insist that Hopkins had come looking for her, but in truth it was the other way around. Once again it was Jack Clarke who probably made the difference. He and Luddy often spent parts of the winter at Uncle Louis Clarke's house in Palm Beach, Florida, where one of the neighbors was none other than Arthur Hopkins. *These Days*, then, was likely one more favor granted to a young woman who'd already had quite a few of them. "I had my whole early career handed to me on a silver platter," Kath would admit, years later, to James Prideaux.

Just when Putnam reinserted himself into her life isn't exactly clear. He hadn't stayed in Canada long; already by September 18 he was back at Davenport's flat on Beekman Place. The difference now was that Kath had moved on, spending much of her time with Luddy. Some friends believed she was using Luddy simply to make Putnam jealous, which has a ring of truth to it. For a time, the two men overlapped in their courting of her. From his letters we know that Putnam was aware of "that bastard Smith"; Luddy was no doubt also aware of Putnam but, given his more easygoing temperament, likely didn't waste as much time on being jealous as his rival did.

When *These Days* opened in Hartford the week before its New Haven run, Luddy had been seated prominently beside Kit in the audience. For Kath, it was an exhilarating moment to step out onto the stage of the Parsons Theatre, where as a girl she'd once sat spellbound watching the tempestuous Anna Held. The *Hartford Times* observed: "Not only her friends but all those who like to see local talent arise and shine, will be interested in the appearance of Katharine Houghton Hepburn at Parsons Theatre." Although Hopkins's publicity saw to it that her local connections were highlighted for the Hartford press—throwing in that she was related to Ambassador Alanson Houghton, then running for the Senate in New York—one significant figure was missing from the auditorium on opening night. Luddy was there, and Kit, and all the children, but Hep, still not entirely forgiving, stayed at home.

Her father's absence, as well as the rest of her family's presence, seems to have elicited some "natural nervousness" in Kath's performance, but the *Times*'s reviewer still predicted "heaps of natural talent . . . may well lead her, in time, to do things in the theater." Kath had the small role of a wiseass boarding-school student whose repeated lines of "Yes, Miss Alstyne" and "No, Miss Alstyne" suggested untold shenanigans.

Phelpie in fact thought she was so good in New Haven he stuck around to see the play again the next night. After the Tuesday night performance, he showed up at F. O. Matthiessen's house on York Place. The next morning, Matty would stumble through classes "bleary-eyed" because Putnam had kept him up past two o'clock. "He is in town seeing some girl who is acting at the Shubert," Matty wrote to Cheney, "and his presence is a complete secret." Put was in high spirits, Matty said, and had read him his latest poem. The next day, they got together again. Putnam planned to return to New York the following morning.

This convivial atmosphere, documented by Matthiessen's letters, disputes Barbara Leaming's description of a tumultuous break between Kath and Putnam at this time. Leaming wrote of an agitated Putnam banging on

Matty's door but finding his friend away, only to be allowed to drink all of his whiskey by someone she identified as "Mrs. Matthiessen," who, of course, didn't exist. In truth, there was no break with Kath; by the time *These Days* opened in New York at the Cort Theatre on November 12, Kath and Putnam had just spent an intense two weeks together back in Davenport's flat.

But in a repeat of the events of the previous summer, as soon as Putnam got what he wanted—Kath—he broke down again. Drinking heavily, he wrote to Cheney that he was "full of poison." Was it merely a wounded ego that had made him want to win Kath back? For now that he had her, he was in the same straits as before, horribly conflicted.

Soon after the play's New York premiere, Kath invited Putnam to accompany her to Hartford, apparently hoping that the change of locale would revive his spirits. "I'm going to beat it," Putnam wrote to Cheney, meaning his depression, "as I've been invited to beat it, before I really go blooey." He gave his address in care of "Dr. T. N. Hepburn" and said he'd stay through the weekend. He hoped Cheney, in nearby Manchester, would visit.

Having seen how effortlessly Luddy had won the affections of both Hep and Kit, Kath was no doubt curious how Phelpie would fare with her family. If it was a test, he failed miserably. All Putnam seems to have done is raise Hep's hackles. Recognizing that his daughter was in love with the moody, married poet, Dr. Hepburn dropped his arm around Putnam's shoulders and guided him out into the English-style, brick-walled back garden. There he looked the younger man in the eye and told him plainly, "If you lay hands on her, I shall shoot you." Putnam returned to New York even more anxious than before.

Dealing with Putnam's shifting moods could not have been easy—especially given the fact that Kath was performing every night on stage. Yet she remained in good spirits through the first few performances of *These Days*, characteristically disregarding the play's negative reviews. At least one, in the *New York Evening Journal*, had singled her out for praise, saying she had played "gorgeously." Her optimism wasn't entirely groundless. Hopkins had an excellent track record; if anyone could keep a play afloat, he could. He'd staged Ibsen, Shakespeare, and Tolstoy, and produced such hits as *Paris Bound* by Philip Barry. Kath would always remember the round-faced producer fondly, calling him "Hoppy." He seems to have taken a shine to her as well. Possibly because of her connection to the Clarkes, Hopkins indulged her with wardrobe expenses and a higher salary than most bit players. When word came that *These Days* was closing after just eight performances, Kath was confident that Hoppy would have something else for her.

He didn't, at least not right away. And so it was that in those immediate weeks after the closing of *These Days*—her first official Broadway show a resounding flop—that Katharine Hepburn took a step no one could have predicted. Once again, a devastated Kath turned to an equally distraught Putnam. Once again, as his letters indicate, he was unable to offer her support. But Luddy was right there waiting, eager to squire Kath around town and buy her gifts. This seems to have had an effect. Less than a month after bringing Putnam home to meet her family, and just two weeks after his correspondence suggests they'd been living together, Katharine Hepburn did what none of her closest friends ever believed she would do. She married Ludlow Ogden Smith.

Did Kit Hepburn ever think she'd see this day, knowing her daughter as she did? Helping Kath slip into the crushed white velvet Babani dress with the antiqued gold embroidery, what was going through Mrs. Hepburn's mind? Downstairs, Luddy's parents sat stiff-backed in the living room, awkwardly exchanging small talk with their son and Hep. It had all happened so fast. Just a little more than a week previous, Kath had announced her plans, and despite Kit's desire for a grander, more elaborate affair, the bride had insisted it had to be on a Wednesday afternoon, at the house, with only the immediate families present. It was almost as if she feared she'd change her mind if they waited too long.

Looking out the windows onto that clear, crisp December day, what did Kath herself contemplate? She'd say she was determined to give marriage a whirl, to try being a wife, to put on the wide-brimmed hat of a conventional society lady. She'd decided, rather abruptly, to quit the theater. She'd abandoned all her ambitions, given up on her cherished dreams. She was planning to move with Luddy to a big white house in Strafford, Pennsylvania, and settle in as Mrs. Smith. At least, that's what she'd tell us was going through her mind on December 12, 1928.

"Nonsense," said Noel Taylor. "Absurd," added James Prideaux. "She never wanted that kind of life," echoed Max Showalter.

Her family was "absolutely stunned," said Bob Hepburn. "Why she did it, none of us knew."

She was not in love with Luddy. That much everyone agreed on. He was her *friend*—probably the best friend she ever had. Even as she took Luddy's hand and turned to face her grandfather Sewell Hepburn, austere in his black suit and tattered prayerbook, it was Phelpie who no doubt remained in her thoughts. Some believed that if Reverend Hepburn had not been visiting when Kath got the idea to tie the knot, she never would have gotten married. But once an idea got into her head, it was well nigh impossible to get her to back down—especially when the minister was on hand.

Since, as usual, Hepburn's version of events is not especially revealing, we must travel back ourselves to those two weeks prior to the wedding if we want to understand what brought her to this point. What we discover is a storm of emotions. Only by considering the full context of her life at the time can we ever make sense of what she did on December 12.

On November 26, a week after the closing of *These Days*, Arthur Hopkins opened his newest production, Philip Barry's *Holiday*, at the Plymouth Theatre. Just days before, he'd hired Kath as understudy for the star, Hope Williams. She'd thrown herself into the effort, learning the lines as fast as she could, watching Williams from the wings and aping her every movement. "I was acting away," she recalled, "secretly convinced that I was much better than Hope in some of the emotional scenes." But this time none of the applause was for her. At the curtain, Katharine Hepburn was not among the players who trooped out and took their bows. Occasionally, some of the actors had to tap her on the shoulder and ask her to step aside so they could make their way out onto the stage.

Meanwhile, Phelpie was sinking deeper into an alcoholic abyss. Luddy, her salvation, got her out of the flat, driving her up to Hartford, where the family marveled at how good-naturedly he allowed her to boss him around. At Bryn Mawr, Kath had had Palache; now, in this uneasy time, she had Luddy, just as she would always need someone at her beck and call for the rest of her life. Certainly Phelpie, as much as she remained drawn to him, wasn't filling that particular demand. Putnam, in fact, expected her to take care of *him*. In time, Katharine Hepburn would learn how to play both roles at the same time, caretaker to some, prima donna to others. But at twenty-one she believed she had to pick one over the other. She chose to be taken care of.

In late November, something dramatic happened to finally push her away from Putnam for good. His letters to Cheney and Davenport reveal a crisis he does not specify: "I have descended deeper than ever before and extinguished whatever light was in my life." Was there a particularly nasty episode of drinking? An angry exchange with Kath? Did he tell her he'd never give up Ruth? Did she find him with someone else?

Whatever it was, Kath's resilient spirit seems to have finally broken by early the next month. In a pique, she barged into Hoppy's office and told him she was quitting the theater. A critic for the *New York Times*, who seems to have had an inside track, wrote at the time that Hope Williams's understudy had "casually retired to marry—or maybe she had retired to marry casually." Looking back, Hepburn herself would gloss over the moment, as if quitting the theater were just an inconsequential speed bump. But it was far more significant. Not only was she abandoning her dream; she was admitting she'd been wrong and her father had been right. The theater was not for her. She should have never taken the risk that she did.

Such a turnaround was—and always would be—completely out of character for Hepburn. Just why she married perplexed even her closest friends. Had she married Luddy but *not* quit the theater, the explanation that some offered might hold more logic: that she didn't want to be subjected to the sexual demands of amorous producers, and that as a married lady she could more easily sidestep the casting couch. But she had *quit*—turned her back on all that—before she ever started buttoning up that crushed velvet wedding dress. Kath's marriage to Luddy was not the calculated, cynical move some tried later to imply. It was an impulsive act of an emotional girl on the rebound.

Six years later, in a similar rash move, she would flee the crises of her life on board the *Paris*. Kath's abandonment of the theater was another cry of the heart, an impetuous bolt away from the troubles at hand. She was a woman who always got what she wanted, who needed to be *the star* at all times—but it was a bottle of whiskey that had ultimately mattered more to Putnam. It was Hope Williams who got the applause at the Plymouth Theatre. Indeed, Kath's first six months as an actress had offered only a chain of disappointments: a company that folded, a firing for inexperience, a Broadway flop, and now this anonymous drill. Kath Hepburn was never one to put up with unpleasant situations for long. She usually found some way out. So she decided to prove that *someone* was devoted to her, that *someone* thought she was a star.

One other motive drove her as well: to break from her father, to slip the ropes that still bound her to him. On the surface, their rift of the previous spring had healed, but it remained ready to bubble up the next time Kath found herself out of work or in need of money. If she quit the theater as an unmarried girl, Hep would have expected her to come home to Hartford, something she was not about to do. Accepting Luddy's proposal meant Kath was at last free of her father—the star of her own show.

But first—there was one final appeal to Putnam. On a cold, blustery night during the first week of December, Mitch Davenport walked into his flat to find that Put, already asleep, had left him a note: "Kate Hepburn Senior told me that she thought the Kid would marry that bastard. She says the Kid is coming around here Sat[urday] to talk to us. In which case, for

Christ's sake, wake me in time to talk a little with you, cher Figaro, before this farewell supper . . . Y'r Phriend Phelps is damned near death."

Apparently, the farewell supper was exactly that: nothing Putnam said could convince Kath that life with him would ever be anything different. The encounter, he told Davenport, was "ghastly," and immediately afterward he set out on a train for Boston—and Ruth.

What had made it so ghastly? Had Kath been hoping he'd promise to divorce his wife and marry her? If that seems unlikely, so too was her decision to marry Luddy. We know that at some point before their marriage, Kath agreed to have sex with Luddy at Jack Clarke's apartment. In her memoir, she made a point of documenting the moment, perhaps to assure skeptics that her marriage had not been in name only. "Luddy and I were alone in the apartment," she wrote, "and there was the bed and there didn't seem to be any reason not to . . . And that was the end of my virtue." She had finally done with Luddy what she had never done with Putnam.

Given her aversion to actual intercourse, sex between the two of them probably wasn't very frequent. But Luddy, his family recalled, was eager to start a family, which would have finally satisfied his father's demands. Just when he and Kath had their first sexual experience is not clear, but it was probably soon after the "ghastly" farewell supper with Putnam. *There didn't seem to be any reason not to,* Kath wrote. Not anymore.

Just a week after saying good-bye to Putnam, Kath was Mrs. Ludlow Ogden Smith. The young woman who'd once insisted she'd never wed, who'd looked askance as her friends walked down the aisle, who'd valued ambition above all else, was now an unemployed married lady.

Three days later, on Saturday, December 15, the newlyweds set sail from the West Fifty-fifth Street pier on board the Furness Withy ship *Bermuda*, heading for Hamilton and their honeymoon. Both Kath herself as well as her brother Bob recalled she played "a lot of golf " on her honeymoon. Indeed, Kath had possibly chosen the destination because of the publicity generated by the Bermuda Open championship, which climaxed that week. On December 17, the day after Luddy and Kath arrived, four American pro golfers gathered for an exhibition at the Riddell's Bay Club, attracting a large audience of aficionados. After two weeks of golf and sun, Kath and Luddy departed the island on December 29, most likely on the *Fort Victoria*, arriving in New York on the morning of New Year's Eve. After spending the holiday in the city, they motored down to Philadelphia to find a house.

In her memoir, Hepburn seemed to really want us to believe that she was considering life as a society matron. Close friends, however, insisted otherwise. George Cukor called the marriage "one of her phases of evolution," which soon left her "bored." Garson Kanin called it "a bad accident." The writer Robert Shaw, a frequent guest at her New York home, said, "I think after the ceremony was over she looked around and said, 'What have I done?' "

Although Luddy, too, could be rash ("I sometimes do things on impulse that I afterwards heartily regret," he once admitted), he seems to have made this particular decision consciously and deliberately, at least in part to silence his father's demands to settle down. Still, marriage to Kath, with whom he had so much in common, held real appeal for him. "I am so tremendously happy with Kate, and I hope she with me," Luddy wrote to his mother soon after the wedding. He could indulge "all the foolish romantic thoughts" he wanted, and instead of having them called impractical, Kate responded with "ideas just as foolish and just as alluring." They'd probably make mistakes in their marriage, Luddy wrote, but they'd have "loads of fun together making them," and in the end he thought they'd "be finer persons, and shall at least have gotten some enjoyment out of life."

It's clear that, while Kath may have acted impulsively in agreeing to Luddy's proposal, she'd at least done so knowing she wasn't taking a terribly dangerous risk. As Luddy's letter suggests, they were making the best of an admittedly impractical situation and could indulge each other's "foolish" ideas. "It was a comfortable relationship," said Luddy's niece Eleanor Smith Morris. "If you marry the boy next door, there are a lot of things you don't have to explain."

Kath's assertions that she was planning to set up housekeeping along the Main Line, however, are just so much hokum—though it *is* true that for the first couple of months of 1929 she lingered in the environs of Philadelphia. However, looking at real estate was hardly her chief preoccupation. Instead, old habits died hard. Slipping off to Bryn Mawr, she sought out none other than Phelps Putnam, who was once again staying with the Mannings. Luddy's accommodating nature was now proven. Within a month of their marriage, he obligingly looked the other way as his wife forged a new relationship with her former paramour. It was, perhaps, part of the "foolish and impractical" approach to marriage they both found so "alluring."

This time around, the relationship between Kath and Phelpie was far less volatile. She was now, like Putnam himself, married. There could be no immediate expectations on either's part. "The Kid was here today," Putnam wrote cheerfully to Davenport on January 22. The three of them were planning to meet up in New York at some unspecified date. During this period, Putnam also finally introduced Kath to Cheney and Matthiessen, with whom she often enjoyed late-night gatherings at Davenport's flat. Freed from the pressures of the previous several months, Putnam seemed a man regenerated. Railing against passionless marriages, he steamed over Davenport's recent nuptials, as impulsive as Kath's, and by the spring he was finally ready himself to agree to a divorce from Ruth.

But Kath wasn't waiting around anymore. She and Luddy had settled into his Manhattan apartment at 146 East Thirty-ninth Street, just a block away from Jack Clarke's residence. Sometime in mid-February, Kath worked up her courage to stick her head into Arthur Hopkins's office and ask for her job back. She couldn't undo what she'd done on December 12—not easily, anyway—but she could maybe make the best of it and get back to what really mattered: her desire to be a star. Like a great round Buddha, Hoppy smiled, folded his hands across his belly, and said he'd been expecting her. By the end of the month, Kath was back to pantomiming Hope Williams's lines behind the curtain at the Plymouth Theatre.

If her marriage had taught her anything, it was to stay the course, to always keep her career ahead of her emotions. A few more crises would be needed before that lesson fully sunk in, but in fact never again after Phelps Putnam would Katharine Hepburn allow herself such unbridled passion. Every subsequent relationship, even those that involved love, would be drafted and maintained according to the dictates of her ambition. Never again would she let herself fall so recklessly in love.

ALL THE SORT OF HIGHBROW CUSTOMS

The fragrance of well-oiled wood still hung heavily throughout the newly remodeled Berkshire Playhouse in Stockbridge, Massachusetts. In its previous incarnation, before it was dismantled and reassembled at the bottom of Yale Hill, the Playhouse had been the legendary Stockbridge Casino, the heart of "dissipation and gaiety" in the rolling, maple-shaped Berkshire hills. To judge from rehearsals of the two-year-old theatrical company that June of 1930, some things hadn't changed.

Up on the stage, Miss Katharine Hepburn, in the bit part of Lady Agatha in James M. Barrie's *The Admirable Crichton,* tiptoed out from the wings, a devilish smirk enlivening her freckled face. As she mimed looking for her friend, she was supposed to utter, "Lady Catherine! Lady Catherine!" But instead she sang out, "Laurrrrra! Laura Harrrrrding!"

For the fifth or sixth time, the young director Alexander Kirkland, an associate of the great Eva Le Gallienne, threw down his script in frustration. Onstage Kath dissolved into laughter. "Miss Hepburn," Kirkland shouted. "You just can't do that!"

"Oh, no?" Kath asked, glaring down at him. "Who's going to stop me?" Behind her, Laura Harding, playing Lady Catherine, bubbled over into her own hysterics. Only after being threatened with dismissal did they agree to shape up and play the scene right.

In modern parlance, that season Kath was a girl gone wild. One look from Laura was enough to break her into giggles whenever the young English actor Robert Coote, who had a facial tic, walked onstage. Kirkland, fuming, would have to stop the scene and start over. Such hijinks incurred the wrath of leading players Geoffrey Kerr and June Walker. Kath stewed over the fact that neither would speak to her. Sharing the stage with Kerr in one pivotal scene, she devised a trick to irritate him. Wearing a hat made of jungle grass, she positioned herself so that every time she turned her head, a spear of grass brushed Kerr's cheek. Spinning around, he'd find Kath innocently fluttering her eyelashes.

After two years of ups and downs, Kath, at twenty-three, was finally having some fun in her chosen profession. That she was earning herself a reputation for insubordination seemed not to faze her—not with the ebullient Laura at her side, forever goading her on. Laura Harding was a gamine beauty, with a cherubic face, short dark hair, and the round button eyes of a doll. They'd met a year or so earlier, at Frances Robinson-Duff's, but it wasn't until they'd headed to the Berkshires, at Robinson-Duff's suggestion, that they'd become good friends.

For Kath, Laura seemed to awaken a mischievous spirit that harked back to her days with Ali Barbour. During their run at the Berkshire Playhouse, Kath and Laura became inseparable. Rooming in a Victorian house on Devon Road in the nearby town of Lee, presided over by the Reverend Edward C. Bradley and his wife, Laura and Kath would sit up all night drinking whiskey with Bradley's three daughters, who ranged in age from nineteen to twenty-four. The dirty glasses, Laura recalled, were left for the maid.

Bradley's was a crowded place. "At one point," Laura remembered, "there were eighteen people in the house—the clergyman and his family, theater folk—and all sharing one bathroom." Even offstage, Kath exasperated her fellow players, taking "endless baths" and holding up the line. With the actor George Coulouris, she charged headfirst into debates about theater and literature. "Sparks flew!" Laura remembered. On one occasion, Kath asked why the poet Francis Thompson "used words of three syllables when he could use two" in "The Hound of Heaven." Coulouris just glared at her and thought, "What a nerve!"

By the summer of 1930, throwing caution to the wind, Kath did indeed have a lot of nerve—or actually hubris, since her confidence far outweighed her experience. With her defiant disregard of makeup and her penchant for disheveled clothes held together by safety pins, she seemed even younger than she was, a smart-mouthed street urchin who'd somehow managed to wheedle her way into a respected summer stock company. Speeding through Stockbridge in her LaSalle convertible, with its long wheelbase and 80 brake horsepower, Kath soon became a familiar sight in the Berkshire town. At her side at all times was Laura, elegant in her white silk kerchief.

One weekend, a man from New York showed up introducing himself as Ludlow Smith, Miss Hepburn's husband. The company was surprised to discover their little spitfire was married. But Luddy didn't stay with her at Bradley's. Instead, he took a room at a local inn. George Coulouris spied Luddy one time washing Kath's hair for her in the tub before he left for the evening. "That, and fetching ice cream," Coulouris said, "was about all he did . . . as far as she was concerned."

Not all. Surely Luddy had also bought her that fancy car, unless it was Laura's. In either case, it was always Kath behind the wheel. The security of having a wealthy husband may explain her aggressive misbehavior in Stockbridge. Striding up to Kirkland, Kath poked a finger at his chest, demanding a larger part in the company's next show. Not one to be coerced, Kirkland relegated her to yet another bit. When the company geared up for its third production, *Romeo and Juliet,* Kath drove everyone mad by running around the house reciting "Wherefore art thou, Romeo?" But once again a lead role failed to materialize.

In a snit, Kath and Laura packed their bags. No way was Kirkland going to renew their five-week contracts, and Kath was *not* going to endure being fired once again. Instead, she extricated herself from this latest unpleasant situation by quitting, the tires of the LaSalle squealing as she tore out of town, leaving the Berkshires behind in her dust.

The world had changed considerably since she and Luddy had said "I do." So had Kath. Traditional married life had of course ended almost immediately, but soon circumstances allowed her to slip out of any kind of cohabitation at all. On March 21, 1929, relaxing in the bathtub after yet another frustrating night understudying Hope Williams in *Holiday,* Kath had heard her husband scream from the other room. To his parents Luddy would explain that he'd spilled kerosene all over himself while lighting a wood fire; instantaneously, he'd ignited like a torch. Leaping out of the bath in a "lightning movement," Kath threw her husband to the floor and wrapped him in a rug, all the while shouting for help. When their neighbor from across the hall flung open their door, he discovered "a beautiful red haired Godiva seated on a young man in flames."

Luddy's right arm was badly burned with "large folds of gray goozy skin . . . and tremendous blisters," as he described his injuries to his parents. Hauling him to Hartford, Kath placed him under the care of Hep, but she herself would not linger long. The next day she received a propitious phone call from Arthur Hopkins, announcing that Hope Williams was ill and Kath would have to go on in her place. "So she has gone off to New York again," Luddy wrote his mother. "Ain't that hell?"

But either Williams suddenly got better or Kath had misunderstood—or lied—for she never did take over the lead in *Holiday* that season. No matter how it happened, with Luddy conveniently in Hartford for several weeks, Kath was able to resume living in New York much as she had before her marriage. Many a glass of white wine was raised after the theater with Putnam at her side, often with Mitch Davenport and his new wife, Marcia, the daughter of the famous opera soprano Alma Gluck and herself an aspiring author. With Mitch's novel *Through Traffic* being readied for publication and Putnam hard at work on his follow-up to *Trinc*, a sense of energy and accomplishment pervaded their circle.

It was far from what Kath was experiencing with Luddy, who still had neither a steady job nor, at almost thirty-one, any specific career aspiration. Even after her husband's return to New York, Kath continued to chart her own course. In May, with Putnam and Palache, she attended Russell Cheney's annual art opening at the Babcock Galleries. At some point, she also sat for a portrait by Cheney, who adopted Put's habit of calling her "the Kid."

That spring was also her political baptism. Often it takes outsiders to drive home the significance of one's family, and that's what seems to have happened for Kath as she sat listening to Phelpie's political friends praise her mother's liberal activism. A potent symbol of her sudden adulthood must have been socializing with Fred Manning, the husband of her former dean, who'd bring a historical perspective to the current affairs debated by Put and his cronies. With Manning, Cheney, Matthiessen, and others, Putnam frequently engaged in late-night free-for-alls on the state of the world—the expulsion of Leo Tolstoy from Russia, the Kellogg-Briand Treaty to outlaw war—all the while passing around a bottle of bootleg whiskey. Matthiessen, an outspoken socialist, believed organized labor was "the chief source of democracy," an attitude that was shared by Put and which seems to have rubbed off on Kath as well, given her pro-union stance early on in Hollywood. While some would say Hepburn was apolitical—and certainly in her later life she learned how to overlook political convictions when it became strategically necessary—this grounding in leftist political thought, affirming her mother's values, would shape her worldview for the rest of her life.

Even Luddy was more liberal than has been supposed, certainly more so than he later became. Still, by the spring of 1929 he and Kath weren't seeing eye-to-eye on many things. As obliging as he was, friends and family believe her time with Putnam surely must have bothered him. That Luddy himself likely carried on his own sideline relationships seems not to have mattered; after all, his time was not being spent with other women but with other men. The relationship with Jack Clarke had continued, and rumors have persisted of a relationship with the publicist Stanley Haggart.

Yet the most significant source of tension between Kath and Luddy seems to have been his frustrating lack of direction and ambition. Despite his personal wealth, which was still largely controlled by his father, he wasn't bringing any money into the household; Kath remained the sole, if inconsistent, breadwinner. Luddy had also recently lost a considerable sum after investing in a failed play produced by Jack Clarke, *Young Alexander*. The story of the early life of Alexander the Great, the play ran for just seven performances—not surprising, given the play's story line: the playwright Hardwick Nevin had dared allude to Alexander's homosexuality, with the conqueror demanding his troops share his abstinence from women. Sniffing out this subversive subtext, mainstream audiences stayed away. For his part, Luddy seemed unfazed, certain that he was about to make it big in the stock market.

When *Holiday* closed after a successful eight-month run—with Kath never having gone on—Mr. and Mrs. Smith took off for France. It was a second honeymoon after the trials of the winter and spring. At every stop, Luddy hustled to find a newspaper so he could keep his eye on the stock market, riffling past the front pages to run an inky finger down the columns of minuscule figures. He was "cocksure," he said, that the tips he'd been given by broker friends were soon to pay off.

With the market hitting its peak in September, Kath headed back to work in an optimistic frame of mind, accepting the challenge to finally go on for Hope Williams in a revival of *Holiday* at the Shubert Riviera Theater uptown. Williams, preparing to take the show on the road the following Monday, didn't want to tax her energies by performing on Saturday, so Kath, the part still vividly memorized, walked onstage in her place the night of October 19. She quickly realized she hadn't been better than Hope after all, for lines that had brought big laughs when Williams said them now fell flat.

At the same time, she was entertaining two other offers, one with the Theatre Guild for its production of *Meteor,* and the other with the newly formed

Professional Players for an adaptation of Alfredo Casella's *Death Takes a Holiday*. After accepting the Guild's offer, Kath changed her mind and began rehearsing with the Professional Players, likely because the part of Grazia, the girl with whom Death falls in love, was a far showier role.

On Thursday, October 24, a burst of frantic selling on Wall Street signaled the onset of the worst stock market crash in American history. Over the next several years, thousands of people would spiral down into poverty. Shocked and terrified, Luddy tried to sell his shares but found it was too late. Speculators like Luddy would be blamed, rightly or wrongly, for having driven stock prices away from their fundamental value, causing the bubble in the market that was so evident that heady summer of 1929. Now Luddy was broke. He had no choice but to turn to his father, who sent five hundred dollars in November to help him through his "fiasco."

Kath wasn't nearly as understanding. She was "furious," she later told her friend Max Showalter, that Luddy had lost so much money in the crash. She pointed to the shining example of her father, who for the rest of his life would brag about how he'd emerged unscathed. That previous spring, despite the urging of friends to invest in the market, Hep had instead paid off his loan for building the house on Bloomfield Avenue. Not only had he gotten out of the market in time; he was spared the harassment of creditors in the bleak years to come. Luddy, on the other hand, had borrowed so much money in order to play around in the market that even his father could not entirely bail him out.

Yet if Kath, angry with her husband, hoped once again to be sustained emotionally by Putnam, she was disappointed. The poet, suffering from asthma, left that winter for New Mexico. Although they would still see each other occasionally over the next couple of years, the intensity of their relationship had fizzled out. In New Mexico, Putnam settled in with a predominately homosexual circle that included Senator Bronson Cutting, a Republican who would quite famously break with President Hoover over Depression-era policy; Witter Bynner, the modernist poet (who also became a friend of Kath's); and Clifford McCarthy, Bynner's young lover who soon switched his affections to Cutting.

As she began rehearsals for *Death Takes a Holiday*, Kath was more alone than at any time since those first two difficult years in college. She was estranged from Luddy, bereft of Putnam and his circle, and her loneliness made her churlish. Fighting with the director, Lawrence Marston, over the interpretation of her character, Kath would retreat to the wings and sulk. She thought Grazia should be a tomboy, but Marston saw her as wraithlike and ethereal.

When the play opened in Washington, D.C., on November 18, Marston's doubts about Kath's performance seemed justified. Several reviews trashed her; the most important, from the *Washington Post*, conspicuously failed to mention Grazia at all. Still, the play generated a good deal of buzz heading into its second tryout in Philadelphia, where Kath's parents came to catch it. It was the first time Hep had seen his daughter on the stage—and he had nothing but invective for her. Charging into her dressing room after the last curtain, Dr. Hepburn was red-faced and fuming. "They're absolutely right!" he shouted as Kath faced him, mouth agape, still in costume. Wagging his finger in front of her face, her father asked, "Who's going to believe that . . . a big healthy girl like you could fall in love with Death?"

To make matters worse, she was fired. Once more, Katharine Hepburn lost her job just before the play reached Broadway, and in another show produced by a Shubert (this time it was Lee Shubert). And once more, the actress who replaced her (in this case, Rose Hobart) went on to win the praise of the critics. Brooks Atkinson thought Hobart brought a "petal-like tenderness" to the part, an outcome not likely had Kath continued to *galumph* (Hep's word) across the stage.

Swallowing her pride, she slunk back to the Theatre Guild, where a meeting with the casting director Cheryl Crawford landed her another understudy job in Ivan Turgenev's *A Month in the Country*, starring Alla Nazimova, which opened the following March. But while the Guild had initially offered her $225 a week to star in *Meteor*, she was now forced to accept just $30 as an understudy. Even after she took over the small part of a maid in April, Kath's request for a five-dollar increase in pay was denied. Humbled and miserable, Hepburn had finally made it back to Broadway, but in yet another bit part.

Other than standing in the wings and marveling at Nazimova's technique, the most memorable outcome of *A Month in the Country* was Kath's friendship with Eunice Stoddard, the actress for whom she'd understudied. After the play closed, the two of them took a quick trip to Paris on board the *Aquitania*, departing New York on May 28. "We had become great friends," Stoddard said, "and it seemed a fun thing to do after the show was over." Luddy, whom Stoddard recalled as "a wonderful man," had no objection to his wife traveling without him. Only a few months apart in age, the two women went steerage, as per Kath's custom, but when the stewardess realized they were of "a different class," Stoddard said, she brought them breakfast in bed every morning. Stoddard stayed on in Paris, but Kath returned after just a week. Later descriptions of the trip would say Kath had gone over to buy the latest Parisian gowns, a story that made Stoddard laugh. "She wasn't interested in any of that," she said.

As far as Kath was concerned, Stoddard had the best of both worlds. Hailing from a prominent New York society family (her real name was Eunice Smith), Stoddard had faced none of the usual parental opposition when she'd decided to become an actress. Defying class snobbery, Stoddard's mother had in fact sponsored the Laboratory Theatre, an experimental off-Broadway company. In the months after her European trip with Kath, Stoddard was part of the movement that founded the Group Theatre, the influential troupe that challenged commercial theater by producing topical, relevant plays by politically inspired writers. At some point, Stoddard brought her new friend Kath to an early planning meeting of the group. Members like Harold Clurman and Cheryl Crawford sat around speaking high-mindedly about the power of theater to change the world.

"That may be all right for you people, if you want it," Kath told them, "but you see, I'm going to be a star." Stoddard said that while the story may be apocryphal, it was true in spirit: "She definitely would do anything that would put her on the up and up."

Although Kath continued to periodically live with Luddy at the apartment on Thirty-ninth Street, it's clear from a close study of her movements in 1930 that she was away more often than not. Rather than seeking a reunion with her husband after her months of engagements in Washington and Philadelphia and the two-month run of *A Month in the Country,* she took off on a European holiday with a girlfriend. Clearly, Kath had other priorities. The friendship with Eunice Stoddard was, in fact, a dry run for her relationship with another prominent society girl. Enter Laura Harding—the most private and most enduring of all of Hepburn's relationships, and the one that, in 1930, made all the difference to a wayward, weary, lonely young woman. "I think it's fair to say," Kath confided to a friend, "that Laura Harding saved my life."

The time: July 1912. The place: Hollywood—not California but rather the exclusive country club of the old-money enclave of Long Branch, New Jersey, where the Monmouth County Horse Show took place every year.

Climbing up onto Phillip, her Virginia Highlander chestnut pony, ten-year-old Laura Harding was determined to ride him into the ring, despite the fact that another young rider had just been hurt in a fall. Only her groomsman's warning that he'd be forced to tell her father of her disobedience brought Laura down from the saddle. Throwing her riding crop across the yard in a fit of temper, she stormed off through the straw in her jodhpurs and riding boots, snapping her fingers at her chauffeur to take her home.

During those late nights sharing whiskey and cigarettes at Reverend

Bradley's house, Kath listened in rapturous fascination to tales such as this, stories of how the very rich amused themselves. One of her favorite stories was the time Laura, heading into a New York society party, instructed Sailor, her chauffeur, to wait for her out front, assuring him she wouldn't be long. When she finally danced back down the stairs at 4:30 a.m., some six hours later, it had started to snow—and there was Sailor, still dutifully waiting for her in the open car, sound asleep with an inch of snow on his cap and shoulders.

Laura Harding grew up in a six-story town house at 955 Fifth Avenue filled with gilded Louis XV antiques, Chinese porcelain vases, and paintings by such eighteenth-century masters as Joshua Reynolds, Henry Raeburn, and Thomas Gainsborough. "When they made the film version of *Holiday*," recalled Laura's grandniece Emily King, "Hepburn used Aunt Laura's life as her model. It was all Aunt Laura—the adult children living in the town house with the elevator and the butler and the organ and the children's room upstairs." With her family's five personal maids, two governesses, three cooks, formal-dressed butler, and houseman-chauffeur, Laura was the perfect model for the film.

Five years older than Kath, Laura Barney Harding was born in June 1902 at her family's estate on Philadelphia's Main Line. Her mother, Dorothea Barney, was the granddaughter of Jay Cooke, the banker known as "the financier of the Civil War" for his handling of U.S. war bonds. Cooke's daughter married Charles Barney, who founded the brokerage firm that later became Smith-Barney; Laura's father, J. Horace Harding, would serve as senior partner for the firm.

Horace would, in fact, serve as director for many companies, but only one of them seemed to matter to Hepburn chroniclers from Lupton Wilkinson to Scott Berg. Through the years, writers would consistently attach to Laura Harding's name the prefix "American Express heiress"—a nagging error that has annoyed the family for decades. "Whatever money my grandfather left," said Robert Harding, Laura's nephew, "only a very small amount of it ever came from American Express."

No matter where it came from, J. Horace Harding's wealth was considerable; at his death, the *New York Times* estimated it as "running into millions." Kath was undeniably intrigued by the world from which Laura sprang; for all the socialist sympathies drilled into her by her mother and her friends, Hepburn would always be fascinated by, even envious of, the very rich. Like the unfolding of a fairy tale, the little details of Laura's life held Kath rapt: summering in Santa Barbara; attending debutante parties at the

Ritz-Carlton; organizing balls for charity; rubbing elbows with Mellons and Rockefellers at the exclusive Jekyl Island Club off the coast of Georgia. In 1921, Laura's attendance at an exclusive dance given by Mrs. William K. Vanderbilt affirmed her place among the top two hundred in the first rank of society.

Such social status would later be presumed for Hepburn as well—an image she thoroughly enjoyed cultivating. In a way, it was Laura she was playing. "She knew all the sort of highbrow customs of the time and I learned the way," Hepburn said. "The Vuitton luggage—the clothes—where to shop—what to buy."

Kath's attraction to Laura was not dissimilar to her early interest in Phelps Putnam, who also offered entrée to a crowd otherwise inaccessible to her. Having grown up feeling ostracized by the "best" of Hartford society, Kath had been chasing after those with the finer things since her days at Bryn Mawr, and the pursuit would forever imprint the path of her life. Never one to hang out with fellow actresses (who were, after all, mostly drawn from the ranks of grocers' daughters and chorus girls), Kath saw herself as someone apart. As was the case with her mother, who could be both socialist and elitist at the same time, there was a part of Kath who believed she was inherently different (*better?*) than her fellow players, especially as she basked in the friendship of Jay Cooke's great-granddaughter.

Of course, the Houghtons were nothing to sneeze at, either; even if Kath's family wealth didn't always measure up, she could legitimately claim her own place within the American aristocracy. Describing herself in her memoir in the third person, Hepburn wrote, "She was . . . old Hartford and very socially OK." In a revealing exchange in 1991 with her friend the columnist Liz Smith, she lamented the fact that no one was "socially OK" anymore. "Nobody," she said, "knows what that means."

The world in which Katharine Hepburn moved, even after she dirtied her boots by going to Hollywood, was *very* socially OK. Her disdain for the film colony, her disinclination to sit with the Zanucks and the Goetzes at the Brown Derby restaurant, went beyond her desire to foster an "elusive" image. Hepburn's private world would always be very small and insular, a contained set of upper-class bohemia. "They all seemed to live in the East Fifties," said the artist Tim Lovejoy, whose mother had been part of that world and a friend of Laura's. "They all swelled around together. It wasn't about fame as much as being well-bred. It was Philip Barry writing *The Philadelphia Story* about his own people, and then Hepburn playing her own people. That's what they did, how they perpetuated themselves."

It wasn't just around class that Kath and Laura gelled. They shared a very similar personal history. Harding family photographs give the impression that Horace and Dorothea had three sons and one daughter. Laura's year-older sister Catherine, known as Cammie, stands demurely in a white lace dress and enormous bow. Only on closer inspection does Laura emerge, her short hair and pants making her resemble Jimmy Hepburn. "Laura wanted to be a boy," explained Emily King, "because her father didn't have time for girls."

And so we meet yet another young woman unhappy in her girl's body and craving attention from a strict, demanding father. Horace Harding would be described by family members as "mean," more interested in acquiring art to add to the Henry Clay Frick collection, of which he was a trustee, than in building relationships with his children, especially his daughters. Compensating for her father's disinterest—once more like a certain red-haired girl some hundred miles northeast in Hartford—Laura developed a strong exhibitionist streak. When not riding her pony or relay-racing her brothers through Central Park, she was organizing family theatrics; one 1914 photograph, when Laura was twelve, reveals the Harding children in a production of *The Admirable Crichton,* the very play she and Kath would giggle their way through sixteen years later in Stockbridge.

At age eighteen, Laura made her social debut, resplendent in a brocaded white gown, taking each step carefully down the grand staircase at the Plaza. As uncomfortable as she must have been in that dress, no doubt she loved the sheer spectacle of it all. Five hundred guests had taken over the Plaza's first floor, decorated with palms, ferns, and hundreds of white chrysanthemums. As she shook hands with her guests, Laura reveled in being the star of the show—much as Kath had once enjoyed being the center of attention at her birthday parties. After supper, Laura led the dancing with her good friend Wilmarth Sheldon Lewis. Other society girls stepped aside in awe as she passed. From Laura's neck, ears, and wrists dangled pre–Civil War jewelry passed down from Jay Cooke.

Her peers would often copy Laura's style, considering her an arbiter of fashion, yet descriptions of Laura as a "clothes horse" and "fashion snob" are wildly off the mark. Her interest in style was never about the accoutrements themselves; in some ways, she didn't give a hoot about clothes. What she cared about was her reputation as the final authority on what was socially correct, her ability to influence and persuade.

This inbred egotism, one more trait she shared with Kath, also compelled Laura's desire for a stage career. But Horace Harding, like Thomas Hepburn, would never have countenanced such an ambition from one of his daughters. A daughter's job, according to Horace, was to marry well, as Cammie did in 1921, marching down the aisle with Lorillard Suffern Tailer, a well-known polo player and scion of the British-American tobacco family. Yet Laura had steadfastly refused to get serious with any suitor, a fact increasingly troubling to her father, who fretted over an unmarried daughter now in her late twenties. But fate stepped in to offer an escape hatch for Laura Harding: soon after the new year of 1929, while Laura was away in Europe, a sudden bout of influenza took the life of J. Horace Harding.

"If her father had lived," said Emily King, "he'd have arranged some financially advantageous match for her, and she would've ended up as some society hostess. How she would have hated that!"

Her mother, who never forbade Laura anything, now encouraged her daughter to seek her dream. Pasted prominently into Laura's scrapbook is a letter from the Berkshire Players, dated June 29, 1929, six months after her father's death, telling her to report to Stockbridge for rehearsals of Somerset Maugham's *Caroline*. At a salary of twenty-five dollars a week, Laura's first season in the Berkshires had her playing bits with the young James Cagney and Jane Wyatt.

In the fall, the Dramatic League of Chicago kept her in the cast of *Thunder in the Air*, first staged in Stockbridge and remounted at Chicago's Princess Theater on October 14. Three nights into the run, however, word leaked to the press that "an heiress to a seven-million-dollar fortune" was playing the bit part of a maid. Furious, Laura cornered the press agent she suspected of giving away her identity and chewed him out in front of the entire cast. Sweeping grandly into her dressing room, she packed her Louis Vuitton bags and announced she was quitting the show. "I do not want any publicity," she snapped at reporters outside the stage door. "I want my work to be judged on nothing but merit. I simply will not have people come to stare at me because they have found out who I am."

The "heiress exposé" story ran in papers all across the country, often accompanied by a glamorous headshot of Laura looking over her shoulder in a backless dress. Despite reports that she was finished with the theater—and Hepburn's later protestations that acting was "just a lark" for Laura—the determined Miss Harding was soon back at Frances Robinson-Duff's studio for more acting lessons. By the end of the year, she had secured another season with the Berkshire Players. Indeed, when Laura and Kath came together, it would have been hard to say whose ambition was greater.

"I think what Hepburn brought to Laura was an awareness of how to be independent," said Emily King. "Laura had the financial freedom to live freely . . . but it was only after meeting Hepburn that she really started making her own decisions about life." For all of Laura's sophistication, she had not gone to college; Miss Porter's finishing school, not far from Hartford, had been her highest education. Unlike Kath, Laura hadn't needed to struggle or find her way in the world. Nor did she have Kath's experiences with men.

As in all of Hepburn's most significant relationships, there was a certain quid pro quo in her friendship with Laura. Indeed, Laura's wealth and social connections enabled Kath, at this precarious time in her career, to flourish. No wonder she'd feel that Laura saved her life. In return, Kath—so driven, determined, and full of confidence—gave Laura a sense of what was possible. She showed her how they could make their shared dreams and ambitions come true.

Laura was the first and in many ways the most equal partner in Hepburn's life. Other accounts have played up their dissimilarities in style and speech, but in fact their personalities and worldviews complemented each other perfectly. "Laura Harding was the most important relationship in her life," said James Prideaux. Another friend echoed with an even more precise assessment: "If Kate had a great love other than herself, it was Laura."

They fell in love—for that's how any great friendship begins—on a warm night in June 1930, after considerable glasses of whiskey shared in Reverend Bradley's living room, under a starry sky unobscured by the bright lights of the city. Outside in the surrounding woods, green tree frogs kept up their high-pitched chatter. Despite having been assigned her own room, Kath found she could not simply say good night to Laura and let it end at that. Rather, as Laura remembered in later interviews, Kath stepped quietly into her new friend's room, closing the door behind her. There she'd remain for the duration of their time in Stockbridge; there, in effect, she'd remain for the next four years.

Several decades later, the author Charles Higham was ushered in to see Laura Harding at her swank, if small, Beekman Place apartment. He was writing the first book-length study of Hepburn's life, and the screen icon herself had arranged this meeting. Seated by a window, Laura, now a silver-haired lady in her seventies, turned to face the young author. "I hope," she said, raising an eyebrow, "you aren't planning on making me a lesbian."

"Only God can make one a lesbian, Miss Harding," Higham replied cordially. A small smile crept across Laura's face. She always did like witty men.

In Laura's view, *lesbian* meant something very specific. It meant the outrageous Louisa Carpenter, a great-great-granddaughter of E. I. Du Pont who used her wealth and class to blatantly seduce beautiful young women like the French singer Milli Monti, promising to make them stars. As a young girl, Carpenter had moved in similar social circles as Laura, who had looked down her perky little nose at the other girl's brusque mannerisms and masculine clothes. As an adult, Carpenter would fly her own plane, captain her own yacht, and stand beside the notorious Broadway star Libby Holman when she was indicted for murdering her husband. It was all just too terribly déclassé for Laura's taste.

In the 1930s, only the most overt "bulldaggers" embraced the connotations within the word *lesbian*. It meant mannish. It meant degenerate. Worst of all, it meant low-class. It meant the defiant dames in Greenwich Village bars and the shadowy, predatory creatures who, in the wake of *The Captive*, lurked as popular villains on the stage and in literature. It meant women who hated men, or men "trapped in women's bodies"—abnormal, sick, perverse. *Lesbian* did not simply mean a woman who loved other women; it meant a particular *kind* of woman, one who bore no resemblance to Laura Harding.

To her family, Laura never divulged the full details of her relationship with Hepburn, and they never presumed to press. But many of them offered thoughtful considerations of what might have been. "It would make sense to me that Aunt Laura was gay," said a grandniece of Laura's, the author Robin Chotzinoff. "Everyone in the family was always speculating about why she had never married, what her real story was. But usually I feel sorry for people who spend their lives in the closet. It was simply not possible to feel sorry for Aunt Laura."

That's because her life was not governed by the strict contemporary construction of sexuality. Laura was never "in the closet" because she didn't see the world in those terms. Sitting there at her window overlooking Fifty-fourth Street, meeting Higham's gaze, she wasn't obfuscating the issue; according to her definition, she was *not* a lesbian, and neither could her relationship with Hepburn be described that way.

Yet it *was* sexual. Hepburn admitted as much to friends like James Prideaux, cutting him off with a shrill "Of course!" when he asked, saying no more as if the subject were simply too obvious and boring to belabor. Another friend recalled: "She would speak to me of Laura in such a way that I *understood*. She knew that I'd get her meaning because I was gay myself." George Cukor, who became nearly as close to Laura as he did to Hepburn, also understood the full nature of their relationship. According to Gavin Lambert, Cukor's friend and biographer and widely considered the dean of Hollywood historians, "[Cukor] knew they were lovers. This he told me . . .

When he mentioned Laura Harding, it was clear he was talking about Hepburn's lover, and that meant *sexually*."

Sex, of course, whether with men or women, was never an overriding determinant for Hepburn's significant relationships. Great shows of affection made her uneasy; extended bodily contact held no appeal. Sex should not be a "pastime," she told one interviewer, especially not for women. Women, she said, were fortunate in that they didn't "have the same need" as men. Two women together, she told several friends, could avoid the dreaded act of intercourse. For her, sex should be gentler, less intrusive. Reminiscing with George Cukor in 1969, a tape recorder running in the background, Hepburn reflected, "[R]omantic magic between two people is what sex should represent . . . [It] goes on forever, because you can't describe it to me and I can't describe it to you. It's the magic of life."

With Laura, she had definitely found some magic. Stepping back, we can examine Hepburn's life in total and obtain a deeper understanding of her relationships. Only then do patterns become apparent. At the end of the 1920s, Kath turned to the companionship of women after being disillusioned by both Putnam and Luddy. It would be a recurring model throughout the decades: after painful, conflicted experiences with men, she would seek refuge with women. It was a natural impulse for her. "I think men and women are more shut off from each other than a woman and a woman," she'd say. With women, Kath could give expression to her most private, most authentic self. She could once again be Jimmy.

This is critical to understand. Hepburn's sense of who she was never had much to do with sexual attraction. Instead, it was defined by her sense of gender—which, as she told Liz Smith, was "not female, certainly." In 1981, she admitted to Barbara Walters, "I put on pants fifty years ago and declared a sort of middle road." No better description explains the essence of Katharine Hepburn. She was, in her soul, neither woman nor man, though it was men—*straight* men—with whom she identified, never women. But it was only *with* women that she could set Jimmy free and be herself; rare was the man who would tolerate such a paradigm.

Cleaving to Laura was in fact a return to the female world of Bryn Mawr, where Kath had been the mischievous tomboy among a group of like-minded girls. And if sexual feelings arose from such intimacy, they were free of the rough, hard, penetrative sex of men, which a boy like Jimmy Hepburn would never, *could* never, tolerate. Bonding them even closer, Laura shared Kath's loathing of intercourse. "She tried it and just didn't like it," said Emily King. "I told her it got better after the first time, but she wanted nothing of it."

Some friends, made uncomfortable by this ambiguous sexuality, would insist Hepburn was asexual, citing her lack of physical affection with people, her reluctance to hug and kiss. But others rejected such a label. "Asexual is just wrong," said Noel Taylor. "Someone who is asexual lacks passion, and Kate was as passionate as you can be."

"I would say [Kath and Laura] were genuinely, deeply in love," said another friend, who knew both women. "I don't know how else to put it. *In love*. It was a passionate friendship, with all the love and expression that comes with it."

James Prideaux had another observation. "Don't you think all great stars are a little bit bisexual?" he asked rhetorically. "It's part of their charisma, their appeal."

Certainly in the theatrical world of the time, the relationship between Kath and Laura would have raised few eyebrows. In fact, in the more sophisticated environs of New York, a fascination for homosexuality had blossomed, with drag balls attracting thousands to the ballrooms of the Savoy and Hotel Astor. Decades before the term *lesbian chic* was coined, worldly circles imbued same-sex love with an exotic allure. Alla Nazimova, Libby Holman, Elisabeth Marbury, and Elsie de Wolfe were all understood to have women as lovers, and a certain cachet swirled around the androgyny of such actresses as Eva Le Gallienne and Hope Williams. "It was in the air," Hepburn said, "that boy-woman. My arrival in the big city was well-timed."

If not "out" in the modern sense, the theatrical lesbians of the period lived within the fluid borders of the "open secret." Hepburn told the writer Helen Sheehy that she knew Le Gallienne (with whom she'd later share Constance Collier as a mentor) was "queer" but never thought "it queer that she was." Sophisticated circles knew and understood such things, but the rest of the world was oblivious, due to the fact that many of these women had husbands who, like Luddy, provided a degree of social currency while intersecting only occasionally in their lives. Yet for all intents and purposes, these women did not see themselves as creatures apart from the culture; private sexual behavior was not yet a determinant of one's public identity.

Against such a backdrop, the relationship between Kath and Laura becomes easier to integrate into our understanding of her life. In 1930, not yet a star, Kath would have felt little need for pretense; the decorum of the "open secret" allowed such relationships accommodation without discussion. Kath and Laura would have feared no scandal or social ostracizing; sophisticated people considered such private matters trivial and irrelevant.

Given such freedom, Kath began spending much of her time with Laura at her house on Fifth Avenue. Although Luddy still joined her for visits to Hartford, Mr. and Mrs. Smith seem to have reached an understanding. Marion Hepburn's diary reveals that Luddy often arrived in Hartford accompanied by Jack Clarke, with whom the Hepburn children also had an affectionate bond. It wasn't uncommon for Kath ("Katty") to travel separately from Luddy and Jack. Yet despite what other accounts have presumed, Laura rarely accompanied her to Hartford. Hep and Kit were far too sharp not to guess her place in Kath's life. For his part, Luddy seems to have accepted Laura's presence with equanimity, just as he'd once made room for Putnam. Indeed, he became good friends with Laura's brother Charles, and the four of them sometimes socialized together.

Once Kath became a celebrity, however, and her story exposed to the masses beyond the urbane world of the theater, such an easygoing, indulgent model could not last. By the time Hepburn decided to carve her legend into stone by writing her memoir and filming the documentary *All About Me*, it was clear that Laura's place in her life needed to be repackaged for public consumption. What was private and immaterial in 1930, shielded by the protocol of the open secret, was now, in 1991, an accepted, even expected, part of public discourse. In this new climate, to ignore the gossip that had proliferated over the years would only make it more incriminating. So, in true Hepburn style, she tackled it head-on.

"It was bound to happen," Kate said in *All About Me*, "that there would be rumors that Laura and I were, how should I say, more than just friends." Her voice quivered with just the right amount of incredulity and amusement, though her claim not to have known about such talk at the time is rather hard to swallow, given the kind of early press she got. (Recall the caption "What kind of queer arrangement is this?") Yet by claiming ignorance of the charge of lesbianism, she could refute it without ever actually denying it. "Ridiculous" is what she called the gossip. "And . . . a bit boring."

In her own way, wiggling out of the label of lesbian wasn't entirely disingenuous. Throughout Hepburn's life she would know lots of lesbians, many of them in her inner circle. From these women she *was*, in fact, different. Unlike them, she enjoyed being transformed into a lipsticked, pancaked love goddess, even if away from the movie studios she still scuffed around in sneakers and jeans. Unlike her lesbian friends, Hepburn relished flirtations with the male sex. And unlike those other women, she adopted all those wounded men, like so many stray puppies in need of a home.

But Laura Harding fit perfectly into Hepburn's world. A battalion of men stood ready at all times to escort Miss Harding to the latest dance or debutante party on the New York social calendar. Like the horses stabled at her farm in New Jersey, Laura's beaux were always impeccably groomed and at the top of their breed.

But just who were these unbilled bit players Kath and Laura called their beaux? Identifying these men allows us to understand better the dynamic between them and their ladies, and between the ladies themselves. For Laura, there was Wilmarth Lewis, the effete, erudite collector of Horace Walpole memorabilia, and Carleton Burke, the glad-handing, gregarious polo player who lived with his sister in the affluent Berkeley Square section of Los Angeles. For Kath, there was Alan Campbell, the wisecracking actor who'd later marry Dorothy Parker. Both women shared Mitch Davenport, who'd just started working for Henry R. Luce at his new magazine *Fortune*. All were men whose charm preceded them, and whose repressed homosexuality made them eminently suitable companions, even if such an arrangement was certainly never acknowledged.

"Laura would always be with these charming, lovely, fascinating, wonderful men," said Emily King, "who for their own reasons were never going to marry her, and of course she knew it and wanted it that way."

Behind all the romantic, magnolia-shaded images of society girls and their beaux was the reality of New York's theatrical elite. Stepping off a private elevator at a town house on East Fiftieth Street, Kath and Laura waltzed into a swell party hosted by Hope Williams, like Laura a graduate of Miss Porter's and a member of the Junior League. Clifton Webb and Gertrude Lawrence were leading the banter, waving around their tumblers of gin. On certain nights Guthrie McClintic, the husband of Katharine Cornell, was there, and so was the mannishly dressed Lillie Messenger, a Hollywood talent scout who lived with two other women in Greenwich Village. Witty repartee and double entendres bounced off the oak-paneled walls, as Williams sat on the edge of a mahogany wing chair, her arm draped around a pretty girl. Hope's "secret" was so open around Broadway that when her latest play premiered, Brooks Atkinson quipped that she strode "manfully through the leading part."

Thanks to Laura's social connections, Kath found herself socializing with Williams and her high-placed theater friends. By 1930, high society was in an uproar over well-bred girls like Hope flocking into the once-forbidden world of the theater. Now, at places like Bessie Marbury's town house in Sutton Place, Vanderbilts and Morgans condescended to mix with Frohmans and Shuberts. When Nadejda de Braganza, the daughter of Princess Miguel de Braganza of Newport, Rhode Island, joined the company of Max Reinhardt in Germany, many had had enough. Starting in January 1930, "society buds" who took to the stage were threatened with the upper classes' version of excommunication: being dropped from the Social Register.

Kath and Laura weren't concerned. In the privacy of Fifth Avenue penthouses, Jacobean crewel curtains shielding them from the outside world, the two ambitious young women sipped champagne with Philip Barry, Beatrice Lillie, Elsie Janis, and Clifton Webb. One night Kath even met Noël Coward. At other times, she mixed with Eunice Stoddard and people from the Group Theatre, notably Cheryl Crawford and her lover, Dorothy Patten. All sophisticated, clever, dexterous types, wise to the ways of the world and the vagaries of love and desire. These people wrote, produced, and acted in plays that poked holes in convention and skewered sacred cows like marriage and motherhood. The world in which the young Katharine Hepburn moved was sexy, provocative, subversive—far from the picture of domestic simplicity she tried to paint in her memoir, sitting at home with Luddy and having their kindly landlord send up their meals by dumbwaiter.

It's true that around such glittering theatrical hotshots, Kath's old shyness and lack of confidence led her sometimes to shrink into the background. But when she did speak up, she managed to impress. Mercedes de Acosta, a lover of Hope Williams and later the paramour of both Garbo and Dietrich, met Kath around this time in a box at Carnegie Hall. "I was impressed by her personality then," de Acosta wrote. "When she became a success in films, I was not surprised."

In those busy months, Laura offered one other important connection as well. Among the dapper, enameled young men who'd led her around the dance floor at her coming-out party had been Leland Hayward, the son of Colonel William Hayward, U.S. attorney. Now an aggressive young agent on the hustle, Leland Hayward would spot the angular, freckle-faced, red-haired girl acting with overwrought intensity on the stage and think, for some crazy notion, that she just might have the makings of a movie star.

THE BEAUTIFUL SCENT OF
ORANGE BLOSSOMS

On the tiny wooden platform at Croton-Harmon some thirty miles north of Manhattan, Kath stood peering down the tracks, watching for the train. Humid and overcast, the late afternoon sky threatened a downpour. Luddy stood nearby, nervously jangling the coins in his pocket, making Kath all the more anxious. For the last few minutes, she'd been walking along the edge of the platform, craning her neck as far as she could. The *Twentieth Century Limited* was famous for being on time, but that didn't soothe Kath's nerves.

Finally, a mile or so off, a whistle sounded. Kath glanced over at her husband.

"You're going to Hollywood," Luddy told her.

It was Sunday, July 3, 1932. In the three minutes it took for the train to connect with its dining car, Kath slipped on board, the only passenger embarking at Croton-Harmon. Almost forgetting to wave good-bye to her husband, she bolted through the blue and white art deco cars in search of Laura, who'd boarded at Grand Central Terminal. As the wheels began to turn, black soot rising from the tracks, Kath was pleased she'd managed to elude the photographers. Who'd have thought the star of the Broadway hit *The Warrior's Husband* would depart for her first film in Hollywood from this obscure little way station? It was the start of a long game of cat and mouse with the press, and Hepburn had won the first round.

When she found Laura, Kath wasn't surprised to see that her friend had insisted on traveling in style. Stacked against one wall of their private drawing-room compartment were at least ten pieces of Louis Vuitton luggage. Throughout the cabin, baby pillows had been strewn across the stiff leather seats. Laura's two dogs, a Scottie and a Shelbourne terrier, started yipping happily at the sight of Kath. Off the drawing room stretched a large sleeping area and a separate toilet annex, filled with flowers.

Gliding along at speeds of up to one hundred miles per hour, the *Twentieth Century* reached Chicago early on the second afternoon. Debarking, Kath spied the actress Billie Burke and her daughter Patricia in another compartment. Although the newspapers had announced that Burke was returning after a long absence to resume her film career with George Cukor's *A Bill of Divorcement*, the same picture for which Kath had been hired, Hepburn would claim not to have known it, and so never introduced herself to the older actress. It seems once again to have been a manifestation of her old shyness—the flip side of her narcissism whenever she found herself in alien environments.

For the second leg of the trip, Kath and Laura boarded the *Chief.* Two hot, grueling days lay ahead before the train reached Los Angeles. Finally nearing the end of her journey, Kath wrapped a Pullman towel soaked in ice water around her head and strode out onto the observation platform. There, a steel filing flew into her eye—a filing that has grown bigger and bigger in every retelling. The story of Hepburn's arrival in Hollywood always begins with the tragicomic anecdote of the young actress stepping off the train with her eye swollen and teary. Myron Selznick, partner with Leland Hayward in the agency that represented Kath, supposedly took one look at her and griped to Leland, "The studio is paying $1,500 a week for *that*?"

And if it wasn't her swollen eye, it was her bony figure; her director, George Cukor, too, was said to recoil when he first met her. "A boa constrictor on a fast," he allegedly moaned to David O. Selznick, Myron's brother and the new head of production at RKO. Adding to the screwball ambience was that crafty mythmaker herself, Adela Rogers St. Johns, who'd later claim to have been there on the day Hepburn first arrived at the studio. "As long as I live I will never forget," St. Johns wrote. "Everybody was in the commissary at lunch when she walked in with Mr. Cukor. Several executives nearly fainted. Mr. Selznick swallowed a chicken wing whole."

In fact, most Hollywood legends start this way: a nearsighted Hollywood exec fails to spy the swan behind the ugly duckling. Bette Davis's story always begins with Universal chief Carl Laemmle tearing up her contract because he thinks she's got "as much sex appeal as Slim Summerville," the gangly comedian. Various versions of Joan Crawford's origins have her stepping off the bus onto the MGM lot as a chubby, frizzy-haired girl, only to be told to turn around and go back home to Kansas City.

Of course, if Kath's eye had really been as bad as all that, there's no way that Leland Hayward—so cunning, so protective of his clients—would have brought her immediately to the studio. Like so much else in the Hepburn legend, the story of the swollen eye began as a humorous anecdote in the first press releases churned out by RKO and was later incorporated into "official" accounts by "official" biographers. Hepburn herself would ultimately carry the story to a screenwriter's dream conclusion: in her version, told in her memoir *Me*, John Barrymore observes her red eyes, assumes she's as much of a lush as he is, and kindly gives her his private bottle of eyedrops.

Cukor would later tell his biographer Gavin Lambert that the story of Hepburn's eye was exaggerated into "a lot of hooey," but the star herself may have come to believe it was true. Writing about her life, she often used old clippings (and the biographies she claimed to loathe) as a way of "remembering" the events of her past—a revealing example of the funhouse nature of public lives.

But all of that was still years in the future. Stepping off the train in Pasadena, Kath was just a wide-eyed, ambitious young woman from the East struck immediately by "the beautiful scent of the orange blossoms" and the dry, clear air: "No smog in those days," she recalled. Dolled up in a sleek gray suit by the New York designer Elizabeth Hawes, complete with a flat-as-a-pancake hat (Laura had chosen the ensemble), Kath posed stiffly for an RKO photographer sent to capture the arrival of the studio's new star. There was no escaping the press now.

With the sun dropping lower in the sky, Leland—who collected his client and her friend from the station—hustled Kath, Laura, and the dogs into the backseat of the yellow Rolls-Royce he drove whenever he was in L.A. He informed them he was taking them directly to the studio, bags and all. RKO was indeed paying a lot for Kath, and Leland was determined to show that she was worth every penny.

Hollywood was in transition. Every week, hundreds of young stage actors from the East were disembarking from trains and buses, eager to enunciate their vowels roundly into the microphone and thereby prove themselves indispensable to the new medium. But these young Turks were eyed suspiciously by many in the old guard: would the Spencer Tracys and Margaret Sullavans prove to have the endurance of a John Gilbert or Gloria Swanson? The old silent stars might have been making fewer pictures, but socially they retained their clout. Douglas Fairbanks and Mary Pickford were still the unchallenged cultural arbiters of the film colony. Swanson still set the style; Gilbert was still viewed as king.

Yet the smell of change was in the air, as definite as the fragrance of orange blossoms. It wasn't just sound that made the movies of the early 1930s so different. A new art form, one that pushed at the edges of form and content, was emerging. A stone's throw from RKO, Paramount was turning out Hollywood's most sophisticated pictures, from the swell comedies of Ernst Lubitsch to the madcap antics of the Marx Brothers. At Warners, gritty gangster pictures exposed the raw underbelly of American life during the Great Depression. All along the wide, palm-lined boulevards, from the opulent Metro-Goldwyn-Mayer out in Culver City to the ramshackle studios of Poverty Row, there was the sense of something new taking shape. And it required a new kind of actor, modern and independent.

At that precarious moment, Katharine Hepburn was exactly the kind of East Coast, well-bred, theater actress producers insisted they wanted—no matter how limited her theatrical experience actually was. Looking into his rearview mirror as he headed out of Pasadena toward Hollywood, Leland saw not a plain, angular woman in a funny hat but a movie star. He was definitely a believer—Kath's first and perhaps most important. If Hepburn owed her career to anyone other than her indomitable self, it was this man. Stepping on the gas, Leland steered the yellow Rolls along scenic Arroyo Boulevard. Before this workday was over, he'd deliver his client to the destiny he fervently believed was hers.

It had been two years of stops and starts. After the debacle in Stockbridge, Kath had languished about in idle luxury at Laura's Fifth Avenue town house. "Little hopes here and there," she'd say of her job prospects, "but nothing real." Then, once again, in November 1930, Jack Clarke played fairy godfather, putting Kath in touch with his friend Richard Aldrich, then working with Kenneth Macgowan on a play titled *Art and Mrs. Bottle*. Kath got the showy role of the daughter who confronts her mother (played by Jane Cowl) after twenty years of truancy.

During the run of the play, Kath proved as impulsive as she'd been in Stockbridge. Quarreling with the director, she also annoyed Cowl by splashing herself with alcohol so that her face would shine in the footlights. Fired once, she was rehired when her replacement showed none of the fire Kath had brought to the part. Yet for all of Hepburn's bratty behavior, the genteel Miss Cowl would obligingly tell Lupton Wilkinson a decade later (when Katharine Hepburn was a far bigger star than she was) that nothing "that child could have done could have turned me against her." Chastened by such civility, Hepburn would offer an apology in hindsight: "Could I possibly have been so rude to so lovely a person?"

Whatever happened backstage, the role brought Hepburn good reviews and her first true hit show. The *Times* credited Kath's "decisive ability," and the *New York World* thought she was "uncommonly refreshing." It all should have led to another part in another production. But Kath, without an agent, watched as the show went on the road in January without her. With nothing to replace it, she went back to sitting around Laura's parlor, the butler bringing in her lunches on trays. It was a curious scenario: here she was, finally a success in a long-running Broadway play, and it had gotten her nowhere. In previous Hepburn chronicles, very little has been made of this period of stagnation, the narrative flowing seamlessly from the closing of *Art and Mrs. Bottle* to her next job—a full *eight months* later. But of course that's the way she wanted the story told, how she shaped it herself in Wilkinson's *Saturday Evening Post* narrative, which would serve as the blueprint for all the writers to follow. Yet Kath's eight-month dry spell, especially after such a good run, deserves a bit more scrutiny. Her reputation for being difficult—not only on *Bottle* but also on previous shows—seems to have gotten around.

It wasn't until August that she worked again, landing a gig with the New York Players at the Cheney Comstock Theatre in Ivoryton, Connecticut, not far from Fenwick. Again, Jack Clarke may have eased her way, as Henry Hull, the star of Clarke's *Young Alexander,* had signed on as the playhouse's guest leading man. Kath came along as well, assigned to leading parts in the company's last four productions: *The Cat and the Canary, Let Us Be Gay, The Man Who Came Back,* and *Young Sinners.* (Kath would erroneously remember the title of the final play as *Just Married.*) Perhaps humbled by her months of unemployment, she behaved herself splendidly overall, retaining an affectionate relationship with the playhouse's founder, Milton Stiefel. "I learned a lot," she said of her month in Ivoryton.

Even her father thought she was pretty good. After a performance of *The Man Who Came Back,* Hep came backstage and told her, "This is the first time I've ever thought you might have some talent." It was also the first time

Kath ever heard such words from her father. Possibly the last, too—at least, she never reported any others.

By now, Hep had grudgingly accepted that Kath wasn't going to give up "her theater madness," and so he was making the best of it. For the first time in three years the family enjoyed some harmony. Kath lived at Fenwick during her stint at Ivoryton. Mornings and afternoons she spent swimming in the Sound and paddling with Dick and Bob in rowboats through the marshes near the lighthouse. Observing their daughter, both Hep and Kit realized that her marriage with Luddy had drifted into a distant, if cordial, acquaintanceship. They were still fond of their son-in-law, as indeed the Smiths were toward Kath; Gertrude Smith told a family member that Kath had proven "a real daughter" to her, one who brought "fresh joy" to her life. Yet despite such affection, neither Luddy nor Kath saw much of their in-laws that summer. Kath was on the road almost constantly, and Luddy had finally found a job, working as an industrial engineer for the John R. Hall Corporation in New York.

Significantly, during this period Luddy ceded control of Kath's financial management to Hep. With Dr. Hepburn directing his daughter to send her paychecks to him, he was acting like most husbands of the era, managing their wives' money and making all of their financial decisions for them. To this arrangement, Luddy offered no objection. Certainly, it served Kath well: Hep invested most of what the budding thespian made, doling out an allowance to her as if she were once again a Bryn Mawr freshman. So much for breaking free of parental control. Yet over the next few years, as Kath's income skyrocketed with Hollywood money, Hep's financial wizardry became apparent. His daughter became "a rich girl almost before she knew it," said Garson Kanin, who gave credit to the "eleventh commandment" that New Englanders like Dr. Thomas Hepburn always followed: "Thou shalt not touch thy capital."

Luddy's absence from Kath's life was noticed in other ways as well. By the summer of 1931, it was no longer Luddy sitting down to dinner with the Hepburn family but the impishly attractive Laura Harding. It was now Laura who read lines with Kath on the front porch, lying with her in the hammock, shoulder to shoulder, thigh to thigh, as family members of both women remember. Their closeness may have made Hep uncomfortable. After staying at Fenwick for a few days that August, Laura rented her own house in nearby Essex, where Kath often stayed after performances. Unlike Luddy or Palache, Laura was never fully embraced into the inner circle of the Hepburn family.

Laura's career had gradually taken a distant second place to Kath's, as she took on the role of cheerleader and personal manager rather than competitor for parts. Kath would later downplay Laura's own theatrical ambitions, but the Harding family insisted Laura had really wanted to be an actress. Her decision to back off and bolster Kath's career was a sacrifice—one she gladly made, but a sacrifice nonetheless. To pursue her own parts would have meant leaving Kath's side, each heading off with a different company, and Laura was not willing to endure such separations. Instead, she packed her Vuitton bags and hitched her dogs to their diamond-studded leashes and trooped after Kath wherever she was sent. In Connecticut, Laura slipcovered the "ghastly" furniture in her rental house and hung imported tapestries on the bare walls. She wanted the two of them to feel "at home." Later she'd tell friends this was when she was the happiest, running around with Kath before she became a success.

In late August came a call from the office of Gilbert Miller, who was producing Philip Barry's play *The Animal Kingdom*, set to star Leslie Howard and open late that year on Broadway. Barry had suggested that Miller contact Kath, whom he remembered from both *Holiday* and Hope Williams's soirees the previous spring. Suggestions that Barry wrote the part of Daisy with Kath in mind are baseless. But when it came time for casting, the playwright thought Hepburn might have some of the qualities he wanted for the character, particularly an edgy independence and bohemian spirit. Kath was thrilled with the offer to audition, convinced this would be the part that would "absolutely" make her a star.

Apparently, she acquitted herself well enough, for after reading for Miller she was hired. Rehearsals were not scheduled to begin for several months, however, so she took the opportunity to join Laura in Europe. Luddy went with her. He had split with Jack Clarke, who'd abandoned his Broadway aspirations to lead a yearlong expedition into the jungles of Brazil, planning to film the adventure and release it as a documentary feature.

With Jack gone from his life, Luddy appears to have been pressing Kath for a reconciliation. His father had just died, and at thirty-two, Luddy was coming to grips with his mortality. "I don't feel any older," he wrote to his mother on his birthday that year, "but I do feel that I am getting nearer the point when my life will mean something to the rest of the world." He had a real job and seems to have wanted a real wife to go with it. Children were next on his list, though, according to Hepburn's brother Bob, Kath had made it clear he shouldn't expect any from her.

She'd later tell friends that she considered divorcing Luddy at this time. Whatever usefulness the marriage may once have had was now gone, and Luddy's desire for children and a more traditional relationship surely made Kath regret her rash decision of three years ago even more. She wasn't dependent on Luddy financially, as many women of the time were with their husbands. For the first time in her life, having signed the contract for *The Animal Kingdom* at the beginning of November, Kath was financially self-sufficient, bringing home $250 a week for the first three weeks of rehearsals and thereafter $200 a week plus 1 percent of the gross. Money was no reason to remain in the marriage.

Then, as if on cue, everything came crashing down. Rehearsals began the last week of November, soon after Leslie Howard's arrival from Europe. Later, Hepburn would insist the trouble stemmed from the fact that she wore high heels on her first day, making her tower over her costar. Given that Howard was a good five inches *taller* than Hepburn, those heels must have been pretty high. Whatever the reason, the two clearly clashed; it's not far-fetched to imagine that, once again, Kath proved difficult and idiosyncratic in rehearsals. By the time the press reported the names of the cast on December 10, Kath had been fired again. For the time being, any talk of divorce was off.

Her arrogance could be off-putting to other company members, who often attributed it, not unfairly, to an attitude of upper-class privilege. Yet Kath was also an ambitious young woman whose assertive behavior might have been looked upon more tolerantly had she been a man. She'd come to see how easily actresses were discarded; she'd given up once, and she was not about to do that again. Asked late in life what advice she'd give to her younger self if she had the chance, Hepburn didn't say, "I'd tell her to be more cooperative" or "less arrogant." Rather, she said she wished she could reach back through time and simply tell that young woman who bounced from job to job, "Don't worry, it'll happen."

And it did. A year earlier, Hope Williams had played in an amateur one-act farce called *The Warrior's Husband* at the Comedy Club. By the time the producer Harry Moses decided to expand it and bring it to Broadway, Williams was committed to doing a "serious" play for Arthur Hopkins. So Moses turned to the young woman everyone said was a "carbon copy" of Hope, even if she had a "difficult" reputation. Kath jumped at the chance. It meant giving up the opportunity to play with the actress she most admired, Laurette Taylor, in a forthcoming production by William Brady, but the part Moses was offering was far showier.

When she reported for rehearsals, Kath quickly proved how she'd earned her reputation. Condescending to the director, Burk Symon, whom she deemed inadequate, she was also querulous with the playwright, Julian Thompson, asking for rewrites and once stalking off the stage. Within a week Moses had had enough and tossed her out of the cast, replacing her with Jean Dixon. But even with all her troublesome behavior, Moses knew he'd hired Kath for a reason. By the first week of February 1932, he'd brought her back.

What made Hepburn so right for *The Warrior's Husband* was what made her so right for *Little Women*, for *Stage Door*, for *The Philadelphia Story*, for *The African Queen*. She was playing herself, setting Jimmy free to romp about the stage. Katharine Hepburn would never be known for possessing a great range as an actress. When she truly clicked, she was playing close to her own skin. *The Warrior's Husband*, loosely based on Aristophanes' *Lysistrata*, allowed her to run, jump, tumble, leap, and scurry down a staircase with a dead stag over her shoulders. As Antiope, the Amazon warrior, she must confront a world that seems quite unnatural to her. In Amazonia, it is the women who hunt and fight, the men who stay home and simper effeminately. "It was very controversial," remembered Phyllis Seaton, the play's stage manager. "The whole thing was a 'sex change'—years before its time."

Kath took to the part with gusto. Every night, she smeared bronze greasepaint all over her face, arms, and legs, since most of the time she was near naked onstage, wearing little more than a short chain-mail tunic and a pair of silver leather shin pads. Finally, strapping on her sword, she bounded out onto the stage like an antelope. "She came down a ramp of great stairs," Seaton recalled, "running onto a platform, then jumping onto the main stage." She literally *leaped* at the audience, causing many of them to gasp out loud. Audiences were instantly struck by her newness, her sense of being *different*. In such a forthright, aggressive, gender-defying way did Katharine Hepburn first burst into public awareness.

Thrust back in his seat, one spectator would never forget that night. Noel Taylor, then a young playwright, could not tear his eyes away from her. "No more ingenues," he thought to himself. "The ingenue was dead—and Katharine Hepburn had killed her."

Reviews for the show were mixed, but everyone loved Kath. Brooks Atkinson called her "excellent." Burns Mantle in the *Chicago Tribune* found himself transfixed by this "fascinating boyish person." Banging on her dressing room door after one performance, Leland Hayward claimed he could make her a movie star. She wasn't quite sure she wanted that—after all, she'd just had her first unqualified success in a Broadway show, why leave now?—but she let Leland in, intrigued by his talk of fame. "I was just full of the joy of life," Hepburn would remember—but even more, as always, it was her "wild desire to be absolutely fascinating" that would determine what she would do next.

Walking into the RKO headquarters in Hollywood with Leland at her side, Kath thought the place seemed more like a gargantuan warehouse than a glamorous movie studio. Unlike the elegant, colonnaded facades of the more established MGM and Paramount, the six-year-old RKO fronted North Gower Street with a plain exterior, two rows of eight windows with simple awnings. Only above the door was there any ornamentation, a pattern of art deco diamonds etched into the stucco behind the name RKO.

The perception of a warehouse wasn't really that far from the mark, for what else were the Hollywood studios of the time but giant factories? Instead of brass casings and ball bearings, they churned out films, celluloid dreams consumed by Depression-weary masses with an energy that is difficult to grasp today. Movies were the primary form of entertainment for most Americans. The theater was beyond most people's financial reach, and though radio had made considerable inroads by the early 1930s, it was Hollywood that still dominated the public imagination. Even in the early years of the Depression, buoyed by the novelty of the "talkies," the movies remained profitable, though by 1932, with the economy reaching its nadir, even Hollywood had begun to feel the squeeze. Just before Kath arrived, RKO had slipped into the red by $5 million.

Aggressively reversing that trend was the studio's executive producer, the young, fleshy-faced, passionately intelligent David O. Selznick. In the name of efficiency, Selznick had charged onto the lot swinging a large scythe, laying off dozens of RKO personnel; those he didn't fire were given sixty days to prove their worth. Under Selznick's management, RKO rearranged itself into a system of production units, each with its own producer and stable of directors. (This model would soon dominate throughout Hollywood.) Two of Selznick's lieutenants, Merian Cooper and Pandro Berman, presided over units intended to upgrade RKO's market value. At the time, Cooper's main project was a big-budget "gorilla picture" starring Bruce Cabot and Fay Wray. Berman had gone a more literary route, taking on a film adaptation of Clemence Dane's play *A Bill of Divorcement,* for which Selznick had approved a staggering $125,000 fee to secure the services of John Barrymore.

Striding into Selznick's office and shaking hands all around, Kath was given a royal welcome. If the terms of her contract weren't as extravagant as Barrymore's, they were still quite extraordinary for a young woman with just one Broadway hit under her belt and no picture experience at all. She'd get a whopping $1,500 a week, with an option to employ her for two additional features after this one, and always with the proviso that she be allowed enough time in between to appear on stage in New York. The fact that she was making as much as George Cukor, the director assigned to *Divorcement,* demonstrates just how much the studio wanted her—and how hard her agent had fought on her behalf. Although in the official versions that came later, it would always be Katharine Hepburn who named her price, pulling the figure of $1,500 out of the air with no expectation of it being met, it was in fact Leland Hayward who negotiated this deal; any attempt to position Hepburn at the center, no matter how necessary to the legend, does a disservice to Leland's enterprising arbitration.

Already by 1932, he was a legend in the industry. Agents at the time were considered sleazy, underworld characters with sweaty palms and heavy accents, hustling for vaudeville comics and burlesque dancers. Leland had captured the fancy of the Hollywood moguls by being markedly different, a polished Easterner who wore linen underwear and furnished his office in Beverly Hills with authentic French antiques. He began asking for, and getting, huge salaries for his clients. George Cukor called him "a buccaneer," but for all that, he was a gentleman too, a rarity in the rollicking, topsy-turvy world of Hollywood in the early talkie era. Leland's ultimate success was ensured not so much by the moguls themselves as by their wives: Frances Goldwyn, Ann Warner, Virginia Zanuck. "All the wives were crazy about him," the director Billy Wilder once observed. "He should have been a captain in the Austro-Hungarian army—something like that. He was certainly miscast as an agent."

Leland had an irresistible appeal to women, with a strong, masculine face and deep-set, pale blue eyes. Smelling of fresh air and bay rum aftershave, he was an impeccable dresser, his suits cut to fit, his shoes always polished to a high shine. When he breezed into a room, he clapped the men on their backs and kissed the ladies on their hands. But what he loved even better than show business, even better than the women he successively proclaimed as the loves of his life, was flying. Only with great reluctance did Leland leave the air to do business on the ground. Usually flying in an open cockpit, his ears buzzing for hours afterward, he once told his daughter Brooke, "I'd give up the agency in a minute, if I could spend the rest of my life in an airplane." Securing his tie to his starched white shirt was a gold clip in the shape of an airplane propeller, a sapphire sparkling at its center. So fond of the clip was he, so much did it announce who he was, that Leland instructed Cartier's to make him twenty identical copies just in case he ever lost it.

Five years older than Kath, Leland had flunked out of Princeton and headed to Hollywood to make his mark. There, as a publicist, he'd shaped Gloria Swanson's femme fatale image, his boss declaring he'd never known "a better exploitation and publicity man." As a lark, Leland arranged for Fred Astaire to perform at the Trocadero nightclub, earning himself his first commission as an agent. "The pickings were too easy," he said. "I decided this was my line of work." While most Americans saw their earnings fall away after the stock market crash, Leland's income doubled between 1929 and 1930. By 1931, he was making more money as an agent than many of Hollywood's top producers.

Just how he first noticed Hepburn is unclear; some reports say Belle Willard Roosevelt, a daughter-in-law of the former president and a doyenne of New York society, was so impressed by Kath in *The Warrior's Husband* that she wired Leland that he "must make this girl a star." More likely the conduit was Lillie Messenger, Kath's friend from Hope Williams's parties and now a scout for RKO. Certainly, once he met Kath, Leland also had Laura's persuasive arguments in his ear. Coming from a similar social background as Miss Harding—one wag called Leland "the only bona fide Park Avenue agent in a business where any Park Avenooers of any description are hard to catch"— Leland and Laura quickly became a team in their promotion of Kath.

For Leland, however, it was about more than just making some young woman a star. Although it hasn't generally been realized, Leland was using Hepburn in order to reengage with Hollywood after several years of being focused primarily on the New York stage. When he signed the contract with Kath on June 17, 1932, he was still affiliated with the American Play Company; by the time he met her at the train in Pasadena a couple of weeks later, he had taken the leap and formed his own business in partnership with Myron Selznick. Katharine Hepburn was the first of Leland Hayward's long, stellar list of Hollywood clients.

He was still married to his wife, Lola, but that didn't prevent Leland from spending hours with Kath, Laura, and his assistant, Miriam Howell, at his swanky duplex penthouse on East Seventy-third Street, planning for their futures. Without fail, they'd be interrupted—five, six, seven times—by the shrill ring of the telephone, the predominant fetish of Leland's life. At Chasen's, a phone was always brought to his table so he could keep making deals as he ate. Often he sent people telegrams just to let them know he was about to call them. No sooner had they opened the cable than their telephone rang.

By the early spring of 1932, Leland was entertaining two offers for Kath from Hollywood. Selznick wanted her for the part of the daughter in *A Bill of Divorcement*, and Paramount was interested in making a movie of *The Warrior's Husband*. Although he'd yet to persuade her to sign a contract with him, Leland arranged screen tests for Kath anyway. For the RKO test, Hepburn turned to friends for help: Lillie Messenger ran the camera, and Alan Campbell fed her lines from *Holiday*. For the Paramount test, a scene from *The Animal Kingdom*, the director listed in the files of the UCLA archive (where the test is held) is none other John Ford. It's curious that Hepburn never mentioned such an early meeting with Ford; might the UCLA record be wrong? In fact, there's only a small window in which the taciturn, bespectacled Ford could have shot this test. Touring the Pacific from October 1931 until the following March, Ford was back in Los Angeles in early May, when he signed to do a film for Universal. Doing a job for Paramount after that seems unlikely. If Ford really did peer through his lens at Kath in 1932, it would have had to have been in late April, the earliest she was likely to have done the test.

Of course, there would be the usual declarations that the tests were terrible, that there was "no spark." Such tales, too, have always been prerequisite in movie-star legends. Bette Davis likewise insisted her screen test was "ghastly." But Selznick and Cukor obviously liked what they saw, because they gave Kath the job in *Divorcement*.

In Kath's mind she wasn't leaving the theater; she was merely supplementing her income. Her pay for the Broadway production of *The Warrior's Husband* had been a comedown, just $100 a week with 1 percent of the gross. In May, she'd been stiffed by the producers of a one-night-only gig in Philadelphia, playing opposite Blanche Yurka in *Electra*. Promised $500, she'd walked away empty-handed. Then, after a week of stock in Ossining in late June, someone absconded with the box-office receipts, and Kath had to take what she could get. Determined to change all that, Leland was demanding $1,000 a week from RKO. The studio balked, calling such an amount "excessive." One RKO exec wrote to Cukor: "I agree . . . that $1,000 a week is too much for Hepburn. As far as I can recall, she has done only three plays."

So it was with utter astonishment that Kath got the final news from Leland two weeks later. After much wheeling and dealing, he'd gotten Selznick up even higher than their original demand, to $1,500. Translated into current dollars, that was about $21,000—a *week*. Even today, that's extraordinary money. No wonder she walked through the corridors of the studio with her nose in the air. No wonder she brought such an air of condescension to her first meeting with Cukor. She was making as much money as he was, after all.

This privileged beginning would forever imprint Hepburn's relationship with Hollywood. She was worth more than most; ergo, she was *better* than most. Just a year before, Bette Davis had arrived at Universal with none of the fanfare with which Kath had been delivered to RKO. No one had even met Davis at the train. Yet she, like Hepburn, had just come off a well-reviewed featured role in a Broadway play. In fact, Davis's production,

Broken Dishes, had run considerably longer than *The Warrior's Husband.* But still Davis was signed at just $300 a week, one-fifth of Kath's salary.

Why such privilege? For one thing, Bette Davis didn't have Leland Hayward fighting for her. And while Davis came from a respectable middle-class background, she didn't carry with her the air of gentility and lineage that her fellow New Englander had learned to cultivate so deftly. From Selznick's point of view, he was getting a bona fide American aristocrat, and that was worth every penny he was spending. Hepburn promised the kind of class so fervently coveted by the Hollywood moguls, most of whom hailed from working-class, immigrant, mercantile backgrounds. It's hardly surprising that Hepburn's early press would name her the daughter of the wealthy capitalist A. Barton Hepburn. It's who Hollywood wanted her to be, who they had paid for, and who she had managed to become.

From across his desk George Cukor stared at these two rather pretentious newcomers. As far as he was concerned, they wore their East Coast schooling and old-money backgrounds as obviously as their weird, avant-garde clothes. Sitting there in a white short-sleeved shirt that revealed his thick, hairy arms, Cukor didn't speak for several seconds. He just peered through his wire-rimmed glasses at the two women in his office. The Hepburn girl grew a little fidgety under his gaze, but the other one, Miss Harding, stared right back at him.

Squat and plump, Cukor was thirty-three but looked twenty years older. Jewish and homosexual and secretive about neither, he was the son of a Hungarian immigrant who barely spoke English, and his schooling had been limited to New York's De Witt Clinton High School. In other words, he couldn't have been more different from these two WASP princesses seated before him, who seemed to consider their very presence in Hollywood as "slumming."

Cukor resented their attitude, for he loved making movies. After several years of directing stock companies, he'd come West to make films for Paramount, quickly establishing himself as a canny director of female stars. He guided Tallulah Bankhead in *Tarnished Lady* and Kay Francis and Lilyan Tashman in *Girls About Town.* But it was Cukor's first film here at RKO, the current smash-hit *What Price Hollywood?,* that had elevated him to the top rank of directors. Starring Constance Bennett, *What Price Hollywood?* was the prototype for *A Star Is Born,* a shrewd insider's look at the demands of stardom.

In assigning Cukor to *A Bill of Divorcement,* the studio was counting on his ability to balance the performance of the nominal leading lady, Billie

Burke, with the showier role of the daughter, played by Hepburn. The true star of the film was John Barrymore, as a man long committed to an insane asylum who comes home to find his wife ready to remarry. Still, it is through the eyes of his daughter—Kath—that the power of the drama unfolds.

Looking at her that first day in his office, Cukor hoped his faith in what he'd seen in her screen test would be justified, though he'd admit later to having doubts. When he finally spoke, it was to show Kath and Laura costume sketches, which Kath immediately declared all wrong. The director was taken aback. He was showing the sketches to this first-timer as a courtesy, not for her opinion. But Kath was gesturing to Laura, sitting beside her.

"I think she should be wearing Chanel," she told Cukor, "like Miss Harding here."

"Oh really?" Cukor replied. "And what do you think of what *you're* wearing?"

She glanced down at her designer suit. "I think it's very smart."

"Well, I think it stinks," Cukor told her. "We can proceed from there."

So began George Cukor's makeover of Katharine Hepburn. Asking her to remove her hat, he saw a face that appeared frighteningly skeletal with her hair pulled tightly back into a knot. Without the hat to shield her skin from the light, Kath's freckles and blemishes popped out in stark relief. Cukor walked around her once, then paused, his hand on his chin as he studied her. Reaching around with his thick, stubby hands, he undid her hair and let it fall to her shoulders. The light caught flecks of red and gold. Calling in his assistant, Cukor ordered Hepburn's hair cut to chin length, then washed with egg shampoos to build up its luster. And her face, he instructed, was to be pancaked smooth, made into porcelain.

Later that afternoon, when she saw the results, Kath was astounded. She might not have been born beautiful, but she was blessed with, as the photographer Cecil Beaton would observe, "the most photogenic bone structure." This, Beaton believed, compensated for what he called her "hooded eyelids" and "horrid skin." That same potential had clearly been glimpsed by Cukor the moment he'd laid eyes on her. When the studio cosmetician turned her around in the chair to face the mirror, revealing her perfect skin, lustrous hair, and lacy lashes, Kath let out a gasp. From then on, she never doubted George Cukor's word.

Filming began about a week later. For all her imperiousness on the stage, under Cukor's direction Kath proved surprisingly cooperative and incredibly industrious. She worked hard, very hard, which gradually won the director's respect. Kath came to understand that acting for the camera was very different from acting on the stage. "At times she'd get too mannered, high-falutin, actressy," Cukor recalled. "I'd bring her down. I'd say, 'Be yourself, draw on your own emotions, keep your voice down. The audience is at your shoulder.'"

To the still distant Laura, Cukor gave the part of an extra in the film's opening party scene. When he called "Action!" she fumbled and accidentally broke part of a banister, ruining the take. Furious, Cukor stalked over and smacked her across the shoulder. Startled by his aggression, Laura burst out laughing at the absurdity of it all, which only made Kath double over in hysterics herself. "Just because you don't know what you're doing," Kath said between gales of laughter, "don't take it out on us." Finally, Cukor had to smile himself. They all became fast friends after that and would joke about the incident for the rest of their lives.

Laura had no intention of staying in a hotel for the month of shooting, so she had her Los Angeles "beau" Carleton Burke find them suitable lodging. What he found was a charming four-room tile-roof cottage nestled in a secluded area of Franklin Canyon. With its rolling hills, tall firs, and lack of palm trees, Franklin Canyon was the closest Kath and Laura could get to the East Coast in southern California. Burke also arranged for a live-in maid and a car, a flashy Hispano-Suiza, which turned heads as Kath and Laura were chauffeured into the studio by a driver chosen for the job because, as one fan magazine reported, "his skin matches the deep brown of the car." It was all quite a different experience from what many of Hepburn's contemporaries endured during their first few weeks in Hollywood. Rosalind Russell slept on a pull-out couch in a cramped bungalow rented by actor friends, and Joan Crawford lived at a seedy hotel that was close enough to the studio so she could walk to work in the morning.

On the set, there was a civil distance between Kath and Billie Burke, perhaps out of the natural tension between an older leading lady and a fresh new face. But with John Barrymore there was immediate rapport. Not surprisingly, given the actor's reputation as a lush and a rake, the legend would insist Barrymore made the obligatory pass at Kath, which she comically rebuffed by shrieking, "My father doesn't want me to have any babies!" In retrospect—for that's when such stories are drafted—it was precisely the kind of provincial, naive image Hepburn liked to impart to her young self. But Cukor told Gavin Lambert it never happened. Barrymore was, in fact, on his best behavior during filming, in high spirits after welcoming the birth of his son. Courteous to his leading ladies, he helped Burke adjust to the microphone—it was her first talking picture—and gave Hepburn pointers, often turning her by the shoulders so that she gave the camera her best view. If he was flirtatious, it was all in good fun, and Kath, hardly the rube she later wanted us to think she was, certainly understood the difference.

What most impressed everyone was how naturally she warmed up to the camera—though it's not really all that surprising when one considers that the camera, this *machine*, could always be counted on to give her its undivided attention, unlike live audiences, who could look this way or that, cough, and get up to use the restroom. "Kate was quite good at rehearsals," Cukor said, "but she didn't really come alive until the camera closed in on her. I had a rough idea she was doing well, but she sprang to life when I saw the rushes. Her odd awkwardness, her odd shifts of emphasis, these were proof of her being alive on the screen."

Though Barrymore and Burke had the titular leading parts, Cukor realized this young upstart would steal the picture from these two seasoned veterans. When a rough print was screened in August, Merian Cooper agreed that Hepburn was "due to be an important star," and empowered Cukor to reshoot her close-ups to emphasize the special quality they both agreed was coming through on the screen.

Watching the film today, one can still see it. Kath moves with a striking newness, her excitement at being in front of the camera obvious in her eyes and in her gestures. We see her first from below, a girl in a white dress on a mezzanine. The camera pans up, and she runs down, straight into the arms of her lover. Off they waltz, twirling through the frame, all in one shot, as fluid and graceful as a piece of music. When we see her up close for the first time, she is glowing with youth and energy. Later, gazing up at herself on the screen, Kath whispered to Cukor that she never thought she could look so pretty.

When the film was released in October, headlines proclaimed Kath "the find of the year." The *New Yorker* called her "half Botticelli page and half bobbed-hair bandit." Philip Scheuer rhapsodized over her "geometrically fascinating face." She was compared to Garbo, called the most exciting new face since Dietrich. Yet she was "far from being a stencil of anyone else," wrote Norbert Lusk in the *Los Angeles Times*. Rather, she possessed "a strange beauty that places her apart . . . Unless all signs fail, Miss Hepburn will withstand the efforts of any studio to trick her eyebrows into disturbing angles or publicize her as a hothouse orchid. Character and intelligence are reflected in every word she utters and every gesture, yet she is human, appealing and girlishly sympathetic . . . forthright, courageous, dignified."

With just one film, Kath's girlhood dream of world-class fame had been achieved. Back in New York, Alice Palache exulted to see her friend's face "all over the Fifth Avenue buses." And in that one gushing review in the *Los Angeles Times*, Norbert Lusk had spelled out all of the most salient traits that would come to define the legend of Katharine Hepburn.

LIKING EVERYTHING ABOUT THE MOVIES

Looking down the hill toward Sunset Boulevard, Kath, the toast of Hollywood, could hardly have known what this stretch of land would come to mean to her in the years ahead. George Cukor had recently purchased these six steep acres in the Hollywood hills, intending to landscape them with gardens and terraces. The simple stucco house where Kath stood now, gazing down from a large picture window, would become a showplace, the site of so many of her most memorable moments in the film colony over the next forty years. As George showed the place off to his bachelor friends, the boy millionaire Alex Tiers and the urbane photographer George Hoyningen-Huene, Kath only half listened to all his grand talk of marble pillars and parquetry floors. She was in her own world, staring down the hill at the dreamscape of Los Angeles, its lights twinkling as late afternoon faded into dusk.

Pull in now for a close-up: She stands there five feet, five and one half inches—tall for an actress, but not unusually so—and weighs 110 pounds—thin, but hardly the boa constrictor of legend. Her hair, thanks to Cukor's egg shampoos, has taken on new body and luster, and even her skin seems to have been much improved by the dry California air. She is, in a word, glowing. Hollywood has been very good to her.

Years later, she'd try to forget how dazzled she was by the experience. In tape-recorded conversations with Cukor in 1969, she'd say (in keeping with the Hepburn legend) that she had never gone in for "any of that nonsense"—hair and makeup and Hollywood glitz. But Cukor simply laughed out loud at her assertion, telling her emphatically, "*You did!*" Reluctantly she had to admit, "Ninety years ago, yes."

In that long-ago time, Katharine Hepburn fell in love with Hollywood. Los Angeles was completely different from New York. For all her later invective against southern California and her undeniable affinity for the East Coast, in the beginning Kath *adored* L.A. For a young woman who could never resist climbing a grassy hill or wading hip-deep into a field of wildflowers, Los Angeles gave her opportunities Manhattan never could. Within minutes she could leave behind the concrete walls and arc lamps of the studio and be surrounded by green pastures and babbling brooks. Back East, it took two hours to drive from New York to Fenwick, but here she could breeze down Santa Monica Boulevard in less than half an hour and find herself at Alex Tiers's beach house, running naked into the pounding surf of the Pacific Ocean. In New York, she spent as much time as she could in Central Park, but so much of the city of Los Angeles was itself a park in 1932. "It was just beautiful," she said of the city. "It really was paradise."

And if some part of her were really as provincial as she liked us to think, she would have enjoyed the sense of the movie capital being a small town. Everyone knew each other in the 1930s. When Cukor first came to Hollywood, he lived next door to Fatty Arbuckle on Franklin Avenue, rented a house in Malibu next to B. P. Schulberg and Kath's old boss Edwin Knopf, and went out on the town with Gloria Swanson. There were no secrets in such a small community, no need for the heavy curtains and brownstone walls that divided New York's sophisticates from the hoi polloi. Hollywood was a haven for people who lived independent lives, whether politically, culturally, or sexually, and that much no doubt Kath savored. Not yet had the film colony turned on itself, pointing fingers and making accusations. In 1932, Hollywood was still a bohemian dream lived out under blue skies and palm trees.

"I liked everything about the movies right from the start," Hepburn would remember—not least of which its work ethic: "You went to work at six o'clock [a.m.]—and I was happy to go to work at six o'clock so long as I could go home at five." For someone who thrived on getting up early and never going to bed too late, it was the ideal schedule. "The theater," she said, looking back, "is more work."

Nor had the theater given her the immediate success that the movies had. Hollywood might not have been in her game plan, but was she ever glad that she came—that men with loud voices and surnames not of the Connecticut variety had given her the chance to be a star. And now they wanted to *keep* her. Soon after *A Bill of Divorcement* was completed, she and Laura drove out to David O. Selznick's house in Malibu. Not only was Selznick picking up her option, but he was also raising her salary to $1,750 for a second picture and $2,000 for a third—which would then be increased to a whopping *$4,000 a week* in the course of filming. Kath was speechless. Leland had made sure Selznick kept the provision allowing for periodic stage work, but the pièce de résistance was persuading the studio boss to cross out a clause that allowed RKO to terminate Kath without explaining why. Few movie performers, even established stars, had it so good.

Heading back East, Kath was dazzled. Laura, however, found the whole experience terribly gauche. At Selznick's house, his parents had been sleeping on the couch, his brother Myron drunk. When Kath asked for a cup of tea, "everyone was in shock," Laura recalled. "They only drank hard liquor and coffee." Laura, for whom $4,000 a week was a pittance, never fell for Hollywood the way Kath did. Watching her friend's eyes light up at the terms of her contract, Laura already seemed fearful of losing her to the glittery allure of Tinseltown.

In early September, Kath took off for her annual trip to Europe, once again going steerage: since she always got seasick anyway, she argued, why waste money being sick in first-class? It would, in fact, be her last anonymous voyage; by the time she returned, *Divorcement* had been released and her name was on everyone's lips. Some friends insisted that Laura accompanied Kath, bicycling with her through Austria and Switzerland. We know for sure that Luddy was with her. "I think during that last trip with Lud she was trying to figure out how, or if, she was going to keep him in her life," said Michael Pearman, who became friendly with Luddy about this time. "She was still tremendously fond of him, but now, being a movie star, I think she saw the difficulties ahead."

Their relationship had settled into occasional visits and stopovers. Kath still kept many of her belongings at Luddy's New York apartment and was forever calling him to bring a coat or a pair of gloves over to Laura's or to the train station as she headed out of town. But if it had been difficult to maintain even the facade of a marriage in New York, it seemed impossible now that Kath was spending considerable time in Hollywood. With that in mind, Luddy's actions upon their return from Europe in October take on some real poignancy. Determined not to let the marriage just crumble away, he began looking for a larger residence, one more appropriate to Kath's new status. Soon after the New Year, he rented a four-story brownstone on Forty-ninth Street in Turtle Bay. "Lud's house is too grand to be true," Palache wrote to her mother. "He has just had it all painted and varnished and it is beautiful." The house was, in many ways, Luddy's last-ditch attempt to save his marriage. He still envisioned a future in which his untraditional union with Kath could survive.

His hopes for children, however, may have been permanently dashed that winter. Previous chroniclers seem to have overlooked, or written off as inconsequential, a series of news reports about Kath's health in early 1933. In late January, in Los Angeles, Laura rushed Kath to Good Samaritan Hospital on Wilshire Boulevard. The press reported she was suffering from influenza, but apparently there was more to it than that. Soon after she was released, Kath hurried back East to be placed under her father's care at Hartford Hospital. On February 25, she underwent a "serious" operation, according to letters Luddy wrote at the time. Pacing back and forth in fear, Luddy had no idea whether his wife would "live or die." To his brother Luddy wrote that he'd given her up for "dead at least a dozen times [while] she was on the table." Once under way, the operation turned complicated, requiring double the usual length of time for such procedures. When it was done, Kath was left with a scar "on her lower anatomy," according to Luddy.

With the scant descriptions that exist, the procedure sounds uterine, especially since we know Kath's appendix had been removed some years earlier. It's really the only explanation for a scar on the lower anatomy. The most probable cause for an incision in this case, doctors say, would be the removal of an ovarian cyst—the first sign of which may have been excessive menstrual bleeding, prompting the first hospitalization. The fact that complications arose while on the operating table in Hartford suggests a more radical procedure, possibly a hysterectomy, was deemed necessary.

Indeed, Kath's long recuperation also points to this idea. A month later, she still wasn't well, with Palache reporting that she grew tired easily, "which is so unlike her . . . something really is wrong." Even a partial hysterectomy would have had profound implications on her life. Hepburn's lifelong insistence that women couldn't have both children and a career—and that she herself had made the decision for the latter—may have hidden a difficult

fact: that not only was she disinclined to have children; she couldn't physically bear them.

Still weak and underweight, Kath managed to attend the New York premiere
of *A Bill of Divorcement* at Radio City Music Hall that March. For the occasion, the house at 244 East Forty-ninth Street was filled with guests: Hep and
Kit, Marion and Peg, Luddy's mother, Gertrude. Tired, overcrowded, as-
saulted by a bitterly cold March, Kath couldn't wait to return to sunny Los
Angeles and the new house Carty Burke had found for her and Laura. While
the New York address would become her cherished domicile for seventy
years, in 1933 she was more excited by the Spanish-style hacienda in Cold-
water Canyon, a hideaway Laura dubbed "Quinta Nirvana." With a swimming pool, tennis court, and a backdrop of the Santa Monica hills, the house
offered Kath a retreat from the crazy pace of moviemaking.

And crazy it certainly was. Upon her return, she was studying for the upcoming *Three Came Unarmed*, the story of a girl raised in the jungle and
then brought to civilization, as well as for a proposed adaptation of Louisa
May Alcott's *Little Women*. But within a month Kath was put into another
picture, the story of a female aviator not unlike Amelia Earhart. Originally
called *The Great Desire*, it would be released as *Christopher Strong*.

In those days, studio contract players, even the stars, didn't choose their
parts. Nor were parts chosen for them to prove their range or skill. The top
brass at RKO wanted a part that would capitalize on the quirky, unique personality that reviewers had discerned in Hepburn upon viewing *Divorcement*. The role they chose for her follow-up feature should therefore call
attention to this "otherness," not deflect it—a decision they'd live to regret,
but which at the time seemed to make all the sense in the world.

In this light, *Three Came Unarmed* would have been an ideal fit: Kath was,
in many ways, a girl raised outside of conventional civilization, an outsider
whose manners and mores often seemed alien to mainstream observers. Yet
Christopher Strong had much the same attraction as well. Here was a part
where the studio could play upon the androgyny Kath had popularized onstage in *The Warrior's Husband* while also highlighting the independence audiences had so admired in *Divorcement*. Someone, probably Pandro Berman,
then had the bright idea of helming the picture with Dorothy Arzner, the only
woman working as a director in the studio system, and hiring as scenarist
Zoe Akins, an eccentric like Kath who shared her home with another woman.
With all that synchronicity, they seemed poised for a terrific hit.

Still, Kath wasn't happy making the film, which began shooting in early

1933. She missed Cukor and found Arzner distant, despite all they had in common. "She wore pants," Hepburn said. "So did I." During her youth in Los Angeles, Arzner had also adopted the persona of a boy, calling herself "Garth." As children, Garth Arzner and Jimmy Hepburn might have been friends, but as adults there was tension. Arriving on the set in her man's coat and tie, her short hair slicked back severely with brilliantine, Arzner was well known as a lesbian, living with the choreographer Marion Morgan in a house they dubbed "Armor," in the same way Pickford and Fairbanks had christened their house "Pickfair." Arzner was precisely the type of lesbian from whom Laura instinctively recoiled, a woman whose obviousness seemed terribly middle-class. The discomfort Laura felt around Arzner (in her scrapbook she referred to her dismissively as "Dotzy") seems to have rubbed off on Kath.

Zoe Akins was even worse. George Cukor, who liked her, considered Akins terribly crass, a prime example of the excesses of the nouveau riche. Many thought Akins had married Hugo Rumbold, son of the eighth baronet, just so she could claim a link to the British nobility. "The marriage to Hugo was one of convenience," said her friend Elliot Morgan. "Zoe's convenience in becoming an aristocrat." After Rumbold's death, Akins resumed living with her longtime companion, the actress Jobyna Howland.

There was also, once again, distance from Billie Burke, cast in her second picture with Hepburn. This time Kath was unequivocally the star, and Burke the character actress. Adding to the awkwardness, rumors abounded that Burke, newly widowed after the death of Florenz Ziegfeld that summer, was being consoled after hours by Arzner. (Morgan was conveniently away at the Yale School of Drama that year.) Laura no doubt insisted they keep their distance from such déclassé goings-on. Still, she showed up on the set to take home movies, which she'd later project for the crew's amusement.

For her third picture, Kath lobbied to delay *Little Women* and substitute *Morning Glory*, another script by Akins that had been originally set for Constance Bennett. Pan Berman was originally opposed to the switch but eventually came around. By now, Selznick had left RKO, lured away by MGM, so it was Berman who took over guiding Kath's career. At twenty-seven, just two years older than his star, Berman was the studio's boy wonder, a hardworking, technically proficient, fundamentally decent man with a passion for making movies. And—critically—he believed in Kath. "He thought that she would eventually become a big star," recalled his son Michael Berman. "He always thought that."

Kath soon convinced the producer that *Morning Glory*, the tale of an aspiring actress, was perfect for her, building upon her image as a "determined thespian." The first scene, in fact, had her mooning over lobby posters of Maude Adams, Ethel Barrymore, and Sarah Bernhardt. The film's production turned out to be far more pleasant than *Christopher Strong*, with Kath liking the director Lowell Sherman's method of filming in sequence, allowing her to build her characterization the way she did on the stage. The title was taken from a speech delivered by C. Aubrey Smith, playing an old actor, on the nature of fame: "Every year in every theater some young person makes a hit . . . Youth has its hour of glory. But too often it's only a morning glory, a flower that fades before the sun is very high." When filming was completed in May 1933 after just seventeen days, Kath could do nothing more than take a deep breath and wait to see whether her own hour of glory would outlast the sun.

In the meantime, she was having a ball.

A starry night over the palatial Beverly Hills estate of the producer Walter Wanger and his wife. From out of the shadows slink three figures in servants' uniforms. Look closely behind their poker faces and discern they are Kath Hepburn, Laura Harding, and Leland Hayward. With nary a glance behind them, the three would-be stooges follow a group of caterers in through the back door of the Wanger mansion, lifting platters of food and carrying them out to the assembled guests in the parlor. Serving hors d'oeuvres to the likes of Charles Boyer and Madeleine Carroll, they nod and bow and scrape, until finally Justine Wanger, peering up at Kath, asks, "Has anyone told you that you look like that new girl in town, Katharine Hepburn?" The jig is up, and they run from the house laughing.

Another time, hiding in the trunk of the director William Wellman's car, Kath and Laura scared the poor man half to death when they jumped out in his garage. Once again the girl who had broken into houses at Fenwick just for fun was acting up, sneaking into the homes of Hollywood's rich and famous and smoking cigarettes on their divans. Laura, brought up within a proper world where such behavior was unimaginable, found it all tremendously exhilarating. "Everyone in Hollywood took themselves oh so seriously," she'd later say, explaining the pranks she pulled with Kath. "We thought they needed a little shaking up."

George Cukor lovingly called them "subcollegiate idiotic." Recognizing this inherent screwball quality in Kath's nature, the studio decided to play it up in her publicity, especially after its initial bid to present her as a Park Avenue heiress failed to take off. "The Marx Brothers' long-undisputed title of Hollywood's champion nuts is threatened at last," one RKO press release trumpeted. "And by Katharine Hepburn, the newest actress-sensation of movieland . . . the screwiest dame we've ever had on this lot!"

Accordingly, while their screwy dame was still being touted for *Three Came Unarmed*, she was handed a shifty-eyed, long-limbed gibbon and told to make herself conspicuous. Someone in the RKO publicity department thought it would be great for the picture if the public believed the actress playing the part of the jungle girl actually loved apes in real life. The resulting photographs, taken during several days in which Kath drove around Los Angeles with the gibbon clinging to her neck, are among the oddest in Hepburn's entire career.

What's significant here is that Kath was *cooperating*. Later, the legend would insist that Hepburn never played photo-op games, never allowed herself to be used for publicity purposes. The very idea would stand in direct opposition to the star image she eventually cultivated. The official line, given by Lupton Wilkinson in 1941, was that she'd marched into RKO's press department when she first arrived in Hollywood and announced, "Publicity? Not for me—none at all!"

Baloney. On a warm day in December, Kath trooped out of her dressing room in a frilly one-piece bathing suit and greeted the handsome Joel McCrea, slated to star with her in *Three Came Unarmed*. Stretching out beside the studio pool, she showed off her firm, long legs; they had served her to good advantage in *The Warrior's Husband*, and RKO hoped to get similar traction out of them now. Kneeling beside her, McCrea flashed a pearly white grin, and the cameras started snapping. The photographs would turn up in the March 1933 issue of *Screen Book* as well as elsewhere. Later, with reporters still milling about, Kath flung herself into McCrea's arms and had him carry her to her car.

The film colony was soon "agog" over rumors of a McCrea-Hepburn love affair. Headlines blared JOEL FALLS IN LOVE. Yet when *Three Came Unarmed* was scrapped, enterprising studio publicists quickly redirected the gossip to the writer John Farrow, an early contender to write the script for *Little Women*. Soon enough, Grace Kingsley was hinting in her column that Farrow was two-timing Maureen O'Sullivan (whom he'd eventually marry) with Katharine Hepburn, called elsewhere "RKO's latest siren."

It's all a far different picture from what the public eventually associated with Hepburn. She would, in fact, block many of these early PR outings from her memory. Later, when she'd say she never indulged in publicity stunts or allowed herself to be "cheapened like a floozy for the fan magazines," she probably honestly believed she was telling the truth. Hepburn had a way of remembering only what she chose to remember. Once again reminiscing with George Cukor nearly forty years later, she'd recall a time when he supposedly tied a ham to the end of a rope and lowered it onto the set as a way of telling her she was overacting. Despite Cukor's repeated insistence that it never happened, she would hear none of it, cutting him off whenever he objected. By that point in her life, Hepburn had grown absolutely certain that her version of history was the only correct one.

What set Hepburn apart from most contract players, however, was that she didn't stick around Hollywood between pictures—and when she was beyond RKO's reach, she tended to mess things up. As the *Bremen* was steaming back toward New York in October, reporters had managed to get ahold of the ship's manifest. They'd very quickly deduced that the "Katharine Smith" returning with her husband was the breakout star of *A Bill of Divorcement*. Assuming that she'd wed while abroad, a pack of reporters hounded Kath down the Fifty-eighth Street pier in Brooklyn, bombarding her with questions. Stunned that Luddy's identity had been discovered, Kath tried to fluff the newshounds off with a joke, but her wit proved a little too sophisticated for the mainstream press. Shouting over her shoulder, she told them that she wasn't married, but she *did* have children. "Two white and three colored," she said, as she ducked into a waiting car and slammed the door.

Some provincial newspapers, picking up the comment from the wires, printed it as if it were true. Even more worldly publications thought she was too flip with her answer, and remained unconvinced by her denials of marriage. With the press buzzing with potential scandal, the studio insisted Kath sit down with reporters and smooth things out. How much RKO knew about Luddy is debatable, but Leland Hayward surely knew the truth, and evidently he was still coaching her that denial remained the best course of action.

"No, I'm not married," Kath lied outright to the columnist Alice Tildesley, who wasn't buying it. If that was the case, Tildesley pressed, was the name of the "supposed bridegroom" simply made up? Kath had to admit it wasn't. Since the star ended the interview at that point, Tildesley was at a loss as how to reconcile the contradiction. She concluded, "So if it turns out later that she *is* married, don't quote me [saying she isn't.]"

Of course, it would have been a lot easier just to admit she was married, but Leland seems to have considered that too risky. A few years before, Claudette Colbert had faced a similar situation when the press discovered she too had a "secret husband" from whom she lived apart. Gossip columnists titillated their readers with accounts of Colbert's "modern, twin-apartment" marriage to the actor and later director Norman Foster, who blithely took it upon himself to explain, "We go where we please and with whom we please." The Fosters' open marriage remained the talk of the town for years.

Though Hollywood had traditionally tolerated such freethinking, Leland seems to have decided Kath's image would not benefit from the kind of European sophistication that swirled around Colbert. Although she was often compared to Garbo, Kath was a much more American figure, and Americans didn't live apart from their spouses. She was also getting ready to star in that most American of pictures *Little Women*, with its celebration of homespun, traditional family values. A part-time husband would simply not do at this point, especially one who, as Leland surely was aware, had maintained a longtime relationship with Jack Clarke, the director of that season's most publicized documentary, *Matto Grosso*, then in the nation's theaters. To come clean about Luddy's identity meant getting too close to too many other awkward truths. By stonewalling a little longer, Leland seems to have been gambling that the questions about matrimony would die down, and Kath could then quietly divorce Luddy and be done with it.

Back in New York, however, her embattled husband was taking a different tack. That spring, Luddy initiated the legal process of changing his name. Later, of course, came the story of Hepburn insisting he change his last name because she didn't want to be confused with Kate Smith, the ample, pie-faced radio singer. This bit of blarney was repeated so often that Hepburn herself started saying it; dozens of her obituaries would include it in the "facts" about her. But the truth is that Luddy didn't begin the paperwork for the name change until the point when reporters first began sniffing out his existence and identity. If Hepburn hadn't wanted to be known as "Kate Smith," she sure took a long time to press her point: when the change was finalized that November, they'd been married for nearly five years.

More likely, Luddy's name change had a more complicated explanation. His family felt certain he couldn't have been bullied into changing his name, no matter how much he wanted to please Kath. There was a great deal of history and pride in the Smith name; in Strafford, Gertrude was horrified and hurt by her son's actions. Luddy adored his mother and would only have taken such a radical step if he believed there was no other choice. With his identity discovered, Luddy knew it would only be a matter of time before reporters tracked him down at the new house he'd found for Kath, making her even less likely to want to come home. Changing his name, then, was Luddy's attempt to maintain a shield of anonymity for himself and his wife. And in those days, before Internet searching of public records, the simple juxtaposition of names—from Ludlow Ogden Smith to Ogden Ludlow—would be enough to throw the hounds off their trail. At least for a little while.

George Cukor's living room, its highly polished parquet floor only recently laid down, was abuzz with the sounds of laughter and tinkling glasses. "It was my first Hollywood party," remembered Elliott Morgan, then a young employee in the research department at Metro-Goldwyn-Mayer. "And I remember Katharine Hepburn was sitting on the sofa with Lilyan Tashman and they were so sparkling, so witty and gay. I thought this is it. This is *Hollywood*!"

Cukor had noticed the young Oxford graduate, working as an assistant to F. Scott Fitzgerald at MGM, and deemed him just the kind of polished, sophisticated young man who'd appreciate the gatherings at his estate on Cordell Drive. Cukor's property was then in the midst of being hewn and shaped by the architect James Dolena and the landscape designer Florence Yoch. Scion of a well-known Los Angeles society family, Morgan recalled Cukor's circle of the early 1930s as being "filled with people who lived more freely than most." Morgan, a homosexual with a winking, campy sense of humor, did indeed mix well with Cukor's crowd.

Significantly, so did Kath Hepburn. We've always had the impression that she didn't "fit in" with Hollywood, but that came later. In her first year in the film colony, Hepburn frolicked with a community of like-minded souls. She might not have been hanging out at the Brown Derby, but she found a place within Hollywood's beau monde. We catch glimpses of her in Malibu, at the house of Alexander Kirkland, her erstwhile director from Stockbridge, who had forgiven all now that she was a star. No matter if Kirkland was a Johnny-come-lately to her charms, Kath adored being invited out to his boat-shaped beach house for a meal cooked by his fabulous Cajun chef. And if she wasn't at the beach, she was on the golf course in Bel-Air, flagrantly disregarding the rule that forbade women to play on Sundays. "Throw me off," she dared the owners. "It's my only free day." Or if not golf, she was on the tennis court, knocking balls around with Harvey Snodgrass, the famous tennis star and coach. In 1933, the Hollywood "in-crowd" found it very chic to say they'd "just played a set with Harvey." The lean, tan, blue-eyed bachelor always made time for Kath.

But mostly, we find her at Cukor's parties, sitting in his oval-shaped parlor and meeting others, like herself, who defied easy categorization: Lil Tashman, William Haines, Fanny Brice, Somerset Maugham, Greta Garbo. Oft told is the tale of Hepburn going for an early morning swim au naturel in Cukor's pool, only to emerge to run smack-dab into Garbo, who barely lifted an eyebrow in surprise. From those languid days around Cukor's pool, Hepburn learned how to do an uncannily accurate impression of the moody Swedish star.

If the Katharine Hepburn who arrived in Hollywood in 1932 was not the person she would later become, neither was Hollywood the place it would be within just a few years. The film colony was still at this point a haven for free-thinkers and free lovers, for political radicals and sexual nonconformists. In many ways, Hollywood was an extension of the "upper-class bohemia" Kath had known in New York's theatrical circles. "No one followed any rules," explained Morgan. "That was what was so wonderful. There were all kinds of people. Men and women who lived together without getting married, two men who lived together, two women . . . Some were socialists, some were cap-italists, but nobody much cared about anything if you knew how to be witty and hold your liquor."

The press had yet to become a real menace. Sure, there seemed to be a growing tendency among some newshounds to dig up juicy tidbits like Kath Hepburn's abandoned husband, but reporters usually proved cooperative and pliant when it came to the stars' private lives—especially if they were given something entertaining to distract them from the truth. For several years now, William "Billy" Haines, MGM's number-one box-office star dur-ing the late-silent and early-talkie period, had openly shared his home with his male lover, Jimmie Shields. Their galas were among the most exclusive in Hollywood, and the guest list always included prominent newspaper colum-nists and fan-magazine reporters. In the late 1920s, Garbo had resided openly with John Gilbert without any fear of public sanction. More recently, Marlene Dietrich had been quite blatant in her affair with Mercedes de Acosta, both women arriving at movie premieres wearing tuxedos.

In letters to friends, George Cukor would look back on this era of indul-gence and tolerance as "La Belle Epoque," fondly recalling the spirit and sen-suality of the times. So enchanted was Cole Porter upon his first arrival in Hollywood that he arranged to live on the Coast for six months of the year, even if his wife chose to stay back East. "It's like living on the moon," Porter gushed.

To a first-time visitor, the sexual energy could be intoxicating. Everyone was flirting with everyone else, and flirtation often led to more. The director Edmund Goulding's orgies were infamous; the screenwriter Frederica Maas recalled "more women and men [being] initiated into more kinds of kinky sexual practices than one can possibly imagine." Some scandals proved too hot to contain: in 1932, the film colony had been rocked by tabloid accusations of sexual promiscuity by the "It Girl," Clara Bow. To the world outside Holly-wood's borders, such reports served either to titillate or to shock. While a conservative, middle-class, time-card-punching element definitely existed in the Hollywood studios, right alongside thrived another world, one where "anything went," Morgan said, "anything and everything in between."

The movies of the period reflected the liberal social outlook of the people making them. Even today audiences are surprised by the sexual frankness of the films of the early 1930s. Sex before marriage, abortion, prostitution, allu-sions to homosexuality—all were frequent plot devices. "Kept women" be-came figures of glamour: Constance Bennett in *The Easiest Way*, Joan Crawford in *Possessed*, Norma Shearer in *Strangers May Kiss*. Cecil B. DeMille, one of the town's most conservative moralists offscreen, nonetheless glorified raw sexu-ality and sadomasochism in films like *Sign of the Cross*. And then came Mae West, bursting onto the screen in 1932 and overturning all sacred cows in her path.

You can see it in Hepburn's first films too. *A Bill of Divorcement* contains the very clear implication that Kath's character has spent the night with her fiancé. Entering the scene yawning and stretching, she is exhausted, with her aunt wondering aloud if the young man ever went home the night before. "I'm not a sinner," Kath declares, though she declines to join her mother in church on Christmas Day. Such unapologetic defiance of social norms and disregard for religion would disappear from Hollywood films just a few years later.

In *Christopher Strong*, there was even more over which to raise eyebrows. Not only does Hepburn, playing the aviator Cynthia Darrington, have an af-fair with a married man, but the message of the picture (shaped by its lesbian, protofeminist director and screenwriter) repudiated the very idea of marriage. Billie Burke, playing the neglected wife of Hepburn's lover, holds no grudge against her, only admiration: "Marriage and children make almost any woman old-fashioned and intolerant," she says.

This is what truly outraged moralists across the nation, who were then beginning to gather petitions against the "sins" of Hollywood. John J. Cantwell, the Roman Catholic bishop of Los Angeles, denounced the "seventy-five percent" of the film colony who were "pagan . . . who care noth-ing for decency . . . living lives of infidelity and worse." Even more galling to the moralists, this 75 percent was foisting upon the nation an underlying message that there were alternative, no less valid ways of living in the world than what church and society had always taught. More than any ribald retort from Mae West, more than any single portrait of a kept woman, it was this pervasive liberal worldview that incited the forces of reaction to rise up against the movies. But it was also, significantly, what made Katharine Hepburn feel right at home when she first arrived in the film colony.

Liberal, sophisticated Hollywood found its epicenter at Cukor's house. Forever under construction during this early period, garden terraces were being pounded out of the side of rocky cliffs. Elliott Morgan recalled that first party as being thrown in honor of Lilyan Tashman, "opening in some play downtown." This can only be *Grounds for Divorce* at the El Capitan Theater, which premiered in February 1933; indeed, we know Kath was in Hollywood at this time, having just finished *Christopher Strong*. Newspaper reports confirm that on the night of February 13, Cukor led a star-studded crowd to the show and afterward gathered his close circle ("Hollywood's gayest," one report said) for a soiree at his house. A week later, the director was whooping it up again with many of the same people, this time at a party at the Hollywood Barn restaurant. Among the regulars: Tashman; her husband, Edmund Lowe; Billy Haines; Gary Cooper; Anderson Lawler, a supporting player and popular Hollywood escort; Blythe Daly, the high-spirited daughter of the renowned stage actor Arnold Daly; Roger Davis, for many years Fanny Brice's onstage "stooge"; Phoebe Foster, a boyish actress Cukor often used for bits; and Tom Douglas, the former film juvenile turned interior decorator.

"If you traveled in George's circle," recalled Cukor's longtime pal Richard Stanley, "you always had to have a collection of amusing stories. It was what the group thrived on. Not really gossip but celebrating the ironies of life. If you think of everything as either profound joy or profound sadness, you'll go crazy. So there was always that twist of lemon that made [Cukor's gatherings] work."

With a revolving cast that also included the actresses Ina Claire and Ilka Chase, the screenwriters John Colton and Rowland Leigh, and the actors John Darrow and David Manners (Kath's love interest in *A Bill of Divorcement*), Cukor's circle was the hip young alternative to the snooty soirees at Pickfair, where crass nouveau riche rubbed noses with dethroned royalty. The *Hollywood Reporter* caught Cukor and his friends slipping out early from one studio luncheon to hurry back to the house on Cordell Drive and "continue the party with their own fabulous kind."

Although her name wasn't often included in such newspaper accounts, it's important to realize that Hepburn was there in the center of it all. "Give my love to all the 'irregulars,'" Billy Haines wrote to Cukor in 1933. "Tom, Andy, Roger and Kathy Hep." When a photographer recorded the arrival of the author Hugh Walpole at Cukor's house, Kath was captured sitting on the couch next to him. She drank little—too much imbibing at Cukor's was frowned on in any case—and sometimes seemed shy when the room filled with bigger-than-life personalities. But she was *there*, her inimitable voice crackling above the din.

Indeed, it was at Cukor's that Kath met so many of the illustrious figures in her life, people like Brice and Maugham and Ethel Barrymore and Tallulah Bankhead—though the last was a little distant in the beginning. Possibly envious of Cukor's burgeoning friendship with this imperious newcomer, Tallu leaned in to the director and whispered, "I think your friend, Miss Hepburn, is a New England spinster," her tone dripping with meaning.

No sexual conformist herself, Bankhead would eventually warm up to Kath after seeing a rough cut of *Little Women*, which finally started shooting in the summer of 1933. Dropping dramatically to her knees, Bankhead kissed the hem of Kath's skirt and told her she was overcome. "She was really darling and terribly moved," Kath recalled, but Cukor just rolled his eyes and quipped, "Tallulah, you're weeping for your lost innocence."

That the sophisticated circle surrounding Cukor was largely gay cannot be denied. Those who weren't tended to be famous ladies with tolerant, world-weary views on sexuality: Chase, Claire, Brice, Barrymore, Countess Dorothy di Frasso. "George's friends were a very bohemian stellar crowd," said Richard Stanley. "They traveled in their own circles and people just minded their own business. It was an era when . . . people respected boundaries more than they do now. There was never an issue about it. If you bought the convertible, you knew the top went down. You didn't have to put it down to know that."

As was the case with all her gay pals, Kath preferred not to see or hear about any sexual exploits. Indeed, Cukor's friends all testify that the director was quite particular about forbidding any kind of sexual horseplay or "inappropriate, crude behavior" at his gatherings; it's what eventually caused a rift with Billy Haines, who had a tendency to drink too much and tweak the derrieres of attractive young men. "George always insisted on a certain decorum, especially around the important ladies like Miss Hepburn," said Charles Williamson, a longtime friend and assistant of Cukor's.

In this, Cukor's crowd was following the pattern of other homosexuals in Hepburn's life. After hours, Cukor might prowl Griffith Park looking for rough trade with Haines and Lawler, but in Hepburn's company he played the eunuch. Not for him would there even be a companion at dinner parties, for—in his view as well as Kath's—that would be "flaunting" it. Indeed, according to Gavin Lambert, Cukor felt that fellow director James Whale was "flaunting his homosexuality" and "asking for trouble" by living openly with his lover, the producer David Lewis.

Of course Kath knew that her friends were gay. Yet by compartmentalizing their lives, they enabled her to live in a world ordered by her own idiosyncrasies. Still, no matter how ostrichlike she was around Cukor and his friends, Hepburn no doubt appreciated the fact that their sexual nonconformity rendered unnecessary any awkward, imprecise explanations about her own relationship with Laura.

"What Cukor gave her," said Elliott Morgan, "was a place she could be herself, no questions asked. I don't think there were many other places where that was true."

Observe her now, with her best friend George, on the set of *Little Women*. Done up in elaborate period costume, Kath is nodding her head as Cukor tells her repeatedly that they have no spare of her dress. She must, he insists, be *exceedingly careful*. A moment later, handed a bowl of ice cream for an upcoming scene, she takes off in a rush—and, of course, spills the ice cream all over the front of her dress.

Cukor would recall slapping her ("Not hard enough," he joked) and calling her an amateur. "Think what you want," Kath retorted, turning on her heel and storming off the set. Yet an hour later they were both in hysterics watching a pregnant Joan Bennett, playing Amy, trying to squeeze into the hoop skirts designed by the costumer Walter Plunkett.

"The best of all [working conditions]," Hepburn would observe, "is to be a very good friend [of the director] because then . . . all guards are down. There's nothing that George could do that would disturb me, and there's nothing that I can do that would disturb him. We know each other much, much too well." Cukor agreed: "There's a complete absence of sham and nonsense between us. A real rapport." Even more than forty years later, working on their final film together, Hepburn could say: "We've the same taste, the same sense of values . . . We work together so closely that I don't know where I begin and he ends."

The film historian Patrick McGilligan wrote that while critics tend to gush over the collaborations of Josef von Sternberg and Marlene Dietrich or William Wyler and Bette Davis, "here was a director-star relationship that cut closer, ran deeper, and lasted longer than any other in Hollywood, off as well as on the set."

"It was as if George and I had been brought up together," Hepburn said. "Total comfort. The same liberal point of view—the same sense of right and wrong."

Yet it was less a sibling relationship than one of father and daughter. With Cukor, she had found the indulgent father she never had. True, he could haul off and smack her—Kath was used to that, growing up with Hep—but Cukor came to trust Hepburn's vision as much as his own, often allowing her to play a scene according to her own instincts. Outside of their own collaborations, Cukor followed Kath's career with parental pride, cheering when she succeeded and despairing when she did not. Her visits to Cordell Drive always gladdened him, with tales of her madcap antics easily reducing him to a quivering bowl of jelly. Even as he tried to insist that he was "shocked," he was pressing her for more details.

Hepburn was the one person Cukor, a devoted lover of gossip, refused to hear stories about. If she were staying with him, Cukor would run around like mad setting up the guest room so it would be just the way she liked it when she arrived. His maid would be set to work slicing dozens of limes so they'd have plenty of Kath's favorite limeade in the icebox. "He was very protective, even to the point of being intimidated by her," said Charles Williamson. "He'd say, 'Don't tell that to Miss Hepburn,' or, 'Don't get Miss Hepburn upset.'" He might smack her on the set, but the rest of the time, when she called, he jumped. "Suddenly I'd see him sit bolt upright in his chair," Williamson recalled, "because outside he'd hear that unmistakable voice coming up the walk, calling 'Jo-udge! Jo-udge!'"

The intimidation Cukor felt is apparent in their tape-recorded reminiscences, made in 1969, in which Hepburn runs roughshod over her old friend, repeatedly interrupting him and co-opting his stories. In contrast, in similar informal tape-recordings with John Ford, she acts far more deferentially. "I have the sense that's how she treated the more obviously gay men in her life," said Gavin Lambert. "Cukor was her best friend, but that also made him her peer. She could tell him to shut up, to let her speak. With men she considered more red-blooded, more manly, like Ford, like her father, she tended to yield and pander."

Cukor, like Kath, thrived on working long days. He preferred to go to bed early and wake up early. And while professing liberal politics and a concern for the "lower classes," Cukor could sometimes be quite pretentious. On the set, he'd frequently fall into French, exhibiting a "*mentalité du bossu*" when actors slipped out of character or applauding the "*garçonne*" in Kath's performance in *Little Women*. Middle-class, the son of Jewish immigrants, Cukor was endlessly fascinated by the ways of the rich, personified by the characters in Philip Barry's plays—and by Laura Harding, sitting right there in his living room. "We're not all great-grandchildren of Jay Cooke," Cukor teased Laura at one point. "All of us aren't socialites, with money to burn." Teasing, yes, but the envy was real. At his dinner parties, everything was quite formal—even "showy," some thought. "We always used to say he went on directing at home," said Elliott Morgan.

This affinity between Cukor and Hepburn meant that the majority of her best film performances would be those directed by him: *Sylvia Scarlett, Holiday, The Philadelphia Story, Adam's Rib, Pat and Mike, Love Among the Ruins.* And *Little Women*, perhaps especially *Little Women*, where Hepburn proved once and for all that playing herself was her fastest ticket to success.

"It rather suited my exaggerated sense of things," Hepburn would say of the film, made in the summer of 1933. The stylized, theatrical nature of the script—and especially of her character, Jo March—reflected Kath's own "exaggerated" childhood. "I could say 'Christopher Columbus! What richness!' and believe it totally. I have enough of that old-fashioned personality in myself."

That she did, though what she also had was Jo's cultural defiance, a defining theme of Alcott's original novel and probably why Hepburn had always adored it. Like Kath, Jo saw herself outside of her own gender, expressing more than once her desire to be "the man of the family." Even when Jo finally marries, it is not a romantic, storybook kind of love, but an egalitarian match with a sexless older man. By not tempering Alcott's depiction of the tomboy Jo, Cukor was taking a risk; the last time Kath had played androgynous, in *Christopher Strong*, she'd flopped with the ticket-buying public. *Morning Glory*, however, released during the shooting of *Little Women*, enjoyed a successful run of several weeks in the nation's theaters, lifting everyone's hopes about Kath's long-term box-office appeal. But Jo March was a far cry from dewy, long-lashed Eva Lovelace. Jo was unapologetically dismissive of anything feminine, a boy resentful of the girls' dresses he is forced to wear. Kath had a marvelous time making the film, jumping over fences and swinging from tree branches. But some at RKO predicted it was just too offbeat to be a hit.

They were wrong. NEW HEPBURN FILM BREAKS EVERY RECORD headlined the *New York Times* when the picture opened in November, beating the previous top-grossing film, *Cavalcade*, at the influential Radio City Music Hall. The studio's fears had been groundless; America loves a tomboy, and Kath gave them one they could take to their hearts. Cukor had reached above the story's inherent sentimentality to embrace something far more profound: the yearning to belong, to be loved, even by those who live a little "outside" of convention. On Kath's face, we see Jo's ache to be noticed, her desire to be applauded, her longing to be loved. But it is really Hepburn's own emotion, her own vulnerability, that we see, and our hearts break for her. We want Jo to succeed—no, it is *Kath Hepburn* we want to win, and on *her* terms, not anyone else's. On such foundations are legends built. This, ultimately, is the most significant, most lasting achievement of *Little Women.*

"A triumph!" crowed Edwin Schallert in Los Angeles. "Radiantly beautiful!" agreed Norbert Lusk in New York, who added that not only was the film the best of the year, but "Miss Hepburn's performance the most brilliant of any American player for a like period."

It had finally happened. All her dreams of fame and glory and recognition had come true. Katharine Hepburn was on the top of the world.

NO SECRETS FROM THE WORLD

While Kath was emoting through the final retakes of *Little Women*, Hollywood's leading power brokers were arriving into the nation's capital in the midst of a sweltering heat wave. Jack and Harry Warner, Frank Capra, Sidney Kent, Will Hays, and RKO's B. B. Kahane were all sighted making their way along the streets of Capitol Hill. "Not a breadline," quipped one Washington wag, "just a few of the millionaires filing in for the hearings on the motion picture code . . . See how happy they look!"

Years of conservative outrage against Hollywood had reached the boiling point—quite literally, it seemed, as Kahane and the Warner brothers tugged at their shirt collars and gigantic electric fans rattled at the front of the hearing room. The movie moguls were in town to testify for the National Recovery Administration's proposed reorganization of the film industry. Though the NRA's main focus was on financial restructuring, reformers from around the nation had also descended on the hearings to insist that the government regulate "moral content" in films as well. Canon William Sheafe Chase, the rector of Christ Church in Brooklyn and a longtime crusader against the movies (he was on record as saying the cinema was "the greatest enemy of civilization"), told the panel, "It will be one of the greatest things the New Deal could accomplish if we obtain moral uplift through the revised Code."

The Production Code had actually been in place since 1930, set up by the Motion Picture Producers and Distributors of America and agreed to by all the major players. Yet the Code had been more philosophy than policy, the studios merely paying lip service to a small but vocal minority calling for reform. Over the next several years, the Code would be ignored and flouted—as when Eva Lovelace (Katharine Hepburn) becomes the "kept woman" of her producer (Adolphe Menjou) in *Morning Glory*. Such instances provoked thundering sermons from the nation's pulpits, decrying Hollywood's lack of morality. With the mood of the country already surly after four years of economic hardship, the reformers' voices seemed to be growing, fueled in large part by resentment of Hollywood's freewheeling millionaires. Fearing church-led boycotts or worse—government-regulated censorship—the studios found themselves backed into a corner. Sweltering in that hot, humid hearing room, Kahane and the rest surely understood that the motion picture industry was facing the most significant upheaval of its short life—even more momentous than the coming of sound.

Breathing a collective sigh of relief, the moguls were pleased when the Washington hearings concluded on September 14, 1933, without federal regulations being imposed on content. But as they boarded the train back to the Coast, they were surely still reeling from the words of NRA administrator Sol Rosenblatt, who demanded "teeth" be given to the industry's enforcement of the Code. That wasn't the end of the pressure the moguls faced, either. In October, the National Conference of Catholic Churches announced a "vigorous campaign for the purification of the cinema," warning of "a blacklist" of films they deemed objectionable.

For Kath, this cut close to the bone. Of her two 1933 releases so far, *Morning Glory* was branded "poor" by the church, and *Christopher Strong* only "fair." Catholic audiences were duty bound, the bishops said, to avoid any film that did not receive a "good" rating—which up to this point amounted to only one, *Picture Snatcher* with James Cagney.

With all of the major studios posting losses in 1933, boycott threats were taken very seriously. Of even more concern, the number of weekly moviegoers had dropped by some 20 million in the first three years of the Great Depression. The moguls had no choice but to agree to enforce the Code. Although it would take another six to seven months to formalize the structure of enforcement, the climate in the film colony shifted as soon as the studio chiefs returned from Washington. "A pall of silence envelops the place," one reporter observed. Press departments were forbidden to admit that pictures were being "laundered" to meet Code requirements, but soon the screen was purged of kept women, sex perversion, and ribald double entendres. The studios were forced to plot a new course, though just what it would be was still unclear. Since its inception, Hollywood had used sex to sell its pictures and its stars. How would it move forward now, strapped with a chastity belt?

What was becoming increasingly clear as 1933 turned over into 1934 was that the Code's reach would extend beyond the screen to the private lives of Hollywood's players. As early as December 1933, the *Los Angeles Times* was proclaiming SEX-APPEAL ERA FADES AS NICE GIRLS COME INTO OWN, and stars and their publicists took heed. In the course of just one year, Ginger Rogers's screen image went from happy-go-lucky hooker to homespun heroine, both on and off the screen. By the end of the decade, Joan Crawford would morph from kept woman to the ideal American mother.

Just what route Hepburn would take wasn't quite as clear. How does one remake an image that had never been very comprehensible in the first place? "The young actress sets a new mark in eccentricities," one report had observed soon after her first arrival, "wearing overalls, the good old denim variety, and generally acting like a picture star doesn't."

For nearly a year, Hepburn's overalls and pants had been a press obsession. "A new sartorial thrill," sniped one columnist after Kath showed up on the set in sweatshirt and jeans. Another sniffed, "Not only does La Hepburn wear dungarees like a common farmhand, but they're patched, dirty, and full of holes." On the set of *Morning Glory*, her overalls were stolen as a prank, and George Shafer wrote it up in his column as big news. When the gossip columnist Jimmie Fidler fired "twenty impertinent questions" at her, he led off with the one uppermost in his readers' minds: *Why did she wear pants?* "They are comfortable and convenient," Kath replied. "And . . . because it seems to amaze people. I like to do unusual things."

That much was already obvious. In 1933, Hepburn seemed like a "queer duck" to the Hollywood press. One columnist in the *Los Angeles Times* thought she was "miscast" as a star: "The world of pictures . . . has its large provincial viewpoint to consider. She will appeal more genuinely to the sophisticates."

Therein lay the problem. Hepburn's most enthusiastic audiences were in major eastern cities like New York and Philadelphia; indeed, though it bombed elsewhere, *Christopher Strong* did a thriving business in New York. On the other hand, provincial audiences, becoming increasingly conservative as the Depression deepened, looked with disfavor on independent, gender-defying women, both in the movies and in real life. Various studies have documented the reaction in the 1930s to the perceived "excesses" of the Roaring Twenties, a time when women, in record numbers, had broken out of the mold of home and family to seek employment and social equality with men—even to smoke their tobacco! Kath, described in many interviews as sitting in her trousers puffing away on cigarettes, was conspicuously out of step with the new, conservative times.

Ironically, her persona seemed defined by her least successful film, the strident, masculine turn in *Christopher Strong*. The film encoded for the first time a fundamental part of the Hepburn image: independent and freethinking, but also wistful and lonely, cut off from an orthodox lifestyle of marriage and family. Yet even her glowing performance in *Little Women*, for all its widespread appeal, had similar overtones, with Jo resenting her sisters' desire for traditional roles as wives and mothers. Such implied social deviance came to define the persona of Katharine Hepburn. Her on-screen performances and offscreen images were conflated in the public mind.

Then there was Laura. Except for the stories about Joel McCrea and John Farrow, which quickly fizzled out, Kath's first year in Hollywood was devoid of gossip about men, a rarity for a new female star. There was only Laura, "Katy's closest, constant, cozy companion," one columnist called her. Another divulged that the two women "shared a secret hideaway, just the two of them, so don't come knocking." According to reports, Laura was as offbeat as her friend: the "inseparable companion of Katharine Hepburn" was spotted on a Beverly Hills street wearing "men's blue denim overalls," a cigarette dangling from her lips. In October 1933, several strange items reported Hepburn and Harding being shot at by "two ruffians" who came upon them in the woods, then blocked their way along the path. No charges were pressed.

Most significantly, in December a prominent article in the *Los Angeles Times* included Laura among the "husbands, wives, and lovers" who acted as "powers behind the thrones." The piece treated Hepburn's "very close friend" as no different from Mrs. Paul Muni, Mrs. George Arliss, or Frank Fay, the husband of Barbara Stanwyck, all of whom worked to make sure their spouses were noticed.

Indeed, Kath's "queer duck" antics were presumed to be Laura's brainstorms. *Photoplay*, the most influential fan magazine, ran a four-page profile on Laura in January 1934, claiming she'd created Hepburn's "prankish personality" and invented "fresh ways of drawing attention to her." By now, Laura's aggressive advocacy of her friend's career had become the talk of the town. Insisting on approval for all publicity photos, Laura also made sure she was in on story conferences and routinely overruled costume designs. In her private scrapbook she kept a letter from Howard Greer, the flamboyant designer on *Christopher Strong*, who sent her a sketch for her approval, signing it "H. Greer, Seamstress Extraordinary to Her Majesty."

Laura proved to be the bane of studio officials, and even of Leland Hayward, who often found themselves frustrated in their attempts to reach Kath after hours. Laura simply refused to bring the star to the phone. Her quip about being "Miss Hepburn's husband" suddenly didn't seem so far-fetched. And while the tolerant film colony took the women's relationship in stride, that didn't preclude the press from making snide inferences about it, or some of the more sophisticated members of the public from recognizing it for what it was.

With the political climate changing across the country, stories of Kath's pants and her cohabitation with Laura rested uneasily in the public mind. Freethinking Hollywood might simply *not care*, but a much different reaction could be expected from the vast provincial readership of fan magazines. Striding across the RKO backlot in her overalls, Kath was certainly aware of the change descending over Hollywood by the autumn of 1933. But there's no way she could have been prepared for the hullabaloo that would erupt when someone actually dared print the name Ludlow Ogden Smith.

Heading down Vanderbilt Avenue toward his office at the John R. Hall Corporation in November of 1933, Luddy quickened his pace, hoping to lose the reporter in the trench coat and felt hat among the morning rush-hour crowd. But this one proved tenacious, following Luddy through the revolving doors into the building and barking out questions that echoed across the marble lobby. It was all Luddy could do, he'd say, to keep himself from turning around and slugging the fellow. Hopping into the elevator, he told the operator to secure the grille quickly and hoist him upstairs.

When reporters had first discovered Luddy's name, they'd acted with relative discretion, peppering Kath with questions but refraining from identifying her husband in print. Now, in the face of her continued intractability, all bets were off. Already by February 1933, various syndicated reports had named "Hepburn's husband" as Ludlow Ogden Smith, though Luddy had outsmarted the newshounds by changing his name and moving to East Forty-ninth Street. Even then, however, he must have known it was only a matter of time. That fall, THE TRUTH ABOUT KATHARINE HEPBURN'S MARRIAGE was splashed across the pages of *Modern Screen*, providing details of their wedding in West Hartford and offering a grim indictment of Kath. "Of all the low forms of life," the article stated, "there is none meaner than the woman who, in the first flush of success, disavows the mate who helped her to triumph."

So began a refrain that would echo in the background of the Hepburn legend, eventually sounded even by the star herself, when she called herself a "pig" for the way she'd treated Luddy. Yet while her behavior was hardly selfless, Kath and her husband had always had an understanding—an understanding that would never have been translatable to mainstream audiences. Therefore it was inevitable that Hepburn would become the villain, Luddy the victim, when neither he, nor Kath at the time, saw the dynamic in those terms.

But the press certainly did. By the end of 1933, they were having a field day with "Hepburn's abandoned husband." An increasing stridency had become evident in the press corps. Emboldened by the temper of the times and frustrated by years of doing the studios' bidding, reporters could no longer be expected to look the other way when stars misbehaved. For one thing, there were simply a lot *more* of them, the early sound era coinciding with the rise of mass-circulation weeklies and the advent of radio broadcasting. Wisecracking, street-smart journalists from Park Row descended on Hollywood in the hundreds. No longer could the studios expect reporters to be as pliable as they were in the days when William Haines hosted Sunday brunches with his boyfriend. The historian Alexander Walker identified the "latent sadism" that emerged in the Hollywood press during this period. This new breed of reporters took delight in ferreting out "scoops," actively rejecting the idea of collaboration with the studios. "The history of American journalism," one asserted, "does not indicate that the public has much interest in an industry's attempt to tell its own story. The public will not be interested in faked smokescreens and there will be no reason for their publication."

Such high-minded ideals, of course, did not prevail. There would always be an element willing to give the studios the kinds of stories they wanted in exchange for access and privilege. But for a while, at least, it was the vogue to challenge and provoke. The article in *Modern Screen* bears none of the standard studio talking points. Rather, its excoriation of Kath ("of all the low forms of life") is quite remarkable and surely sent her, Leland Hayward, and the RKO press department scurrying for damage control. For now they maintained a policy of silence, apparently hoping the stories would sputter out and die. Instead, they proliferated, with several newspaper accounts calling Kath "a liar" outright.

It hurt. "She didn't let things just roll off her," Laura Harding told Charles

Higham. "This was a very difficult time for her." Hepburn's friend James Prideaux said that the negative publicity over Luddy flattened her. "She had no idea how vicious the press could get," he said. "She was at a loss as to how to respond about something she saw as so personal."

Blood in the water always attracts sharks. In an effort to counter the images of a pants-wearing errant wife living with her gal pal in a secret Hollywood hideaway, RKO began releasing the first "official" biographies of the star. Churned out on mimeographs and distributed to the press, the studio's account admitted Kath was "an unusual girl" with an "abstruse" personality—but that was only because she had integrity and refused to be caught up in the Hollywood "social swirl." The nonsense about A. Barton Hepburn was finally jettisoned and Kath's real father named, with Adela Rogers St. Johns and others beginning their chronicling of the Hepburn legend. St. Johns even got the star to finally acknowledge Luddy, with the observation that it wasn't "easy to conduct a marriage at such long range." But new fictions emerged. For the first time, two years were lopped off Kath's age, making her twenty-three instead of twenty-five, a ruse that would endure for decades.

Leland wanted even more. He argued Kath should submit to what she'd so far managed to avoid: a fashion spread for the fan magazines. Once again, it would be a photo shoot conveniently forgotten, but in various libraries the irrefutable proof has been preserved: KATHARINE HEPBURN'S STYLE SECRETS. There she stands in stark black and white, posing this way and that in a French flannel suit and a big floppy hat as if she were Marion Davies or Norma Shearer. But when Leland suggested she slip into a gown with a plunging neckline, Laura quickly snatched it away. "No more cheesecake," she insisted—though Kath's meager bosom wouldn't have filled out the dress anyway. In the final magazine spread, the most skin she shows is an exposed arm. With Kath's facial expressions failing to conceal her boredom, the whole tedious effort to feminize her image had little effect.

Neither did her next film, a curio entitled *Trigger*, about a mountain girl who may or may not have healing powers. Hepburn would try to shift blame for the film onto RKO officials, but with Leland out in front fighting for her, she was actually more involved than many stars in selecting her vehicles. ("I used to have quite a say," she later admitted; when the interviewer suggested that wasn't usual for most stars, she said, "It was usual for me.") Trying to capitalize on the star's offbeat public image, the script for *Trigger* had Kath speaking in a dialect so peculiar that half the time she's completely unintelligible. No chemistry sparked with her costars, Ralph Bellamy and Robert Young, and with her director, John Cromwell, she had little rapport. When the film wrapped in November 1933, Kath just wanted to get out of town—a 180-degree change in her attitude from the previous year, when she was happily sipping cocktails poolside with George Cukor and his cronies.

In fact, as she left town, she wired Cukor not to expect her back. That telegram is terribly poignant to look upon all these years later. Here she was, her dreams finally achieved—but the success of *Little Women* proved fleeting as the political climate shifted in Hollywood. Kath was still young enough not to be jaded, innocent enough to be hurt by the savagery of celebrity. For all her bravado, she was crestfallen as the criticism of her mounted. "She could be an arrogant girl, no question about it," said her friend Robert Shaw. "But she really could never imagine being cruel to someone just for the sake of being cruel. So it hurt her—astounded her—when people in the press seemed to be so needlessly cruel to her."

Kath's threat not to return may have been more than mere hyperbole, as she had yet to sign a new contract with RKO. She may have been thinking that the movies had made her a star, and now she could return triumphant to claim her proper place on the New York stage. In fact, by late 1933, she had every reason to think this might be her destiny; the famed producer Jed Harris had hired her to star in *The Lake,* set to open in Washington the following month and move to Broadway before the end of the year.

Boarding a Western Express airplane at the Burbank airport, Kath turned on the tarmac, held her chin high, and seemed to offer a defiant parting gesture to the censorious climate of Hollywood. With her was the actress Elissa Landi. Wearing matching fur coats and cat-that-swallowed-the-canary grins, the two women were photographed obtaining their tickets, boarding the plane, and settling into their seats. Other than the fact that Landi had starred in the film version of *The Warrior's Husband,* the classically beautiful actress and occasional author had little connection to Hepburn. *The Warrior's Husband,* after all, had been made at Fox, and stars from different studios rarely socialized. Nonetheless, the two of them gladly posed for the camera together. No running from photographers here.

Rumors of an affair between Hepburn and Landi have persisted for decades, supposedly explaining Laura's abrupt departure for the East ahead of Kath. At the time, columnists were hinting strongly that Landi lacked interest in men, another example of the new aggression being shown by the Hollywood press. But there is no evidence, aside from a few photographs, of an affair. Rather, what's significant about their brief planeside encounter is Kath's willingness, in the face of her own recent troublesome headlines, to flaunt her association with a woman perceived as a lesbian by the press. Perhaps she was telling reporters, in effect, that Hollywood might be reforming, but she wasn't playing that game.

Upon her arrival in New York, however, Kath seemed to revert to Leland's playbook. Almost immediately she was greeted with the news that she and Luddy were being dropped from the Philadelphia Social Register. Though neither of them cared about such niceties, the announcement rendered moot any further dissociation from the marriage. It wasn't some gossipy fan magazine reporting the news this time, but the *New York Times*. The dynamics of her situation now fundamentally altered, Kath faced facts: she could no longer proceed with an inconvenient, untraditional marriage always lingering in the background, especially not with the new political mood in Hollywood. Steeling herself, she sat down with her husband and told him they needed to separate, which seemed—given their lives—an odd choice of words.

To Kath, the move was clearly a prelude to divorce, though Luddy seems to have resisted. "I think they're [sic] decision to live apart an extremely wise one," Palache wrote to her mother after arriving to offer Kath moral support. "He thinks it only temporary. I'm not so sure. But in any event I think it's the very best thing that could have happened."

Not surprisingly, Luddy's mother didn't agree, immediately writing her son that Kath had humiliated and shamed him by forcing him to move across the street to a rooming house—insult piled onto injury after the disgrace of the Social Register. "You are mistaking the symbol for the substance," Luddy cabled back. "Nothing is changed, only an undistinguished label which can only be superficial." He meant the separation, and in some ways he was right; for years, he and Kath had mostly lived apart, and even now, they still planned to spend part of the holidays together in Hartford. "Humiliation and shame," Luddy told his mother, "are words which don't evince much comprehension of my real feelings."

Still, he seemed very sad to fifteen-year-old Marion Hepburn, who traveled with him back to the city by train on New Year's Day. "He asked me if I had fallen for anybody," Marion wrote in her diary. "I said no . . . he said that he thought I was wise not to." Fearful that "Katty" was planning to divorce this "very nice" man, Marion read Luddy's palm and saw two marriage lines. "Oh, dear," she wrote. "I hope that there is nothing in palm reading."

Kath, meanwhile, was busy settling into Luddy's former house, finally making it her own. Turtle Bay was, and is, an enclave of isolated gentility bounded east and west by bustling city thoroughfares. The owner of the house was Mrs. Maud Knowlton Smith, no relation to Luddy, but a prominent society name in her own right. Her previous tenant had been Linsley

Dodge, son of the wealthy exporter V. Atherton Dodge. Along the block lived architects, bankers, and physicians, all with maids and cooks and governesses. "Set back in its own affluence" was how the writer Philip Hoare would describe the house. Indeed, it was tall and stately but largely unornamented, separated from the street by an iron gate. No matter the smells of the East River slaughterhouses that sometimes wafted up to Kath's windows, this particular stretch of Forty-ninth Street bespoke a storied history. Lillian Russell was believed to have lived here in the late nineteenth century, taking vocal lessons from Leopold Damrosch.

Kath simply adored the place. As soon as Luddy left, she and Laura began redecorating, hauling in Turkish carpets and antique chairs, hanging Oriental tapestries on the walls throughout. A steep, narrow staircase led from the first-floor kitchen to a double parlor, then to a formal dining room and finally the bedrooms above. Sitting in the bay windows at the rear of the house, Kath could look out onto a tangle of trees in the courtyard, the fabled Turtle Bay Gardens, with their benches and sculpted cherubs and Medici-inspired fountain. Here artists and writers set up their easels and scribbled in their journals, snatching an hour of quiet in the tranquil green, birdsong replacing the bleating of taxicabs.

Kath, too, would come to see her New York address as a refuge. More than anyplace else, even more than Fenwick, she considered Forty-ninth Street home. It was here she would come to escape the demands of Hollywood; it was here she would live for nearly seventy years, taken away only when she was too frail to get up and down those narrow steps. But in late 1933, she took them three at a time, filled with excitement to be back in New York and on the stage. Jed Harris was telling her she was going to be a smash in *The Lake*. To hell with Hollywood. Kath had nothing but high hopes and confidence that her return to Broadway would be a triumph.

Then she started rehearsals.

Around Broadway Jed Harris was known as "the Vampire." Part of the reason was he looked the part. His hooded eyes were dark and hypnotic under peculiarly arched eyebrows, his face perennially stubbled with five-o'clock shadow, his voice a low whisper that reminded many people of the hiss of a snake. But the epithet was earned even more by the bloodthirsty approach he took to producing plays: driving his cast and crew to their breaking points, cruelly tongue-lashing his stars, and usually seducing (and then abandoning) his leading ladies. George Cukor he certainly wasn't.

Only a few days into rehearsals at the Martin Beck Theatre, Kath was a wreck. Harris was shouting that she was horrible, that she had no talent, that she should go back to making movies, "where art doesn't count." After courting her for the play, making the trip up to West Hartford to woo her, Harris was now convinced she was all wrong for the eerie, moody story of a woman who grieves for a husband she never loved, a husband who drowns on their honeymoon. "I could see she was hopeless," Harris remembered. "I begged her to stop posing, striking attitudes . . . to stop being a big movie star and feel the lines, feel the character. I was trying the impossible, to make an artificial showcase for an artificial star."

Kath came undone. "Jed was horrible to her," Laura Harding remembered. "Kate was struggling so hard to do the play . . . It was a hideous moment for her, the whole ordeal."

For a girl who'd been raised never to show self-pity, Kath's tears during rehearsals are quite profound. She'd start off by reacting to Harris's insults with anger, storming off the stage. In the past, she might have been fired, and that would have been the end of her torment. But now too much was riding on the play; neither Hepburn nor Harris could afford to abandon the project. As a result, Kath would be forced to come back out on stage for more of the producer's abuse, her chin quivering as she tried to hold back the tears. Afterward, alone with Laura, she'd break down completely. "She was still just a girl," Laura said, as indignant in 1974 as she was forty years earlier, "and Jed Harris was a monster to her."

"She needed sensitive treatment," said the play's director, Worthington Miner, who tried to give it to her until Harris fired him. Storming up and down the aisles of the theater, the producer berated every line Kath spoke during rehearsals. When Laura showed up to sit in back as moral support, Harris threw her out. Never in her career had Kath been treated like this. For the rest of her life Hepburn would wonder what Harris "thought he was accomplishing by tormenting and thus rendering useless a poor amateur kid."

Part of Harris's abuse may have stemmed from a bruised ego. When he'd gone to Hartford to meet with Kath months earlier, he'd clearly been hoping for a sexual conquest. When her parents returned home just as he was making his move, Harris was put off, and Kath never did sleep with him the way most of his leading ladies did. Resentment lingering for more than forty years, the Vampire told the author Charles Higham elaborate tales of Kath throwing herself at him, crying about how she might have loved him. In these stories, which sound nothing like Kath, it is Harris who does the rejecting. Rewriting history, it seems, is standard showbiz practice.

Born Jacob Horowitz, Harris was particularly obsessed with tall, patrician women like Kath, though at the time he was living discreetly with the actress Ruth Gordon—feisty, diminutive, and the daughter of a factory worker—with whom he had an illegitimate son. Kath met Gordon at this time, liking and admiring her; Gordon had been her inspiration for Eva Lovelace in *Morning Glory*. But Harris's passion was reserved for the actress Margaret Sullavan, like Kath a more genteel figure, and who by now Harris fervently wished was playing the lead in *The Lake*.

Word got back to Hepburn of Harris's obsession with Sullavan, who, again like Kath, was known for wearing jeans and eschewing Hollywood glamour. The two women seemed destined to be rivals. Both were iconoclastic, headstrong, and upper-class, but Sullavan was infinitely more feminine and sympathetic. On-screen and onstage, she'd be known for heart-searching emotion, while Hepburn was revered for outward strength—exactly why Harris wished it was Sullavan up there on the Martin Beck stage. If Kath *did* make overtures to Harris, even flirt with him, it was because her own ego was wounded. The idea that a producer of hers would prefer someone else was simply unbearable.

She also had some history with Harris, having auditioned for him years before for some show she never specified. He'd turned her down, which clearly stuck in Kath's craw: "He never thought anything of me as an actor." By proving herself to Jed Harris now, she'd also be proving herself to all the other producers and directors who'd failed to see her talent: Knopf, Marston, Miller, the Shuberts. Wowing Hollywood hadn't been enough. Kath was determined to finally do the same to Broadway. Yet as Harris's sadistic assaults withered her a little more each day, her confidence began to sink, and she felt ever more desperate.

For all of Harris's pettiness, however, he was still a brilliant producer, and his observations that Kath was wrong for the part should be given consideration. The part of Stella Surrege in *The Lake*, in fact, required the actress playing her to exhibit introspection and modesty, two qualities rarely seen in Katharine Hepburn, in her roles or in her life. Four decades later, watching her bluff her way through Tennessee Williams's *The Glass Menagerie* on television, Harris shook his head and thought she hadn't changed at all. "She was still babbling with a fixed smile on her face," he said, "the way she did in *The Lake*."

Still, as a movie star, Kath was a draw, and the show did bang-up business when it opened in Washington at the National Theater on December. Hep and Kit were in the audience, along with Aunt Edith Hooker and Margaret

Sanger, with whom Kit was now actively campaigning for legalized birth control. But on stage Kath was shrill and unsteady. "I could actually feel the attention of the audience recede like the tide," she said.

She was not yet the cool, collected, confident Katharine Hepburn of popular memory. She was just a terrified girl—even if she gamely tried to hide the fact. "The first thing to learn," she said, looking back on the experience, "is that nobody must ever know how terrified you are. You've got to be absolutely cool . . . although you may be dying."

After that, the story of *The Lake* becomes something of a "he said, she said." Hepburn would insist she wanted to tour longer with it, improving her performance before opening in New York. Harris would say just the opposite, that she pressured him to open in New York as soon as possible because she was eager to conquer the Great White Way. The fact is *Variety* had already announced on November 28 that the play would open in New York in late December and that the Martin Beck Theatre was sold out. Enthusiastic fans were eager to see the star of *Morning Glory* and *Little Women* in person, and Harris, no matter his low opinion of Kath as an actress, was clearly thrilled with her box-office draw.

Even after *The Lake* had premiered on Broadway on December 26 and the critics had begun their work of delectably savaging it, the show continued to do good business. Yet the full houses barely registered for Kath. The occasional bouquet tossed her way, like the one from the *New York Sun* that called her face "impossible to forget," was eclipsed by the widely quoted poison barbs from Dorothy Parker and Brooks Atkinson, and the glee so many seemed to be taking from her failure. Parker's quip about the "gamut of emotions from A to B" did the most damage, because it simply wouldn't die. Picked up by other writers, it quickly became part of the lexicon. By the spring, a critic for the *Washington Post* was referencing it as part of a book review, and a character in the short-lived play *After Such Pleasures,* based on Parker's book, actually spoke it onstage. For Hepburn, the insult clearly rankled, though she'd try to make a joke of it in later years. Pronouncing *gamut* with the accent on the second syllable, she'd say that's what she was in *The Lake,* a "big mutt."

She wasn't laughing at the time, however. Even after Suzanne Steell had come backstage and begun her impassioned coaching and encouragement, Kath found herself spiraling down into depression. Going onstage every night became agony. "A slow walk to the gallows," she called it—especially after the box office plummeted dramatically, word of the enormousness of the flop discouraging even enthusiastic movie fans from buying tickets.

She'd claim she didn't know Harris was planning to take the show on the road after its final New York performance in February—once again, hard to believe, since the newspapers had announced tour dates for Pittsburgh and Chicago a full month before. Still, the legend of Hepburn buying her way out of her contract is likely true. When she asked Harris what it would take to get out of the tour, the wily producer supposedly responded, "How much have you got?" According to the stories, she wrote him the full amount in her bank account—$13,675.75—and he canceled all scheduled bookings. Once again, Hepburn's family wealth and privilege proved beneficial; such an option was certainly never available to Bette Davis or Barbara Stanwyck in similar difficult situations. While Hepburn would say she was "never much interested in money," it did come in handy when she needed it.

If she'd hoped the close of the show would give her some respite from the storm of criticism, however, she was wrong. The first week of March, *Trigger*—retitled *Spitfire*—opened in New York, and although Mordaunt Hall at the *Times* thought Kath was "vital and persuasive," most other critics used words like *tedious* and *excruciating*. *Time* called the film "queer." In some ways, Kath was doomed trying to follow up *Little Women*, by now among the top twenty most successful films ever made. *Spitfire* was not held over after its first week at Radio City Music Hall. Around the country, it was the same story. In Chicago, the premiere was marred by an incompetent projectionist, who let the screen fall blank between reels. In Los Angeles, the buzz was all about how the picture could never make back its costs. Within two months, *Spitfire* had vanished from the nations' theaters. It was hardly ever seen again.

With the twin catastrophes of *The Lake* and *Spitfire*, the press declared open season on Katharine Hepburn, almost as if they'd been lying in wait for the chance.

"Hepburn does as she pleases," one reporter wrote, "but it's all with one eye on old demon publicity." In later years, such articulated suspicion about the veracity of her public image would be rare indeed. But in early 1934, such talk was all over the place. "Anything for publicity," *Collier's* wrote. Pare Lorentz, the film critic for *Vanity Fair*, said she was "constantly sticking out her chest and saying, 'Look at me, I can chin myself with one hand.'"

Hepburn claimed she didn't care what critics said, that all she wanted was privacy. "If I cannot be interviewed without confessing how I sleep, whether I bathe daily or weekly, or what I think of love," she told Jimmie Fidler, she'd stop giving interviews altogether. "Interviewers . . . pry until actresses have no secrets from the world."

Assigned to get a photo of the star, one reporter became frustrated when Kath kept covering her face with her hands. Finally, he snapped, shouting that maybe *she* was secure in her job, but *he* wasn't. Some long-ago chord of class sympathy instilled by her mother seems to have been struck, for Kath let him take the picture. Likewise, after a preview of *Little Women*, she hid out in an alley rather than wade into a crowd of fans and photographers. When a torrential downpour hit, she was discovered wet and shivering on a basement stair. The next day, the story of the ungrateful star played out in headlines in the *Los Angeles Herald*. Edwin Schallert called Kath the "top-notcher" when it came to "snooty stars."

She'd make lots of noises about privacy, and friends would cite her essential shyness. Yet in truth she *thrived* on the chase. It was how she played the game. Attempting to sneak aboard a flight to New York, Kath was pursued down the tarmac by a news-service photographer. When she realized she'd been too successful in eluding him—all he'd gotten was the back of her head as she ducked into the plane—she came back outside. "Well, come here," she called, "and get a good one of me anyway!" When the photo was published, there she was, arms akimbo, staring into the camera, in tweed jacket and men's pants. "Her whole attitude expresses one thing," another reporter observed. " 'Try to find out anything about me.' "

The press didn't appreciate such double-dealing. By early 1934, with her drawing power in doubt, many writers turned openly antagonistic. Edwin Schallert in the *Los Angeles Times* led the chorus, with his "ha, ha, ha!" response to her box-office appeal. But others were also hopping on the anti-Hepburn bandwagon. "Haughty Hepburn thought she was tops," one columnist ranted, "but we knew her reign wouldn't last, and how right we were."

Certainly the "poor little rich girl" image hadn't played well in the provinces. The fancy car and shabby clothes seemed staged and pretentious. When out of principle Kath refused to pay a nickel to the wardrobe department for sewing a patch onto her dungarees, the press called her cheap, and much of the public, struggling to get by without her high-figure salary, agreed. More negative coverage came her way when, for a day's overtime on *Spitfire*, she insisted RKO pay her *ten thousand dollars*—about ten times the average American annual income. It was one thing for Jean Harlow or Joan Crawford to demand that much money, for they at least spent their big bucks on glamorous clothes to entertain their fans. Hepburn, by contrast, gave nothing back to the public that had made her fame possible.

The nastiest press came from the West Coast newspapers, which were generally more provincial-minded in their coverage than their counterparts in the East. This was a very real problem, for these were the newspapers Pan Berman and B. B. Kahane found waiting for them at their breakfast tables. As the New York columnist Walter Winchell once pointed out, West Coast editors required writers to turn their stories of divorce and romance over to the city desks, where they were slated for the front page. In Los Angeles, scuttlebutt and scandal were *news*. And that would prove debilitating to Kath's career.

From the dazzling heights of *Little Women* just a few months earlier, Kath's stock with the public had fallen precipitously by early 1934. Her press, once rhapsodic, was now, after *The Lake* and *Spitfire*, almost uniformly negative. RKO had tried to stem the tide by arranging for the first authorized career articles. Some, like Adela Rogers St. Johns's seminal piece, hewed close to the publicists' blue mimeographs, but others ended up more part of the problem than the solution. A two-parter in *Modern Screen* endeavored to make Kath's "exhibitionism" sympathetic by featuring her as a plain-Jane everywoman who'd always yearned to stand out from the crowd. But the author consistently refers to Hepburn as a "young boy" and ends up concluding she's "about as sexy as a washboard," surely making the RKO publicists want to turn in their typewriters. Likewise, a largely sympathetic article in the *Pictorial Review* declared Hepburn "feminine to a glamorous degree," but then the editors slapped the sensational title "Hollywood's Strange Girl" onto the piece and ran a photo of Kath in pants perched on a wall looking like one of the Dead End kids.

In many ways, Hepburn had only herself to blame. Taking the traditional glamour route had seemed beneath her. As a proud daughter of a patrician New England family, she wasn't about to model her fame on eager shopgirls like Joan Crawford and Ginger Rogers. Her quick success seemed, in the beginning at least, to confirm the wisdom of her approach: fame apparently *was* her due. Yet the demands of it all took her by surprise. She hadn't counted on needing the fan-magazine base to sustain her. She hadn't figured on catering to those hundreds of thousands of devoted moviegoers, mostly women, mostly working-class—two demographics for which Hepburn had little empathy or understanding—who wanted their stars to reflect, not contradict, their own dreams and desires.

Of course, Kath wasn't the only female star to wear pants. A photo of Garbo and Dietrich wearing pants ran in *Vanity Fair* under the banner MEMBERS OF THE SAME CLUB. Yet despite their cultivation of androgyny, Garbo and Dietrich also projected an undeniably erotic allure. Hepburn, by contrast, was angular and sexless. Her tomboy gimmick had worked as an attention grabber, but it had nothing to offset it, nothing to convince the public that she was, deep down, a woman—as the 1930s defined the role. With *Time* magazine reporting in early 1934 that she lived with Laura Harding "on a chicken farm," Hepburn seemed about as feminine as Gertrude Stein, then touring America in her crew cut and men's suits.

The conservative Code clampdown occurred just as Kath was facing her career low point and was therefore most vulnerable. Taken together, these various forces didn't augur well for her future in pictures. With the coming of the Code, any whiff of deviancy was being purged from the screen, from limp-wristed "pansies" to overly masculine, "trousered women." Meanwhile, *Variety* was blaming "sophisticated" stars and pictures for a decline in movie attendance. As the Production Code Administration clamped down on screen content, so too did the studios put pressure on stars to change their images. If Leland Hayward was urging Kath to make a clean break from Luddy and even distance herself from Laura, we can be sure it was coming from somewhere, that he was feeling the squeeze from Pan Berman and B. B. Kahane. While divorce was also condemned by the Catholic Church, it was better than implications of open marriages and sexual perversion.

There was another consideration at this particular moment as well. On January 18, 1934, Kit Hepburn, mother of the star, raised her right hand to give testimony to the House Judiciary Committee in Washington, exhorting legislators to allow the wide dissemination of information on birth control. "I have ceased to worry about people being shocked," Kit told the panel. Such unapologetic defiance was vintage Kit, but when she said religious opposition was based on "superstition," even some of her colleagues were taken aback. For in truth she was pitting herself directly against the Catholic Church, in the person of Father Charles E. Coughlin, a priest from Detroit and host of a popular radio program, who testified for the other side. One headline read: RADIO FATHER VERSUS MOVIE MA.

Any further attempts by RKO to obfuscate the nature of Kit's activism were now pointless. For nearly a week, studio officials picked up their morning newspapers and read all about "the mother of Katharine Hepburn, screen star" going head to head with the power behind the Production Code. Squaring off against a priest and calling religion "superstition"—how much more awkward could it get? For her part, Kath was annoyed that newspapers referred to Kit as her mother, protesting it should be the other way around, that her mother was more important than she was. But friends felt her annoyance stemmed from another source as well. "Certainly, she was never ashamed of her mother's work," said one very close friend, "but I think she must have wished she wasn't in the headlines at that particular time, when she herself was at a turning point in her own career."

It was, in fact, the most significant crisis Kath had faced in her twenty-six, almost twenty-seven, years. She was certainly finished on Broadway; no producer would hire her now. She also had no immediate prospects in Hollywood; the fact that a new contract was still not signed by May suggests some hesitancy on RKO's part. Meanwhile, Leland was telling her to dump Luddy, dump Laura, and certainly dump Suzanne Steell, who had moved in, carrying meals up to Kath's bedroom since she refused to go out. From her usual support network she'd cut herself off: Luddy was too painful to see, Laura was miffed about Steell, and Palache's letters bemoaned the fact that Kath was in town but unavailable to see her.

Finally, with even the Oscar for *Morning Glory* failing to cheer her, Kath sailed off on the *Paris*. She was running away. Where she planned to go, what she intended to do, who she thought she might become—we'll never know. Because two weeks later, after that galvanizing visit to Jo Bennett, she was back, with ruby-red lips, Ernest Hemingway on her arm, and a confident new glint in her eye—one that said she was ready to do whatever it took to get back on top.

A TERRIBLE PRICE FOR FAME

Carlos Menendez, sitting with a cup of café de olla at an open-air restaurant, couldn't help but notice the two *mujeres Americanas* hurrying down the street, their high heels clattering against the cobblestones. *Turistas*, he thought, until he got a closer look. As editor of *El Diario*, the daily newspaper for the Mexican state of Yucatán, Menendez had been following a breaking story out of Hollywood. The sharp-eyed editor thought the taller of the two women, despite her wide-brimmed hat and the preponderance of freckles across her face, looked very familiar. But why would she be here, in Yucatán's picturesque capital, Mérida?

"*Perdone, señora,*" he asked, standing as they passed. "But aren't you . . . ?"

She turned and gave him a broad smile. "Yes," she said, "I'm Kate Hepburn."

She didn't cover her face, run away, or deny who she was. Instead, Kate cheerfully shook Menendez's hand and introduced him to her friend, Miss Harding. Menendez asked why she was in town. Could it have anything to do with reports that she was about to divorce her husband? Kate just smiled, insisting they'd come to see Mayan ruins. Leaving Menendez in a swirl of suspicion, she resumed her walk down Paseo de Montejo, the city's main boulevard, lined with palatial homes of white stucco and red-tiled roofs.

But as she pulled open the heavy mesquite door of the Hotel Itza, surely her painted smile faded. She had lied to Menendez. She had indeed just come from the second civil courthouse of Mérida, where she'd filed a suit of divorce against Luddy—the first step in ridding herself of the baggage of Kath's old life and establishing *Kate* in the public mind. Though the distinction between the two nicknames was not a conscious change, it's remarkable how often the press began calling her "Kate" in the weeks and months after her return from Paris. Gone were the "Katharines" and the "Katys" and the "Kittys," and in their place was the short, affectionate, down-to-earth "Kate," the name by which she'd become a beloved national icon. Though this nickname had been used by Palache, Luddy, and Laura for years, only now did the press and public pick up on it. And while Hepburn would increasingly use "Kate" to introduce herself and to sign her letters, she'd continue to think of her private self as "Kathy" or "Kath"—the flip side of the public "creature" who was spearheading her career.

Kate's first order of business had been to sail on April 21 on board the *Morro Castle* to Havana, arriving on the twenty-fourth and hopping on a plane for the short flight to Mérida. With her was Laura, everything patched up between them now that Suzanne Steell was gone. Though Leland Hayward would profess he didn't know why Kate had gone to Mexico, his daughter, Brooke, believed he'd planned the trip. "Of course he did," she said. "He was her agent and knew how to fix things up." Fixing things up, in this case, meant getting rid of Luddy.

Whether Luddy was aware of her trip is unclear. When a reporter cornered him, pressing him on whether he'd become an "interference" in his wife's career, Luddy seemed still in denial. "I do not expect Katharine to interfere in my career," he replied, "so why should I interfere with hers?" A hundred miles south, reporters had converged outside Sherraden and found Luddy's mother fighting mad. "I can't believe it is my daughter," Gertrude said when informed of reports that Kate had arrived in Yucatán. "She has not gone to Mexico and she is not divorcing her husband." With that, she slammed the door in the reporters' faces.

Back in Mexico, waiting to be called before the judge, Kate and Laura made the most of their visit. They toured the ruins at Chichén Itzá and the hemp plantations at Mukuyche. She was "favorably impressed with the culture and civilization of both ancient and modern Yucatán," she told one reporter, still making a concerted effort to be friendly. It wasn't easy. Wherever she went, she was followed; Menendez had filed a report with the Associated Press, and soon Mérida was thronged with journalists. On April 30, they were clustered outside the courthouse as Kate and Laura made their way in to see the judge. She asked for a divorce on the grounds of "deep disagreements to life," adding that since they spent more than three hundred days apart a year, they were in effect already divorced. Summoned to appear, Luddy instead hired a local attorney, Francisco Arcovedo Guillermo, a freedom fighter in the Mexican Revolution some twenty years earlier, who told the court his client had instructed him simply to "assist Miss Hepburn in any way possible." The judge agreed to consider the case.

Without making any statement, Kate and Laura took off for Miami. Stopping to refuel in Havana, the women were besieged by reporters as they briefly deplaned. "Did you accomplish your objectives in Yucatán?" one shouted. "I saw the ruins," Kate said. "That's what everyone goes there to see." In Miami, they were again bombarded. Trying for sympathy, Kate asked, "Would *you* have anything to say about such a personal matter?"

Back in New York, Luddy had vacated his office, leaving the secretary at the John R. Hall Corporation to repeat "no comment" over and over again as an endless stream of reporters burst into the office throughout the day. Kate met the siege head-on. Stepping off the plane after touching down in New York, she parried with the newshounds: "Who is this Mr. Smith you keep asking me about?" Mr. Smith, of course, no longer existed. He was Mr. Ludlow now, though most reporters seemed clueless about the name change.

The divorce was granted on May 8. Kate (and Leland Hayward) had chosen to pursue the case in Mexico because of the likelihood of a swift decision. If they'd hoped the distance might also give them some cover from the press, they were wrong—though it's remarkable how well Kate rolled with it, fending off reporters' questions not with her usual hostility but with wit, humility, and grace. In fact, she and Leland probably counted on getting some press attention: after months of disinterest, *Katharine Hepburn* was the name once again on everyone's lips. Just weeks ago, conventional wisdom had written her off as finished. Now RKO was announcing a whole new set of pictures lined up for her, starting with *Joan of Arc*.

That doesn't mean she was without feeling about what had just transpired. She regretted hurting Luddy. When a furious Gertrude demanded her "dearest daughter" write a letter taking responsibility for the breakup of the marriage, Kate willingly did so. For years, Gertrude held the letter in safekeeping, yet when her papers were donated to the American Philosophical Society in 1992, the epistle was not among them.

But there's no doubt her actions left Luddy crushed. To his brother Sam, he wrote he'd been "very close to the end of everything during the past few months . . . whether it is weakness or not, I can only carry on in my own way." Even without the possibility of children, he believed Kate still represented his best hope for marriage. "I think the whole thing is a horrible mistake," he wrote. "I don't think [Kate] knows what she wants." His mother's wrath didn't make things easier. "It would help me tremendously," Luddy wrote to Sam, "if when I see you and Mother, you refrain from discussing the subject . . . Mother doesn't realize that intellectualizing doesn't help a very painful situation."

If Gertrude Smith wanted nothing further to do with Kate, the corollary wasn't true when it came to Hep and Kit, who insisted that Luddy remain a part of their lives. For the next several years, he'd still show up for weekends and holidays in West Hartford and Fenwick, easing into a cordial, comfortable relationship with his ex-wife. Always, in the back of his mind, there was hope for a reconciliation with her. Their conviviality was enough to prompt the occasional rumor in the press that "Kate Hepburn and her former husband" were getting back together.

But of course Kate had never married Ludlow Ogden Smith. That had been another girl, rash and impractical. Kate would never have done such a foolhardy thing.

Back in Hollywood, Leland was cooking things up. On June 1, Kate signed a new two-year contract at fifty thousand dollars per picture—a remarkably good deal, especially after bombing so badly with *Spitfire*. But although she made some color tests for the *Joan of Arc* film, her next picture turned out to be an adaptation of J. M. Barrie's *The Little Minister*. For the next several weeks, under the direction of Richard Wallace, Kate ran around the RKO backlot dressed as a gypsy agitating rebellion among Scottish millworkers. That her other option had been a film on the life of George Sand suggests that neither the studio nor Leland nor Kate had yet settled on just what kind of image she should be projecting on-screen.

Offscreen, however, they had a clearer idea. Beginning in June 1934, the rapacious hordes of movie journalists had a new Hepburn upon which to feast, a romantic creature who held her own with Crawford and Harlow in the gossip columns. In previous narratives, this is the point where stories have arisen of Kate falling "head over heels" for her swashbuckling agent, where we've been treated to tales of imminent wedding plans and secret lovers' getaways. But in truth such stories were simply regurgitated from the columns of Louella Parsons and Florabel Muir many decades after they first saw print. True, Kate herself, looking back, would include Leland among her beaux, but her use of that word, as we've seen, was cagy. What she wanted the public to *think* she meant wasn't exactly the way it was.

"Hepburn had some woman she was living with, and there was an image problem," said Brooke Hayward. "I'm sure there was calculation in their romance. But Father was crazy about her, so he was glad to do whatever [he could] to help her."

Significantly, the first whiff of romance between Kate and Leland appeared in the press only after the divorce from Luddy, never before, even when reporters didn't know she was married. Likewise, mentions of Leland in Palache's letters prior to this point suggest only a friendly business relationship, never any romance. But when the Mexican judge dispensed with the usual ten-month restriction on remarriage, gossipmongers were certain this was done so Kate could quickly marry Leland, whose own divorce had conveniently just come through as well. Though Kate occasionally protested she had no plans to remarry, Leland just winked and smiled and tipped his fedora when reporters asked him about Kate.

For the rest of 1934, the romance between Katharine Hepburn and the dashing agent-aviator Leland Hayward was among the hottest buzz in Hollywood. Marriage always seemed just around the corner. Hidden behind sunglasses, they were spotted with a carafe of wine at the Beverly Derby (Prohibition was finally lifted) and picnicking alongside the Los Angeles Reservoir. Finally, a good news cycle for Kate. In *Photoplay*, George Cukor was recruited to give her an even bigger boost, pronouncing Hepburn's future in films "unlimited."

Though her savvy agent could take most of the credit, Kate was also learning how to play the game herself. In the days following the divorce, a Persian kitten had escaped from her New York house. Calling to one of the reporters positioned in front, Kate asked him to fetch it back, and, in turn, gave him a few minutes of her time. Letting him into the street-level front room of her house, Kate confided that it had become "almost impossible to enjoy life after success in pictures." She was paying "a terrible price for fame," she said, stroking the kitten and worrying how a hostile press might "shorten" her career. Clearly, she eliminated any hostility from this particular newshound. In the ensuing article, widely syndicated, Kate comes across soft and vulnerable, like the kitten she held to her bosom.

It wasn't all a charade. In her plaintive lament about the price of fame, there is a clear echo of the agony that had propelled her across the Atlantic just two months before. And in this difficult period, it was Leland who was her savior, who stepped in to play the part of personal and professional champion that Kate always seemed to need in her life. He was indeed crazy about her. Leland was a man who loved women, who genuinely preferred their company to men. To be sure, he loved them sexually—his youthful diaries are filled with passion for a long list of women—but he also loved making them laugh, making them blush, making their eyes widen with excitement when he handed the controls of his airplane over to them. And Hepburn—especially this new, fiercely determined creature she'd become—was like no woman Leland had ever encountered before. She wasn't demanding; she wasn't jealous. She loved his stories and his gossip. He had more good, plain *fun* with Kate than with any other woman in his life, his daughter believed.

Late in life, Hepburn would make much of the fact that Leland's last wife, Pamela Churchill, supposedly told her, "He loved you more than he loved any of us." Most observers found that absurd, insisting Margaret Sullavan was the great love of Leland's life. But as Brooke Hayward said, "There was no bitterness with Kate, no rancor, so of course he could keep his feelings intact for her."

No bitterness, no rancor—because, unlike with Leland's other women, there was probably no sex. What started as a convenient scheme to improve Kate's image in the press blossomed into an intense friendship, but one where, friends insisted, there was no physical intimacy. The headlong romantic passion she'd felt for Putnam, and later for John Ford and Spencer Tracy, simply wasn't there for Leland. Some who knew the two of them thought the reason for that was plain. "Leland just wasn't tortured enough for her," said Daniel Selznick, son of David O. and Irene Selznick.

Hollywood hostess and former actress Jean Howard, who worked with Kate around this time and knew Leland for years, observed, "She adored Hayward, absolutely adored. But she never, *ever*, wanted to sleep with him."

Even Hepburn's own description of their life together seems to point to the same conclusion. By the middle part of 1934, Leland split his California time between living with Kate and staying at the Beverly Hills Hotel. "I could see very quickly that I suited Leland perfectly," Hepburn wrote. "I liked to eat at home and go to bed early. He liked to eat out and go to bed late. So he had a drink when I had dinner and then off he'd go. Back at midnight. Perfect friendship." They were, she said, "like an old married couple"—and like many old married couples, sex wasn't necessary to keep them together. "Life with Leland had no problems," she concluded. "We just enjoyed—enjoyed—enjoyed."

Of course, what's missing from these stories of happy cohabitation is Laura Harding. In fact, she was still there, accommodating Leland as much as he accommodated her. "[Leland] liked Laura," Kate said, "which was lucky." Lucky indeed. After all, he had moved into her house, monopolized her telephone, and strewn papers all across her living room. It may have been why Laura secured a larger residence for the three of them, a luxurious house owned by the director Fred Niblo on Angelo Drive on the top of the hill overlooking Benedict Canyon.

Still, by the beginning of 1935, Laura was fast fading into the background of Kate's life, replaced by the glamour and excitement Leland was offering. "Here's why Kate always remained so fond of Leland Hayward," said one close associate of Hepburn's. "She was never in love with him the way a woman loves a man, with all those messy dramas and jealousies. They were *chums*." Like Luddy, Leland was her friend; she never lost her head over him the way she had with Phelps Putnam. Rather, in the daredevil Leland, Jimmy Hepburn had found his ideal companion, a globetrotter whose thirst for adventure matched his own.

"Hang on!" Leland shouted above the roar of the engines.

Strapped into the seat beside him in the cockpit was Kate, her blood racing as the plane sped down the runway of the airport at Newark. Propellers spinning, wind whistling, the "Thunderbird," as Leland called his personal airplane, took off at a nearly forty-five-degree angle into the gathering dusk.

"Sixteen hours!" Leland shouted over at Kate. That was the record he wanted to set; his previous best had been seventeen. It was nearly six thirty. They would fly all night.

First stop, Columbus, at nine o'clock. By now, it was dark; Kate had watched the sun set from ten thousand feet, the sky in front of her a swirl of reds and golds and greens. Back up into the air they soared, temperatures dropping. From under the seat Leland pulled a blanket, which Kate wrapped around herself. Soon after midnight, they stopped to refuel in Wichita, but Kate wasn't tired. Not many people in 1935 got to see the earth from the air or managed to get from the East Coast to the West in under a day. One last stop, in Albuquerque, around two in the morning, then Leland took the plane as high as he could go, thirteen thousand feet, crossing the mountains. Below, long red shadows stretched across the painted desert as the sun rose ahead of them. Not a wink of sleep all night, just a continent-wide stretch of conversation and laughter. Finally, in a cascade of bright morning sunlight, they landed in Burbank. It was nine thirty. Kate let out a whoop. They'd made it in *fifteen*!

Years before Howard Hughes, Leland was Hepburn's first aviator, enabling her wish to keep her ties to the East even as she became a first-rank movie star in the West. Several times a month, Leland flew the route, Kate his frequent passenger. In New York, she'd turn over the model airplanes he kept on his desk, fascinated. Running a finger across the brightly colored maps on his walls, she'd trace the air route from New York to Los Angeles. Everything about Leland had come to fascinate her. With his black hair slicked down, a flower always decorating his lapel, he was the kind of man Kate would have been herself had a few chromosomes been different—dashing, cocky, irresistible. She may not have fallen in love with him the way a woman falls in love with a man, but she was besotted with him nonetheless. Leland was, in many ways, how she saw herself, what she wished she could be.

Yet as much as he enjoyed her company, Leland was a lusty man, and if he wasn't getting sex from Kate, he'd go elsewhere. He thought she was beautiful—toward the end of his life he'd include her among his top ten—but hers wasn't a beauty that quickened his pulse the way other women's did. The way Maggie Sullavan did, for example, with her dainty, heart-shaped face and small mouth contrasting with fiery, intelligent eyes. Leland's pursuit of Sullavan (and other women) was not a secret to Kate; just a few weeks after the columns had reported on Hayward and Hepburn at the Beverly Derby, they also spilled the beans on Hayward and Sullavan dining at the Vendome. If it bothered Kate at all, it was more about public perception; she did not want people to think she was being two-timed.

But all that talk about marriage was just that. Kate was being honest when she said that after her divorce she was certain she'd never marry again. If Leland proposed as she said he did, it was because he never took marriage all that seriously in the first place (he'd wed five times) and saw it as a good career move for both of them. In the wake of the Code, everyone in the film colony seemed to be getting respectably hitched—or, in the case of Claudette Colbert, respectably divorced. Following Kate's footsteps to Mexico, Colbert purged herself of her own inconvenient husband and was soon remarried to the upstanding Dr. Joel Pressman, with whom she projected a far more traditional union.

By the second half of the decade, marriage had become a strategy for survival in Hollywood, a way to bring stars into compliance with the conservative canon. Consider the August 1938 issue of *Modern Screen*. Gone was the town's "life of the party," the magazine observed, replaced by early risers and stay-at-homes. Tyrone Power and Merle Oberon were portrayed as longing for domestic bliss, while Spencer Tracy had found it: if it "weren't for the grace and grit of his wife," he told readers, he might not ever have become a star.

Kate could have joined their ranks by marrying Leland, earning herself a social stamp of approval. Yet with equal parts obstinance and integrity, she never went that route—though if others thought she might, she didn't mind. She deliberately floated the idea of marrying Leland at a party for George Cukor soon after the divorce was final, knowing the story would quickly get around. Her own family was left to wonder. Obfuscating and dissembling when confronted about it, Kate made her sister Marion so distraught that the teenager agonized in her diary over the prospect of trading Luddy for Leland as a brother-in-law. The Hepburns liked Leland—Hep would take him under his care late in 1934 when he required hospitalization—but they never cozied up to him as they had Luddy.

What's fascinating to chart are those precise moments when the Hepburn-Hayward marriage rumors flared up in the press. Dormant for months after the initial flurry in the summer of 1934, stories of Kate's impending nuptials were suddenly rampant again that winter—just as *The Little Minister* was failing to live up to expectations. Tales of Kate and Leland flying back and forth across the country, however, diverted the public from the film's failure. Using romance to help a star's career was common, called for what it was ("free advertising") by Alma Whitaker in the *Los Angeles Times*, but still largely swallowed whole by the public. Likewise, when Kate's next picture, *Break of Hearts*, was released in May, the columns were again filled with reports of her and Leland "sneaking off" together. "Maybe those two coy lovebirds will finally take the big leap," wrote one easily distracted columnist, who failed to mention that *Break of Hearts* was yet another critical and commercial bust.

Three flops in a row—and offscreen, her press was getting tedious, with reporters crying wolf so often on the topic of marriage that they were starting to sound absurd. Clearly the image makers still had work to do. Kate would not be built in a day.

Standing on the deck of the *Bremen*, watching the skyline of New York recede into the distance, Laura Harding hoped the sea might bring some relief from the heat and humidity that had gripped the city. But not for two days, well out onto the Atlantic, did the temperature cool down, and then it started to rain. Ferocious sheets of water washed across the deck, confining

Laura to her stateroom. The weather seemed determined to prevent her depression from lifting. Ever since leaving Hollywood two months previous, Laura had been in a funk, and no amount of excited chatter among the first-class passengers, most heading to London for Ascot week, could bring her out of it. Not even the maharaja of Kapurthala, also on board, quickened her pulse. Laura kept to her room, penning doleful letters to Mitch Davenport.

"I feel very much between two worlds, a little light-headed," she wrote. Davenport, an avid amateur astrologer, was charting her horoscope. "I think my planets are all distressed beyond astrological terms. Neptune is probably in such ascendancy that he has become all dried out." Even after her arrival in London, Laura remained "uncomfortable and . . . very lonely, wondering is it my luck or is it me—are they the same thing?" This tendency for introspection, revealed in her letters, puts Laura in stark contrast to her friend Kate, who would never have taken time to ponder such things nor "poured out her feelings" in a letter the way Laura admitted to Davenport she was doing.

But she couldn't help it. What's clear is how adrift Laura felt, suddenly bereft of her companion of five years. "I have had that unbelievable sensation of waiting for the telephone to ring ever since I got here," she lamented to Davenport. For three days she stayed in bed; even after she forced herself up she continued to feel "half-dead." Her friends in London—even a "special friend who has married an Englishman, whom I more or less expected to be glad to see me"—weren't able to rouse her from her depression. Despite the "very nice things" they said, "not one eye has lit up," Laura bemoaned, "and it is slowly killing me."

Reading Laura's letters, one can't help but feel her heartbreak. For although she was ostensibly in Europe to meet with Elsa Schiaparelli about designing some costumes for an upcoming picture, in truth she'd been sent into exile, dismissed from the court of Kate.

If Hepburn thought divorcing Luddy was all she'd needed to do to improve her image and secure her career, she was badly mistaken. The winking little asides about Laura had continued unabated in the press, threatening to derail the stories about Leland. From shouting ringside at the fights with Ernst Lubitsch to driving that old pickup truck across the RKO lot as she brought Kate her lunch, Laura's activities remained juicy news for the columns. When the gossip writer Dan Thomas compiled a roundup of Hollywood's "gal pals," he listed Laura alongside Sandra Shaw, "closest friend" of Dolores del Rio, Madeline Fields, "inseparable companion" of Carole Lombard, and Elizabeth Wilson, "constant chum" of Claudette Colbert—all of whom faced their own underground lesbian scuttlebutt.

None of those ladies, however, could match Laura's frequency in the press. And so, a short time later, she was sent off on her "special job" to Europe. From Leland, kisses and wishes of Godspeed; the dogs licked Kate's face sloppily as they all said good-bye. The move was just temporary, everyone insisted. But Laura seems to have been well aware that she'd never return to Hollywood to live. "It had become obvious," she admitted later, "that I did not belong at the center of [Kate's] life."

In fact, sexual relations between the two women had likely tapered off some time before. Kate's flirtation with Elissa Landi and her escapade with Suzanne Steell suggest the amour had ended with Laura. Many friends believed that by 1935 the relationship between Hepburn and Harding had become nonsexual, though the intensity and commitment remained. "Kate never could sustain that kind of [sexual] interest in anyone, man or woman," said a very close friend.

Yet it may, in fact, have been Laura who initially steered the relationship away from sex; the class-conscious Harding was always more sensitive to the whispers of lesbianism than Kate. When Liz Smith, decades later, pressed Kate on whether the gossip had bothered her and Laura, Kate answered cockily, "Well, it bothered *her*."

Still, even if Laura was content to end the sexual aspect of their relationship, there's no doubt she remained emotionally attached to Kate and did not want their connection severed. As pressure mounted to build a new image for Kate in the public mind, Laura found it painful to be told to "stop living Kate's life for her"—a remark that can only have come from Leland, who'd been advocating for her dismissal for almost a year. But by early 1935, Laura herself could read the handwriting on the wall. She knew it was time to go.

"People kept sympathizing with me and with [Kate]," Laura said, "saying that it must have been a terrible wrench for us to be separated after our intense friendship." Forty years later, however, she'd insist it had all been for the best: "I traveled, went to Europe, found a new string of beaux, and got back into my kind of society. Unhappy? No. I had come home."

Her letters from Europe, however, tell a very different story. "So many moods have swept over and through me this summer," she wrote to Davenport from France. The deal with Schiaparelli had fallen through, and she fretted that Kate would be upset. Just as Palache's letters always centered on Kate, so too did Laura rarely write a page that didn't somehow reference her friend and the longing she felt for her. Davenport had prepared a horoscope that prophesized a project that would one day engage him, Laura, and Kate together, and Laura clung to the belief that the stars promised a reunion with her "dearest Kate." She wrote, "[A]ll of us together, all working for one thing—a picture, I suppose it will have to be—but it is something we must do. My God, it would be fun."

The stars were wrong. Laura returned to the States that December, tired of "battling it out" in Europe. She'd buy an apartment on Fifty-second Street, not far from Kate's house on Forty-ninth, and remain in her movie-star friend's life whenever Hepburn was in New York. But never again did they work together. Never again did they share a household except for brief visits. Though she'd occasionally join Kate on trips abroad, Laura was essentially from this point on an outside observer. "I hear rumors of Kate and Leland," she wrote to Davenport late in 1935, "but in my one letter from her not long ago she never even mentioned his name! Rather ominous."

Laura herself contemplated marriage a few times. Mitch Davenport professed to be in love with her and probably would have divorced his wife if Laura had given the nod. But Mitch's anguish over the suicide of his friend Parker Lloyd-Smith, with whom he admitted he'd been "more than intimate," seems to have given Laura pause. Though Mitch's grief was in fact what made him so empathic with Laura's own heartache, empathy alone does not make a good marriage. A few years later, Laura gave more consideration to the proposal from the artist and set decorator Allen Saalburg. She paid for Saalburg's divorce, in fact, and promised to meet him in Silver City, Nevada, to tie the knot. All the way across the country Saalburg drove his little two-seater Ford, only to be stood up by his lady love, who had sailed to Europe rather than say "I do." Still, they remained friends; Saalburg decorated Laura's New Jersey farmhouse.

There was also a courtship by David O. Selznick, from whom Laura had initially recoiled in Hollywood. But, lonely in New York, she now welcomed his companionship, which earned her the enmity of Selznick's estranged wife, Irene. "I really loved him," Laura recalled for the writer David Thomson, possibly because, to her great relief, Selznick "never made a pass."

"I think Laura would've been happier had she been gay," said her grandniece Emily King. "She ended up living her life as a heterosexual woman who didn't like sex. With men, she liked the flirtation and the wining and the dining. But that was it. Then she'd flutter away."

Like Palache, Laura seemed to come most alive when Kate suddenly dropped back into her life, taking her on a trip or decamping at her farm for a much-needed holiday. "The bond was there," said King. "It was a large part of who Laura was, and it never went away."

In the dark theater, Kate slid down in her seat, watching Bette Davis verbally tear into Leslie Howard—"Yew cad! Yew dirty swine!"—and she felt her heart sink. At the end of 1933, the *New York Times* had proclaimed Katharine Hepburn's performance in *Little Women* the most brilliant of the year. Six months later, her crown had been snatched away by this pop-eyed creature. *Life* magazine crowed that Davis's acting in *Of Human Bondage* was "the best performance ever recorded on the screen by a U.S. actress." Not just that year. *Ever.*

Kate could never have played the Cockney tramp that Davis so vividly brought to life. Certainly, she didn't covet the part. But *Of Human Bondage* was an RKO film, directed by her *Spitfire* director, John Cromwell, who was being lauded for eliciting such a powerful performance. Kate stewed. Why hadn't he helped *her*? Why was the most heralded actress on the lot a loan-out from Warners? "Kate would never admit it, but she was jealous of Bette Davis from way back," said Robert Shaw, who knew both women. Other friends concurred. "When Kate was in her worst slump," said one, "Davis was being trumpeted as Hollywood's great actress. The fact that they were both from New England made it somehow worse."

All along, the one consistent positive in Hepburn's press had been her "brilliance" as an actress. Critical reaction to her first four pictures had supported that idea, but now, after three flops in a row, Kate's virtuosity seemed a forgotten, even faulty, notion. With Luddy and Laura both gone, what Kate's career needed next was a hit picture.

The problem with her last two films was that neither established an appealing, popular image for her in the public mind. In the 1930s, stars needed immediately identifiable personas: Barbara Stanwyck's earthy grit, Jeanette MacDonald's operatic elegance, Bette Davis's fiery temperament. Hepburn's early image as the enigmatic "American Garbo" was now in shambles, and nothing she'd tried since *Little Women* had struck a chord with audiences. In *The Little Minister*, her schizophrenic turn as the gypsy-cum-gentlewoman left people confused (and her second attempt at a weird dialect, this time a Scottish burr, didn't help either). *Break of Hearts* was even worse. The film's director, Philip Moeller, was instructed to cast Hepburn as a softer, more feminine, more traditional leading lady, who sacrifices all for her man (Charles Boyer) even after he cheats on her and takes her for granted. But Kate was always at her least convincing when she played sob sisters.

If either film left any kind of lasting impression, it was *The Little Minister*, and what it told us about Kate was hardly what the studio or Leland Hayward would have wanted us to know: that she was a lurking insurrectionist. Her rebellious, tomboy ways now seemed merely cover for a seditious zealot who turned workers against management and questioned the authority of

church and state. Her gypsy woman even dares to sing on Sunday, a dog-
matic violation of her strict Presbyterian village. Of Katharine Hepburn's
early screen subversion, there can be no more potent symbol: she stands accused of desecrating the Sabbath—an extremely tenuous position in this
cautious, conservative era.

For the public, this insurgent image took hold, for after they'd left the
theaters and picked up their newspapers, they saw Kate doing the same thing
in real life. Not only was her mother taking on the church in Washington,
but Kate herself was seen as fomenting unrest in the state of California. In
the gubernatorial race of 1934, she came out for the Democratic candidate,
Upton Sinclair, the muckraking author of *The Jungle* and a man pilloried as
a rabble-rousing communist in the conservative press.

It was a time of grand political struggle. The Depression had set the dis-
enfranchised lower-middle classes against an old order desperate to retain
power. Sinclair's radical plan to turn idle factories into worker-run coopera-
tives led the *Los Angeles Times* to denounce him as an "admirer, defender
and self-proclaimed instructor of Communist Russia" who intended to "so-
vietize California and destroy her businesses and industries." The movie
moguls, staunch capitalists all, launched an all-out campaign to destroy Sinclair. Fake newsreels played up fears that he would wipe out churches and
take away private homes. Studio employees saw large chunks of their paychecks docked to help fill the Republican war chest. Word went out through
the studios: support Sinclair and lose your job.

When campaign literature for the Republican candidate, Frank Mer-
riam, showed up in her dressing room, Kate had a fit. Back home in Hartford, her mother was ecstatic over Sinclair's candidacy, hopeful that his
populist fire would catch on. Kate shared her views. With George Cukor,
an ardent Democrat, egging her on, she marched into B. B. Kahane's office
to protest the studio's partisan politics. She was ordered to hold her
tongue.

Someone, possibly Cukor, took the tale to the state Democratic Party. A
few days before the election, party lawyer David Sokol filed a formal complaint with the district attorney's office, requesting a grand jury investigation
into studio intimidation of employees. Katharine Hepburn, Sokol charged,
was "an example of an employee so threatened."

The news spread across the nation. Here was Kate, in the midst of a bid
for public rehabilitation, aligning herself with communists and traitors. In
the waning days of the campaign, the tide was turning against Sinclair; it was
clear that the studio-led smear tactics had had an impact. Furious that Kate

had been linked to Sinclair, Kahane demanded she deny the charges. Instead, she went into hiding. That night, when an investigator from the district attorney's office came out to RKO to question her, the star was nowhere to be found.

It was left to her father to make things right. "Nonsense," Hep called the charges of intimidation, greeting reporters outside his door for once without fisticuffs. (Just a few months before, during the height of the divorce frenzy, he'd smashed a photographer's camera.) "She has no intention of voting for Sinclair. . . . On the contrary, she will vote exactly the opposite."

The fact that Kate was not a registered voter in California was immaterial to Hep's statement. Bob Hepburn thought his father had been asked to speak by either Kate or Leland, thereby absolving them of any need to go near the issue. Given his own politics, Hep was only too pleased to put the kibosh on the notion that his daughter would support a communist. Inside the house, however, Kit was cringing. So must have been Kate, whose instinctive support for workers' rights harked back to Heterodoxy meetings.

The Sinclair episode would teach her a valuable lesson: principle sometimes needed to make way for ambition. For all the forces marshaled against him, Sinclair lost by just nine percentage points; supporters believed if a few more prominent names had spoken up in support, he could have won. Yet even through her silence, a perception of Kate's political radicalism seeped into the public mind, bolstered by her agitation of those millworkers in *The Little Minister*. Among more reactionary elements of the public, her sins would not be forgotten.

By the middle of 1935, the naysayers were creeping back into Hepburn's press. *Photoplay* decried her lack of traditional glamour, judging that Ziegfeld would have shouted "No sale!" had he ever gotten a look at her. Four months later, the same magazine asked, "Is Hepburn killing her own career?" Cowed by the Sinclair brouhaha, Kate had reverted to ducking reporters and refusing to answer questions. This, then, was the press's revenge.

The studio countered with some fluff pieces: an extra girl tried to humanize Hepburn in the July issue of *Movie Classic* by revealing how she ate lunch with the crew, and the actress Jean Parker, a costar of *Little Women*, went to bat for Kate that same month in *Movie Mirror*. "People think Kate doesn't care about clothes the way other girls do, but she does," Parker reassured moviegoers. "She cares all right about boys and clothes and things." Parker had even fixed her up on a date with a boy she knew: "Kate had sort of a crush on [him.]"

For all that malarkey, what Hepburn really needed was a picture that would distance her from subversion and rebellion, a picture that would, once and for all, establish her as feminine and warm and humble and nonthreatening. It was a prodigious task, to be sure, but the perfect vehicle was at last found. That spring, Kate began work on *Alice Adams.*

Folding his big bear arms across his barrel chest, George Stevens refused to be intimidated. Katharine Hepburn might be a big star. She might be making more money on this picture than he was. But *he* was the director, after all, and the shots were supposed to be called by *him.* The thirty-year-old California native had a lot riding on *Alice Adams.* With a résumé consisting mostly of two-reelers and Wheeler and Woolsey programmers, Stevens had been hired to direct because William Wyler, Hepburn's first choice, was too expensive. Stevens was under contract, collecting a regular weekly salary, so Pan Berman took a gamble. And the young director wasn't about to blow the chance—not even if it meant losing a whole day's shooting because Hepburn had barricaded herself in her dressing room, furious with Stevens for overruling her on a scene.

The scene in question: a pivotal moment in the story, where Alice Adams reveals her softness, her vulnerability, her femininity. Stevens remembered, "Katharine had been a great success being strident and strong on-screen, but she had never really been feminine before. It was time for her to do something a little different."

Part of her problem stemmed from the fact that she was playing a lower-middle-class girl. Stevens recognized right away the class divide the actress faced. "Which side of the tracks people lived on was tremendously important" during the 1930s, the director explained. "An individual's economic background [could make] him superior to another." Kate, Stevens observed, had a distinct lack of empathy for Alice Adams. "She didn't know these kinds of characters at all. [She] couldn't understand that a girl would have to withdraw into the corner and hope for acknowledgment. In her experience, these kinds of people just didn't exist."

In fact, Kate *was* aware of the lower classes, at least theoretically; she had, after all, been a Sinclair supporter. But to actually *play* one of them, to inhabit the life of a simple working girl, was her greatest acting challenge yet. Luckily, for the first time since George Cukor, she found an understanding director—even if sparks flew at first.

The legend has told this story in two ways: one, that Kate wanted Alice to cry on the bed after her disastrous experience at a neighbor's party and that Stevens objected, wanting her to cry standing at the window; and two, that both agreed on the window but that Kate, unable to cry on cue, threw a fit and demanded to do it on the bed, so no one could see the technical difficulties she was having with her performance. In either event, Stevens insisted she play the scene at the window, tears or no, and she stormed off in defiance.

Hours later, she emerged. "There's a limit to stupidity!" she screeched. But Stevens proved as implacable as before. Refusing to be countermanded, he threatened to quit if she didn't play the scene as he ordered. Ultimatums might be fine for Kate herself to throw out, but when they were thrown back at her she flew into a rage. Under her breath, she called Stevens a "son of a bitch," and finally the director lost his cool. "*Who's* a son of bitch?" he shouted. Steely eyed, he asked one last time that she play the scene at the window. Later, Kate would credit the fear and anger of the moment with inducing the tears she needed. She'd also credit Stevens's "brilliance." From that moment on, they were good friends.

From his star the director elicited her finest screen performance to date, eliminating those scenes where, he said, she was trying to telegraph to the audience, "I am a fine actress." In so doing, Stevens made her one. With *Alice Adams*, we get the first inkling that Kate might be an artist as well as a movie star, that the craft of acting might be as important as the drive for fame. Hepburn's previous tendency to play too big and mannered was tempered by the sleepy-eyed yet ever-watchful direction of George Stevens. Together, they brought out Alice's innate grace and bravery by having Kate play down those very qualities, letting the audience discover them on their own.

"Above all," Stevens said, "I had to guide her in the love scenes. She had always thought that to play a love scene with a man involved standing up straight and talking to him strong, eye to eye." Instead, he taught her about "quiet assurance," that "she didn't have to bulldoze him into submission." Later, there'd be talk that the married director had fancied his temperamental leading lady—stories Hepburn did nothing, of course to quell.

Whatever the exact nature of their chemistry, it left behind a remarkable residuum on the screen. Little moments are what make this film so memorable: the look on Alice's face when she realizes she'll be a wallflower the entire night, the little "okay, okay, okay" she utters when her mother persuades her to invite her suitor (Fred MacMurray) to dinner, and, indeed, the scene where she cries at the window, her sorrow emphasized by the melancholy rain. Hepburn may have had nothing in common with these people socially or culturally, but she knew what it meant to be an outsider. She'd been a wallflower, too; she'd felt the sting of being an ugly duckling; she, too, must have begun to wonder if she'd ever find lifelong love. Only recently, she'd said good-bye to Laura, her soul mate, and turned her back on her good friend Luddy. If Hepburn's best film performances were always those where she essentially played herself, the resonance she found with Alice Adams was not any external parity but a kinship of the heart—the most promising sign yet of her development as an actress.

Near the end of production, the front office, its eye on the box office, insisted on a new, more upbeat ending. At the conclusion of Booth Tarkington's novel on which the film was based, Alice is still alone but she is climbing the stairs at Frincke's Business College. "The steps at the top were gay with sunshine," Tarkington wrote—an unmistakable feminist message, no doubt the reason Kit had given the book to her daughter to read as a girl. But Pan Berman wanted Alice to get her man: "Our chance with this picture," he wrote in an inter-office memo, "lies in the satisfactory conclusion of the love story."

To Kate's credit, she fought for the original ending, but Berman bolstered his case by bringing in George Cukor, whose good friend Mortimer Offner had written the final version of the script. After viewing the rushes, Cukor agreed with Berman. With "Maestro" Cukor swaying both Kate and Stevens, a new ending was shot. The picture fades out as Fred MacMurray arrives just in the nick of time to take Hepburn into his arms.

Artistically, it may have been a compromise, but Berman's instincts were right; without the happy ending, *Alice Adams* might not have been the tremendous success that it was. At a preview on Sunset Boulevard, "there was much excitement, and the picture was received with loud acclaim," wrote Palache, who was visiting Kate. Palache pronounced it "the best she's done"— a sentiment echoed halfway across the globe, when Laura saw the film in London. "I am left speechless with no criticism," she wrote to Davenport. "I loved it."

Alice Adams would be the fourth-highest-grossing film in the nation during its month of release. The critic Nelson Bell thought it should have been even higher: "It just goes to show what a figurative black eye, such as *Break of Hearts*, will do for a star even when she belongs in the first flight." The picture would be among the top ten moneymakers that year.

The fan magazines hailed Kate's comeback, showering her with accolades. TOPS AGAIN! blared the headline in *Modern Screen*. "Those old meanies who whispered that the Hepburn crown was slipping have had to eat their words," the magazine's reviewer enthused. "After Kate's tender, sympathetic portrayal of poor, silly, pathetic Alice Adams, she can snatch back that seat on the top of the Hollywood heap."

Kate was jubilant. All of the struggle, sacrifice, and compromise of the past twenty months seemed to be paying off.

But then she and George Cukor had the brilliant idea to make *Sylvia Scarlett*.

A YOUNG MAN WEARING LIPSTICK

With waves crashing against the rocks along Trancas Beach above Malibu, George Cukor called "Action!" Ripping off her dress, Kate plunged into the surf.

It was, in fact, one of the few moments in the picture where she actually had a dress to rip off. For most of *Sylvia Scarlett*, Kate played a girl disguised as a boy, a con artist roving around the English countryside in trousers and derby hat, swindling gullible folk and stirring up confusion wherever she goes. But here on the beach, Sylvia was—for once—out of her male drag, walking around in a frilly dress and high heels. Suddenly, she spots her rival, played by Natalie Paley, drowning in the rough surf, and feels obliged to rescue her. Good swimmer that she was, Kate had insisted on doing the scene without a double. But that day in the late summer of 1935, the undertow was particularly strong. Everyone assembled onshore watched in horror as Kate went down once, then a second time.

"Help her!" Cukor shouted, and half a dozen crew members dove in fully clothed.

In moments, they had their star back on the rocks, wrapping a towel around her shoulders. Kate looked up at Cukor. "Just thought I'd see if you were paying attention," she said, teeth chattering. Both of them broke into relieved laughter.

In a replay of *Little Women*, Kate and Cukor were having a splendid time working together. "Every day was Christmas on the set," Cukor recalled. Hepburn often sunbathed on the rocks and organized picnics along the beach. Much of the film was shot on location, near the beach house of Cukor's friend Alex Tiers, where the crew sometimes repaired for lunch. Far away from interfering studio executives, Cukor and his pal Kate were not only having fun but also making the most outrageous film of their careers, a story that upends gender expectations and exposes the fluidity of sexual desire. Kate proves to be quite fetching in her short hair and tailored suits, arousing passions in both men and women, a situation that allowed for many farcically titillating moments. At one point, Sylvia's trampy new stepmother, played by Dennie Moore, is overcome with desire for her "stepson," while a bohemian artist (Brian Aherne) also finds himself irresistibly drawn to "Sylvester." He gets "a queer feeling," he says, whenever he looks at him.

Very hot stuff indeed—and we need to remember that the movie had been Hepburn's brainstorm, even if she'd deny it later. Rushing into Cukor's house with a copy of Compton MacKenzie's novel *The Early Life and Adventures of Sylvia Scarlett*, she'd announced it was the perfect picture for them to make together. Cukor had readily agreed.

The film's producer, Pan Berman, wasn't so sure. "I despised everything about it," he'd recall. "It was a private promotional deal of Hepburn and Cukor. They conned me into it and had a script written. I said to them, 'Jesus, this is awful, terrible, I don't understand a thing that's going on.' They were hell-bent, claiming this was the greatest thing they had ever found."

The writer they'd engaged for the script was the British novelist John Collier. Together, the three of them crafted one of the most subversive films of the 1930s. The newly empowered censors were expected to balk, and they did. In August, after reading the script, Joseph Breen, chief of the Production Code Administration, fired off a letter to RKO chief B. B. Kahane citing nearly fifty objections to "sex confusion." Clearly exasperated, Breen wrote, "It is difficult to make any specific criticism or suggestion, as it is the general flavor . . . which is open to objection."

Most objectionable to the powers-that-be was the scene with Dennie Moore: "We suggest that thought be given to the danger of overemphasizing . . . any possible relationship between Sylvia and another woman based upon the fact that she is masquerading as a boy." Breen ordered no physical contact nor "any horrified reaction on the part of Sylvia."

What was Kate thinking? After all the compromise of the year before—returning to Hollywood, divorcing Luddy, banishing Laura—here she was, practically daring the press to start the rumors all over again. With good reason, Leland Hayward was reportedly against the whole project. He'd spent considerable effort to soften and feminize Hepburn—which she seemed now to be tossing aside.

"Then I *won't* be a girl," Sylvia declares in the film's opening scene. "I won't be weak and I won't be silly." In pants, she's happy and lighthearted, an echo of a boy named Jimmy (or a girl named Kath). When she slips back into a dress, she's decidedly uncomfortable: "I keep wanting to put my hands in my trouser pockets."

Toward the end, Natalie Paley poses the question: "Are you a girl dressed as a boy, or a boy dressed as a girl?" One scene suggests an answer: Sylvia/Sylvester is barred from both the men's room and the ladies' room, underscoring the fact that she/he belongs to neither. It's one more bit of autobiography layered onto celluloid. "I think . . . her whole ambiance is in that film," Kate's niece Katharine Houghton would reflect. "It's just quintessentially who she is."

Berman, however, was appalled. Already the press was having a field day on the subject of the star's shorn hair, and the film wasn't even released yet. Driving down Sunset Boulevard in her convertible, Kate noticed odd looks from people on the street. "It was terribly embarrassing," she admitted to one reporter. "They apparently thought I was a young man wearing lipstick" (the only makeup she ever wore offscreen).

The columnist Dan Thomas thought she looked like a cross between a "close-cropped goat and Julius Caesar," and took the opportunity to remind readers that, except for Luddy, Hepburn's "name has not been linked with any other man"—suggesting Thomas didn't give any weight to the stories about Leland Hayward. Certainly *Sylvia Scarlett*, once the public saw it, wasn't going to help matters, though Hepburn and Cukor seemed either not to realize it or not to care.

So what was behind this insurrection on Kate's part, this relapse into the mind-set that had led to her crisis of a year before? "I think it took her a while before she learned just what she really needed to do to be a successful [movie star]," said her brother Bob. Sure, she'd made some compromises, but she wasn't about to start playing demure females like Norma Shearer or Janet Gaynor. She could also, significantly, still be quite naive. Caught up in all the in-jokes and sophisticated tomfoolery (Cary Grant, who costarred in the picture, would later grumble that "the whole joke was far too private"), Hepburn (and Cukor) may have really believed the film would have mainstream appeal. If *they* found it so hilarious, why wouldn't everyone else?

In her recollections of the film, Kate would be inconsistent, insisting in one interview that she feared the film would lead them to ruin, in another stating she'd had no idea it had the potential to be a disaster. Looking back, Cukor thought there was "something gallant and foolhardy about the whole thing."

What's clear is that, by the middle of 1935, Hepburn honestly had no clue what kind of screen image would work for her. Tops at the box office were women with whom she had very little in common: Joan Crawford, Claudette Colbert, Jeanette MacDonald. At RKO, Kate was well aware that Ginger Rogers was the queen of the lot. But at the moment, the nation's most popular star was a little curly haired moppet named Shirley Temple.

Alice Adams was still in postproduction when Kate began work on *Sylvia Scarlett* in late summer 1935, so its formula for success—self-effacing, feminine girl wins her man—had yet to be proven to her. So she barged on ahead, not as reconstructed as everyone thought, still apparently hoping to forge an untraditional path in Hollywood. If any further evidence of that is required, we need only to step behind the camera during the *Sylvia* shoot and see who she was inviting back to her house on Angelo Drive to play sixteen-ball Kelly pool in the enormous game room in the basement. It wasn't Leland Hayward, the man the press said she was about to marry. Instead, it was a group of women in stylish pleated pants and short, boyish haircuts like Kate's. George Stevens, her *Alice Adams* director, called them her "stooges." Others in Hollywood weren't nearly so kind.

For her entire life, Katharine Hepburn despised being alone, a legacy perhaps of those first two harrowing years at Bryn Mawr. From that point forward, Kate was always surrounded by an entourage, a court of devotees. The moment after Laura left, she'd been on the phone with Alice Palache, pleading with her old friend to fly out and visit. Arranging to get three weeks' vacation from her job at the Fiduciary Trust Company on Wall Street, Kate's devoted college chum had left Newark on the night of July 12, 1935, and arrived in Los Angeles the next morning. The letters she wrote back home offer a remarkable snapshot of Hepburn's life that summer: a swim before breakfast, tennis with Harvey Snodgrass, a party at Cukor's ("crowds of celebrities of screen and stage, all talking about themselves exclusively but fascinating to watch just the same"), dinner with Edna Ferber—crowned by a lunar eclipse from Kate's balcony "in a serene and limitless sky."

Kate's house above Benedict Canyon took Palache's breath away. "It's way up on the top of a mountain overlooking the valley," she wrote to her family. "At night the lights are like a fairy coverlet as far as you can see." Writing all this on stationery monogrammed *LBH*—Laura Barney Harding—Palache seemed convinced Kate's life was a walking dream.

Despite his annoyance over *Sylvia*, Leland was still around—he flew Palache up to see her aunt in Carmel for a few days—but that didn't stop Kate from assembling a loyal sorority around her who essentially lived, worked, and spent most of their time together. Among them were Trudy Wellman, an extra who'd worked in several Cukor films and for whom Kate paid the bills when she was briefly hospitalized, and the Doyle sisters, Adalyn, Patsy, and Mimi, daughters of a prominent Los Angeles attorney, all of whom variously worked as Kate's stand-in.

With Adalyn, Hepburn grew especially close, insisting that her friend be with her on the set at all times. So ubiquitous did Adalyn become that the press took to calling her "Kate Hepburn's good-luck girl." Known as "Murph," Adalyn Doyle was a wisecracking, boyish, freckle-faced Irish girl, whose ambition to become a full-fledged actress impressed Kate. Accordingly, the star helped Murph land a part in *Finishing School*, RKO's adaptation of the play *These Days*, as well as other roles. For *Home Sweet Home*, a Broadway tryout being staged in Greenwich, Connecticut, Murph changed her name to Eve March—a tribute to her favorite stand-in part, Jo March in *Little Women*, and to the woman who played her. For Murph's East Coast stage debut, Kate asked her parents to drive down from Hartford to cheer her on.

Playing duenna to this group of spirited young women was Emily Perkins, a brisk, efficient Englishwoman. In her early fifties, Em had just as much energy as the girls she nurtured, and not a little of their ambition as well; she was always pleased when she got a chance to grab an extra part and mug for the camera.

Born Emily Stephenson in Leeds, Yorkshire, Em had come to the United States in 1911 with her fiancé, a well-to-do young man whose family had not approved of their son's working-class sweetheart. According to Em's stories, which have a certain melodramatic, silent-movie ring to them, her swain then died, leaving her no choice but to accept a proposal from an older man, Arthur Perkins, who worked in a mill in Sanford, Maine. Theirs was largely a loveless union, though it did produce a son, Blynn, born in 1914.

Soon after, Em's husband died, freeing her to seek her fortune amid the bright lights of New York. There, she made costumes for chorus girls until Hollywood beckoned. By 1930, Em had found herself ensconced in the wardrobe department at RKO. As early as *A Bill of Divorcement*, Kate was enchanted by Em's tough-but-tender, no-nonsense ways. When she thought the star was acting haughtily, Em told her so—but she was also quick to wrap a shawl around Kate's shoulders if she thought she might catch cold. After Laura left, Kate hired Em to be her personal secretary-dresser-companion. What she really wanted was someone to live with her and take care of her. For fifteen years, Emily Perkins did just that.

But for the moment the most important member of the group was a handsome, bespectacled, serious woman by the name of Jane Loring, a film editor Kate had first met while making *Break of Hearts*. Loring, seventeen years Kate's senior, was renowned for her expertise at cutting film to match the sound track, a valuable skill during the transition to talking pictures. First at Paramount, then at RKO, Loring was so respected that she was often given the title of associate director. This was the case on *Break of Hearts*, where she taught the newcomer Philip Moeller about camera angles. Peering through the lens, she locked eyes with Hepburn, and from there an intense friendship grew.

A Colorado native, Loring never spoke of any family, and indeed the name she used in Hollywood may not have been her real one. Barely out of her teens, she'd headed to New York equipped only with a violin and loads of ambition, landing a part in a musical revue. Married very briefly to the pioneer film director Lansdale Hanshaw, Loring decamped to Hollywood on her own, taking a room at the Plaza Hotel on Vine Street and a job with Al Kaufman, general manager of the Grauman theaters. From there it was a quick leap onto the Paramount lot, where a friendship with Dorothy Arzner brought her into the cutting room. By 1934, she was Pan Berman's assistant at RKO.

"She was a Hepburn type," Berman's son Michael recalled of Loring. "She used to wear slacks and overcoats and men's hats . . . She was very good with details, talking to people and working things out. Hepburn liked her and would listen to her." Jane became a trusted conduit between producer and star. "She'd give Kate some time to digest things and think about them and then Dad would talk to her. Jane was [good at] smoothing things."

In her beret and rubber-soled shoes, Jane hurried about the set, speaking only when necessary, huddling with Berman then rushing to confer with Kate. In winter she invariably wore blue trousers, in summer white flannel slacks. "She is so busy," one reporter surmised, "she has no time to buy dresses."

Loring made no pretense about being a lesbian. "She was as obvious as one could be," recalled Jean Howard, who worked with her on *Break of*

Hearts—an opinion confirmed by those who knew Loring later in life. "She was very forthright," said one friend. "She might not have shouted it from rooftops, but she didn't need to. It was plain and clear."

Indeed, the cutting room was traditionally a very hospitable place for freethinking women, an oasis of opportunity in an otherwise sexist system. Dorothy Arzner had also started out as an editor, mentored herself by an older woman. Columnists spotted Loring sharing a hamburger at a drive-in with Arzner and hunkered down on the lot with Eda Warren, another "single miss" from the cutting room. Another time, she was observed strolling with Fred de Gresac, one of the most overt lesbians in the film colony, with her men's ties and short-cropped, flaming red hair. On her own from a young age, forced to earn a living for herself, Loring fit a model identified by the historian Lillian Faderman: the self-identified lesbian. Socially and economically independent from a husband or family, these women "could live out [their] attachment to women for the rest of [their lives]."

In other words, she was precisely the kind of woman Laura Harding wanted nothing to do with. But with Laura gone, Kate seemed intrigued by Jane and the alternative path she was charting through life, an echo of Mary Towle and Bertha Rembaugh and the women of Greenwich Village. It was the same fascination that had drawn her the year before to Suzanne Steell. "I remember how friendly Hepburn got with Jane Loring," said Jean Howard, present on the set of *Break of Hearts* when the two women met. "There was a whole circle around [Loring] of women who were very masculine, and Hepburn was a part of it."

Sometime after Laura's departure, in between all the stories about marrying Leland Hayward, Kate began an ardent companionship with Jane Loring. Jean Howard called them "inseparable." Forty years later, for the author Charles Higham, Loring herself would recall sitting with Kate in a field weaving daisies through each other's hair—a lovely little reverie, though Higham chose not to include it in his own biography of Hepburn. But the friendship didn't go unnoticed by the press; *Modern Screen* commented on how much time the two spent together. George Stevens, in fact, thought Loring exerted undue influence over Kate, who turned to her new friend for advice in the way she had once done with Laura.

Whether their affair was of the heart or the flesh—or both—is impossible to know. Certainly Loring, even at forty-four, was the physical type of woman Kate always seemed to prefer: slim and boyish. What's undeniable is that for much of 1935, Kate and Jane were devoted to each other. Loring's friend Teddy Smith, who knew her in the 1970s, recalled a photo of Kate on

Loring's table and notes from the star bundled in a drawer. "Jane told me Hepburn was very special to her," Smith said. "Their affair was wonderful, but she understood when Hepburn had to end it. Jane could live the way she wanted, but Hepburn had an image to maintain."

It wasn't just the demands of stardom that pulled Kate back, though of course that would always be an issue. In this case, there was another consideration. Throughout her life, Kate often had the impulse to follow these independent women, admiring their disregard of rules and expectations. In the company of these unapologetic lesbians, the part of her who was still Jimmy could come out and relax. Yet despite this tendency, in the end Hepburn never really followed through with this sort of woman. After a brief flirtation, she'd think twice and pull away. A voice seems to have kicked in—the voice of her class—for, in truth, these bourgeois women were very different from her. Arzner was the daughter of a restaurant owner, Steell a social climber. Jane Loring's background was mired in mystery. They were nothing like Laura, Kate's unattainable social model. And so Kate's sense of her place and her class ultimately stood in the way of her ever really settling in with these "alternative" women—though she'd continue to engage in the occasional dance with them for the rest of her life.

For her part, Jane Loring would find another companion, a woman with whom she shared her life and who inherited the bulk of her estate when she died in 1983 at the age of ninety-two. Though she apparently retained fond memories of Hepburn, Loring (like Suzanne Steell before her) did not remain in Kate's orbit. They simply moved in incompatible worlds.

One other factor was at work here as well. Eight years earlier, enmeshed in another tight bond of female friendships at Bryn Mawr, Hepburn had sent her women companions an unmistakable message that she was not going to be easily categorized. She began her aggressive flirtations with Eugene O'Dunne and Robert McKnight and her eventual affair with Phelps Putnam. Something similar took place now. Just weeks, maybe even days, after Laura's departure, Kate found herself in a parked car with her *Break of Hearts* costar, Charles Boyer—"flirting," she said later. Lupton Wilkinson, without identifying Boyer, turned it into a make-out session, placing Kate and a "beau" in "the middle of a kiss" when George Stevens came by to knock on the window. Nothing was made of this flirtation in the press, since the flop of *Break of Hearts* rendered any romantic gossip about Hepburn and Boyer pointless. Still, the stories lingered. Kate would tell Scott Berg that although she never had an affair with Boyer, it wasn't "for her lack of trying." What's significant is that at the same time she was weaving daisies through

Jane Loring's hair, she was also playing the flirt with Charles Boyer. At least, she wanted us to think so.

And it may, in fact, be true. After all, until the charming Boyer, most of Hepburn's leading men—David Manners (*A Bill of Divorcement*), Colin Clive (*Christopher Strong*), Douglass Montgomery (*Little Women*)—had been homosexual. For a woman who craved attention, it must have been exhilarating to finally have a costar who might conceivably be attracted to her. It's quite easy, in fact, to picture Kate sitting in a parked car playing the coquette with Boyer, even if the story's real purpose, as told in the various Hepburn chronicles, was to segue into her affair with *another* man, George Stevens.

That knock at the car window had led to a meeting in which Stevens was named director of *Alice Adams*. Catching Kate in flagrante delicto with Boyer allowed director and leading lady to "meet cute" and begin their supposed love affair. According to some stories, the tempestuous relationship between Hepburn and Stevens on the set of *Alice Adams* had led to an equally passionate offscreen coupling. But in truth, there is not a peep, not so much as a blind item, about any romance between them in any contemporary account. The stories of their affair are all *after* the fact, springing from a single, imprecise source: Pan Berman's opinion, given in 1974, that Hepburn had agreed to Stevens as director because "she found him very attractive." That's even less basis than we have to presume an affair with Jane Loring, but traditionally the relationship with Stevens has been accepted, the one with Loring denied or ignored.

That doesn't mean there wasn't *something* with Stevens. Looking back, Hepburn would recall the director as being similar to Spencer Tracy, both the same "sort of very male members of society." Indeed, Stevens was the kind of man who always intrigued Kate and inspired her devotion. "In private life and in movies," said her friend the director Anthony Harvey, "what attracted Kate was big, strong, tough men." For all her fascination with women who lived autonomous lives free of male authority, a sensitive, masculine, *married* man—like Stevens, like Tracy, like Phelps Putnam—was irresistible to Hepburn. Such men would always arouse her most passionate attachments. Within the company of women she might take comfort, support, and refuge, but the great passions of her life—the florid expressions of feeling and emotion, even if they didn't involve sex—were always reserved for men.

"Previewed our little love child last night," Cukor wired Kate in West Hartford after an advance screening of *Sylvia Scarlett* in December. "Audience interested if a bit confused." He was overly optimistic about their interest, while severely underestimating their confusion.

At another screening, Kate sat in horror. Despite her pratfalls with Cary Grant on-screen, the audience remained frozen in a stubborn, angry silence. Her face growing hot, Kate realized that the transgressive humor wasn't going over. As Michael Pearman remembered, she retreated to Cukor's house, pacing around his oval sitting room, trying to figure out how they might "cook it up"—how they might save their skins. It was at that moment that the full weight of the changes in Hollywood seems to have hit her, how much against the grain they'd gone with this picture, and just how massively she'd bungled her chance to reclaim her fame.

Cukor survived the devastating reviews of *Sylvia Scarlett*—the *Chicago Tribune* called it "a queer sort of picture, a fantastic, unhinged sort of thing"—because he was safeguarded within his new contract with MGM. Hepburn wasn't so lucky. Still contracted with RKO, she had one film left to go before the studio decided to keep her or dump her. And as 1935 turned over into 1936, with *Sylvia* being yanked quickly from theaters, her days seemed numbered. After all, hadn't Brian Aherne called her in the film "You oddity, you freak of nature"—exactly the image she and Leland had been trying so hard to eradicate?

If Kate thought her press was bad after *The Lake*, she had woefully underestimated its venom. Eleanor Barnes wrote in the *Los Angeles Daily News*, "Shutters shudder[ed] and neighbors pull[ed] down their blinds" whenever they saw Hepburn approaching. Back were the criticisms that the star double-dealt the press, that she was rude and arrogant. No insult was too low for Katharine Hepburn. "She looks like a gargoyle on vacation without any makeup," snarled Harry Lang, the critic for *Modern Screen*. After *Sylvia*, no amount of spin seemed able to convert her cheek into charm. Several reviewers quipped that Hepburn had made a better-looking boy than she did a woman.

One last effort was made by Leland to help. In November, just before *Sylvia Scarlett* was released, rumors of their impending marriage had flared up again. Possibly anticipating the reaction to *Sylvia* (and possibly to offset industry buzz about Jane Loring), Leland had tossed the press a bombshell. Flying with Kate to New York and making what he called an "emergency landing" in St. Louis, he appeared impatient with reporters who gathered around the plane, snapping that he was "not a celebrity or a screen star but only her husband." Elbowing each other out of the way, journalists raced to the phone to call in their scoop.

The next morning, Hepburn's name topped every column in the country. She was still leading the news the next day, too, as waiting photographers caught a dramatic moment upon her arrival in Newark. Trying to slip away from the crush of reporters, Kate ran under the plane's fuselage and reportedly missed the whirling propeller by inches. HEPBURN DODGES DEATH blared the headlines. Coupled with the speculation about whether or not she was married, this particular news cycle was a fairly positive one for Kate, generating interest and sympathy. A week later, she and a "mystery man" (identified in some reports as Leland) were conspicuously shopping for furniture in New York.

Problem was, such good spin couldn't last. Shortly thereafter, *Sylvia Scarlett* premiered, and on January 24, Leland shipped out on the *Bremen* for a lengthy trip to Europe—sailing, in a sense, out of Kate's life. Although she'd remain his client for several more years, by the time Leland came back, she had moved out of his sphere of influence. For his part, Leland would focus his attention on Margaret Sullavan upon his return.

Ironically, the ship he sailed on was the same one that had taken Laura Harding out of Kate's life six months earlier. And like Laura's similar quip about being Hepburn's "husband," Leland's statement had been intended to send a message—that it was he who was Hepburn's great love, despite any rumors to the contrary. That message was lost, however, in the free-for-all that ensued in the press following *Sylvia Scarlett*. Kate's brief comeback in *Alice Adams* was now seen as an aberration. After *The Lake,* she'd been able to coast a little on her Academy Award for *Morning Glory*. Nominated again for *Alice Adams*, this time she lost—and to Bette Davis, for *Dangerous,* whose reputation as Hollywood's preeminent actress was now cinched. Katharine Hepburn was sliding into the nadir of her career.

For all her arrogance and presumption, she was at heart still a frightened little girl. In her late twenties, she was in different ways both older and younger than her years. Agreeing to a face-to-face interview with Edwin Schallert of the *Los Angeles Times*, Kate was attempting to neutralize one of her strongest critics. But in that piece we catch a glimpse of the softness that friends insisted lurked under Hepburn's hard shell. Her words to Schallert reveal her fear of deficiency, her lifelong sense of being inadequate, which harked back to the days of being snubbed in Hartford. Usually a brittle arrogance camouflaged this insecurity, but during times of stress or challenge— like her first two years at Bryn Mawr and indeed here in Hollywood—it sometimes burst through her imperious demeanor. To Schallert she admitted, quite honestly, "I'm so dreadfully afraid of boring people that throughout my career I have always sought to avoid any contacts." This humbler side of Haughty Hepburn touched the columnist; the resulting piece definitely tipped in her favor.

Of course, narcissistic personalities often arise out of inferiority complexes, and one fan-magazine article tried to psychoanalyze Hepburn exactly that way. Yet while her dread of inadequacy was real, dating back to her childhood, her difficulties in Hollywood can also be explained by the class divide she faced on the RKO lot. With the studio laborers—the electricians and carpenters—she had an upper-class liberal's easy rapport. But with the time-punching middle class, who comprised most of the studio employees (and the press), she was often at a loss. Laura had looked down her nose at them, but where Laura could be a classic snob, Kate was driven more by a sense of *displacement*. She simply didn't know how to *act* around these people, which only fueled her sense of inadequacy even more.

With keen understanding, the reporter Helen Louise Walker honed in on the problem Hepburn faced. "She is possessed of no such give and take of small talk, and it scares her to death . . . Katie's friends will tell you that she is shy. I don't believe it. No really shy girl could've made her way with such stubborn determination through so many setbacks."

Hepburn's "shyness," while true enough, was really a reflection of her outsider status. An upper-class girl among the parvenu. A bohemian among the bourgeois. An adventurer, one who "strayed from the beaten track" (as the introductory title card for *Sylvia Scarlett* had proclaimed), stranded among a community of middle-of-the-roaders. Dropping her arm around the shoulders of a visitor was not her style, nor was "calling him by his first name and becoming his fifteen-minute pal," according to one observer. Such was unthinkable behavior for this Connecticut Yankee. Joan Crawford might invite reporters in for tea and biscuits, but that's because she wanted them to think she had class. Hepburn had no need for such parlor games. That whole routine was completely alien to her.

What characterized her best during this difficult time was restlessness and impatience. Hurry up and make things right. That was always her credo: "Why sit around fretting why things are the way they are when you could be out there changing them to what you want them to be?" Admirable, but also avoidant: on the cusp of thirty, she'd never had a lasting, successful relationship (few Hollywood figures had). Despite the glimmer of humanity that comes through in the interview with Schallert, at this stage in her life Hepburn was still maddeningly self-absorbed. Her single-minded focus was on staying famous—everything else be damned. In his letters, Luddy had called

Kate confused about what she really wanted out of life. Indeed, to one interviewer, she herself admitted: "I can't think farther ahead than a few months. Who knows really what's best?"

Yet unlike the career crisis of two years previous, this time Hepburn did not fall into the depths of depression. There would be no impulsive tantrum, no running away. In the wake of the *Sylvia Scarlett* disaster, she appeared determined to stick it out, to do whatever she needed to do, recommitting herself to her girlhood goal of being the most famous person in the world. She had come precariously close to losing that dream.

So once more she smiled prettily, her lips full and red, her hair coiffed elegantly. Once more she made herself "adorable." Sitting down with hostile interviewers like Schallert, she did her earnest best to win them over. But the girl named Kath—with all the softer, more thoughtful, more authentic characteristics that had defined her—seemed exiled alongside Luddy and Laura.

Soon after the New Year 1936, Phelps Putnam ran into Hepburn in Hartford. He barely recognized her. "I had cause to wonder anew," he wrote to Davenport, "at what the passions can do." What he'd once seen in her was now unfathomable. "She looked and felt to me like a sort of etiolated cheesestick, one of the things you have with tea or a glass of beer. It was quite different while I was imagining the poem [about her]. Or perhaps the Hollywood life is a death to growing and immature girls."

Yet for all the hardness she presented to Putnam, in Kate's quieter moments, she was lonely. "Solitude hurts," she admitted to Schallert. "The criticism that goes with it hurts too." Untethered, unsure, shorn of her most long-lasting relationships, Kate Hepburn was ready, no matter what her former paramour thought, to fall in love again.

THINKING A THOUSAND THINGS

On a bright morning in March 1936, wearing jodhpurs and riding boots, Kate Hepburn bounded into the RKO commissary, having just dismounted from a gallop around the backlot. Waiting to meet her was the humorist Frank Scully, assigned by *Screen Book* magazine to do a story about her latest film, *Mary of Scotland*, directed by the esteemed John Ford. With Ford, Scully was already well acquainted, often spotted at the Brown Derby raising a glass of beer—or two or three or ten—with the director. But so far Scully had never met Hepburn, "that willful bundle of beauty," he wrote, "who acted as if she thought a picture queen could do no wrong, and even if she did, they'd better praise her for it, or else."

With some hesitation, then, did Scully extend his hand to greet the star.

Kate grasped it, shook it solidly, and asked the writer to join the crew for lunch. As Scully took his seat, Ford ribbed his pal: "So you wouldn't shake hands with me, eh?"

"I had a clean glove on," Scully parried back.

Kate nearly fell out of her chair in laughter. "I've been trying to think of a crack as mean as that for weeks!"

Ford gave her a dramatic leer, puffing on his clay pipe. Dressed in a patched tweed jacket, old gray trousers, and tennis shoes, he challenged Kate to a game of golf. "If you lose," he said, "you'll agree to come to this studio at least one day dressed like a woman."

"And if I win," Hepburn countered, "will you agree to come to the studio at least one day dressed like a gentleman?"

"Listen, Dudley," Ford said, turning from the star to the screenwriter, Dudley Nichols, "let's put that unhappy ending back on this picture. Let's behead the dame after all."

Surely their banter was enacted partly for Scully's benefit, and surely the writer, known for his humorous books and articles, also polished up their dialogue to make it crackle. But the fact that Scully was a drinking buddy of Ford's suggests it wasn't all an act. The woman Scully was watching his friend flirt with wasn't just another of his leading ladies, but someone who had quite obviously captured his heart.

On a bright Sunday not long after this, Kate—this time wearing shorts and sandals—trooped across the gangplank of the *Araner*, Ford's 110-foot, gaff-headed yacht. By now their intimacy was plain and undisguised. Sitting cross-legged on the deck at Ford's feet, Kate smiled wide into a photographer's camera, her mouth outlined in lipstick, while she gave the man she loved a foot massage.

"Oh, Sean," she wrote at one point, affectionately addressing Ford by his Irish name, "it will be heavenly to see you again—if I may—and if I may not, I can drive by . . . in an open Ford and think a thousand things. In my mind and heart your place is everlasting."

At the start of 1936, Kate was once more smitten with a moody, heavy-drinking, married man who—again like Phelps Putnam—was thirteen years her senior. They certainly made an unlikely looking pair, she sharp and thin, he round and thick. Six feet tall, Ford had been known as "the human battering ram" when he played high school football. Now, at forty-four, after decades of hard drinking, he looked ten years older than he was, his face craggy and jowly. From behind round black eyeglasses, his hooded eyes watched everything with the sharpness of a hawk. From his lips protruded a clay pipe, almost a permanent attachment. When it wasn't clamped between his teeth, it was in his hand, waved about as he told his actors how to move. To approach John Ford was to inhale the tangy fragrance of pipe tobacco, another quality he shared with Putnam—and indeed with Dr. Thomas Hepburn.

Observe him on his boat, tanned and leathery, not long before beginning

Mary of Scotland, heading down to Mexico with his cronies Hank Fonda, Duke Wayne, and Ward Bond. Docking at Mazatlán, they trooped off into the village, hopping from one bar to the next, downing shots of tequila, trailed at all times by a hired mariachi band. The next morning, head throbbing, Ford staggered off to Mass. When he returned to the *Araner*, he had the priest in tow and, in front of Fonda and Wayne, signed a pledge to give up drinking. They celebrated the signing with a round of champagne. A little later they brought out the brandy. To Kate, Ford's drinking was part of his allure. It was the sign of a real man.

Indeed, for more than twenty years, Ford had been one of Hollywood's most famous debauchees. From his days as an actor in the early silent films, when he'd donned a white sheet to play a clansman in *The Birth of a Nation*, he'd stepped up to director, making a name for himself with Harry Carey westerns and other aggressively macho vehicles. He could always be counted on to drink until he dropped, usually taking the whole bar down with him.

The son of an immigrant saloonkeeper, Ford had been taunted as "shanty Irish" during a brief stint at the University of Maine, leading to his withdrawal before the end of his freshman year. His Irish identity would imprint his entire life. Always partial to the Gaelic form of his name, Sean Aloysius Feeney, Ford remained a devout Catholic all his life. Yet he was drawn to blue-blooded women like his wife, Mary McBryde Smith, whom he married in 1920, and Kate Hepburn. Such women seemed to hold an almost magical attraction for him.

With Mary, Ford had two children, a son Patrick and a daughter Barbara. "Our family life was pretty much that of a shipmaster and his crew," said Patrick, whose browbeating by his father eventually left them estranged. "He gave the orders, and we carried them out."

On the set, Ford expected much the same obedience. Dorris Bowden, who worked for the director in *The Grapes of Wrath*, remembered being humiliated by him over the public address system for a very minor infraction on her part. "Part of his mercurial personality was to do something he knew was mean or mischievous and then try to justify it," Bowden said. She compared him to another director she'd worked for: Kate's nemesis Jed Harris.

Yet despite the horror stories, Hepburn was thrilled to be working with Ford. At the moment, he was the hottest name in Hollywood, having just won the New York Film Critics prize for *The Informer*. (In the course of shooting *Mary of Scotland*, he'd also win an Oscar for it.) But Maxwell Anderson's blank verse, ruffles-and-velvet play was a far cry from Liam O'Flaherty's gritty tale of working-class Irish rebels. It was a talky, stage-bound vehicle with lots of posturing by Mary, her lover Bothwell, and the firebrand religious reformer John Knox. Still, Pan Berman was hoping that the property, a succès d'estime for Helen Hayes on Broadway, might restore Kate's standing with the public after the debacle of *Sylvia Scarlett*, especially if it were helmed by the most acclaimed director in Hollywood.

Like clockwork, studio publicists kicked into overdrive, saturating the press with stories of RKO's "greatest actress" working with its "greatest director." Press releases hyped the old Hepburn family lore of being descended from Bothwell, though Kate didn't cooperate, shrugging off the possibility of royal blood when reporters questioned her about it. She was quick to point out that Bothwell left no legitimate heirs.

If she were going to play games, she'd play ones of her own choosing. On the first day of production, done up in her high-collared sixteenth-century costume, Kate assembled her girls around her, all of them puffing away on clay pipes as Ford walked onto the set. He barely lifted an eyebrow, just continued past them without saying a word.

But he was tickled. Soon Kate had won him over with her impish ways, getting away with things Ford would have tolerated from no one else. Stopping in the middle of one scene, Kate would motion for Patsy Doyle to stand in for her while she ran around peering through the camera and checking the construction of the shot. Another time, annoyed with Ford's direction, she snapped at the twenty-year veteran that he was throwing away the scene. "Direct it yourself then," Ford replied, placing his old felt hat on his head and walking out. Hepburn went ahead and shot it on her own, telling the cameraman Joe August where to stand and when to zoom in. While it was the kind of scene Ford loathed—an impassioned moment between the queen and Bothwell, played by Fredric March—observers were stunned that he had so quickly and willingly relinquished control in that way.

Clearly Kate had Ford eating out of her hand. Once again, she was doing her best to be "adorable." She quickly became the director's confidante. No one could remember Jack Ford ever warming to an actress like this before. Known for taking siestas in his dressing room during lunchtime, now he was regularly trooping over with Kate and the Doyle sisters to the commissary, sitting beside his star and laughing uproariously at her jokes.

With Leland and Laura gone, with Eve March off to Broadway, Kate was lonely—and in need of a new champion. Actively encouraging Kate in her pursuit of Ford was Em Perkins, who called the director "Shoney," a diminutive of Sean. Ford was quite fond of the sassy Perkins as well, bonding with her over their shared roots in Maine. Part of the reason Kate developed such strong feelings for Ford was how "unsnobbish" he was toward Em.

By the middle of the shoot, director and star had become inseparable. Now it was Ford whom Kate huddled with at lunch, whom she invited up to the house to play pool in the game room. Jane Loring hadn't disappeared completely; Ford entrusted her with editing the final print of *Mary of Scotland*, and so pleased was he with the result that he made only minor changes before sending it off to be scored.

But Loring's place in Kate's life was now filled by Ford. Unlike the highly publicized back-and-forth with Leland Hayward, this affair, far more authentic, never made the papers. In fact, the public didn't learn of it until Ford's grandson, drawing upon the director's personal papers, wrote about it in his 1979 biography *Pappy*. Still, ever since then, the legends of the Ford-Hepburn romance have sprouted like wildflowers. Film buffs have enjoyed speculating that the screenwriter Dudley Nichols based *Bringing Up Baby* on the "madcap" (it was hardly that) affair between Ford and Hepburn. Other scribes, in an attempt to reconcile competing legends, devised a jealous feud between Ford and Spencer Tracy. But the most outrageous claims came in Barbara Leaming's 1995 biography of Hepburn, which tried to posit the affair with Ford as the central relationship of Kate's life.

Yet even with all that, there's no question that for about ten months during and immediately after *Mary of Scotland*, an intense connection existed between Ford and Hepburn. Despite her love of genteel, cultivated men like Luddy, Cukor, and George Hoyningen-Huene, Kate considered "he-men" like Ford—like her father—the truly superior beings. "For Kate," said her friend Robert Shaw, "a real man, as she defined him, was quite the wonderful thing to find, especially in effete Hollywood. A real man, like John Ford, like Spencer Tracy, like John Wayne—part of her just looked at them as gods."

Indeed, in her estimation, Ford was the epitome of what a man should be: aggressively masculine, staggeringly talented, painfully sensitive. Yes, he could be crude and mean, but underneath, Kate sensed, he wasn't as uncultured as he liked people to think. Still, it was Ford's public disdain for refinement that Hepburn found so appealing. The director never made any great airs about being an artist. Instead, he saw himself as a *craftsman*—"like a carpenter or something like that," Kate said—and she liked that image just fine.

For all her iconoclasm, for all her tendency to seek home and comfort from women, part of Kate still venerated the traditional male-female relationship. It was the way her parents had lived, the way "it should be," as she said more than once. With Ford, she could indulge the fantasy of being a tra-ditional woman in a traditional relationship. Like a schoolgirl, she clipped photographs of her sweetheart from fan magazines and pinned them up in her dressing room. No doubt her feelings were real—even if the illusion sur-rounding them was not. Ford was, after all, a married man who was never going to leave his wife.

But that, too, was fine with her. To carry the fantasy that far would have been her undoing, and she was smart enough to know it. Besides, being a married man's inamorata was seductive. As "the other woman," she could feel *better than* the man's wife, more attractive, more exciting—an intoxicating brew for a woman whose ego constantly craved affirmation. "She liked being the other woman," said Robert Shaw—whether opposite Ruth Putnam, Mary Ford, or Louise Tracy. "It made her feel alluring and special."

There's also a hint of some leftover childhood rebellion in her relation-ship with Ford. Bringing the director home to meet her parents, Kate had to know how they'd react to him, given their anti-Catholic bias. Just recently the *Catholic Transcript* had editorialized against Kit and her birth control work, suggesting no attention be paid to a woman "so depraved and so disgusting" that she allowed her children to witness the act of childbirth. Kit called it an "old and slanderous lie," forcing the paper to apologize. To the Hepburns, Catholics were hopelessly anachronistic, the inhibitors of progress.

So it was with suspicion that they greeted Ford. Sitting around the din-ner table, the family—including "Auntie" Mary Towle—did their best to make the director feel out of place. Kit orchestrated a great show of shock when she learned he came from a family of thirteen. "Your people are Irish Catholics?" she asked, prune-faced.

"This sort of nonplussed her," Ford remembered—an understatement.

Later, on the golf course, he found Kate could be as imperious as her mother. She played aggressively, beating Ford with such giddy pleasure that it nearly ended their affair. "You are a split personality," he told her years later, "half pagan, half puritan." Most times, he said, she was "sophisticated," but often she acted "like a little girl of eight or ten."

For all their passion, *Mary of Scotland* turned out to be a dreary, tedious picture—with one important exception. Whenever the camera moves in close on Hepburn, the film sparks to life. As the Catholic queen, she is in-fused with a religious ecstasy that is almost sexual in its power. In this film, Ford gave Hepburn her most luminous, erotic screen presence yet; compar-isons to Garbo no longer seemed so far-fetched. The shimmering result is testament to Ford's enchantment and enduring evidence of their ten months of rapture. "*Mary of Scotland* is less noteworthy as a movie," Ford's biographer Joseph McBride wrote, "than as visual evidence of the grandest romantic passion Ford ever pursued."

Yet how intimate were they? It always comes down to that question when discussing Katharine Hepburn's relationships, whether with men or women. Of course, no one besides the two of them—two "secretive New Englanders," Kate said—could ever truly know the answer. But evidence does exist that allows us to draw some conclusions.

"Some people thought John Ford and I were involved," Hepburn said in *All About Me*, before adding a resounding "Not true!"

Of course, her statements always need to be taken with a grain of salt, but Kate's fabrications tended to be ones she could rationalize. She and Laura weren't *lesbians* because the word meant something very specific to her. Leland Hayward was a *beau* because beaux were gentlemen escorts, not necessarily men with whom she was in love. In the same way, she could say "not true" about being involved with Ford, because to her, "involved" meant *sex*.

And with Ford and Hepburn, as their letters document, it was the *feelings* that mattered, not how they were acted on. "You know what I'm trying to say," she wrote to him, "though it's more feeling than saying—because I guess that is always the way it will be with me about you and things that happen to you."

In Ford's papers, there exists an extraordinary letter that sheds further light on their affair. More than a year after Kate's relationship with Ford had ended, one of her girls, Mimi Doyle (Eve March's sister), wrote a letter to the director that gives us a glimpse, however skewed, into Hepburn's thinking at the time. Mimi quotes Kate as admitting that Ford "never made a pass" at her. "I think Jack loved me," Kate told Mimi, and the fact that he never made a pass "proved" it to her.

Until now, Mimi's letter has been a mystery for historians. The identity of its author, who signed her name merely "Mimi," was unknown. Still, this single source seems to have been Barbara Leaming's basis for much of her account of the Ford-Hepburn romance, including her bold assertion that Ford planned to leave his wife and marry Kate.

As a source, Mimi does have some real authority. Part of Hepburn's inner circle at the time, she was privy to intimate conversations. But this particular letter, while revealing, needs to be treated with some caution; it is clear that, by the time she wrote it, Mimi—a "gingery miss," according to the *Los Angeles Times*—was in love with Ford herself.

"My darling," she wrote, "I've been putting this off until I got the proper Noel Coward mood." In playlet form, she proceeds to describe a private conversation between "Miss Katie Hep," "Miss D" (Mimi), and "Miss M" (presumably Eve March). Mimi quotes Hepburn: "I thought a great deal about marriage with [Ford] or living with him, but decided against it . . . I think I could have forced the issue—but then I don't know really. Every time we talked of it, he would just smile. But this you can be sure of—if he wouldn't divorce for me, he would do it for no one."

Clearly, Mimi was trying to goad Ford into getting angry with Hepburn. Under her pen, Kate comes across as coldly presumptuous: "If anyone could have made Jack happy, I am that person." Mimi's bias, however, becomes evident at the end, when she tells Ford that she thinks of him constantly and looks at his picture to keep from getting too lonely. "I love you like mad," she wrote, "love me?" For good measure, she added that she'd like to "kick Miss H. in the pratt." By attempting to turn Ford against his famous former lover, Mimi may have been hoping to secure some kind of future of her own with him.

Other than this one somewhat fanciful, obviously biased letter, there is no real evidence that Ford considered divorcing Mary for Kate. Leaming's assertion that Hepburn offered Mary $150,000 to leave her husband apparently comes third-hand from a niece of Ford's, whose reliability has been questioned by Ford's grandson and confidant Dan. Given that Kate wasn't above using money to buy her way out of uncomfortable situations, it wouldn't have been completely uncharacteristic; but it does seem a horribly crass gesture, and that much *was* unlike Hepburn. Besides, admitting to a rival that a conflict existed was never Kate's style. To acknowledge such would be to put herself equal with her rival, and that was something she would never do.

In his biography of the director, Joseph McBride refuted most of Leaming's conjectures, so there is no need to go over all of them again here. But given Kate's own history, a few other considerations about the exact nature of her relationship with Ford still need to be made. For, upon closer study, there may have been one more thing that Ford had in common with Phelps Putnam.

Maureen O'Hara, the star of some of Ford's most famous pictures, made the surprising claim in her 2004 memoir that she'd once caught Ford in a lip-lock with an unnamed male actor. Her disclosure of what happened on the set of *The Long Gray Line* in 1954 took many readers by surprise: *John Ford, homosexual?* The director of so many macho, all-American pictures, the buddy and mentor of John Wayne?

Indeed, O'Hara seemed to relish giving away Ford's secrets. The stunt-men in the Ford stock company, she said, routinely warned newcomers to "stay away from the old man after dark." Quoting a passage the director had once sent her about loving a man but being torn with guilt over it, O'Hara said she'd been confused at first by its meaning, but after seeing Ford kiss the actor, it seemed "much clearer."

Of course, O'Hara had her own biases. She'd long resented Ford, blam-ing him for all sorts of abuse and misdeeds. Her stories about him have the feel of scores being settled. That doesn't mean, however, that there isn't some truth to them. In fact, Ford's biographers often depicted him, despite his macho reputation, as somewhat ambivalent about women. Sexual passion, according to McBride, was never "high on Ford's agenda." Some have called Ford's attitude toward sexual relations "puritanical," and certainly his devout Catholicism may have kept him from cheating physically on his wife. But his avoidance of intimacy with women might be characterized as much by dis-interest as disapproval.

All his life, Ford would struggle with a perceived tension between being artistic and being masculine. On some level, the former football player known as "Bull" Feeney believed he could not truly be both. His reputation as a "man's director" was, therefore, well earned. Reminiscing with Ford late in life, Kate observed he'd made a choice to direct the kind of pictures he did, as opposed to the more woman-oriented films of George Cukor. Ford replied that Cukor could never have made the kind of films he did (read *manly*, read *superior*), to which Kate readily agreed.

Yet neither did George Cukor live with the kind of torment Ford did. He did not drink himself into oblivion. He did not chew his handkerchiefs until they were rags, which Ford was famous for doing. If Ford did have homo-sexual tendencies, he would have struggled to reconcile them with his tradi-tionally masculine interests in sports, boating, and fishing. The prevailing image of gay men in 1936 was stereotypical and demeaning, largely what Ford himself put on the screen in *Mary of Scotland* in the character of Lord Darnley. Effeminate and conniving, Darnley runs around in makeup and earrings and pouts when the queen's ladies call him a "wench." Eventually, he gets blown up with dynamite, and the audience is glad to see him go. By put-ting Darnley on such display, Ford could clearly demonstrate he had noth-ing in common with such a creature.

If Ford was indeed struggling with internal demons similar to Phelps Putnam's, his turmoil may be seen in a new light. Compensating for his homosexual desires, Putnam acted out with excessive braggadocio and womanizing, drinking until he was unconscious on the floor. Ford's way was to posture aggressively (Kate called him "over, over masculine"), sometimes turning cruel and sadistic, humiliating Dorris Bowden and browbeating his son. Drinking seemed the only escape. If what O'Hara claimed about Ford is true, he would certainly not have been the first, nor the last, repressed homosexual to act out in this way.

This image of Ford links him to a discernible pattern among all of Hepburn's serious male romantic attachments—a fact not realized by Ford's biographers, who did not have Kate's full history before them. The biographers also presumed Hepburn would be *open* to a sexual relationship with Ford, because they were unaware of her own aversion to sexual intercourse.

This idiosyncrasy of hers may, in fact, be why Ford felt so strongly for her. In Hepburn's very independence, the director found liberation for himself. He could be a man, venerated by a woman who adored him, but also freed from all the expectations women usually had of men. He could indulge a passionate attachment away from his wife without any of the Catholic guilt actual adultery would have wrought. In a way, what Ford and Hepburn were doing was playing house, casting themselves in the leads of the Good Husband and the Good Wife, roles they knew they could never play in life.

What all this means for Ford's story must be reserved for future studies of the director; it is not the matter at hand here. What *is* significant for our understanding of Katharine Hepburn is that, once again, a man with whom she fell in love has left behind suggestions of sexual conflict in his own life. It seems to have been an unconscious prerequisite for her. The suffering of these men, their confusion and anguish, seems to have inspired in Hepburn the caretaker sort of feelings she once brought to her relationship with her brother Tom.

Consider the following story she tells in her memoir. Ford was on a bender, holed up at his house in the Hollywood hills, and the producer Cliff Reid asked Kate to intervene. "So I went over to Ford's house and somehow I got him into my car and I drove him to the RKO lot where I had a nice big dressing room," she said. "And somehow I got him to drink a lethal dose of whiskey and castor oil." Of course, he got sick all over the place, and Kate worried she'd killed him. But she let him sleep it off and then took him over to the Hollywood Athletic Club, where he got dressed and cleaned up. She had saved him. She had made things right—at least for the moment. In the end, that was all the intimacy she seems to have needed with a man.

If she talked about marriage, she was daydreaming, playacting. No wonder

Ford just smiled when the topic came up. To each other, they likely never articulated the reality of their situation; with them, remember, it was always "more feeling than saying." In truth, Kate was content to simply spend leisurely days with Ford on board the *Araner*, basking in the sun, helping him attach the riggings and reel in especially large yellowtails. And as the sun set, she'd settle down at his feet, imagining she and Sean were just like any other woman and man in the world. Like her mother and father, in fact, Kit so strong and independent but submissive, too—the way it was "supposed to be."

According to Mimi Doyle, Mary Ford discovered their getaways and thought Kate had "double-crossed her." Kate had met Mary briefly, and the two women were friendly. But Mary may have been less concerned than Kate liked to believe. Mrs. Ford likely sensed that nothing permanent, certainly nothing sexual, would transpire between her husband and Katharine Hepburn.

Indeed, the star's own public statements about Mary of Scotland offer insight into who she was and how she was thinking at the time. The queen of Scots, Kate averred, was a "ninny"; it was Elizabeth of England whom she really admired. With the sappy Mary, lamenting how she'd "loved as a woman, lost as a woman," Kate had nothing in common—even if, as the years went by, she sometimes wanted us to think she did. Rather, it was Elizabeth's line "I've loved no man, only my kingdom" that reflects the truth of Katharine Hepburn. Her kingdom was her career.

The audience at Boston's Colonial Theater was going wild. For the third time in a row, Kate grasped hands with her costars, Dennis Hoey and little Patricia Peardon, and headed back onto the stage. This time, the throng was on its feet. The applause rang up to the rafters. Kate was smiling so hard her cheeks hurt. Repeated curtain calls, common today, were a rare thing in 1937. But for the past two weeks, the cast of *Jane Eyre* had trooped out three, four, and five times a night. Kate could definitely get used to this.

Going back to live theater was, after the debacle of *The Lake,* a gutsy move on her part. It's to Kate's credit that she risked the poison pens of the critics once more, who were clearly waiting for her to trip and fall on her face. Plans to return to the Ivoryton Playhouse the year before in *Dark Victory* had collapsed under myriad problems during rehearsals, not least of which may have been Kate's own fear of trodding the boards once again. Live audiences terrified her still, leaving her trembling behind the curtain and hoping to "drop dead" before she had to walk out on stage. Motivating her, however, was "a sort of Puritan streak," she said: "If it hurts, it's doing you good, or if it's hard, it's better for your character."

Her holy grail remained success on the stage. Until she'd managed that, she'd never feel fulfilled. And given the state of her movie career, a backup plan was a smart idea.

When she was approached by the Theatre Guild to star in Helen Jerome's adaptation of the Brontë novel, Kate was still reeling from the disaster of *Sylvia Scarlett*. She met with the Guild's directors, Theresa Helburn and Lawrence Langner, and stipulated that if she were to do the play, she reserved the right to keep it on the road as long as necessary until she felt confident about a New York opening. She might be taking a risk, but there was no need to be foolhardy about it. Even in the matter of billing, she was practical. Furious when she spotted an ad for the play in which her name was printed larger than that of her costar, the English actor Dennis Hoey, she demanded that Langner make the names equal. When he told her she was being generous, she laughed. "I just don't want to stick my neck out!"

In the meantime, she signed a new contract with RKO. *Mary of Scotland* hadn't been a disaster like *Sylvia Scarlett*—few pictures were. It had, in fact, opened strong in its first month of release but then dropped off precipitously amid lukewarm reviews. Still, Pan Berman kept the faith. Despite Kate's largely unsuccessful tenure with the studio, he believed she'd eventually find her groove. "She kept going back to Broadway, and Dad kept calling her back," said Michael Berman. "[He kept] trying her again and trying her again."

Her new contract, signed in July 1936 and running through November 1937, called for four pictures, five if there was time. First up was *Portrait of a Rebel*—an apt enough title for the Kate everyone knew, though the script transforms her character rather quickly from a freethinker to a typically heartbroken Victorian heroine. Indeed, she spends most of the film changing into twenty-two—count them—*twenty-two* lavish hoop-skirted costumes.

Going after the female demographic was a strategic move. *Portrait of a Rebel* was intended to feminize Hepburn once and for all, but with her costar Herbert Marshall there were fizzles instead of fireworks. The director, Mark Sandrich, seemed utterly at a loss with the material, which gives Kate an English accent that is even worse than her Scottish brogue in *The Little Minister*. Changing the name to *A Woman Rebels* didn't help, and the picture disappeared quickly in the autumn of 1936.

Kate's advisers were clearly in disarray. In retrospect, it seems they should have realized they ought to get her out of period clothes and stop trying to remake *Little Women*. But off she marched in bodice and bustle to play Phoebe Throssel in an adaptation of James M. Barrie's *Quality Street*. By reuniting her with George Stevens, the studio was hoping to recapture the magic of *Alice Adams*. Yet once again, sparks failed to ignite with her leading man, Franchot Tone, who the press reported was put off by Kate's rudeness to reporters.

After so many flops, the critical pans couldn't have been a surprise to anyone. "Phoebe Throssel needs a neurologist far more than a husband," Frank Nugent snarled in the *New York Times*. "Such flutterings and jitterings and twitchings, such hand-wringings and mouth-quiverings, such runnings about and eyebrow-raisings have not been seen on the screen in many a moon." The stylized playing was aimed at urban sophisticates; the provinces, as usual, stayed away. The film ended up $248,000 in the red.

Part of the problem was that Leland Hayward was gone. Although he still negotiated the terms of her contracts, he was absent from the daily management of Kate's career and image. Leland had always known how to "cook it up," how to launch a favorable news cycle, how to drum up interest, how to distract the public from her failures. But these days, Leland was far more interested in guiding Margaret Sullavan's star. By the summer of 1936, the columns were filled with sightings of the two of them, and unlike the travels with Kate the previous year, there was nothing stage-managed about their romance. That fall, Maggie learned she was pregnant with Leland's child. On November 15, Kate heard the news that they'd married over the radio, and the next morning she opened her *Los Angeles Times* to see the headline: MARGARET SULLAVAN WEDS KATHARINE HEPBURN MANAGER.

She hit the roof. George Cukor was perplexed by her attitude—understandably so, since she was, at the moment, enmeshed with John Ford. Still, others—like David and Irene Selznick—called Leland "a scoundrel" for the way he'd handled the whole thing, having thoroughly believed in the authenticity of their romance.

Kate certainly played the part of the woman scorned when she saw the Selznicks and others. The latter-day assumption has been that she was brokenhearted over Leland's "abandonment," but that ignores the relationship with Ford. In reality, what put Kate in such a dander was the media's implication that Sullavan had stolen her beau. That was simply intolerable. "I don't think [the marriage] particularly bothered her," said Brooke Hayward. "She had other things she was up to. But she was afraid of what the world would think."

What was particularly galling to Kate was that Leland, once so sensitive to every little peak and valley of her public image, would do this without telling her. The response she chose to Leland's marriage echoed her actions after being fired from *The Big Pond*, when she'd showed up at the theater to say good-bye and shame everyone with her apparent graciousness. This time, saving face meant sending Sullavan a telegram. "Dear Maggie," Kate wired. "You have just married the most wonderful man in the world."

Sullavan was outraged. "Mother was so incensed," Brooke Hayward said, "that she burned the cable right in front of Father. He *loved* it. He told that story all the time."

Raconteur that he was, Leland no doubt enjoyed stirring up the rivalry between the two women. But it was Kate's ego that was wounded, not her heart. For now, the latter was still in the hands of Jack Ford, even if they were seeing less of each other. Kate was back East, rehearsing for *Jane Eyre* in New Haven. Plans were to open in New York on January 1, after a series of tryouts in Boston, Washington, and elsewhere. Meanwhile, the London production of the play opened to terrific reviews, with the relatively unknown Welsh actress playing Jane, Curigwen Lewis, hailed as the find of the year. For Kate, the pressure was on.

She fit in well with the Theatre Guild set. The Welsh-born Lawrence Langner had roots in Greenwich Village, having helped found the Washington Square Players. He was also a lawyer, with a keen mind for business, having set up the patents provisions in the Treaty of Versailles after World War I. His wife, Armina Marshall, was a delicate beauty, part Cherokee, the daughter of an Oklahoma sheriff. The Langners were close with Laura Harding as well; their letters to Kate were often sprinkled with little updates on Laura.

Finally, there was Langner's partner, Theresa Helburn, Bryn Mawr class of 1908. A small, stocky woman with heavy eyebrows and gray-streaked hair pulled back in a bun, Helburn "seemed never to be still," observed Oscar Hammerstein II. "Always prodding, like a very small shepherd dog, pushing you relentlessly to some pasture which she had decided would be good for you." Though Helburn was married to an English professor, most around her knew she was a lesbian. Living in France, she'd been the protégée of both Gertrude Stein and Isadora Duncan. Later, she was close with Katharine Cornell and Dorothy Arzner.

Could that partly explain the tension that always seemed to bubble just below the surface between Helburn and Hepburn? In truth, despite the potential for a simpatico collaboration, more than just a single consonant separated the two women. Terry could be embarrassingly mannish. In Hollywood, she was often spotted on the tennis courts with Arzner. Though Kate sometimes brought other "obvious" lesbians into her inner circle, she always kept Helburn—another of those women whose style she could never embrace—at arm's length. Terry, baffled and hurt, would feel compelled on occasion to ask Kate why she was so distant. "Will your illusive [sic] highness please telephone me?" Helburn wired at one point. Another time, she wrote, "What are you up to that you keep changing your phone number? I will guard your secret if you will send it to me."

Here they were, embarking on a major partnership, and Kate was keeping a distance, not only with Helburn but to a lesser degree with Langner as well. It suggests the walls were already going up around her private life. Indeed, with the Guild, Kate always acted the star. Nearly a decade before, while she was toiling on *A Month in the Country* with Nazimova, the Guild had denied her a measly five-dollar raise. Now seats were booked well in advance for *Jane Eyre*, all on the strength of Kate's movie-star name.

Ironically, the Guild was on record as opposing the star system. "With us, the play was always the thing," Helburn said. "We fought for ensemble acting, which projected the meaning and beauty of the script as a whole." The Guild had been created by directors and playwrights dedicated to producing plays of high quality in order to challenge audiences rather than pander to them for commercial gain. Still, with its profits down by the end of the decade, the Guild didn't mind bending its philosophy for a little star power if that meant filling its coffers for riskier productions. And certainly Kate often played the diva, storming out of meetings if she wasn't happy; afterward, the Guild would follow up with solicitous letters filled with flattery. It was all probably a strategic move on her part, making sure the Guild never treated her in the bureaucratic manner of a movie studio.

Usually, the Guild's serious, literate reputation—"snooty," one Hollywood columnist called it—tended to mean staging plays by Shaw and O'Neill. Of the merits of Helen Jerome's script for *Jane Eyre*, Helburn was never convinced. She also had doubts about Kate's abilities, fearing her Hollywood training had rendered her unable to truly build a character over three acts. Yet under the direction of Worthington Miner, who'd initially helmed *The Lake*, Kate eventually won over Helburn, who thought she was "wonderful" in the part.

The critics largely agreed. The show opened at the Shubert in New Haven the day after Christmas. Eight years earlier, Kate had played her small part in *These Days* here, with Phelps Putnam sitting in the audience. This time, it was the whole Hepburn clan watching her from beyond the footlights, including her brother Dick, now a playwright himself. The New Haven critics weren't keen on the play but thought Kate was marvelous.

On New Year's Eve, the curtain went up on the show's first night in Boston, where the local critic thought Kate played "her not too exacting role with much simplicity and straightforward intelligence." In Chicago, where the play opened at the Erlanger Theater on January 11, reviews were the best of the show's run. "Word from Chicago," wrote one New York critic, "is that Katharine Hepburn is giving an excellent account of herself." That's just the spin Kate and the Guild wanted as the show rolled ever closer to Broadway.

Later, Worthington Miner would insist that Kate had played Jane Eyre in a much more confrontational manner than Joan Fontaine did in the more familiar screen version. Following this lead, Barbara Leaming wrote that Kate was "bold and provocative," insisting, without any basis, that her performance was based on her relationship with Ford. In fact, reviews from the time reveal a much different flavor to Kate's performance. A New Haven critic praised Hepburn's "tinkling piquancy and . . . elfin delicacies." Her success in the part, other critics observed, came from her "simple ingenuousness" and "ladylike deportment," and the fact that she used "no star tricks to force herself into the center of the picture." It sounds very much as if she played Jane like Alice Adams, allowing the audience to discover on its own the courage behind her primness.

Indeed, it seems that Kate made a very conscious decision to tone herself down, to go soft and "ladylike" for this stage outing. Tellingly, when she signed with the Guild, she'd been weighing one other stage option, a revival of *Peter Pan*. (Maude Adams, one of her revered idols, had made the part famous; more recently, it had been played by Eva Le Gallienne.) No doubt Hepburn would have made a memorable Pan—quirky, defiant, subversive. But those were the very qualities from which she needed to distance herself. Her strategy seems to have paid off. One critic, thrilled by how "thoroughly feminine" Kate was, announced grandly, "We forgive Miss Hepburn many of her past, and most of her present sins . . . On the whole, we like Miss Hepburn better than we have in two years."

Kate was learning what worked. And she was smart enough to know she needed something else in the mix as well. Two years earlier, when her Hollywood box office was at a similar low point, she and Leland had kept interest in her alive by jetting back and forth across the country together, giving the press a juicy little romance to feast upon. That wasn't something she could do with Jack Ford. But there was another man out there just waiting for the chance.

Kate first met Howard Hughes in the late summer of 1935, when he'd landed his Sikorsky amphibian airplane along Trancas Beach during the *Sylvia Scarlett* shoot. Later, the legends around Hepburn would twist the story to imply that the famous aviator and film producer was a besotted fan of the actress's and had staged the dramatic landing to impress her. But his intention that day was actually to show off in front of his pal Cary Grant—and show off he certainly did. The sun sparkling from its wings, the plane buzzed low over the beach then landed expertly just below the cliffs. The crew burst into applause. Hughes came trudging up the beach in his leather flight jacket, breeches, and cordovan boots, his goggles dangling from around his neck. "Nervy and rather romantic," Kate would recall, "in a bravado sort of way."

But over lunch she found him a bit of a dolt. She was unnerved by having to repeat everything she said due to his near deafness. But there's no hint in any of Kate's recollections that she was romantically interested in Hughes at this point, no matter how much biographers of both would try to turn that first meeting into a fateful encounter. After lunch, Hughes simply replaced his goggles, got back in his plane, and flew off. Kate went back to work.

She likely didn't see him again until more than a year later. At some point during the fall of 1936, soon after *Quality Street* had wrapped, Kate was playing golf at the Bel-Air Country Club. She'd just reached the seventh tee when the air around her suddenly whipped up into a minicyclone. Overhead a low-flying plane was attempting to land between two trees on the perimeter of the green. No question she was impressed with Hughes's spectacle, though she made a show of berating him for his boorish behavior when he landed. The exact nature of that golf-course meeting, immortalized in the film *The Aviator*, has never been clear. Was Hughes pursuing her? Was he there to see someone else and then noticed Hepburn on the green? Or was their meeting prearranged, designed to kick-start the most sensational publicity Kate had yet known?

Her relationship with Hughes, just as she was setting off on tour with *Jane Eyre*, was extraordinarily well timed. Soon after she opened in Chicago, the newspapers were filled with stories of Hepburn and Hughes, which certainly didn't hurt the box office; the play was extended for a week in the Windy City. No matter how much she'd complain about the press hounding her on the tour, she—and the Theatre Guild—certainly appreciated the reams of free publicity the romance with Howard Hughes was generating. Despite the fact that she remained mired at the bottom of the Hollywood box office, Katharine Hepburn routinely led off nearly every gossip column in the country for the first several weeks of 1937.

Looking back, she'd be surprisingly insightful about the relationship with Hughes. "He was sort of the top of the available men—and I of the women," she said. "It seemed logical for us to be together . . . We each had a wild desire to be famous."

Over the next eighteen months, both of them would take that fame higher—*literally*—than it had ever been before.

PEOPLE WHO WANT TO BE FAMOUS

On a warm, clear night in July 1938, Kate Hepburn and Howard Hughes took off from an airfield in Westhampton, Long Island, soaring into the indigo skies. Below them, the lights of Manhattan glittered and pulsed as the propellers of their S-43 Sikorsky amphibian airplane whirled noisily through the night air. Ahead of them was the Fifty-ninth Street Bridge.

"Do you want to take over?" Howard called to Kate.

He'd taught her the basics. Even though flying over the city was new to her, Kate didn't hesitate. As if the cameras were rolling, she cried, "Let's go!" and gripped the cold metal controls in her thin hands.

The plane dipped. With Howard guiding her, it surged forward and, in a long graceful arc, swooped under the bridge. Both of them let out a cheer.

In some places below them, the streets were still littered with ticker tape from the parade in Howard's honor, celebrating his round-the-world flight. What a day that had been. Hughes, America's hero, had broken all records, and thousands had crowded onto the streets to cheer him. Kate's block of Forty-ninth Street had been swarmed with people, expecting to catch a glimpse of the aviator with his sweetheart. Hughes and Hepburn had dodged the crowds by holing up at Laura's flat on Fifty-second Street. Now, looking up, people on the street would have noticed the plane buzzing low through the air. If only they knew who was at the controls.

The most famous man and woman in America.

At the moment, anyway. That summer, their faces graced dozens of fan magazines and newspaper articles. Reporters dogged them everywhere. Radio announcers broke into programming to inform the nation that Howard Hughes had just been spotted with Katharine Hepburn at a party on Long Island. Even the staid *New York Times* was speculating when the two of them might marry.

In the summer of 1938, the world was hungry for heroes. The Depression was ending, but across Europe, war was rumbling like fast-approaching thunder. As Spain was torn by civil unrest, German troops were mobilizing; Hitler announced the annexation of Austria. Hollywood responded by filling the silver screen with upstanding, heroic figures: Clark Gable, Errol Flynn, Robert Taylor, Gary Cooper, Spencer Tracy. By now, American filmmaking was at its zenith. The talkie revolution complete, the great directors of the golden age were working at the top of their craft: Frank Capra with *Lost Horizon* and *Mr. Deeds Goes to Town*; William Wyler with *Dodsworth* and *Jezebel*; Michael Curtiz with *The Adventures of Robin Hood*; Victor Fleming with *Captains Courageous*; and of course John Ford, who at the moment was working on his masterpiece *Stagecoach*.

For all the heroism on-screen, however, Americans were more enthralled with a real-life hero, Howard Hughes, whose daring round-the-world flight had reestablished the United States as the world leader in aviation. Yet not for Hughes any boast or swagger. Standing at the microphone after completing his flight, he appeared shy and bashful. The public took this boyish thirty-two-year-old to their hearts. Hughes seemed one of them—even if he'd come from wealth beyond the dreams of most Americans.

Fittingly born in Humble, Texas, Hughes had grown up believing the world was his oyster. His father had invented the dual cone roller bit, which made oil wells easier to drill. It also made him a multimillionaire. Howard Junior inherited his father's ambition, declaring as a teenager that he'd be the world's best golfer, the world's best movie producer, and the world's best pilot. He made good on the last and came pretty close on the others.

Like Leland Hayward and John Ford, Howard Hughes never earned a diploma. He'd attended prestigious preparatory schools, but after the deaths of his parents—his mother when he was sixteen, his father two years later—Hughes dropped out of school. After all, he'd inherited $17 million and at nineteen was CEO of the thriving Hughes Tool Company. His money and connections enabled him to open a movie production unit; established producers looked askance, but Hughes released a string of hits in the late 1920s. He stunned Hollywood by pouring several million dollars into the production of *Hell's Angels*, which showcased his love for aviation. *Scarface*, which he made in 1932, was another blockbuster, riding the gangster vogue in the pre-Code era.

A year and a half older than Hepburn, Hughes had been married once and divorced. Since making *Scarface*, he'd spent most of his time building, testing, and flying airplanes, setting records for speed and distance in the process. For his downtrodden nation, Hughes was an extraordinarily romantic figure. The *New York Times* described him as having "the face of a poet and the shyness of a schoolboy." That combination of aggressive masculinity and cultured sensitivity was catnip for Kate. They seemed perfect for each other. Both were from privileged backgrounds, both were ambitious, creative, and adventurous—and both had that wild desire to be famous.

Yet that desire, she'd say, in one of her rare moments of true introspection, wasn't necessarily a virtue. "People who want to be famous are really loners," she mused, many years later. "Or they should be."

When Hughes first began courting her, being alone was the last thing either of them had on their minds. Coming together, they must have sensed they'd set the world on fire. With surprising alacrity in late 1937, Kate transferred her emotions from Jack Ford to Howard Hughes. While playing in *Jane Eyre*, Hepburn met Hughes for dinner in Boston. Within days, Hughes was cabling her in Chicago, the tour's next stop, calling her "Darling" and signing himself "Dan," as in "Dynamite Dan," one of Kate's nicknames for him. ("Dynamite Dan" Sullivan had been a colorful character in the 1920s, blowing up tree stumps for farmers and known for walking around with a stick of dynamite in his back pocket. Eventually, he blew himself up by accident. To Kate, the daring, cavalier Hughes was asking for the same thing.)

Of course, such derring-do was why she found him so attractive. Some aspect of her wished that she, too, could strap herself into a streamlined fast plane and zoom through the skies breaking records. But she contented herself watching from the sidelines, much as she had with Tom all those years ago when he'd troop off with Jimmy Soby to walk the roof of the Mark Twain house. Into her life, when she was at a low point in her career, Hughes brought excitement and adventure. Tall and lanky, his dark eyes forever cast downward, his flight suit emblazoned with the American flag, Hughes was perhaps the most idolized man in America in 1938. And at his side was Kate, loving every minute in the spotlight.

It all happened very quickly. After accosting Kate on the golf course in the fall of 1936, Hughes had stuck around Hollywood long enough to get photographed with Ginger Rogers at a nightclub. Back and forth across the country he flew a couple of times after that, crashing an amphibian cabin ship on Long Island after being caught in a tailwind and walking away without a scratch. Wrecking planes was like changing shirts to Howard Hughes; with wealth like his, he just ordered new ones. New Year's Eve was spent with Cary Grant in Los Angeles, socializing with Alfred Gwynne Vanderbilt, Cesar Romero, and the Darryl Zanucks. The next day, bright and early, he was testing his clipped-wing pursuit plane in the blue skies over Burbank, pushing it to speeds of 300 miles per hour. On the ground, crowds gathered to watch and cheer. Howard Hughes was getting ready to break another world record.

Indeed, on January 19, he rocketed through the skies in his "silver bullet" faster than anyone had ever flown before—332 miles an hour—setting the record from Los Angeles to Newark in seven hours and twenty-eight minutes. "I'm tickled as a kid," he announced, still shivering in his fleece-lined jumpsuit.

"Howard Hughes has done it!" crowed the *Los Angeles Times*. "No one can say this is the limit . . . If this progress in speed keeps up . . . a man will be able to fly from New York to Los Angeles and arrive before he starts."

As tired as he was, Hughes wasn't finished traveling for the day. There was a certain lady in Chicago he just had to see. Wiring Kate at the Ambassador Hotel, he told her he'd be arriving on the train around six the following evening—"probably not in time to see you before the theater so will try to contain myself until eleven-thirty."

That telegram guaranteed that within twenty-four hours, the whole world would know about the Hepburn-Hughes affair. Kate's later protestations that they'd wanted to keep the relationship a secret are distinctly difficult to believe. In his telegram, Hughes had made no attempt to disguise either his or Hepburn's identity. As soon as the wire went through, Western Union workers were blabbing the story to newspaper reporters. The following day, Hughes, quite ostentatiously, took a suite at the Ambassador Hotel on the same floor as Kate. Both of them knew exactly what they were doing.

A rumor soon ignited that the flying ace had come to Chicago to marry his movie-star girlfriend. County Clerk Michael J. Flynn arrived at his office dressed in his Sunday best, telling reporters he would "hand out the license personally and congratulate the glamorous couple in the name of the county of Cook." By midafternoon, some three hundred people had jammed the corridors of Flynn's second-floor office, waiting for Kate and Howard to arrive. Newsreel cameras stood poised to capture the couple coming down the street. In response, Kate issued a statement late in the day that seemed designed to feed the furor: "I won't make any statement, either to confirm or deny marriage plans."

"Seems like just a publicity stunt to me," grumbled one fan as the crowd dispersed.

That night, leaving the hotel for the performance, Kate wrapped a fur coat around her maid, Johanna Madsen, and sent her out through the crowd into their limousine. Then she clambered down a fire escape only to find it didn't go all the way to the ground; she had to climb back up and sneak out a side door into a waiting cab. After the show it was more dodge and pursuit. Newspapermen followed the company to a nightclub on East Walton Street, outside of which they cooled their heels for about an hour, excited by reports of a man called "Appleby" who was allowed inside to meet the star. Afterward, Kate's limousine tried to shake newspapermen by driving all the way out to Evanston, to no avail. Arriving back at the Ambassador, they found more than three thousand fans congregating in the street. Struggling through the crowds that surged against the blue barricade of Chicago policemen, Kate hid her face as photographers tried to snap her picture. Her costar Dennis Hoey rushed one reporter and knocked his camera to the ground, leading to fisticuffs. The next night, Hoey would walk onstage with bruises and cuts on his face.

All this attention for an actress at the bottom of the box office. Even Shirley Temple, the top star in America, didn't draw crowds like this. By hitching her star to Hughes, Kate had found a way to keep herself on top—and front and center in the public eye.

Some in the press were wise to the game. "The Katharine Hepburn–Howard Hughes romantic drama continued to receive good press notices today," observed an International News Service reporter a day after the brouhaha. "Still unwed, the couple refused to state when a marriage, if any, will be staged . . . Miss Hepburn and Mr. Hughes apparently have decided it would not be good theatre to tip-off the finale."

That much of Kate's affair with Hughes was indeed "theatre" doesn't mean real feelings weren't involved. Their telegrams to each other reveal authentic passion behind the headlines. The diamond-and-sapphire jardiniere brooch Hughes gave her may have been showy, but it was heartfelt. Yet relationships between public figures are rarely spontaneous combustions. There's a meeting, a recognition of the mutual benefits of coming together, and then the relationship begins. Still, it's remarkable how strong and passionate that recognition of mutuality can be, especially for people with "wild desires to be famous." Together, they realize, they can rule the world.

From there it is but a quick somersault into being in love—exhilarating, intoxicating, even sexually arousing. It's actually quite believable that when Hepburn spoke of Hughes to Scott Berg, she'd glow with the remembrance of "the lustiest relationship of her life." No one else ever called up such "a glint in her eye," Berg said. That's because Hughes, more than any other man, had made her dreams come true.

Whether their affair was actually sexual is, as ever, a matter of opinion. Berg clearly thought it was, and others agreed. "I think [Hughes] was the one she had the most passion for," said James Prideaux. Certainly the aviator had a "ladykiller" reputation, and it seems unlikely that he'd have stuck around for as long as he did if he'd never scored some intimacy. That Kate may have overcome her dislike of sexual intercourse speaks volumes about her passion for Hughes.

Of course, Hughes had his own problems in that department. Despite his lothario image, he was often impotent, if the stories told by several of his girlfriends, as recorded by Hughes's biographers, are to be believed. Some of these other women coaxed him along to achieve the desired result, but Kate likely wouldn't have minded his inability to perform. Some friends concluded that, for much of the time at least, the relationship with Hughes stopped just short of intercourse. "Between her reluctance and his ineptitude, I'd say there was probably little actual sex," said one close associate of Hepburn's.

Besides, said Elliott Morgan, who knew the aviator in the 1930s, Hughes, like Putnam, was never entirely faithful. "There were always other women for Howard," Morgan said. "He would certainly never have felt deprived if he wasn't getting any from Hepburn."

There were also, possibly, other men. Yet again, the pattern holds for Katharine Hepburn's male lovers. Stories of Hughes dallying with his airline mechanics have long persisted among Hollywood's gay underground, although there is no real evidence for them. At least one female lover, the socialite Brenda Frazier, declared Hughes had homosexual tendencies, but that was based on his inability to perform sexually with her. All that can be said with certainty is that Hughes was quite comfortable in the gay subculture. Often spotted at B.B.B.'s Cellar in Hollywood, a drag club with a regular gay clientele, Hughes was part of a sophisticated Hollywood crowd, from Tallulah Bankhead to Clifton Webb, which openly partook of the "pansy nightlife," as the *Hollywood Reporter* called it.

Yet no matter the particulars of his sex life with Kate, there's no question that the relationship between them was romantic and passionate. Indeed, their desire for each other burns through their telegrams even now. From the Bahamas, Hughes wired that he missed Kate "too damned much." Desperate to return to her, he called himself "an impudent and . . . slightly demented young fool." Wiring her after the *Jane Eyre* company had moved on to Kansas City, he told her to expect a telephone call: "[F]orgive me if I should awaken you with only a second to say what you already know so well." Another cable, arriving for her debut in Cleveland, stood in for "one large, luscious, hand-picked, personally selected magnolia with extra special smell," Hughes said, since customs officials in Nassau wouldn't allow him to send her flowers.

And then this, on February 16: "Would you care to know what takes place in my mind as the rattler rattles on? A sample then. How dreadful I like your everyday use of curse words normally considered so violently expressive and your saving for special occasion, I hope, my little 'gee whiz.' " ("Gee whiz" was Kate's endearing final line in *Alice Adams*.)

With her curse words and free spirit, Kate had left Hughes entranced, and the feeling was mutual. "Certainly I felt that I was madly in love with him," Hepburn remembered. But while Hughes thought little about leaving behind Ginger Rogers—or Ida Lupino or Nancy Belle Bayly, other women he'd squired around in the weeks before Hepburn—Kate had a few more qualms about what she'd left abruptly unfinished. In a name: Jack Ford.

"My dear miss Katharine," Ford wrote on January 16, "I am looking forward with great anticipation to the day I see you again so that I may give you the goddamnest kick in the ass you have ever received and which you so richly deserve."

He was joking. Ford, in fact, was still unaware at this point of how close Kate and Hughes had become. He did not know, at that very moment, that the aviator was gearing up his plane so he could fly back East and work his way to Kate's side. Rather, Ford's "goddamnest kick" was his tongue-in-cheek response to Kate's cable to him that same day, thanking him for the gift of winter underwear. (Chicago was in the midst of a deep chill.) She'd kidded him that next time she'd really prefer "one-hundred percent wool." Signing the telegram "Love and Kisses," it seems she hadn't yet told Ford a thing about Hughes.

Turned out, she didn't need to. A few days later, like everyone else in the country, Ford picked up a newspaper to read all about the frenzy in Chicago over the Hepburn-Hughes marriage rumors. There, in stark black and white, were photos of the lovebirds departing (separately of course) from the Ambassador East Hotel. County Clerk Flynn, still spiffed up in his tweed jacket and bow tie after three days of waiting, was heard griping, "I wish those two would make up their minds. Are they or aren't they? I want some peace around here."

Jack Ford wouldn't have minded a little peace himself. Clearly hurt by Kate's actions, but unwilling to admit it up front, he wrote an ironic letter pretending to be a suitor of Emily Perkins's, thrown over for a sailor who he claimed had a "girl in every port"—a clear reference to Hughes. When he got no response, Ford tried phoning, but Kate avoided his call, leaving Em to write to "Shoney" and make excuses.

"I know you are cross with baby," Em wrote, explaining that Kate had been unavailable to take his call because she was in an important meeting with the Guild. "I know you are too cross to write her again," Em told Ford, "but this is the truth." Encouraging the director to try one more time, Kate's companion seemed to be championing Ford, who'd been so attentive to her, against Hughes. "We miss your letters," Em insisted.

An exchange of amusing telegrams followed, with Kate calling Ford "Wee Willie Winkie." The tone of the cables suggests the two did speak and make some peace. Ford then wrote what Kate called "the best letter I've ever had from anyone"—though, unfortunately, Ford did not keep a copy of it in his files. Whatever he wrote, however, touched Kate deeply enough to force her to address head-on what was happening in her life.

"I can only say," she wrote to Ford, "that I am facing (and have been for a time) the first crisis in my life." In attempting to assuage Ford's pain, she was exaggerating a bit—certainly there had been many crises before. But nonetheless there was truth to her words. Closing in on her thirtieth birthday, Kate's dilemma was existential. She wanted to make sure, she said, that "the next thirty [years] fit with the last."

The loneliness that had come through in the interview with Schallert was no passing thing. Hughes was filling up a very real void in her life, though her conscience was torn by how Ford might feel. "I don't want to become a mess," she continued in her letter to the director. He had given her strength and understanding, she said, and he'd always be her dearest friend. As gently as she could, Kate was trying to explain that her ardor for him had evolved into something else. "I know that you do understand me," she added. "Please do always, because a lot of what I'm planning looks very odd in my mind's eye."

What was she planning to do that seemed so "very odd"? What was she asking Ford to understand? If we look at her actions over the next several months, she would become increasingly public with her relationship with

Hughes—something she'd never done before with anyone. Given the status of her film career, there was likely some professional calculation to her actions. But there's also the hint of something more personal going on. While calling her situation a "crisis" may have been her way of soothing Ford's feelings, assuring him she hadn't thrown him over cavalierly, it might also suggest that, at thirty, Kate was looking down the corridor of her own mortality for the first time. Was the rest of her life going to be like the last several years? Alone and lonely? Or might she listen to the cries of all those fans in the streets of Chicago and marry Howard Hughes?

Later, she'd claim she *never* wanted to marry Hughes, and no doubt part of her did hold on to that sense of herself, that she was not the sort of woman for whom marriage made sense. But in her memoir there's also the suggestion that, however briefly, she did toy with the idea—the point when all of their antics "came right down to 'What do we do now?'" That deliberation seems to have occurred here, in March 1937, referenced in her letter to Ford. To be Mrs. Howard Hughes—the idea was heady. What heights they might scale together.

And she was, after all, "madly" in love with him. There were far worse futures than being married to a man she admired this much. Hughes's enormous wealth had allowed him to chart his own singular path through life, to indulge his iconoclasm and feed his inexhaustible yen for fame. He took risks, defied convention, broke rules, and shattered records. Howard Hughes was, in short, cut from the same cloth as Katharine Hepburn.

Not since Leland had she had this much fun. Flying in Hughes's seaplane over Long Island Sound, she'd suddenly announce she wanted to take a swim. Howard would land the plane on the water, dropping the anchor while Kate stripped off her clothes and jumped into the sea from the wing. Over the course of the next several months, she'd hop into whatever plane Hughes happened to be flying that day. Sometimes she'd find herself in Newport for the boat races, or up in Maine to see Em Perkins's family, or on a private Long Island estate. Once she and Howard island-hopped through the Caribbean.

After more than a decade of the playboy life, Hughes was ready to give it all up and marry Kate. At thirty-two, he was still, at heart, a lovesick little boy. He clung to this strong, free-willed woman who was so unlike the gum-snapping skirts he'd been chasing for the last ten years. Indeed, the women who truly mattered in Howard Hughes's life were always those who were strong enough to play caretaker, standing in for the beloved mother who'd died when he was sixteen. Even now, there were flashes of the mental illness that engulfed him late in life. Overcome by a bout of paranoia, Hughes would sometimes refuse to meet with a group of officials who had gathered to greet him, hiding in the dark of his room. Kate would have to tiptoe into the darkness, crouch beside him, and whisper a few sentences into his ear. Only then would she be able to gently coax him outside. When he'd drink too much and start to cry, she'd convince him he was the strongest, bravest hero in the world, and for a while, he'd believe her. It seemed her life calling was to boost the egos of fragile men.

Once again, Hepburn rose to the occasion when a man she loved was faced with "the endless life struggle," the generic catchphrase she'd use, time and time again, to describe the personal torment of all of her men. Like John Ford before him and Spencer Tracy afterward, Hughes was simply too "sensitive," Kate insisted, to deal with what life had to offer. Tracy's agony she'd blame on his son's deafness; Hughes's problems, she believed, were due to his own. "Howard's deafness finally did him in," she said, blaming the aviator's hearing problems for eventually turning him into an "oddball." Finding simplistic answers to problems was always her way. By avoiding deep introspection, she could ignore the larger, more pervasive conflicts that kept Ford, Hughes, and Tracy in eternal turmoil.

It's no surprise, then, that Hughes would want this strong, vital, mother figure to marry him, to commit to taking care of him for the rest of his life. And when he wasn't stricken with his obsessions and paranoia, he seemed Hepburn's ideal mate as well. In the spring of 1937, Kate was faced with two decisions: whether to marry Hughes and whether to take *Jane Eyre* to Broadway. She eventually made the choice to do neither, and in both cases, her reasoning was the same.

On the road, *Jane Eyre* was a hit. The box office had exceeded the Theatre Guild's hopes; the play smashed all road-show records by pulling in $340,000 by the end of its run. Provincial critics might have withheld their highest praise, pointing out the flaws inherent in the script, but most were awed by Kate's movie-star fame and overflowed with personal accolades for her. Kate knew, however, that critical quibbles in Cleveland and Kansas City would be turned into headline-making condemnation in New York. The Guild put out the story, not entirely false, that it had kept the show on the road because it could make more money that way. With Kate due back in Hollywood on May 1, there was no time for a Broadway premiere, though the Guild hinted she might return to the show for a New York opening in the fall. Her old nemesis Edwin Schallert, however, voiced what many were thinking: that Hepburn was clearly not confident enough "to risk the critical darts and arrows" of the New York critics. He was right. She was quitting while she was ahead.

The same could be said of her decision not to marry Hughes. Why mess with a good thing? Why allow marriage to ruin the good run they'd been enjoying so far? In an unusually reflective letter to Jack Ford soon after *Jane Eyre* ended, as she and Em enjoyed a few days of holiday in Florida and the islands, Kate wrote: "[W]here human relations, of a passionate nature, are involved . . . one must say yes or no, but not maybe. Maybe is a feeble way of saying no . . . Clarity is a necessity as everyone gets so mixed up, they don't know what is important to them. I used to be a great exponent of clarity and I shall try to be again."

Not only was she telling Ford that their relationship was definitely over; she was also coming to the conclusion that she had to say no to Hughes's offer of marriage as well. No doubt, as she wrote that letter, she was on her way to see him: she was planning to visit Jamaica and Nassau, she told Ford, where we know Hughes had arrived sometime before. (In Nassau, Kate began to paint, which became a favorite pastime; her earliest paintings, of Nassau Harbor, date from this period.)

Whether she gave Hughes her final answer then or at some point thereafter, her decision seems to have been accepted with equanimity. Their relationship continued, to the enjoyment of both. Hughes kept his Kate; indeed, when she returned to Hollywood, she'd live in his house. Meanwhile, Hepburn was able to continue coasting along on the publicity their romance generated, keeping her name in the news and her face on the covers of fan magazines. Indeed, her connection to Hughes likely provided the heft she needed to snatch top billing away from Ginger Rogers in her next picture, an adaptation of the Broadway hit *Stage Door*, even though Rogers had been the more reliable moneymaker for the studio.

Hughes even accompanied her back to Hartford to meet her family. Hep and Kit clearly preferred the single, Episcopalian Hughes to the married, Catholic Ford, even if he antagonized them by his use of the telephone, missing out on their roundtable discussions.

His phobia of germs also puzzled the family. At the time, Fenwick had only outdoor showers, and Hughes recoiled at the thought of washing himself on sand only a few yards from the shore. To accommodate him, Kate paid for the house's only indoor shower to be installed. Problem was, she didn't lock the door. The weekend of Howard's visit, her sister Marion had also invited her fiancé, Ellsworth Grant. With Grant came two of his friends from Harvard, Tom Calhoun and Caspar Weinberger, later U.S. secretary of defense.

"The Hepburns were in an uproar," Calhoun recalled, "because Kate's friend Howard was coming." Weinberger, unaware that the shower was reserved for a guest far more privileged than he, stepped onto its sparkling clean tile and turned on the water. "All of a sudden comes this woman's voice," Calhoun remembered. " 'Who the hell is in the shower?' The voice was Kate's, and she took off like a Roman candle. 'Get out, get out, get out! That's for Howard!' And there was Caspar throwing all those germs down the drain."

Though the Hepburns may have preferred Hughes to Ford, that didn't mean the world-famous aviator could measure up to Kate's ex-husband. Bob Hepburn said the legends are true that Luddy, still present at most family gatherings, filmed home movies of Hughes as he played golf on the Fenwick green. Finally, Hughes glared up and told Luddy he was interrupting his concentration. Removing his pipe, Hep came to his former son-in-law's defense. "Howard," he said, "Luddy has been taking pictures of all of us for many years before you joined us and he will be taking them long after you've left. Go ahead. Drive. You need a seven iron." In a fury, Howard complied—and sunk the shot in two.

"Not bad in a pinch," Kate remembered.

While Martin Scorsese's film about Hughes may have condensed several of his visits to Fenwick into one, the spirit of the sequence was true. Hughes couldn't wait to get out of there. Far better to have Kate on his own turf. Moving into his mansion at 211 Muirfield Road in Los Angeles, Kate took over the suite once occupied by Hughes's wife. Much has been made of their living together, yet it was really two different households. They never shared a bedroom. Even with his wife, Hughes had maintained separate living quarters. It was simply a practical and convenient arrangement. Kate needed a place to stay in Los Angeles while she made the next two films on her contract, and Hughes, with all the space in the world, suggested she move in. So she did—complete with her own maid, chauffeur, and cook, not to mention the ever-present Em Perkins.

Each side (and their staffs) struggled to maintain a sense of independence and authority. Kate and Howard took to calling each other "Boss," an affectionate nod to their debate over who was the true head of the household. Of course, living with either Hughes or Hepburn would never be easy for anyone. It helped that Hughes was gone much of the time, planning his next flight. And when he *was* in town, he wasn't always with Kate. In May, he was spotted with the actress Grace Bradley; two days later, he showed up at a party at Henry Wilcoxon's estate in Triunfo Canyon with both Bradley *and* Hepburn.

No matter their jostling for control of the household, their bond remained strong. When storms in March 1938 produced flooding throughout southern California and sewer mains were found to be leaking, Hughes, in Nassau, wired Kate not to drink anything but "bottled Arrowhead or Poland water." If she wasn't feeling well, she shouldn't go to work, he insisted. "Miss you terribly," he signed the cable. "Love, Boss."

Just as their joint household would prompt considerable overheated comment from the various Hepburn chroniclers, so too were Kate's departures from Muirfield heralded as the "beginning of the end" of their affair. Not so. In fact, Kate always left Hollywood between films. After she finished *Stage Door,* the latest picture on her contract, she flew back to New York to finally buy her rented house on Forty-ninth Street (for ten dollars and "other good and valuable consideration"). She then returned to Muirfield to make *Bringing Up Baby* for Howard Hawks in late 1937. By early 1938, her long hiatus between films had begun, so staying in Los Angeles was pointless. There was no dramatic break when she left Muirfield for the last time, as Scorsese's film depicts. She simply packed up and left, as she had all of her previous temporary addresses in Hollywood.

As Hughes was preparing for his historic round-the-world flight, the one that would climax with Hepburn at the controls swooping under the Fifty-ninth Street Bridge, Kate was at Fenwick, lounging on the rocks and canoeing through the marshes. She told Jack Ford that she planned to remain at her family's beach house "until his nibs leaves for his great adventure." From Paris, Moscow, and various stops across Siberia, Hughes telephoned Kate at Fenwick, where most houses still had party lines. The Hepburns' ring was one long, three short. Neighbors picked up when they heard this telltale sound, eavesdropping on the aviator reporting in from across the globe.

When word came that Hughes had made his last stop in Minneapolis, Kate instructed her driver, Charles Newhill, to take her into New York. Pushing through the crowds that had assembled outside her building in the early afternoon of July 14, Kate didn't seem resentful. Rather, she too was caught up in all the excitement. Setting her radio at the window, she adjusted the volume loud enough so that the crowd below could follow the late-breaking developments. At exactly 2:37 p.m., Hughes landed his twin-engine Lockheed 14 at Floyd Bennett Field. A mob of admirers immediately rushed the plane, bearing the unshaven, greasy aviator over to a platform where he was officially welcomed by Mayor La Guardia.

"Seven million New Yorkers," the mayor said, his voice floating from Kate's radio out over Forty-ninth Street, "offer congratulations for the greatest record established in the history of aviation." The mob cheered as Hughes accepted the praise with a shrug and a few simple words. After a round of press interviews, he snuck away, causing much consternation among officials, who weren't quite through with him yet. According to legend, he hailed a cab to take him to Hepburn's house, but as he neared her block he realized the crowds had anticipated his move. He went instead to the Drake Hotel and crawled into bed, alone and exhausted.

The next day, the city went mad. Driven down Broadway in an open car amid a constant shower of ticker tape, Hughes was cheered by more than a million people lining the sidewalks and hanging from windows. It reminded many of the city's freewheeling days before the crash of 1929—giving hope that the long national nightmare of the Depression really was coming to an end. But for a man of Hughes's idiosyncrasies, such public hysteria was nerve-wracking. Biting and licking his lips, constantly removing his hat and putting it back on, he was anxious to be done with it, despite how much he loved the adulation.

When it was over, he hurried to Laura Harding's, where he and Kate finally had some time alone. It was the pinnacle of their fame together. Nothing could possibly top this. It was also the end. They didn't know it, but when Hughes left for Washington, D.C., on July 19, it was, in effect, for good.

Just a short time before, Kate had roared onto the RKO lot driving an old Ford beach wagon with wood-paneled sides. On the running board, risking her million-dollar legs, was Ginger Rogers, laughing uproariously with her *Stage Door* costar over some private joke. Screeching to a halt in front of one of the soundstages, the two actresses hurried inside, followed by a menagerie of barking dogs. Hoping to nab a "scoop," Gladys Hall, a writer from *Modern Screen,* waited for the girls to reappear. When they did, they were still laughing and chattering together. Kate slid back behind the wheel of the car and Ginger once again hung on to the side. Into a cloud of dust they disappeared as Kate zoomed off, ignoring the five-miles-per-hour limit for driving on the lot. But not before Gladys Hall had written it all down in her reporter's notebook.

This carefree little scene was no doubt staged by the studio, intended to give the lie to stories of a feud between Hepburn and Rogers. Rumors were rife during production of *Stage Door* that the plebeian Rogers, a former flame of Howard Hughes, had clashed with her patrician costar Hepburn, who supposedly resented Rogers's inclusion in the film as box-office insurance. Making the rounds was a delicious story of Kate tossing a glass of water on Rogers's mink coat, snarling, "If it's real mink, it won't shrink." According to Gladys Hall, who attempted to defuse the story in 1937, the water had been spilled by accident by a studio exec, and the remark was made by Ginger, not Kate. Still, it was one of those stories so good it refused to die. Nearly fifty years later, Rogers even repeated it in her memoir. Whether or not the story was true, Rogers had obviously come to believe it was.

The two stars' animosity worked to the film's advantage, however. Their characters, both aspiring actresses in a theatrical boardinghouse, detest each other at first sight. Playing up their feud could only heighten interest in the film, an adaptation of the Broadway smash starring another of Kate's rivals, Margaret Sullavan. Indeed, Sullavan's excellent reviews in the part ratcheted up the pressure on Hepburn: not only did she need a hit picture; she needed to beat the critical bar set by Sullavan. It was a big task. For the first time since *A Bill of Divorcement*, Kate was working as part of an ensemble. Each member of the cast had her moment to shine: Gail Patrick, Andrea Leeds (who actually won an Oscar), Lucille Ball, Eve Arden, Ann Miller, Constance Collier. And Ginger Rogers's part, as written, was equally as important as Kate's.

That didn't sit well with Hepburn. She'd recall flipping through the script and thinking, "What the hell is going on here?" Ginger, as the wisecracking chorus girl, was clearly intended to grab the sympathy of the audience; Kate, as the arrogant debutante, would be far less likable. Rather than make a fuss, she said, she simply went along with everything the director Gregory La Cava told her to do: "I had brains enough to shut up, and he handed me the whole end of the picture."

La Cava, who'd risen to the top rank of directors with Carole Lombard's screwball comedy *My Man Godfrey* the year before, seemed smitten with Kate. "To win her," he mused, "to beat down that proud, impervious hauteur, is a challenge only the most virile and dominant male could afford to take up. That's the sort of man who should play opposite her . . . and if he were strong enough to make her melt—oh!—that would be worth filming. She's never had a leading man like that. They've always let her be the master."

That formula, of course, would eventually figure mightily into the Hepburn legend, but La Cava, much to his regret, had no virile, dominant costar playing against Kate—unless one counts Ginger Rogers. History has, however, proven La Cava wrong. While the box office would indeed respond to a dominant male melting the impervious Hepburn, the truly worthwhile filming of Kate's career was being done right here by La Cava himself. *Stage Door*, with brilliant dialogue from Morrie Ryskind and Anthony Veiller and crackling, straightforward performances from its ensemble cast, was Kate's finest picture to date.

She is superb. Crisp, confident, she has the courage to lampoon her own shortcomings, mocking the "monotone" she was often criticized for using on stage. Playing on the heavy melodramatics of *The Lake* in the play-within-the-film, Kate gives us as close a rendition of her performance in that disaster as we're ever going to get. We watch as she delivers the immortal line "The calla lilies are in bloom again" in a grating, amateur manner until, moved by Andrea Leeds's death, she says it beautifully and convincingly. It is a wonderful demonstration of Hepburn's own acting prowess by 1937. Her range might be limited, but she could be very, very good when playing close to her own life.

"I'm beginning to feel there must be something definitely wrong with me," she says at one point in the film, after the other girls have turned their backs on her. "You're different, that's all," Leeds tells her prophetically. "They'll get to understand you after a while."

True—but not quite soon enough for RKO. *Stage Door* did well in its first weeks of release but dropped sharply during the holidays. It was too sophisticated for the masses, too New York for Peoria. Its humor was the oh-so-dry urban variety: HEPBURN: "And I use the right knife and fork, I hope you don't mind." ROGERS: "All you need is the knife." What Kate really needed was a picture where she could connect with the heartland.

Pan Berman's first idea was to pair her once more with Rogers in an adaptation of Kate Douglas Wiggin's play and novel *Mother Carey's Chickens*. A sentimental turn-of-the-century tale of two sisters who survive family hardships and make their way in the world, the film was perfect for mainstream appeal. Ginger had been announced for the part as early as June 1936; Kate was mentioned as her costar during the production of *Stage Door*. Although the Hepburn legend would later insinuate that this was a B picture (and therefore beneath Kate's standards), there was no way the studio would have put Rogers, its top-ranked female star, in an inferior vehicle. If Hepburn objected, it was probably due to the fact that it was another ensemble project and she wanted to be front and center again.

So Berman pulled out his next idea: a film based on a short story in *Collier's* called "Bringing Up Baby." It was the tale of a screwball rich girl who loses a tame panther in her upscale Connecticut neighborhood. Nothing like a couple of pratfalls to loosen up the studio's haughty ice queen, Berman thought, and Kate agreed, noting the popular success Carole Lombard and Irene Dunne had had in the screwball genre. Assigned to write the screenplay was Jack Ford's buddy Dudley Nichols, and Cary Grant was brought back as costar. As director, Berman enlisted Howard Hawks, who'd helmed *Scarface* for Howard Hughes. It seemed the ideal team.

As good as she was in *Stage Door*, Hepburn is a revelation in *Bringing Up Baby*. Her Susan Vance goes beyond anything she'd done on-screen before. Here we get the goofball she could be in real life among her closest friends, when she snuck out on the town in male drag with Palache or broke into dinner parties with Laura and Leland. In *Bringing Up Baby*, she is madcap, manic, irrepressible—and yet, as one critic pointed out, so utterly reasonable in her arbitrariness, so Harpo Marxian, that she seems almost surreal.

In *Sylvia Scarlett*, the chemistry with Cary Grant had largely been wasted, diverting her with the less interesting Brian Aherne. Here Grant and Hepburn bounce off each other like rubber balls. Nichols's dialogue is fast and furious, and the stars deliver it with overlapping ardor. (GRANT: "Susan, you have to get out of this apartment!" HEPBURN: "I can't, I have a lease.") Later, when Baby the leopard (changed from a panther) gets loose, a panicky Grant tells Kate: "Now, don't lose your head." To which Hepburn, with utter deadpan logic, replies, "I've got my head. I've lost my leopard!"

Still later, in an ad-libbed scene, we get a wonderful glimpse of the off-screen imp Hepburn could be—a moment of Kath instead of Kate. Limping after she's lost the heel of one shoe, she says, more to herself than anyone else, "I was born on the side of a hill," then cracks up at the quip. It's one of the most endearing moments in the film.

Hepburn enjoyed the production, gamely climbing into the leopard's cage for one scene. When the swinging tabs on her skirt drove the big cat a bit crazy, the trainer had to whip it away from springing at her. Impersonating a gangster moll ("Swinging Door Susie") was a kick, even if her nasal Brooklynese still sounded very New England. And although her friend Noel Taylor said she never much cared for Cary Grant in later life, probably reflecting Cukor's low opinion of the man (not the actor), here Kate was thrilled by Grant's playing and the ease with which they worked together.

Yet for all this goodwill, the film bombed. "If you've never been to the movies," Frank Nugent declared in the *New York Times*, "*Bringing Up Baby* will be all new to you—a zany-ridden product of the goofy farce school. But who hasn't been to the movies?"

Nugent's review—a brief, dismissive few paragraphs intended to convey the unimportance of the picture—set the tone for the "official" response to *Baby* in the press. By the middle of March, just two weeks after the film's release, conventional wisdom held that Hawks's picture was old hat, part of a declining genre, one that had peaked a full year earlier with *The Awful Truth* and *Nothing Sacred*. In syndicated question-and-answer columns, fans were weighing in against screwball comedies: "Maybe I'm just a crank, but I think it's getting unbearably silly." The columnist Ed Sullivan asked his readers what was next: the dignified Edna May Oliver tossing a custard pie?

By March 21, the prevailing opinion against Hepburn and *Baby* had spread across the country, with Norbert Lusk opining in the *Los Angeles Times* that RKO had made a mistake in casting the star in a "goofy comedy." Repeat something often enough and it becomes the truth. After that, there was no way to salvage *Bringing Up Baby*. Although no evidence exists, the legend insists that Howard Hughes, with whom Kate was still sharing a house, stepped in to pay for the film's continued distribution after RKO threatened to pull it from theaters. Even if true, it did little good. The film lost more than $300,000 for the studio.

Bringing Up Baby would eventually become a favorite of film buffs. But in 1938, it was a dud. Everyone concerned was mystified. Here they'd been urged to bring Hepburn down a peg, to show her warm, human, funny side—and the picture had flopped. Clearly, they'd jumped on board the screwball craze too late. Although a few classics in the genre would still be made, the vogue was now for spicy, adult comedies like *The Women*. Just as when she'd clung to a pre-Code persona in 1934, Hepburn was once again out of step with the times. RKO decided it could do no more.

Across town, Bette Davis had gone on suspension from Warners for refusing to play in substandard pictures and was roundly applauded for her courage and integrity. Desiring a similar spin for her exit from RKO, Hepburn would tell Lupton Wilkinson a few years later that it was the prospect of *Mother Carey's Chickens* that had forced her out. It was a story that, like so many others, would be repeated over and over until it was gospel. Kate never mentioned that the film had been planned as a big-budget vehicle for her and Ginger Rogers. Rather, with its cornpone title conjuring up images of Ma and Pa Kettle, the picture was presumed by many readers to have been a low-budget programmer. Of *course* the Great Hepburn would refuse such a part. Like Bette Davis, she was a *serious* actress. She had *standards*.

The truth was that by the time *Bringing Up Baby* had been released in March, Joan Bennett and Anne Shirley had already been cast in *Mother Carey's Chickens*. Although Bennett withdrew sometime in early April, Hepburn couldn't have been seriously considered to replace her, at least not for very long. By April 22, she had left the studio.

Kate would insist she paid RKO $220,000 to buy back her contract. Although such a payment is not indicated in her studio files, it's probably true, as the studio would hardly walk away empty-handed. What the files do include is her debt for $22,740.43—overtime pay for *Bringing Up Baby*. To cancel out this last obligation, Kate admitted she placed a call to Hartford and asked her father to send a check. She wasn't going to put up a fight like Bette Davis. She just wanted to be done with it, and with her means and privilege, she could be.

Anxious to get away from movies for a while and plan a new stage vehicle with the Theatre Guild, Kate was just as glad as the studio to call it quits. In fact, her departure from RKO might have been treated as rather routine by historians had an advertisement not been placed a week later in the *Hollywood Reporter* by the Independent Theater Owners' Association. On May 3, B. B. Kahane, Pan Berman, and the other RKO brass opened the trade paper to the headline WAKE UP! They went on to read a tirade bashing the studios for keeping stars "whose public appeal is negligible [while] receiving tremendous salaries." The irate exhibitors named names: Dietrich. Garbo. Crawford. Mae West. Katharine Hepburn.

That day, after two weeks of sitting on the story, RKO announced that Hepburn's contract had been terminated. It was the studio's way of assuring the exhibitors, angry over being forced to show films even "when they drive people away from the box office," that at least they wouldn't have to worry about Katharine Hepburn anymore.

In her six years in Hollywood, Kate had been called many things. Now, there was one more, the most damning of all: "Box office poison."

THEY SAY SHE'S A HAS-BEEN

Just a few moments into the second act of *The Philadelphia Story*, onstage at the Shubert Theatre on Broadway, Joseph Cotten, playing C. K. Dexter Haven, bounds out to confront his ex-wife, the socialite Tracy Lord, played by Katharine Hepburn. He lashes out at her, accusing her of not being tolerant enough of him, insisting that whatever abuse she may have suffered at his hands was her own damn fault. His drinking, his carousing—she'd simply been impatient with "any kind of human imperfection." It is *she,* therefore, who is responsible for the breakup of their marriage. He bears no culpability whatsoever.

Her long red hair falling seductively to her shoulders, sheathed in a white dress that hung delicately down her lithe, feminine body, Hepburn did not play Tracy as she'd played Jo March or Susan Vance. Either of those two hell-cats would have responded with their trademark, diaphragmatic "Heeey!" and charged the bully in their own self-defense. Instead, as the brittle, haughty, glamorous Tracy, Hepburn played her next few scenes on the verge of tears. When her father, played by Nicholas Joy, reproached her for being a bad daughter, for lacking "an understanding heart," she stuttered and muttered and ran her hands through her hair. It was *her* fault, her father tells her, that he cheated on her mother—*her* fault that he neglected his family. If he'd had "the *right* kind of daughter . . . one who loves him blindly," he wouldn't have had to go off in search of love. Even Alice Adams wouldn't have taken such abuse. But as Tracy Lord, Kate simply breaks down and cries.

A roaring, cheering, standing ovation greeted her when it was all through. *The Philadelphia Story* was sold out for weeks, and the critics—*the New York critics*—loved her. Brooks Atkinson, who five years earlier had said Hepburn was "not a full-fledged dramatic actress yet," now celebrated her "grace, jauntiness and warmth." She moved across the stage, Atkinson said, "like one who is liberated from self-consciousness."

From the chrysalis of the last year Kate had indeed emerged a different creature. Taking her lumps onstage was worth it—if it meant standing alone in front of the curtain, basking in the waves of applause and affection from the audience.

Philip Barry had written the play with her in mind, having spent weeks at Fenwick observing her and her family and the constant parade of friends and associates passing through. Indeed, Tracy Lord *is* Kate Hepburn, even if she's a far cry from Kath or Jimmy. But Barry never knew his star's alter egos. All he knew was the aggressively ambitious Kate—who could not tolerate being called box-office poison for long, who was determined to get back on top, who hadn't spent more than a decade fighting and grappling with fame only to watch it slip away through her fingers.

That's what it had been, one long fight, and Kate was weary of fighting. Once before she'd set her mind to come back, to do what was needed to secure her fame. She'd made compromises. She'd played the game. But always she'd held back just a little part of herself, never fully giving in. It was the part of her that had felt called to make *Sylvia Scarlett*, the part that couldn't go through with actually marrying Howard Hughes. But such reticence, Kate seemed to believe now, had held her back from the heights. Now she was ready to push on full speed ahead and this time get it right. For keeps.

It had been a long road to the applause at the Shubert Theatre. A year before, when a reporter had confronted Kate about the "box-office poison" label, she had tried to play nonchalant. "They say I'm a has-been," she said. "If I wasn't laughing so hard I might cry."

She insisted she had five better offers than the deal she'd had at RKO, but she was lying. Despite the fact that Joan Crawford was also on the box-office-poison list, MGM had just renewed her contract for more than a million dollars. To Hepburn, however, the studio offered just $10,000 for a one-picture deal. Later, the legend would tell stories of Hepburn and Marlene Dietrich bantering over which of them was *more* poison at the box office. But privately Kate was not amused. It bothered her terribly, her friends and her brother Bob recalled. She was determined to make the exhibitors eat their words.

First, she faced an immediate problem, one not shared by Crawford or Dietrich. She had a picture to promote. Just a few weeks after the box-office-poison gambit in the *Hollywood Reporter*—which of course had generated further headlines in newspapers and magazines throughout the country—Hepburn's film *Holiday* was released. She'd gotten the chance to play the part she'd understudied for so long when George Cukor arranged a loan-out from RKO, soon after production had wrapped on *Bringing Up Baby*. Following her over to the Columbia lot was Cary Grant, who played her love interest once more.

As good as they were in *Baby*, here Hepburn and Grant play together with an intelligence and sexiness Kate never again found with a leading man. In *Holiday*, they both reject a life defined by status and riches, leading a mutiny out of a pretentious party to the playroom upstairs. "Don't make fun of Leopold," Hepburn says, holding up a toy giraffe. "He's very sensitive. Looks like me." Turning in profile to prove it, we see another conflation of real and reel life. In that moment, we see more evidence of the softness under her shell.

Indeed, guided by the trusted hand of George Cukor, Kate made Philip Barry's spunky rich-girl heroine entirely her own, obliterating the memory of Hope Williams in the role. But, like *Bringing Up Baby*, acclaim came only in hindsight. With her name rarely mentioned without the suffix of "box-office poison" these days, Kate watched regretfully as *Holiday* sank even faster than *Bringing Up Baby*. Which meant very quickly indeed.

Columbia didn't give up without a fight, however. Within days of the box-office-posion ad, stories of an "imminent marriage" between Kate and Howard Hughes were suddenly in the news again. Meanwhile, the studio was busy cranking out press releases that declared a "New Hepburn." Two hundred fifty billboards were erected throughout Los Angeles that asked the six-feet-tall question: IS IT TRUE WHAT THEY SAY ABOUT KATHARINE HEPBURN? Of course, the studio was playing coy: lots of things had always been said about Hepburn, and publicists let people wonder just what the billboards meant. Launched just before *Holiday* was released, the campaign was intended to jump-start curiosity about the star, but after six years the public seemed bored by the topic of Katharine Hepburn. In truth, people really didn't care anymore if what they said about her was true.

Critics, however, liked *Holiday* far better than *Bringing Up Baby*; even as tough a sell as Edwin Schallert declared Kate "quite stunning." But audiences stayed away. And in some ways Frank Nugent's review in the *New York Times*, despite its favorable assessment, thrust Kate right back to square one. "The 'New Hepburn,' " Nugent said, was "very mannish."

In the wake of the box-office-poison brouhaha, all of Hepburn's old negative press came roaring back. "She is almost masculine in her indifference to her surroundings," wrote *Modern Screen*, aghast at the lack of interior decoration in her house. In an open letter in *Screenland*, the editor Delight Evans called her "Hep" because it was clear she didn't "want to be a little lady—so why should anyone address you as 'Miss Hepburn'?" Evans went on: "This is just to tell you that what was once sincere admiration has turned to amusement, and not with you but *at* you . . . [T]he astute businesswoman I believe you to be, if not the artist I hoped you were, is seemingly blind to signs and portents. Wear slacks under a mink coat; cover your face if you wish. But you'd better be good on the screen."

And so: enter Philip Barry.

Sitting on the old jetty at Fenwick, their legs dangling above the swampy waters, the actress and the playwright discussed the story at hand. What it needed to say. How Kate—Tracy Lord—would come across. How she might click. How she might *come back*. As Barry set to work writing the play, Kate flew up by seaplane at least once to brainstorm with him at his retreat at Dark Harbor, Maine. Later, when Barry was writing the last act in Hobe Sound, Florida, Kate was in frequent communication with him by phone. In "Sea-Air," Dick Hepburn's rarely read, long-suppressed play about his sister, we see this process quite plainly. The character based on Barry colludes with the character based on Kate, both of them eager to whip up a confection of fluff and pretense.

While Kate and Barry connived in Connecticut, across the country Joan Crawford was battling her own bad press with a very different strategy: by playing the star. "I'd lose ground," she said, "if I ever stopped working for a minute. I've got to improve my own performance to keep faith with my fans . . . I've got to watch my health, my face, my voice, my figure, my carriage, my make-up . . . The only real physical luxury I allow myself is breakfast in bed every Sunday morning. I work with my fan mail all the rest of the day."

If she read that, Hepburn would have blanched. She'd never answered a single fan letter herself in her entire career. Not for her, either, were worries about her figure or her carriage or her makeup. That wasn't how she'd fight this challenge to her fame. Rather, she invited Philip Barry to her family's summer home and got him to write her a play.

Barry had always been enamored by the upper classes. Born to middle-class Irish-Catholic parents in 1896, he'd found himself among the sons of America's Protestant elite at Yale. After graduation, he enrolled in George Pierce Baker's theater workshop at Harvard. *The Jilts,* later retitled *You and I,* one of the plays Barry wrote under Baker's direction, became his first success on Broadway.

Married with two sons, Barry moved easily in his adopted class, living part of the year in a villa in the south of France. Sparkling Broadway come-dies like *Holiday* made him the darling of the American aristocracy. In the last several years, however, Barry had been trying his hand at weightier fare, like his *Hotel Universe* for the Theatre Guild—work that was largely met with failure. His most recent play, *Spring Dance,* for Jed Harris, had run for just twenty-four performances.

Everyone, then, had a stake in the success of *The Philadelphia Story:* Kate, Barry, and the Guild itself, tottering on the brink of financial disaster. Kate felt obliged to return to the Guild after *Jane Eyre.* Although there had been talk Howard Hughes might back her in a play about Amelia Earhart, Kate knew she needed something different. Earhart was too spiky, too androgy-nous. Rather, Kate was drawn to Barry's idea about a wealthy Main Line family whose privacy is invaded by a magazine writer.

Originally, Barry based the beautiful Tracy Lord on the socialite Helen Hope Montgomery, the wife of his friend Edgar Scott, but as the rewrites went on, Tracy became more and more like Kate. Redheaded, hotheaded, she'd been to Bryn Mawr and got naked at the drop of a hat. "Make her like me," Kate instructed, "but make her go all soft." Those may have been the smartest words Katharine Hepburn ever uttered, at least in terms of her career.

In the marshes beyond Fenwick, Kate was desperately trying to keep her ca-noe from tipping over. An offshore breeze had stirred up the waters, and she was yelling and cursing and waving her arms for balance. All at once she looked up and discovered Luddy had caught all her wild gesticulations on film. She threw an oar at him.

It was the summer of 1938, and for the first time in six years, Kate had no schedule. Her time was completely her own. At Fenwick for the summer, in between brainstorming sessions with Barry, she lazed about in an ill-fitting rubber suit on the beach, "getting sunburned and then coming in and get-ting unsunburned." Late afternoons were spent whacking balls with Eve

"Murph" March on the tennis court, swearing nonchalantly whenever she missed a shot—"which is somewhat frequently," one observer said.

For the Fourth of July, the whole borough gathered to watch the fireworks. "Someone dropped a punk into the barrel and the whole thing went off," Kate recalled—rockets whizzing down sidewalks and roman candles exploding through windows.

The next day brought excitement of a different sort. As Fenwickians cheered wildly, Dr. Hepburn won the annual Fourth of July tennis tournament. "Conservative Hartford insurance (Fenwick) has finally accepted us," Kate crowed to Jack Ford. Her sister Peg, however, gave Katty the real credit for "redeeming" the family in the eyes of the world.

Residents of Fenwick, "conservative people who can be trusted to do the well-bred thing in any circumstance," gave Kate plenty of space that summer, her first extended period at home since she'd become an actress. Neighbors, shopkeepers, well-to-do visitors from Hartford all tried not to stare or ask too many questions. "Some of them even feel a little sorry for Mrs. Hepburn," one observer said, "because she has a daughter in the movies."

In and out of Saybrook village Kate breezed, wearing shorts and a kerchief knotted "peasant-style" under her chin. Her only concession to her stardom was her shiny, expensive town car, driven by Charles Newhill as she lounged on the spacious leather backseat. Every now and then she'd poke her head through the open top to wave to a family friend.

For all her insistence on normalcy, however, some things had changed. Practicing her once-famous dives off the pier, she found it took eight tries to get it right. Jimmy Hepburn was out of practice. He was also over thirty. "First I landed on my face with my eyes opened and lacerated my eyeballs with my lashes," Kate lamented to Jack Ford. "Then I landed on my 'bosom' and what was so little has simply disappeared, perhaps never to rise again"— not that she would have spent much time grieving for it.

Howard Hughes visited Fenwick a few times that summer, flying his plane over the golf course and dipping its wings before landing at nearby Essex. Once, when word got out that Hughes was expected, newspaper planes circled over the Hepburn house for hours, infuriating Hep and the neighbors. Hughes, perhaps tipped off, never showed. After his round-the-world flight that July, his visits to Connecticut had in fact become increasingly rare; surely Kate knew he was seeing other women in New York and Hollywood.

Some days she had Newhill take her into the city for a little infusion of cosmopolitan life: dinner with Edna Ferber, a meeting with the Guild, a happy reunion with Palache. But all Kate really wanted to do was hang around Fenwick, enjoying "the summer waves and breezes and burning my nose"—a lovely reverie after six frantic years, even if she'd regret all that sunburning later on. From her brother Dick's room came the constant tapping of typewriter keys. Whether Kate ever poked her head into his room and asked him what he was writing, we don't know—but she'd find out soon enough.

At twenty-six, Richard Hepburn was a dreamy, visionary poet who'd wander for hours along the beach talking to himself as he juggled plots and characters in his head. Retreating to his room, he'd spend days behind closed doors, banging out all his wild ideas on his typewriter. From his father Dick had inherited stunning good looks, and he shared with his elder sister a burning desire for fame. But what Dick lacked was their discipline and determination. While his younger brother Bob was completing his internship at Hartford Hospital, Dick hadn't held a job since graduating from Harvard.

"Dick was from another planet," said his son Kuy. "When it was a beautiful day, he'd say, 'Go take a walk. Don't stay inside and do your work.' That was Dick. Enjoying life, doing what you want. But . . . when you have to pay the rent, you can't take a walk."

Kate recognized Dick's shortcomings, just as twenty years ago she'd recognized Tom's. Once again she became her brother's champion. Every month a stipend for $125 arrived for Dick from Kate's account in order that he might devote all his time to writing. Generous by nature, Dick ended up sharing the money among his bohemian friends—poets and playwrights like himself with big dreams and short résumés, who'd gather for card games and gin drinking and spirited late-night pontifications on the state of the world.

A few years before, Dick had seemed on his way. His play *Behold Your God*, a satire of corporate values, was produced in April 1936 by the acclaimed Hedgerow Theatre in rural Pennsylvania. Although Dick always insisted he'd make it on his own talent, he wasn't shy about exploiting his famous sibling. To Hedgerow director Jasper Deeter, he offered to display busts of both himself and Kate at the theater "in order to bring out the relationship and maybe tap the movie public." In order to drum up interest, he suggested the theater company hint that Kate was flying East to see the play— "a terrible lie," he admitted.

Dick liked to see himself as cut from the same cloth as his sister. In his self-written playwright's biography for *Behold Your God*, he mused, "His family have always been respectable, but his sister and he seem to have broken the spell." Dick often linked himself with Kate in this way. "We are both donkeys to be in this business," he told Deeter. "We both plan to leave it and set up a bakery shop and sell things like Nabiscos and Parcheesi."

He might as well have. *Behold Your God* flopped terribly. "Ineffective satire," chided the *Philadelphia Inquirer*. *Variety* opined, "Even the name of Hepburn as author is unlikely ever to persuade any ambitious producer to give it a Broadway presentation."

Undeterred, Dick kept writing. Holed up in a small New York flat, paid for by Kate, he finished another play, this one about the conquistador Hernan Cortés, but Hedgerow promptly rejected it. Heartbroken, Dick moped around Fenwick, penning pitiful letters to Deeter begging for another chance. Then, after one of Howard Hughes's whirlwind visits, an idea struck him. Fired once more by a burst of creativity, Dick spent the remainder of the summer banging out a new play called "Sea-Air." It concerned a famous actress, Elizabeth Lascelles, who must decide whether or not to marry her aviator beau. Walking in dizzy circles around her are an eccentric ex-husband, a pompous agent, and a snobbish WASP family. It was a quirky house of mirrors: as Kate and Barry were busy fictionalizing Kate's life, Dick was equally hard at work fictionalizing them doing it.

With all that was on Kate's mind that summer, it's a good thing she didn't know exactly what her brother was up to. By late summer, she was in a frenzy over David Selznick's forthcoming production of *Gone With the Wind*, allowing Leland to submit her name as a possible Scarlett O'Hara. Bette Davis had been the presumptive first choice, but now that Warners had taken her out of the running, *Photoplay* was calling Kate's casting "inevitable." The novel's author, Margaret Mitchell, though protesting her neutrality, did admit she thought Kate had "looked pretty in the hoopskirts in *Little Women*." Others blasted the very idea of such a staunch Yankee playing the quintessential southern belle, though with George Cukor set to direct, some thought Hepburn had a lock on the part.

Kate herself wasn't so sure. "*Gone With the Wind* is in again, out again," she wrote to Ford. "I really don't imagine that I'll get it but it is the only interesting thing out there from my point of view." But when she finally met with Selznick, his lack of enthusiasm was obvious. Privately the producer admitted, "The more I see of her, the colder I get on her." Reportedly he told associates he couldn't imagine Clark Gable chasing her all those years. Her ego wounded, Kate backed out before she could be rejected. Howard Hughes relayed her opinion to Selznick that any actress who took the part was "sticking her neck out . . . if she is less than sensational she will get nothing out of it but a lot of criticism." Kate had been hoping all this might lead to a long-term contract with Selznick, so it was a bitter disappointment.

"Everything for me at the moment is at loose ends," she wrote to Jack Ford. "It is impossible to say anything definite." Except for *Gone With the Wind*, her Hollywood prospects had all dried up. "I've probably bitched myself up plenty waiting so long but what I've been offered has been so dull that I couldn't screw myself into accepting."

Everything hinged on what Barry was writing up at Dark Harbor. Pacing around Fenwick, Kate was preoccupied with thoughts of the play. She probably didn't read the newspaper or listen to radio reports about a hurricane that had sideswiped Florida's east coast a few days before. Even if she had, she'd have been reassured that the storm had turned out to sea. On Wednesday, September 21, the weather forecast called for heavy rain. But it was still dry that morning when she played a round of golf with their houseguest, Jack "Red" Hammond, then took a swim. She did notice the wind was getting strong and the waves were rather high. The sand was blowing off the beach, stinging as it hit her face.

Taking refuge inside, Kate and Hammond sat down at the table as Fanny, the cook, served them tea and toast. Kit and Dick came downstairs to join them. (The rest of the family was in West Hartford.) Dick's son Mundy recalled the family lore about what happened next: "The waves were crashing against the windows. My grandmother kept saying, 'Don't worry, it's just another storm.'" All at once a car flew by their window and landed in the lagoon. Then, from below, came a long groan of wood. The house was shifting on its piles. Taking one last sip of tea and replacing the cup in its saucer, Kit looked around the table and said, quite calmly, "Well, I suppose we should move along to higher ground."

In those days before satellite meteorology, no one could have predicted the hurricane of 1938. The extreme storm surge killed at least six hundred people and caused $306 million in damage—about $3.5 billion today. Due to the buffer of Long Island, the Connecticut coastline was spared the enormous tidal wave that engulfed Rhode Island and southeastern Massachusetts, but still the waters of the Sound rose twelve feet above normal. Wind gusts of up to 183 miles per hour flattened houses all along the coast and carried away steeples, factories, farm animals, and automobiles. Those who lived through it described the high pitch of the wind as one long horrible scream.

Climbing out a window, Kate and the others waded knee-deep through the surging waters, taking shelter at an inn safely perched on a hill. Looking back once, they saw their beloved home turn, twist, then float away. In an instant, a whole chunk of Kate's childhood was gone—Jimmy's half-gainers, Tommy's sneakbox races, the Inghams' fishing shack, lazy afternoons on the porch. Later, Kate and her siblings would dig through the sand to recover most of the family silver and china. But everything else was gone.

Except for a copy of "Sea-Air" that Dick had managed to stuff inside his jacket.

For the next ten years, Katharine Hepburn's life would be a story of rebuilding. Rebuilding Fenwick. Rebuilding her career. Rebuilding her personal life. Everything from her private style to her public image would be remade from scratch.

"I think we all come to town from the village with a certain amount of goodies," she'd reflect, looking back. "And when you first get there, everyone wants to buy them . . . And then when you look in and find that the box is practically empty, why then you know you've got to fill it up again somehow."

With *The Philadelphia Story*, Kate's box would be filled to overflowing. She had influenced Barry's words to such a degree that today it seems absurd when any other actress attempts to play the part of Tracy Lord. Tracy isn't really a literary character; she's simply a doppelgänger of Katharine Hepburn, a means to an end. If Barry's play had failed to meet her approval, Kate would have pulled out; she didn't sign a contract with the Guild, in fact, until December 29, 1938, when she was sure Barry had met her requirements. She also insisted on approval over her director. Kate ended up choosing Robert Sinclair because he was strong enough, she said, to keep her from going "well—fancy."

For the reborn Katharine Hepburn, fancy would no longer do. Fancy was highfalutin. Fancy was subversive. Fancy was Sylvia Scarlett and Susan Vance. Fancy women thought they could get away with things, like telling men what to do. In *The Philadelphia Story*, one very fancy woman gets put in her place—by not just one man but three different men. Yet it was this very comeuppance that ensured *The Philadelphia Story* would be "full of the hit atmosphere," as Kate recalled in her peculiar syntax. Audiences seemed to enjoy watching Tracy—Kate—humbled for her past sins of arrogance and indifference. Or self-esteem and independence, depending on one's point of view.

The Philadelphia Story opened in New Haven on February 16, 1939. Critics adored Kate and the play. Good buzz followed the show during subsequent tryouts in Philadelphia, Baltimore, Boston, and Washington. Nelson Bell in the *Washington Post* thought the play was a "personal triumph" for Kate, that her "stock would soar." And unlike the reviews for the Theatre Guild's production of *Jane Eyre*, such praise wasn't couched in qualifications over the script; Barry was hailed as loudly as Kate.

On the basis of this early success, Kate agreed, with some trepidation, to open in New York after just a month of tryouts. Her gamble paid off when *The Philadelphia Story* premiered at the Shubert Theatre on March 16. Summing up the conventional theatrical wisdom, Brooks Atkinson wrote that by "surrender[ing] to the central part in Mr. Barry's play," Hepburn had "at last found the joy she has always been seeking in the theater."

Kate was ecstatic. Noting Tallulah Bankhead's concurrent success in *The Little Foxes,* she wrote to Cukor, "Your girls seem to have redeemed themselves finally." To John Ford she wrote, "For once everything seems to be hunky. I am very happy . . . and slowly recovering from my surprise and pleasure at the reception—so unaccustomed."

The applause echoing up to the rafters after every final curtain convinced her she was on the right track. In Hollywood's classical era, few stars sat in the driver's seat of their careers with as much authority as Kate Hepburn. Even Bette Davis lost her court case against Warners and came back like an indentured servant to sulk her way through a series of substandard pictures. Hepburn, on the other hand, seized control of the reins in late 1938 and never let go. From here on, her career and public image would be carefully planned and maintained by the star herself. Despite her seeming indifference to the star system and all its trappings, Hepburn—having been burned once too often—would spend the rest of her life in single-minded control.

The first stage in her reconstruction was now complete—and a resounding success. She was a hit in New York; her long tilt at the windmills of Broadway was over. She'd achieved the one goal that had always eluded her, one that many had believed unattainable, even foolhardy. Now, having conquered Broadway, some thought Hepburn might remain there, settling in as the new Katharine Cornell perhaps, or as a rival to Helen Hayes. But instead she was looking westward over her shoulder. She had one more score to settle.

Howard Hughes, wisely, had advised her to buy the movie rights to *The Philadelphia Story*. With Hepburn still considered poison at the cinematic box office, producers were sure to snatch up the hit and slap someone else in the lead role. Indeed, Louis B. Mayer had already eyed the play as a vehicle for Norma Shearer. But while Hughes's advice was sound, Kate, out of work, didn't have the immediate cash to purchase the rights. With a millionaire as a beau, however, it hardly mattered. For thirty thousand dollars—pocket change—Hughes bought the rights and presented them to Kate as a gift. After two years of expensive trinkets, it was the most welcome gift he'd ever given to her. It was also his last.

For the past six months, they'd hardly seen each other. After the hurricane, as Kate and her family dug through the sand to salvage a bit of their home, she'd looked up to see a familiar Sikorsky seaplane coming in for a landing. Running over to greet it, she discovered the man whose head poked out of the hatch wasn't Hughes, but one of his pilots, delivering bottled water. Then and there she knew that she and Howard had become friends instead of lovers. "Love had turned to water," she said. "Pure water. But water."

It wasn't an easy acceptance on her part. Always before—with Putnam, Laura, Jane Loring, Jack Ford—the end of the relationship had come from Kate, no matter how mutual the decision ultimately became. With Hughes, she seemed less willing to let go completely. Part of it, as ever, was ego; his dalliances with other women had become public, most notably a brief but tempestuous affair with Bette Davis that autumn. As with her pique over Leland Hayward's marriage, Kate did not appreciate this kick to her public image, especially when she was down—and Davis, who'd claimed the top of the box office (and another Oscar) with *Jezebel*, had taken quite enough from her already.

Yet the distance from Hughes was caused as much by Kate's own self-absorption these past few months as her beau's wandering eye—a fact that left some in her inner circle scratching their heads over her woeful attitude toward the breakup. "I can't understand her behavior," Mimi Doyle wrote to Jack Ford. "She is so upset over the 'Black Prince.' So confusing. Oh, well— you figure it out."

Still, some part of Kate understood her relationship with Hughes had simply run its course. There was nowhere else for them to go. She knew the public expected these things to end in marriage, and she could never give them that kind of happy conclusion. People who want to be famous are really loners, as she'd say—or they *should* be. From the affair with Howard Hughes—the only romance she ever allowed the public to see while it was actually taking place—Hepburn learned she could never again cede control to the gossip writers and newspaper columnists. To be linked romantically again in public would mean enduring another go-round of the marriage questions, for which she knew she'd never be able to give the public the answer they wanted. From now on, then, the perception of Katharine Hepburn would be that she was married to her work.

It would be, at times, a lonely road. Having gotten the last of what she needed from Hughes—the movie rights to the play—Kate withdrew from him. After opening night in Boston, she came back to a waiting telegram calling her "terrific"; but Hughes also expressed the wish she "might say something nice" to him amid all the "cleverness" of her last cable, which had made him feel "lonesome." She doesn't seem to have obliged. The next day he sent her another wire, telling her how much he missed her and how much he was yearning for a reply. Using the nicknames that had characterized their relationship, Kate finally wrote back: "Missing, one Boss. Lonely, one Mouse. Empty, one Conkshell." Immediately, Hughes cabled back, hoping to "remedy empty conkshell situation."

But they were friends now, as Kate said, not lovers, no matter how melancholy and lonely it made the "Mouse" feel. Hughes was soon back to pursuing Ginger Rogers and asking Joan Crawford out on dates. Hughes didn't pine for Kate the way the film *The Aviator* portrayed; within the year, he'd give Rogers an engagement ring. Still, he remained quite fond of this woman who'd offered him such efficient caretaking; when he could, he still enjoyed shuttling her between coasts. Once, in late 1939, he had both Hepburn and Group Theater director Harold Clurman as passengers. When Clurman grew anxious over some turbulence, Hughes told him to look over at Kate, placid and undisturbed by all the bumps and shakes. "I feel better now," Clurman reportedly said. "Nothing can happen to *her.*"

Seven months into the run of *The Philadelphia Story*, Kate was confronted by her brother Dick's urgent demand that she read his new play right away. It was October 1939. Kate had just arrived from New York at the newly rebuilt house at Fenwick, a much grander structure than the previous one. The wood still smelled fresh and new as Kate took the script from Dick's hands and settled down at the dining table to read. It didn't take long for her to let out a shriek that recalled the wind of the hurricane.

"Sea-Air" was far more autobiographical than even *The Philadelphia Story*. Reading it today, we can easily see why Kate's first reaction was horror—and a conviction that her brother was trying to "ruin her life." The lead character is capricious, self-absorbed, and mad for fame. Her father is arrogant and autocratic. The playwright of her latest hit, obviously an alter ego for Philip Barry, is effete and obsequious, eager to do his star's bidding at any cost. The most sympathetic character is the one based on Hughes, who feels at times he has wandered into a house of lunatics.

Red-faced, arms akimbo, Kate called Dick "either a fool or a fiend." She demanded he burn the play. Hep backed her up, shouting "dreadfully." When Dick told them Jasper Deeter at Hedgerow Theatre had expressed interest, Kate hit the roof, calling the producer "another Jed Harris thrilled to spoil her career." Then, her brother said, she wept with shame.

Taking her son aside, Kit explained that "Sea-Air" could hurt Kate's "business relationship with Howard." She admitted, however, that the play had merit. Indeed, it's well-written satire, likely the best work Dick ever committed to paper. Garson Kanin compared it to Noël Coward's work. "It seems to me," Kanin wrote, "a fascinating and entertaining portrait of a kind of American family . . . It may have been written before its time."

Yes—before Kate was dead. "I am faced with smothering a work on which I have spent almost a year," Dick wrote to Deeter. He put forth the argument that "Sea-Air" wouldn't damage Kate but would actually *help* her. He went so far as to suggest she play the lead. Even more galling than Kate's theatrics, Dick felt, was the fact that his father instinctively took her side in the matter, underscoring Dick's belief that she was Hep's favorite.

Kit continued to be more understanding. Never all that impressed with her daughter's career, she considered *The Philadelphia Story* so much fluff. She was intrigued that Deeter thought Dick was an important emerging playwright; might she have given birth to the next Shaw or O'Neill? To stifle true artistry to protect commercial interests, Kit believed, was the real shame. She told Dick to wait. Kate might still come around.

Not likely. Dick became embittered by what he saw as his sister's hypocrisy. "I never believed K could feel all these moral things as business," he wrote to Deeter. "I guess all this moralizing about private life, etc., is largely a cover for plain commercial deals . . . I now begin to see she is commercial—and has thrown up a lot of sentiment around it which she feels the play makes fun of." In other words, "Sea-Air" exposed the fictions she was using to create her public image. Dick Hepburn was nothing if not percipient. He had no sympathy for his sister's point of view. "It isn't the gossips who would ruin her business," he wrote. "It's herself—but she doesn't know it."

Wracked with sciatica, felled by depression, Dick spent the next several months planning for a cruise around South America. He wasn't giving up on his dream yet, however. He wrote Kate that he was going ahead with "Sea-Air," and if she planned to sue him, he asked that she do so before he'd invested all his savings in the cruise.

With considerable chutzpah, Dick mailed a copy of the play to Lawrence Langner at the Theatre Guild, who lost no time getting such a hot potato off his desk. "There is no possibility whatsoever of the Guild . . . producing this," Langner wrote, "for the simple reason that we do not think it would be 'fair play' on our part to do so. Your sister Kate has always treated us in the most sportsmanlike manner and we would not be a party to anything which would hold her up to public censure or profit by a scandal in which she is involved. After reading your play, I feel that not only Kate but your whole family and her circle of friends are easily recognizable. Knowing what a decent, fine girl Kate is, we could never associate ourselves with anything that took advantage of her in this manner."

Though Dick sputtered on a while longer, eventually "Sea-Air" was put aside, locked away in a drawer. Over the years, it would be seen only by a handful of insiders. Instead, Dick sent a script called "Spirit" to George Cukor, who seemed leery to touch anything Dick wrote. Six months later, Dick was writing to ask for the play back, as he'd given up any hope of hearing from the director. When finally another play of Dick's was mounted, *Love Like Wildfire*, it disappeared as quickly as *Behold Your God*. After that, there was a long fallow period for the playwright Richard Hepburn. Many believed his best work, the work that could have put him on the map, was hidden away in his drawer.

He'd keep dreaming, but he never quite shook the feeling that his sister had stomped out his creative fire, backed up by the powerful forces around her. Langner would continue to read his plays but never produced anything Dick sent him. At home, Hep called his son a failure, instructing the more industrious Bob to watch out for his brother. "Dick's insane," Kuy Hepburn quoted his grandfather as telling the family. "We have to take care of him."

And, Kuy said, "Aunt Katty *did*. Dick would have been muddled on his own, but he had her help." The allowance continued. As the rest of the family married and moved on, Dick remained at Fenwick, always laboring over some play he hoped would fulfill his conviction (and his mother's) that he was destined for greatness. Kate's financial support seems to have been, at least in part, compensation for suppressing "Sea-Air."

Certainly her reaction to it was understandable. Few public figures would condone a family member penning a "tell-all" play—at least one not perused first with a blue pencil, the way Kate had done, figuratively, with Phil Barry. "Sea-Air" hardened her resolve for control. Around her, Hepburn's inner circle assumed a defensive posture, echoing Langner's commitment not to do or say anything to offset the image of Kate as "a fine and decent girl." No one dared step out of line until Garson Kanin wrote his memoir in 1971—and even that would be a spin on the *legend*, not a look at the real woman the way "Sea-Air" had been.

By the early 1940s, Kate had learned the necessity of convincing the world that her public and private selves were the same. Yet her brother's words about "all this moralizing" being used as a cover for commercial interests ring down through the decades. "Throwing up a lot of sentiment" became Kate's way of staying on top. In fact, from here on, Katharine Hepburn would become one of the best sentiment throwers Hollywood had ever seen.

A gigantic silvery close-up of Katharine Hepburn in *The Philadelphia Story* fills the screen. Her chin quivers, her eyes well up with tears. She's learned her lesson. Her heart has softened. Audiences, enchanted by the sight, responded by making the film one of the top ten box-office champions of the year. Exhibitors hailed the new and improved Kate.

The hurricane had washed away more than just her childhood home. Gone with its winds was everything that had made Hepburn such a peculiar, troublesome star. Gone was the "youthful spikiness" identified by David Thomson, the "sense that she was living dangerously, exposing her own nerves and vulnerability along with her intelligence and sensibility." By contrast, *The Philadelphia Story*, for all its charm, feels calculated and contrived— because it *is*. If there's anything spiky about Tracy Lord, it's there only so it can be filed down to a smooth, glossy finish while the audience watches. At the end of the film, released in late 1940, Kate's in a frilly dress getting hitched to her man in a lavish society wedding—a standard close for many Hollywood pictures, but a first for Katharine Hepburn.

How different were her films of the 1930s. Life was lived in them on her terms. Collectively, Hepburn's early work offered, in the words of one modern critic, the "tomboy as life force." That's apparent in *Little Women* and *Sylvia Scarlett*, of course, but also in *A Woman Rebels*, where she reacts strongly when a teacher claims women are inferior to men, and in *Quality Street*, where femaleness was revealed as merely a masquerade. When Fay Bainter calls Joan Fontaine a "silly goose," Hepburn replies cynically, "It's what gentlemen prefer."

With women, this early Hepburn was always soft and vulnerable; with men, she was guarded and aggressive. Despite all her attempts to feminize herself on-screen for the last five years, she'd still left an impression of sexual ambiguity. In the final clinch in *Quality Street*, she says to Franchot Tone, "Sir, Susan, too," and pulls Bainter into the embrace as the film fades out. Audiences were frustrated by this seeming disinterest in sex both on and off the screen, until at last Kate gave them the highly publicized romp with Howard Hughes.

When she *did* show interest in men on the screen, she was usually the aggressor. In *The Little Minister* she frightens John Beal so badly he runs off and shuts himself safely inside his house—the way a maiden might hide from a male rascal in other films. Of course, no better example of this is

Bringing Up Baby, where she chases after Cary Grant in a complete upending of the traditional male-female pursuit. Men, in fact, are often rather masochistic in these early Hepburn films. In *Baby*, Hepburn totally destroys Grant's life, symbolized by her destruction of the brontosaurus skeleton he's spent years creating—but he's happy about it, falling into her arms with a breathless, "Oh, Susan, dear." It's Hepburn who teaches men lessons about life in these early films, not the other way around.

That's why Thomson called *Bringing Up Baby* "so serious a film—without ever losing the status of being one of the funniest." *Baby* was the best evidence so far in the Hepburn canon that there were alternative ways of living in the world—a theme that percolates throughout her 1930s work, the alchemy of her own sensibility meshing with those of her directors and writers. In *Baby*, Howard Hawks makes us see the folly of Grant's life by asking who the crazy person really is—the free spirit played by Kate or the guy trapped by convention?

Holiday is arguably even more subversive than *Bringing Up Baby*. The whole film is a rejection of the status quo, with Cary Grant choosing a life of freedom and wanderlust over the security of a high-paying job. His fiancée can't see his logic, but her sister, played by Hepburn, finds it liberating. In a remarkable scene, she tells her brother (Lew Ayres) that she'll save him from "the reverence of riches." She'll be "back for him." It's a line men have said to women for ages: "I'll be back for you." It defines, in fact, the position of male and female. But here it is Hepburn who is in the position of strength.

This tweaking of convention is what made *Holiday* such a hit on Broadway in the Roaring Twenties, but its message was rejected by movie audiences in 1938 still reeling from the Depression. In their eyes, Grant was an insensitive clod to walk away from a good job, not an oracle for a better way to live. Yet more than sixty years later, *Holiday* provides a very satisfying coda to Hepburn's body of 1930s work.

With *The Philadelphia Story*, however, Hepburn was consciously—even cynically—responding to every fan-magazine criticism she'd endured for the past decade. "She had to do some kind of self-abasement to stay on the good side of the audience," said the critic Molly Haskell, who called *The Philadelphia Story* "really quite mean." Indeed, the film's very first scene (not in the play) has Cary Grant placing his hand square over Kate's face and pushing her down to the floor. Take that, Jo March—and Cynthia Darrington, Sylvia Scarlett, Terry Randall, Susan Vance, Linda Seton.

In that one gesture, the spiky, subversive Hepburn had been vanquished. The film spends the rest of its 112 minutes making sure audiences get the point. Grant tells her he left her because he didn't want to be "a high priest to a virgin goddess." Later he literally backs her into a corner, and though she tries to stand up to him, she's eventually intimidated. It's almost painful to watch today, this humbling of Hepburn, but in 1940, mainstream audiences were reassured that she'd no longer pose a threat to their conventional values. Yet Cary Grant—just as culpable as Hepburn in *Sylvia, Baby*, and *Holiday*—gets off scot-free, the prerogative of being male. When at the end of the film Hepburn pledges herself to him ("I'll be yar now, I promise to be yar"), Kate's former partner-in-crime looks decidedly uneasy about the whole thing—"as if they'd both stolen something," according to the film critic Dan Callahan, "but only she was to be punished for it."

For all that, there's no denying the film's snappy dialogue and the obvious chemistry among its stars. In addition to Grant, who replaced Joseph Cotten, Kate sparred memorably with a young, acerbic James Stewart, who deservedly won an Oscar.

She'd originally wanted Clark Gable and Spencer Tracy, however, and had tried unsuccessfully to make their casting a condition for giving MGM the film rights. But accepting Grant and Stewart in their place was the only concession she made. Sitting down with Louis B. Mayer in his office in Culver City, Kate held her chin high. Thanks to Howard Hughes and the fact that she owned the rights, she was in the driver's seat. Mayer found himself obliged to grant her request that George Cukor direct and Donald Ogden Stewart adapt Barry's script. The autocratic MGM chief would learn very quickly that Kate Hepburn drove a hard bargain. She sold the rights to the play for $175,000 and demanded an additional $75,000 for her to star in the picture.

Yet for all the control she wielded off the screen, she had to know how fundamentally she'd compromised herself on-screen. David Thomson, having interviewed her, felt she was "doubtless aware" of the irony of being lauded for her post-1940 work while her "dazzling achievements" of the 1930s had merely hardened audiences against her. Hepburn's close friends agreed that with *The Philadelphia Story* she made a very conscious decision to sacrifice, at least on-screen, the prickly independence that had once characterized her. "She did it because she knew she had to," said James Prideaux. "And she was very smart about always knowing what to do to stay on top."

Of course, she'd never admit it in so many words. She could be maddeningly obtuse about her own actions and motivations. Part of her likely rationalized *The Philadelphia Story* as simply a great script, patting herself on the back for finally finding one that worked. For the rest of her life, she'd call most of her early work "dogs"—and only when certain films like *Sylvia Scarlett* or

Bringing Up Baby were reclaimed by cineasts would she suddenly come around to seeing their worth.

Yet the decisions she made in 1939–40 sprang from her deeply rooted commitment to fame. At that critical point, Hepburn wanted what Bette Davis had: two Oscars, box-office clout, the industry's acknowledgment. No doubt her loss to Ginger Rogers (of all people) at the Oscar ceremonies in February 1941 was particularly irksome, preventing the symbolic crowning of the Hepburn comeback—not that she would have shown up to collect the award.

But it wasn't just ambition that drove her. In 1940, Katharine Hepburn was thirty-three years old. She was alone. Never again after the experience with Hughes would she come so close to considering marriage; it's likely she understood now that she'd never marry again. If anyone was going to take care of her and her career, it would have to be herself. With her family money and her earnings well invested by her father, it's true that Kate may have had more options than other actors confronted with similar rough patches in their careers. But as a woman in Hollywood—especially a woman of a certain age—she was distinctly at a disadvantage. What she did, she did to survive.

Barging into Mayer's office, she laid out her terms. Take them or leave them. In her own hands, she took control of her career, her image, her pocketbook—because if she didn't, she'd be left on the side of the road with so many other, once-popular stars. Who remembers Ruth Chatterton or Kay Francis today? Sure, Hepburn could have retired comfortably. But what man would be expected to retire at the age of thirty-three?

Kate Hepburn may have made some compromises, but in doing so, she ensured her survival. She found the formula that worked and ran with it. No one can blame her for that.

Nor could anyone blame her for insisting her next picture pick up squarely where *The Philadelphia Story* left off. She had found the perfect follow-up project to consolidate her new position and public image, dreamed up by a young, ambitious writer who seemed uncannily clued in to her needs. His name was Garson Kanin.

And this time, she wouldn't settle for anyone else as her costar but Spencer Tracy.

SIMPLY AHEAD OF THE TIMES

T hat *can't* be her," said the young man, turning his face from the silver screen.

"That's *her*," said his equally wide-eyed companion. "That's Kate Hepburn."

Stretching her shapely leg across the screen, Kate adjusts her nylon stocking with all the brio of an Ava Gardner. Her luminous eyes flick up as she suddenly becomes aware of being watched—not only by Spencer Tracy, who's just opened the door in the scene, but by millions of movie fans, struck dumb in their seats by the transformation of Katharine Hepburn into a love goddess.

She is, in a word, breathtaking. *Woman of the Year*, released in January 1942, sexualized her in a way no film had ever managed before—more so than *The Philadelphia Story*, where she was brittle and arch, and more so even than those glorious close-ups in *Mary of Scotland*, where she was unapproachably divine. Here she's a *temptress*, playing with that stocking and showing off her leg. True, she's still an intellectual and a bit of a snob; but now, layered onto that, she's downright sexy as well. Clearly somebody had been paying attention to the critic Frank Nugent's paean to Kate's gams in

Bringing Up Baby, in which he'd realized, for the first time, "that Miss Hepburn was human."

That's the whole point of *Woman of the Year*. After being defrosted in *The Philadelphia Story*, here Kate is a living, breathing, flesh-and-blood woman—pursued by an equally carnal, down-to-earth man. No one was ever going to mistake Spencer Tracy for the effete sophisticates who'd made up the roster of Kate's previous on-screen suitors.

Kate's latest reinvention had come at a very propitious moment. The Japanese had attacked Pearl Harbor just days after the film's first preview, and by the time *Woman of the Year* made it to the nation's screens, the United States was at war. All over the country, soldiers and sailors were queuing up outside theaters before trooping off to battle. Those two moviegoers gazing rapturously up at Kate (as reported in a Sunday newsmagazine supplement) were a couple of GIs on a night off from their base, preparing to be shipped across the Atlantic the very next week. *Woman of the Year* may have been the last movie they ever saw.

Finally, the times were catching up with Katharine Hepburn. With images of Wacs and Waves in their Jeeps now a frequent sight in newsreels—and with posters of Rosie the Riveter in rolled-up sleeves emblazoned in workplaces—Kate Hepburn in her slacks was no longer such a jarring image. In fact, her independent, can-do nature fit the patriotic vogue, as women were increasingly keeping the country running as men headed off to the front lines. Not surprisingly, when the Office of Emergency Management planned its documentary *Women in Defense*, extolling the ways in which women assisted the war effort, it was Hepburn they turned to as narrator. The unmistakable authority of her sharp, intelligent voice, reading the words of Eleanor Roosevelt, was just what the Pentagon needed.

Temper that strength and accomplishment with the sexuality of *Woman of the Year* and Kate had found, at last, a winning formula. Metro-Goldwyn-Mayer knew how to make movie stars, and the studio gave her the full star treatment. The famed couturier Adrian carefully veiled over the fractious, edgy Hepburn of the past with gowns designed to flatter her small waist and long legs. The stylist Sydney Guilaroff spun Kate's hair into gold thread. Her skin was burnished to its highest sheen by the makeup artist Jack Dawn. Thirty-four-year-old Katharine Hepburn emerged—for the first time really—as a classical movie star. By signing with Metro, she joined the ranks of Gable and Garbo and Shearer and Crawford at Hollywood's most glamorous and most prestigious studio.

MGM fit her sense of herself: Katharine Hepburn of Hartford, Connecticut, belonged only with the best. Striding through the Culver City studio—catching glimpses of Clark Gable and Lana Turner filming *Honky Tonk* and Mickey Rooney and Judy Garland filming *Babes on Broadway*—Kate pretended not to be impressed. Later, however, she'd admit to being "thrilled" as she wandered across the fabled backlot. Coming to Metro was a triumph for Hepburn, the culmination of a dream. From "has-been" to "have-it-all," from lower-rung RKO to the top of the Hollywood ladder.

What's remarkable is that Kate had managed most of it entirely on her own; she and Leland had amicably parted, and for several years she represented herself. With the producers at Metro—men like Joe Mankiewicz and Lawrence Weingarten—she forged strong friendships, which served her well when time for negotiations rolled around. She also shook hands with the studio's publicity chief, Howard Strickling, understanding that a certain amount of spin would be needed to realign herself as a star under the MGM aegis.

Indeed, Metro had the world's smoothest, slickest, most efficient publicity machine. Beginning in May 1939, when the preproduction hoopla had begun in earnest for *The Philadelphia Story*, MGM had waved its wand and suddenly there appeared a rash of articles recasting Hepburn as a star transfigured. "Sweetness and light have come to the little spitfire," wrote Jack Gould in the *New York Times*, offering the first major biographical profile since Adela Rogers St. Johns and concluding, "All may be forgiven and forgotten." The same sentiment was echoed in a four-page spread in *Life* titled "The Hepburns." Even so staunch a conservative as Hedda Hopper lauded the clan's virtues in her column: "They're quite a family, those Hepburns."

Working from mimeographs prepared by Strickling, the fan magazines followed suit. Gladys Hall, in *Silver Screen*, quoted an electrician on the set as saying Kate came "right down to the good earth with the rest of us." And whereas Hepburn's trousers had once caused consternation, now James Reid wrote in *Modern Screen* that "every girl in her right mind" was wearing slacks. "I was simply ahead of the times," Hepburn told Reid—clearly following the talking points set out by the publicists for this press cycle.

Their spin was obvious. It was Hollywood's fault, not hers, that Kate had failed in the past. The industry simply hadn't been ready for her. "Hepburn came to Hollywood eight years too soon," one scribe wrote. "If she had waited until 1940 to make her entrance into the celluloid city, her presence would have caused no unfavorable comment." The "phony elegance" of Ruth Chatterton and Kay Francis had given way to the no-nonsense of Bette Davis, who drove around town in the same kind of station wagon for which Hepburn had once been criticized. Davis, the queen of the box office, didn't go in for all that "trussed up glamour" either; she was often spotted in kerchief and jeans.

Yet for all the "unfair" treatment she'd received, Kate assured the fan magazines she held no grudge. "Despite all the rumors to the contrary," she said, "I happen to like Hollywood very much." What wasn't to like, with two smash hits in a row?

With *Woman of the Year*—the nation's top moneymaker for several months in early 1942—the legend of Hepburn kicked into high gear. Lupton Wilkinson's influential series, with Kate's behind-the-scenes cooperation, began running in the *Saturday Evening Post*, and worshipful spreads appeared in *Look* and *Reader's Digest*. For the first time, Hepburn was called "Kate the Great" rather than "Hepburn the Haughty." Out of the headstrong deviance of the 1930s, Kate emerged as the archetype of the strong yet feminine woman, whose battle of the sexes was not really a threat to the status quo but merely a search for love. *Woman of the Year* set the standard: Tess Harding, the brash, independent newswoman (named, in an inside joke, after Laura), falls in love with Sam Craig, the crusty sportswriter. Let the fireworks fly—but make sure to fade out with a kiss.

Hepburn knew what she was doing when she chose the "very male" George Stevens as director of *Woman of the Year* over her pal George Cukor—who, she said, didn't know "a baseball game from a swimming match." For this critical picture, Kate wanted a man who understood "manly" things, who had direct experience with the sexual dynamic between men and women. Indeed, that's what this film is all about: uppity women coming to the realization that their real place is a step or two behind their men. Even a character reminiscent of Auntie Towle, an unmarried suffragist played by Fay Bainter, finds she's tired of winning prizes and wants to be "a prize" herself. So she gets married—the implication being she'd been unhappy all those years on her own.

In *Woman of the Year*, the age-old conflict between men and women takes on quite profound implications. Sam Craig goes so far as to call Tess Harding's independent way of thinking a threat to "our American way of life." While the first half of the film is fun and sexy, the second half—in which Tess learns her "lesson"—often feels dated to audiences today, especially at the moment when Bainter gets married and Tess realizes no woman should be "above marriage." Accordingly, for the last ten minutes of the picture, we're treated to the spectacle of this formerly independent hotshot trying (unsuccessfully) to cook breakfast for her man as he waits in bed.

The fact that she fails—the coffee bubbles over, the toast gets burned—

actually saves the picture from being a complete capitulation. Sam tells Tess he doesn't need to domesticate her on every front. How princely of him. By having Kate play both independent and submissive at the same time, MGM was able to capitalize on her reputation as a career woman (so marketable during the war years) while subverting it at the same time.

Promoting *Woman of the Year* with the kind of vim and vigor she'd never thrown behind her RKO films, Kate summed up its message this way: "The picture ought to throw some light on the problem of the modern woman who is financially independent of a man. For her, the marriage problem is very great. If she falls in love with a strong man, she loses him because she is concentrated too much on her job. If she falls in love with a weakling she can push around, she always falls out of love. A woman just has to have sense enough to handle a man well enough so he'll want to stay with her. To keep him on the string is almost a full-time job."

That, in a nutshell, is *Woman of the Year*. A woman has to be smart enough to keep her man from leaving her. That's all. Not smart enough to have a life of her own—just smart enough to keep her man "on the string." It was a formula that satisfied most everybody, preserving a veneer of Hepburn's old spunk and independence while at the same time harmonizing her with the sexual politics of the era—a brilliant strategy that ensured a continuing role for her to play in public life.

She was, in many ways, moving into uncharted waters. Until now, the career of a movie star had rarely lasted more than ten years. Only a rare few—Chaplin, Pickford, Swanson—had sustained their stardom for more than a decade. Even then, their celebrity was based largely on the memory of past greatness. By 1942, Hepburn may have sensed that her fame could be a lifelong thing—that if she learned to adapt, she could keep herself relevant and working, transcending the very nature of conventional Hollywood stardom.

That is, if Kate could keep Kath from messing things up.

Delaware state trooper Joseph Shannon thought he was pulling over an underage driver for speeding along the highway to Baltimore. So he was completely unprepared for the ripsnorting, fire-breathing redhead who charged out of the driver's seat at him.

"You have no right to be stopping me!" Kate Hepburn shouted, wagging her finger in the trooper's face. "I'm being detained without cause!" Behind her in the car, Eve March, Em Perkins, and Perkins's bandleader son Blynn hid their faces in embarrassment.

Trooper Shannon was not awed by the fact that he'd just pulled over a movie star. When Kate informed him she'd left her license in Hollywood, he took her in to see the magistrate. After much high-pitched complaining (what the papers called "shrieking"), Kate was arraigned at the Wilmington courthouse before Magistrate Alfred J. P. Seitz. Posting a $13.50 bond, a sum equal to the fine of driving without a license, Kate tore out of town—though this time *under* the speed limit and with Eve at the wheel. When she failed to appear at a subsequent traffic violation hearing, Seitz called her an "irresponsible, spoiled child," the precise headline that appeared over her photograph in dozens of newspapers the next day.

All this occurred just before her latest reinvention for *Woman of the Year*, but it was precisely the sort of eruption for which Kate's new handlers at MGM were constantly on the alert. More headlines shouting "spoiled" could derail their careful campaign for rehabilitation.

Another fear haunting the publicists was that Kate's politics might again get her in trouble the way they had in 1934 when her support for Upton Sinclair had caused considerable comment. Nearly seventy years after the fact, much of Hepburn's political activity has been forgotten, obscured by chroniclers who have seemed determined to present America's heroine as neither too liberal nor too conservative. But in the 1930s and 1940s, Kate's political activities and opinions frequently made the newspapers—a rarity among movie stars then. The same month as her arrest, Hepburn made headlines for refusing to cross a picket line of striking hotel workers in Washington, D.C. A short while later, she spoke out in support of the Associated Actors and Artistes of America in their fight with the stagehands' union. Like her championship of Sinclair in 1934, Kate's solidarity with labor grew out of a deeply ingrained sense of social justice, instilled by her mother and burnished by friendships with Putnam and others.

Indeed, so pervasive was Hepburn's image as union activist by 1940 that one critic used her name as a rallying cry. "I often wonder if Katharine Hepburn, the great advocate of organized labor, ascertains if every purchaser of a ticket to her shows is a union laborer," the anonymous "Skilled Carpenter" wrote to the *Washington Post*. "Surely she would not want to receive any money but union money."

Hepburn's pesky little tendency to get political was explained away by the MGM publicists with one simple word: *democracy*. Free speech was, after all, a foundation of American life. The spin didn't always fly, especially in the more reactionary years to come, but for the time being it largely canceled out any negative buzz about Hepburn's politics.

Such shrewd press agentry made Howard Strickling and the MGM publicity department the acknowledged masters of the industry. One article from this period offers an extraordinary window on the efforts to rehabilitate Hepburn in the buildup to *Woman of the Year*. Although the star in question isn't named, it's clear the article is about Kate. Studio publicists are depicted as coercing editors to run interviews with her as personal favors. "Nobody tells the star [she's being interviewed only] because the press agent is a good guy and deserves a break." When reporters troop onto the set, "the star, who has high-hatted newspaper and magazine writers in the past, has a sudden attack of graciousness. She woos you with every trick she knows. She dresses as she thinks you'd like her to dress. She works hard at perfecting a good act . . . Sometimes, at such enforced exchanges of courtesy, the star and the interviewer remind you of two fighting cats with arched backs, just preparing to unsheath their claws. The anxious representative of the company stands by and hopes for the best."

But if Kate was cooperating, so, too, would the press. Unlike the constant chatter about Laura Harding's presence in the early days, the MGM Kate was rarely dogged by such insinuations, despite the fact that everyone remained well aware of the constant circle of women still surrounding the star. "Of course we knew the truth about [stars'] private lives," said the longtime MGM publicist Emily Torchia, who spent her last years as a freelancer helping protect the secrets of Rock Hudson. "We knew about Hepburn, about her unconventional life, and the press knew, and there was an unspoken arrangement that we never would say anything that might reveal [the truth about her life]."

Once again, in her relationships with men and women, Kate had behaved according to pattern. Just as she had after her break with Phelps Putnam, she followed her split with Hughes by retreating to the comforting embrace of a community of women. First, it was Eve "Murph" March who was her most frequent companion. "For several weeks this season," one reporter observed, before MGM leaned in to control what was written, Kate "had as her houseguest the very pretty young woman who serves as her stand-in and to whom she is now quite devoted." Whether there was an actual romance with Murph, who was touring in a repertory version of *Stage Door*, is unclear. By the middle part of the decade, Murph had married Ian MacDonald, a doctor at the University of Southern California, and borne two children. She named her daughter after Kate, who also served as the girl's godmother. Later divorced, Murph would remain in Hepburn's orbit; in *Adam's Rib*, she'd play her secretary.

But it was the presence of two new women in Kate's circle that raised the most speculation in the Hollywood rumor mill. Whenever Hepburn traveled back East, she often had Nancy Hamilton or Frances Rich at her side. Neither woman ever married, nor did they put up smoke screens about male beaux. Look-alikes, both Hamilton and Rich wore their hair short and boyish, eschewed makeup, and were rarely seen without ties and trousers. To look upon either of them was to imagine that Sylvester Scarlett had nimbly stepped off the screen.

Two years younger than Hepburn, Nancy Hamilton had been Kate's understudy in *The Warrior's Husband*. Within a couple of years, she'd become a successful lyricist, hailed by critics as an acerbic Cole Porter. According to one acquaintance, Hamilton was "a prodigious maker of plans and planner of junkets, an indefatigable mixer, collector, and maker of friends." She was also the lover of the actress Brenda Forbes, with whom she often hosted Kate for supper at their apartment on East End Avenue. A few years later, when Hamilton became the devoted companion of Katharine Cornell, the friendship with Hepburn cooled somewhat. Kate was never keen to move in circles where she had to share the spotlight with a star as important as herself.

More constant through the years was her friendship with Fran Rich, whom she'd met through Jack Ford. The daughter of the actress Irene Rich, Fran was on her way to becoming a well-known sculptor, having studied with Carl Milles and Malvina Hoffman. During World War II, she served as a lieutenant in the navy's Women's Reserve. Possessed of a sharp wit, Fran— a Smith graduate—had fired off a few cutting comments about "that old Bryn Mawr" when she'd first discovered Ford's affair with Hepburn. But she could also be sentimental, crying "real salt tears" over a Chaplin film with her friend Noel Sullivan, a San Francisco arts patron. Rich's soul, said one acquaintance, was "alive with the great gothic vibration."

Kate was clearly enchanted by Fran. "We were very close for a time, always together," Rich acknowledged, though she declined to characterize the relationship further. But Rich's friends remembered the fondness she used in describing her travels with Kate, and from Hepburn's own anecdotes it's obvious she adored sitting on a stool posing for Fran, who would sculpt half a dozen likenesses of her over the years. Sometimes the attention came double, as Rich would arrange for their mutual pal Robert McKnight, Kate's erstwhile "beau," to bring over his hammer and chisel as well.

Both Hamilton and Rich were part of the "upper-class bohemian" world that defined Hepburn's inner circle. But as always, however, the private reality of Kate's life wouldn't play to the masses. A great deal of insulation would be needed, a buffer zone of protective fiction.

Enter one very enterprising writer named Garson Kanin.

To understand the role Kanin played in Hepburn's life and legend, we must go back to a night at George Cukor's house in 1939, just as Kate was enjoying her comeback onstage in *The Philadelphia Story*. Larry Olivier was refilling her brandy snifter when his lady love, Vivien Leigh, swept up behind them in a sparkling dress with a wiry young man on her arm.

"I want you to meet Garson Kanin," Leigh announced, presenting the small (five-foot-six) director with the thinning hair and boyish grin. Kanin was then the talk of Hollywood, having just helmed *Bachelor Mother* with Ginger Rogers and starting on *My Favorite Wife* with Cary Grant and Irene Dunne. He was eager to meet Hepburn. As he extended his small hand to her, his grin stretched across his face like a jack-o'-lantern's. Looking over at him curiously, Kate observed Kanin's head seemed too large for his diminutive frame. But she took his hand—and there was destiny.

That night, or one soon thereafter, Gar would share an idea he had for her. The story of how *Woman of the Year* came to be is in fact the genesis of so much of the legend of Katharine Hepburn.

Just twenty-eight, Kanin was fired with an ambition similar to Hepburn's, even if their backgrounds were remarkably dissimilar. The son of a Russian Jewish immigrant who worked as a building contractor in Manhattan, Garson had dropped out of school to help support his family during the Depression. Running around as a Western Union messenger, stocking shelves in the silverware department at Macy's, he never lost his dream of being an actor. Scraping together his savings, he enrolled at the American Academy of Dramatic Arts. But upon graduation in May 1933, he found Broadway wasn't exactly waiting with open arms. There wasn't much call for short, balding Jewish boys except as comic foil.

When he heard that the producer George Abbott needed a redheaded actor for an upcoming play, Gar dyed his hair and showed up early. He didn't get the part, but Abbott did take him under his wing as an assistant. The influential producer thought highly enough of the scrappy Kanin to recommend him to Samuel Goldwyn, who brought the young man out to Hollywood in June 1937. Spinning his own legend, Gar would say he was hired because he looked like Irving Thalberg, and Goldwyn wanted his own "boy wonder." Still, Kanin would prove himself after he jumped ship and headed over to RKO. Arriving just after Kate's departure, he directed a handful of hit pictures.

Kate was immediately taken with Gar's kinetic energy, his fist-clenching enthusiasm. That oddly shaped head of his was always cooking up scenarios. As the story of *Woman of the Year* fell into shape—with all sorts of little business designed to tear the highfalutin Tess off her pedestal and "human- ize" her—Kate began to trust Kanin's vision more and more. Gar fit well into her clique at Cukor's. Impeccably urbane in his manner, Kanin was renowned as a mixer of superb dry martinis. He was also a die-hard liberal. "We are all hypocrites," he once charged during a night out on the town. "Here we sit, drinking in a bar that won't serve Negroes. Yet I'm a guy who says he believes in equal rights."

"His sympathies are always with the underdog," one observer said, "but he thoroughly enjoys being in the higher income brackets." In this, as in nearly every aspect of his life, Gar was perfectly in sync with Kate.

Not surprisingly, MGM press agents, with their subjects' tacit coopera- tion, cooked up a romance between Kanin and Hepburn. "They are the newest pair of exciting dates in cinemaland," Ruth Waterbury gushed in *Movie Mirror*, pointing out that Gar and Kate had stood up for Olivier and Leigh at their wedding. Could they be next? Kate was mum, but Kanin wasn't exactly throwing cold water on the idea. "We are at that telephone stage," he told Waterbury, "that small-gift stage . . . This thing between us is either too important or not important enough . . . We'll have to wait and see."

The thing between them was indeed important enough; but it would be Ruth Gordon whom Kanin would marry a year later, in a madcap ceremony in Washington, D.C., after the last curtain of Gordon's play *The Three Sisters*. Ruth Gordon—spunky, quirky, campy, so homely she was almost beautiful, and sixteen years older than Gar.

"What does that tell you about Kanin?" the sageful Gavin Lambert asked rhetorically. "No red-blooded heterosexual man of twenty-nine is going to marry Ruth Gordon at forty-five."

"Garson was a winking kind of queen," said Elliott Morgan. "He winked and thought all the boys' talk was great fun, but he always left with Ruth be- fore things got out of hand."

Kanin once told Lambert that he'd managed to have it all: a wife and so- cial respectability, on the one hand, and a connection to gay life through Cukor, on the other. "He'd show up in his velvet suits with his little old lady wife and was really convinced he'd fooled people," Lambert said. "Well, some people. He knew he didn't fool all of us."

Kanin's reverence for his various mentors is also telling. Conscious of his lack of formal education, Gar liked to say he'd attended "the college of Thornton Wilder." The renowned playwright had once considered marrying Ruth Gordon himself; to Ruth, "Thornie" was her "guide and mentor, dream boy and friend." Wilder became even closer with Ruth's husband, who surely was aware of the playwright's private life. Terribly conflicted over his homosexuality, Wilder routinely engaged in brief, guilt-ridden affairs with men that were, according to his biographer Gilbert Harrison, "so hurried and reticent, so barren of embrace, tenderness or passion that [they] might never have happened." Kanin's close friendship with and affinity for Wilder suggests that the playwright's attitudes toward sex and sexuality might offer windows onto Garson's own.

Yet that very suppression of his basic nature was what made Kanin so attractive to Hepburn. He met her criteria for nonromantic male friends: homosexual but undeclared, sophisticated but unfailingly discreet. He brought to their friendship an awareness of the fluid parameters of her own life without either of them ever needing to articulate anything. Even more, Kanin demonstrated an uncanny ability to anticipate the needs of Kate's public image. Indeed, for the next thirty years, Garson Kanin became the most important mythmaker in the Hepburn legend—even, in some ways, more than the star herself.

Drafted into the army before production on *Woman of the Year* could begin, Gar entrusted the basic narrative to his brother Michael and his collaborator, Ring Lardner. Kate pushed the script through at MGM. Yet Garson's imprint remained. "After all," he'd insist later, "I was the one who thought up the [Tracy-Hepburn] team."

Later he claimed he'd had to convince Kate of the wisdom of using Spencer Tracy over Cary Grant, but this seems another example of Kanin spinning his own legend. Hepburn had, in fact, been after Tracy for months. Instinctively, she knew he was precisely what the film needed—the kind of "virile, dominant male" Gregory La Cava had once envisioned melting the "impervious" Hepburn.

Kate had first seen Tracy on Broadway in 1930 when he was performing in *The Last Mile,* a grim prison melodrama, and had admired him ever since. Tracy, on the other hand, had never seen any of Kate's pictures—or at least, that's what the legend would later insist, keeping them both in character, she the fawning enthusiast, he the indifferent topliner.

Tracy had *heard* about her, however—enough to think she might be a lesbian, Kate later recalled. During their first chance meeting outside the Thalberg Building, he noticed she had dirty fingernails. Kate quoted Spencer as saying, "How can I do a picture with a woman who has dirt under her fin-gernails and who is of ambiguous sexuality and always wears pants?"

That he should still consider her "ambiguous" in the wake of all that hul-labaloo with Howard Hughes suggests that the industry had noticed Eve or Fran or Nancy. It may be why later chroniclers would reinsert George Stevens into the narrative at this point, insisting that he and Kate had re-newed their affair when he was tapped to direct *Woman of the Year*. Al-though the director and his leading lady were seen around town together several times, there is, once again, no evidence of an affair between them. The story of Stevens graciously withdrawing when he noticed the chemistry between Hepburn and Tracy on the set seems merely an attempt to provide a segue between two chapters of the legend.

But the chemistry between the two stars of *Woman of the Year* was nonetheless real—clear to everyone who viewed the rushes and still obvious today. There's a moment on a stairwell when the electricity between Hep-burn and Tracy nearly crackles on the sound track. At another point, when Sam walks Tess to her door, the cabbie asks if he should wait. A sexually charged moment of silence follows. Tess tells the cabbie to go, and invites Sam upstairs. Rarely did so much sexual tension permeate a post-Code film. It's clear Tess wants to sleep with Sam, but he upholds traditional morality by slipping out of her clutches. If the public still harbored suspicions similar to Tracy's about Hepburn's "ambiguous sexuality," they were quickly dis-pensed with after seeing this film. Kate racked up more kissing scenes in this single picture than she had in all the rest of her films combined.

And it was plain to see that Hepburn and Tracy loved every minute of filming them.

When Spencer Tracy was born, on April 5, 1900, his father, a trucker, the son of Irish immigrants, went from tavern to tavern in downtown Milwaukee to celebrate the event. John Tracy, like his son later on, would be enshrined as a decent sort of man, salt of the earth. He worked hard as general sales man-ager for the Sterling Motor Truck Company—"kind of a truck himself," Spence once said. He also liked to drink. And so, from the start, the bottle figures strongly in Tracy's story.

Although tales of street brawls would later lend a Bowery Boys backdrop to Spencer's childhood, the Tracys were respectable and middle class. John Tracy's wife, Carrie, was the daughter of Edward Brown, who owned a chain of mills throughout the Midwest and Northeast. Although some of the fisticuffs later publicized were real, Spence was hardly the hellion imagined by Hollywood press agents, who hoped to associate him with the urchins of his popular film *Boys Town*. In truth, the young Spencer preferred, like Kate, to stage little playlets with his friends.

Indeed, part of Tracy's legendary devotion to the Catholic Church was the theatricality of its ritual. As a boy, he regularly attended Mass; with his older brother Carroll he received all of the Sacraments. With his pal Bill O'Brien, who later became the well-known actor Pat O'Brien, Spence attended Marquette Academy, a Jesuit prep school, where the priests were his heroes. "You know how it is in a place like that," he told Kanin. "The influence is strong . . . Intoxicating." For a time he considered becoming a priest himself, and a part of him always felt he'd have been happier in his life if he had. Whenever he'd play a priest in the movies, he told Kanin, putting on that priestly collar always felt "right."

Instead, he slipped into a soldier's uniform in 1917, training in Norfolk, Virginia, during the last months of World War I. Like Luddy, he never saw any actual fighting. After the war was over, Spencer entered Northwestern Military Academy at Lake Geneva, where he thrived on the discipline and became a model student. Like Phelps Putnam, he developed intense friendships with his schoolmates, especially the smart, outgoing Kenneth Edgers, who encouraged Spence to consider college. Together, after graduation from Northwestern in 1921, the two young men entered Ripon College in central Wisconsin. Family members of both commented on how intensely committed Spence and Ken were to each other, particularly Spence.

At Ripon, Tracy's dreams of the stage were revived. Acting in college productions fired him up on the idea of New York, and he left Ripon after his sophomore year for the American Academy of Dramatic Arts, a few years before Garson Kanin showed up there. His father thought Spence was "softheaded" to pursue a stage career, but he paid his way nonetheless. In the stories of Tracy's life, his father seemed not so different from the actor's own on-screen image, an ordinary guy who didn't go in for highfalutin nonsense. After one of Spencer's stage performances, his father reportedly told him that while he performed well enough, he'd do even better sitting in the driver's seat of a new five-ton truck.

But for all of John Tracy's good-father image, at every opportunity he reminded his son how homely he was, how that pug face of his would keep him from becoming a matinee idol. The elder Tracy drank hard; he withheld praise; he voiced disappointment in his son's career. Was this part of the pain Spence carried around? Despite all the stories of a happy childhood, the camaraderie of friends, and the support of his teachers, Spencer Tracy inexplicably emerged into young adulthood—as every account of his life describes—an unhappy, tormented man. "He was forever running away from something," said one old friend, though just what he was running away from was never made clear.

Living on West Ninety-sixth Street with Pat O'Brien, Spence was already drinking heavily. Despite encouragement from his acting teachers, he lacked confidence in himself and his abilities. By nature he was a pessimist. An insomniac, he'd toss all night, getting drunk sometimes just so he could fall asleep. Returning to church, Spencer seemed to be seeking some kind of absolution. Sometimes he prayed for hours on his knees, his Rosary beads dangling from his hands.

In 1923, he married the actress Louise Treadwell, who thought him brilliant—and made it her life's mission to get him to think so, too. Their courtship was marked more by admiration than ardor: "I loved him," Louise said, "because he was so earnest, so attentive, and such a good actor."

Nine months after their marriage, their son John was born. A year later they learned he was deaf—one more excuse for Spence to wander out to the taverns. Since coming to New York, he had rarely *not* been drunk. Sometimes he even walked out onto the stage with a slight, numbing buzz. To Garson Kanin, Spencer admitted he'd been drunk continually "for twenty-five years . . . just enough to cushion the shock of life."

To his friends, he was a decent man, never unnecessarily cruel or mean— at least when sober. "When Spence wasn't drinking, he had the softest heart in the world," said one old friend. "He could be a sentimental guy, buying a balloon for a kid who was crying—and what a kick he'd get seeing the kid's face light up." Those who knew Spence often commented on what an expert listener he could be; he seemed genuinely interested in other people. "When he listened to you," said his friend the director Jean Negulesco, "he made you want to be at your best."

Unlike Kate's attraction to the theater, Tracy's own ambition wasn't about fame or applause; the narcissism that drove Kate ever onward simply wasn't present in Spence. Rather, acting offered him an escape from his torments. "For a little while, he could be someone else," said his old friend. "He didn't have to be Spencer Tracy." But again, just *why* he needed an escape wasn't clear.

His big break came in *The Last Mile* (1930), playing a cold-blooded killer. Tracy's powerful performance caught the eye of John Ford. At the Lamb's Club, the two bluff Irishmen often drank themselves into oblivion, a fond memory that stayed with Ford all his life. Their camaraderie led to a leading part for Spence in Ford's latest picture, *Up the River*. Subsequent films like *Me and My Gal, 20,000 Years in Sing Sing*, and *The Power and the Glory* turned Tracy into a major star, usually playing gangsters or tough guys.

Yet for all his success, "the shock of life" could still prove too much. Hollywood in those pre-Code years offered many temptations for a man with Spencer's addictions. When police were called to the scene of an accident on Sunset Boulevard before dawn on September 21, 1933, they found Spencer Tracy, star of the current hit *Shanghai Madness*, snarling and throwing punches at them. So belligerent did Spence become that he had to be restrained with both handcuffs and leg irons.

Even worse, stories reached Louise of her husband's patronage of brothels, but friends discounted such tales. Indeed, the producer Joe Mankiewicz said the last thing Spence thought about when he was drinking was sex.

Still, the rumors alone were enough to flatten Louise. Too many nights were spent pacing the floor wondering if Spence was going to come home. Shortly before Spencer's crack-up on Sunset Boulevard, the Tracys had separated. To reporters, Spence expressed the hope that living apart for a while might do them some good. Meanwhile he was seen around town with Loretta Young, his costar in the film *Man's Castle*. Given that Spence was a married man, it's surprising how frequently the gossip columns mentioned his dates with Loretta: dancing at the Beverly-Wilshire, laughing at Will Rogers's show at the El Capitan, listening to Gene Austin's band at the Cocoanut Grove.

Yet as much as they enjoyed each other's company, the Tracy-Young affair was likely never sexual. Spence himself called it "all platonic." Indeed, Loretta was even more devoutly Catholic than he was; her tryst with Clark Gable a year later would clearly be an aberration. In contrast, her affair with Spencer was passionate yet guilt-free, something both of them could live with. Their companionship lasted for about a year. It seems to have ended by late 1934, when columnists reported that a reconciled Spencer and Louise showed up for Thanksgiving dinner at the director Harry Lachman's house. Loretta was there, too—alone.

Despite their conflicts, the Tracys continued to be drawn back to each other. Whenever a new film was released, it was Louise's opinion Spence valued above all others. Her championship of his career was already legend by 1935, when a fan magazine trumpeted BECAUSE SHE LOVED HIM SO MUCH—a tribute to Louise's "grace and grit" in the face of Spencer's perennial "melancholy and moroseness." Spence was quoted as saying that with "a wife like Louise— loving, confident, and always proud of me—I just have to make good."

The article was clearly an attempt to prove to the public that their marriage was back on track. Soon thereafter, the couple bought a brown-stucco hacienda in the San Fernando Valley that they called "The Hill." On their twelve acres they raised chickens and goats. It meant a long commute over the mountains to work, but Spence found the privacy worth the effort. A daughter, Susie, had been born in 1932.

Part of Spencer's decision to move his family to such a remote location stemmed from a kidnapping threat he'd received on February 23, 1934. Unless eight thousand dollars was paid, the extortionist, known only as "Rattlesnake Pete," vowed to kidnap either Tracy, his mother, his "baby" (presumably Susie), or Loretta Young. "Going away won't help you a dam [sic]," the note read. "We got you." With memories of the Lindbergh baby kidnap-murder still fresh, Spencer was understandably concerned. The FBI began an investigation, but no suspect was ever caught. Two years later another threat was made; again no one was apprehended.

Yet the parade of suspects that Spence identified for the FBI led some in Hollywood to wonder about the sort of riffraff the actor called "friends." One former Tracy employee told federal investigators he often accompanied the actor on nightlong visits to the "various bootlegging and drinking joints throughout Los Angeles." (When Spence first arrived in Hollywood, Prohibition had still been in force.) Throughout the industry, stories were rampant of the actor's recurrent dashes across the country onboard the Chief, in which he'd hide out in hotels in Chicago or New York and drink until he'd used up all his credit.

During the first week of March 1935, having just finished the last scenes for his film *Dante's Inferno*, Tracy barreled out of town with Hugh Tully, a jockey from the Bel-Air stables, where he kept several racehorses. That Louise was scheduled to compete that week with the women's polo team at the Riviera Country Club seemed not to matter. The two men ended up in a hotel room in Yuma, Arizona, where they proceeded to get stinking drunk. A phone conversation with Louise left Spencer in a rage, and he began hurling dishes against the wall. People in the next room complained, and soon police were on the scene.

Spencer could be a mean, belligerent drunk. Cursing and shouting, he threw a chair at the cop who entered the room. He and Tully put up a good fight, but they were so intoxicated that the single officer was able to subdue and handcuff them both. Released after posting fifteen dollars bond, they promised to pay for the hotel damage. When Louise showed up the next day to bring her husband home, Spencer and Tully had already hightailed it for Nogales. No one was surprised when, a few months later, Tracy's contract with Fox was not renewed.

What *did* raise some eyebrows was MGM's decision to add the volatile actor to its galaxy of stars. Then again, that studio's lean, mean publicity machine could rein in Spencer's public image in a way Fox never could. The canny publicists at Metro knew they needed to find a reason to "explain away" Tracy's bad behavior. A scapegoat was required, and they found one very close to home. In the same article that heralded Louise's "grace and grit," little Johnnie Tracy's deafness was, for the first time, named as the cause of his father's bad behavior. "When you understand that," the magazine declared, "it's easy to see how a man can go berserk now and then, break loose, try to forget."

The fact that Johnnie was thriving seemed immaterial. Working with specialists, Louise had taught the boy to speak and to read lips. He was doing well in school and seemed bright and happy. But the "tragedy" of his deafness—played up in the years to come in hundreds of articles—brought a wave of sympathy for Spencer in the popular press.

Not surprisingly, MGM turned Tracy into their populist hero. "I'd like to know where else in the world people could make what we make here," Spence was quoted as saying of Hollywood. "When a producer is paying a man some $150,000—which is $149,900 more than he'd get for any other job—why shouldn't the producer be entitled to ask the actor to postpone his dinner hour a few minutes?" Actors, he said, needed to "get off their high horses and down on their knees where they belong."

The public loved it. "It is refreshing to find a modest man," noted the usually acerbic columnist Jimmie Fidler. "[Spencer] is changed not one iota since he was an unknown bit player. He cannot get the idea through his head that he has become a man of importance."

By 1937, the former bad boy was being hailed not only as a "regular guy" but also as the movies' finest actor. He won the Screen Writer's Guild award twice in succession, for *Fury* and *San Francisco*. Academy Awards followed, also twice in succession, for *Captains Courageous* and *Boys Town*. By the end of the decade, Metro had turned Spencer Tracy into the movies' biggest star, outpolling Clark Gable by half a percentage point in a Roper poll. A trip to London in April 1939 confirmed his popularity. A riot of more than a thousand fans broke out when the most popular star in the world stepped off the train at Waterloo Station.

No wonder Kate Hepburn wanted him as costar. "Spencer's face was really familiar to the public," she said. "It was Irish and solid and strong. He was a man. He was the American man with an Irish background. It represented MAN in capital letters."

And not just his face. She also went into rapture over his neck. "A bull neck," she proclaimed. "Size 17 is a *man's* neck." She also loved repeating the story that Tracy, unlike most actors, never wore makeup.

Just as she'd once sat at John Ford's feet, she would now sit at Tracy's. *Woman of the Year* would do more than just reposition Katharine Hepburn's public image. It would also introduce her to the relationship that, for better or worse, came to define her life. Once again, Hepburn would leave behind the more comfortable, reliable association of women for a man of bluff and swagger with alcohol on his breath—and enough demons to keep her entranced for a very long time.

WHAT WAS IT, SPENCE?

The man slipping into a rear aisle seat in Pittsburgh's grand old Nixon Theater didn't go unrecognized by one reporter. All through the first act of *Without Love,* the Theatre Guild's new play starring Katharine Hepburn, Kaspar Monahan kept an eye on the man slouched down in his seat. At the intermission, he nabbed him.

"Mr. Tracy?" the reporter asked.

A crooked grin stretched across Spencer's face as he realized he'd been caught. Tracy admitted he'd snuck in to see if the play might make a good film—and yes, after the tremendous success they'd had in *Woman of the Year,* he might make it with Miss Hepburn. But he didn't have time for any more questions, he told Monahan. He was leaving for the Coast immediately after the performance, though the reporter doubted the story. "I noted at final curtain that he was not in too great a hurry to get out of town," Monahan wrote, "or to neglect to run backstage and congratulate Miss Hepburn."

It was May 1942. *Woman of the Year* was still on the nation's screens, one of the most popular pictures of the year. Its stars were officially just good friends; after all, Spence was a married man. But Tracy's presence in Pittsburgh, one of the last stops on Hepburn's tour, set tongues wagging. It may explain why Kate seemed so tense; at one point during the Pittsburgh run, she lashed out at a cameraman waiting outside the theater and knocked his camera to the ground.

The fact that she was smitten with Spencer was apparent to everyone around her. Indeed, watching *Woman of the Year*, movie buffs have long imagined that it's the first rush of intimacy between Kate and Spence they're witnessing as Tess Harding and Sam Craig fall in love, and they may be right. The glow in the stars' eyes isn't just the result of trained spotlights.

Yet their attraction did not turn serious right away. On *Woman of the Year*, there simply wasn't time or opportunity. For part of the shoot, Laura Harding was Kate's guest at her rented Spanish hacienda in Beverly Hills, and most nights, Spence retreated over the mountains to be with his family. After the film wrapped, Kate almost immediately headed back East while Spence remained in Hollywood to make *Tortilla Flat*. Although the spark had been lit, by the time Kate left there was no clear indication where their flirtation was going, if anywhere at all.

Of course, the fact that Spencer snuck off to meet her in Pittsburgh, and perhaps other cities as well, suggests the feelings engendered on the set hadn't gone away. Yet while Kate, as always, adored attention from an amorous man, she didn't yet view herself as linked exclusively to Tracy. That's evidenced by letters from the period, which make no reference to Spencer, and by certain actions she took during the run of *Without Love*. The play, once again written by Philip Barry expressly for her, bowed that February of 1942 in New Haven. The next month, at a time when the legend has always insisted she had eyes only for Tracy, Kate was in fact meeting a handsome, besotted fan after the show for drinks.

During the Broadway run of *The Philadelphia Story*, David Eichler, a twenty-nine-year-old Harvard graduate student, had tossed notes into Kate's car, sent messages through her driver, and presented her with a book of poetry by Edna St. Vincent Millay. His pursuit resumed during *Without Love*, when he followed her from Wilmington to Boston to New York. Every night, huge sprays of flowers arrived at her dressing room with notes of affection from Eichler. Today a star might call the police about such a persistent fan, but Eichler's letters, filled with the kind of extravagant flattery Kate never could resist, led her to meet him for a drink after one show in April 1942. They ended up talking and flirting well into the night. Kate found the young man charming; not long after, she invited him for a weekend in West Hartford. The flirtation with Eichler had an added benefit: he provided long, detailed analyses of the strengths and weaknesses of *Without Love,* which Kate passed on to Phil Barry.

That spring, the play went on hiatus without opening on Broadway. Reviews had been lukewarm, and a scathing assessment from none other than George Bernard Shaw had deflated the Guild's faith. *Without Love* was a strange hybrid of politics and romance, the story of a man conducting secret war work while marrying a woman purely out of intellectual attraction, or "without love." The man (played by Elliott Nugent, whom Kate despised) spouts off tangentially on Irish politics, a favorite topic of Barry's. Kate never found her way into the part; it's not surprising she was eager to hear Eichler's critiques. Even after rewrites, she remained dissatisfied with the script. That fall, she'd try to renege on a promise to return to the part, huffing out of a Guild meeting and remaining "incommunicado" for several days. Her behavior prompted a letter from Terry Helburn, who reminded the star that she'd be responsible for paying all salaries due to the cast under their Equity contracts.

When the play finally got back under way and opened on Broadway in November 1942, Kate's fears proved justified. Brooks Atkinson thought she gave "a mechanical performance . . . not without considerable gaucherie in the early scenes." The production, he said, was "theatre on the surface of a vacuum." Another critic thought Kate "was not born for the stage." How quickly her laurels from *The Philadelphia Story* had been forgotten.

Without Love closed in February 1943, and Kate was glad to see it end. She told Cukor that when people came backstage—*if* they came back at all— they always jumped to the subject of her elaborate costumes, "which is a dreadful sign." Anxious to get back to Hollywood, she'd come to the conclusion that the theater was "one hell of a tying-down job."

But before she could head back to the Coast, there was a lingering matter from her past that required her attention. One evening, returning to her father's house in West Hartford, she found Luddy waiting for her. At his side was his pretty, twenty-four-year-old fiancée, Elisabeth Albers, daughter of the dean of Boston University's Law School. Since the divorce, Luddy hadn't had an easy time. His employer and close friend, John R. Hall, had jumped to his death in 1936 from the sixteenth floor of the Hotel Roosevelt. Since then, Luddy had been at loose ends, spending time with Michael Pearman and the "idle rich." When the war began, he took a job as a naval engineer, moving to Bethesda, Maryland. He later became a lieutenant commander in the Navy Reserve.

Not confident of the legality of the 1934 Mexican decree, Luddy told Kate that he was planning to file for another divorce. Kate agreed to sign several deeds, relinquishing any claim she might have on Smith family assets. Within days a summons was brought to her at her father's house to appear at Hartford Superior Court on June 2. Of course, by mutual agreement, she ignored the summons and never appeared.

In filing his case, Luddy was charging that Kate had deserted him in December 1933. When Judge Patrick O'Sullivan heard arguments in *Ludlow v. Ludlow* on September 18, he was unaware of the identity of the principals. Finally realizing who "Mrs. Ludlow" was, he expressed doubt that Connecticut was Kate's legal residence. Luddy had anticipated this problem, which is why he had Dr. Hepburn sitting beside him in the courtroom. Hep swore that Kate's tax returns were made from Hartford. Satisfied, Judge O'Sullivan banged his gavel and ended the nearly fourteen-year union of Kate and Luddy. Eight days later, Luddy married Elisabeth Albers in Alexandria, Virginia.

Kate, meanwhile, was heading back to Hollywood—and Spence.

A soft glow from the fire in George Cukor's fireplace fell across the faces of the four people sitting in front of it. Like petty kings at a summit conference, Spencer Tracy and Joe Mankiewicz held forth from their wingback chairs, engaged in a spirited discussion of MGM studio politics. At their feet, on the floor, mostly silent, were their acolytes, Kate Hepburn and the twenty-one-year-old Judy Garland. Occasionally the two women rested their heads on their lovers' knees.

It would be a rosy memory for all involved. "I was happiest then," Judy would tell friends. Her boss, Louis B. Mayer, would be furious when he discovered that one of his producers was dallying with the young, emotionally fragile star. But at George Cukor's, Judy and Joe found a haven where no questions were asked—one of the few places in Hollywood where the truth was allowed.

It was the same for Kate and Spence. The undefined, mostly flirtatious courtship they'd enjoyed since *Woman of the Year* had deepened into a powerful commitment during production of their second film, *Keeper of the Flame.* Filmed during Kate's hiatus from *Without Love,* the picture, amiably directed by Cukor, offered them the time and opportunity to really fall in love. After a long day's shoot, the two stars would retire to the sanctuary of their director's house on Cordell Drive.

If so much else about her relationship with Tracy would parallel her experiences with Phelps Putnam and John Ford, then we can presume Kate fell for her costar in a similar impulsive, rapturous manner. "Hit over the head with a cast-iron skillet" was how Hepburn described falling in love with

Tracy. "He was so steady and I was so volatile . . . [W]e challenged each other, and that was the fun of it."

Her legend would telescope their moment of falling in love down to a single episode on the set of *Woman of the Year*, when Kate accidentally knocked over a glass of water in the middle of a scene. Rather than stop the cameras, Spencer handed her a handkerchief to wipe it up as if it were part of the script. "You old so-and-so," Kate thought, and tried to knock him off stride by getting down on her knees to mop up the water as it dripped from the table. But Spence just smiled and stayed in character. In that moment, both were enchanted by each other's spirit. In many ways, the image of Kate on her knees offers a fitting start to the Tracy-Hepburn affair—at least as it was concocted for the public.

Yet Gavin Lambert, who knew how to separate fact from fiction, insisted that it wasn't until *Keeper of the Flame* that the romance really took off. Only here did they really have the time to fall in love. With wartime rationing of gasoline, Spencer had found the long commute home over the mountains every day to be too expensive, so he took a third-floor suite at the Beverly Hills Hotel. The hotel essentially became his home—and afforded him and Kate the kind of privacy and leisure they hadn't had on *Woman of the Year*.

Their affair was perhaps inevitable. Spencer, with all his secret pain masked by a gruff, masculine exterior, was precisely the sort of man Kate could never resist. Just as she had with Ford, she could sit at Spencer's side and imagine they were an ordinary couple in a traditional relationship. To one interviewer, she said it was "just easy to be with Spence." To another, she'd say it was a relief to find someone who wasn't "curious," someone who didn't press her with too many questions or expectations or presumptions. It suggests that others (Laura? Hughes? Luddy?) had maybe pressed too much.

In many ways, this essential lack of curiosity sums up Hepburn's approach to her emotional life. Externally, she was curious about everything, from the workings of airplanes to the mating habits of Australian lyrebirds. But in matters of the heart, she preferred not to answer—or to ask—too many questions. She was not someone for heart-to-heart confessions, and she was thrilled to discover Spencer wasn't either.

Yet Tracy did not, in fact, share Kate's aversion to emotional contemplation. If anything, he contemplated *too much*—hence his drinking. So preoccupied was he with his own ruminations, he never tried very hard to figure Kate out. He never pressed her for information or asked her to draw any conclusions about herself. There was no need. The only things that mattered to Spence about Kate were readily apparent. She was available for him in a way Louise hadn't been since before the children were born.

Sitting at Spencer's knee in front of the fire at Cukor's, Kate would quickly be on her feet when he suddenly announced he needed a refill of his drink. With Judy Garland tagging along behind her carrying Mankiewicz's glass, Kate would refresh Tracy's drink and then hurry back to her place, never once considering that perhaps Spence had had enough. Unlike Louise, Kate never asked Tracy to stop drinking. She believed he drank because he *had* to; like Putnam, like Ford, a real man *had* to drink if he were to survive in the effete world of the arts. This was something Mary Ford and Louise Tracy had never understood. But Kate did. To her, the man knew best— hadn't even her own mother believed it so?

"In my relationships," Hepburn would say, years later, "I know something has to give. I never think the man is going to give . . . so I do. I just deliberately change. I just shut up—when every atom in me wants to speak up. Mother used to say, 'You can't change anybody else, but you really can change yourself.' "

And so, once again, Kate Hepburn—struggling against her atoms— deferred to her ideal of a real man. "You see," she told Dick Cavett in 1973, "a woman can give a man enormous confidence." No comment on what a man might give a woman.

Their friend Jean Negulesco thought the Hepburn-Tracy relationship was based on "a very solid and ideal foundation. Kate was doing the spoiling and Spence simply accepted . . . From the beginning she understood that devoting her life to him was the only course that would make caring for each other a lasting arrangement."

It wasn't a new revelation for her; it was the way she'd treated Putnam, Ford, and Hughes. Yet for all the admiration of Negulesco and others, in many ways the Tracy-Hepburn pairing was less than admirable: it was often an immature man craving attention from a maternal figure. "Spencer was like a little boy in so many ways," said a longtime acquaintance. "Kate took care of him like a mother."

Still, more than that drew them together. Tracy and Hepburn were in fact quite alike in a fundamental way. They were "highly civilized people," Garson Kanin said, "who held firmly to the enlightened principle of live and let live." Liberal in life as well as in their politics, Kate and Spence moved in a world that passed no judgments on private affairs. In front of Cukor's fireplace, they could discuss theater and art with people of various backgrounds and lifestyles—sophisticated people living among other sophisticated people.

It's fitting, then, that their romance should blossom on the set of *Keeper of the Flame*. No love story like *Woman of the Year*, without any of that film's romantic clinches, *Keeper* is instead a gothic thriller with a leftist political message. During the progressive Roosevelt years—and with the Soviet Union an ally against fascism—directors and writers like Cukor and Donald Ogden Stewart found it easier to express liberal themes on-screen. Based on a novel by I. A. R. Wylie (Kit's friend from Heterodoxy days), the film warns of the dangers of nationalism. After the American hero is revealed to be a bigot and a traitor, Tracy says, "Of course they didn't call it Fascism. They painted it red, white and blue and called it Americanism."

Not surprisingly, conservatives hated the picture. Hedda Hopper blasted it as "*Citizen Kane* with all the art scraped off." Several Republican legislators in Congress complained to Will Hays about the film's "Communist propaganda"—further identifying Hepburn as seditious in the minds of many conservatives.

Liberal politics would, in fact, prove another bond between Kate and Spence. The legend, trying to tie Tracy to his screen character, would make him either conservative or apolitical, forever blustering about actors staying out of politics, with Kate perennially quoting his pithy remark, "Remember who shot Lincoln!" That may have been true later, but during the progressive war years, Tracy was glad to support Democratic causes. Perhaps influenced by the cosmopolitan world at Cukor's, Spencer seems to have transcended his conservative, religious roots to embrace a more liberal worldview, at least politically. To his longtime friends Edith and Loyal Davis (mother and stepfather of First Lady Nancy Reagan), Tracy was very vocal in his support for civil rights for blacks.

Kate, as ever, was even more public about her politics, stumping for Roosevelt, lending her name to Russian war relief efforts, delivering the key patriotic speech in the all-star *Stage Door Canteen*, and narrating the antiracism film *American Creed*. Already she was defending Vice President Henry Wallace, the darling of American liberals, against his critics. "The more high-minded and intent a man like Mr. Wallace is, the simpler it is to make him appear ridiculous," she told a reporter in February 1943. "It's always easy to satirize greatness."

But her real focus at the moment was on another man she considered great. By the middle of 1943, Hepburn and Tracy had become inseparable. Kate might have recommitted herself to her career, but that didn't mean her old loneliness had gone away, or the need to recreate the ideal of her parents' union. In Spence, she seemed to find not only the perfect career match, but a fitting personal complement as well.

Since her own daily routine was a model of efficiency, Kate insisted

Tracy's become one, too. Early to bed, early to rise. Cold-water baths, she told him, were best to keep the body at peak physical health. Together they took long walks along the Los Angeles Reservoir and flew kites on the beach at Santa Monica. Setting up an easel, Kate taught Spence how to paint. It became a lifelong shared pastime. If they didn't paint outdoors, they'd paint from the window of his hotel. She brought him books to read, compiling an entire library of mysteries and detective novels in his suite.

Spencer's rooms became models of order and cheerfulness. Spence liked to play classical music, so Kate played records for him, even if music held very little appeal for her. All her life she'd prefer a roomful of silence to a roomful of music, and that meant any kind of music, from classical to show tunes. But if Spence liked it, she indulged him. Her own passion had always been for flowers, which only got stronger as she got older. (She was now thirty-six to Spencer's forty-three.) Accordingly, every room in Spencer's suite was brightened with strategically placed bouquets, often picked by Kate herself.

Her obsession with cleanliness, also increasing with every year, meant she frequently scrubbed Spencer's rooms all over again after the maid had left. Though he might grumble when she insisted one of those ice-cold baths would cure whatever ailed him, he submitted to her care. For his cooperation Kate would reward him with a box of chocolates or a box of cigars. Tobacco was another shared pleasure; Kate smoked constantly in those days. A cloud of blue smoke perpetually hovered at the ceiling of Spencer's suite, as Hepburn puffed on her cigarettes and Trace chewed on his cigars.

This is the point where chroniclers usually stop to ask why Spencer didn't divorce Louise and marry Kate. Traditionally, the answer has been that Spencer was a Catholic and didn't believe in divorce. Sometimes that got twisted around to say that Louise was the Catholic and therefore the culprit, when in fact she was Episcopalian. But Spencer's friend the reporter James Bacon said it wasn't religion at all that prevented Spencer from getting a divorce. Instead, it was "guilt over his deaf son"—yet again an example of poor Johnnie being used as a scapegoat.

In fact, none of that is true. Marriage was a consideration only in retrospect, raised not by Kate and Spence themselves but by chroniclers desperate to reconcile truth with mainstream presumption. If Tracy and Hepburn were so much in love, it was reasoned, wouldn't they quite naturally want to get married?

Left out of consideration was the essential sophistication of Kate and Spence. Within their sophisticated community—the homosexual Cukor, the unmarried Mankiewicz and Garland, the unorthodox Ruth Gordon and

Garson Kanin, among others—there was no requirement for the conventional parameters of marriage.

Yet eventually all the latter-day speculation would force Kate to address the issue herself. Writing her memoirs, she tried, as ever, to walk a fine line between maintaining the myth and outright lying. "I was complacent," she said. "I didn't push for action. I just left it up to him. And he was paralyzed. I must say it taught me a lesson—one must figure out how much you care for this or that. Then put up a fight. Or don't." She ended this reverie with what seems to be an unfair jab at Louise, suggesting the idea for a divorce should have come from her. Such an action, Kate said presumptuously, would have been "ennobling" for Mrs. Tracy.

If her fans wished to take from these words the belief that Kate would have married Spence if only he—or Louise—had made it possible, that was fine by her. But the truth was very different from what she implied. Joan Fontaine, whom Spence saw socially in the 1950s, would recall him telling her, "My wife and Kate like things the way they are." According to Lee Gopadze, the son of Spencer's close friend and longtime assistant Dorothy Gopadze, everyone involved "accepted the situation as it was . . . Louise understood what was going on. She was resigned to it anyway."

Indeed, in other interviews, Kate would seem to contradict the impression that she'd ever wanted to marry Spencer; usually she'd insist she had never wanted to marry *anybody*. That was the truth the way her friends remembered it. "She *never* would have gotten married," said Noel Taylor. "That wasn't her goal."

When her friend Robert Shaw first met her in the early 1950s, Kate told him point-blank she wasn't "the marrying kind." Rather, Shaw believed, she was perfectly content to keep her relationship with Spencer exactly as it was. "Not for one moment," Shaw insisted, "did she ever sit around wishing she was 'Mrs. Spencer Tracy.'"

Neither did Spencer want to completely sever himself from Louise. She was his wife, the mother of his children, and he could see no one else in that role. On Sundays, he still enjoyed going back to the Hill, their secluded home over the mountains, where after dinner he'd stroll around the farm with John, Susie, and their dogs. Never once did his children see Spencer take a drink. "He was a very good father," said Lee Gopadze, who as a boy was often taken by his mother to see Spencer and his family. Though Louise could take the lion's share of the credit for Johnnie's care, Spencer was actually quite involved in his son's life. They'd play ball and hike into the mountains. Sometimes he brought Johnnie to the studio to watch him filming a picture. To both his children, Tracy was devoted. Susie was sometimes his escort to industry functions, and Spencer made sure to be at every parents' event given by her school, the prestigious Westlake.

Indeed, Louise and Kate occupied very different places in Spencer's life. There was no reason they had to be incompatible. In fact, except for Kate's exhibitionist impulse (which Louise did not share), the two women were quite similar. Both were smart, proper, enormously disciplined East Coast WASPs with deep wellsprings of loyalty and devotion.

Yet Kate's devotion, unlike the more perceptive Louise's, was inspired less by the man than by his image: the strong, masculine hero and great actor whose talent humbled her own. After meeting Spence, Kate said she came to see "a certain sort of cheapness" in her own craft. "My concentration was not anywhere near as good as his," she said. In her opinion, Spencer was "a God-given artist," and there were precious few of those; Kate usually cited Laurette Taylor as Spencer's only peer. Such thinking kept her forever in Tracy's thrall. Louise, on the other hand, remembering the struggling actor he'd been, was more grounded in reality. When Spencer wanted an honest opinion of his work, he went to his wife. Kate would just gush and say he was wonderful.

"He was a subjective actor," Garson Kanin observed in 1971. "She is a cerebral actor. She wants to think everything through—every line, every move, every gesture. He just wanted to get out there and do it."

With an attitude similar to Jack Ford's, Spence did his job like a skilled craftsman. "Just learn your lines and don't bump into the furniture" was his legendary advice on how to act. It was precisely that manly disregard for pretension for which Kate loved him. In her eyes, he could do no wrong as an actor—an attitude that prevailed in their personal lives as well.

"Where Spencer was concerned, Kate lived in a kind of dream world," said Robert Shaw. "No matter what he did—no matter how destructive—he could do no wrong."

She wasn't unaware of her blind spots. Hepburn would admit she never understood her men fully. Late in life, reminiscing with Jack Ford, she said she'd never known how he'd react to "this or that." The same held true for Tracy. She'd claim she never even knew how he really felt about her.

Yet the plain fact of the matter was, she didn't *want* to understand. To give names to her lovers' demons was unthinkable. "Kate didn't believe in that sort of thing," said James Prideaux. "She was strictly New England, and you didn't have mental problems in New England. Work and exercise took care of that."

With all her men, Kate seems to have tried to get them to follow her example—or the examples of her strong-willed women friends like Laura Harding or Fran Rich or Nancy Hamilton. Buck up! Put all troubles out of your mind! Crying is for sissies! Too much brooding, Kate believed, was unhealthy. After all, look at what happened to Tom.

This emotional tug-of-war would define the relationship between Kate and Spencer for all of their years together—he spiraling down, she trying to yank him up, neither of them ever asking the other why or how. As with Ford, it was always "more feeling than saying." Adoring Spencer was enough. Only later, after he was gone, did Kate give any thought to understanding him.

Pacing around the kitchen at Fenwick, Spencer felt like a caged dog. No matter the breeze from the beach or the soothing sound of the waves, he wanted out of the Hepburn house as much as any of his predecessors had. Kate's niece Kathy Houghton would recall the family lore of Spencer standing there awkwardly "twisting his hat around" in his hands.

Certainly Hep and Kit weren't thrilled with this latest Irish Catholic married man their daughter had brought home. Finding a place to sit off to the side, Spence listened edgily as Dick read some of his esoteric poetry and the rest of the clan pretended to pay attention.

What happened next would be dramatized by Kanin in his memoir as if it were a scene straight out of *Woman of the Year*. Every Hepburn biographer has lifted it and replayed it verbatim. Yet while the story was certainly dressed up by Kanin's screenwriting skills, there is no doubt some underlying truth to it.

As the family was discussing what Kanin called "the rights of the poor," Dr. Hepburn suddenly charged out of his seat and onto the porch, shouting threats to a trespasser on the beach. In that moment, Spencer seems to have decided he wanted nothing to do with Kate's family. He'd soon bid them all good-bye, with the Hepburns shaking their heads over his abrupt departure. "I don't think he ever really felt as if he fit in," said Bob Hepburn. For the next two decades, Spencer would return to the Hepburn homestead only a handful of times.

Of course, Kate could see nothing incongruous about Hep's actions. One could want to help the poor without letting them trample across private property. But Spence, having grown up in a very different class structure, had little tolerance for patrician liberalism, which he considered hypocrisy. For two such different emotional temperaments, some adjustments were clearly going to be required if their relationship was to succeed.

Kanin remarked that Kate's world was always "expanding." Hopping back and forth between coasts, she was always meeting new people and trying different things. Spencer's world, on the other hand, grew ever smaller, especially during the last thirty years of his life. Afraid of flying, he didn't like to travel. As friends died or moved out of his sphere, Spencer didn't replace them. His old crowd of Pat O'Brien, Jimmy Cagney, and Frank Morgan—Hollywood's hard-drinking Irishmen who met regularly at Romanoff's in the late 1930s and early 1940s—was eventually supplanted by the more sober, less raucous presence of Kate, Cukor, and the Kanins.

Look in now on one of Cukor's fabled dinner parties, courtesy of a mid-1940s guest list, a menu, and a series of snapshots. Twelve women, twelve men. Hepburn is paired with Tracy. Ethel Barrymore sits next to Cole Porter. Her son Sammy Colt sits with Billie Burke. Constance Collier is paired with Clifton Webb, Lady Mendl (Elsie de Wolfe) is on the arm of Somerset Maugham. And of course the Kanins sit with each other.

After the last crème brûlée has been served and the final bottle of Radicchio poured, the only ones left sitting in front of the fire are Kate and Spence, Ruth and Gar, and Cukor himself—the "Entente Cordiale," as the director dubbed their little group. In the 1940s and early 1950s, this was the heart of Kate's inner circle. The five friends all had deep roots with each other. Spencer and Garson had been friends for several years before Kate arrived on the scene. Gar had also been close with Cukor at least by the late 1930s. Kate had known Ruth for years, admiring her work. They also had horror stories of Jed Harris in common.

What defined the Entente Cordiale was the sparkling compatibility of its members. Kanin could nudge them into serious conversation—"I think the theater ought to be a place where you *learn* something," he'd say—while Ruth could break them all up by countering, "The theater's just somethin' where all the girls are gorgeous and all the boys are cute." With her street-slangy habit of dropping her final consonants, Ruth was forever reminding them that—with the exception of "Miz Hepburn here"—they all came from "workin' people."

But what truly bonded them was a shared love of creature comforts. Spence liked expensive cars (Lee Gopadze recalled a shiny red Cadillac) and Kate had a preference for imported chocolates. Ruth bought her clothes "whole hog" from the expensive designer Mainbocher, and Gar—that ardent socialist—showered his wife with so much jewelry that Cecil Beaton thought she resembled "a little Burmese idol."

From this rarefied quintet would spring *Tracy and Hepburn*, Kanin's seminal memoir of the Spence-and-Kate legend—though he'd slice Cukor out of much of it, giving the impression the clique had consisted of two couples rather than five friends. Such an image, of course, served Kanin's mission to present the "great untold love story" of America's favorite movie couple, with he and Ruth benefiting from the backlight. Yet even within Kanin's mythmaking there exists truth. The iconic image Kanin presents of Hepburn sitting at Tracy's feet is as much a part of her persona as her defiant, jaw-thrusting turn as Jo March.

As she told Scott Berg, Kate had spent her first thirty-five years living essentially "for me, me, me." Now, instead, she was putting someone else's needs first. Of course, there had been similar interludes before, but none compared to her time with Tracy. At the Beverly Hills Hotel, she enjoyed cooking Spencer's meals—roast beef and potatoes, even if she herself still mostly ate salads. When Tracy was drunk, she put him to bed. When once he accidentally struck her as she was doing so, she never breathed a word of it to him.

With women, Kate's relationships had always been predicated on a certain degree of equality, even if Kate, the star, was maybe a bit more equal. But with Laura—her most important relationship next to Spence—there existed a deep-seated respect and mutual give and take.

Yet the kind of devotion that Kate showed to Spencer could be given only to a man, and a very particular kind of man at that: one who combined the strong masculine image of her father with the tortured vulnerability of her brother. With such a man, Kate seems to have put Jimmy aside for a while and imagined herself the sort of woman she sometimes, deep down, thought she ought to be.

There's a moment in *The Little Minister* when Hepburn's free-spirited gypsy admits that she could love a man who *compelled* her to do his bidding. "He must rule me," she says longingly, "be my lord and master." If Kate didn't truly believe such words, it seems that a part of her *wanted* to. She wanted to honor the traditional male-female paradigm the way her mother had done. But mother and daughter had always been very different creatures. Kit empathized with women. She'd seen herself as *one of them*. Kate, meanwhile, spent her life balancing uneasily along the fence between the genders. Indeed, if any line from her movies might articulate her thoughts and fears, it was the insult Sam Craig hurls at Tess Harding: "The outstanding woman of the year isn't a woman at all."

With Tracy, she could put such fears aside. She could *be* a woman, precisely because he was such an elemental man. "He's like an old oak tree," she once mused, "or the summer, or the wind. He belongs to the era when men were men." Later, making *Rooster Cogburn*, she'd make a similar, even more pointed comment about John Wayne: "It was like leaning against a great tree . . . A man's body. Rare in these gay times." What she was doing was distinguishing these "real men" from her homosexual male friends—and in doing so, distinguishing herself as well.

Yet, as ever, we must eventually confront the inevitable question, just as we have for every significant romantic relationship in Kate's life: just how far did she go in playing the woman to Tracy's man?

Joan Fontaine told one interviewer that Tracy had described his relationship with Kate to her as "platonic." Late in life, when Garson Kanin was challenged about the authenticity of his account of the Tracy-Hepburn love affair, he responded defensively, "I never said they *made* love, did I?"

Most of Kate's intimates felt similarly; they concluded that Hepburn and Tracy loved each other without needing to express their feelings sexually. "The relationship with Tracy wasn't physical," said James Prideaux. "I truly question how much sex was ever involved. But as far as the admiration and the caring—absolutely."

"Knowing Kate, knowing Spence," said one man, who first met the couple in the late 1940s, "I'd have to say no, their relationship was not [sexual]. At least not after the first year." Another friend said, "Any scene that puts [Kate] in bed with Tracy, even just to sleep, is pure imagination. Tracy was an insomniac. Kate would never have put up with that." Indeed, Kate herself, whenever she'd describe her bedroom ministrations to Spence, always placed herself on the floor.

Irene Selznick, one of the great wise women of Hollywood and later one of Kate's closest friends, had a very definite opinion on the subject. "I never believed that relationship with Spence was about sex," she told Scott Berg. When Berg objected, arguing that a "sexual animal" like Tracy wouldn't have stuck around if the relationship hadn't included sexual relations, Selznick countered by saying Berg was too young to have known all the (lesbian) women in Kate's life. She added, "You can't drink as much as Spence did, and maintain a relationship built on sex."

But Spence didn't drink constantly. That's important to remember. There would be bad episodes, sometimes weeks long, but then months would pass when he was sober. Surely, in the beginning, in the new throes of love, there was time and opportunity for Kate and Spence to be intimate. They had time alone at the Beverly Hills Hotel, a luxury Kate had never enjoyed with Ford. If it's possible that she overcame her dislike of sexual intercourse with Howard Hughes, it's also possible that she did the same for Tracy. In fact, none other than Laura Harding herself believed that the relationship between Hepburn and Tracy was sexual. After the couple stayed at her New York apartment one weekend, Laura told friends that their lovemaking had been so strenuous that they'd knocked over several glass pieces in her foyer. (Of course, wanting to distance herself from the lesbian rumors of a decade before, Laura may have believed that spreading tales of Kate's amorous adventures with Spence would contribute to the effort.)

"All this talk about whether they were intimate or not is pointless," said Kate's friend Max Showalter. "The kind of love Kate and Spencer shared— her taking care of him, the two of them painting landscapes together, going for walks, having fun—if that's not intimate, I don't know what is." Quite possibly, it was all the intimacy they needed.

Daniel Selznick, while still a boy, would watch Hepburn and Tracy when they came to play tennis at his parents' private court. "It was like a scene out of [their film] *Pat and Mike*," he recalled. "They laughed, they joked with each other, they lost their tempers. It was, watching it, like a variation on making love. It was a very romantic lesson for my adolescence."

No matter how often they slipped between the sheets, the passion they felt for each other in these early years was real. Spencer called her "Kath," an indication that he recognized the private woman behind the public image.

Lee Gopadze said that his mother explained Hepburn and Tracy were in a "difficult situation," but they did the best with it, finding real sustenance in being together. When Jean Negulesco met them, he found them very content in their domesticity. "They looked and were the way I imagined them to be," he said, "simple, warm, ready with friendship. She served a good cup of tea with homemade cookies, and he talked."

Whatever their own personal motivations, Kate and Spence found a formula that worked. "It may not have been the traditional hearts-and-flowers kind of romance it was later portrayed as being," said Gavin Lambert, "but it was a lovely alliance that made them happy to be together, and whenever people find that, it's wonderful."

Though Hepburn would claim she never knew how Tracy truly felt about her, his actions when she visited the set of *The Seventh Cross* (1944) suggest he could get quite jealous over her. Watching as Kate flirted with Hume Cronyn, Spence grew sullen and angry. When Cronyn gallantly leaned in to light Kate's cigarette, Spence barked, "Why don't you two find a bed somewhere and get it over with?"

According to Cronyn, Tracy was drinking that day, which refutes all the stories that said he never drank while working. Kate, getting ready to leave for New York, had come to check on Spence. In fact, part of the reason she'd tried to renege on returning to *Without Love*, then scheduled to open on Broadway, had been concern over Spencer's welfare. Writing to Philip Barry that Tracy was "a wreck and cannot sleep and is feeling as though he might go mad," she hoped Barry might allow Spence a holiday at his house in Hobe Sound, Florida.

But back on the set, Tracy didn't seem much better. "How are you doing, old man?" Kate asked when she saw him. "On my ass," he replied. "Problems?" Kate asked, but she got no answer. No doubt she was just as glad not to have one.

Later, faced with the task of recording the myths for posterity, Hepburn had to finally consider the question of *why* Tracy drank. She argued that it wasn't "a voluntary thing," that some people just couldn't stop drinking (even if *she,* of course, could). She had a point. Alcoholism is a disease, an addiction. But to preserve the legend in amber, she seemed aware that the question needed a little more thought.

Her response was characteristically facile. Concluding that peace of mind was difficult to come by for men like Spencer, she explained that he was plagued by "an oversensitivity to life." Spencer's problem, she said, was a "peculiar combination" of his Catholicism, his imagination, and his artistry.

Once more, it was the idea that a real man *had* to drink when he found himself trapped in the feminized world of Hollywood. "I've known several men who drank too much," she said, almost boastfully, "and they were all extremely interesting." To her way of seeing things, alcohol wasn't the problem. Hep always said if you drank when you were happy, you became happier; if you drank when you were miserable, you only became more so. The trick, then, wasn't to stop drinking; it was to become happy. That was how she'd tried to fix things for all of her men. If she could only get Spence to buck up and be happy, all his problems would be solved.

When, on rare occasions, she allowed herself to ponder Tracy's demons, it was his work in the film *Dr. Jekyll and Mr. Hyde* that intrigued her most. The story had fascinated Spence. "Either because of drink or dope or who knows what," he told her, "[Jekyll] would become . . . Mr. Hyde. Then, in a town or neighborhood where he was totally unknown, he would perform incredible acts of cruelty and vulgarity."

But just what possessed Jekyll to take the potion that turned him into Hyde was never really made clear. For all of Hepburn's attempts to understand Tracy's demons, she was ultimately left frustrated. "Why the escape hatch?" she asked in her rambling open letter to Spencer at the end of her memoir *Me*. "Why was it always opened—to get away from the remarkable you? What was it, Spence? I meant to ask you. Did you know what it was?"

It seems quite likely that he did.

His hands covered in grease and oil, the gas station manager hooked the nozzle into the tank of the black Dodge four-door sedan and counted out a dollar's worth of gasoline.

"Care to come up later and take a dip in the pool, Scotty?" the driver of the car asked. Scotty smiled and said sure.

Scotty liked George Cukor. "George hated to drive," he remembered fondly some six decades later. "So I always knew he really wanted it when he'd drive down the hill."

On the corner of Hollywood Boulevard and Van Ness, now the site of a freeway entrance ramp, Scotty's Richfield gas station has become part of filmdom's underground legend. For decades, an interview with Scotty—called by the *Los Angeles Times* reporter David Ehrenstein Hollywood's "famous male madam"—has been passionately sought after by historians. He represents a vanished world, a living link to a secret Hollywood.

Some sixty years ago, on any given night, fifteen to twenty cars might have been lined up outside Scotty's gas station, but their drivers were nowhere to be seen. Inside the station, behind the oil-smudged axles and piles of rubber tires, Scotty's customers were paying for more than just gasoline. The mechanics at his station were invariably handsome young bucks, just home from the war, and for twenty dollars they were happy to wash their hands (or not) and take a trip with a client to the back room.

"The vice squad would drive by and wonder why all these cars were always lined up at this station," Scotty said, laughing. "But we never got busted."

A farm boy from Illinois, Scotty had spent three years in the Marine Corps during the war. But now, in the summer of 1945, the war was over and hordes of young men were descending on Los Angeles, footloose and fancy-free. Such an influx was bound to shake things up. The screenwriter and playwright Arthur Laurents remembered the postwar years in Hollywood as extraordinarily sexual. "It didn't matter if you were straight or gay or bisexual," he said.

The enterprising Scotty recognized a good opportunity. It wasn't just the boys at the station. He also had girls fanned out across the city to meet some very rich and powerful men. He insisted he never asked for a cent for making such introductions. But if Howard Hughes wanted to send him a $3,000 tip for sending over a pretty girl, Scotty wasn't going to send it back.

A compact, hard-muscled man with tight curls and a ready smile, Scotty quickly became popular with high-profile clients who required a little more privacy than the gas station offered. Happily bisexual, Scotty reported having a long, happy association with Vivien Leigh. He could be equally accommodating with men. With his refreshing, unabashed love of sex, he was adored by homosexuals. Cukor often invited him to dinner when it was just a small handful of gay friends. Arthur Laurents recalled the evenings. There'd be a "cast of just four," he said. "Me to converse with George, an old queen to reminisce with George, and a hustler [to sleep with] George." Other times, Cukor might ask Scotty to wait in the guest room as a surprise for visiting friends.

And one night, soon after the end of the war, one of those friends was Spencer Tracy.

"That was the first time, but it went on for years," Scotty said. "Tracy would always be drinking when I arrived. He'd get so loaded. He'd sit there at the table drinking from five o'clock in the afternoon until two in the morning, when he'd fall onto the bed and ask me to join him . . . And in the morning he'd act like nothing happened. He'd just say thanks for staying over."

For all the occasionally unsavory aspects of his work, Scotty was—and still is—held in very high esteem in Hollywood. A frequent bartender at private parties for stars like Errol Flynn, Rita Hayworth, and Charles Laughton, Scotty would have his trustworthiness affirmed by many. "He was known as discreet and always professional," said Michael Childers a friend of Cukor's and the longtime partner of the director John Schlesinger.

Gavin Lambert agreed. "I've never known Scotty not to tell the truth," he said. "He was always incredibly discreet, and has turned down offers to tell his story for pay. He had nothing to gain by telling what happened. And the fact that George Cukor trusted him—that's saying a lot. George, as shrewd as he was, had a good sense of character. That he'd ask Scotty to dinner was significant. If one can use the word *classy* for the work Scotty did, I'd say that's just what he was."

Scotty's recollections allow for a deeper understanding of Tracy's story. Indeed, they show that Spencer fits the profile of Kate's other significant male relationships. Like Putnam and Ford, he found particular fulfillment from impassioned friendships with men, from his college years through adult life. Like those men as well, the many stories of Tracy's indiscriminate womanizing do not hold up under scrutiny. Scott Berg called Spencer a "sexual animal" presumably because that's how previous accounts had portrayed him, complete with tales of brothels and prostitutes. Like Kate's other men, Spencer drank himself unconscious because she said he was "oversensitive" to life. But to *what* was he so sensitive? That's the question that's never been adequately answered—indeed the cliffhanger with which Kate herself ended her memoir: "What was it, Spence?" Once again, a clue to the answer may be found in the stories of Putnam and Ford.

Certainly, Spencer had plenty of demons. In the war years, there was his guilt over not being in uniform when MGM's other top stars—Clark Gable, Jimmy Stewart, Robert Taylor—had all enlisted. Spence could have joined up, but he blamed ill health. His doctors had told him he had a weak heart, likely because of his drinking. One night, at the fights at the Hollywood Legion Stadium, a group of sailors began taunting Spence as a coward. Stone-faced, he watched as the drunken servicemen were hustled out of the building. Later, devastated, Spence slunk out the back door. In years to come, the legend would play up the tale of President Roosevelt supposedly asking Tracy to deliver an important secret message to European allies. Roosevelt died before he could ever tell Spence what that message was. The anecdote may have been highlighted at least partly as a way of alleviating some of Tracy's guilt over his nonparticipation in the war.

Of course, the traditional explanation for Spencer's torment has been Johnnie. Despite the assessment of all who knew him that Spencer was a good father, his tendency, as always, was to focus on his shortcomings, especially when compared to the enormous accomplishments of his wife. With backing from the University of Southern California, Louise had founded the John Tracy Clinic "to find, encourage and help, by every means at its disposal, the parents of deaf and hard-of-hearing children." From then on, "Mrs. Spencer Tracy" was canonized by the press. Hedda Hopper wondered "if Louise, with her good deeds, won't be remembered longer than Spencer Tracy, the star." Like Phelps Putnam's guilt in the face of his wife's nobility, Spence may have felt Louise's shining example pointed up his own failures—not only as a father, but as a man.

The implication has been that Spencer believed "the sins of the father" had been visited upon the son. For a devout Catholic, such Old Testament–style punishment wasn't so far-fetched to believe. Yet why should Spencer's son be punished when the offspring of other drinkers and carousers were left untouched? What was it about Spencer that singled him out for special sanction? Without an answer to that question, stories of Tracy's self-flagellation over his son's deafness have always seemed a bit suspect.

In fact, his torment stretched back years before Johnnie. To several people (including Kate's niece Katharine Houghton), Spencer said he was convinced he was going to hell—a debilitating belief for a devout Catholic to live with. No wonder he was tormented. Yet why was he so sure of his eternal damnation? God didn't send people to hell for drinking too much; hell would be overrun with artists and theater people. Infidelity to one's wife might be enough to gain entry, but Tracy's lack of hope implies he was struggling with something which no amount of prayer or penance could undo.

"We knew Spencer wrestled with homosexuality," said Elliott Morgan, Cukor's friend and head of research at MGM. Morgan remembered the topic being discussed in hushed tones at the studio, though it was off-limits at Cukor's. "George was very good at protecting Spencer, because [homosexual tendencies] were so against [Tracy's] public image. I'm convinced that's why he drank so much."

"It was one of those very deep, dark secrets of Hollywood," said Gavin Lambert. "It always seemed so odd, because I never felt any gay vibe watching Tracy on-screen. But the stories were told by people in George's circle I trusted. I think it's really the only way to fully understand why Tracy was so troubled."

One of those people in Cukor's circle was Richard Gully, aide-de-camp for Jack Warner, who called Tracy in one interview a "bisexual" who was "never sober." Gully added, "I don't think he functioned as a man." A trusted confidant of many in Hollywood, Gully knew "everybody everywhere," according to Hedda Hopper. For Gully, the essential nature of the Tracy-Hepburn relationship was quite plain: their chemistry, he said, played out "only on-screen."

That's not entirely true. Whether they were sexual with each other or not, Kate and Spencer shared an authentic emotional connection, even if part of it was based on a pattern that today's substance abuse experts might call "codependency." Kate was always there to pick up the pieces for Spence so he didn't have to do it himself. It was the kind of caretaking she thrived on, the kind he needed to exist. Such idiosyncrasies only brought them closer.

Among the Entente Cordiale, Spencer had two models. One was Cukor, who chose a life of undisguised bachelorhood. The other was Kanin, who found a spouse to give him heterosexual credentials without the demand for anything more than a devoted companionship. It would be Kanin's model that Tracy chose over Cukor's. But Kanin, a nonpracticing Jew, was free of the concept of "sin," which seems to have kept the devoutly Catholic Tracy emotionally imprisoned.

Yet occasionally he broke free. Several in Cukor's crowd pointed to Spencer's friendship with Thomas "Tim" Durant, a sportsman well known in polo circles, as a possible romantic involvement. "They were always together," said Elliott Morgan, "racing horses, playing polo. We definitely thought there was something between them." Concurred Michael Pearman, that shrewd witness to so many behind-the-scenes stories of Hollywood and Broadway, "George told me stories about Tracy and Tim Durant. But only with the most hush-hush."

Durant served as head of the United Hunts Club, where he cut a debonair figure astride a horse. One friend praised his "rare quality of masculine charm tinctured with friendliness." Divorced from a daughter of Marjorie Merriweather Post and her first husband, banker Edward Close, Durant had been a New York stockbroker, but the crash of 1929 sent him from Wall Street to Hollywood. Hedda Hopper was soon calling him "one of our better bachelors." Indeed, Durant was a regular name in the columns, photographed with various ladies on his arm, though his most frequent companions were Marlene Dietrich and the aged Constance Collier.

Though he was primarily a rich playboy, Durant occasionally dabbled in moviemaking. As a friend and financial adviser to Charles Chaplin, he worked on the script of *The Great Dictator*. But his primary role seems to have been to usher pretty women into Chaplin's bedroom. (Durant introduced the famous comedian to Joan Barry, who later slapped Chaplin with a paternity suit.) Notably, when the columns started linking Durant to actress Carole Landis, it was only a matter of time before Landis was dating Chaplin.

"Tim Durant was the procurer of girls for Chaplin because he was so debonair," said Michael Pearman. "He wasn't interested in them himself." Indeed, the columnist Jimmie Fidler, known for his bitingly sharp tongue, labeled Durant and the gay actor Bruce Cabot two "peas in a pod," while other reports placed Durant at Ciro's with the notoriously homosexual New York columnist Lucius Beebe.

It was at the Bel-Air stables, where they both kept horses, that Durant first met Spencer. Cheering at the chases, placing their bets at the Santa Anita racetrack, the two men became tight friends. At Durant's swank bachelor home in the hills, Spence swam in the saltwater pool and sampled freely from Tim's well-stocked bar. After they shared a table at Ciro's and ate lunch at the West Side Tennis Club, their friendship was remarked upon in the columns several times. "Two men about town," Hedda Hopper called them. In July 1936, photographers caught Spencer and Louise arriving at the Trocadero with Durant, whose right arm was occupied by Rosalind Russell and his left by her sister Betty Jane. In 1939, Durant took the cabin next to the Tracys' on their transatlantic voyage to Europe.

That year, he was also involved in managing Spencer's career. In May, a letter from the Theatre Guild asking Spencer to appear in Shaw's *The Devil's Disciple* was answered by Durant, who said Spence might be interested. "Spencer and I may come on this next weekend for a week and if so we will certainly get in touch with you," Durant wrote. Later, Terry Helburn would send greetings to "Mr. Durant" in her letters to Spencer.

By the time Kate entered Spencer's life a couple of years later, however, Durant was gone, and her presence seems to have prevented him from coming back. No further mentions of Tracy's friendship with Durant appeared in the columns. Just as she had with Putnam and Luddy, Kate shooed away any homosexual associations in Tracy's life—for a while anyway. In this light, it's impossible not to recall the scene at the end of *Woman of the Year,* when Sam (Tracy) literally kicks his new wife's effeminate secretary (Dan Tobin) out of their lives. The public pairing of Tracy and Hepburn needed to be free of all deviance and subversion. It was strictly an all-American kind of thing.

Spencer's devils wouldn't be so easily discarded, however. In the autumn of 1945, he returned to the stage in Robert Sherwood's play *The Rugged Path,* based loosely on the life of the war correspondent Ernie Pyle. Kate was right behind him all the way, supporting him and encouraging him through rehearsals, convinced his great artistry should be seen on the legitimate stage. Garson Kanin was directing the play. Though Tracy was surrounded with friends, he was terrified; it had been fifteen years since he'd acted on the stage. *The Rugged Path* kicked off in Providence, Rhode Island, on September 28 and set into motion one of the most difficult periods of Spencer's life.

Down on her knees scrubbing his dressing room, opening all the windows to let in fresh air, Kate was determined that Spence's return to the theater would be a triumph. And she had every reason for optimism. The Pulitzer-winning Sherwood was a great admirer of Spencer's, and Kanin was directing him with special tenderness. He was fully aware of Spencer's lack of confidence. As a substitute for drink—Spence hadn't touched any alcohol since he began rehearsing—Kate fed him a steady supply of chocolates.

Yet Kate was aware of Tracy's increasing anxiety at every performance. She told John Wharton of the Playwrights Producing Company, the backers of the play, "It will take a lot of courage to open in New York, and Spencer hasn't got that kind of courage."

She helped him find it, however. That November, the play did open on Broadway, though by now Spencer was at odds with Sherwood over the script. Even he and Kanin were on the outs; the experience of *The Rugged Path* would derail their friendship for more than a year. With reason, too: Spencer's insecurities were making him behave like a spoiled star. Through the intermediary of his brother Carroll, who acted as his manager, Tracy had been threatening to quit for weeks. He seemed to Kanin to be deliberately sabotaging his success.

Kate, too, was at a loss to understand his actions. Every night after the show, while Spencer held court with visiting theater people in his room at the Waldorf, she sat gazing up at him in silent adoration. But after the visitors left, Spencer paced the suite, unable to sleep. Kate tried to boost his spirits. She told him how brilliant he was. She told him he was better than Laurence Olivier, considered the finest actor onstage. Why didn't he believe her? Why wasn't her faith in him enough?

The Rugged Path closed on January 19, 1946. Soon after, Kate returned to Hollywood to make a picture, while Spence used the occasion to go on one of the worst benders of his life. For months he was out of touch with everyone. Michael Pearman heard tales of Spencer hiring hustlers to come up to his room in the Waldorf, where furniture was destroyed and housekeepers routinely hauled out trash cans filled with empty bottles. The actor Don Taylor told of seeing Spencer twisting and turning inside a straitjacket at Doctor's Hospital; a few months later, Tracy was hospitalized again in Chicago as a patient of his old friend Dr. Loyal Davis. "There was a very private floor at Passavant [Hospital]—the top floor," Davis's son Richard remembered. "He was there maybe six weeks getting dried out." Through all of this, the head of security at MGM, Whitey Hendry, managed to keep the press from finding out.

But no one could stop reports from getting back to Kate, who understood now it was a matter of life or death. "Tracy . . . would have died many years before he did had it not been for Hepburn," said the MGM publicist Esmé Chandlee. This much of the legend is real. For the next five years, Kate put aside "me, me, me" and devoted herself to keeping Spencer alive.

SILENCING THE MOST ARTICULATE VOICE

A windy, foggy night in Los Angeles in May 1947, and the thirty thousand people crammed into Gilmore Stadium were getting restless. "Wallace in Forty-eight!" they chanted. But instead of the former vice president—an ardent liberal many suspected of being a socialist who was considering a run for the White House—a thin woman in a bright red dress walked out onto the stage.

A murmur went through the crowd. *Could it really be her?*

A day before, Louella Parsons had mused in her column, "I wonder if it's true that Katie has agreed to appear with Henry Wallace. I hope it isn't."

Louella's hopes were in vain. For yes, indeed, that was Katharine Hepburn up there striding confidently across the stage. The crowd went wild. That a movie star of her magnitude would show up in support of a man being pilloried as a socialist by both Democrats and Republicans seemed unbelievable. But these were extraordinary times.

Not two weeks before, Representative J. Parnell Thomas, chairman of the House Un-American Activities Committee, had arrived in Hollywood to initiate an investigation into Communist activity in the film industry. Two days ago, he'd announced he was "amazed" at the extent of "Red infiltration" in the movie studios. He called for immediate hearings in Washington.

Kate was outraged. Grabbing hold of the microphone, she barely waited for the applause to die down before she launched into a ringing denunciation of what she saw as a witch hunt. "I want to speak to you about the attacks on culture," she said, her unmistakable voice crackling out of the stadium's loudspeakers. "I speak because I am an American and as an American I shall always resist any attempt at the abridgement of freedom."

A thunderstorm of cheers crashed all around her as Kate went on, her voice rising, growing more powerful. "The artist, since the beginning of time, has always expressed the aspirations and dreams of his people. Silence the artist and you have silenced the most articulate voice the people have."

Once more she was interrupted by applause. As ever, she took strength from it, allowing the surge of affection from the audience to sustain her and carry her along. The screenwriter Arthur Laurents may have written her speech, but the passion and the strength she brought to it were undeniably her own. She believed every word she was saying. Laurents would recall she was euphoric afterward, proud of what she had done.

To those in the audience, Kate's presence on stage was "like an angel in a red dress." Her confident, aristocratic demeanor gave them hope that their cause would prevail. Whoops and whistles continued punctuating Kate's words as she laid out a radical vision of America. She lambasted President Truman's call for a loyalty test, comparing him to the "thought police of imperial Japan." She excoriated the State Department for censoring American paintings abroad, likening it to Hitler's suppression of art. She condemned the segregation that tried to silence the actor Paul Robeson, "an American citizen," she said, "a great artist, the most articulate voice of the Negro people [and] an obvious threat for the men who would ignore the meaning of the Bill of Rights."

Then she turned her attention to the crisis at hand. "Today J. Parnell Thomas is engaged in a personally conducted smear campaign of the motion picture industry. He is aided and abetted in this effort by a group of super-patriots"—laughter from the audience at this point—"who call themselves the Motion Picture Alliance for the Preservation of American Ideals." Still more derisive laughter. "For myself, I want no part of their ideals or those of Mr. Thomas." The cheering lasted for a full five minutes.

But out beyond the stadium, Hollywood already was cleaving in two. The alliance that Kate slammed in her speech had produced fourteen "friendly" witnesses for Thomas, people like Robert Taylor, Lela Rogers (Ginger's mother), Rupert Hughes (Howard's uncle), and Adolphe Menjou, who'd appeared with Kate in *Morning Glory* and *Stage Door*. All willingly named names of suspected Communists. While some studio heads initially struck a defensive posture—"No half-ass Congressman is going to tell MGM how to run its business," Eddie Mannix huffed—Jack Warner behaved like a man with a gun to his head, blurting out the names of every liberal he could think of, Communists or not.

The brief flowering of progressivism in Hollywood, which had produced such films as *Crossfire, Gentleman's Agreement,* and Hepburn's *Keeper of the Flame,* was now being challenged by a backlash not dissimilar to the political storm that had swept the Code into power in the 1930s. Back then, Hollywood had been charged with a lack of moral and social conformity. Now it was the charge of political subversion. Yet ultimately it was the same instinct: to safeguard traditional values and stifle social change.

The postwar backlash wasn't against communism so much as it was against the liberal intelligentsia that had held power throughout the long Roosevelt years. Gunning for subversives would be common sport for the next decade, and the hunt ultimately mattered more than the kill. Hollywood, showy and influential, was an obvious target for the forces of reaction, though not the ultimate goal. "We were simply window-dressing," said the actor Will Geer, later blacklisted, "for a major drive on the part of Congressmen and people in power who wanted to stop all sorts of thinking on many scores. They were really after the scientists, the teachers, and others."

But for now it was Hollywood in the crosshairs. In these first few months of the great inquisition, the outrage felt by liberals in the film colony could barely be contained. Not yet was there a feeling of hopelessness. Not yet had the great machine of the federal government squashed its opposition into silence. In May 1947, most on the left believed Thomas's smear campaign was a temporary aberration wrought by a cocky, revenge-minded Republican Congress, which had just won back power in the last election. Surely this could not succeed. The *New York Times* reported in May that only "the most determined alarmists" felt HUAC would truly do any harm to the film industry. Kate believed that if enough people spoke out, Thomas would be exposed as a fanatic, and rational people had to agree. "The House committee seemed only stupid," agreed the screenwriter Walter Bernstein, who was later blacklisted. "I understood their bigotry but not their power."

It was a regrettable underestimation. Roosevelt was dead. Truman was yanking the Democrats away from the liberal policies of his predecessor. Red-baiting was now a strategy for both parties. Only Wallace, then exploring a run for the Democratic nomination, rejected the trend. "If I fail to cry

out that I am anti-Communist," he said, taking the stage after Kate had finished, "it is not because I am friendly to Communists but because at this
time of growing intolerance, I refuse to join even the outer circle of that
band of men who stir the steaming cauldron of hatred and fear."

The crowd loved him, but others felt Wallace was either a patsy or a traitor. Both labels would soon be used for Kate as well. Naively, she had
thought she was scandal-proof. "Edward G. Robinson was supposed to make
that speech," she recalled, "and I thought, 'Well . . . he's Jewish and very left
of center, so he would be suspect by that committee.' My ancestors were 'on
the Mayflower.' There's nothing that they can tack onto me." (Apparently she
had forgotten how easily her critics had found things to tack onto her in the
1930s.)

Indeed, she had some reason to fear being targeted. Thirty years earlier, Kit
Hepburn had come very close to joining the Communist Party. At the very
time of her daughter's speech, there were dozens of books and pamphlets in
Kit's study that J. Parnell Thomas would have found very incriminating. "That
speech was for Mother," Bob Hepburn believed. But when we listen to Kate's
voice, fortunately preserved on tape in the records of the Hollywood Democratic Committee, it's impossible not to believe it was as much for herself. This
was the young woman who'd sat in thrall at another lover's feet, listening as
Phelpie debated capitalism and socialism with Matthiessen and Davenport.
This was the fiery independent who'd rebuffed her studio's interdict against
supporting Sinclair, who'd refused to cross picket lines, who'd spoken out for
the rights of workers. Sure, it was for Kit. But it was for Kate, too.

This was also a woman who had just turned forty, who had spent the
past year and a half in largely selfless activity, getting Spencer on the wagon
and his career back on track. Her speech for Wallace was something for *herself*—a burst of the young Kath coming through. At a recent party, she had
been appalled when the twenty-six-year-old actress Gene Tierney described
herself as a conservative. "At your age?" Kate asked. "Heaven help you."

Yet it would be Kate who needed the help. Her career was once again in a
slump, and her rash decision to deliver that speech, as noble and admirable
as it was, could only make things worse. While nowhere near the severity of
her problems in the 1930s, Kate's professional life had lost some of the momentum of the one-two punch of *The Philadelphia Story* and *Woman of the
Year*. *Keeper of the Flame* had failed to set a fire at the box office. Offers from
the Theatre Guild to take on another play went unheeded because they
would have meant leaving Spencer, who was still drying out, day by day, in
his suite at the Beverly Hills Hotel.

But Kate's real problem was that her success had boxed her in. The new Hepburn, to be popular, had to be a brittle career woman taken down a few pegs by a man. She could not be, for example, a Chinese peasant fighting heartless Japanese invaders. That's what she had played in *Dragon Seed*, based on the novel by Pearl S. Buck and helmed by the director Jack Conway. Kate's black wig and typical Oriental makeup weren't enough to disguise her high New England cheekbones. She's miscast even worse here than she was in *Spitfire*, shuffling along behind her husband (Turhan Bey). It didn't help that Conway collapsed halfway through the picture and had to be replaced by the undistinguished Harold S. Bucquet. Still, the film offered Kate a reunion with Pan Berman and Jane Loring, who'd moved their base of operations over to MGM. And, in fact, it wasn't the complete box-office failure it's been presumed. Released in the summer of 1944, *Dragon Seed* was among the top ten moneymakers for September, its ringing war propaganda guaranteeing an audience.

Critics were less impressed, however. What they were waiting for was another *Woman of the Year*, and Hepburn had now disappointed them twice. It was with open arms, then, that they welcomed *Without Love* the following March. The film marked the return of the comedy duo of Tracy and Hepburn, with Spencer taking over Elliott Nugent's part in the adaptation of Kate's play. By snipping out all of Phil Barry's Irish politics, however, the screenwriter Donald Ogden Stewart deprived the script of any gravitas it might have had. Once again a listless Harold Bucquet was in charge (he died less than a year after the film was released), with the result being an uneven, often incomprehensible farce.

Yet critics seemed to overlook the film's obvious flaws, so pleased were they to have Kate and Spence back where they wanted them. "They play contrasting, dominant characters in remarkably finished style," wrote Bosley Crowther in the *New York Times*, offering the first critical analysis of the Tracy-Hepburn team. "They strike sparks when they're thrown together."

Without Love turned out to be a smash. Even if there had been no personal connection between them, the careers of Hepburn and Tracy were now forever intertwined. The irony is, for all of Crowther's admiration for the sparks they gave off, *Without Love* lacks the playful sexuality of *Woman of the Year*. Lucille Ball, in fact, steals the show as the wisecracking sidekick, though Kate does get to deliver one memorable in-joke. "I like Dorothy Parker, too," she says, finally secure enough to tweak her past problems at the box office.

She may have laughed too soon. Greeting her director, Vincente Minnelli, on the set of her next film, *Undercurrent*, Kate made him feel as if it was *her* picture, not his. She didn't like Minnelli, probably biased in her opinion by Cukor, who loathed him. But worse, Kate found him weak and ineffectual, a capital crime in her book. "When I've had a director I could smother," she said, "and I've had one or two who shall be nameless, I have really suffered, because I knew I was pushing them around, and it was more painful for me than it was for them."

Jayne Meadows, who had a small part in the film, remembered Hepburn "bossing" Minnelli on the set. Kate had just seen the director's latest film, *The Clock*, and despised it. "You better not make any of those mistakes in this movie," Meadows recalled Kate telling the director, "or you'll be on the next Super Chief back to New York."

He may as well have bought a ticket. The film ranks among the worst in both of their careers. Kate didn't like her costar, Robert Taylor, very much either—feelings confirmed by his testimony to HUAC just a few months later. Kate's part of a meek bride was better suited to Joan Fontaine. The RKO Hepburn would never have resorted to such a role, but film noir— what *Undercurrent* had pretensions of being—was all the rage, and Kate wanted a hit.

What she got was a moderately successful picture, even if the critics hated it. But moderate success wasn't enough for a female star of Kate's age. She needed another blockbuster like *Woman of the Year*. Bette Davis, Ingrid Bergman, Betty Grable, and even little Margaret O'Brien were all well ahead of Hepburn at the box office. If her fame was going to be of the lifelong variety, she was going to have to recommit herself to the task.

Problem was, she had a few other things on her mind.

The inner sanctum of Louis B. Mayer's office was not a place many at the studio ever got to see. Plushly carpeted, its expensive antique furnishings always smelling tartly of wood polish, the room emanated a sense of power and authority. The little man in the round glasses seated behind the enormous desk struck terror in the hearts of even the biggest he-men on the lot. No matter the bravado with which she later told the story, Kate Hepburn no doubt felt at least a twinge of trepidation as she headed to Mayer's office on the day after her speech at Gilmore Stadium.

Louis B. Mayer despised liberals. Kate would describe him as "not on my side of the fence at all." So the headlines in the morning newspapers about Kate's performance at the Wallace rally would certainly have raised his blood pressure. The *Los Angeles Times* described her dress as "a sweeping scarlet gown." With Parnell Thomas ready to paint the whole town as Red Commies,

Kate had just given him a head start. Why, Mayer demanded, had she made that speech?

Despite her boss's politics and autocratic nature, Kate liked Mayer. He was a gambler, and she liked men who gambled, who trusted their own judgment. Mayer also loved making movies, and Kate respected him for that. So she reasoned with him that day in his office rather than argued. She told him that she didn't blame him for being upset. She understood the dilemma he now faced in trying to promote her pictures. But, Kate argued, if she had told him in advance that she was going to make the speech, he would have forbidden her, wouldn't he? And she would have done it anyway. That, she said, would have been even worse.

Telling the story later, Hepburn depicted Mayer as rather befuddled by all her fast talking, caught off guard by her admission of wrongdoing and her suggestion that he drop her from the weekly payroll. "If you presume to take a weekly salary from someone," she reasoned, "maybe you haven't got a right to go out and walk naked down the street." Using an argument Mayer should have been using on her, Hepburn wanted us to believe that she left her boss scratching his head as she departed, rather like a comic scene from one of her films.

More likely, Mayer let her off the hook for other reasons. Just as her social prestige had carried her through dark days at RKO, Hepburn's distinction as a "high-class" star gave her considerable leeway with the class-conscious Mayer. He also genuinely liked her. "To him, she was proof that one could have talent without temperament," recalled his daughter Irene Selznick. Mayer told colleagues that Hepburn was a woman of her word.

But for the studio chief, there may have been one other, even more important consideration in treating Kate's indiscretion lightly. She was succeeding at a task where all others had failed. She was keeping Spencer Tracy on the wagon.

Ever since Spence had returned from New York, Kate had devoted herself to getting him back on his feet. For the first time since she started making movies, she spent more time in Los Angeles than she did in the East. Her decisions to make two bad films, *Undercurrent* and the later *Song of Love*, can't be seen outside this context. They kept her in Hollywood and within easy reach of Spence at the Beverly Hills Hotel. For a woman whose decisions had always been self-motivated, this was a remarkable change.

It was tough, however. Every few months the Theatre Guild sent another letter cajoling her to do a play. Shakespeare's *As You Like It* was the carrot they dangled most often, but when Kate's hopes for luring Garbo back to the screen for *Mourning Becomes Electra* were dashed, Lawrence Langner suggested they do it on the stage. In May 1946, Langner sent another play he thought worthy of Kate's consideration; if she didn't want to do it, he was going to send it to Bette Davis. No doubt he hoped that might get her goat, but Kate didn't bite.

What she really wanted to do was Shaw's *Saint Joan*. "I wish you could really do something about that," she told Langner, pushing him to talk to "G.B.S." The play—which suggests Joan of Arc needed to be killed because the world wasn't yet ready for her—suited Kate's sense of herself. She'd wanted to play Joan now for more than a decade.

The Guild did talk with Shaw, but he wasn't making any commitments. In truth, it's unlikely Kate would have left Spencer anyway. When Langner learned she was mulling over signing a new contract with MGM, he pleaded with her not to "sell [herself] into slavery for another five years," when she could be supporting the Guild (and Spencer) by doing *As You Like It.* Though Kate had once admitted to getting more and more "sog-brained" the longer she stayed in Hollywood, nothing could induce her to leave Spencer by this point. In September 1946, Kate signed on with MGM again with a weekly salary of $3,512.59.

It was Spencer's progress that motivated her decision. She'd made an undeniable difference in his life. Not for more than a year had he touched a drop of alcohol. In his daily logbooks, Tracy began recording little marks of progress: "One week without a drink." "Two weeks without a drink." Yet his withdrawal from alcohol had left him with a host of related illnesses, some real, some imaginary. Leave it to efficient Kate to know what cured a stomachache or soothed sore joints. Moreover, she knew the best pharmacy to deliver it at any hour.

Much of Hollywood knew Spence was out of commission during this period, but the columns kept his name in rotation, reminding the public that despite being replaced by Robert Walker in *The Romance of Henry Menafee* (the film was never made), Tracy was still lined up for several projects, including *Sea of Grass* with Kate. Meanwhile, Kate told the Guild that if it really wanted to work with her, it needed to find a play she and Spence could do together. Langner had suggested O'Neill's *Lazarus Laughed,* but Kate couldn't make sense of it—and while she might be "quite dumb," she said, Spencer didn't get it either.

In June 1946, Langner had proposed an idea that almost took off: a repertory company headed by Tracy and Hepburn that would "set the country on fire by bringing back some of the real, old-time theater." Ideas tossed around were *Dodsworth, The Master Builder,* and *Desire Under the Elms.* The Guild proposed forming an independent picture corporation in which Spence and Kate would each have a share. That fall, during a trip East, they met with the Guild to talk it over, but nothing eventually came of the idea. After the experience of *The Rugged Path,* Spence wasn't eager to go back on the stage, and Kate figured the confines of a movie studio were safer for him than being on the road.

Her lack of fulfilling work was, for the moment, worth it. She was over-joyed with helping to turn Spencer's life around. Never before had she been able to rescue the men she loved. She had failed Tommy, lost Putnam, and turned her back on Jack Ford. With Spencer, Kate was determined to have lasting success. The image that has seeped into the public consciousness is of one long battle, with Tracy always drunk and Hepburn always picking him up off the floor. But after the debacle of *The Rugged Path,* it was not that way at all. Spencer was sober for several years, and the warm, funny human be-ing he could be came through from under all his layers of pain and conflict.

When his personal assistant, Dorothy Griffith Gopadze, got married, Spencer sent down a crew to barge in on them as a prank during their hon-eymoon in Palm Springs. He spent considerable effort planning the joke, knowing "Miss G.," as he called her, would be amused—but then Miss G. and her new husband stayed in a different room, foiling Tracy's plan. The two laughed about it for years. When Gopadze's son was born, Spencer sent her a telegram: "Miss G., I didn't know you had it in you."

"You have to understand what a sense of family there was around Spencer," said Gopadze's son Lee, to whom Tracy was a gruff but avuncular presence. "He treated my mother as his equal. He didn't put on airs. He was a very down-to-earth man."

One day, when he was about six or seven, Gopadze was with his mother on the MGM lot when Spencer drove up in his brand-new red Cadillac con-vertible. He gave the wide-eyed boy a ride around the lot, letting him wave to everyone from the flashy car. "Spencer had a soft spot for children," said one of his friends. "He'd rather sit and talk with a kid than most adults."

If he could make someone laugh, he considered the time spent well worth the effort. Tracy liked to tell jokes, and he could be the most amusing storyteller, leading his listeners through long and deliberately rambling monologues before coming to the surprise punch line. He was also a bril-liant mimic, performing dead-on impersonations of a snooty Laura Hard-ing or a befuddled George Cukor. "He wasn't always this tormented creature," said his friend. "He could sometimes be a very jolly old boy, sitting there making faces behind Kate's back and winking at us, a devilish twinkle in his eye."

Of course, sometimes his lighthearted teasing could take on an edge. His often callous treatment of Hepburn was sometimes harsh enough to leave observers dumbstruck. "Who the hell are *you*?" Spence might bark if Kate ventured an opinion that departed from his own. Her nurturance was sometimes taken for granted, with Tracy growling out orders to get him a glass of milk or to haul in some firewood.

At least one of Tracy's friends thought the verbal abuse of Kate didn't really begin until after *The Rugged Path,* when Spence was on the wagon and often irritable from lack of sleep. "Without booze, he often lay awake all night, and then he'd be very grouchy the next day," said the friend. "And he took it out on the person closest to him—Kate."

She never complained, never put up a defense. Like Tracy Lord, she took what the men in her life had to give. "She would take anything from [Spencer], even his mockeries," said Jean Negulesco, adding that some of those mockeries were "pretty hard to take."

Joe Mankiewicz ventured the opinion that Hepburn put up with such behavior because she took it as a sign of affection. It was well known that Spence chose to ignore people he didn't like. If he abused you, that meant he liked you.

Yet even worse, in some ways, was what Tracy *didn't* say. "I don't think he ever complimented Kate to her face," Mankiewicz added. "He would say wonderful things *about* her, but never *to* her."

Kate took it all in stride. "She excused Spencer's meanness toward her," said Robert Shaw, "because she felt he didn't really mean it, that he was struggling with staying sober and always exhausted and so she needed to be sympathetic."

It was also, in many ways, the way she had been raised. Kate had taken her father's criticism much the same as she now took Tracy's. It was a sign that he was paying attention to her—precisely what little Kathy Hepburn had craved from her earliest days.

It was during this period that Hepburn and Tracy were most a couple. These years would, in fact, later be inflated to encompass the entire period of their knowing each other, giving the impression that for twenty-six years they'd lived in steady domestic companionship. But only here, from roughly 1945 to 1949, was there any truth to that image. Their togetherness is documented in letters to Kate from the Guild, which never failed to send "love to Spence" at the end of every missive. Often Kate and Spence were invited to join Lawrence Langner and Armina Marshall at their house in Connecticut. Terry Helburn always addressed her Christmas greetings to the both of them during this period, and Christmas cards to George Cukor were signed "Kate and Spence."

Yet they never lived together, despite everything the legend has implied. Spencer still resided at the Beverly Hills Hotel, while Kate had settled into the former John Gilbert house at 9897 Beverly Grove, her longest period of residence at any address in California so far. Em Perkins still bustled about efficiently, if a little slower these days, watching over Kate and the household. Laura still arrived for extended visits, as did Palache, Murph, and Fran Rich.

No matter their separate residences, however, in many other ways Kate and Spence were like a married couple—an *old* married couple, content in a certain compatible routine. At long last, Kate had been able to sustain her funhouse version of the traditional male-female relationship, a dream that had eluded her in the past. The vigor with which she lived the part, the sheer commitment she brought to it, bespeaks how dear it was to her.

Sipping sherry in Cukor's suede-walled oval room, sharing bon mots with Ruth and Gar, the fact that the five friends of the Entente Cordiale were anything *but* traditional seemed not to matter. For a girl who'd grown up with a sense of theatrics, who knew from a very young age how to playact, who'd always been "a very good fairy-tale teller," the illusion was enough—especially given the truth of the feelings.

Such a carefully constructed existence would have been shattered if Kate and Spence ever considered marriage. Returning from a weekend with his wife and children, Spence didn't share much of this other life with Kate, Cukor, and the Kanins—his family of choice—just as he certainly never spoke of Kate to Louise. Indeed, the dynamics of the Tracy-Hepburn relationship were such that not a lot of intimate conversation of any sort ever passed between them, not if Kate could say later on that she never knew Spence or how he felt about her. There's a certain, upside-down logic to it. Too much intimate talk might have destroyed their intimacy, upset their delicate make-believe, brought their castles down from the air. Neither of them wanted that, especially now, when they'd achieved some semblance of order in their lives.

At forty, Kate was desperate to keep Spence sober and functioning. Looking back, she would have seen a long winding trail of ambition in her life, but until she'd dried Spencer out and created this little domestic life for the two of them, she'd been alone. Not once in all that time had she found any sustaining fulfillment in a relationship with another human being. Laura had come closest, but life with Laura had proven impossible.

To see what she was missing, all Kate had to do was go home to Connecticut. After nearly fifty years, her parents were still deeply in love. Of her siblings, only the dreamy Dick was still without a mate. Even Palache had settled down, marrying her longtime friend Russell Jones and moving to upstate New York. "She really envies us this place," Palache said. "The stability and the security. She never says so, but I know she does."

Jayne Meadows recalled a moment on the set of *Undercurrent*, when word came that Judy Garland had just given birth to Vincente Minnelli's daughter Liza. Kate became quite emotional. "That must be the greatest thrill in the world," she told Minnelli, congratulating him despite their differences on the picture. It was the emotion behind what she said that was affecting, recalled Meadows, who couldn't comprehend what had caused the usually strident star to suddenly go soft.

Some writers have concluded that during this period Kate began lamenting the fact she'd never had children. Barbara Leaming, in her book on Hepburn, insisted Kate tried to persuade Palache to have a baby so she could raise it, although there is no specific attribution for the story. But Kate's wistfulness at this point in her life wasn't about being childless. It was about the fear of being *alone*, about not having any permanent connection. For all the routine she shared with Spence, she knew the eggshells under their feet could break at any time. Spence's sobriety could unravel, and she'd be on her own again, and another year older.

Of course, *sober* is a misleading word. While Spencer may not have been drinking, he continued to suffer from terrible insomnia. With so little sleep, his frequent grouchiness and disorientation on the set aren't surprising. Guzzling coffee all day to keep himself alert, at night he'd pop any number of the different barbiturates his doctors had prescribed, including Seconal. He also was reportedly taking Dexedrine—speed—to combat his depression. It only aggravated his insomnia, keeping the vicious cycle in motion. Even without alcohol in his system, Spencer still lived with a constant jangle of nerves.

Increasingly, Kate bore the brunt of it. Late one night, Signe Hasso, who had starred with Spencer in *The Seventh Cross*, received a phone call. It was Spencer, insisting she come over right away. Concerned, Hasso made a beeline over to the Beverly Hills Hotel, where she walked into the middle of an argument between Spence and Kate. Kate, however, wasn't doing any of the arguing. She was just sitting there, listening as Spencer berated her about the way she'd played a certain part. Mimicking her Bryn Mawr voice perfectly, Tracy flounced about the room, waving his hands. Suddenly, he turned and asked Hasso to act out the part with him. Reluctantly, she went along. "You see?" Spencer shouted at Kate when they were finished. "Now this is a *real* actress!"

Just as, decades earlier, Kit had found her escape hatch from the pressures of her marriage to Hep, Kate found her own release from Spencer's volatility. On the set of *Dragon Seed*, she encouraged the eager attention paid to her by the twenty-one-year-old Turhan Bey. Fifteen years her junior, Bey, the son of a Turkish father and Czech mother, was just starting out, thrilled to be appearing opposite Katharine Hepburn. Love letters from Bey began arriving for Kate, who gave them to Em Perkins for safekeeping. (She'd still have them twenty years later.) When Louella Parsons reported in her column that orchids were showing up in Kate's dressing room, Kate was forced to gently ask Bey to send no more.

Yet the best distraction for Kate was always work. In the summer of 1946, the team of Tracy and Hepburn was back in front of the cameras, toiling in a turgid melodrama based on Conrad Richter's novel *The Sea of Grass*. The director, Elia Kazan, on just his second major picture, recalled watching Spencer "squeeze" out of the studio car. Under Kate's care, Tracy had plumped up considerably. No alcohol meant lots of food—mostly sweets—and it showed. Spence was the heaviest he'd ever been in his life.

He'd also aged quite a bit since his last appearance in *Without Love*. At forty-seven, Tracy looked at least ten years older. More white than russet now colored his hair; his face had folded and creased into hundreds of lines. To Kazan, Spencer resembled one of the horses he was slated to ride in the film, the story of a nineteenth-century cattle baron. The director worried Tracy wouldn't be up to the task. For her part, Kate in her early forties still looked fresh and young, if a bit gaunter since the height of her sexiness in *Woman of the Year*.

But neither seemed inspired by the script. Spence sat in his chair, waiting to be called. When he was, he did what Kazan observed he always did to prepare himself, simply smoothed his forehead with an open palm. When Kazan tried to give him direction—some of that "Method" business Spence found "hocus pocus"—he was brushed aside. After doing his bit, Spencer wandered back over to his chair and sat down heavily. "Perfectly believable as an actor," Kazan remembered, "completely unbelievable in the scene." Not yet with any studio clout himself, Kazan called "print" and moved on. He didn't know what else to do.

Kate was no help. Whenever Spence would finish a scene, before Kazan could offer an opinion of his own, she'd burst in with "Wasn't that wonderful! How does he do it? He's so true! He can't do anything false!" The resulting film was a disaster, and MGM knew it, sliding it onto a shelf and hoping to forget about it. But the bigger disaster was still to come.

Leo McCarey was fighting mad. The director of *Going My Way* and *The Bells of St. Mary's* had wanted Kate for his upcoming picture, *Good Sam*. But as one of Thomas's "friendly" witnesses, McCarey was still piqued at the spectacle Hepburn had made of herself in her red dress a month earlier at Gilmore Stadium. So he leaked to a *Variety* reporter that her "political outbursts" had cost her a job.

While Louis B. Mayer may have let her off the hook, others weren't so forgiving. Once again Kate was a lightning rod for conservative anger. Ronald Reagan, then head of the Screen Actors Guild, would denounce her speech as "a word-for-word copy of a CSU strike bulletin several weeks old"—referencing the Conference of Studio Unions, a federation of craft unions then being accused of communist sympathies. One correspondent to the *Hollywood Citizen-News* claimed Kate had made a "plea for the Communists" in her speech at Gilmore Stadium. It was her red dress (even if few of her critics had actually seen it) that seemed to expose Hepburn's political beliefs for what they were. One outraged letter writer described the dress as "flaming." It was like a red flag waved at a pack of bulls.

Then, just as it seemed the furor was dying down, syndicated political columnists got wind of the "Lady in Red" story and began wiring it across the nation. "It was Henry Wallace who made the headlines," wrote Drew Pearson in a dispatch that reached dozens of papers in the Midwest and South, "but it was movie actress Katharine Hepburn who really stole the show." In his widely read column, Jimmie Fidler said McCarey was right to can her from *Good Sam*: "Her recent . . . extremely hot political speeches may queer her at the box office."

Of course, Kate made *one* speech, not "speeches." But such was the way the story was building. By early September, Drew Pearson's syndicated column reported that "inside sources" had confirmed Hepburn would be subpoenaed when HUAC convened its hearings in Washington the following month. Although Charlie Chaplin and other well-known liberals were also named, it was Kate's picture that adorned Pearson's column.

Her top-rank celebrity kept her in the spotlight. Nearly every newspaper article about the hearings carried her picture, and usually above the fold—a bit of movie-star glamour injected into dry political discourse. Again, so much of this coverage has been forgotten today—obscured by a legend eager to preserve its heroine from charges of sedition. "They were very cagey about me for a while" was all Kate shared with Dick Cavett in 1973, though she did admit "Hepburn a Communist" was "a favorite cry" for a time. Indeed it was. In the late 1940s, the constant headlines about Kate and her red dress allowed that perception to seep into the public mind.

Nowhere is this better illustrated than in a piece in the *New York Times*. Kate's image happened to fall above a paragraph outlining conservative opposition to the film *The Farmer's Daughter*, which was based on a book called *Katie for Congress*. Directly beneath Hepburn's photo was the conservative nickname for the film: "Katie for Communism." A quick glance gave the impression of a caption.

She was never a Communist, of course, though her sympathies leaned in that direction. Safe in front of the crackling fire at George Cukor's, Kate often listened to long, impassioned sermons from Ruth and Gar about the promises of socialism for America, even as Ruth's jewels glittered in the firelight and Cukor poured them another round of expensive imported champagne. But what truly set Kate's blood boiling in the spring and summer of 1947 was the attack on artistic freedom. "I thought that somebody should make that speech and I thought that somebody should be me" is the way she'd remember explaining herself to Mayer. "I think the situation is idiotic and out of hand. People are being crucified who can't afford it, and I can afford it."

Give her laurels when they're deserved, and she definitely wins them here. She had the courage of her convictions. She may have argued she was merely coming to the aid of free speech—Wallace had been denied a forum at the Hollywood Bowl—but she had to know any association with a man who challenged conventional wisdom about communism, segregation, and other hot topics was a risky move for a public figure.

Her optimism about being able to "afford" the publicity initially seemed to be confirmed when she was not among those issued a subpoena on September 27. Instead, nineteen "unfriendly" witnesses, mostly writers, were called as the hearings got under way in Washington. Chubby little Parnell Thomas perched himself up on two telephone books so the newsreel and television cameras could get a good view, while two future U.S. presidents—Richard Nixon, a member of HUAC, and Ronald Reagan, a friendly witness—milled about looking officious.

Liberal Hollywood, meanwhile, was hoping its glamour could offset the committee's image. At Lucey's restaurant on Melrose Avenue, Philip Dunne met with John Huston and William Wyler to found the Committee for the First Amendment. Kate signed on, though she never attended a meeting. Neither did other stars like Humphrey Bogart, Myrna Loy, Fredric March, and Danny Kaye. Their name and celebrity were all that mattered.

To support the nineteen "unfriendlies," the CFA sent off a planeload of stars. Photographs of Bogart, Lauren Bacall, and Marsha Hunt disembarking in the nation's capital appeared in newspapers all across America. With the threat of a subpoena still hanging over her head, Kate declined to join them. It was just as well. The stars' highly publicized trip backfired. When one of the nineteen, the screenwriter John Howard Lawson, let loose a diatribe of outrage against HUAC, public opinion turned against the liberals, especially when Thomas produced evidence, some fabricated, of Lawson's Communist involvement. Bogie and his pals seemed to have flown all that way simply to support a dirty Red.

From then on, the tide was against anyone who spoke out against HUAC. The Hollywood press, always conservative, turned savage. Cleaning "the scum out of the industry" became a rallying cry of the *Hollywood Reporter*. Hedda Hopper made it her personal mission to expunge every last liberal from the film industry. "[She] took it upon herself to badger all of us who had protested the hearings . . . to make *our* loyalty suspect," said Marsha Hunt. "The very people who had defended the industry were now being made suspect in the industry. It was an unbelievable turnabout."

Yet just like Hollywood's capitulation under the strong arm of the Production Code in 1934, this too was a surrender to forces more market driven than politically inspired. Winding its way through the courts that fall was the government's case to forcibly divest the studios of their theater chains. The Hollywood moguls were well aware of the economic disaster that augured. Coupled with the growing popularity of television, the threat the studios faced that fall of 1947 was very real. Movie attendance was declining; by 1948, it would be down more than 10 percent. With the *Hollywood Reporter* warning of "acute anemia" at every box office in the country, the moguls knew that if they appeared to be on the side of Communists, to be harboring them within the studio confines, they could very likely bring about the end of American moviemaking as they had known it.

Accordingly, the standard line moved from defense to cooperation. "We know there are Communists in Hollywood," Eric Johnston, head of the Motion Picture Association of America, told Thomas's committee. "But we are alert to this threat . . . We agree that the proper way to fight Communism in this country is to expose it fearlessly. Turn the spotlight on a Communist and he becomes ineffective. Like any termite he works best in the dark."

Over the next months, many more would be called before the committee. Hepburn, despite having been the first—literally and symbolically—to
wave the red flag of defiance, was not among them. That didn't prevent her
photo from continuing to illustrate the newspaper coverage, however. The
director Sam Wood, still seething over her ostentatious display, told the
committee on October 20 that Kate's appearance at Gilmore Stadium had
raised more than eighty-seven thousand dollars. "You don't think that money
is going to the Boy Scouts, do you?"

The threat Kate faced was never as specific as a subpoena. It wasn't even
about being blacklisted. It was about public perception, and throughout the
fall of 1947, the insinuations about Hepburn's "loyalty to her nation" grew
exponentially with every newspaper story around the country. The *Chicago
Tribune* ran her picture under a boldface subhead proclaiming ORDERS IS-
SUED FROM MOSCOW. Provincial newspapers made the association even
plainer: NOTED ACTRESS APPEARED IN BEHALF OF FELLOW TRAVELERS ran
the headline in the *Times-Recorder* of Zanesville, Ohio. In Mexia, Texas,
Kate—"she of the tiptoeing voice"—was listed under a heading HOLLYWOOD
REDS. Though her speech might have been old news in Hollywood, it was
still making headlines throughout America's small towns.

Sometime that fall, J. Edgar Hoover at the FBI quietly opened a file on
Kate. Coverage of her speech was clipped from the *Daily Worker*. A government agent in Paris got hold of a French Communist paper that had reprinted
the speech in full. Just how seditious her words were has never been realized by
the general public, as the full text of her speech was never published. But to
read excerpts from it in her FBI file is to understand how radical Hoover
would have found her. Hepburn had, after all, compared the president of the
United States to Japanese fascists. The fact that such inflammatory words had
now been distributed abroad made the situation even more tenuous for Kate.

And it got worse. A few days later, on November 24, at a meeting of motion picture leaders, Eric Johnston revealed that an audience in Chapel Hill,
North Carolina, had actually stoned the screen of a theater showing a Hepburn film. Most likely the film was *Song of Love*, a dud of a picture Kate had
made the previous winter, which had screened at the Carolina Theatre in
Chapel Hill the week of October 24. While neither the local newspaper nor
the files of the police department have any record of the incident, it's likely
the theater owner would've turned first to the Motion Picture Association
anyway. He didn't want negative publicity. What he wanted was to be relieved of the burden of showing Hepburn films.

In an echo of the exhibitors' rebellion against Kate as box-office poison, this latest incident suggested she was again considered unsuitable fare. The Chapel Hill patrons who'd tossed stones at the screen weren't angry about the film's boring plot. They were riled up by photos of Kate in local papers linking her to the subversives in Washington. At a time when the industry was fearful of losing control of its theaters, the studios would have paid very close attention to exhibitors' concerns over Hepburn's liability.

Indeed, she had little clout at the box office to make a stand in her defense. *Sea of Grass* had finally been released, and while it had performed moderately well, *Song of Love*, with Kate playing Clara Wieck Schumann, had disappeared overnight. A mishmash of genres, the film suffered from its director, Clarence Brown, tossing a bit of everything into the mix: music, melodrama, screwball comedy. Yet what likely sunk the picture faster than any of its artistic shortcomings was the political controversy swirling around Kate. One exhibitor in Indiana was quoted as saying he refused to show any picture starring the "Lady in Red."

Enter Spencer Tracy. Kate had saved him—now he could return the favor.

Early in the year, months before Kate's speech, Spencer had been negotiating with Frank Capra to make a film called *State of the Union*, based on Howard Lindsey's play about a crooked politician running for president who gets a lesson in values and morality from his estranged wife. The picture would be made by Liberty Films, Capra's independent company, and released through MGM. Capra wanted Kate to play Spencer's wife, but after some early announcements that she was in, by April it was reported she had opted out, with Claudette Colbert replacing her. By October, however—just before the committee hearings got under way in Washington—the roles had been switched again. The stated reason for Colbert's departure was Capra's refusal to grant her request for a daily 5:00 p.m. quitting time. Yet Colbert's work habits may have simply been an excuse to get Kate back into the film. "Spencer made a deal to get Hepburn into *State of the Union*," said the MGM publicist Emily Torchia, "because she was in trouble and he thought the picture could help her."

State of the Union was the perfect film to revive Hepburn's battered image. Rather than run from politics and hide out in another melodrama like *Song of Love* or *Undercurrent*, she played what she was, a woman of strong convictions. Indeed, she becomes the conscience of the film. *State of the Union* is the only one of the Tracy-Hepburn films where *she* teaches *him* the lesson, the only one besides *Guess Who's Coming to Dinner* where Kate, not Spencer, is the voice of reason. With typical Capra populism, the film walks a careful line between conservative and liberal. Grant and Mary Matthews

(Spence and Kate) are, in fact, Republicans, but the film sidesteps any partisan philosophy. Grant offends both big business and labor leaders alike.

The film makes the point that true patriots are defined by honesty and compassion. That appeal to America's independent voters allowed *State of the Union* to take some potshots at the anti-Communists. In Tracy's epiphany at the end of the picture, he speaks of all the "simmering hates" in the nation, "all the petty warfare undermining our unity." And he thinks he knows the cause of it: "It's fear. Fear of the future. Fear of the world. Fear of Communism." Watching his impassioned speech, Kate becomes all misty-eyed, anticipating a similar emotional moment in *Guess Who's Coming to Dinner* nineteen years later.

Lest the film be accused of being too critical of the investigations going on in Washington, all Capra needed to do was point to Adolphe Menjou's presence in the cast. If Kate had become a lightning rod for the right, Menjou attracted much of the enmity from the left, having been an eager informant for HUAC. Though Kate loathed him, she no doubt saw the wisdom of making a picture with him. Jimmie Fidler reported that neither spoke to each other off the set—which is what their individual partisans wanted to hear, of course. Kanin, however, said they all maintained a "reasonable and professional" relationship while making the picture.

It may have been even more cooperative than that. The question needs to be considered: why was Katharine Hepburn never subpoenaed to appear before HUAC? In September, it had seemed all but certain that she'd be called. The fact that the FBI had begun compiling a dossier on her suggests a subpoena was being planned. Several pages from the script of *Keeper of the Flame* had been pulled, potential evidence in any case against her.

But at some point during the making of *State of the Union*, the right-wing radio commentator Fulton Lewis Jr. announced on the air that Kate wished to recant her actions. According to Lewis, Hepburn said she didn't know what she was signing when she joined the Committee for the First Amendment, and that she'd had "no idea of the type of speech" she was reading at Gilmore Stadium. Meanwhile, according to Kate's FBI files, Adolphe Menjou told a government official (from either the FBI or HUAC—the name has been blotted out) that Spencer Tracy insisted "Hepburn wanted to make a statement in order to clear herself with the American public." Menjou claimed the force behind this was Frank Capra, whose reputation for American values was unassailable.

This mea culpa, despite being secondhand, seems to have satisfied investigators. Kate was never called by HUAC. What the records suggest is that her nemesis Adolphe Menjou, in association with Tracy and Capra, got the committee to back off. Quite possibly it was also Menjou, cajoled by Louis B. Mayer, who approached Fulton Lewis and got him to make the radio announcement exculpating Hepburn.

Indeed, Lewis would later say Hepburn's recanting was a trick played on him by MGM publicists. Among conservative circles, word spread that Kate had "furiously denounced all the heads of MGM" when she learned of the broadcast. Quite possibly she did—but the fact remained that the noose had been untied from around her neck. How much she knew about these back-room deals on her behalf is debatable. Of course, she'd already proven more than once before that she was amenable to compromise if it meant saving her career.

In later years, Hepburn would try to cast herself as less of a radical than she actually was. "At first I was going to wear white," she recalled, referring to her controversial wardrobe onstage at Gilmore Stadium. "And then I thought they'd think I was the dove of peace . . . How could I have been so dumb?"

No matter what she'd have us believe, however, her dress that day was no accident—not for a woman who always wore slacks in public. That day, she decided to wear a *dress*—and a dress of a very particular color. All one has to do is listen to that speech and hear her voice to know everything about that day was deliberately provocative.

And despite Spencer's insistence that Kate "wanted" to make a statement, she never officially did. That's important to review. Unlike so many others— Humphrey Bogart wrote a piece for *Photoplay* titled "I'm No Communist"— Kate never offered any official retraction of her political activity. In many ways, *State of the Union* was all the statement she needed to make. Released in the spring of 1948, the film was a gigantic hit—possibly because, for all of Mary Matthews's nobility, the film ends with her over her husband's knee, getting "one good smack on [her] south end." Once more, Hepburn submitted to an on-screen punishment for her nonconformity.

Still, the spanking didn't satisfy all her critics. Kate might have been safe from HUAC, but not from Hedda Hopper, who was compiling her own dossier. Included among Hopper's papers were letters from readers, like the one from a Pasadena woman who made it her "policy to never attend any moving picture in which Miss Hepburn appears." When *State of the Union* turned out to be a hit, Hopper was obliged to write, "Although I dislike Katharine Hepburn's political policies, I will admit that she does a beautiful stretch of acting." After years of receiving boldface mentions in Hopper's column, Kate was now limited to the rare snide remark. When Hopper heard Hepburn was being considered for a film about underpaid teachers, she quipped, "Katy may look hungry, but never underpaid"—her way of calling Kate a hypocrite for her socialist sympathies. In March 1948, the columnist reminded her readers, in case they'd forgotten, of Hepburn's perfidy, wondering when she'd "take the stump" for Wallace's presidential campaign.

Hopper wasn't attacking Kate simply for supporting Wallace. Surely she was aware of the full contents of Hepburn's speech, even if the vast majority of the public had heard only a few buzzwords. Hopper knew what mainstream America did not. Kate hadn't just voiced her support for an increasingly unpopular candidate. She'd also decried segregation and called for an end to censorship. For staunch conservatives like Hopper, Katharine Hepburn stood for a set of values that was completely antithetical to their own. It's why, though Kate may have breathed a sigh of relief when she wasn't called before HUAC, she had to realize she was not yet completely out of danger.

In November, plays by Clifford Odets and Lillian Hellman were banned in the joint U.S.-Soviet-occupied Berlin, on account of Communist accusations made about them before HUAC. This caused the *New York Times* to wonder "whether films featuring Charles Chaplin, Frank Sinatra, Humphrey Bogart, and Katharine Hepburn also will be banned." When the liberal-leaning columnist Sheilah Graham tried to write sympathetically about Kate, she was cut down by letters to the editor challenging her to print the full text of Hepburn's speech. One accused Kate of picking up "the Communist cry for 'unity.'" When the Hungarian Communist newspaper *Szabed Nep* came to the defense of Kate and other liberal stars, it did far more harm than good, with critics saying it showed the celebrities' "true stripes."

Although *State of the Union* had gotten her film career back on track, around Hepburn there still existed an air of subversion. What Kate faced by early 1948 was the realization that film success was now no longer enough. She could still be brought down by legislators, columnists, or public opinion. In the past, a hit picture had solved everything. Now, to keep the fame she had spent half her life cultivating and maintaining, she needed to craft an image that went beyond movie-star celebrity. Film personalities came and went, but Katharine Hepburn had intentions of sticking around. The only way to do that was to become an institution.

FANCY HER, A HEROINE

There she stands, proud and imperious, towering over an unshaven Humphrey Bogart who refuses to take his boat, the *African Queen,* down the river and torpedo a German ship.

"In other words," Kate says, all icy indignation, "you are refusing to help your country in her hour of need."

Until now, the world had known her as Katharine Hepburn the tomboy, the rebel, the independent woman. Now observe as one more shading is layered onto the legend.

Katharine Hepburn the Patriot.

Of course, she persuades Bogart to sail down the river with her and blow up the enemy ship. Through Hepburn's courage and evergreen morality, Bogart is a man transformed. "I'll never forget the way you looked going over the falls," he tells her, in awe. "Head up, chin out, hair blowing in the wind—the living picture of a heroine."

Cut to a close-up of Kate. She is glowing. "Fancy me," she says, "a heroine."

The African Queen would be the single most important film in Hepburn's career. There were others that were better, others that made more money. But *The African Queen* made possible everything that was to follow. Without it, even this book would not exist.

Beginning in the late 1940s, Hepburn took the first steps toward her secular canonization. *The African Queen* was the crowning achievement of this process, establishing her as an American exemplar despite the fact that she played a British subject. The film, and the image she gained from it, guaranteed her place in the public sphere, putting an end to the crises that had flared up repeatedly in her career. The battle she faced during the HUAC years was the make-or-break one, and on some level, she surely knew that. She may have escaped being blacklisted, but it was no longer just about making movies for her. At forty-one years of age, Hepburn had her eye on her legacy.

On a day in June 1949, sitting in the shade of a palm tree on the veranda of her house on Beverly Grove, Kate glanced down at her morning paper. KATHARINE HEPBURN NAMED AS RED APPEASER. She had escaped the national noose, but California had its own Committee on Un-American Activities, chaired by State Senator Jack Tenney. Daring to go where Parnell Thomas had not, Tenney listed some of the biggest names in Hollywood as "following or appeasing the Communist party line over a long period of years." Kate was in good company. Not just the usual Chaplins and Bogarts and Kayes. Now there was also Pearl S. Buck, Lillian Hellman, Lena Horne, John Huston, Gene Kelly, Myrna Loy, Fredric March, Dorothy Parker, Gregory Peck, Frank Sinatra, Donald Ogden Stewart, Orson Welles.

Some chose to deny feverishly. Others reacted with contempt. Huston called the charge yet another example of Tenney's "vicious campaign to smear the names of his betters." For her part, Kate chose not to say anything. An MGM spokesman simply told reporters who called that she refused to dignify Tenney's accusation with a reply.

But within a few months she'd no longer be a studio employee. Her contract was up, and she wasn't renewing. Neither was MGM asking her to do so. At the moment, she had no offers, no plans—the first time Kate had found herself at liberty since the summer of 1938. If it hadn't been for Spence, she'd have gone back East, where she could have had another glorious summer at Fenwick. But Spence was here—he was still under contract—and so Kate was, too, idling her days in a Hollywood that was once again changing from underneath her.

These days, if the topic wasn't blacklists, conversation at the Brown Derby buzzed mostly with talk of TV. The restaurant's maître d' saved the best tables for Milton Berle and Sid Caesar. Everywhere there was a sense that moviemaking was changing, even as the studios struggled valiantly to prevent it from doing so. As feared, the U.S. Supreme Court had forced the studios to give up their theater chains. In one year (1947–48), MGM saw its profits drop from $10.5 million to $4.2. With more people staying home these days to watch *The Goldbergs* than there were going out to the movies, the studios had little hope of reversing the trend.

Sitting on her veranda, Kate surely understood that the next phase in her career would need to be very different from anything before. She wasn't alone in facing an uncertain future. While the men—Gable, Cooper, and of course Tracy—had more options, most of Kate's female contemporaries were in trouble. Davis had lost her box-office appeal, Stanwyck was making lower-budget films, and Crawford had been off the screen for two years. For a while, they'd all believed they'd be the first generation to keep their fame for more than a decade. Were they wrong? As with the silent stars before them, was their time now up?

Kate wasn't ready to concede quite yet. The first thing she needed to do was polish up her image. While Tenney's committee proved more scare tactic than anything else, it did keep her name linked to communism in the press. Early hopes that all this would blow over quickly now seemed terribly naive. Private lists of those who had been called "appeasers" were drawn up by the American Legion and circulated to producers and exhibitors with a request that they take action against the people named. Kate's name was on a good number of these lists, which have been preserved in various archives. At the same time, well-thumbed copies of *Red Channels*, listing the names of all those suspected of "un-American values" (actually merely compendiums of Hollywood's liberals), were on every studio executive's desk. Once again, the name Katharine Hepburn was often found in these reports.

Even more reactionary than *Red Channels* were the booklets published by Myron C. Fagan. *Red Treason in Hollywood* came out in 1949, with a follow-up, *Documentation of the Red Stars in Hollywood*, a year later. Fagan, a frustrated playwright, wasn't buying reports of Kate's change of heart. At a rally of anti-Communists at the El Patio Theatre in Los Angeles, Fagan got up on the stage and announced, "Katharine Hepburn's love for Joe Stalin is no secret." The larger newspapers ignored him, but the tabloids gave Fagan plenty of coverage.

Myrna Loy, another star so slandered, sent her lawyers after Fagan. But once again Kate's response was no response. Though Fagan would slap five stars after her name in *Red Treason*—indicating the highest level of Communist support, right up there with the blacklisted screenwriters now serving time in prison—Kate understood that to protest would simply draw more attention. The tactic enraged influential right-wing columnists like Jim Tarantino, who wrote that Kate's silence simply implicated her in the charges against her. She and others, Tarantino said, were being "charged with betraying their country, classed as spiritual traitors . . . Yet [they] sit idly by and do absolutely nothing."

In fact, Kate was anything but idle. Just weeks after Tenney's committee named her a Red appeaser, she began work on a film written specially for her and Spencer by Ruth and Gar. *Adam's Rib* would be the film that defined Hepburn and Tracy as a couple in the public mind, the picture that convinced the world their lives were the same off the screen as they were on. As rival husband-and-wife lawyers, Kate and Spence bicker and provoke, but remain deeply and profoundly in love.

After five films together, they'd finally gotten their rhythm down right. They'd finally grasped that what audiences wanted was the romantic battle-of-the-sexes of *Woman of the Year*, not the lumbering melodrama of *Sea of Grass*.

Yet it's impossible to see *Adam's Rib* outside the context of Kate's real-life controversies. With Cukor as director, the film sprung from the fireside intimacy of Hepburn's private circle. Originally called *Man and Wife*, the script had been a collaborative process. The Entente Cordiale came as a package, and it took the producer Lawrence Weingarten (who was also an occasional guest at Cukor's) less than forty-eight hours to sign on. Just as she was in *State of the Union*, Kate is full of high principles here. But as Amanda Bonner she's also quirky and eccentric. Still, her husband, Adam, loves her—*and so should you*, the script was telegraphing the audience.

Take the classic rubdown scene, for instance, where once again Tracy slaps her south side for being so impertinent.

AMANDA: You meant that, didn't you? You really meant that.
ADAM: Why, no, I . . .
AMANDA: Yes, you did. I can tell. I know your type. I know a slap from a slug.
ADAM: Okay, okay.
AMANDA: I'm not so sure it is. I'm not so sure I care to expose myself to typical instinctive masculine brutality.
ADAM: Oh come now.
AMANDA: And it felt not only as though you meant it, but as though you felt you had a *right* to. I can tell.
ADAM: What do you got back there? Radar equipment?

All of which was to say: she might spit and she might spar, but she was harmless. With dialogue crafted by the Kanins intended to make the public fall in love with her, Kate took a giant step toward her eventual apotheosis. *Adam's Rib* was a huge hit, the biggest Tracy-and-Hepburn film so far. Making its debut in November, it pulled in $3 million during just the last six weeks of 1949, securing itself a place among the top twenty moneymakers of the year. Continuing strong into 1950, *Adam's Rib* became one of that year's biggest blockbusters as well.

"I think on film we came to represent the perfect American couple," Kate reflected, years later. "Certainly the ideal man is Spencer: sports-loving, a man's man. Strong-looking, a big sort of head, boar neck, a man. And I think I represent a woman. I needle a man. I irritate him . . . yet if he put a big paw out, he could squash me. I think this is sort of the romantic, ideal picture of the male and female in the United States."

She seemed aware of the artificiality of what they were presenting; she saw herself as "representing" a woman, after all, instead of authentically *being* one. Yet by playing the submissive on-screen, Kate was in effect also disempowering her offscreen image. That strident woman in the red dress? Don't worry about her. Underneath, she's just a pussycat.

The films with Tracy all make this point. Even in *State of the Union*, where she was uncharacteristically the wise one, it's Spencer's epiphany that is the heart of the film, his speech that lifts the audience—and the spanking at the end signaled that the two of them were now back to their proper roles. *Adam's Rib* took this not so subliminal message even further. It's not a film about women being equal to men, as some have remembered it. Amanda might make a giant squawk about the issue, but the film ends up affirming the traditional male-female relationship—strong man, submissive woman.

Kate didn't see any of this as capitulation. One simply did what one needed to do to get back on top. That had always been her mantra. Never admit defeat. "You could push her down," said her friend James Prideaux, "but she'd always get right back up."

In this light, see her elbowing her way past the reporters gathered outside Judy Garland's house. The night before, distraught over being fired from MGM, Judy had tried to slash her throat. With all the crisp efficiency of a high school gym teacher, Kate now stood over her young friend's bed and insisted Judy come live with her. "Oh, dear, here comes Hepburn health," Judy would later recall for friends, shuddering at the thought of what Kate had in mind for her. Cohabitation wasn't to be—neither's schedule permitted it—but Kate would always feel she could've straightened Judy out had she been given the chance. It was similar to the way she once tried to cure Ruth Gordon's fear of heights, driving her high up into the Hollywood hills along narrow roads to make her confront her fears.

But such direct, head-on confrontations with those who were accusing her of communism would have backfired, as Kate and everyone around her now understood. Speaking out was no longer an option. In the face of reactionary broadsides by the likes of Myron Fagan and Fulton Lewis, liberals found themselves denouncing communism as strongly as conservatives—even more so at times. By 1950, the voice of organized liberal opposition to the great inquisition had effectively been silenced.

So Kate decided to make *The African Queen*.

The way she'd tell it, she was simply lounging about Irene Selznick's house in the fashionable foothills above Sunset Boulevard when the telephone rang. It was the producer Sam Spiegel, who said he was doing a picture with John Huston based on C. S. Forester's novel *The African Queen*. Did she know of it?

Kate said she did not. Spiegel asked if he could send it to her. "Thank you," she told him, stretched out on a chaise beside Irene's pool. "I'll read it right off."

Maybe that's the way it really happened. Maybe she really had no idea at this point what the part could mean for her. But after reading the book, Kate quickly grasped why Huston was so gung ho on the project. Though she'd insist she accepted the part only after Spiegel sent her flowers and champagne, what surely convinced her far more than orchids and bubbly was the chance to play Rose Sayer—the most laudable, lionhearted role to ever come her way. A woman who risks her life for her country. A true patriot, in fact.

"*The African Queen*," said Max Showalter, "was Kate's way of coming back after all the problems with the Red scare."

"Of course she chose that film consciously," said James Prideaux. "With Kate and her work, *everything* was a conscious choice."

Her brother Bob thought that after *The African Queen*, Kate "sort of became a heroine to everyone." Indeed, when Hepburn's career is considered in the full context of her life and her times, it's impossible not to see *The African Queen* as a response to her political woes—problems she shared, in fact, with her director and her costar. No coincidence, no mere chance, brought Hepburn, Huston, and Bogart together at this time. Though they may never have articulated the film's connection to their current problems, surely Kate, at least, understood the script's rehabilitative potential. Just as she'd selected *The Philadelphia Story* as a response to critics' charges that she was too cold, unfeminine, and independent, she chose *The African Queen* as a way to transcend what was being said about her now. If the film clicked, no one would ever call her a traitor again.

First, though, she needed to finish up her run in the Shakespearean play *As You Like It*. Kate's decision to tackle Shakespeare for her next Theatre Guild project can also be seen as a response to her recent trials. She was getting out of Hollywood—a move that would end up having a serious impact on her relationship with Spencer—and returning to a venue less controlled by popular opinion than the movies. But she was also taking a real professional risk. Most of her contemporaries, faced with their own middle-age career crises, either lapsed into inactivity or tried to recycle old formulas. Joan Crawford, when she came back to the screen, was still playing variations on Mildred Pierce well into the 1950s. Admirably, Hepburn, at forty-two, embraced a brand-new challenge, one few others of her station would have dared.

Indeed, Rosalind is the longest woman's part in all of Shakespeare's plays. Serious preparation was going to be needed. Ringing Constance Collier, a Shakespeare veteran, Kate asked if she might become her student. Collier agreed to help her master the rhythm of Shakespeare's dialogue. Meeting with her in New York, Collier taught Kate to speak the lines naturally for their meaning. Life was imitating art. Collier had played the drama coach in *Stage Door*.

Kate also made sure she was in top shape for the strenuous part. Jogging through Central Park at dawn, she'd have Charles Newhill follow in the car, honking the horn if he spotted a fan or a photographer approaching. At the other end of the day, Kate would crawl out onto a rock promontory overlooking Belvedere Castle and sit studying her lines, lifting her eyes occasionally from the script to gaze off at the great lawn and Turtle Pond below. This was her "secret spot," a place she'd held dear since the days before she was a star. Here, for a few hours before dusk, she could revert to being just Kath, an actress learning her lines.

Once again, in *As You Like It,* she was a girl playing a boy. Cukor offered his services to direct, but the Guild chose the twenty-nine-year-old Michael Benthall, the wunderkind of the Old Vic in London. Benthall and Hepburn hit it off immediately, agreeing on a very romantic vision for the play. Rosalind would be airy and feminine, they decided, with none of the "garçonne" Cukor would have instilled in the part. At first, Terry Helburn worried Kate might find Benthall's ideas "a little too delicate and fancy," but she was in fact delighted.

As You Like It would mark the first lengthy separation Kate had had from Spencer in more than three years. Tracy seemed on solid ground; Kate didn't need to fear leaving him the way she had just a few years previous. Arranging for her brother Dick, still without any real success of his own, to work as assistant stage manager, Kate insisted the show open in New Haven, as had become her custom. There the first-night audience on December 8 included her parents, Gar Kanin, and Thornton Wilder. This home-state crowd demanded six curtain calls from its favorite native daughter.

Word spread quickly, however, that Kate's legs, still as shapely as they had been in *The Warrior's Husband,* were the best parts of her performance. Although she gets an A for effort, in the end, Kate failed to master Shakespeare at this point. The ill-conceived decision to play Rosalind soft and frilly only made her mannerisms more pronounced. When the play opened at the Cort Theatre in New York on January 22, 1950, Brooks Atkinson scolded her for the "romantic and disarming graces" that were simply not part of her nature. She was not, and never would be, Atkinson said, "a helpless, moonstruck maiden." No matter how hard or how often he tried, Jimmy Hepburn was never comfortable playing the dainty girl.

One night, unbeknownst to Kate, Margaret Sullavan sat in the audience with the three children she'd had with Leland Hayward. Sullavan frequently took Brooke, Bridget, and Bill to the theater so they could see great performances and learn about their parents' profession. This experience, however, was going to be a little different, Sullavan explained. "Tonight," she told her children, "you'll see an example of a really *horrible* performance."

Still, as was the case for all of Kate's Guild plays, *As You Like It* was a box-office success. It ran for almost six months, closing on June 3. That fall Kate took it on the road again. Driving through Oklahoma the star had another run-in with a cop unimpressed by her celebrity. "That policeman was so unpleasant," she later confided to George Cukor, "I told him I'd hate to be his wife." Another shrill scene followed in the courthouse, where Kate singed her mink coat on a stove. "This coat cost fifty-five hundred [dollars]!" she shouted. The shrill socialist in the mink coat provided more fodder for the tabloids.

It didn't matter. Within a few months she'd be hard—very hard—at work on *The African Queen.* Her efforts would eventually ensure that negative press like this would virtually disappear.

From the beginning, Kate had insisted the film not be shot on any backlot. It was her one chance to see Africa, she said, and she wasn't going to miss it. On April 6, 1951, she set off on her journey, first to London and then to the heart of the Dark Continent. Hurrying down the West Fourteenth Street pier, Kate chattered animatedly with Constance Collier while Collier's companion,

Phyllis Wilbourn, pushed their luggage behind them. Their ship, the *Media*, was smaller than most vessels Kate was used to, and, as ever, she got seasick. A week later, they docked at Liverpool, where a Rolls-Royce hired by Spiegel met them and drove them to London. Kate was thrilled that Spiegel had splurged on Claridge's, her favorite hotel in London, even if she felt the film's budget couldn't afford it.

Indeed, she was beginning to worry that the production was getting off on the wrong foot. Huston proved maddeningly unwilling to talk with her about the script. Bogart assured her that was simply the director's style. Still, to protect herself, Kate asked her father to send her a letter of credit for ten thousand dollars in case she needed to make a fast getaway. Even at forty-three, Kate still sent her father all her paychecks and depended on him to pay her bills.

Early in May, Kate left London for Rome, where the company was scheduled to rendezvous before heading to the Congo. There she enjoyed two reunions. The first was with Fran Rich, who'd set up a studio in Rome, trying her hand at bronze liturgical sculpture. The two women hadn't seen each other in some years. Meeting Kate at the airport in her little Fiat Giardinetta wagon, Fran zipped her along the old Appian Way, both of them talking a blue streak and laughing a great deal. "We always had so much fun together, and I had missed her so much," Rich remembered. After several years of playing hausfrau to Tracy, Kate seems to have been energized by this reconnection with a close woman friend. That night, Fran treated Hepburn to a moonlight tour of Rome. The next day they picnicked at Ostia Antica at the mouth of the Tiber River, picking wildflowers at the ruins of the Neptune Baths. "It was just so lovely to be together again," Fran would recall.

But Kate's reverie with Fran was short-lived. On May 13, Spencer arrived in Rome for a meeting with Pope Pius XII, a lifelong dream of his. It had been several months since he'd last seen Kate. If we read between the lines of Kate's memoir of the shooting of *The African Queen*, it seems their months apart had left a mark on the couple. Kate found Spence distant, but as usual, she did not pry into what was bothering him.

The papal meeting was scheduled for a week later at a special reception in Vatican City. Forty other pilgrims, including the Scottish writer A. J. Cronin, would take part. In the meantime, Fran played guide for Tracy as well, touring him around churches and the Roman countryside, though not in her little Fiat. Spence insisted they use the limousine provided by MGM. At her apartment, littered with bronze shavings, Fran cooked dinner for Kate and Spence. Afterward, she drove Tracy back to his room at the Grand Hotel. Kate, as ever, did not join him but stayed with Fran.

When, immediately after his audience with the pope, Spencer left without saying good-bye, Kate was hurt. "Did he leave because he was bored or did he leave because he couldn't bear to say goodbye?" she asked, years later. "The eternal question."

Kate presumed he left for London to fly back to the States, but in fact he stopped in France for a tour of the Alps. Kate also seemed not to know that Louise was being given an honorary degree from Northwestern University on June 11, and Spencer wanted to be home by then. If she had been hoping he'd stick around Rome until she left for Africa, Kate was disappointed. Fran Rich would later wonder if Tracy liked her; she could never tell, she admitted. Had he, possibly, been uncomfortable with her friendship with Kate?

A short time later, Kate set out for the Belgian Congo. Nearly four decades later she'd document the harrowing shoot in her memoir *The Making of the African Queen, or, How I Went to Africa with Bogart, Bacall and Huston and Almost Lost My Mind*. That last was a bit of hyperbole—no surprise—but in fact there would be sickness and insects and snakes and mud. Still, Kate would always be glad she'd nixed the backlot.

In Léopoldville, a village along the Congo River, the *African Queen* company was greeted by natives with painted faces performing a tribal dance. "The natives didn't know what we were about," remembered Lauren Bacall, Bogart's wife, who went along for the adventure. "When a match was struck and a flame followed, they'd mumble in Swahili."

Any initial doubts Kate had about Huston were soon allayed as she developed an abiding respect for the director. He was, after all, the kind of man she worshiped: cultured in literature and art but raw in his masculinity. Stepping through swamps as he hunted elephants and wild boar, Huston made little fuss about grooming or unnecessary bathing—hardly an attitude Kate could have expected from her two most recent directors, the fussy George Cukor and Michael Benthall.

Once again between the lines in her memoir, she gives the clear (and not surprising) impression that she was attracted to Huston. Was it, like the less intense flirtation with Turhan Bey, a momentary escape from the heaviness of the relationship with Spencer? Sitting with Kate on top of the paddleboat watching the eyes of the hippos in the water, Huston would recall talking with her "about anything and everything." When she became sick with dysentery—ironic given how insistent she'd been about drinking only bottled water—it was Huston who came to her hut and gently massaged her body. "Took the trouble from me," Kate would recall. "It is true—the laying on of hands. So quiet—so sweet—soothing." Leaning over her on the bed, Huston rubbed her feet, her hands, her back, her head. He purred gently into her ear, "Just stay asleep, Katie dear. Stay asleep." It is the only recorded moment of a man physically taking care of Kate instead of the other way around.

Huston's advice that she play the role as if she were Eleanor Roosevelt is not insignificant. With this movie, Kate was transformed into a tower of strength. In fact, *The African Queen* accomplished even more than that, convincing audiences that Hepburn was actually to be *admired* for her eccentricities. Take the moment when she goes shoulder to shoulder with Bogart in the leech-infested water to pull the boat through the muck. No movie queen had ever dirtied her hands—and the rest of her—in this way before.

While it may have been the Union Jack that she was hoisting as they set off down the river, for American audiences it was Yankee common sense and self-reliance that Rose was displaying, qualities for which Kate would soon be venerated. And no matter what flag she was sailing under, the fact of her allegiance to it dispelled any notion that she might be a godless Communist. At one point, Rose even prays to God, and He listens, sending a rainstorm to free the boat from the muck. The message was plain. If God listened to Katharine Hepburn, so should the world.

She could never have made this film with Tracy. For all their popularity, the Tracy-Hepburn films could go only so far in creating the kind of image she needed to establish herself as an institution—to make herself, in essence, invulnerable to criticism and the vagaries of public opinion. With Tracy, she was required to be deferent. Here, Rose and Charlie truly are equals, trudging together through the mud.

It's that sense of equality that makes Hepburn's performance in *The African Queen* so wonderful. The morning after she, the stiff-backed missionary, makes love to Bogart, the crusty sea captain, Kate displays no shame; there is no scrambling to restore conventional order to their relationship. Rather, she's *ecstatic*. The famous scene of Hepburn rolling her lover's name around on her tongue—"Charlie, Chaaarlie, what a wonderful name"—is perhaps the moment when the public really forgave her for everything that came before and took her to their hearts as their heroine.

The acclaim that greeted the film made all of her hardships in the jungle worthwhile. Critics thought Kate's performance "the deftest thing one is likely to see this season." Audiences agreed. *The African Queen* was the sixth-biggest moneymaker for 1952.

How different Kate's press suddenly became. After Rose Sayer, she was "Dynamic Katharine" and "Katie the Magnificent." All of her old faults were spun into positives. "An unapproachable person?" asked one reporter. "Very often, especially to the press. Yet . . . it is part of her complex, unpredictable personality. It is also part of her fascination and sparkle."

Of course, spinning that complex, unpredictable personality into an asset rather than a liability meant the public legend surrounding her needed to be updated. A new bible was required to supplant Adela Rogers St. Johns and Lupton Wilkinson, now hopelessly démodé. *Time* magazine delivered the goods, putting Kate on its cover on September 1, 1952. KATE HEPBURN, read the cover line. HEADLONG INTO A TREE. No need anymore to hide or explain away her bullheadedness. Now it was celebrated on the cover of the nation's most well-known newsmagazine.

"It's a peculiar thing," the article quotes George Cukor, "but the movie audience is hostile to Kate at the start of a picture. You can almost feel the hostility. By the middle of the picture they're usually sympathetic and, by the end, they're rooting for her."

Yet this new spin was careful not to portray Hepburn as *too* ambitious. In the 1950s, traditional gender roles had once again become sacrosanct. The idyll of the nuclear family of husband, wife, and children was celebrated nightly on television in shows like *Father Knows Best* and *Donna Reed*. Kate had to be careful about not seeming too career-minded. She was, after all, an unmarried, childless woman, an image often mocked in 1950s popular culture.

And so was born the myth that Hepburn really cared little about her career, that she was indifferent to ambition and stardom. The new "Hepburn Story" in *Time* ends with our tough, resilient heroine musing, "I've always had a strange and strong dream that if I stopped and went back to Hartford, I wouldn't remember a thing about my acting career." She stops and pauses meditatively before adding definitively: "Not one damn thing."

It was, of course, pure hokum. If Kate ever dreamed about ending her career and going back to Hartford, one friend said, "she would've awakened in a cold sweat and screaming." Yet as time went on, she sometimes tried to convince her friends of this alternate vision of herself. Robert Shaw, who occasionally stayed with her in New York during this period, remembered her once musing about giving up her career. "I really ought to get out of the spotlight and go work in a garden somewhere," she said. Shaw told her she was fooling herself, that she could never give it up. She grinned and admitted, "Yes, I know."

What made Kate's resurgence in the middle part of the 1950s so remarkable was that she pulled it off in middle age. When *The African Queen* was playing in the nation's theaters, she was forty-five years old. Gone was the glamorous sex goddess of *Woman of the Year*. Indeed, her latest screen incarnation had layered another image onto her: the spinster. Physically, Kate looked the part of Rose Sayer, growing thinner and sharper, her hair now usually pulled into a knot on the top of her head. Because of her frequent exposure to the sun, her lifelong battle with her skin blotches had only gotten worse. She was particularly self-conscious about the loose skin of her neck, rarely being seen without a scarf or a turtleneck.

Yet, in fact, this gaunt, wrinkled middle-aged spinster had just made one of the biggest moneymakers of the year and would follow up with several other hits in the 1950s. Kate's generation of stars proved remarkably resilient. Just as they were about to be written off, stars like Hepburn, Crawford, Stanwyck, and Rosalind Russell showed they could hold their own at the box office alongside younger stars. One article even hyped that Kate made middle age fashionable. "Hepburn's birthdays only add more glamour," another article boasted—though, of course, it presumed her to be forty-three, rather than forty-five.

In every way, Kate had triumphed. While the blacklist intensified, she had become a paragon of virtues. That didn't stop the long arm of the inquisition from creeping right into the heart of the Entente Cordiale. Both Kanins were accused of being Communists. In April 1952, Garson sued the *Hollywood Reporter* after it made Red allegations. When Ruth acted in a radio drama for the Theatre Guild, letters flooded in denouncing her as "a female Com-rat." But Kate was safe. Her public life now seemed protected by an impenetrable shield.

If only the same could have been said about her private life.

Shortly before she'd left to make *The African Queen*, Kate had spent a few days in West Hartford. On an unseasonably warm St. Patrick's Day, she and her father, now seventy-five, took a drive down to Fenwick. Physically, Hep had hardly changed a bit. Yet he'd mellowed somewhat about his Kath and her career. He still might not ever say "good job," but he was always ready with advice and opinions, encouraging his daughter to tackle Shaw now that she'd finally done Shakespeare. When they arrived back in West Hartford late in the afternoon, they found the maid had set the table for teatime. The pot on the stove was filled with freshly brewed tea. But Kit was not there. Indeed, an awful quiet had settled over the house.

They found her upstairs, stretched out on the bed. From what they could determine, Mrs. Hepburn had taken a bath when they'd left for their drive.

Afterward, pinning up her hair, she must have felt weak and decided to lie down. In seconds she was dead from a cerebral hemorrhage.

Once before, on another unseasonably warm St. Patrick's Day, Katharine Hepburn had run away from her heartache. Now, she was forced to confront it straight on. Her mother may have often seemed like a distant deity in her life, an idealized, unattainable model of womanhood. But that had only made Kate venerate her more. "I can't be philosophical about parents dying," she'd written, several years before, to console John Ford over the loss of his father. "I don't know what I should do or think if mine did. I should be completely lost."

What Kit had kept alive for her daughter was a link to a past that seemed increasingly unfamiliar as the years went on—a link to Tom, indeed, to Kath. Standing at the gravesite, beside the plain marker that bore her brother's name, Kate watched as her mother's ashes were lowered into the open earth. Glancing over at her father, she observed his struggle to stay stoic. Stiff upper lips remained the Hepburn rule. But Hep was unable to completely disguise the grief that furrowed its way across his ruddy face. Kit had been his beloved, the mother of his six children. His passion for her had never died.

Kate later told friends that her mother's death was a turning point. "She realized she'd never have the kind of marriage her mother had had," said Robert Shaw. In that one, devastating glance at her father standing at the gravesite, Kate seems to have understood that what her parents had shared for nearly half a century was fundamentally different from what she had with Spencer. No longer could she keep up the pretense of comparison. Compared to her mother, Kate had always come up short. Now, in middle age, she understood that difference to be immutable.

Various Hepburn chroniclers have described this moment in Kate's life. Christopher Andersen, wanting to boost the romantic image of the Tracy-Hepburn connection, claimed Kate called Spence in Hollywood to tell him of her mother's death and he offered to get on the next plane to be with her. According to this story, Kate turned down Spencer's loving offer, but still he called several times a day to console her. Barbara Leaming, whose book was largely unsympathetic to Tracy, painted a directly opposing picture, saying Kate was hurt by Spencer's failure to fly immediately to her side.

In fact, there is no evidence for either position. Most likely, part of Spence's reason for meeting Kate in Rome a few months later was to see her in the aftermath of her mother's death. But it was Laura Harding, arriving from New York, who was there for Kate in the days leading up to the funeral. Kate would not have expected Spencer to come East. He feared flying, for one thing; for another, it would have risked publicity. Besides, Spence had *never* rushed to her side. It was not in the nature of their relationship.

That much had become abundantly clear. Sailing for London with Constance and Phyllis soon after her mother's funeral, Kate must have at least started to realize that the illusion of her life with Spencer, which she had fought so hard to maintain for the past several years, was beginning to unravel. Both Max Showalter and Robert Shaw believed Kit's death was the first turning point in Kate's relationship with Spence. The suggestion of uneasiness between them in Rome tends to support this idea.

What their months apart had done was delineate the fantasy of their union. For a while, it had been enough—the feelings between them were real, and the routine they found together was fulfilling. But, in truth, Spencer had never stopped seeing Louise on the weekends. When Kate was away, he thought nothing of asking other women, like Joan Fontaine, to dinner. Even if his intentions were merely social, Spencer's extracurricular activity exposed the fact that what he and Kate shared was amorphous and indefinite. Not at all like what Hep and Kit had shared all those years. And that's what Kate's friends believed she was beginning to understand.

That may explain, in part, Kate's unexpected reaction to her father's remarriage only a few months later to one of his nurses, Madeline Santa Croce, who was more than twenty years his junior. While others in the family were angry that Hep had replaced Kit so quickly, Kate was complaisant. She seemed satisfied that her adored father would continue to enjoy the kind of domestic contentment that so far had eluded her. (Hep also burned all of Kit's socialist literature, a move his daughter, after her recent trials, may have supported as well.)

Meanwhile, Kate's adventure in the Congo seems to have galvanized a wanderlust within her. Returning to New York, she hung tribal masks on her walls and wore African pendants around her neck. According to Robert Shaw, she was ambivalent about returning to the settled existence she'd known in Los Angeles. Kate had given up quite a bit to devote herself to Spence; some part of her, quite understandably, seems to have wanted to get back to "me, me, me." With the studios in decline, Kate understood her work would continue to take her away from Hollywood. What that meant for her relationship with Spence was uncertain, but she seems to have been ready to give it a try.

In some ways, being away from Spence for so long had reawakened her sense of herself and her own possibilities. It's critical to understand that since leaving Spencer's side two years previous to do *As You Like It,* Kate had spent no more than five months cumulatively with him, and rarely more than a few weeks at a stretch. She had rediscovered her own routine; as much as she loved Spence, it seems to have been rejuvenating.

For a time, she'd try to bridge the two worlds: Spence and her need for stimulating professional work. On the lookout for projects they might do together, she was encouraged by the Guild's idea that they take on Eugene O'Neill's *A Touch of the Poet*. But the playwright had expressed unfamiliarity with Tracy (and possibly with Kate as well). "It is hard to believe that people can be so ignorant about moving pictures," Lawrence Langner lamented. Even after a screening of Spencer's film *Captains Courageous*, O'Neill seemed unimpressed.

On another front the Guild had more success. But *The Millionairess* by George Bernard Shaw was for Kate only, with no opportunity for Spence. After much cajolery, Shaw had finally agreed to Hepburn's taking on the play, considered one of the playwright's minor efforts. *The Millionairess* had never been mounted as a major production in the United States. In considering Hepburn, Shaw had demanded to know what kind of athlete she was, concerned because the lead character is a vibrant expert in judo. Only after Armina Marshall assured him that Kate played tennis every morning and was the most athletic actress she knew did the playwright give his consent.

Fired with the excitement that she was finally going to fulfill her parents' dream of playing Shaw, Kate arrived on the Coast in late 1951 for a reunion with Tracy. Once again, their time together would be brief. Rehearsals for *The Millionairess* were slated to begin early the next year in London, where she'd open for the producer Hugh Beaumont before taking the show to New York.

By now, Spencer had moved into a bungalow on Cukor's estate, four little rooms with a driveway on St. Ives Drive. This is the house that many writers have tried so earnestly to portray as a little love nest for Kate and Spence. But no matter what else has been written or presumed, Hepburn never lived there with Tracy. Nor did she even think to *stay* there during her visits. Her correspondence with Cukor attests to this fact. When Irene Selznick's house on Summit Drive wasn't available, Kate stayed with Cukor in the main house in one of his guest bedrooms. Once she offered to "go down the hill [to Tracy's bungalow] to all meals," but the director would hear nothing of the kind. She'd get "three wholesome meals," he insisted, at "Pension Cukor."

The fact that she didn't live in the bungalow, however, certainly didn't prevent Kate from making decisions about the place. Walking in for the first time, she found Spencer's little house austere and depressing. Indeed, Cukor would call Tracy's bedroom "a monk's cell . . . [with] the air of a place where a man might do penance." Spence called it the "last stop before the Motion Picture

Relief Home." Rubbing her hands together, Kate set about changing things. On the floor of the living room she laid a white and red wool rug that Cukor had bought in Spain. On the brick walls she hung her own paintings of seagulls and lighthouses. Eventually she'd dangle from the ceiling a wooden sculpture of a swan in flight, a gift Spencer especially cherished. He called it his "goose."

Since she'd last seen him, Tracy had grown even heavier. He was also drinking again, beer and wine, though it didn't appear to be a problem. Still, they had a picture to make, *Pat and Mike*, so Kate put him on an exercise regimen. It wouldn't do for Spencer to look out of shape—especially since Kate would be appearing in tiptop form as a professional athlete in this one. Every morning they'd emerge in sweatpants and baseball caps, marching up the steep incline of Doheny Drive, Spence groaning with each exertion of his big tree-trunk legs.

Pat and Mike was a happy production, with Cukor coining a new nickname for the quintet behind it: "The Kids from Kordell." Their little group had grown even tighter, with the Kanins buying a place next door to Kate's town house in New York. Perhaps to prove to Shaw just how athletic Kate really was, Ruth and Gar made sure there were plenty of opportunities in the script to showcase her physique in short skirts and tennis shorts.

True to form, they'd also written the dialogue with such a smooth pen that the world continued to assume that Hepburn and Tracy were simply playing themselves. *Pat and Mike*, in fact, encapsulates in one single scene the entire Tracy-Hepburn myth. The hangdog Tracy looks over at the beaming Hepburn and tells her, "I don't know if you can lick me or I can lick you, but I'll tell you one thing I do know. Together we can lick 'em all."

To which Kate replies, "You bet."

It's a touching scene, coming after ninety minutes of sexual tension. And yet, after they finally admit their love for each other, this is the payoff we get: *they shake hands.*

An alert moviegoer might well have wondered at that point when the last time was that Hepburn and Tracy had kissed on the screen. In our collective memory, of course, we seem to recall lots of affection—*smooching* even, in *Adam's Rib*, where the passion between Adam and Amanda Bonner is key to the plot. But look back at the film. When Adam and Amanda kiss, they move *offscreen*. It's a deliberate, even jarring moment, leaving the viewer to stare at an empty room for several seconds before they return into the frame. Later, we know they've been smooching only because Adam has lipstick on his face.

It's a pattern that becomes obvious only in retrospect. Consider their films together. No physical connection of any kind exists in *Keeper of the*

Flame. In *Without Love*—where the whole point is to nudge the two leads from platonic friendship into romantic passion—there's no climax to their final fade-out clinch. He kisses her neck; she kisses his cheek. (In the stage version, even though Kate hated Elliott Nugent, there'd been a long, passionate kiss.) In *State of the Union*, the reunion of our two stars is capped not by a kiss but by that infamous spanking. In *Sea of Grass*, Kate sits demurely on Spencer's lap, but they never once touch lips. In fact, you'd need to go all the way back to *Woman of the Year* for a real kiss—the first and only time Tracy and Hepburn were overtly sexual on the screen.

Maybe that's because it was the only time they were overtly sexual with each other in real life. This pattern of nonaffection with Tracy becomes glaring when we see how willing Kate was to lock lips with other actors during the same period. She kisses Paul Henreid several times in *Song of Love*. Even in *Sea of Grass*, she gives Melvyn Douglas, playing her lover, a full-mouthed kiss. But with Tracy in the same film—even when their characters are supposed to be happy together—it's never more than cheek-to-cheek.

Many felt it was a conscious decision on their part. "The word was that the writers were not to put in any love scenes for them," said Elliott Morgan, then head of the research department at MGM. If, in fact, their real-life relationship had become platonic, too much kissing may have been embarrassing for them. Certainly, the Kanins, their closest intimates, seem to have accommodated them by writing offscreen smooching scenes and chaste handshakes at the fade-out.

"Everyone at Metro knew the truth about Kate and Spencer," said Elliott Morgan. "They knew that they were together but that it wasn't a sexual thing. I always laugh when I hear people say, 'Oh, wasn't it good of Hollywood not to gossip, to be so respectful of their affair.' But nobody was gossiping because they knew there was nothing to gossip *about*. Everyone knew that they were just good, devoted friends."

Of course, it was difficult for people to understand—then as well as now—that a relationship could be intense and passionate and important without being sexual. The love story of Tracy and Hepburn should not be minimized just because sex (at least for much of the duration) was not a defining characteristic. For nearly a decade, whether they slept with each other or not, Kate and Spencer had loved each other and considered themselves a couple. Only by 1950, after Kate's long absences, did their sense of each other gradually start to change. But Hollywood kept nattering on, drawing its own conclusions.

Elliott Morgan referenced one of the primary myths of the Tracy-

Hepburn story: that although people knew about their relationship, the press never wrote about it. Yet this is simply not true. Columnists like Hedda Hopper, Earl Wilson, and Mike Connolly signaled their awareness of a connection between the two stars by often including their names in the same sentence. Connolly's "blind items"—like the one about Kate meeting an "old flame" at the Mayfair in London—were easily deciphered by those "in the know." Another columnist asked, "Who is the craggy married star Katie Hepburn sees first whenever she gets to town?"

In 1948, *Movieland* had come right out and named him. The magazine quoted a typist from the Aetna insurance company in Hartford as saying, "She's been madly in love with Spencer Tracy for years. Everyone knows that. But Mrs. Tracy won't give him a divorce." During the run of *The Rugged Path*, both the *Boston Globe* and *Life* magazine had reported on Hepburn's presence backstage, suggesting she was calling the shots and implying a personal relationship between the two. The myth of how respectful reporters had behaved toward Kate and Spencer was largely a latter-day attempt by the press to pat itself on the back.

In fact, with the rise of the scandal magazines in the 1950s, Kate and Spencer found themselves prime targets. In 1956, *Inside Story* would put them on the cover, trumpeting the UNTOLD STORY OF SPENCER TRACY AND KATHARINE HEPBURN. "To the world," the magazine reported breathlessly, "Good Guy Tracy and Haughty Hepburn are models of virtue. But the inside story about this pair has Hollywood gossips wagging their wicked tongues." Illustrating the piece with photos of Kate, Spencer, and Louise, the magazine revealed, "Like an iceberg, seven-eighths of which lies hidden beneath the surface, there is much more to Spotless Spencer than meets the eye . . . This exemplary family man and model citizen has for years carried on movie-town's biggest secret romance."

Many of the key elements of the Tracy-Hepburn legend can be traced back to this spurious piece. According to *Inside Story*, Kate was desperate to marry Spencer; the reason she spent so much time away from Hollywood was that she was "haunted" by being "the other woman." The piece sets up the heartbreaking ménage à trois that would come to prevail in later accounts of the Tracy-Hepburn story.

But the heartbreak was never so simple as that.

Washing Tracy's dishes for him at his bungalow, Kate was interrupted by a knock at the door. It was Scotty, Cukor's friend from the gas station. While she'd been gone, Scotty had once again become part of Spencer's life. Stepping aside, Kate allowed the young man to enter. At the table, Spence had opened a bottle and was pouring himself a drink. (Scotty never drank with him.) Kate dried her hands and left them alone.

For all the abuse Spencer could give Kate, Scotty recalled she could also land a mean blow when she was angry. "She'd tell him he was a fool to just sit there and drink," he said. "She could be very cutting to him. Then she'd walk off and leave us alone to have sex."

Kate had to have known they weren't just buddies. Yet she had always been an expert at compartmentalization. She could be very blind when she wanted to be, especially involving the men in her life. If something troubled her, she could push it right out of her mind. For all her celebrated strength, her approach to life was never so much about confronting her fears as it was finding the resourcefulness to step around them. "Fear," she told one interviewer, "is no builder of character."

What's clear is that Kate's obtuseness in recognizing the true nature of Spencer's turmoil was a willful choice on her part. On a late Sunday afternoon, staying in Cukor's guest room, she was surely aware of the young men gathering around the director's pool. Because the household staff had Sundays off, Cukor and his friends, mostly young, unmarried men, carried the food out from the kitchen themselves. Sliced meats, caviar, and exotic fruits were arranged poolside on a buffet table. Famous faces weren't to be found on Sundays, but rather behind-the-scenes people like Elliott Morgan, the editor Bob Seiter, and the publicist Robert Raison. With them they brought young men they'd met on movie sets or at the Hollywood Athletic Club. Kanin said Sundays were "sacrosanct" to Cukor. He and Ruth never attended. Neither did many of the director's other high-profile friends, which only made them all more curious. "Mr. Cukor has all these wonderful parties for ladies in the afternoon," observed the baroness d'Erlanger. "Then in the evening naughty men come around to eat the crumbs."

Kate had another term for them. "I always forget those little boys' names," she said once, introducing George's friends to Irene Selznick. She'd stopped when she got to the screenwriter Arthur Laurents, drawing a blank. Laurents was offended by Hepburn's use of the term *little boys,* feeling she was hostile to Cukor's gay Sunday crowd.

Perhaps with reason. Glancing up from the buffet table one Sunday, Elliott Morgan saw the red face of Spencer Tracy appearing over the edge of the hill, hauling himself up the steep, cliffside staircase. A few times, "no more than two or three," Morgan recalled, Tracy was present on a Sunday, lured from his lair by the sounds of merriment. Without anyone making a fuss, Spence tottered over, slightly out of breath, to join the party around the pool.

When Kate left Los Angeles after completing *Pat and Mike*, sailing a few weeks later to start rehearsals for *The Millionairess* in London, she was, in effect, putting an end to one phase of her relationship with Spencer. The "couplehood" that had characterized them during the 1940s was over. There was no announcement. But those around them knew something was happening. The columnist Doris Lilly understood Kate was "seriously considering breaking it off " with Spencer; this was echoed by James Bacon's observation that "Hepburn walked out on Tracy and went back East." Max Showalter said this was the period when Kate had "taken all she could and had finally seen the light." Robert Shaw recalled Kate returning to New York after *Pat and Mike* with a face more pained than he could ever remember. Sitting down hard opposite him, she said, "If I can't have what my parents had, why have anything at all?"

Shaw presumed Spencer was drinking too much. It's what everyone presumed. But Tracy's renewed drinking was only part of the story. If it had just been drink or pills or illness, Kate would've stayed forever. It wasn't even Scotty, not really, even though every time Kate let the young man into Spencer's bungalow she gave him the same hard, humorless face, snapping at Spencer and calling him a *fool*—the word Scotty remembered her using the most. Maybe she used the word so often because she herself had begun to feel that way. In the end, that's what really caused her to leave: the sense, gradually realized, that she had been living a fantasy. She could never be her mother. And Spencer was certainly not Hep.

Later, Kate would try to forget this period. In her memoir, she'd rewrite history to insist that no matter how difficult it got with Spence, she hung in there. "I can only say that I never could have left him," she said.

But in fact she did. Sailing on the *America* on March 21, 1952, with Constance Collier and Phyllis Wilbourn once more at her side, Kate was leaving Spencer behind—along with all the illusions she'd allowed herself to believe were real.

SOMEHOW VERY RIGHT ABOUT THINGS

Against the backdrop of the majestic Blue Mountains of Jamaica, Kate Hepburn and Irene Selznick were watching Noël Coward's dog give birth. The playwright-songwriter-raconteur hadn't even known his mangy mutt was female until she began waddling around obviously pregnant. Now, presented with four unexpected puppies, Coward and his long-time friend Lesley Cole exclaimed in wonder, their voices echoing across the sun-dappled half-moon cove of Blue Harbour, Coward's island retreat. Celebrating with champagne, the worldly group of friends named the newborns for the Brontës: Charlotte, Emily, Anne, and Bramwell. Emily took to Kate immediately, gazing up at her with adoring eyes, which made them all laugh.

Kate was glad for the laughter. She and Irene had arrived on the island in early March 1953, both of them exhausted and demoralized. Kate had just emerged from a long, grueling experience with *The Millionairess,* Irene from the flop of a play she'd produced, *Flight into Egypt.* The trip to Jamaica was "escape thinking," Irene told her friend Hugh "Binkie" Beaumont, the British theatrical producer. Kate had needed to take Irene "by the scruff of the neck" to convince her to go on holiday. But Irene was savvy enough to know Kate's idea of a holiday would be very different from her own. "I have warned her not to be too energetic around me," Irene told Binkie, "not to galvanize her poor tired old friend into any kind of strenuous or athletic activity. I'm taking my tennis racket along merely for appearance."

Yet for all Kate's gung ho itinerary planning, Irene sensed her friend wasn't as strong as she let on. "My position is that she's overtired and doesn't know it," she told Binkie. "While her job may be to perk me up a bit, it will be my job to bring her down a peg."

It had always been Hepburn's way to cloak her problems with frenzied activity. To sit around and mope was unthinkable. But shrewd, compassionate Irene saw through the early morning calisthenics and ambitious plans to motor across the island. She was well aware of what Kate had been through during the past year. Bringing her down a peg, Irene may have believed, would allow her some time to heal.

For Kate, the wounds of the past few years went far deeper than just the professional and the political. Her decision to leave Spence hadn't been as easy to live with as she may have hoped when she sailed off for London almost exactly twelve months before. Looking back, George Cukor would express some regret that he hadn't been fully aware of the crisis Kate was going through at this time. He later came to understand that "she was having misgivings about her life" during this period, and for inspiration she turned to Ethel Barrymore, whose seventieth birthday they'd all recently celebrated at Cukor's house. In Barrymore, a woman who'd never remarried after her divorce in 1923, Kate may have found a model for how she now envisioned her life: on her own, making her own decisions, charting her own path.

But it wasn't easy. Soon after her arrival in London, Kate wrote to John Huston that all she wanted was "a complete separation from reality." She was feeling nostalgic for the "long grass . . . and early morning light" of Africa. Instead of going onstage in *The Millionairess,* she told Huston, she just wanted to "get out, clear out"—once more her urge to flee, an echo of her impulsive escape on the *Paris* eighteen years earlier.

Running away wasn't an option this time. She had a twelve-week engagement with Beaumont's Tennent Productions to do *The Millionairess* in London. The play started off promisingly enough, with huge crowds turning out during the tour of the English provinces before the London opening. For an American performer to tour England in this way was unprecedented, but Kate proved her appeal transcended national borders. Once again, Michael Benthall was directing, and this time they seemed to have struck the right note in the performance. Kate played the lead character of Epifania—whom

Shaw had called "an awful, impossible woman"—at the top of her voice, flailing across the stage as if she were swinging a scythe. The *Daily Express* called her "a human hurricane."

Shaw had died a few months before, so he never got to see what Kate did with the part. After the show opened on June 26, 1952, at the New Theatre, St. Martin's Lane, the *Times* trumpeted Hepburn as a "force of nature." Yet all her shouting and gesticulations merely covered up the essential emptiness of the part of Epifania, a domineering, unhappy shell of a human being. "Shaw could not make a woman of her and Hepburn does not try," the *Times* said. "Every now and then she is quiet for a space and the effect is that of a sudden shutting off of power in a boiler factory. This is magnificent in its way, but it is still not acting."

For a woman who tolerated no self-pity, who indulged few expressions of pain or grief, Epifania's character served as a sort of relief valve for the existential, midlife, possibly even menopausal crisis Hepburn was facing. The part didn't require her to act, as the *Times* had noticed. All Kate needed to do was *vent*. "The worse your private life," she admitted later, "the pleasanter it is to go into the never-never land" of the theater.

Sweltering in an unusual London heat wave, each night Kate seemed to walk out onto the stage a little crazier than the night before, and soon all that screaming and shouting left her with laryngitis. Beaumont, fretful that audiences would brook no understudy in the part, insisted Kate keep absolutely quiet except for her time onstage. Her days were passed in a silent, surreal, slow-motion existence, only to explode into rage and savagery every night.

And then Spencer Tracy showed up.

In London to shoot final scenes for his film *Plymouth Adventure*, Spencer found time to take at least one walk in the park with Kate, who captured the afternoon on canvas in one of her most melancholy paintings, called *A Walk with Spencer*. She rendered the trees roughly in dark, dull greens with little sunlight coming through them; the lone figure of a man—opposite a dark, dismal house—is dwarfed by the enormousness of the forest.

That there had been a change in their relationship is made clear when we consider with whom Spencer was spending most of his time in London. Despite their walk in the park, it wasn't Kate, but rather his *Plymouth Adventure* costar, the exquisitely beautiful Gene Tierney, thirteen years Kate's junior. Spence was enchanted with Tierney; he'd reportedly asked her to marry him, although there had been no change in his own marital status. As proof, Tierney would show Kirk Douglas, her former beau, a "saccharine letter" that Tracy had written to her outlining how "they could go off together." Yet at dinner in Grosvenor Square, Tierney believed Spence was always on the lookout for Kate, his eyes flicking toward the door whenever someone entered. (Hepburn was staying just above the square at the Connaught Hotel.)

Tierney didn't know it, but Tracy was also spending time with the Australian model June Dally-Watkins, in a date arranged by none other than the Kanins. After they attended the ballet at Covent Garden with Prince Aly Khan and his date, Dally-Watkins detected a "spark" between her and Spencer "that culminated in a kiss." Since he was leaving soon for the United States, the two arranged to meet in Los Angeles in a few weeks. In the interim, Dally-Watkins was bombarded with telegrams from her ardent suitor. "Have [you] run off with handsome stranger?" Tracy cabled. "If not, when coming? Lovely house, homely man waiting. Much love, Uncle Sam."

"There did not appear to be anyone in his life at all," remembered Dally-Watkins, who spent time with Tracy at George Cukor's house during the fall of 1952. "Certainly he never mentioned Katharine Hepburn." Despite the spark between them, Dally-Watkins said Spencer never made any moves on her. "There would be champagne before dinner and a kiss on the cheek afterward. That's all."

Spencer was not "cheating" on Kate with Tierney and Dally-Watkins in the way some chroniclers have portrayed him. Hepburn's departure after *Pat and Mike* had marked a clear break between them—one that was obvious to their close friends if the Kanins were fixing Spence up with an Australian model. Still, hearing about her former lover and other women was no doubt painful for Kate. The decision to leave may have been her idea, but it surely hurt to see Spence moving on without her.

Of course, Tracy may have been acting out with Tierney and Dally-Watkins, either to make Kate jealous or to soothe whatever conflicts existed within himself. In any event, it's highly doubtful he would have divorced Louise as Tierney seems to have hoped. Tierney's own mother, talking religion with Spencer, found him "the most tormented man she had ever met." Kirk Douglas was angry at what he perceived to be Tracy's manipulation of the gullible actress. "I don't know what was in Spencer Tracy's head," Douglas remembered.

Spencer's presence in London no doubt exacerbated the roiling emotions Kate was required to display every night onstage. Bewailing the tragedy of her life, Epifania breaks a chair and tosses her costar, Cyril Ritchard, to the ground, calling him "vermin." When the show finally ended on September 20, Kate was in no mood for niceties. With fans blocking her car after the performance, she shouted to the driver, "Drive on! We'll sweep up the blood later!" No need anymore to worry about her voice—or what Londoners might think of her. The next day, the tabloids bannered the remark, but Kate was on her way to New York.

Despite their overlapping London schedules, there's no evidence Kate and Spencer saw each other more than a few times. That hasn't stopped writers from imagining romantic interludes between them during this period. Indeed, elaborate scenarios have been constructed to keep alive the image of the Tracy-Hepburn relationship as a constant, unchanging thing—even during the first half of the 1950s, when Kate was usually a world away from Spence. Of course, for the legend to be maintained, this kind of invention was crucial. Accordingly, in previous narratives, we've been treated to images of Tracy feeling rudderless without "his Kate." Hepburn, meanwhile, has been portrayed as forever fretful over Spence's welfare, anxious to hurry back to his side. Without any evidence, writers have imagined transatlantic telephone cables crackling with overuse. Some chroniclers even imagined couriers posted in the depths of the African jungles to ferry out regular letters from Kate to Spence.

Yet in fact, for much of this period, communication between Hepburn and Tracy dwindled as each recognized the relationship, as they had known it, was over. Cukor's letters to Kate during this period reveal that while there was no apparent animosity between the former lovers, interaction in each other's lives had virtually ceased. Kate often had no idea of Spencer's activities until Cukor told her about them. "My elusive tenant turns up at his little home from time to time, unexpected and unannounced," he wrote to her at one point. "Before I know it, he's gone again."

Where Spence was off to, Kate could only imagine. But it was no longer her job to keep track. Both, in their own ways, had moved on: Tracy with Tierney and Dally-Watkins, Kate back to the comforting friendship of women, like Irene Selznick and Constance Collier.

Just as she had in London, Kate subsumed her emotions into *The Millionairess* when it opened at the Shubert Theatre in New York on October 17. The actress Marian Seldes, then just starting out, recalled seeing Kate in the "very difficult part." Seldes was glad she had never studied the play before, "because [Kate] created the part . . . She had that magnitude where people just wanted to see her."

Yet Broadway critics were less impressed than their West End counterparts had been. Walter Kerr in the *Herald-Tribune* said Kate's performance began and ended in the larynx. Once more, New York critics seemed determined to prove her success on the stage with *The Philadelphia Story* had been a fluke. Kate tried to be philosophical. "American vitality has a great appeal to the British," she mused to *Time*. "But back home, vitality is not so bloody unique."

The Millionairess closed a few days after Christmas 1952. It was Kate's last project with the Theatre Guild. By that point, she was at a serious low point. In a memo shortly before the closing of the play, Lawrence Langner had expressed concerns that she was "under a strain," and indeed, almost immediately after the last performance, Kate reportedly checked herself into Columbia-Presbyterian Hospital. She was run-down, exhausted, and under-weight. Such a move reflects just how dispirited she was; for a Hepburn to resort to hospitalization and not rely on supposedly boundless reserves of inner strength was a major concession.

Kate may have been depressed, but she was far from suicidal, as some have suggested. In fact, she was soon out of the hospital and driving up the coast to Fenwick with Robert Helpmann, Michael Benthall's lover and her costar from *The Millionairess*. There, wandering across the frozen beach, Kate decided what she really needed was a holiday. She was quickly on the phone to Irene.

They blew into town in a snazzy little convertible, their gauzy headscarves flying in the breeze behind them. Upon seeing their car, Noël Coward fretted that they'd burn themselves or suffer sunstroke in the hot Caribbean sun. But Kate and Irene—he called them his "two belles"—pooh-poohed his fears, exulting being in the open air. Soon Coward had switched his closed car for a convertible as well.

Coward was delighted by their visit. "There is nothing whatsoever to do but lie on the beach, read bad books and look at the view," he promised them. "Witty conversation is not the order of the day before 11:30 a.m. when I emerge from my toils, then of course I expect the dialogue to scintillate. The rock bathing is fairly uncomfortable, which Katie will adore, but there is enough glorious white sand to comfort more sedentary types."

They spent their days in luxuriant laziness, swimming and beachcomb-ing. While Irene could be spotted "lying in a lump" in a beach chair, Kate was clambering over rocks and diving into the harbor from great heights. In the afternoons, they did indeed parry words back and forth with Cow-ard. From London, Binkie Beaumont wired he presumed the three of them would soon be founding "the Royal National Jamaican Theatre," and that their first production would be *Design for Living*.

For much of 1953, Irene would be a boon companion for Kate, who had just turned forty-six. When Kate wasn't with Irene, she was with Constance

Collier and Phyllis Wilbourn, or at dinner parties with Nancy Hamilton or Eve March. Once more, after a difficult stretch with a man, Hepburn had returned to the camaraderie of women for sustenance and renewal. In the first few weeks after leaving Tracy, she took great comfort in that platonic communion. Collier wrote to Terry Helburn that Kate hadn't looked "so well in years." The change, Collier said (without specifying what change she meant), was "doing her so much good."

Though her appearances in most Hepburn biographies have been infrequent, Irene Selznick was in fact one of the great friends of Kate's life. To emphasize Irene's presence, of course, or any of Kate's other close companions, would be to marginalize Spencer at this point, which most chroniclers seem to have been loath to do. But in fact, Irene would prove to be one of the key figures in Kate's story. Just a month separated the two women in age, but everything else about them seemed distinctly mismatched. Jewish, dark, and sharp-featured, Irene looked like the pixieish screenwriter Anita Loos "if Anita Loos had been ground in a pencil sharpener," according to Irene's (and Kate's) friend James Prideaux. Forever griping about some pain, real or imaginary, Irene nevertheless became the inseparable companion of the red-headed, eternally healthy, New England Yankee Kate. Unlike most of the other women in Kate's life, Irene was a mother with two children, Jeff and Danny, who adored Hepburn as a kind of eccentric maiden aunt.

As the daughter of Louis B. Mayer and the former wife of David O. Selznick, Irene had enjoyed a privileged ringside seat in Hollywood for her first four decades. But in midlife, in circumstances not so dissimilar from Kate's, she found herself on her own and in need of reinvention. Out of the long shadows cast by the towering men in her life, Irene emerged as one of Broadway's top producers, having gambled on a risky (some said unstageable) play by Tennessee Williams called *A Streetcar Named Desire*. She followed *Streetcar* with another hit, *Bell, Book and Candle*, and already had her eye on Enid Bagnold's *The Chalk Garden*. Irene was hoping Kate would play Miss Madrigal.

Although they'd first met as far back as *A Bill of Divorcement*, the two women didn't really click until a party at George Cukor's in the mid-1940s. For years, Cukor had nurtured friendships with both of them but never brought the two together. "George had a firm grasp on us," Irene recalled, "one in each hand and never the twain shall meet." Finally, at one swank dinner party on Cordell Drive, Cukor sat them together "below the salt"— meaning "the last two seats at the wrong end of the table." Hepburn and Selznick were quick to take mock outrage. "What a nerve he has!" Irene announced. "Look where he puts the people he cares for!" Within minutes, she and Kate were fast friends.

"We entered a lifelong conspiracy which we haven't yet either defined or implemented," Irene said in 1983. Theirs was one of the rare, genuine friendships of Hollywood. When Louis B. Mayer died, Kate stood steadfastly at Irene's side: "She is not what I would call frivolous or undependable," Irene wrote to Binkie Beaumont. It was Kate's loyalty to Mayer that cemented her friendship with Irene, especially as others seemed to relish attacking the late studio chief's reputation.

Irene was, in fact, one of the few to socialize with Kate and Spencer outside the Entente Cordiale. Arthur Laurents recalled a trip on a rented yacht, from Balboa to Catalina, on Memorial Day weekend, 1947. The twenty-nine-year-old writer was Irene's escort. Tracy sat in a chair as Kate patted pillows behind his back. It wasn't a very pleasant excursion, with Laurents getting seasick, Irene obsessing about her husband, and Kate worrying about Spence falling overboard. On their own, without their men to distract them, the two women had much better times.

Yet it's a wonder, really, that they got along so well. In her deep, husky voice, Selznick bossed those around her with an authority that was not unlike Kate's in its efficiency, always insisting whatever she said was for the person's own good. "With your head on my shoulders," Kitty Carlisle Hart once quipped to Irene after being given some trenchant advice, "I will go far."

In fact, there was much between Kate and Irene that was compatible. Both ladies could be snobs, and if Irene's snobbery was more obvious (she graded Hollywood's parties and told Arthur Laurents he should never be seen at one below a B), it was also more honest. In fact, Kate turned her nose up at certain names, like Joan Crawford's—though it would be bad for the image if that attitude ever became too apparent, especially post–*African Queen*.

Laurents called both Kate and Irene "completely humorless" about themselves. It's true that Kate and Irene took their places in life very seriously. Certainly Kate never enjoyed laughing at herself, nor allowing others to do so in her presence. "They were two women who were uncomfortable with being women," said Laurents. "It made them peculiarly dissatisfied."

Together, however, Kate and Irene could jettison those parts of womanhood that didn't fit. They traveled together, hiring their own cars and deciding when to stop, where to go, whom to see. Together, these two supposedly "humorless" ladies knew how to have fun. One of Irene's favorite memories was scaling walls with Kate in Beverly Hills and swimming in people's pools when they weren't home, an echo of Kath's long-ago antics with Ali Barbour and Laura Harding. After the heaviness of the last few years with Spencer, Kate was once again having a ball.

In New York, she and Irene would frequently sit and talk for hours, sometimes all through the night, just the two of them, smoking cigarettes, Irene's throaty crackle of a laugh breaking through the rat-a-tat-tat of Kate's constant chatter. Often Irene would stand behind her friend, her strong hands massaging Kate's neck and shoulders. Irene prided herself on her deep massages. Friends and actors in her productions were often the grateful recipients.

Yet there's no evidence, as some have suggested, of a sexual affair between the two. Irene was far from the boyish, athletic, Protestant type Kate was always drawn to in women. Years later, in fact, Irene would express surprise to Scott Berg after witnessing an exchange between Kate and a woman she didn't recognize that implied "a level of intimacy she had never allowed herself to believe." Until that point, apparently, Irene had never considered Kate's sexuality to be as fluid as it really was.

Even if Kate didn't disclose all facets of her life to Irene, she found with her a fulfilling replacement for the intimates she had left behind in L.A. During this period, the Kanins were mostly living in France, and although Garson would imply in his memoir that Kate visited, he was imprecise (as usual) about exact dates. Clearly, he stitched together anecdotes to make it seem as if the happy foursome of Tracy and Hepburn and Kanin and Gordon were never far apart from each other. But it's unlikely that, for most of the first half of the 1950s, Kate saw much of them. Even with Cukor there was distance, though affectionate letters back and forth remained.

It wasn't just the Entente Cordiale that had disappeared. Other important figures were passing out of Kate's life as well. In addition to her mother, she'd lost Phil Barry to a sudden heart attack, a "dreadful" shock for Kate, according to Irene. There was also heartache over the death of Fanny Brice, one of the Cukor regulars, who'd been able to make Spence laugh as few others could. In some ways, however, the most wrenching loss was that of Em Perkins, who'd retired to Maine in 1949. In her late sixties, Em's health had been declining for some time. But what a ride she and Kate had had together. All over the country they'd journeyed, and how thrilled this former seamstress had been to play small parts in both the stage and film versions of *Without Love*. But try as she might, the feisty Em simply couldn't keep up with Kate's jet-set lifestyle anymore. Retiring to Ogunquit, she ran a teahouse for several years. Although Kate visited, she deeply missed the daily doses of Em's maternal nurturance.

In many ways, Constance Collier was Em's replacement, though she was certainly no paid companion. Collier was an imposing, regal figure, standing with as much grandeur at Kate's side as she'd once stood beside the noted English actor Beerbohm Tree on the London stage. Yet she was also an extremely nurturing and maternal figure in Kate's life. Collier coached her in Shakespeare, in all sorts of theatrical technique, but even more important, she provided Kate with the model on which she now fashioned her life.

The first thing that struck the forty-seven-year-old Kate about Venice as she, Constance, and Phyllis Wilbourn entered the city that day in the summer of 1954 was the stench—the raw, acrid smell of the polluted water. The second thing she noticed was the heat—how when she stepped from the launch onto a gondola, the temperature seemed even hotter than in the equatorial jungles of Africa. At the Palazzo Papdopoli (chosen because it was reportedly the only place in Venice with air-conditioning), Kate turned to Constance and wondered if they'd ever make it through the shoot of David Lean's film adaptation of Arthur Laurents's play *The Time of the Cuckoo*. Constance was there to provide moral support, and she came through now: "Acting," she said, "is always about rising above."

To Collier, acting was everything, "the essence of her existence," according to the columnist and raconteur Lucius Beebe. Born in England in 1878, Collier came from a long line of actors and dancers. Her real name was Laura Hardie—perhaps proof she was fated to play a role in Kate's life. With dark, exotic features inherited from a Portuguese grandmother, Collier was considered one of the great beauties of the early-twentieth-century stage. In fact, her appearance was quite masculine, with heavy eyebrows, an imperial nose, and a prominent chin. During her heyday, most every photograph taken of her was shot from below to soften her imposing features. Tall and broad-shouldered, she had the hands of a man, which were nonetheless incongruously graceful when she spoke, gesturing as she made a point. People said Collier had the air of a duchess.

No one influenced the second half of Hepburn's life more than Constance Collier. Kate's determination, rather late in the game, to push herself and her craft was a direct result of her friendship with Collier. With her husky, contralto voice, Collier had played just about every role in the theater, from Sweet Nell of Old Drury to the Queen of Denmark. Performing was in her blood. As a baby, she'd been wrapped in a blanket and left among the greasepaints by her actress mother, and was fed between acts. She first toddled out onto the stage at the age of three, playing Peaseblossom in *A Midsummer Night's Dream*.

Telling tales of her past, Collier fired Kate's imagination. Acting—performing—was one's *life*, one's *art*. Until now, Hepburn's ambition, her fierce drive, had largely been motivated by a desire for fame. Now, finally, there was a sense of something bigger. "Constance made her see that she could be an artist," said Noel Taylor. During the late 1940s and the first half of the 1950s—Kate's most aggressive period of challenging herself artistically—Collier was always at her side.

The older actress had other, more personal influences on Kate as well. "There was no man in her life, and Connie never pretended there was," said the costume designer Miles White. "She'd look at you with those heavily lidded eyes, daring you to say anything about it."

For several years around the turn of the century, Collier had been rumored to be engaged to Beerbohm Tree's brother Max Beerbohm, the drama critic and onetime habitué of Oscar Wilde's circles. Asked once why she had never wed Beerbohm, Collier laughed. "Ah, poor dear Max," she said. "He had carpet slippers in his soul."

But, like Hepburn, Collier did marry once. Her husband was the Irish actor Julian L'Estrange; aspects of their unusual marriage would be echoed in Kate's union with Luddy more than two decades later. As a young woman, Collier had had "no desire, no intention" of marriage; "I felt I needed to be free and that career was the only thing that mattered," she said. L'Estrange— her "good friend," the way Kate always called Luddy—persuaded her otherwise, even if they weren't in love.

Although they rarely lived together, L'Estrange spoiled Collier with gifts and attention, much as Luddy would do with Kate. All the while, L'Estrange was frequently traveling about the countryside, both in England and the United States, in the company of Albert Morris Bagby, a young pianist who'd trained under Franz Liszt. To Collier's great relief, she found that "marriage didn't affect [her] in the least." She could still come and go as she pleased, while her "gay and beautiful husband" proved a "wonderful companion" on those rare occasions when they saw each other. In New York she stayed at the Algonquin; he had an apartment on West Fifty-second Street. It was there that L'Estrange died of influenza in 1918.

By the time Kate got to know her, Collier was well into her second career as a Hollywood character actress and drama coach—one of the legendary grandes dames. Noël Coward recalled her presiding over a roomful of people from her bed, wearing a pink dressing gown with a dog in one hand and a cigarette in the other. Lucius Beebe remembered the old racing prints on Collier's saffron walls, the brocade-covered daybed, and six of the largest brandy inhaler glasses he'd ever seen—and he had seen plenty.

Since the 1930s, Collier, a diabetic, had been tended to by a devoted companion, an English girl named Phyllis Wilbourn. "In those days, they called them *be-withs,*" said Noel Taylor. Collier preferred the term *secretary,* but everyone knew Phyllis did far more than answer telephones. She was there to eat breakfast with Collier, to read the newspapers to her, to clasp her diamond necklace for her on those evenings they went to the theater. In return, Collier gave Phyllis—a rather simple girl from a small town in Essex—access to a sparkling world. "I spent my life with an angel," Phyllis later told Hedda Hopper.

They came as a pair, and everyone respected that. When Kate asked Collier to travel with her to London for *The Millionairess,* she was dismayed to see that Binkie Beaumont had paid for only two transatlantic passages. Knowing Constance would never leave without her Phyllis, Kate exchanged the two first-class tickets for three fares on a less expensive ship.

Some friends assumed that, early on, Constance and Phyllis had been lovers. By the 1950s, however, when Collier was over seventy, their relationship was devoted yet platonic, according to Noel Taylor, who knew both of them. Still, Collier had always been close with some of the theater's best-known lesbians. She was an early mentor and lifelong intimate of Eva Le Gallienne, and she often socialized with Mercedes de Acosta. Some friends believed Collier first met Hepburn in the early 1930s at a party given by Hope Williams. Such a Sapphic association swirled around Collier that Alfred Hitchcock hired her in 1948 specifically for the lesbian air she'd bring to a small part in *Rope*—though Arthur Laurents said Hitch later worried that her husky voice might actually be pushing it too far.

With this unconventional mentor did Kate now spend much of her time. "[Constance] had a real zing and a zest for all that was good in life," Hepburn said. After the gloom of her last days with Tracy, Kate blossomed under Collier's nurturance in a way she had done only twice before in her life: in her last two years at Bryn Mawr and in her first two in Hollywood. She looked better; she sounded better; she moved through the world better.

"This was the Kate I knew," said Robert Shaw. "This was Kate living the way she wanted, not like that person we saw in the movies, bossed around by Spencer Tracy. She was completely her own person, and I think that's when she was the happiest in her entire life."

From Collier, Kate learned a design for living that imprinted the rest of her days. From here on, women formed her basic family unit. What Constance had with Phyllis was admirable, Kate thought. "They are two such gay and strong characters," she told Cukor. "Absolutely idiotic but somehow very right about things. They have such a happy point of view."

It had been some time since Kate had been happy or felt right about things. For too long she'd been trying to nail the square peg of her personality into the round hole of life with Spencer. Now, at age forty-seven, with Constance, with Phyllis, with Irene—with living in New York, traveling to Europe, pushing herself as an actress—she was starting to *live* once again. Summing up *The Chalk Garden* for Irene, Constance wrote, "Human beings cannot flourish in the wrong soil for our souls." She might have been describing her friend Kate.

"With women, Kate found a sense of home," said one longtime friend, a woman, who remembered a community around Hepburn "who really took care of one another." Indeed, when Kate was discouraged after a long, fruitless struggle to find the backing for a film adaptation of *The Millionairess*, Irene proved solicitous. With Kate heading for London, Irene wrote ahead to Binkie Beaumont to make sure he offered "particular warmth and companionship [to Kate] the next few days." Collier was also on hand to offer consolation and support. It was the kind of nurturance Kate rarely received from the men in her life.

Yet what was missing for Kate was a romantic attachment. After Spencer, she seems to have sublimated that need into her work and her friendships—and into a series of encounters with a young woman she met in early 1952, as she was finishing *Pat and Mike*.

Walking into Cukor's house, Kate had spotted Scotty tending bar. Rarely did she ever speak to him, Scotty recalled, but this day, she approached him. He looked up into her well-scrubbed shiny face. She wasted no time on pleasantries. Did he know of any young woman who might like to go hiking with her? Scotty said he did. The next day a thin, dark-haired, athletic eighteen-year-old met Kate at the Los Angeles Reservoir, and they hit it off.

"She was good to me . . . a wonderful person" is all the woman, now a grandmother living outside L.A., would say about Hepburn. Scotty said he understood they saw each other often over the years, and that the woman sometimes accompanied Kate back East. Might Scotty's friend have been the woman Irene Selznick saw, but didn't recognize, in an "intimate exchange" with the star?

That Kate could so compartmentalize her romantic life in this way—confining her most intimate expressions to a woman who came and went—suggests a resignation to never finding a fulfilling relationship that might bridge her public and private lives. She seems to have accepted that emotional sustenance would come from the circle of platonic friends, largely women, she had drawn around her.

"I think people like Irene and Constance and others understood Kate better than any man ever did," said her longtime friend who, for a while, was also part of the female circle around Hepburn. "It wasn't a feminist thing. They just accepted her, and she accepted them. And Kate was every bit as loyal as they were."

Indeed, among her inner circle, Kate was known for her loyalty and her generosity. Even those on the periphery, like Ethel Barrymore and the aged actor Lionel Pape, an old friend of John Ford's, were beneficiaries of her financial and emotional support. "She's extraordinary in that respect," Palache told an interviewer in 1985. "Once she's your friend, she's your friend for life and you can do no wrong."

For all her competitive spirit, Hepburn was free of the petty jealousies that typified other major stars. She never viewed younger actresses as threats. In a crucial scene in *Adam's Rib*, Kate gave the rising star Judy Holliday the spotlight, sitting off to the side with only her shoulder in the frame. Few other stars were ever as generous with the camera. "Kate wasn't in competition with women in that way," said one of her friends. "She didn't worry about who was prettier or if a younger actress had more close-ups. That wasn't how she thought."

Certainly there was little room for vanity in her latest project, the film version of Arthur Laurents's *Time of the Cuckoo*. Playing the plain, lonely spinster who finds unexpected romance on a Venetian holiday, Kate looked her age, gaunt and brittle. Her appearance fit the part, and indeed, she gives one of her best (Scott Berg thought most self-revealing) performances in the film, ultimately retitled *Summertime*.

Indeed, standing on the balcony of her hotel, Kate is heartbreaking as she watches the young lovers around her. As Jane Hudson, she remains outside all that, barricaded against emotion. Yet when Rossano Brazzi makes love to her, the transformation that takes place is magical. Lying in the grass with her hair down, Jane looks almost like the young Kath Hepburn of Bryn Mawr.

Laurents wasn't happy with how she played the part, claiming Kate's movie-star wattage blindsighted director David Lean. Indeed, Hepburn's description of working with Lean as a "treat" suggests she was able to get her way during the filming. Yet there's no mistaking the power of the last scene, when Jane leaves her lover, exuberantly waving good-bye from the train. After spending the first three-quarters of the picture longing for love and connection, Jane finds it, only to give it up when she realizes she's okay on her own, that she's good just as she is. Rather than a mawkish, tearjerker ending, *Summertime* gives us the rare portrait of a woman who decides the love of a man isn't necessary to make her whole.

The message no doubt resonated for Kate. At one point during the shoot, Tracy visited, upsetting her careful equilibrium. To her dismay, he was either drinking again or else overly agitated by his medications and insomnia. No matter the source of his discontent, Spencer seems to have temporarily upended Kate's time in Venice. The MGM publicist Emily Torchia said Kate "didn't want [Tracy] around" that summer. Though Kate had written to Cukor in March that she hoped Spence would visit, her former lover's periodic appearances in her life during the 1950s always seem fraught with some kind of tension or melancholy.

Still, after he left, Kate's letters to Binkie Beaumont gave the impression she was "very lonely." Hepburn and Tracy had spent nearly a decade together, and the feelings hadn't disappeared completely. The sweltering heat also made Kate miserable, and her famous fall into a filthy canal during one scene only made things worse. (She developed a staph infection in her eyes.) Snapping at the crew, Kate was excluded from their evening jaunts, which left her angry and resentful.

The saving grace was David Lean's twenty-eight-year-old script girl, Maggie Shipway. Kate befriended the unmarried, tweedy Englishwoman, bringing her back with her to London as her personal secretary. "Maggie was good for her," said one friend. "She just let Kate be Kate."

In her next picture, an adaptation of the Richard Nash play *The Rainmaker,* she was once again cast as a spinster, "plain as old shoes." Yet while Lizzie Curry is more of a traditional old maid, Kate still manages to strip most of the pity away. When her brother suggests she try harder to please a man, her father defends Lizzie's lack of femininity by saying, "That's the way Lizzie is. She can't be anything else"—rather like Kate herself. Indeed, the highlight of the film is Lizzie's imitation of a girly-girl, stuffing her bra and batting her eyelashes. It's hysterical, for what Kate was really doing was parading her own rejection of traditional femininity. "I was playing me," she told Scott Berg.

In many ways, Kate's spinsters of the 1950s, starting with her transformative Rose Sayer in *The African Queen,* harked back to the deviance of her early RKO films. More than one critic has observed that Jane Hudson might be Alice Adams in middle age. The public, of course, read such parts as merely extensions of Kate's real life as an unmarried woman, presuming upon her the kind of longing her characters felt: Lizzie Curry wishes for a husband who will order her to press his suit and scratch his back. Yet in truth, Hepburn was more like Jane Hudson, turning away from all that—in fact, waving good-bye to it with an exuberance that was as much relief as it was acceptance.

"I wouldn't give you ten men for any one woman," Hepburn told Arthur Laurents at the time. "All men are poops." For the first half of the 1950s, that seemed to sum up her life.

For much of 1954 and 1955, Kate lived in London. Her world there returned her to the kind of urbane, sophisticated circles she had known in New York before going to Hollywood. Once again, many of her closest friends were homosexual men: Noël Coward, Binkie Beaumont, Michael Benthall, and Bobby Helpmann. What made these men different from previous friends was their more obvious lifestyle. Beaumont lived openly with a male partner, and few in London didn't know that Benthall and Helpmann were lovers.

Michael and Bobby were rare in another way. The possessive Kate embraced few couples of any stripe; if a friend had a significant other, she often didn't want to know about him or her. Michael and Bobby were the exception, though it didn't start out that way. When Benthall was directing her in *As You Like It,* Kate had made it quite plain she had no interest in sharing him with his lover. "I felt I was on the outside, looking in," Helpmann recalled. "When we were all together, a sort of tension grew up between the three of us. I didn't feel at ease with her. I don't think she felt at ease with me." Kate made sure she sat next to Benthall at meals and rode to the theater with him— alone. Often she seemed not to even notice that Helpmann was in the room.

Part of it was likely Bobby's flamboyance, especially compared to the masculine, Eton- and Oxford-educated Benthall. Two years younger than Kate, Helpmann was the son of a meat exporter from southern Australia. As a boy, he horrified his father by lisping through the part of Juliet and pirouetting better than any of the girls in his ballet class. From the taunts of his schoolmates, Bobby found refuge at age fourteen as a student in Anna Pavlova's company. Coming to London to dance with the Vic-Wells Ballet, he was soon the principal dancer, renowned for his work with Margot Fonteyn and Frederick Ashton. Helpmann was also an actor, performing in drag at the Ambassadors. More recently he had played with the Oliviers in *Antony and Cleopatra,* directed by Benthall.

By the time Kate met him, stories about Helpmann were already legend. There was the time he performed the entire balcony scene from *Romeo and Juliet* at two in the morning from the first-floor gallery of a Manchester hotel. Another time, he showed up at a party given by Gerald Lord Berners dressed as a minor European princess, complete with wig, satin dress, and a hat made of silk stockings. With his pop eyes and extravagant hand gestures, it was immediately apparent upon meeting Bobby Helpmann that he was homosexual. Until now, the gay men in Kate's life, like Cukor, had gone to great lengths to shield her from their sexual carousing. Bobby was flagrant about it. The *Times* called him "a homosexual of the proselytizing kind" who "could turn young men on the borderline his way." It was no wonder Kate wanted nothing to do with him at first.

Yet Helpmann and Benthall moved in a world where other undisguised homosexuals—people like Coward, Beaumont, Ashton, John Gielgud, Oliver Messel, Benjamin Britten—held considerable sway and influence. To ignore Bobby forever would socially imperil Kate in London. After accepting Benthall's suggestion that Helpmann take a part in *The Millionairess,* Kate soon developed a tight bond with him. Bobby ended up spending Christmas with her at Fenwick that year. "He's delicious to know," Kate admitted.

Various letters offer a panorama of her life in London. There she sits with Coward and Graham Payn sharing an aperitif at a party given by Nancy Hamilton for Alfred Lunt and Lynn Fontanne. On another day, she talks Shakespeare with Peter Brook and his wife, Natasha, to whom she lends her house in New York. In April 1955, there's a warm reunion with Irene Selznick, in London to talk with the actress Siobhan McKenna about taking the lead role in *The Chalk Garden,* which Kate has finally turned down. Days later, she's sipping cocktails with Binkie, Gielgud, Vivien Leigh, and Laurence Olivier at a party for Clifton Webb.

Far away from Red-baiting Los Angeles, Kate had found a glamorous safe harbor. Though Britain was in the midst of its own period of conservative reaction, the great expanse of the Atlantic Ocean put a distance between Kate and her difficult political battles.

She adored everything about England. The theater. The countryside. Stopping for tea in the middle of the day. Truck drivers whistled at her when she wore slacks on the street, even if Claridge's made her use the back entrance. No matter; it was the no-nonsense, can-do attitude of the British that won her over. "They're the toughest race in the world," Kate said. "They can go through anything and have a passionate belief in themselves."

Michael Benthall had succeeded Tyrone Guthrie as director of the Old Vic in 1953. One of his stated goals was to perform within five years all thirty-six plays in the first folio of Shakespeare. As part of this plan, Benthall was putting together a tour of Australia with *The Taming of the Shrew, Measure for Measure,* and *The Merchant of Venice* in rotation. Just as she had with *The African Queen,* Kate jumped at the chance to see a part of the world she might otherwise never have visited. When she returned from Venice, she signed on to play Katherine in *The Taming of the Shrew,* Isabella in *Measure for Measure,* and Portia in *The Merchant of Venice.* Benthall would direct; Helpmann would costar.

Kate was fully cognizant that the tour would require her to spend more than six months on the other side of the globe—and after that, she was committed to return to England to make a movie with Bob Hope. That meant she'd be away from the United States for nearly a year. Her frequent sojourns away from her native country may have reflected her distaste for the political climate. (The Army-McCarthy hearings were being broadcast on television during the early part of this period.) But it's also possible that Spencer's latest unsuccessful foray into her life convinced Kate that keeping her distance was a good thing.

There's one other consideration—perhaps the most important one—that explains her decision to stay away from home for so long. For several years now, Constance Collier had been encouraging her to push herself as an artist. Here was an extraordinary opportunity to take on not one but *three* Shakespearean parts in the company of close friends whose artistic sensibilities she trusted. Once again, we see Kate embarking on a new artistic challenge when so many of her contemporaries were either retired or working in substandard projects.

As she set off on her adventure in the spring of 1955, Kate's high spirits were tempered only by news that Collier had died in New York, where she'd been coaching Marilyn Monroe. Her cherished mentor would not see her play Portia, a crushing disappointment for Kate. Unable to return to New York in time for the memorial service, she stopped by on her way to Australia and invited the bereaved Phyllis Wilbourn to accompany her on the tour. Phyllis was grateful for the offer, but she and Marjorie Steele, wife of the grocery chain heir Huntington Hartford, were taking Constance's ashes back to England for burial. Kate assured her that the tour would be her own tribute to Collier.

On May 5, Kate departed on Qantas Airlines for Australia. Never as big a star "down under" as she was in the United States and Britain, she found herself confronted by some tough, cynical reporters, the likes of which she hadn't had to deal with since the 1930s. Wearing beige gabardine slacks and a white polo sweater, she sipped a whiskey and soda as she tried to keep up with their questions. Was she temperamental? Why did she wear pants? Were she and Helpmann romantically involved? Apparently, the Australians hadn't caught up with the fact that she now expected to be treated like an institution. Kate effectively ended the press conference with a rambling nonsense monologue: "Your water here is wonderful. New York City water is fine. Hartford water is good, Middle West water not so good, but Atlanta, Georgia, water is very good. I went there and immediately had a bath and washed my hair because the water was so good."

The Old Vic tour began in Sydney and ran through Brisbane, Adelaide, Perth, and Melbourne. Though reviews were mixed—many critics compared Kate unfavorably to Vivien Leigh, who'd appeared in a similar tour a few years before—business was excellent. Kate liked the enthusiasm of Australian audiences, finding a spirit of "defiance" and "unconventionality" that seemed to match her own.

She also found some new friends. One night, Maie Casey, whose husband, Richard, was a former ambassador to the United States (and later Australia's governor-general), came backstage to invite Kate, Michael, and Bobby to dinner at the Casey estate in Berwick. Kate hit it off immediately with the perky, silver-bobbed, blue-eyed Maie, an old friend of Noël Coward's. As the wife of a diplomat, sixty-four-year-old Maie was required to preside over her share of society teas, but, much to Kate's delighted surprise, she was also a daredevil pilot. Strapping herself into Maie's plane, Kate soared up into the air over vast stretches of the Australian backcountry. It was as if she were back with Leland or Howard. Only now a *woman* was at the controls.

Kate and Maie shared more than sheer joie de vivre. According to her biographer, Maie had cultivated "discreet but intense romantic attachments to other women" for several years, apparently with her husband's unspoken blessing. One of these attachments was with her former assistant, the journalist Pat Jarrett, who also became a friend of Kate's. Sturdy and blond, her hair slicked back in an Eton crop, Pat was a former cricket player now serving as editor of the women's pages at the daily *Sun News-Pictorial*. Living on a portion of the Casey estate, Pat was devoted to Maie, but their relationship seems not to have been exclusive—given what transpired with Kate.

"My sense was there was a short romance with the Australian girl," said one friend of Kate's, a woman who for a time was a part of Hepburn's circle. After several years of suppressing her romantic drive, Kate seems to have let loose a bit in the wilds of Australia. Her affair with Jarrett was not serious, but the affection between them was quite real.

"I hope that you do not have to be told how I feel about you," Kate wrote in a letter of thanks to Pat after receiving a bouquet of roses and lilies of the valley from her. "You are nice on the face of it and even nicer in the heart of it."

Four years younger than Hepburn, smart and vivacious and as boyish as they came, Pat was definitely Kate's type. A few days after the roses, she again proved supportive in some way, for Kate sent her a note to thank her for being "so *there* . . . you are a solid angel."

Pat wasn't the only one to give gifts. Kate presented her with a watercolor she'd done of Port Melbourne Pier. When, on November 8, Pat sent flowers to the Hotel Esplanade in Perth for Kate's birthday, Kate was obliged to write back and admit the date wasn't the correct one: "I just lie because I am secretive," she said.

Yet, in fact, a world away from Hollywood, Kate didn't need to lie. Her various memories of her trip to Australia would be infused with a deep sense of nostalgia, as if what she had found there was never replicated anywhere else. In Australia, Hepburn had the freedom to be herself—a seven-month holiday during which Kath could come out and play. One of her favorite pastimes while in the country was to wander along the paths of a rain forest outside Melbourne. Within the deep, mysterious gloom pierced here and there with shafts of sunlight, she wasn't recognized by a soul, and she loved it. Once, coming upon a group of children, she sat with them to listen peacefully to the kookaburras singing in the trees.

Her trip to Africa would be the one glamorized and immortalized, but that was a trip taken by the public Kate, the mythmaker of *The African Queen*. To Africa she'd traveled with public friends like Bogart, Bacall, and Huston, not with intimates like Michael and Bobby. In Africa she met villagers who spoke no English, but in Australia she met people like Maie and Pat, who touched her soul. In truth, it was this journey down under—usually relegated to just a few paragraphs in previous accounts—that seems far more profound. A consideration of the paintings she did while there seems to bolster this idea. They are lighter, happier, more colorful than many of her others, with lots of sky and green grass. One depicts Bobby Helpmann jauntily sitting on a beach in a bathing suit.

Of course, Kate knew that she had to go back to America eventually. The tour wouldn't last forever. Even if she made the picture with Bob Hope in England, she couldn't remain an expatriate for the rest of her life.

But for the moment, all that was in the future. Wandering through that lush Australian rain forest, she was intent on finding a lyrebird, that strange, elusive creature no bigger than a peahen. It's not surprising that Kate would always express an affinity for the bird. To attract a female, the male lyrebird unfurls its magnificent tail and conducts an elaborate song and dance as if to say, "Look at me!" To Bobby Helpmann, she confided her earnest hope that before the tour was over, she would find a male lyrebird and watch it dance. Now, following its telltale scratchings along a path through the forest, she would remember the excitement building inside her.

Finally, she came upon one of the birds in middance. Strutting back and forth on a mound of dirt like a little stage, showing off its sixteen bright tail feathers, the lyrebird was mimicking the calls of other birds, producing a sound that was both broken and beautiful—not unlike Kate's voice, in fact. Watching the bird, she was enraptured. "A thrilling, rib-tingling experience," she said, "like a sexual, exciting play."

For weeks thereafter she took Bobby Helpmann back to the same place, hoping for a repeat performance, but not until after many disappointments did they have any luck. And what luck that was. They stumbled upon not just one specimen but dozens, all dancing on mounds of earth, each of them displaying its glorious plumage. They were enchanted.

Obsessed with the lyrebird, Kate began to read up on it. She learned that a lyrebird mated for life; but when a mate died, the male bird would go live with other males and the female bird would go live with other females. The elaborate courtship ritual—with all its squawks and thrusts and flashes of feathers—never had to be repeated again. The birds could live out their lives in peaceful contentment with their own kind.

Nine years later, Helpmann would create a ballet inspired by the lyrebird. He would dedicate it to Kate.

QUALITY COMES FIRST

I n the fall of 1961, on the porch of a faded old Victorian, Kate Hepburn was shivering in a white antique-lace gown. A chill wind had picked up off Eastchester Bay, and while the film crew slipped into their parkas, Kate went on pretending it was a cheerful summer morning, as the first scene of Eugene O'Neill's monumental tragedy *Long Day's Journey into Night* called for. It was the first but hardly the last feat of acting she'd push herself to do on the film. Over the course of several weeks that fall, Hepburn's brittle, delusional Mary Tyrone would disintegrate magnificently before the cameras. As Kate writhed on the floor, Mary's madness near complete, one prop man was heard to mutter, "When did this dame get to be so *good*?"

In the late 1950s and early 1960s, Katharine Hepburn became an Actress. After some thirty plays and thirty films in thirty years, she managed to rise up from her provenance of movie stardom to achieve a gravitas few would ever have predicted for her. The girl who made *Spitfire* and *The Lake* was playing Shakespeare and O'Neill.

Ever since her return to full-time life in America, Kate had been on a singular journey toward artistic recognition. With a bag of clothes strung over her shoulder, she'd clomped down the wooden pier of the Housatonic River in Stratford, Connecticut, taking up residence for the summer of 1957 in a fishing shanty owned by Lawrence Langner. There, as local fishermen tied up their boats and dumped their slippery, smelly catch right on the wharf, Kate practiced her scenes for the two plays—*The Merchant of Venice* and *Much Ado About Nothing*—she was doing for the American Shakespeare Festival. Her shanty had once been a bait shop, and at times Portia's pacing back and forth was interrupted by a knock at the door. "Do you have any worms?" a fisherman would call through the screen. "Sorry not today," she'd call back. Kate was fifty years old, and she'd remember it as the happiest summer of her life.

"Our friend Kate has had a very happy time of it at Stratford," Irene Selznick wrote to Binkie Beaumont. "She's worked like a dog, is very skinny but beaming all over as there is not a ticket to be had for the rest of the season."

Finally the critics were starting to come around as well. Reviewing Kate in *Much Ado About Nothing*, Brooks Atkinson found her "beautiful, debonair, piquant," and opined "her Beatrice is one of her best characterizations."

Despite quarrels with her costar, the overbearing Alfred Drake, Kate relished her new reputation as the leading American Shakespearean actress. Constance Collier had done some very fine mentoring. John Houseman, Hepburn's director at Stratford, believed Kate had learned at Collier's knee "that stardom is achieved . . . through the bravura that an audience comes to expect from its favorite performers."

For years, Kate had considered her talent less than Spencer's, but in fact Tracy never pushed himself or his craft the way she did. With her noble, iconic film roles of the 1950s, Hepburn had established herself as an American heroine. Now, she was polishing that image with the veneer of an artist.

Her commitment is even more admirable when one understands just how terrified she remained of the task. Her niece Katharine Houghton, reflecting on her aunt's "greatest weakness," suggested it was her "lack of self-confidence." The world saw a tough, independent woman, but underneath, Houghton said, she was "an absolutely delicate violet." Instead of getting better, opening nights got "steadily worse," Kate said, and the New York critics retained their power to strike terror into her heart. To the world Katharine Hepburn might be a paragon of strength, but walking onstage, she was still that little rejected girl from Hartford trying to prove herself. "Honestly," she said, "I'd like to own a theater in Brooklyn and just never open on Broadway."

Yet despite her fears, two summers later she returned to Stratford to do it all again, this time taking on *Twelfth Night* and *Antony and Cleopatra*. And it was as Cleopatra—Kate's first tragic role—that she finally seemed to convince the critics once and for all that she had what it took. The *New York Times* praised her for hewing close to what the Bard had intended: "Hers is a Queen of the Nile who is one of the great coquettes of history, a woman of passion and temperament . . . This is a many-faceted Cleopatra and a good one."

For a woman in her fifties to play a convincing coquette was quite an achievement. Reviewing her Viola in *Twelfth Night,* Walter Kerr of the *New York Herald Tribune* observed, "Miss Hepburn has always been one of the most fetching creatures to have been bestowed upon our time." No, not always—but a new generation of critics didn't remember the scathing criticism that had dogged her in the past. What they knew from that period came from television, late-night broadcasts of *The Philadelphia Story* and *Woman of the Year*—Kate Hepburn at her most Hollywood beautiful.

Kate was, in fact, aging quite gracefully, all those years of exercise paying off. Her main problem continued to be her skin blisters, which James Prideaux called "pinkish and peeling." From the audience, however, these were undetectable. Hepburn—with her small waist and long legs—did indeed seem quite the fetching creature.

It wasn't just Shakespeare who called during this period. In June 1959, she returned to London to play the monstrous Violet Venable in *Suddenly Last Summer,* Joe Mankiewicz's film adaptation of Tennessee Williams's "dramatic poem" (the playwright's own description). It was another chance to prove her depth as an actress, but in the course of production, Kate's long friendship with Mankiewicz took a fatal hit. In addition to photographing her as harshly as possible—nothing fetching about her here—the director infuriated the star with his very literal adaptation of Williams's metaphorical play. While Kate didn't appreciate the juxtaposition of herself as an old harpy with the springtime beauty of the twenty-six-year-old Elizabeth Taylor, more egregious was appearing in a vehicle that lingered so literally over such gruesome themes as incest and cannibalism. "She told me she didn't like my script," said the film's screenwriter, Gore Vidal. "She said she was too much of a lady to play such a part."

Yet the worst offense of all was the bullying Kate perceived Mankiewicz gave to the tormented, alcoholic Montgomery Clift, still in pain and depressed from a disfiguring car accident. "Kate was wonderfully supportive of Monty during that time," said Clift's longtime friend Jack Larson, who recalled how she tried to boost Monty up with pep talks on the set. During breaks in the filming, Kate took Clift for long walks to get him as far away as possible from Mankiewicz. Nearly every account of *Suddenly Last Summer* ends with her spitting at the director for how he treated Monty. For once, the legend is true, although she spit on the *floor*, not in Mankiewicz's face, as she sometimes told the story.

As much as she disliked the film, what mattered was the growing perception in the public mind that Hepburn was now a serious *actress*. Kate had the validation of Tennessee Williams himself, who called her "a playwright's dream . . . She makes dialogue sound better than it is . . . She invests every scene—each bit—with the intuition of an artist born to her art." Her only equal among actresses, Williams declared, was Laurette Taylor—which must have thrilled Hepburn to no end, since Taylor had long been her idol.

So smitten, in fact, was Williams with Kate that two years later he insisted she was the only one who could play the aristocratic Hannah Jelkes in his *Night of the Iguana*. After initially turning him down, Kate came around after the playwright convinced her that he needed someone who understood "cool, strong ladies of New England." In the spring of 1961, they seemed to have reached a deal, until Kate announced she couldn't possibly commit for longer than six months. The play's producer, Charles Bowden (who'd later admit he'd wanted Margaret Leighton in the role all along), squashed the entire deal, calling Kate's terms unacceptable.

In one of those great might-have-beens, *Night of the Iguana* would have teamed Kate with Bette Davis, cast as the earthy Maxine Faulk. What alchemy might have been brought forth on that stage between high-bred Hepburn and down-to-earth Davis must be left to the imagination. Davis, who had a notoriously bad time with Leighton, would certainly have appreciated Hepburn's professionalism. But the most interesting footnote, told by the play's costume designer Noel Taylor and implied also in Garson Kanin's memoir, is that Kate later insisted Williams had wanted her for *Maxine*, and that he had settled on Bette only after Kate proved unavailable.

Of course, the idea of Kate Hepburn playing Maxine, with her plunging necklines and bawdy sense of humor, is ludicrous. Did Kate really remember things that way? Maybe she thought her reputation as an actress had advanced so far by 1961 that she could indeed play *any* part. Or maybe she just liked thinking that Bette Davis, once seemingly ahead of her at every turn, was now taking her leftovers.

Both Hepburn and Davis would be nominated for Academy Awards in 1962, Kate for *Long Day's Journey into Night* and Bette for *What Ever Happened to Baby Jane?* (Neither won.) Despite how much fun *Jane* is (and how much money it made), in the public's mind it was clear who was in the more prestigious vehicle. The position of the two actresses relative to each other had flip-flopped since 1934. Twenty-eight years earlier, it had been Kate in the lightweight commercial vehicle (*Little Women*) while Bette claimed the acting honors in the succès d'estime of the year, *Of Human Bondage*. Now it was Kate staking a claim for artistry.

Long Day's Journey, which Kate began shooting in the fall of 1961 instead of heading onstage in *Iguana*, would be the crowning achievement of her half-decade pursuit of dramatic challenge. All of the film's actors—besides Kate, they were Ralph Richardson, Jason Robards, and Dean Stockwell—worked for minimum pay, simply because they believed in the project. Only by keeping the budget low would the producer Ely Landau ever get the picture made, since at three hours of unrelenting destruction, O'Neill's autobiographical play was not destined for big box office. The director Sidney Lumet's decision to adhere to the structure of the play (indeed, O'Neill himself fashioned the script) may have been cheered by purists, but it certainly wasn't going to help the film's commercial prospects. Ultimately, none of that mattered. As the horrible, heartbreaking Mary, Kate proved herself an *artist*—and, for the moment, the greatest living American actress.

"From being perhaps America's most beautiful comedienne of the thirties and forties," decreed the influential Pauline Kael, Hepburn was now "our greatest tragedienne."

Critics struggled for words to describe her brilliance in the role. "Marvelous and miraculous," pronounced Philip Scheuer in the *Los Angeles Times*. Arthur Knight in the *Saturday Review* declared, "Her transformations are extraordinary."

Kate, never one for false modesty, tended to agree. Scott Berg said *Long Day's Journey* was one of the few performances he ever heard her brag about.

Certainly, her Mary Tyrone is exceptional. In the course of a single speech, she moves from flashes of convent-girl innocence to morphine-induced manipulation. All the classical technique she'd learned in the last eight years—from Collier, from Benthall, from Houseman—is apparent here. Her mastery of words, timing, and inflection is indisputable. With uncanny precision she navigates the peaks and valleys (mostly valleys) of Mary's disintegrating existence. Yet the question must be asked: how much is technique and how much is feeling?

Hepburn's best roles, her truly great performances—*Little Women, Alice Adams, Bringing Up Baby, The African Queen, Summertime*—were always those that seemed to defy technique, that just put Kate, body and soul, on the screen. Here, for once, she was not playing a variation on herself; Mary Tyrone, with all her self-pity, is about as far away from Katharine Hepburn as possible. That in itself is an achievement. Yet at times that dissonance seeps through her carefully constructed performance. There are times Mary feels artificial, when the actress playing her feels too blueblood, too Protestant, to truly understand the conflicts of this weak convent girl who once dreamed of being a nun.

Yet who can deny the raw emotion that Hepburn brings forth, both in her character and in those watching her performance? Any one of those ravaged close-ups, in which we see all of Mary's pain, degradation, anger, and self-debasement, is sufficient testimony to Kate's new maturity as an actress. In what is arguably the greatest female role in the American theater, no one yet has come close to what Hepburn managed here.

"The thing is," she told an interviewer some years later, "I just don't like to be half-good. It drives me crazy to be mediocre . . . I'm willing to do anything to try to be really good."

In her drive to become an Actress, that meant taking low salaries or accepting second billing to a woman (Elizabeth Taylor in *Suddenly Last Summer*) for the first time in her career. It also meant, as she quipped to one reporter, playing "strange aberrations of nature" like Mary Tyrone and Violet Venable—though Kate could certainly content herself that neither was as strange or as aberrant as the grotesqueries then being played by Davis, Crawford, Stanwyck, Joan Bennett, Tallulah Bankhead, or Olivia de Havilland, all of whom were reviving their careers in the gothic horror genre.

"Quality in material comes first," Kate told Hedda Hopper. Such an attitude established herself one notch above her contemporaries. For all the acting accolades and artistic maturity, Hepburn's new position also gave her something else. It placed her above reproach in many ways. She was an actress of repute; the others were just old movie stars trying to hang on. And so, one more step toward apotheosis.

A panoramic shot across Hollywood. The backlot at MGM is mostly empty. A portion of the roof of the Andy Hardy house has caved in. The soundstage where *Woman of the Year* was shot has been torn down. A few old lots that had been gathering cobwebs have been refitted with television lights. At Musso and Frank's on Hollywood Boulevard, the booths are filled with fast-talking TV producers and writers, lately transplanted from New York. Men like Ely Landau and Sidney Lumet, in fact—men who picked up the reins of filmmaking from the old guard in this new, independent, post-studio Hollywood.

But these men were a fundamentally different breed. "Where the old time film director sported puttees and riding crops," observed *Time*, "the TV director wears blue jeans and sneakers—and gets impressive results under tight schedules and pressures that [would] frighten veteran moviemakers."

The Hollywood Kate returned to after her long absence was barely recognizable. At last, the climate of persecution was over, even if the careers of many people were in ruins. Katharine Hepburn, for all the vitriol tossed at her a decade earlier, would not be one of them. In many ways, *The Iron Petticoat*, the film she made in England with Bob Hope, had been an olive branch to her native country. Playing a Russian Communist who wants to defect to the United States, Kate delivered a clear message: she wanted to come home. "Deep down she's sore as a boiled owl at the Commies," a colonel says about Kate's character—and once again, audiences no doubt conflated the on- and offscreen Hepburn in his words. In the role of a comic Russian (with perhaps the worst accent of her career, which is saying a lot), Kate successfully lampooned any image that she might be a scary Communist. Released in early 1957, the film quickly flopped, but the word to the press was "Katie is back."

Yet few were left to greet her. Looking around at the empty lots and the unfamiliar faces, some of the veterans of the old studio system seemed distinctly nostalgic and ready to make peace. "I don't know why we can't be friends," Hedda Hopper wrote to Kate, soon after Hepburn's triumph in *Long Day's Journey*. "Perhaps you do. But I'd like to be able to call you up once in a while and say hello and perhaps reminisce a bit and promise not to put a word of it in the column." Hopper told Hepburn that she'd always admired her, that she had "a gaiety, a gallantry, a gentlemanly way of expressing" herself that no one else ever had—not even Garbo. As she grew older, Hopper wrote, she found herself mellowing, thinking about days gone by. "You were a big part of that era," she wrote, "and I miss you."

Had Kate not made a comeback, of course, that letter would never have been written. Hopper's outreach, as she neared the end of her influence, seems sad, even a little pathetic. But Kate was generous. "You and I are friends, Hedda," she said. "Time has seen to that." They were both survivors, Kate told the columnist, so there was a kind of "natural admiration" between them. Not for Hopper's politics, Kate insisted, nor for her profession, but rather for her personally—"your stride and your looks and capacity to get on with it—your character on your terms—and that is, I think, what you admire about me."

Of course, despite Hopper's promise not to print what Kate told her, she was surely digging for a scoop, for by the time she wrote that letter, all of Hollywood—what was left of it—knew that Kate was back to taking care of a rapidly failing Spencer Tracy.

While Kate had been traveling the world, rediscovering her sense of personal freedom and artistic challenge, Tracy had been on a downward spiral. For a while, Kate had managed to keep her distance from him and his troubles; but by the time she set off for Australia, she seems to have known it would only be a matter of time before she'd have to step in again and save him from himself. Spencer had come to England to watch her rehearse for the Old Vic tour with Benthall and Helpmann (Hedda Hopper actually reported it in her column), and Kate would have seen he was struggling again with drink and illness. Indeed, while Kate was staying at the Bellevue Hotel in Brisbane, the proprietor, George Adman, remembered "a mass of phone calls" from Tracy to Hepburn. Spence was having a particularly difficult time on the set of his film *Tribute to a Bad Man*, and was turning to Kate for support just like old times. Sending her a photo of himself sitting on a cliff calling into a canyon, he wrote on the back: "Calling Old Kath!" Halfway around the globe in Australia, Hepburn heard Tracy's desperate calls for her to come back.

Perhaps all this explains the wistfulness Kate felt in Australia, the particular joy she attached to her carefree romps with Pat Jarrett and Maie Casey. She was enjoying the freedom while she could. She knew she was returning to the States to resume a life she thought she had left behind.

That's not to say she returned to Spence unwillingly. As ever, the caretaker side of Hepburn could not resist the call of a wounded man in need. It was not so different from her impulse with Monty Clift. Kate believed she could have saved Clift from his downward spiral if only he had listened to her and bucked up. But Clift was "weak," Kate said. "Simpatico but weak."

Not so Spencer Tracy. She'd never think Spencer was weak, no matter how much he drank. What convinced her of this fact was that, unlike Clift, Spencer was willing to *listen* to her. Of course, her advice was never to seek help or to confront his essential conflicts. To Kate, the answer was always to take a hike or a bath, or spend a few days in the country. And Spence was only too happy to keep avoiding his problems in this way. He was grateful to have Kate, this strong maternal and endlessly reassuring figure, back in his life.

With the disastrous shoot of *Tribute to a Bad Man*, directed by Robert Wise, the husband of Kate's old friend Patsy Doyle, Tracy's life had changed forever. In the summer of 1955, on location in the mountains of Colorado, Spence was reclusive and moody. Some thought he should have been, instead, in the best of spirits: John Tracy and his wife, Nadine, had just had a baby boy, named Joseph Spencer Tracy. Yet instead of celebrating being a grandfather, Spence was drinking heavily. "To this day," Robert Wise told the reporter Bill Davidson in the 1980s, "I don't know what was inside the man to make him so nervous and upset."

Eventually, Wise requested that Tracy be fired. The new MGM studio chief, Dore Schary, agreed, terminating the studio's twenty-year relationship with one of its biggest stars. When Spence got the news at his hotel, he wept.

As word spread through Hollywood about his firing from MGM, Tracy sought to escape the pity by packaging his first film as a freelancer. For some time now—at least since scoping out locations in the Alps on his way back from Rome—Spence had had his eye on filming Henri Troyat's novel *The Mountain*. As costar, he insisted on the twenty-four-year-old Robert Wagner, whom he'd met at a Golden Globes ceremony a couple of years before. Approaching Wagner, Spence had told him he liked his work. "Kid, I want you to play my son," Tracy announced, and just like that the starstruck Wagner found himself with a role in Spencer's film *Broken Lance*. "[Spencer] couldn't have been more kind to me," Wagner said, "teaching me a lot about acting that has stood me in good stead to this day."

With *The Mountain*, Spence was looking forward to a reunion with Wagner. But he was unprepared for his reaction to the high altitudes, and once again, partly to offset the discomfort he felt, he began drinking heavily. After a harrowing experience being trapped for two hours in a funicular cable car high over the French village of Chamonix, Spence let loose. According to the film's makeup man, Frank Westmore, the star turned surly at the hotel bar that night, tossing a brandy snifter into the face of a waiter. Just what provoked him was unclear, but Wagner tried to intercept the snifter, breaking it and cutting his hand in the process. Blood was everywhere, Westmore recalled, but Tracy seemed oblivious. The next day, he remembered nothing.

Over the years, Wagner has repeatedly refused to comment on the incident, except to say he never blamed Spence. In interviews, Wagner expressed only the greatest admiration for Tracy. Like Clifton Webb, another of Wagner's mentors, Spence took a real interest in the young actor's career; like Webb, some believed, he may also have had a bit of an infatuation. "Bob Wagner was the best-looking actor in Hollywood in those days," said Elliott Morgan, George Cukor's friend and the head of research at MGM. "He had Webb and Tracy and God knows who else in love with him."

Gavin Lambert, a good friend of Wagner's, agreed Tracy may have been infatuated with his younger costar, but said he did not know how Wagner would have felt about it. Wagner himself declined to answer when asked directly whether he thought it possible Spencer had romantic feelings for him.

Whatever turmoil Spencer was struggling with on *The Mountain*, Kate was kept apprised of it in Australia. Frank Westmore reported that their script girl, Maggie Shipway, Kate's friend from the *Summertime* shoot, routinely informed Kate on Tracy's welfare. The phone calls Kate took at the Bellevue Hotel may have been from Maggie as often as from Spence.

When Kate finally returned to the States, one of her first activities was to turn around and leave again—accompanying Spencer to Cuba in the spring of 1956. He was filming Hemingway's *The Old Man and the Sea*, which was being produced by Leland Hayward. No doubt Kate was hoping her long friendship with Leland might make this a smoother production for Spencer, and of course she also knew Hemingway ever since their shipboard encounter in 1934. But even with her moderating influence, the shoot was a nightmare. Hemingway took an unexplained, instant dislike to Tracy, calling him a "rich, fat actor." Poor Spence, struggling to show the world he could be a star outside the gates of MGM, was once again miserable.

Hemingway was right on one count: Spencer *was* fat—and now he was also very old, far older than his fifty-six years. His hair was pure white, his face the texture of weathered tree bark. Propping pillows behind his back, rubbing his feet, Kate found herself caring for him the way she once did. It was as if no time had passed at all.

Yet their relationship was not, in fact, what it once had been. In books, years can fly by without the reader ever really feeling time passing. But not since 1949 had Kate and Spence spent more than a few months at a time together. In life, such long separations fundamentally change personal relationships. In 1956, Kate was not the same person she had been seven years before. Within a community of women, she had found the kind of emotional nurturance that Spence had never been able to provide. While he was spiraling downward, she was in ascent—pushing herself ever higher in her pursuit of her art. The Hepburn who returned to Tracy's side was stronger and more grounded.

Consider the images we have of her from these years. Kate might be spotted knitting on the set of Spencer's film *Inherit the Wind*, but soon she was jetting off back to England with Phyllis Wilbourn to make *Suddenly Last Summer*. Just because she'd made room in her life for Tracy again doesn't mean she gave up her independence or artistic ambitions.

The nuanced truths of her life were recognized by those closest to her. On a September night in 1957, Kate and Spence sat with Maie and Richard Casey in Kate's New York town house, sharing cocktails and hearty conversation. As Australian foreign minister, Richard was to deliver a speech the next

day to the United Nations. "Spence and Dick at their best," Kate would remember in a letter to Maie. "What charm." But part of the bond between the
two couples was the familiarity they shared, the untraditional relationships
both enjoyed.

In previous accounts, this is where the legend of Tracy and Hepburn
picks up again in earnest, continuing on as if no break had ever occurred. In
late 1960, both Kate and Spence traveled to Hawaii. Tracy was filming *The
Devil at 4 O'Clock* on location there. The trip would be romanticized as a secret retreat for Kate and Spence away from the eyes of prying reporters. In
fact, though Kate met up with Tracy and enjoyed spending time with him,
she was traveling with Fran Rich, as postcards she sent to John Ford prove.

"Kate never traveled with Tracy alone," said one of her friends. "There
was always Fran Rich, or Phyllis, or someone. And it wasn't about secrecy or
propriety the way it's been assumed. It was just how they lived. They'd all
have dinner together, then Kate would go off with Fran on a boat. Kate might
go with Spencer to some shindig with the film crew but then she'd go back to
Fran or Phyllis or whichever one of her girls she'd brought along."

But she also made sure she was there when Spencer needed her. When
Kate reentered his life, Spence was close to hitting rock bottom once again.
She had no choice but to save him one more time. "When people's paths
cross and life sort of throws you together," she believed, "you have an obligation to those people."

In August 1957, John Tracy and his wife divorced. The press feasted on
the case, with headlines blaring SPENCER TRACY'S DEAF SON DIVORCED BY
WIFE. Nadine Tracy testified that John had refused to be intimate with her
after their son was born. Struggling to understand the judge's questions,
John explained his only income was one hundred dollars a month from his
father. Living back home with Louise, he'd "never maintained employment,"
he told the court, but he hoped someday to make a living as an artist. Photos
of the thirty-three-year-old John in his thick glasses accompanied by his
mother were run in all of the papers, which also made much of the young
man's limp, the result of a childhood bout with polio.

Soon after John's divorce, Spencer went on a long drinking binge. Kate
was at Stratford performing in *Much Ado About Nothing*, awaiting a visit
from him. According to John Houseman, Spence somehow got lost driving
to the Burbank airport and missed his plane. Whether it was because he was
drinking or not, Tracy never saw Kate perform at Stratford.

He did come East soon afterward, however. Clearly concerned, Kate insisted that Spencer spend time with her in New York. This was the period in

which they hosted Maie and Richard Casey. Here we are afforded a glimpse of a telling contrast in Spencer's life. On the same night that he and Kate and the Caseys were lifting their cocktails in front of the fire on Forty-ninth Street, Louise Tracy was alone in Sacramento, accepting the Citizen of the Year award from the Military Order of the Purple Heart. Certainly, Louise had long gotten used to accepting awards without Spencer present, but this time, so soon after their son's latest heartbreak, the contrasting images make her husband seem very selfish indeed.

Yet if he was selfish, it was the selfishness of a child, who found it difficult to put anyone else's needs ahead of his own. Taking refuge at Kate's, playing his tough old curmudgeon role in front of the Caseys, Spence could wrap himself in a comforting fiction of normalcy. Only this time, Kate seems to have avoided the trap of sharing his delusion. True, when he got drunk and barricaded himself in a motel room, she sat outside in the car for hours waiting for him to emerge. She had done similar things in the 1940s. But the difference now was that she had Phyllis Wilbourn with her, bringing her lunch, and then dinner, the two of them together waiting out the stubborn child behind the locked door. Sitting there eating her chicken-salad sandwich with Phyllis, Kate may have recalled these words of Constance Collier's: the "best you can expect from any man" is to have him run after you "like a little boy."

When Hollywood seemed ready to give up on him, Kate kept Spencer working. For years she was convinced she was responsible for getting him a role in John Ford's *The Last Hurrah*, until Ford himself told her directly that she'd had nothing to do with his decision. Still, there's no question that Kate's agreement in early 1957 to make *Desk Set*, a tepid return to the typical Tracy-Hepburn formula, was her way of keeping Spencer on the screen. The lightweight project, directed by Walter Lang, was completely incongruous to the acting challenges she'd been taking elsewhere.

But *Desk Set* did send a message to the public (and to the industry) that "Kate and Spence" were back. When Kate, as yet another spinster, tells Joan Blondell they should move in together and raise cats, Blondell snaps, "I don't like cats. I like men, and so do you"—just in case anyone was still wondering. Once again, the film fades out without any clinch between Tracy and Hepburn. He just puts his arm around her, as if they were buddies. It wasn't so different from the companionate relationship the fifty-year-old Kate and fifty-seven-year-old Spence now enjoyed together in real life.

In this light, consider her response a few years earlier after seeing Peggy Ashcroft in Terence Rattigan's *The Deep Blue Sea* in London. The play tells the story of a woman's obsession with an idealized love for a man. Kate considered adapting the play for a film, with herself in Ashcroft's part and John Huston as director. To her way of seeing things, the woman in the play simply longed for a true, pure love—while the more carnal Bobby Helpmann, sitting beside Kate in the theater, insisted cynically it was *lust* that drove the character. "But, gosh," Hepburn wrote to Huston, "lust gets scarce as the years come on and it's no use sitting around moaning if you don't get it."

While "lust" might not have been exactly scarce for her, it seems to have been confined to the occasional visit with Scotty's friend or to a brief intimacy with Pat Jarrett. Certainly, it was not what drove the most significant relationships of the second half of Kate's life, with people like Irene Selznick and Phyllis Wilbourn—and indeed, with Spencer himself. Kate's insistence on seeing Rattigan's heroine as seeking love and companionship, rather than sex and conventional romance, is actually key to understanding Hepburn herself.

Wooden beams were being pulled apart, nails clattering like rain onto the floor. As stagehands broke down the set of *Much Ado About Nothing* in early 1958, Kate Hepburn came trudging through the sawdust, taking one last look around the theater.

She was always wistful when a show ended. Years later, she'd dramatize a moment like this in the autobiographical screenplay she wrote, "Me and Phyllis." Placing herself on the empty stage as the set was being pulled down around her, she indulged in a rare moment of reflection: How fleeting the theater was, how ephemeral. The cast and crew, so close, were now going their separate ways. Had it all really happened, this magic they made on the stage?

At that moment, in the screenplay, Hepburn wrote a bit part for a stagehand, who comically interrupts her reveries. But she also wrote a line for Phyllis Wilbourn, standing raptly off to the side, who tells her she could listen to her forever.

Phyllis had plenty of opportunities to do just that. Secretary, assistant, companion—Phyllis was called many things. But the bottom line was simple. For forty years, as Garson Kanin said, Phyllis was "inextricably woven into the fabric of Kate's life."

On a road trip, Kate was at the wheel of the car, squinting her eyes to read a sign ahead of her. Phyllis was in the passenger's seat, looking at a map. When Kate misread the name on the sign, Phyllis gently corrected her, taking no offense when Kate refused to agree. The prim Miss Wilbourn just waited until they were at the exit and the sign was clear enough to read before pointing out that she had been right. "But that's what I was saying all *along*, Phyllis," Kate snapped, unwilling to admit her error. Phyllis was smart enough to let her win.

That was the secret to their success. Phyllis let Kate be Kate. "Yesterday Miss Hepburn drove 585 miles from Detroit to St. Louis in eleven hours," Phyllis wrote to George Cukor's secretary during the Shakespeare Festival tour. "It is all so organized, that when we stop to gas up, I literally run in and order coffee and milk, then we dash for the ladies' room, I pick up the drinks, and off we go with a four-minute stop, eating our box lunch on the way."

Little Phyllis—she was very slight, standing no more than five-five, less as she got older—was either very bright or very dull. Once, at dinner with Kate and Phyllis, Scott Berg struggled, as many did, to keep up with Hepburn's fast pace of eating. He'd barely finished his soup, and Kate was calling for dessert. Leaning over to Phyllis, Berg commented that the guests of emperor Franz Josef used to grumble because their half-eaten portions were removed as soon as the fast-chomping emperor was done. "What are you two muttering about over there?" Kate demanded. Phyllis looked up and replied, "Oh, Mr. Berg was just saying that he thinks of us as royalty."

With her short brown hair, heavy eyebrows, and precise manner of speech, Phyllis fit the image of the classic spinster. Four years older than Kate, she was born in Rochford, Prittlewell, Essex, in May 1903, the middle of three daughters of Horace and Florence Wilbourn. "Faded gentility," the family was called by Janet Jordon, whose nanny was Phyllis's sister Jeannie. Horace Wilbourn may have rolled his sleeves up as a trader on the Baltic Exchange, but his wife's family had a distinguished pedigree of service to the Crown: Sir George Pocock, an admiral in the Royal Navy, was interred in Westminster Abbey.

By Phyllis's generation, however, the family had been reduced to moving from town to town—from Westcliff to Teddington to Malden—as Horace struggled to find work. Yet even as they bowed to the reality that their three daughters would need to find jobs, so conscious of their heritage did the family remain that the girls were not allowed, according to Janet Jordon, "to enter a profession which would have required the wearing of a uniform." While it's been written that Phyllis received nursing training in England, Jordon said that was not true; a nurse's uniform was forbidden. Rather, Phyllis was sent to secretarial school.

This sense of pride and place in society recommended Phyllis to Hepburn. So did her ambition. Of the three daughters of Horace and Florence Wilbourn, "the only one who showed any 'go' was Phyllis," according to her cousin George Andrew Pocock. Her sisters, who also never married, became nannies. Phyllis had other ideas. In 1925, the ambitious twenty-two-year-old somehow came to the attention of Constance Collier, then one of the most popular actresses on the London stage. Soon Phyllis was part of a dazzling, cosmopolitan world. Her cousin George remembered being taken backstage to meet Collier and Ivor Novello. In 1931, Phyllis even played a small part in *Peter Ibbetson,* which Collier directed on Broadway.

When Constance died, Phyllis's world had come to a crushing standstill. Her grief was overwhelming. "I have never had any contact with death before," she wrote to George Cukor, "but now I find myself remembering the oddest little things and the wonderful wisdom and humor." What brought Phyllis out of her depression was "a wonderful talk" with Miss Hepburn. "Miss Garbo wanted me to look after her," Phyllis later told Scott Berg, "but then Miss Hepburn stepped in and swept me away, thank goodness."

Exactly when Phyllis became Kate's steady companion is unclear. She may have joined her for the last part of the Australian tour. By February 1957, during the filming of *Desk Set,* Louella Parsons reported that Phyllis was "now with Katie." Hepburn said, "Isn't it from the sublime to the ridiculous? Constance was so social-minded and loved people and had so many visitors, and I live so quietly and see almost no one."

Becoming a U.S. citizen in 1957, Phyllis understood her life was now inextricably bound with Kate's. She cooked, cleaned, and typed letters, and for miles and miles of highway she sat beside Kate and endured her moods. She was simply *there* for a woman who could not, ever, abide being alone. "She is a totally selfless person," Kate said in her memoir, "working for a totally selfish person." Kate wasn't totally selfish—her ministrations to Spencer prove that—but once she'd made him his dinner and seen him safely tucked into bed, she'd come back home to Phyllis and expect her own dinner to be waiting for her. And it always was.

Spencer's sharpness toward Kate was, in fact, mirrored in Kate's treatment of Phyllis. Lamenting how "imperious" her old friend had become in her later years, Palache thought Kate treated Phyllis "like a dog." She actually found it "embarrassing" to watch the way Kate spoke to her devoted companion.

There was an echo not only of Spencer but of Dr. Hepburn in Kate's treatment of Phyllis. As submissive as she might be to Spence, on her own, in her own house, Kate was the master. When guests were present, Phyllis always referred to her as "Miss Hepburn," even if letters reveal that in private she called her "Kate." Yet Phyllis was never a mere lapdog. She could handle any situation that arose, whether it meant standing up to an ornery repairman or making small talk with a pompous politician. Not once did she ever ask for a vacation from her duties. "Phyllis was renowned for her ability to keep her counsel and other people's secrets," said Janet Jordon. "She never betrayed a confidence."

Kate and Phyllis were not, as some have presumed, lovers. Though Phyllis was with Kate from sunrise until late at night, she maintained her own apartment on East Seventy-second Street, which, at least for a time, she shared with another woman. When it came to the word *lesbian,* Phyllis could be as touchy as Laura Harding. Introducing Phyllis to Scott Berg, Kate called her "my Alice B. Toklas," prompting great umbrage from Phyllis, who complained the description made her sound like "an old lesbian." Kate was amused. "You're not what, dearie, old or a lesbian?"

"Neither," Phyllis insisted. Those who remembered her relationship with Collier, however, thought she may have been protesting too much.

With Tracy, there seems to have been a bit of rivalry. Although Kanin would insist Tracy was fond of Phyllis, he also described how cruelly Spence could mock her, imitating her accent and mannerisms, sometimes to the point of Phyllis retreating from the room blushing a deep shade of red. One story is telling. In the spring of 1961 (after a tour of the Middle East in which they'd visited Iraq, Egypt, and Jerusalem), Phyllis was with Kate in Paris when they met up with Spencer, who'd just finished making *Judgment at Nuremberg.* Fran Rich was also with them, working on another sculpture of Kate. At one point, Tracy and Hepburn went off together with the Kanins to a fancy Parisian pastry shop. Spotting a tray of napoleons, Phyllis's favorite dessert, Kate insisted on bringing one back to her friend. Spencer, however, grew increasingly displeased with all the fuss she went through to get it. In Kanin's recollections, though they're meant to be humorous, Spencer comes across as resentful—possibly even jealous—that Kate was thinking of someone else other than him.

"You see," said Robert Shaw, "Spencer was used to Kate waiting on him, and he just couldn't get why Phyllis waited on Kate. It sort of made him think of Kate differently, as somebody worth waiting on in her own right. And I don't think he liked that very much."

Three days before Christmas, 1961, Kate, Phyllis, and Spencer disembarked from the liner *United States,* arriving home after the gala Berlin premiere of *Judgment at Nuremberg.* In Germany, Spence had been reported to be suffering from a kidney ailment. Struggling down the gangplank at the West Forty-sixth Street pier, he looked pale and weak. Hedda Hopper reported he'd been on the ship with Kate, along with Noël Coward.

As frail as Spence had suddenly become, Kate was forced to leave his side when word came that her father was fading. Over the next several months, she'd spend considerable time at her father's house, in the room always considered "hers." Hep, now eighty-one, was still as stubborn as ever, even if he had shriveled in stature. Not long before, he'd ruptured his gallbladder, though no one had known of it for weeks, so determinedly had Hep borne the pain. When Bob Hepburn found his father one day on the couch, his face gray, his stomach distended, he knew Hep was near death. It was only Bob's quick action that saved him. The fabled Hepburn forbearance had become downright foolhardy.

Meanwhile, there was Dick, still struggling to make a name for himself. Kate had been present for the New York opening of his play *The Sudden End of Anne Cinquefoil* in January 1961. Dick had toiled on the work for years; he considered the tale of a female revolutionary in eighteenth-century South Carolina his masterpiece. Indeed, the Theatre Guild had considered staging it at one point in 1954, but the project fell through. Richard Barr had finally taken a chance on the play, opening it at the East End Theatre. Cameras flashing, Kate smiled uncomfortably as she stood next to Dick after the show, even as reviewers were rushing back to their typewriters to savage the production. *Anne Cinquefoil* closed after its second performance. It was Dick Hepburn's last try for glory.

Over the next two years, Kate would spend much of her time in West Hartford with her family. Though her father continued to decline, she did find time to travel with Fran Rich, who offered refuge from her family pressures. "Seen a lot of Kate at Hartford," Fran wrote to John Ford. "[O]ld boy is failing rapidly . . . Mind you, he doesn't miss much. . . . [He's] as sharp as a tack when he makes the effort. But this will permit the body to keep on and on. Very tough on all concerned."

It was a long, painful end for Dr. Thomas Hepburn. After months of struggle, he finally died on November 20, 1962, with his children and second wife gathered around him. Unlike the decorous Kit, Hep went out as he'd lived, with an audience. "Dad had a stink of a time for nine months," Kate wrote to Leland Hayward. "He said, 'Thank God it was me and not your mother.' He heaved a sigh and was gone."

Once, he'd slapped his daughter's face for being a show-off, for defying his will. Yet for all of his curses, for all of his withholding of praise, Kate knew she had made her father proud. When John Huston's father died, Kate had written, "I hope you know how rare it is for a son to make his father happy—this is usually left to daughters." Daughters like herself. She'd risen above the lightweight film fare her parents had always dismissed and proven herself with Shaw and Shakespeare. Just a month before he died, Hep had read the glowing reviews of Kate's interpretation of O'Neill. If part of her life's motivation had been to fulfill the dreams her father thought he had lost when Tommy died, Kate had succeeded, magnificently.

All of his children respected Thomas Hepburn. All were grateful for his gifts. But some would have a difficult time forgetting the side of him that had sometimes terrorized and bullied them. Dick said he shed not one tear at his father's death. In her family history, Marion would be quite sharp in her criticism of the Hepburn patriarch. Bob, the one to follow in Hep's footsteps as a doctor, admitted his father was "not an easy one to have."

But their sister Katharine was different. This man had defined her sense of self, taught her how to see the world. His form of love—sharp, smashing down, imperious—was what she came to expect from men and, indeed, was how she herself often showed affection to those closest to her. Her barking of orders at Phyllis was simply an echo of the way her father had spoken to his family. It had meant he *loved* them. Kate could see that, even if her siblings couldn't. Kate would spend the rest of her years telling the world that Dr. Thomas Hepburn was the wisest, most sagacious man who ever lived.

Now it was time to head back West, where another man seemed to be drawing ever closer to his final days. It had taken six months for Hep to let go. This time, Kate's life would be on hold considerably longer.

DEAR, DEAR FRIEND

Up on the screen—bigger and wider in 1967 than in the old days, and saturated with a deep, rich Technicolor—there's Spencer Tracy, looking like an old albino lion in heavy black eyeglasses. His face fills the wide screen. He's telling Katharine Hepburn how much he loves her. No matter that the film, *Guess Who's Coming to Dinner*, is ostensibly about interracial marriage. The public knew this final speech was really about Tracy and Hepburn.

"There is nothing," he tells the father of the man who wants to marry his daughter, "absolutely *nothing* that your son feels for my daughter that I didn't feel for Christina . . . The memories are still there—clear, intact, indestructible, and they'll be there if I live to be a hundred and ten."

The memories were still there for the public as well. Matt and Christina Drayton could be Adam and Amanda Bonner of *Adam's Rib* eighteen years later. The camera turns to Kate, her eyes famously brimming with tears.

"In the final analysis," Tracy says, in the moral, absolute, commonsensical way only Spencer Tracy could say it, "it doesn't matter a damn what we think. The only thing that matters is what they feel, and how *much* they feel, for each other." Again a shot of Hepburn, now with a spotlight to make her glow. "And if it's half of what we felt—that's everything."

A legend was materializing right in front of our eyes, and the process left even critics awestruck. Richard Schickel declared that the performances of Tracy and Hepburn in this film were "beyond the bounds of criticism"—an exalted, untouchable place Kate had been striving to attain all her career, maybe even all her life. The venom of critics was now a thing of the past. Here, at the apogee of her partnership with Spence, Katharine Hepburn had transcended criticism.

Everyone involved knew *Guess Who's Coming to Dinner* would be Spencer's last film. That he made it through the shoot surprised many observers. For the past five years he'd seemed to be hanging on by a thread. But Kate was with him that whole time, her career on hold, her sole concentration his well-being. The story of the five years previous to *Guess Who's Coming to Dinner* is a moving testament to her commitment to Tracy.

Since 1962, Spencer's health had been declining rapidly. Everything seemed to be shutting down on him: his heart, his lungs, his joints. Once again putting aside "me, me, me," Kate withdrew from professional activity to take care of her "dear, dear friend." In 1964, John Ford attempted to lure her away for *Seven Women*, but Kate turned him down. For John Huston, she'd tried to find a way to do *The Lonely Passion of Judith Hearne*, considering how she might bring Spencer with her to London while they made the film. But then Seven Arts, the film's backer, nixed Kate in the part, insisting she was too old.

Indeed, at fifty-six, Kate was becoming increasingly sensitive about her appearance. The skin of her neck had become loose and wobbly ("my turkey gullet," she called it), and she refused to be photographed without high collars or turtlenecks. Costume designers knew Hepburn's neck had to be covered at all times. Then there was the ever-present problem of her skin. Since 1953, when she'd had several small melanomas burned off her face, Kate was constantly worried about skin cancer. Her blotches, which continued to plague her, now came under increasing scrutiny. She was notorious for examining marks on the skin of her friends, insisting they be looked at by doctors. For the next thirty years of her life, Kate would be in and out of clinics having moles and dark spots removed from her face.

For a woman used to feeling eternally youthful, it was a difficult transition to old age. There were some things she never could get used to. "I always thought it odd that for a woman of her years, she still had our father handle all her finances," said her sister Peg Perry. Indeed, until a year before his death, Hep had continued to pay all of Kate's bills, make her investments, and figure her taxes. After he died, Kate felt it was too late to learn how to balance a checkbook, so she turned all that business over to Palache. "Part of her just didn't want to grow up," said her sister, "or maybe it was just that she didn't want to grow old."

It was also that she simply couldn't be bothered with money; like the queen of England, Kate never carried cash in her handbags. That was left to Phyllis. "Kate never cared about money matters," said Noel Taylor. "Money had no interest for her, provided it was there when she needed it."

It was Palache who arranged the rental of Kate's latest house in Los Angeles. With Spencer needing more constant care, Kate understood she would once again need a regular base on the West Coast; and if she was forced to spend time in L.A. during the summer, she wanted to be on the beach. Palache settled on the publicist Frank McFadden's house on Broad Beach Road at Trancas Beach, not far from where Kate had shot *Sylvia Scarlett*.

It might not be Fenwick, but McFadden's beachfront house was perhaps the coziest of all of Kate's West Coast addresses. A paneled living room was arranged around a large fireplace, the kitchen finished in knotty pine. Glass doors opened onto an enormous deck overlooking the dunes and the Malibu coastline. From their perch up in the Hollywood hills, Spencer and George Cukor frequently made the trip down to join them.

Later this house would be described as a "hideaway" for Kate and Spence. The Associated Press journalist James Bacon called it the "house [Tracy] shared with Hepburn," where they "carried on one of Hollywood's great illicit romances." But Fran Rich said it was she, not Spencer, who was there for much of the spring and summer of 1963. Still, any visit from Spencer was enough to set tongues wagging, including that of the house's owner, Frank McFadden, who apparently gave Bacon the impression of a Tracy-Hepburn secret love nest. Of course, if Kate and Spencer had really wanted to be secret, they'd have simply stayed put at the bungalow on Cukor's estate, where complete privacy was assured. The fact was that the house at Trancas Beach simply reflected Kate's desire to be on the water.

The renewed gossip about Tracy and Hepburn was not surprising, given a very strange article that had appeared about a year before in *Look* magazine. In late 1961, the reporter Bill Davidson had met Tracy at Chasen's restaurant for an interview. To Davidson's surprise, Tracy was accompanied by the press agent Pat Newcomb, who was best known for representing Marilyn Monroe. Davidson suspected Newcomb was there "at the behest of Kate Hepburn, as Tracy did not have a paid publicist of his own." In the course of the interview, Spencer stunned Davidson by speaking freely about Hepburn, calling her "my Kate" and revealing how often they traveled together. Neither he nor Newcomb, Davidson insisted, asked that any part of their conversation be kept off the record. So, in the January 1962 issue of *Look*, Davidson delineated Spencer's world for the public, carefully balanced between Hepburn on the one side and Louise on the other. It was the first time a mainstream publication had so explicitly described the situation.

Although it would later be said that Kate and Spence were outraged about the article, it's difficult to believe they could have been surprised by it. Tracy, usually tight-lipped, had talked a blue streak, with Pat Newcomb—one of the canniest publicists who ever worked in Hollywood—at his side. Yet why would Spence (with Kate's apparent knowledge) stoke the rumor mill in this way? Perhaps it was a variation of the old trick Kate had played with Leland Hayward to keep interest alive in between pictures. Perhaps it was to convince the industry that Spencer was truly off the sauce, and that *Judgment at Nuremberg* was just the beginning of a second career. But they had to have known it would hurt Louise. In any event, the article in *Look* was the earliest example of Kate giving the public what it seemed to want in terms of her and Tracy: an offscreen romance as heartfelt as the one in the movies.

If there was a larger game plan at work, it hit a speed bump in the summer of 1963. Stories of Spencer calling his costar "my Kate" were one thing; it was quite another to give the impression they were cohabitating at the Trancas Beach house. On July 21, a lazy Sunday morning, Spencer was reading the newspaper during one of his visits when he suddenly complained of chest pains. Planning to take him to the hospital, Kate got him out to Fran Rich's car, but then Spence slumped over, unable to breathe. Assuming it was a heart attack, Kate called the fire department. Paramedics arrived to give Spence oxygen, then rushed him to St. Vincent's Hospital. At that point, Spencer's brother Carroll took over, and Kate faded into the background. That night, it was Louise who told the press that Spencer was resting comfortably after a pulmonary edema.

Yet Davidson's article had brought the reality of Spencer's marriage to light. Louise was now referred to by the press as his "long estranged wife." Several articles about Tracy's hospitalization pointed out the fact that he'd been "close to" Hepburn (called "a divorcee") since 1941. Even the story Kate gave to explain his presence at the house—that they were getting ready to go on a picnic—had a certain romantic ring to it. And so the myths of the great Tracy-Hepburn love affair began to take shape in the public mind.

Spencer was released from the hospital on August 3. Outside his bedroom at the bungalow on Cukor's estate, an oxygen machine was set up, its constant wheezing the first sound people heard when they entered the place. Kate was in and out, barking orders at the private nurses they'd hired. In September, complications sent Tracy back to St. Vincent's, forcing him to drop out of John Ford's upcoming film *Cheyenne Autumn*. Friends believed the end was near.

Kate, characteristically, wouldn't hear any of it. Rolling up her sleeves, she insisted Spence would get better. He may have been frail, but he was only sixty-three—her father had lived nearly twenty years longer. "Just give me a chance," Kate told one friend, "and I can get him back into shape." She'd done it before—and after all, Spence hadn't had a drink in some time. His last episode was probably the one described by the journalist James Bacon in his memoir, when he'd found a semi-unconscious Tracy at a Hollywood bar and driven him back to the Trancas Beach house. Kate chewed Bacon out for being a "bad influence." From that point on, she determined to keep all such bad influences far away from Tracy's recovery.

Later, Kate would say she moved into Spencer's bungalow at Cukor's. Various chroniclers, including Scott Berg, followed her lead, saying she lived "full-time" with Tracy in the guesthouse. But it's simply not true. "There were three bungalows on the estate," said Cukor's assistant and friend Tucker Fleming. "Spencer lived in one with an entrance on St. Ives. Hepburn and Phyllis took one [with an entrance] on Cordell. During the day, Hepburn was often at Tracy's bungalow, but at night she would go back across the way to sleep." In an interview in 1992, Kate admitted as much: "[Spencer] stayed in one house on George Cukor's estate and I stayed in another nearby." But the impression of cohabitation was already out there from her memoir, in which she'd called Tracy's bungalow "our house." Her admission had little effect on the legend.

No matter where she placed her head at night, however, Kate's caretaking was the talk of Hollywood. "Katharine Hepburn could have her choice of several Broadway plays," Dorothy Kilgallen wrote in her column soon after Spencer's latest release from the hospital, "but she's turning down all New York offers to stay near ailing Spencer Tracy in Hollywood. Her devotion to him for more than two decades has been absolutely selfless."

Kilgallen's words have the unmistakable ring of a publicist (Newcomb?) "leaking" some inside information to a reporter. But no matter how much Kilgallen's spin helped fuel the mythic image of Tracy and Hepburn, Kate's caretaking was hardly just a publicist's invention. "There was total, complete dedication," Palache observed of Kate's last years tending to Spencer. "Nothing . . . could interfere with anything that had to do with their relationship or with him—nothing, nothing, nothing."

Indeed, Kate's devotion not only extended Spencer's life but improved the quality of it. She oversaw his diet. She got him on an Exercycle twice a day. With his frequent need for oxygen, the sixty-three-year-old Spence was forced to quit smoking; that alone made him feel better, he told George Cukor. But Kate wasn't about to give up her own cigarettes in solidarity. She was often spotted by Cukor's assistants sitting out on the stoop by herself having a puff.

The one thing she couldn't do was help Spencer sleep. Still the hopeless insomniac, Tracy often sat up all night watching old films. When he'd catch one of his own, he'd talk back to the tube, critiquing the performances of a young man he no longer recognized as himself. Sometimes Kate would spy his light on and head across the yard with Phyllis, wrapped in their robes, settling down on Tracy's floor to watch *Libeled Lady* or *Boys Town*. From the main house, Cukor, too, could see the lights blazing, and occasionally he headed down the hill with a pot of tea and a tray of French pastries.

"I gather Kate and George are doing yeoman work," Binkie Beaumont wrote from London to Irene Selznick, "but I imagine from the rumors I hear they have their hands full."

In August 1965, Spence was hospitalized for prostate surgery. Afterward, a chemical imbalance threatened his recovery, and he was placed on the critical list. But once again the old man rallied, and by the end of September he was reported to be recuperating at home.

When he was up to it, he may have gone back to the Hill for a time. But returning to Louise for any full-time care was simply not an option. It would have cut Spence off from the family that sustained him at Cukor's. Ruth Gordon and Garson Kanin frequently made the trip from New York to see him, and now there were also a handful of others. Chester Erskine, who'd directed Spence in his Broadway breakthrough *The Last Mile*, often visited with his wife, Sally. Lawrence Weingarten, who'd produced *Adam's Rib* and *Pat and Mike*, was another frequent visitor, as was the director Jean Negulesco.

By now, Spence had also warmed to Fran Rich, who welcomed him and Kate to the home in Palm Springs she shared with another woman. It was there that Kate sculpted her famous three-inch bust of Spencer. Painting, sculpting, swimming in Fran's pool, Kate and Spence loved Palm Springs. Under a purple desert sky, ringed by the San Jacinto Mountains, they'd sit with Fran and her friend, talking late into the night.

Like the community that had surrounded them at Cukor's in the 1940s, the friends who now gathered around Tracy and Hepburn were rarely coupled in traditional relationships. With the exception of Ruth Gordon and Tracy himself, none of them had children. Those who were married—like Maie and Dick Casey—lived with a worldly disregard for convention. Chester Erskine was undeniably devoted to his wife, but he was also often spotted by the director John Schlesinger at "hippie" gatherings on Fire Island with a young man. Lawrence Weingarten, after divorcing Irving Thalberg's sister, lived for many years as a bachelor before marrying Dr. Jessie Marmorston of the University of Southern California. Again, while devoted, the Weingartens lived very independent lives.

Perhaps only such nontraditional friends could offer the kind of affinity Kate and Spence required. In their company, Spencer thrived emotionally, even if his body continued to fail. "He was like a different person," said Charles Williamson, who often saw him on the estate, painting at an easel, waving jauntily up at Cukor from the bottom of the hill. In these years, Spence acquired a dog, a black German shepherd named Lobo, to whom he became devoted. Lobo would bound across the yard when Spence called, happily licking his face.

Kate saw to it that Spencer's every whim was indulged. During one of his hospitalizations, he confided to her that what he wanted when he got out was a "snappy little sports car." Kate made sure to have one waiting for him outside the hospital on the day he was discharged. As all the nurses watched, an excited Spence maneuvered himself behind the wheel. But the car failed to start. Undeterred, Kate threw open the hood and claimed she was able to jump-start the motor with a bobby pin. "All the nurses started applauding," she told James Prideaux. "I took a bow. And we drove off in a blaze of glory. It was my finest hour."

During these five years (1962–67) of professional inactivity, Kate's romantic dream of life with Tracy returned. It's easy to see why. Spence wasn't drinking. Though he grew short of breath easily, he was stable, and seemingly happy. Scotty no longer came around; there were no dinner dates with Gene Tierney or Joan Fontaine. Nothing interfered with the image of domestic tranquillity Kate had created. Setting up an easel, she painted alongside Spencer, once rendering her man reading a newspaper, ensconced in his chair, just as she'd always remember him. Another time she sketched the two of them together in profile, drawing little squares all over her own caricature to indicate her blotches. The resulting sketch is like a grotesque, modernist *American Gothic*.

In some ways, that's just how Kate had come to view herself and Spence, as figures not unlike Grant Wood's iconic couple. Except that their abode was no midwestern farmhouse. It was a couple of bungalows around the swimming pool of a homosexual Hollywood director. No matter the distinctions between illusion and reality; Kate had found the kind of contentment with a man she'd been striving for ever since she'd shared an apartment with Putnam back in 1928. Painting with Spence, watching him play with Lobo, fixing him dinner, and then sitting cross-legged on the floor to watch him eat, Kate was happier than she'd been in a very long time.

"Kate is in absolutely smashing form," Irene Selznick wrote to Binkie Beaumont in September 1966. "There would be not a chance in a million that she would do anything at all on the stage at this time. She won't even do a film unless possibly one with Spence. He is fine, but that is her decision and I can't imagine anything shaking her."

At fifty-nine, Kate seemed content to settle into uncomplicated domesticity. "She took care of Spencer by inches," said her brother Bob. Added her sister Peg Perry, "She was glad to give him that kind of care. She finally got the chance to play the good wife."

Indeed, it would be these five halcyon years that would color Kate's memories of her entire time with Tracy. Relayed in her old age through misty eyes and quivering lips, these would be the happy images that would obscure everything else, that made her forget all the pain of the past. She had saved Spencer's life. For the first time, she had actually saved one of her men—and that gave her a contentment she'd never known before.

And so they decided to make one more film together. *Guess Who's Coming to Dinner* was filmed in the spring of 1967. Stanley Kramer, who'd directed Spence in three previous films, was careful not to push him too hard. Kate was even more solicitous. Lee Gopadze and his sister Tina visited one day and were struck by how tenderly Kate followed Spence around the set, helping him sit and then get back on his feet. After watching Spence struggle through one difficult scene, Tina Gopadze began to cry. "Don't let him see you," Kate whispered. "He won't be able to handle it."

On-screen, Kate was playing the same kind of "good wife" she played at home. When, a year later, she'd win an Oscar for it, she cabled her thanks to the Academy, expressing her opinion that the "good wife" was "our most unsung and important heroine." Forget all those militant feminists burning their bras as the political unrest of the 1960s intensified. Kate told the Academy she was glad the good wife was "coming back in style." Christina Drayton, she said, had been based on her mother—Kit Hepburn without all those causes to distract her, Kit Hepburn with only her husband's welfare on her mind. Whether or not Kit would have wanted to be remembered in that way, it was the legacy her daughter held most dear.

On June 10, 1967, just two weeks after he'd shot his last scene in *Guess Who's Coming to Dinner*, Spence rose before the sun was up. Still unable to sleep, he scuffed out to the kitchen and made himself some tea. Sitting down at the table to drink it, he slumped forward and died. The cause was a heart attack. He was sixty-seven.

That night, Kate was sleeping in the maid's room. The fact that she was staying at Spencer's bungalow when her own cottage was just a stone's throw away tells us she was particularly worried about him that night. Writing about Spencer's death a few days later to Maie Casey, Kate reported hearing a noise at about 3:00 a.m. and getting up to investigate. "He gave a sigh," Kate said of Spence. "There was a crash and that was it." The crash was apparently the teacup, or perhaps Spence had fallen from his chair. Their long drama was given a fitting final scene, as Kate would describe it in her memoir: "I crouched down and took you up in my arms—dead. No life—no pulse . . . Dear, dear friend—gone."

The romance of their story demanded such a theatrical ending. It's almost like the last scene in a Shakespearean tragedy. And while it's tempting to believe Kate mythologized the moment the way she mythologized so much else about their time together, her account of Tracy's death appears to be largely true. Although press reports had Spencer's maid discovering his body a little after six, Kate's memoir tells the same story as her private letter to Maie Casey, written just days after the fact. The story about the maid was clearly concocted out of respect to Louise.

"Spence was tired out and it was good that he didn't linger around half here," Kate wrote to Pat Jarrett. "He just went out like a light."

Apparently with the help of Cukor's groundsman, Kate got Tracy's body to his bed. Carroll Tracy was then called. For a moment, Kate considered vacating the premises before Louise arrived, but then she decided to stay. And so we have the scene of Louise Tracy arriving and delivering her immortal line upon seeing Kate at Spencer's bungalow, "I thought you were a rumor."

How those words infuriated Kate. Indeed, their intention seems to have been to trivialize her, to devalue her place in Spencer's life. Kate was stung. She had spent five years in devoted caretaking. When one nurtures and takes care of a dying loved one, the actual death can seem like the closing of a play—a mix of grief, triumph, relief, and confusion. Louise's words hurt because they came in the midst of all those feelings. The main focus of Kate's life for the past five years—the reason for her existence during that period—was now gone, and here Louise Tracy was, calling her a rumor.

Yet Louise can be forgiven for being surprised to see Hepburn playing the widow, welcoming people at the door, making coffee, telling the undertaker what clothes Spence should be dressed in. Louise was a shrewd woman. According to many observers, she had always understood the nature of her husband's relationship with Hepburn. *All of it*: the fact that they were together and had a deep, abiding commitment, but also the fact that, for much of the time, the relationship had been both passionate and platonic. Never before had Kate presumed to usurp Louise's particular role in Spencer's life; for one thing, he would never have allowed it. So it's not all that surprising that Louise told Kate that Spencer's burial clothes should be *her* decision. She was standing her ground as Spencer's wife.

But Kate Hepburn was never one to step graciously to the sidelines. Outwardly, she appeared to back off in the days after Tracy's death, letting Louise be front row center (Stanley Kramer, the director of *Guess Who's Coming to Dinner,* called Kate "a class act" for declining to attend Spencer's funeral). But in private, she was *stewing*.

"If Louise Tracy made *such* an effort to pretend that that marriage still held together when it was . . ." Her voice trailed off, shaking in anger during a tape-recorded conversation with John Ford a few years later. The spite was coming through loud and clear in Kate's voice as she spoke of Louise. "Everybody knew that it *hadn't*," she finished, nearly spitting the last word.

After all her caretaking of Tracy, Kate's pique isn't hard to understand. She believed she had offered her hand in friendship to Louise and been rejected. Had Louise simply thanked her for her care, given her some form of acknowledgment, the entire Hepburn legend might have been fundamentally different than we know it today.

But, as it was, Kate's grief seemed to push her into needing more. Psychologists say that the caretaker's mix of feelings after a loved one's death is almost always succeeded by a shattering depression and feeling of powerlessness. Kate was feeling irrelevant, and it hurt. Having snuck into the funeral home with Phyllis to pay their respects privately, Kate waited out the actual ceremony at Spencer's bungalow. Afterward, their circle of friends came by to see her. She told Chester Erskine to sit in Spencer's black leather rocking chair so it wouldn't be empty. She explained she was pretending that Tracy had just gone around the corner to buy a newspaper. But when she walked Jean Negulesco out to his car, she could no longer keep up the brave front. In an extraordinary expression of grief, Kate broke down and sobbed on Negulesco's shoulder, "all her poise forgotten," he said.

As for Spence, for all the apparent contentment of his last years, he seems not to have escaped the private turmoil he'd lived with all his life. In *Guess Who's Coming to Dinner*, his character kids a priest that the Catholics were "still preaching hell," as if that were just an old fairy tale. But in real life Tracy firmly believed he was one of the damned. On the set, he'd waxed philosophical with Katharine Houghton, Kate's niece who was playing his daughter in the film. He asked her what she thought happened when a person died. Houghton replied that she didn't believe in heaven or hell.

Tracy was surprised. "You don't think I'm going to pay for my sins in hell?" he asked. When Houghton said no, he pressed, "What do you think is going to happen to me?" She told him she believed his spirit would live on, but that he didn't face any kind of punishment—"because I think that you've had that here."

In the weeks to come, Kate began to experience anger in addition to grief, again not an uncommon emotion. Needing a scapegoat, a place to vent her feelings, Kate chose Louise. "I never went out with Spencer in Los Angeles in the almost thirty years I knew him out of deference to *her*," she complained to John Ford. Of course, she never went out in Los Angeles anyway, and for much of that time she wasn't even on the West Coast. But now she made it seem as if she'd made an enormous sacrifice in never traipsing down to the Brown Derby or Chasen's with Spence.

It was the sidelining Kate was forced into after Spencer's death that eventually determined how she'd tell the story of their life together. Had she not felt so marginalized, she might have memorialized their relationship as it truly was—a devoted, loving, sophisticated, complex friendship-partnership. Instead, she began to remember it the way the romanticists liked to imagine it, seeming determined to prove to Louise—and the world—that she'd been much, much more than a rumor.

After Tracy's death, something seemed to shift for Hepburn. Except for *Guess Who's Coming to Dinner*, which wouldn't be released until several months after Spencer's death, she'd been idle since *Long Day's Journey into Night*. Taking care of Spence had prevented her from the travel that so nourished her soul. Now Kate channeled her grief and pent-up ambition into a frenzy of work; but the change that came over her was even more significant than that. The sense of personal contentment she had known since the early 1950s seemed to crumble. Her friends felt she was adrift, trying to find a new definition for herself now that her focus of the last five years was gone. "She was angry all the time," George Cukor told Gavin Lambert about this period. "I never knew what about."

Kate's rapaciousness took many friends by surprise because it was so markedly different from her previous down-to-earth attitude. Palache thought Kate became increasingly "difficult" after Spencer's death. "She wants things her own way and in her own way," she said. "She doesn't want an argument about it. It just becomes easier to do it her way—whatever it is—rather than argue about it."

Palache acknowledged that much of Kate's obstinacy stemmed from her profession, where someone was always waiting to indulge her whims. Indeed, many celebrities become eccentric as they settle into the privileges of their fame. Yet while Kate had always had a tendency to be imperious, now her narcissism seemed increasingly to define her personality. After 1968 or so, Robert Shaw stopped seeing Kate because she became too "difficult and demanding." Another friend observed, "I think Kate started to believe that she was the greatest star in the world—and the Widow Tracy to boot."

Denied any ritual, any public expression of her grief, Kate searched for affirmation in private. From her friends she expected the kind of acknowledgment Louise had denied her—and she seemed to be keeping a checklist of those who had (and had not) paid their respects. On June 23, Irene Selznick was frantically writing to Binkie Beaumont to let him know Kate was wondering why she hadn't heard from him.

Of course, the savvy Irene understood very well what was expected of her. Heading to London, she rented a flat rather than a hotel room in case Kate wanted to get out of Hollywood for a while and join her. "I felt it unimportant whether or not she came," Irene wrote to Binkie, "only that she had an option, knew that she was welcome, and that I had a roof for her. Poor darling."

Kate was, in fact, ready to get out of town, but it wasn't Irene with whom she took refuge. Telling Phyllis to pack their things, she first retreated to Martha's Vineyard with the Kanins and Nancy Hamilton. Offers were flowing in, including a return to Broadway in a musical comedy, something that Kate at first thought absurd. Still, she was eager to get back to work. From Martha's Vineyard she set off with Laura Harding for Europe, where she'd make two films, *The Lion in Winter* and *The Madwoman of Chaillot*. In Ireland, where part of *Lion* was filmed, she visited John Huston and sent postcards to George Cukor, which show that her spirits revived, as usual, once she was abroad. "Miss Harding has bought all of Dublin," Kate joked. Afterward she flew to the south of France for more filming.

One morning, sitting on the terrace of a villa on the Côte d'Azur, Kate opened an envelope from Cukor. Inside was a photograph of Spence and herself. She wrote Cukor a note of thanks. "I shall love having it and looking at it and thinking of our good friend and his stark, pure taste," she said. "Sad he's dead. What are you going to do with the house?"

With George, who knew her better than most, Kate couldn't get away with playing the bereaved widow too long. The director knew Kate wanted to vacate her own bungalow and move into Spencer's. Part of it was certainly sentiment. But Tracy's cottage, as Charles Williamson pointed out, was also "larger and had better sun." Cukor agreed she could have it.

When Kate returned to Los Angeles, she finally moved into the place she could now, in all honesty, call "our house." Writing to Cukor, she joked, "I feel sure you will rue the day that I decided to take the house and land like a ton of bricks on your kind heart." In truth, he loved that she planned to stay on his property and not return full-time to New York.

Kate hadn't been mentioned in Tracy's will—hadn't expected to be—but now she had his house and the things he had left behind. Cukor's friend Richard Stanley remembered how Kate wore Spencer's old clothes, stitching them up when they started falling apart so she wouldn't have to throw them away. One sweater, Stanley said, was "more holes than yarn." From the ceiling of the bungalow, Spencer's wooden "goose" still dangled; his books remained on the shelves. Kate had also inherited his dog, Lobo, to whom she became attached, the first and only pet she ever really cared about.

Released late in 1967, *Guess Who's Coming to Dinner* was a huge box-office hit, the biggest of Kate's career, grossing $70 million worldwide. Audiences flocked to see a white woman (Houghton) kiss a black man (Sidney Poitier.) But for many it was also the final act of the ballad of Tracy and Hepburn. A few days after Spencer's death, the critic Charles Champlin gave the legend its coda, in effect packaging the Tracy-Hepburn love story for the decades to come: Spence and Kate, Champlin wrote, had given us "a remarkable legacy of an association as beautiful and dignified as any this town has ever known."

Yet in truth, their last outing together hardly measures up to their best work. Bosley Crowther in the *New York Times* wrote that the script, by William Rose, was "structured to suit the convenience and convention of the cinema." Poitier is not only a doctor but a magna cum laude from Johns Hopkins and a Yale professor. Years later, Katharine Houghton would rightly say that the film was "mainly for white people."

Still, the film had *relevance*, that crucial buzzword of the late 1960s.

Guess Who's Coming to Dinner may not have been a profound treatise on civil rights, but it was groundbreaking nonetheless. Houghton reflected, "I think that [for] anybody who's ever been involved in an interracial marriage of any sort, or even a gay relationship, any kind of relationship that's not approved of, that movie became a metaphor."

What it also did was make Katharine Hepburn, at age sixty, "one cool chick," according to a long-haired young man in a poncho standing in line to see the film in Times Square. America's gutsy heroine had proven that she was hip to the social changes of the times. The *New York Times* went so far as to declare that when Hepburn first started making movies, she'd been "the very first Mod—a very round peg in the square hole of Hollywood." Thirty-five years later, her iconoclastic screen persona—for all the trouble it had sometimes caused in the past—assured a new generation that Kate Hepburn was "very Now." Not only did her final film with Tracy confirm our admiration for her; it also proved she was "with it."

By 1968, all the various components of the Hepburn image had been established. Independent, heroic, and critically, for 1968, *relevant*. On top of all that, she was still the foremost actress in America—maybe even the world. If people had doubts, all they had to do was consider her back-to-back Oscars, one for *Guess Who's Coming to Dinner* and the other for *The Lion in Winter*, released in late 1968. A cover of *Life* that year announced THE COMEBACK OF KATE. Six months later, *Look* headlined her as THE UNSINKABLE KATE.

"She stands apart," wrote the *New York Times*, "singular and magnificent, an unchallenged First Lady, the first player of either sex to take three starring Oscars . . . Miss Hepburn has always aimed high. Like James Thurber's moth that scorned streetlamps and pursued an unreachable star, she has climbed higher than any of her own kind."

Hepburn, it seemed, could do anything. Yet even her closest friends were surprised when she told them she'd decided to accept that Broadway musical comedy offer. "Singing and dancing onstage," James Prideaux said incredulously. "*Katharine Hepburn?*" In the end, however, *Coco* would expose much more than Kate's chutzpah.

KISSING HER IN THE STREET

Summer 1967, a dockside restaurant on Martha's Vineyard. The yacht *Honey Fitz* was pulling in from Hyannisport with the musician and Kennedy crony Roger Edens on board, the man who'd taught Judy Garland how to sing. With Edens was a bevy of Kennedy women who wanted to meet America's favorite movie star, Kate Hepburn. In their white shorts and colorful scarves, Pat Lawford, Jean Smith, Eunice Shriver, and Ethel Kennedy paraded onto the pier, waving their arms and hallooing as they caught sight of Kate. Garson Kanin, who was there, thought the Kennedys and Kate were "sisters of a sort, made of the identical fine human material, understanding the same rules of the game." Among this sorority of upper-class New Englanders, Kate allowed herself to be flattered, cajoled, and finally convinced that what Edens had done for Garland, he could also do for her.

While contemporaries like Joan Crawford and Barbara Stanwyck toiled in cheap horror films or the daily grind of television, Hepburn was winning Oscars and planning to star in a major Broadway show. No project at the time had as much buzz surrounding it as *Coco,* the Alan Jay Lerner–André Previn musical based on the life of the Parisian couturiere Gabrielle "Coco"

Chanel. It was Kate's first reinvention of herself post-Tracy, and it would reveal both the durability of her fame and the fragility of her own sense of herself. The best of times, and the worst of times, as they say. As such, it is worth considering in depth here.

Late that fall, at Irene Selznick's suite in the Pierre Hotel, a handful of New York's theatrical elite gathered for a little concert given by Kate Hepburn, intended to dispel any doubts about her singing voice. With Edens tinkling away at the piano, Kate "talk-sang" her way through a Cole Porter medley. At the end of "Miss Otis Regrets," she was greeted with kisses and kudos—even if most present were actually appalled. "She sounded like Donald Duck," groaned *Coco*'s producer, Frederick Brisson, to his friends.

Brisson didn't want her. The show was supposed to star his wife, Rosalind Russell, but Lerner had pushed for Kate, sneaking her a script. The lyricist also secured Chanel's seal of approval—though some wags thought when the aged designer said she wanted "Hepburn" to play her, she meant Audrey. Chanel's widely publicized support, however, meant the part was Kate's, leaving Brisson feeling duped and furious and Rosalind Russell chagrined. Kate tried to soothe any bad feelings. "An incident like this turns to a feather when weighed against a career such as yours," she wrote to Russell. "Nevertheless, embarrassment is bad enough and I am determined to find a way to reduce it to the palest blush possible."

Coco had seemed right up Russell's alley, for she'd scored a huge hit on Broadway a few years back in the comedy *Auntie Mame*. But it was a peculiar turn for Hepburn, whose career over the last decade had striven for ever-greater acting challenges.

Indeed, the two films she'd made in Europe in 1968 had followed this highbrow pattern. Based on James Goldman's searing play about loyalty and revenge, *The Lion in Winter* cast her opposite such acting heavyweights as Peter O'Toole and Anthony Hopkins. Playing Eleanor of Aquitaine, presiding over perhaps the most dysfunctional royal family of all time, she is majestically confident. Goldman's screenplay, based on his own play, is less about history than it is about deception, power, and revenge, and Kate—all jaw and teeth—snaps out his sharp dialogue as if wielding a rapier. "There is something about an actress with this degree of presence . . . that gets her through even misplaced weepy or extravagant scenes," wrote Renata Adler in the *New York Times*. The film's director was Anthony Harvey, a thirty-six-year-old Englishman and former film editor who stunned Hollywood with his brilliant command of the material. He and Kate became devoted friends.

Likewise, *The Madwoman of Chaillot* was another adaptation of an intellectual play, though Jean Giraudoux was far more esoteric than Goldman. "Oh, no," Hepburn said to the press after she'd read the script. "What's all this about? I'm a simple, nice person. I like to make Christmas wreaths, sweep floors. I don't understand all this complicated stuff." Yet despite such provincial pretenses, she was eager to throw herself into Giraudoux's parable of an eccentric countess who saves bohemian Paris from corporate butchers.

Through it all, however, the anger that Cukor had identified seemed ever-present. Kate was fighting all the time, alienating even old friends like Charles Boyer, with whom she shared a poignant scene in the all-star film. Another fellow actor, Yul Brynner, thought she was "an intolerable bitch" when she imperiously ordered him off the set after he tried to take a candid snapshot of her. There had been similar moments on *The Lion in Winter*. When O'Toole detained a makeup man, Kate marched in and physically struck her costar—"as hard as I could hit!" She stormed out, shrieking, "Next time I want a makeup man, send him down right away!" Nevertheless, O'Toole has only sung her praises in public.

Of course, such outbursts of temper were nothing new for Hepburn, as any number of policemen in the Midwest could attest to. But such moments were now everyday ocurrences. When Phyllis broke her leg falling off a bicycle during the filming of *Chaillot*, Kate berated her in front of the entire crew, as if her hapless companion had done it as a personal affront to her.

James Prideaux, who met her at this time, thought her flurry of professional activity was an attempt to keep her mind off her grief over Spencer, grief that was often manifested as anger or irritation. When the recently widowed Dorothy Gopadze visited Kate in 1975, she was embraced by the star with great emotion, and told that only those who had been through a similar loss could understand their grief. Eight years after Tracy's death, Hepburn still felt like his widow.

Work was Kate's best distraction. Besides *Coco,* the one project that really seemed to fire her up at this time was "Martha," an adaptation of two novels by Margery Sharp. The film would be the story of a rule-defying woman who pursues a career as an artist. Kate formed a partnership with Irene Selznick, who agreed to produce. But this time Kate didn't plan to act; she wanted to *direct*.

With Spencer's death, Kate's drive for ever-greater artistic challenges resurfaced, and the prospect of directing a film was terribly exciting. "The ideas Mother and Kate had were fabulous," said Daniel Selznick. Inspired by Norman Jewison's *The Thomas Crown Affair* (1968), Kate was talking about using split screens to tell the story from multiple points of view. "Martha" was announced in the press, and according to letters in Irene's private files, there was considerable studio interest. Irene was after Lynn Redgrave for the lead and Jean Renoir to play an important supporting role. James Prideaux, then a young unknown, helped draft a screenplay, though eventually the script was turned over to William Rose, who'd written *Guess Who's Coming to Dinner* and, in the process, become a close friend of Kate's.

"Rose's script was really wonderful," said Daniel Selznick. "It would have made a really great picture." Much to Irene's chagrin, however, Kate was continually distracted from the project by planning for *Coco*. Eventually "Martha" fizzled out, despite Kate's frequently expressed wish to return to it "someday." "I think there was a real sense of regret on both their parts that the film never happened," Daniel Selznick observed. Sadly, we're left only with imagination and conjecture for what Kate might have accomplished as a director.

By late 1968, there was little time in Kate's life for anything but *Coco*. According to notes taken by Brisson, she was cocksure about her ability to do the part—and even more certain of the amount of business she could bring in. At her first meeting with Brisson, she told him that despite having given it "all up for Tracy," every film she'd made in the last six years had brought her an Academy Award nomination. That proved, she insisted, she still had box-office clout. "They really want me," she boasted of her public appeal. It was from such a position that she proceeded to negotiate with Brisson.

From the start, she made exorbitant demands. All of Phyllis's transportation expenses were to be covered by the producer in addition to her own. Directorial approval needed to rest in her hands, and Kate was holding out for Jerome Robbins. When Robbins proved impossible to get, Brisson sent Kate a list of possible other choices. She refused to make up her mind, dragging out the process. "You will just have to be patient," she wrote grandly to Brisson.

Yet patience was not a virtue she herself was prepared to offer. When rehearsals were delayed because Lerner was still working on rewrites, Kate began sniping about the lyricist behind his back. When Lerner heard about it, he fired off a letter confronting Hepburn on her hypocrisy. "I was surprised," he wrote, "because . . . you didn't seem to be worried about [a delay] when I saw you." He assured her that "[b]arring crippling illness, atomic war, planetary collision or your wishes," rehearsals would begin that November of 1968.

The tension between Kate and Lerner, her onetime champion, dispels the notion that her erratic, sometimes unprofessional behavior on *Coco* was an invention of Freddie Brisson, who had a rather acrimonious reputation himself and who might be suspected of carrying a grudge over the treatment of his wife. Indeed, during the long experience of *Coco*, Kate had few friends in the production. Even longtime pal Michael Benthall (who was eventually hired as director at her insistence) frequently complained about her demands to Brisson, whose notes include mentions of Benthall being "in the doghouse" with the star.

As much as she might be demanding, however, no one could say Hepburn didn't work hard. Indeed, she threw herself into the part, training with Edens as well as with the vocal couch Sue Seton and the pianist Laura Dubman Fratti. In anticipation of all the singing and dancing she'd be doing, Kate also quit smoking—ambition doing for her what even Spencer's oxygen tank could not.

Coco was not, as many have assumed, the first time Hepburn sang professionally. In *Desk Set*, she'd performed a tremulous but passable rendition of "Night and Day." And of course she'd warbled "I Can't Give You Anything But Love" in *Bringing Up Baby*. But *Coco* presented a challenge even the most capable singers would have found daunting. Lerner, without his longtime partner Frederick Loewe, seemed adrift. He never really gelled with André Previn, who, in London for most of their collaboration, paired Lerner's straightforward lyrics with often nonmelodic, modernist music. Songs like "The Money Rings Out Like Freedom" were never destined to be catchy show tunes.

Still, Kate proved passionate about the project. After meeting the real Coco in Paris, Hepburn felt born for the part. "We're not so different," she told Kanin. Indeed, part of the reason Brisson had been so fascinated with Chanel was because, as a young woman, the couturiere had "cut her hair, smoked in public, [and] worn pants." To the press, Brisson echoed Kate's sense of affinity with Chanel: "Both women are extraordinarily independent and vulnerable and feminine. Both lead lives according to their own standards."

There was something else they had in common as well. The story of *Coco* turns on the couturiere's love for Noelle, her protégée, and the triangle that develops when Noelle decides to marry. Considering hairstyles and costumes with the designer Cecil Beaton, Kate insisted that Noelle not be made into a copy of her. "That would be too lesbian," she told him, "and we can't introduce that element into the play. As it is there have been rumors about me, because I have some very good friends like Laura Harding and we wear trousers."

When Beaton lifted an eyebrow, she went on: "Oh, it's been said millions of times and Chanel, too, she had that reputation."

A week later, Kate was still sensitive about the subject, calling Noelle's hairdo too "lesbian." Her real objection, Beaton thought, was that the younger woman's hair made her own look "skimpy." Ironically, the actress playing Noelle was so "nauseatingly sycophantic" (Beaton's words) that some in the company whispered she was Kate's girlfriend. The fact that Hepburn had secured a small part for Eve March in the show also caused some gossip.

For all her distancing from *Coco*'s subtext, however, Kate had clearly been chosen, at least in part, for the enigmatic sexuality she'd bring to the role. That was no secret among some observers. Writing to the screenwriter-composer Leonard Gershe, Claudette Colbert regretted not getting the part herself, insisting she had all the requirements to play Coco: she was French, she was the right age, she could do accents, and she could "also sing quite well, which means a helluva sight better than Miss K. Hepburn." There was only one problem, Colbert said: "*I'm* not a lesbian." It was an ironic comment, of course, yet another example of the dissonance between the word *lesbian* and high-class ladies like Colbert, who spent much of her life with female companions. Apparently, however, Colbert thought the word *did* fit Hepburn.

As the date for the first rehearsals drew near, Kate's need for control only intensified. Unhappy with the venues being proposed, she vetoed the Broadway Theatre ("It's terrible!") and insisted she'd find the right space on her own. On a day in June, she barged unannounced into the Majestic Theatre on West Forty-fourth Street, upsetting the cast and crew of *Fiddler on the Roof* when she demanded a backstage tour. The outraged management called Brisson to complain.

Of more immediate concern was her leading man. Kate campaigned for Douglas Fairbanks Jr. but told Brisson she "wouldn't say no" to Paul Henreid. In the end, she got the lesser-known George Rose, which she brooded about for weeks.

She continued acting out. In July, after Brisson had nixed a wardrobe-fitting session with Beaton in London, Kate went anyway, sending the bill for her (and Phyllis's) first-class airfare to the producer. Infuriated, Brisson accused Lerner of giving Hepburn the go-ahead. Lerner, by now leery of their volatile star, agreed to pay the bill.

In London, Beaton was, at first, impressed by Hepburn's "directness." But the two of them probably never had much of a chance to become friends. For one thing, Beaton could be anti-Semitic, which Kate would have loathed, and for another, his flamboyant homosexuality (Cukor called him an "effeminate dandy") would definitely have put her off, no matter how comfortable she'd gotten with Bobby Helpmann. But Beaton's worst crime was that he had offended her friends. Irene was still bitter toward him since their battles on *The Chalk Garden* thirteen years earlier, when Beaton had said she'd "defiled [his] London house by her presence." More recently, Beaton had also clashed with Cukor during the filming of *My Fair Lady.* Cukor called the Englishman "publicity-seeking and ungenerous and terribly pretentious."

Yet pretension was precisely the sin Beaton found so intolerable about Hepburn. Writing about her in his diary, he seemed to use vitriol instead of ink. His remarks about her are among the most withering invective he ever penned—and for a man of Beaton's spleen, that's saying quite a bit. He caught Kate at her worst, at a time when she was unusually insecure and thus excessively overbearing. Ordering him around, refusing his invitations to his country house, Kate forfeited any chance of winning the designer as her ally. To Beaton, she was a "complete egomaniac . . . a school ma'am, a Victorian sportswoman or suffragette . . . a woman without a vestige of humour." As she left his studio, Kate noticed he was smiling, and asked him why. "I didn't tell her it was with relief," Beaton wrote in his diary.

Kate's anxiety and ill temper were ratcheted up that summer by news that her sister Peg's son, Army Specialist Thomas Hepburn Perry, age twenty-seven, was reported missing in action in Vietnam. "Disastrous family news," she told Brisson, had made "life close in on her." (Tom Perry would eventually be declared dead, but not for several years.) Yet Kate's discontent predated the tragedy. She had been fuming and fighting for two years now, ever since Spencer's death—though every once in a while she seemed to recognize just how difficult she was being. "I don't want to make you suffer, Freddie," she told Brisson over the phone at one point in June. "You have problems enough." But in fact his problems with Kate had only just begun.

When rehearsals finally got under way that fall, a retrospective of Hollywood glamour photography featuring Hepburn opened at the Museum of Modern Art. The late 1960s were a time when the surviving stars of Hollywood's classical era were being feted as living legends, and Kate assumed that air quite consciously.

Presented with the proposed newspaper ad for *Coco,* she rejected it outright because the type size used for her name was too small. She insisted on equal weight with Lerner and Previn. It was a far cry from her days with the Theatre Guild, when she'd actually had her name *shrunk.*

A few weeks later, when she saw Beaton's caricature of her—all chin and hair—she threw a royal fit, sending the image flying across the room. "I look like a *monkey!*" she screamed to friends. Demanding that Beaton draw something else, she was met with a firm refusal from Brisson. "There is no way of us controlling what Beaton draws," he told her.

The most egregious offense, however, was Beaton's signature. Large and dark, it seemed like a bird flapping behind her. Kate called it an insult. "She was offended because it made Beaton seem as prominent as she was," said one of her friends. Hepburn threatened to sue for breach of contract if the signature ran as it was.

By now Brisson was barely speaking to her. "Please tell Kate that I will have our advertising agency try to get it lighter and less conspicuous," he wrote to her agent, but to Beaton, he called Hepburn "dishonest [and] rather disturbed." After watching Kate kiss Beaton on the lips, Brisson called it "an act of Judas."

In a ploy as old as Kate's RKO days, much of the advance press for *Coco* referred to Hepburn as "feminine." If enough people said it, Brisson seems to have been hoping, maybe the public would believe it. Yet the woman Beaton observed at rehearsals was anything but feminine. She had "the manners of an old sea salt," he said, "spreading her ugly piano-calved legs in the most indecent positions . . . being in every gesture as unfeminine and unlike the fascinating Chanel as anyone could be."

Beaton wasn't exactly unbiased toward her at this point, but even Kate's friends agreed that she had become especially mercurial while working on *Coco*. "I'd like to think it was menopause," said Robert Shaw, "but surely this was too late for that." At sixty-two (the world thought she'd just hit the sixty mark), Kate seemed to be alienating everybody.

"When she's rehearsing a play," Palache explained, "you can't get through . . . That makes life very easy for her. She has to make almost no decisions. It's very surprising how that is, but it takes a toll of everybody else."

Her state of mind wasn't helped by the drubbing *The Madwoman of Chaillot* received from the critics just before *Coco* opened. *The Lion in Winter* had been a surprising hit, with critics agog over her fierce Queen Eleanor. But *Madwoman* was a hodgepodge; its director, Bryan Forbes, had been unable to translate the stylized whimsy of the play onto film. Kate herself is an over-the-top cartoon. Vincent Canby of the *New York Times* derided the sentimental "spectacle of Katharine Hepburn . . . gently clenching her perfect teeth, looking into the middle distance and weeping through her tears." It had been a long time since any of Kate's film roles had been reviewed so harshly. One would have to go all the way back to *The Iron Petticoat*, thirteen years previous, to find such universally appalling reviews.

"Kate didn't like it one bit," Robert Shaw said. "She'd come to expect raves for every film she did by that point, just because she was Katharine Hepburn."

She had also just been through yet another surgery on her face. Her skin was deteriorating faster than anything else about her, though makeup still disguised that fact from the public. Not so for Beaton, who got a close-up look. "Her skin is revolting," he said, "and since she does not apply enough makeup . . . she appears pockmarked." He called her "raddled, rash-ridden, freckled, burnt, [and] mottled . . . It is unbelievable, incredible that she can still be exhibited in public."

But in the public Kate very much remained, flailing about on the stage, trying to keep up with the much-younger chorus girls as they sweated through their numbers back and forth across the huge revolving set. After Benthall, who was then in the midst of a long, sad slide into alcoholism, began reeking of so much whiskey that Beaton declared him "a fire danger," authority seemed to pass from the director to the twenty-eight-year-old hot-shot choreographer Michael Bennett. Kate was not pleased. She seemed to resent taking instruction from someone as young as he was. "Kate would not allow me to direct," Bennett recalled. "I blocked scenes like painting with numbers. I ran around and directed the people who *would* take direction."

Yet Bennett was also sympathetic to Kate's neuroses. "She often burst into floods of tears, saying 'I can't do it, I'll never do it, I'm making an ass of myself' . . . Every day she cried. She would come on every day at nine a.m. seventeen days old, full of life and gaiety, and at the end of the day she'd be a woman of sixty. She was maddened by the fact that her mind didn't work as well as she'd like, that her body wouldn't do what she wanted to do."

During previews in November, Beaton remembered Benthall trying to rouse the cast, "blinking like a mechanical owl, [clasping] his fat hands together and [saying], 'We've all got to be kind to Kate . . . We've got to tell her how good she is.'" Her self-doubt had only grown with each rehearsal and was by now apparent to everyone in the cast.

Yet preview audiences seemed pleased with her performance. Certainly, she didn't *look* like Katharine Hepburn anymore, in her high heels, short skirts, and page-boy haircut. Beaton was "greatly relieved to say goodbye to her Victorian landlady topknot." But her singing had not improved much, even after all those lessons. In tears, she apologized to the cast after one preview, saying she'd let them all down. Beaton wasn't moved. "K.H. can expect sympathy from no one, certainly not me," he wrote. "She'll get $1 million for being herself on her own terms, and if she's overwrought and wondering if she's as good as she's pretending to be, then it's all grist to her mill. It's her way of filling an empty life."

Beaton was right on at least one count: *Coco* was a smash no matter that Kate couldn't sing. People came to see *her*, not the show. Opening night on December 18, 1969, was "one of *those* opening nights," Garson Kanin said, with people flying in from all over the world. Kate's family was there, Dick wearing a blazer over bright red pajamas. Close friends, past and present, showed up: Laura, Irene, Bobby Helpmann, Robert McKnight. Cecil Beaton arrived with Princess Lee Radziwill. On André Previn's arm was his girlfriend, Mia Farrow, in a red velvet maternity dress. Stars of stage and screen—Rosalind Russell, Danny Kaye, Martha Graham, Lauren Bacall—mixed with high society—Gloria Vanderbilt, Betsy Bloomingdale, Mrs. John Hay Whitney.

Kanin wondered what could possibly take place onstage that would compete with the spectacle in the auditorium. "It is at times such as these," he mused, "that the theater, which after all is meant to be a forum, becomes instead an arena, a bull ring. The spectators have come to see whether the matador or the bull will triumph."

Kate, the matador, "conquered the bull in a series of brilliant thrusts," Kanin averred. Indeed, even Beaton was touched by the affection that flowed from the audience toward the scrappy lady in the funny hat. Ovation after ovation greeted her at the end.

Critics, too, just as they had with *Guess Who's Coming to Dinner*, overlooked the flaws of the vehicle to heap praise on its star. Clive Barnes, one of the new breed of critics Beaton had worried they'd have a hard time winning over, gushed in the *New York Times* over the "well-scrubbed and gallant radiance of Katharine Hepburn." Everything else about the show he hated, but he adored Kate. No matter that her voice cracked and popped, no matter that she stumbled over lines and laughed in the middle of speeches, Kate—America's sweetheart—could do no wrong.

"Thank God the opening 'went,' " she wrote to Brisson. "I think we're just lucky they didn't turn on 'St. Katharine.' "

She didn't stay saintly for very long. During the recording of the *Coco* cast album, Kate was asked to start a song without her traditional spoken lead-in. When she wasn't accommodated, she got "violent" (her word) and stormed out of the studio. Jetting off for a quick New Year's holiday at her friend William Rose's house on the island of Jersey, Kate penned a letter of protest to Brisson and Lerner. Her handwriting shows her agitation, growing larger from first to last page. "To have made this decision without consulting me," she wrote, "is the most insulting and careless act I have ever had committed against me by any management."

Her rhetorical flourish was plain to anyone who knew even a little about her career: The recording session was worse than being fired? Than having her salary docked? Than being labeled box-office poison? But Kate was filled with resentment. "To be treated like a kitchen maid is not my idea of how I should be treated."

By now, it was Brisson and Lerner who were the really resentful ones. Even with the long lines that *Coco* drew every night to the Mark Hellinger Theatre, the troubles with Kate increasingly did not seem worth the aggravation. Brisson, "fed up with K.H. and her temperament," had resigned himself to bribes "to keep the bitch happy."

That proved increasingly difficult. Once back in New York, Kate griped about Beaton's design for the souvenir program. She went around calling him "a pig, an outrageous character." Yet even more problematic was Kate's refusal to commit to how long she'd stay with the show. "I am sorry to be dillydallying you," she wrote to Brisson, "but I am dillydallying myself too." Contractually she was free to go after April, but after the box office proved steady, she agreed to stay on through June.

Of course, she made sure that Brisson knew just how much of a sacrifice she was making. According to Brisson's notes, Kate told him if she stayed any longer than June, she "would die!" Her doctors had "passed out" when she told them she was staying that long. But as June approached and the delirious applause continued, Kate suddenly announced she felt well enough to stay through the rest of the summer. To Brisson, she admitted she saw Coco as "her part." With a rare burst of honesty, she said, "I don't want someone else to play it."

Yet if she still insisted on leaving eventually, Brisson explained, they'd need to start negotiating with other actresses as her replacement. Kate wasn't happy with any of the ideas suggested. Claudette Colbert wanted it desperately, asking mutual friends like Irene Selznick to lobby for her, but Kate scoffed, calling her "sweet but uncadential"—as if her own cadences were any better. Even worse was the idea of Maria Callas. "Freak!" Kate shouted.

Her greatest hostility, however, was reserved for Danielle Darrieux, who was French, ten years younger, and potentially a more dynamic Coco. The only name Kate seemed to countenance at all was the ten-years-*older* Gloria Swanson, who came in to audition that spring. "Wonderful, but can she take it?" Kate asked Brisson, predicting, "She'll be trouble."

Not as much trouble as they were used to. Behind Hepburn's back, Brisson began talking with Darrieux. Beaton wasn't even sure Kate was serious about leaving, believing all she wanted them to do was beg her to stay. He'd observed her reaction to the thunderous ovations: "It may . . . suit her to stay on to receive the applause of the multitudes. Her whole life is devised to receive the standing ovation that she has had at the end of her great personality performance. As the play nears its end and she is sure of her success . . . the years roll off her, and she becomes a young schoolmistress."

She made a great show of not minding when she lost the Tony that spring to Lauren Bacall in *Applause*—"I don't really feel robbed because these things don't mean much to me . . . Betty is so happy that I can't help being happy for her"—but in fact when Brisson tried to give her the nomination plaque she said sharply, "I don't want it. Keep it." In private meetings, Kate rued the loss because it would have meant a new rush of momentum for the show. Soon after this, she announced she was leaving to make a picture.

But when Kate learned that Danielle Darrieux had been cast, she had a "terrible fight" with Brisson. The producer insisted that she had known since January (when she'd first expressed doubt about how long she could stay with the show) that she would have to be replaced. Back then, Brisson said, she had accepted the fact without qualms. "We also told you when it became a fact then it would be necessary to publicize and advertise it," Brisson wrote. Here he soothed her ego a bit, hoping she'd still take the show on the road for them. "No one will ever be Coco but you. Alas to our deep regret, you have to leave us and I can only hope that you will be coming back to us very soon."

In a snit, Kate refused to commit to the tour. In a way, Brisson had called her bluff. She had no choice but to take her final bow on August 1. Those last few weeks were hell for Kate, with the company off rehearsing with Darrieux. The cheerful strawberry-blond star would slip into Hepburn's dressing room during the day and wear her costumes. Once, discovering her props had been moved, Kate flew into a rage, cornering the stage manager, Jerry Adler, against the wall and screaming that she felt as if she were "dead and in a morgue." Her voice echoing throughout the theater, she bellowed about her bones "being picked like a dead horse!" She wanted "the show closed, the theater burned down!" Everyone, she bellowed, had deserted her!

But screaming got her nowhere. Two weeks later, Kate's worst fears came true when Darrieux's first show was a smash. "For all her artistry and force," opined the *New York Times*, "Miss Hepburn is neither French nor very musical. As of last night, Danielle Darrieux is Coco." Even more important to the *Times*, however, was Darrieux's "overpowering femininity . . . She is all woman." The implication, of course, was that Kate was not.

Pacing across the beach at Fenwick, Kate was stewing. "She really missed that applause," said her sister Peg Perry. "She'd gotten used to hearing it on a daily basis." Another friend joked that if it would make her feel better, he'd come over every night and clap for her.

Kate had other ideas. One night, not long after Kate had left the show, Alan Jay Lerner answered his phone to find Garson Kanin on the other end of the line. Lerner liked Ruth and Gar, and was delighted when Gar suggested they all have a drink. Lerner thought it was a social call. He was unprepared for the news Kanin had to give him.

According to Gar, Kate wanted back in. She wanted Brisson to fire Darrieux and announce that Katharine Hepburn was returning to *Coco* by "popular demand." She'd thought it over, Kanin told Lerner, and decided she'd been a little hasty about leaving. Lerner asked about the film she'd supposedly left the show to do. Wasn't happening, Kanin informed him. Lerner just sat there, at a loss as to what to say.

When word got around the *Coco* crew about Kate's change of heart, Michael Benthall took Brisson aside and told him to pay no attention to her. She was under an "emotional strain," he told the producer, "eaten with jealousy." Benthall was still part of Hepburn's inner circle, and he was privy to the endless rantings that took place at Fenwick and on Forty-ninth Street ever since Kate left the cast. With utter exhaustion, Benthall would later say that the only place for Kate was "Bellevue Hospital in a straitjacket."

Why had it turned out this way? Why had Kate, so renowned for her professionalism, turned into such a diva? Why, after being so admired in the past for her lack of typical star jealousies, did she become consumed with envy whenever Darrieux's name was mentioned? Indeed, it was with real glee that she told friends that, despite the praise of the critics, the show's box office had declined steadily after her departure. *Coco* would close that October, just three months after Darrieux took over. To Kate's gloating satisfaction, Brisson and Lerner were forced to come after her with outstretched arms, asking her to take the show on the road for them. With much pretension of noblesse oblige, Kate agreed.

Hepburn might be forgiven for feeling so proprietary over a role she created. But her behavior during the run of the show—throwing star tantrums and making life difficult for those around her—was surely the most unprofessional of her career. In the past, she'd been a trouper even under the most difficult, humbling conditions. She'd trudged through provincial midwestern theaters for the Theatre Guild, the jungles of Africa for John Huston. She wasn't immune to fits, but they were always timed so as not to disrupt the work. Even on *Suddenly, Last Summer,* she'd waited until the very end before spitting at Joe Mankiewicz.

Part of it may have been lingering grief over Spence, but even more, it was her perennial lack of self-confidence, especially when she found herself in uncharted waters like musical comedy. Despite the crowds, Kate knew she had never truly mastered the form. "If I could describe to you the terror—the sinking inadequacy—the blank horror which I felt every night before I went on," she wrote. "A mouse posing as a lion." For a while, her brother Dick's new wife served as her assistant, and she'd remember Kate regularly coming off the stage (not only in *Coco* but in other shows as well) with a plaintive "Was it any good?" Some believed Kate was simply fishing for compliments, which of course she was; but her need to hear praise (from her underlings, from her producers, from her public) can be explained by insecurity as much as it can by ego.

Yet for a performer who in many ways remained a little girl starved for acclaim and a pat on the back, *Coco* had been a revelation. It hadn't mattered that she couldn't sing. The public had loved her anyway. They'd lined up in droves to see her. At the height of the craze, Laura Harding wrote to George Cukor suggesting they call a meeting "to discuss running Miss Katharine Hepburn for President." No wonder Kate wanted back into the show. No wonder she seemed to want to play Coco forever. The girl shunned by society for her family's maverick ways was now embraced—adored—for those very same unorthodox traits. The woman who'd been nearly tarred and feathered for her quirky habits in her early career was now being lauded simply for being herself.

For in the end, that's what Kate's Coco was—no matter the high heels, glasses, and haircut. Kate's Coco was far more the tomboy from Hartford than the couturiere from Paris. Every mannerism, every toss of her head, every stern shaking of her finger was quintessential Hepburn. And audiences couldn't get enough.

Later Kate would say that *Coco* changed her relationship with the public. Peering through the curtains watching the theater fill up every night, she saw the excitement on the people's faces. Many of her fans returned night after night, usually fervent young men who waited for her outside the stage door, smart enough not to ask for an autograph but merely content to see her up close. "People kiss me in the street," she wrote in wonder to her friend and director Tony Harvey. "Just go by and say 'I adore you.' So terribly touching . . . [T]hey simulate a hug or throw a kiss. It is really quite extraordinary."

She'd never known anything like this before. Even with all the accolades that had begun with *The African Queen* and continued up through *Long Day's Journey into Night* and *Guess Who's Coming to Dinner*, Kate had never really felt the *affection* of the public. Yet onstage in *Coco*, the love had come rushing at her in waves "across the footlights," she said. She felt her public was telling her, "That's all right, Katie. So you can't sing but we get it—we hear you—we feel—we know you." After spending most of her career misunderstood by the public, Hepburn was now indulged—and the sensation was heady.

After her last performance in *Coco*, Kate had walked out onto the stage and displayed perhaps the most authentic emotion she would ever allow the public to witness. "You cannot imagine what an enormously confusing feeling it is," she said, "to have to leave something in the middle which means as much to me as this play did—*does*!"

She was near tears, thanking everyone who'd helped her, from Alan Lerner to Roger Edens. (Notably, Freddie Brisson was not among them.) Yet her deepest gratitude, Kate insisted, went to her fans. "I have had you people," she said, her voice breaking. "It has taught me a great lesson—"

At that moment, someone shouted from the audience, "We love you!"

"You love me," Kate repeated, as if thunderstruck by the words, "and I love you."

Overcome, she bowed to their momentous applause and left the stage in tears. Little Kathy Hepburn had finally found the public acclaim she'd sought all her life.

But now, without *Coco*, where would she continue to find it? No doubt, this was the heart of the anxiety that had compelled Kate to slash and burn her way through *Coco*. She knew she was faced with the task of yet again reinventing her public image, but she also knew that the machinery of that process—studios, columnists, publicists—had irretrievably broken down. Indeed, many of the old guard of Broadway and Hollywood felt out of step in the new era of the late 1960s. The struggle over civil rights and the war in Vietnam was transforming the culture; a new generation of brash young artists, playwrights, and filmmakers had wrested creative control for themselves. In Hollywood, the old Production Code shattered under the artistic weight of new films like *Easy Rider* and *Midnight Cowboy*; on Broadway, *Hair* and *Oh! Calcutta!* made nudity commonplace on the stage. After seeing *Midnight Cowboy*, Cecil Beaton came away feeling "old-fashioned [and] out of date . . . suddenly allied to a world that has long gone."

Many of Hepburn's contemporaries would choose to retire rather than attempt to keep up in this new, youth-oriented arena. Yet after forty years of relentlessly chasing the limelight, it's no surprise that Kate had no interest in following their lead. What she needed to determine, however, was just what kind of career she might have in this new world order. Ruth Gordon had made a splash in *Rosemary's Baby*; she was set to star in one of the era's most definitive films, *Harold and Maude*. But Ruth was a character actress, with room to move, to grow, to change. Stars were more locked into their images.

Kate found her answer in the waves of love that flowed from the audience watching *Coco*. She came to understand that she needed to cultivate a "friend-ship" with her public, she explained. "You have to have that, you know," she said. "You have to have them say, 'You're nice. We like you.' Up till then, I really thought they were my natural enemies and were waiting for me to fall down or break my neck." Now she understood the public might actually *root* for her—but only if it appeared she was rooting for them as well. In the past, she often just "tore up" her fan letters. But now she marshaled a battalion of secretaries to make sure every single letter sent to her was answered on her personal stationery, KATHARINE HOUGHTON HEPBURN embossed at the top.

And so emerged one more incarnation of the Hepburn public image—the Survivor. She was indestructible. No matter the changing times, Kate would always have a place.

Part of her survival was also due to the embrace she'd been given by the youth culture, not only for her liberal turn in *Guess Who's Coming to Dinner* but for a career marked by an iconoclastic difference from the mainstream. Hepburn's legendary independence was now claimed by the emerging feminist movement, her face stenciled onto placards at one "women's lib" rally in New York in 1969, the captions WOMAN HERO printed above her head. Indeed, in February 1970, *McCall's* magazine named Kate "Woman of the Year," putting her strong, scrubbed, smiling face on its cover. "We honor Katharine Hepburn as woman, not actress," the editors wrote. "Miss Hepburn has the traditional feminine virtues in untraditional ways. She is a raving individual. We should have more like her."

Which of her contemporaries, increasingly being put out to pasture, wouldn't have *killed* for such a placement? The *McCall's* tribute has the fingerprints of a shrewd press agent all over it—and if Kate didn't have an official press agent, she still had Garson Kanin, who wrote the piece. In the late 1960s, Kanin seems to have resumed his old role of unofficial advance man for the Hepburn career. In private, recorded conversations with Jack Ford, Kate admitted she'd given Kanin the go-ahead to do the *McCall's* piece.

One anecdote in particular shows Kanin (who may have already been thinking about writing a book about Hepburn) at work manufacturing publicity for his friend. In September 1969, the newspapers were filled with stories of the sensational kidnapping of the teenage son of Dr. Simon Ramo, a wealthy Beverly Hills aerospace executive. The boy was taken into the woods near the Los Angeles Reservoir and tied to a tree, while his kidnappers demanded a huge ransom from his father. Kate, on one of her walks, encountered a policeman who'd been called by the reservoir keeper. She pointed the way to the keeper's house, but with no awareness of the Ramo story, she simply continued on her walk.

Kanin, upon hearing Kate's story, realized she'd had a brush, however tangential, with the headlines. Obviously the police had been at the reservoir to rescue the Ramo boy. The wheels seem to have started turning in Kanin's mind. Since he would recount the Ramo story in detail in his book, it was most likely Kanin who placed calls to various columnists telling them of Kate's "involvement." Within days, Kate was being heralded in the press as a "private eye," likely the phrase Kanin was using to spin the story. Although she'd done nothing more than point the way to the reservoir keeper's house, now Leonard Lyons and others had her leading the team to rescue the boy. KATIE AND THE CAVALRY read one headline.

Garson Kanin proved a very good mythmaker. So did Hepburn herself, even if her special skill was to make it seem as if she was doing nothing of the sort. Yet when she said she was "cultivating a friendship" with her public, what she was doing, in truth, was building her legend and guaranteeing her immortality. Those around her saw this quite plainly. They saw just how determined— and how conscious—Hepburn was to make sure her fame continued into old age and beyond. "Kate was never going to give up," George Cukor told one interviewer. "She'd find a way to be remembered, one way or another."

If *The African Queen* had halted the barrage of poison arrows Kate had been dodging until then, the transformation she experienced in the late 1960s meant that from here on, Hepburn could do no wrong. Even a hysterically bad performance as Hecuba in the international all-star film *The Trojan Women* (1971) brought mostly kind words from critics—even if fellow actors like John Gielgud felt she "doesn't act anymore, only cries in every close-up . . . false and theatrical."

Her public didn't see it that way. "People have just gotten used to me," Hepburn told *Time*. "Now I've become like the Statue of Liberty or something. Now that I've come to an age where they think I might disappear— they're fond of me."

Thirty years earlier, Terry Helburn had written to Kate that she knew there was "nothing allegorical" about her: "I know you are a girl," Terry told her, "and not a Statue of Liberty." Kate herself wasn't so sure. She actually seemed to like the comparison, remembering it for the interview with *Time* and using it often in her later years.

Maybe, in fact, she didn't mind being an allegory. Maybe an allegory was exactly what she wanted to be, if it ensured her legend would emerge triumphant, if the version of her life she increasingly put forth after Spencer's death would be accepted as truth. But while Kate might become "the Great," the girl Terry had referenced—a girl named Kath—was pushed farther and farther into the background until some people never even knew she'd been there.

PROVING SHE'S THE BEST GUY

Jo-udge! *Jo-udge!*"

Asleep in his chair, a newspaper in his lap, George Cukor was startled awake by the slam of his back door and a familiar voice. Sitting next to him was his friend the actor Lon McCallister, who looked up to see the sixty-four-year-old Katharine Hepburn rushing down the hallway with all the force of a hurricane. She brushed past the Georges Braque and Juan Gris hangings and nearly knocked over the bronze bust of Tallulah Bankhead. In khaki pants and black turtleneck, Hepburn was in quite the state, her face red, her arms flailing about.

"He's done it, Jo-udge! That *bastard!* Gone and done it!"

Cukor stood awkwardly, trying to calm her down. "Who, Kate? Who's done what?"

"Garson." Garson—their friend, a survivor of the Entente Cordiale—had written a book about her and Spence. Irene Selznick had called her with the news.

"You must be as mad as a hatter," Kate had told Irene. "He *couldn't* be writing a book, for Christ's sake, about *me.*"

But in the spring of 1971, galleys of a 307-page book titled *Tracy and Hepburn: An Intimate Memoir* made their way into the hands of well-placed New Yorkers, Irene among them. Soon theatrical circles were abuzz. Released late that year by Viking, *Tracy and Hepburn* was an instant best seller, trading the number-one slot back and forth with Joseph Lash's book on another iconic American couple, *Eleanor and Franklin*. Kanin's tome was also excerpted in *Vogue* and serialized in the *New York Daily News*. Across buses and billboards its cover was plastered, and its author interviewed on radio and television. In early 1972, Kate couldn't open a newspaper without seeing a spread for the book.

Kanin would say he hadn't anticipated Kate's outraged reaction. Writing the book, he'd seen it as a valentine to her. In fact, he wasn't doing anything all that much different from what he'd done in the past, as her screenwriter or unofficial press agent. He was shaping and disseminating the Hepburn legend the way he had for years, and always before, he'd received her blessing. Indeed, *Tracy and Hepburn* grew out of the article Kanin had written about Kate for *McCall's*, for which the star had, after some prodding, given a thumb's-up. But Kanin must have known a book would be pushing the envelope, so he kept mum as he put it together.

No doubt, Kate had seen the *McCall's* piece as she had other key coverage. Like Adela Rogers St. Johns, Lupton Wilkinson, and others, Kanin had provided the latest blueprint for a new-and-improved Hepburn legend. "Keeping Kate up-to-date," he said of his efforts soon after the article appeared. In this latest incarnation, Kate was more than just a heroine. She was almost superhuman, "one of those enviable creatures who can learn to do anything," Kanin wrote. She was tough, resilient, a brilliant actress, and a good cook, too. Kanin even credited Kate, in a roundabout way, for the success of *Hello, Dolly!*—simply because she'd once let Tyrone Guthrie (the producer of the original play) stay at her New York house.

But Kanin had to know that Kate was not about to embrace his book the way she had his article. His editors at Viking had pushed for "the scoop" on Tracy and Hepburn, and Gar had done his best to deliver. In his pages, Kate and Spence interact in closer company than they'd ever been shown doing before. Kate cooks his meals. She cleans his house. She seems to be living with him.

Turning in the manuscript, Kanin may have harbored hopes that Kate would eventually come around to seeing its public relations benefits. But no doubt he knew her initial reaction would be negative. Why else would he have kept it a secret from her? Alerted by Irene that spring, however, Hepburn immediately wrote to Garson and asked him to kill the book, even at that late stage. He refused. "Now then I think that is *wrong*," Kate fumed.

It's hard to dispute her charge that it was all about money. Kanin once told Dick Hepburn, "When I write a line and I don't hear a dollar sign go off, I erase it"—and in the late 1960s, there weren't a lot of dollar signs going off for Kanin. The films and plays he directed had all bombed, and while Ruth was riding high as a character actress, the nearly sixty-year-old Gar, even with his long hair and love beads, saw little opportunity for himself. A book on Tracy and Hepburn had the potential to change his fortunes—and it did. "Gar Kanin advertising his book on Fifth Avenue," Kate groaned to Tony Harvey. "Oh, oh, wicked."

Kanin was clearly aware that this "valentine" had its sharp edges—not in its depiction of Kate, for she came off without surprises—but in its implications about her life with Tracy. Gar may have reasoned that since others were cashing in on the speculation about the famous Hollywood pair, he should do so as well; after all, as the couple's original screenwriter, he believed he'd created the team. In March 1969, a biography of Tracy by Larry Swindell had given the distinct impression that Spence and Kate had been lovers. But it lacked the up-close observations intimate friends could offer. Kanin aimed to fill in the gaps.

Actually, he did more than that. He created the archetype of "Spence and Kate," writing them as if they were their screen characters. In Kanin's book, Tracy calls people "chowderhead" and Kate creates words like *zulac* simply because she likes the way they sound. Tracy is bullish, stubborn, wise. Kate is fluttery, stubborn, wise. Basing his tales on old clippings (themselves often the creations of studio publicists), Kanin encoded the various myths that would become gospel for other writers over the next thirty years. Such stories would be repeated endlessly: Kate unexpectedly takes a shower at a house she's considering renting just to test the water pressure; Kate silences a Manhattan construction crew from interfering with matinees of *Coco*; Kate wears platform shoes to intimidate men.

All of Kanin's considerable screenwriting talent was brought to bear on the narrative of *Tracy and Hepburn*. In stream-of-consciousness style, he moves in and out of the lives of his two famous friends, his vignettes like scenes from familiar movies. Kate and Gar stand up for Laurence Olivier and Vivien Leigh in a wacky wedding ceremony straight out of Howard Hawks. Tracy postures as a common man not unlike Jimmy Stewart in *Mr. Smith Goes to Washington*. A page of dialogue is set in an RKO dressing room, circa 1938, with Ginger Rogers, Barbara Stanwyck, and Lucille Ball all discussing Kate. It reads exactly like *Stage Door*. ("She's so *gorgeous*. How can she miss?" "Takes more than gorgeous, sugar.")

Two-thirds of *Tracy and Hepburn* is dialogue, most of it from the mouths of Kate and Spence themselves, sometimes twenty or thirty years after the fact. There are long reflections on life from Tracy, quirky ramblings from Hepburn. Gar would tell interviewers these pithy remarks had all been written down, verbatim, in his journals. In truth, Marian Seldes (whom Garson would marry after Ruth Gordon's death) confirmed that Kanin's journals were not nearly so specific. Instead, he was writing as the talented scenarist he was, turning real people into characters. The Tracy of *Tracy and Hepburn* is not the tormented, childlike man his friends knew. Rather, he is the sturdy, sagacious, on-screen Tracy.

Even in the 1940s, there was a sense that Kanin wasn't a stickler for the truth. *Pageant* magazine observed, "Once in a while, Kanin's love of story runs away with him." Kanin's private letters prove this tendency. He'd write to Cukor or Wilder or Felix Frankfurter in story form, often with dialogue and sometimes from the point of view of a third character—his dog, perhaps, or some great star of the past, like Sarah Bernhardt or Eleonora Duse. Inconvenient facts were never allowed to spoil the fun. For example, in *Tracy and Hepburn*, Kate might be eccentric, but she's *never* narcissistic. She's simply "true to [her] personal vision"—like Thoreau or Jane Addams, Kanin tells us.

With such flattery, Kate might have been expected to greet Kanin's book with open arms. But while she no doubt recognized its expediency—the book was billed as "a joyous tribute to two extraordinary people"—she was uneasy with how Kanin had substantiated long-held presumptions about her relationship with Tracy. It was one thing to let people think what they wanted. Now Garson had pushed the stories of Kate and Spencer right to the edge.

"There I was in the house with Spence," Kate grumbled in private conversation with John Ford, "and I was doing the cooking and everything else and it would be hard to miss the fact that we weren't rather close *friends*, just to put it mildly." Of course, in giving the impression that Tracy and Hepburn were lovers, Kanin knew exactly what he was doing—even if, when challenged on the veracity of his account in later years, he'd react with his defensive "I never said they *made* love" statement.

Much of Kate's pique with Kanin seemed to stem from her vaunted sense of privacy and propriety. "After all," she told John Ford, "Louise Tracy is still alive." But there were likely other reasons for her unease as well. She was canny enough to know there were people still living—Louise among them—who would see through Kanin's mythmaking, people who understood the more nuanced truths of the Hepburn-Tracy relationship. To Ford, Kate admitted that most of what Kanin wrote was "a lot of nonsense."

Close friends were left shaking their heads over the book's implications of a romantic, sexual intimacy. Irene Selznick was reportedly aghast. One friend of Tracy's asked, "Why not tell the story like it was? Why imply more than the truth? Tell the story of two people who had a wonderful friendship and shared a great deal together, but who came to live like brother and sister." According to Gavin Lambert, George Cukor called the book "one last Tracy-Hepburn screenplay from the pen of Garson Kanin."

"I think Kate was embarrassed by Kanin's book," said the publicist Alan Cahan, who worked with Hepburn in the 1970s, "because she knew people would think it was gilding the lily. I think Spence would've been stunned by it."

But no matter what insiders said, the press and public bought the package without reservations. "As a hopeless Tracy-Hepburn buff," wrote the critic Bob Cromie in the *Chicago Tribune*, "I found myself fascinated by this backstage glimpse of what they were made of." Even the usually discerning Vincent Canby of the *New York Times* wrote a long, glowing account of "the love affair between The Baked Potato and The Dessert"—terms Kate had used to describe Tracy and herself (or rather, that Kanin had *said* she'd used). Few critics questioned Kanin's account of Spence and Kate. Charles Champlin thought he'd brought us "closer to their privacy than we have ever been." *Publishers Weekly* said it simply: Kanin had proved "Tracy and Hepburn were *real*."

What was real was the crush of reporters. To Kate, it all seemed rather like an echo of the old days, when the newsmen chased her down the pier and she teased them with quips about colored babies. Back then, they hadn't gotten her sense of humor, but now they seemed to enjoy their romps with her—but not nearly as much as Kate enjoyed them herself.

On a spring day in the early 1970s, her devoted friend and fan David Eichler at her side, Hepburn scrambled from cab to cab trying to keep ahead of a photographer. Bubbling over with laughter as she slid across the taxi seats and out the doors on the other side, Kate finally could keep running no longer, and turned to face her pursuer. They shook hands. Snapping her picture, the photographer called her a "good egg."

Another time, in London, Kate ran all over the West End with Phyllis trying to outwit one tabloid's henchman. Unbeknownst to her, the wily shutterbug managed to snap a blurry photo of her as she hurried from a car.

The next day, seeing it on the front page, Hepburn was playfully peeved. "He *did* get a picture of me after all," she cried. "He could have saved us the gas!" More luck was had in Camden Town when she shook off another newshound. "Now I'm one up on them," she crowed, puffing up her chest the way Jimmy was so fond of doing. "I love winning. I like to prove I'm the best guy."

For all her griping about Kanin's book, Kate seemed to enjoy the renewed attention it brought to her. The *Coco* tour had ended several months before, with no immediate projects on the horizon. *Tracy and Hepburn,* however, kept her square in the public eye. If she'd had any worries about keeping her fame alive post-*Coco,* they were proven pointless now. The increased media attention on Hepburn in the early 1970s seems to have chased away some of the depression and anger that had consumed her since Spencer's death.

Yet there was no getting away from the fact that Gar had transgressed, and he had to be punished. Never before had one of her inner circle been so indiscreet. What was left of the Entente Cordiale now crumbled, with George Cukor taking Kate's side. "Reports tell me your friend and mine, Mr. Kanin, has been suffering from migraine headaches," Cukor wrote to Kate. "I don't think it's all conscience but I don't remember him being troubled by them before *Tracy and Hepburn.* Nothing, however, seems to slow him down in hustling his book . . . When I think of all the fun we had, I'm inclined to be sentimental, but then something happens and my heart hardens agin' him."

Cukor's hostility stung. Kanin told friends he thought the real reason for the director's ire was the fact that he hadn't been "sufficiently noted" in the book. Gar did try to salvage the relationship. "Before we permit our thirty-five-year-old friendship to expire ignominiously," he wrote to Cukor after the book's publication, "I think we should add a half hour to it and exchange our views." As best as can be determined, Cukor did not respond to the letter. Ruth and Gar were, in fact, iced out by all of Kate's inner circle.

Yet when John Ford suggested she sue, Hepburn refused. "They are great friends of mine," she protested. "They still are. I'm very fond of them."

On some level she must have known Kanin had given her a great gift, though it was one she could never acknowledge to anyone as such. David Eichler said she "loathed" the book not for anything it said but because of "how Garson came to write it." Not once, in fact, did Kate condemn the book in the press. "Why should she?" Kanin asked one columnist. "The story was written with taste."

But he was clearly aware of the real issue many insiders like Cukor, Irene

Selznick, and Joe Mankiewicz had with the book. In at least one interview, Kanin was on the defensive. "At the end you still [don't] know whether or not those two people were ever lovers," he said. "And you know why? Because I don't know. They were close friends of mine. We worked a lot together. But what else went on, I just can't tell you."

Yet he'd done more than anyone else to give a certain impression. In fact, Kanin seemed particularly determined to dispel those pesky rumors of bisexuality. He makes a point to tell us that Tracy had few interests: "Theater, literature, Catholicism, politics and the opposite sex." As for Kate, he writes that she started painting because she was having "man troubles." ("Absurd," said James Prideaux. "She started painting because she liked to paint.")

In the *McCall's* piece, Kanin was even more specific. "A lady cannot wear [pants] habitually without—shall we say?—'causing talk.' I have heard some of that talk, and so has Kate. I get mad, but it makes her laugh. The notion that she is anti-feminine, that she wishes to compete, that she is a tomboy can be held only by the snide or ignorant. As for her, she couldn't care less. She knows she is a belle. If not, how come she has had so many beaus?"

Though much of the *McCall's* piece was lifted verbatim for *Tracy and Hepburn*, this little spiel didn't make it into the book. Kanin later admitted that Kate—his "belle"—had pointed out "a few things [in the article] of which she did not approve." This was likely one of Kate's objections, and so Kanin nixed it. Somehow arguing that Hepburn was *not* a tomboy seemed the height of absurdity.

Even more absurd was the infamous story he told, also in *McCall's,* about Kate's refusing to accept the possibility of male homosexuality. "I don't believe it," Kate supposedly said. "Don't believe what?" Kanin replied. "What you say about men and men," said Kate. "I mean, what would be the point?"

Whereupon, Kanin—with the help of Spencer Tracy—explained to Kate ("like high school biology teachers") the facts of gay male sex.

Kanin knew how to create compelling scenes. "We all sat there, quite still, for about two and a half months," he wrote facetiously. "Life slowly returned to Kate's face. She lit a fresh cigarette, inhaled, exhaled, and said calmly, 'I don't believe it.' "

"You don't huh?" Tracy asked.

"No, I don't," Kate supposedly replied. "It's too ridiculous."

The conversation, as Kanin described it, seems extremely unlikely. Yet there *is* some underlying truth. Not only did the anecdote serve to distance Tracy and Hepburn from lingering whispers of deviance, but it also pointed out a very real characteristic of Kate. Though she was hardly as clueless as Kanin made her sound, she once admitted to John Huston she could be "kind of naïve about these things"—these things being sex. Always proficient at seeing only what she wanted to see, Hepburn remained at least partly in the dark about Bobby Helpmann's life, writing in the foreword to his authorized biography that she "didn't know who or what Helpmann was." Similarly, she had never been able to grasp what *Suddenly, Last Summer* was all about—reportedly refusing ever to see the film and rarely mentioning it in recollections of her work. And when, years later, James Prideaux took her to see the gay-themed film *Maurice*, she squirmed in her seat. After so many years with sexually conflicted men, Kate was distinctly uncomfortable with seeing an affirming, unapologetically gay love story on the screen.

For all its obfuscations and distractions, what Kanin's book did was create the paradigm of Kate and Spence that the world took to their hearts—and which Kate herself would try to live up to for the rest of her years. Like everyone else, she seemed to succumb to the book's vision. Even before Kanin had taken pen to hand, Kate had begun to romanticize her life with Spence. Conveniently forgotten were all the troubles and long separations. To Maie Casey, she wrote that she'd been "totally engrossed in [Spencer] for almost thirty years." She now believed she'd been "so much luckier than most."

For a woman easily susceptible to the illusion of traditional domesticity, the myth of her relationship with Tracy as presented by Kanin was irresistible. "She looked back on [her time with Tracy] with a lot of romance and rose-colored glasses," said her sister Peg Perry. "She remembered the good, not the bad. And who wouldn't? You think back, you remember, and you make [the past] what you want it to be."

Part of her *wanted* to believe in Kanin's version of the past. Indeed, for a time, Kate seemed to jump on the bandwagon he'd set into motion. On the set of *The Trojan Women*, for example, she was particularly revealing to one reporter: "I have only had one big love in my life, as everyone knows, even though we never married . . . I don't speak of erotic exaltation, that soon passes . . . Spencer and I succeeded in creating something more than ordinary love. We had a secret understanding, a total understanding."

Straight from Kate's mouth, this description of her relationship with Spencer was more honest and accurate than anything Kanin had written. It wasn't "erotic exaltation"; it was "more than ordinary." Since the world was talking about her and Tracy anyway, Kate seems to have decided to put in her own two cents—and then some. For the next year or so, despite impressions to the contrary, Tracy was not a forbidden topic in interviews with the star. In late 1973, the writer Charles Higham approached Hepburn for an article for the *New York Times* and found her only too glad to chat about Spence. When Higham told her he was using the interview as the basis of a book-length biography, she did not protest, but rather provided him with the phone numbers of her friends. In August 1975, she gave a long interview to *Ladies' Home Journal*, showing off the photographs of Tracy she kept by her bed and the little sculpture she'd made of his head.

Her cooperation with the press is not surprising. By the early 1970s, Kate was basking in the glow of romantic legend. If Louise had called her a rumor in 1967, half a decade later Kate had been shown to be anything but. The world now regarded her as Tracy's unofficial widow; Louise, by contrast, was the unyielding spouse who had kept them apart. One article said Kate had been forced to live out a "back street" kind of existence, but she'd done so with dignity and honor—and most of all with *love*. In death, Spencer belonged to her in a way he never had in life.

The public took their story to heart. "It was common knowledge," the critic Julia Whedon wrote in the *Washington Post*, "that the affection and admiration we witnessed on-screen was also the real thing. Having carefully trained ourselves to disbelieve in True Romance, Tracy and Hepburn made us believe all over again."

Suddenly, members of the press were congratulating themselves for the "quite astonishing and favoring reticence" with which they had treated Tracy and Hepburn for all those years. Charles Champlin thought it was due not just to the "impeccable taste" of Kate and Spence but also to the fact that "the writers understood that they were in the presence of an association at once so beautiful and genuine and so shaded with a sadness that a kind of conspiracy of compassionate silence was the only conceivable response."

Forgotten were the blind items in the columns of Hopper and Connolly, the sensational article in *Inside Story*, the revealing piece by Bill Davidson in *Look*. Forgotten, too, was the more sophisticated understanding of the Tracy-Hepburn relationship that had once permeated Hollywood. Pronouncements like Whedon's and Champlin's led one friend of Tracy's to remark that if Spence had lived longer than he did, "and could see what his relationship with Hepburn was made into, he wouldn't have recognized it."

But by 1976, Kate suddenly stopped talking about Spencer. Reportedly, she'd heard Louise was upset. No doubt she understood why. For a few years anyway, whenever Kate spoke about Spencer, it was about the *actor*, not the man. In truth, she didn't need to say any more. Kanin's book—and the dozens of articles that appeared in its wake—had said it all.

On the screen, Kate Hepburn is packing a pistol and wearing a cowboy hat. "I suppose," she says, looking into the camera, already starting to shake with the family tremor, "I grew up more forceful and independent than a woman should be."

They were the words of Eula Goodnight, Kate's character in *Rooster Cogburn*, the 1975 picture she made with John Wayne. But they pretty much summed up Hepburn's own core beliefs—a view she'd held of herself and her gender since her earliest days. Women, she believed, could make out fine on their own if need be. Both Eula Goodnight and Katharine Hepburn were proof of that. But the natural order gave authority to the man. Now, approaching seventy, Kate seemed determined to make a case not for the independent way in which she'd lived her life but for the way she believed she *should* have lived it.

In one of the most ironic twists in Hepburn's life, just at the moment when she seemed finally in step with the zeitgeist—hailed as "the first Mod"—she repositioned herself squarely against the times. It was as if she didn't know how to be anything other than contrary. Always, when conventional wisdom said up, she said down. If friends called something green, she called it blue. But Kate's rejection of the more liberal parts of 1970s culture went deeper. Her sister Peg thought she became "more conservative" as she got older. In fact, Hepburn's latter-day conservatism was merely a manifestation of what she'd always believed—and what she now hoped, through the stories of her life with Tracy, would be her legacy. Even if she hadn't lived a conventional life, she might still get credit for one.

Hepburn knew the dangers of being too political. The early 1970s were shaping up to be very much like the late 1940s. A conservative government was targeting a liberal intelligentsia. With good reason, Kate was not eager to be caught in that net again. Ever since *The African Queen*, she'd tried to transcend politics. During the *Coco* tour, she was no doubt pleased by one reporter's assessment: "Although Miss Hepburn has always been her own woman, done her own thing, dressed as she liked and been a complete individualist, she has never been identified with causes." Twenty-four years later, Henry Wallace and that flaming red dress had largely been forgotten.

In fact, Kate was proving yet again she was her father's daughter, not her mother's. She shared Hep's repugnance for the welfare state. "We have gotten into a terrible situation in the world today where the law is representing the weak," she railed in a tape-recorded conversation with John Ford. "[It] is protecting entirely the moron, and the worthy person who's sort of hewed the line and dug the potato patch and planted the potatoes and kept the thing going is absolutely disregarded because they say, 'That poor little thing there has such a problem.'" When Ford's grandson interjected that he thought Kate was more liberal than that, she said, "I'm liberal, but . . . I think we are bringing up an irresponsible group of people."

She'd been raised, she insisted, in an age of heroes. "Now they make movies about anti-heroes. Anti-heroes are bores. Now they write about the dust under the rug. If you're so damned complicated that I can't understand you at all, then I don't want to know you."

In public, however, her liberal reputation remained. Both *The Madwoman of Chaillot* and *The Trojan Women* had espoused leftist philosophies, the latter being a forceful parable against the Vietnam War. The filmed version of Euripides' play was dedicated to "all those who oppose the oppression of man by man." The film was used, in fact, as leftist propaganda in some places. Just as President Nixon was launching heavy air strikes against supply camps in Laos and Cambodia, the *Washington Post* wrote, "The state of human affairs being what it is, the reasons for seeing [*The Trojan Women* are] compelling."

Yet Kate's reputation for liberalism would be increasingly at odds with how she really felt about things. She never spoke out against the war in Vietnam, for example, perhaps out of consideration to her sister Peg, who had little tolerance for the war's critics since her son had gone missing. In May 1970, when four students were killed at an antiwar protest at Kent State University, Kate—then at her height in *Coco*—had been strongly opposed to saying anything about the tragedy onstage. Furious with her attitude, Kate's costar Rene Auberjonois had turned on his heel and slammed into his dressing room. "All right, all right," Kate said, banging on his door. "Write me a speech." After the final curtain, she asked the audience to stand while she read a treatise on the sanctity of life. She was careful, however, to avoid making a direct political statement.

Hepburn's discomfort with the cultural changes of the 1970s wasn't so much a repudiation of her traditionally liberal politics as it was merely a reflection of how she'd always seen herself and the world. The sexual revolution horrified her. "Everyone's jumping into bed with everyone else," she said. "It's the fastest way of dissipating one's self." For a woman who'd always found the sex act rather unpleasant, all this focus on sex was mystifying. James Prideaux remembered her angrily storming out of a film when a nude scene came on.

And as ever, women's issues seemed utterly foreign to her. Some feminists expected the daughter of Kit Hepburn to be outspoken in her support for women's liberation, but Kate would have nothing to do with it. In her autobiographical screenplay, "Me and Phyllis," she wrote a scene in which she's stranded with a flat tire. As cars speed past, she sarcastically thanks "women's lib." When asked about her support for the women's movement, she tended to dodge the question. "Not for or against it," she told one reporter, adding, "Women don't want to be liberated from love."

This was her new mantra, and the underlying message of *Rooster Cogburn*, a film that would establish a new, conservative Katharine Hepburn. By agreeing to make a film with John Wayne, known for his far-right politics, Kate left many in the counterculture feeling betrayed. They had loved her, called her one of their own. Now she seemed to stand for something very different. She appeared only too glad to take part in a picture that glorified an aggressive vigilante who is "proud to shoot killers." Though Hepburn plays a strong, feisty woman, the film is hardly a treatise on equality between the sexes. When, at the end, Eula Goodnight tells Rooster Cogburn (Wayne) that he's a credit to his sex, he doesn't return the compliment. Maleness is something to be admired; Eula is simply there to pay homage to how well Rooster embodies it.

Of course, Hepburn had made similar films—nearly all of them with Tracy—that had subverted her presumed feminist image before. What was different now was that the world had moved on. Real feminist films were being made. There was an audience for movies that offered a more modern message, and Kate could have made them. She was still riding high in the industry's esteem; she could have worked with one of the new filmmakers. John Schlesinger, for example, who received the Oscar for Best Director in 1970 for *Midnight Cowboy*, was interested in working with her, but she never returned his calls.

Instead, she chose the old-fashioned *Rooster Cogburn*, produced by Hal Wallis, with whom she'd made *The Rainmaker* back in 1956. Little more than *The African Queen* set in the Wild West, but without any of that film's true egalitarian spirit, *Cogburn* seems to have been Kate's attempt to repeat her success of twenty years before. Girlish and fluttery around her costar, she gushed over Wayne in interviews. One reporter revealed how her eyes "shone with admiration" as she gazed up at the Duke, a comment surely intended to conjure memories of the heartfelt look she gave to Tracy in *Guess Who's Coming to Dinner*. MISS HEPBURN SAYS IT'S LOVE read one headline about the pair. Rushing to Wayne's side, she told him, "I was *born* to be your leading lady." Then came her oft-repeated comment to *TV Guide* about the manly Wayne being so refreshing "in these gay times."

By 1975, Kate had clearly made a choice in the great cultural divide. She was no longer interested in being considered radical. Eccentric, maybe, but eccentric in the way the American frontier woman had been: tough and resilient, able to chop wood and haul it home on her back, but always walking a couple of steps behind her man. She was more Betsy Ross than Susan B. Anthony—or indeed, Kit Hepburn. Not anymore did she embrace current political movements. She'd been burned once before doing that, and besides, true heroes were above politics. Heading into her seventies, Hepburn had her eye on history, seeming determined to prove she and Lady Liberty might hold the same torch after all.

On a cold, windy April afternoon, Kate pointed out to David Eichler the daffodil, tulip, and grape hyacinth bulbs pushing through the soil of her garden, tucked behind her New York town house in the Turtle Bay courtyard. In fallow periods of her career—increasingly common by the late 1970s—one could find her here, kneeling in the dirt, planting her bulbs, weeding out the grass, snipping flowers to place in great bunches throughout her house.

Getting up and down might not have been as easy as it once was, but for a woman in her seventies she was still incredibly agile, especially considering she'd had hip replacement surgery in early 1974. Daniel Woodruff, a young man she'd met through George Cukor, recalled taking a bike ride with her around this time during one of Kate's stays in California. When he heard a noise, Woodruff turned to see Hepburn's bike run into a gulley and the great star fly over the handlebars. Horribly alarmed, the young man hurried to her side, but Kate simply got up, dusted off her khakis, and started riding again.

As ever, her chief physical complaint was her skin. Various treatments had never quite put an end to her recurrent melanomas and blotching. In December 1971, a letter from Chester Erskine reported she'd had a "treatment to her face" and was recovering well. A year later, she wrote to Tony Harvey, "I'm putting the potion on all my spots and hope they'll disappear." She looked "a bit frostbitten and red," she said, and was heading to Massachusetts General Hospital for another treatment. Afterward, observed James Prideaux, she'd be covered in black scabs that itched terribly.

Despite the public image that Hepburn had no vanity, she *hated* the ravages of age. She once screamed at Prideaux when he dared call her a "senior citizen." Many of her face surgeries were more cosmetic than medically necessary. In her autobiographical screenplay, Kate penned a poignant scene at a mirror, tenderly addressing her reflection as "dear," lamenting her freckles and liver spots and shaking head.

In time, this trembling would become her predominant physical condition. One can first detect her quivering ever so slightly in *Long Day's Journey into Night*, when she was only fifty-six. The public didn't really notice, however, until she was onstage in *Coco*. During the run, the columnist Jody Jacobs left a message for Freddie Brisson reporting she'd heard a rumor that Kate's "Parkinson's disease" was so bad that she'd be leaving the show. For the next two decades, the story that Hepburn had Parkinson's would often be reported as fact.

In truth, Kate's shaking was diagnosed as essential tremor, an inherited neurologic disorder. Her paternal grandfather, Reverend Hepburn, had shaken so badly toward the end of his life that he could barely lift a glass to his mouth. Essential tremor usually affects the hands but can also cause the head to shake, as it did for Kate. Still, she integrated the condition into her life and work fairly well in the beginning; it seemed to underscore the tremulous nobility of her characters. One actor actually asked her how she did it, thinking it was "a great bit of business."

For the most part, the tremors were disguised in Kate's two, nearly back-to-back films in 1973, adaptations of Edward Albee's *A Delicate Balance* and Tennessee Williams's *The Glass Menagerie*. The first, the story of a family's disintegration when two houseguests overstay their welcome, offered Hepburn a reunion with Ely Landau, who'd produced *Long Day's Journey*. The film's director, Tony Richardson, thought Kate was perfect to play the "inflexible, authoritarian" matriarch Agnes. Kate herself admitted to similarities with the character: "I'm a very private person. Here were these people [in the play], miserable though they may be, and they wanted to keep their 'shell' intact. When two people came in and established a position in the household, they became threatening. The intruders expressed opinions. You don't want people to express opinions in your house. You only want your own opinion to be expressed. I think all of us banish people when they intrude in any sense."

But where she was perfect for Albee, she was hopelessly miscast in Williams. She'd been reluctant to take on a part originated by her idol, Laurette Taylor, arguing she was too thin, too sharp, too New England to play a former southern belle. But *Menagerie*'s producer, David Susskind, was determined. When her good friend Tony Harvey signed on as director, Kate finally agreed. The production also allowed her to remain in London, where she'd shot *A Delicate Balance*, and she jumped at any chance to stay on longer in a country whose manners and sensibility she much preferred to her own.

Perhaps it was Kate's fear of competing with the sanctified memory of Taylor that led her to take the extraordinary step of trying to alter Williams's dialogue. Letters to Harvey reveal whole stretches of dialogue she was attempting to rewrite herself, in the hope she could make the character more her own. It did little good. Kate's Amanda Wingfield is one of her weakest characterizations. Never good with accents, she based her southern drawl on her father's Virginia cousins. It comes and goes, sometimes in the middle of a speech, as if Kate suddenly remembered she was supposed to be playing southern.

Except for Christina Drayton in *Guess Who's Coming to Dinner*, Kate never managed to play convincing mothers; her best-known parents, Violet Venable and Mary Tyrone, were anything but maternal. Here, as the faded beauty trying to relive her life through her adult children, Kate never makes us believe she is Amanda, despite how much she bats her eyelashes. Throughout, she remains Katharine Hepburn, an actress trying very hard to play something other than herself. Reviewers were kind—rarely were they ever anything but by this point—though John J. O'Connor of the *New York Times* felt obliged to point out that Amanda was "occasionally, only occasionally, overly dominated by . . . a strong-willed, intensely mannered actress named Katharine Hepburn."

Still, *A Delicate Balance* and *The Glass Menagerie* marked Kate's last attempts to really push herself as an actress. After this point, James Prideaux said, she seemed less interested in expanding her craft than in maintaining her fame, a return to the mindset of her youth. No longer could Prideaux be honest with her about what he thought of her performances; she only wanted to hear praise. "She was all ego in that regard," he said. "The legend of Katharine Hepburn had begun to take over the person Katharine Hepburn."

But concern for keeping her career alive was very real. Starring roles for older actresses were rare, and while the best ones usually went to Hepburn these days, even Kate felt the pinch. *A Delicate Balance* was released to a few selected theaters in December 1973; considered an "art-house" film, it soon disappeared, later being aired on television. *Menagerie*, on the other hand, was seen as a television production from the start, Kate's first for the medium. Broadcast on Sunday night, December 16, the film was hailed as a "special TV event," interrupted by only one commercial break. But, despite a repeat showing on January 20, television was a fleeting art form in those days, and *Menagerie* was soon just a memory. Kate wouldn't have been amiss to fear the same for her career.

If she wasn't going to be seen on the screen, she'd keep the spotlight on her by *talking*. "For a while there, it seemed you could never open a magazine or turn on the television without seeing Kate," said James Prideaux. "There were times when I wanted to say, 'Enough already! Shut up!' "

Alan Jay Lerner thought Kate talked "for talking's sake." In fact, she talked in order to keep herself in the public eye, to sidestep the obscurity that enveloped other stars her age. Shortly after she finished *The Glass Menagerie*, Hepburn accepted an offer to be interviewed on *The Dick Cavett Show*, a favorite late-night talkfest. Arriving early, she found lamps hanging limply, cords tangled across the stage, chairs not yet set up properly. Expecting her later that evening, the crew wasn't prepared, and Kate was not happy. "Don't tell me what's wrong," she snapped at some underling. "Just fix it." She was unaware that the cameras were already turning, preserving a record of the offscreen Hepburn to counterpoint the charming woman millions would watch later on Cavett's show.

What came out of that soundstage, of course, was the interview that defined Katharine Hepburn from the 1970s and beyond, a video version to supplant Adela Rogers St. Johns and Lupton Wilkinson. "Do you want to hear the story of my life?" Kate barked at Cavett. "I presume that's why I'm here." The host never quite recovered from the storm of her entrance, fumbling and fawning throughout. But in the course of 180 minutes, broadcast in two segments over two successive nights, October 2 and 3, 1973, we got the whole, magnificent Kate Hepburn story, from her glorious bohemian childhood, complete with the collected wisdom of Hep and Kit, through her great film triumphs, achieved not through any ambition for fame on her part (not her!) but simply through luck and hard work.

The Cavett interview would be best remembered, however, for its presentation of Hepburn as sage, an image of the star that defined her later years. She became, according to her friend John Dayton, "the grandmother of the world," known for dispensing her wisdom. Indeed, the *Washington Post* would headline its review of the Cavett show as HEPBURN ON LIFE AND DEATH—not on art or acting or movies. Kate had become a visionary: "Without discipline," she intoned, sounding like a preacher in a pulpit, "there's no way to live."

Without a studio audience, Kate was playing just to Cavett, the crew, and Phyllis. It didn't matter. She acted the part of Kate with as much charm and effervescence as if she'd been on a Broadway stage. Her friends said that's just how she could be in small settings at home as well, completely dominating the conversation, steering it only where she wanted it to go, but remaining charming and fascinating nonetheless. That was certainly the case on Cavett's show. She enchanted *millions* on two nights—by far, her biggest audience yet.

It wasn't all an act, either. In her own way, Kate was being very honest in how she saw herself. "Cold sober, I find myself absolutely fascinating" is the line that's been most quoted. But another offered more insight. When Cavett said he felt very "in tune" with her, Kate replied that was "her business." Cavett seemed surprised. "Do you mean," he asked, "when you smile at me, it's acting?"

"Puttin' on the charm," Kate quipped.

The stint on *Cavett* was definitely part of her "business." It was intended to keep interest alive in "the Creature"—as Hepburn had already begun calling her public self. Critically, this time the publicity would be on *her* terms. If Kanin had co-opted her fame for his own ends, now Kate would compel the same kind of media attention on her own, keeping control in her own hands. True, she had Ely Landau's publicists helping her along (the interview was ostensibly to promote *A Delicate Balance*), but the entire Cavett experience was largely her doing. She showed up at the studio with only Phyllis at her side. She took over the host's job and basically interviewed herself. Wisely, she chose to sidestep the hot-potato issue of Spencer, except to talk about his acting. Instead, Kate concentrated on herself, on presenting Hepburn the Survivor to a new generation. "Smartest thing I ever did," Kate would tell James Prideaux, after the interview generated considerable praise and interest.

The business of being charming didn't end with Cavett. There was a long interview in the *Times* of London with David Robinson around the same time. In 1974, there were dozens of pieces about the making of *Rooster Cogburn*. In March 1975, *McCall's* excerpted Higham's book, putting Kate on the cover and using her cooperation with the author to banner: THE TRUTH ABOUT HER 25-YEAR LOVE AFFAIR WITH SPENCER TRACY. In August, Kate held a long, detailed conversation with *Ladies' Home Journal*, and in January 1976, she sat for a lengthy face-to-face interview with the *New York Times*. All that—and still she was called "reclusive."

But immortality, after all, demanded effort. In the mid-1970s Kate reversed the direction of her public life. From here on, challenging herself as an actress—her hallmark for the last twenty-five years, what had set her apart from the others—would no longer be her motivation. Instead, she would play only *herself*—Kate the Survivor, the Sage, the Beloved Character. Writers and directors proved accommodating to this goal. Explaining to George Cukor how he'd written the lead for Kate's proposed film *Travels with My Aunt*, based on

Graham Greene's novel, Chester Erskine said, "The character of Aunt Augusta in my script can be easily explained: she is Katharine Hepburn."

Kate never made *Travels with My Aunt*—her delays eventually caused her to be replaced with Maggie Smith—so it would be *Rooster Cogburn* that marked the beginning of this new phase in her career. *Rooster* was no "art-house" pretension like *A Delicate Balance*, doomed to disappear within days of its opening. Rather, it was released into dozens of theaters nationwide, advertised in print and on the radio. Even more important, *Cogburn* showed Hepburn not as some brittle actress striving to display her "art" but as the female version of John Wayne's all-American hero. Indeed, *Time* magazine noted that the film's conservative crew had adorned their cars with bumper stickers reading GOD BLESS JOHN WAYNE. On one of them someone had scribbled an addition: "And Sister Kate too."

To Cavett, she'd called herself "uncomplicated," and with her aversion to introspection, in many ways she was. Yet neither was her life as straightforward as she wanted us to think. In Hepburn's last decades, the distinction between her public and private lives was starker than ever. No wonder she had felt such empathy for the matriarch of *A Delicate Balance*, who was willing to do anything to "keep her shell intact." For the next twenty years, Kate would try to do the same.

ALWAYS DISCREET UNTIL NOW

When West Hartford police were called to the Hepburn house on Bloomfield Avenue in the middle of a cold February night, they found Kate in the kitchen pacing back and forth, her right hand wrapped in a bloody towel. A middle-aged black woman sat on the floor, her coat torn in several places. She said nothing as Kate, Phyllis, and Dr. Hepburn's widow, Madeline, began bombarding the four officers with their account of what had just occurred.

"She was hiding in a closet," Kate shouted, holding up her bloody hand. "You see? She bit me!" So deep was the bite, Kate believed, that she might lose her right index finger.

Looking down at the woman on the floor, the police asked her name. "Louella West," replied the small, handsome woman, before insisting that Kate and the others were lying. Nonetheless, after being helped to her feet, West was arrested for breaking and entering.

Meanwhile, Bob Hepburn had arrived to take Kate to the hospital. "Will this make the papers?" Kate asked a policeman. She was told there was nothing they could do to stop it.

The incident with Louella West occurred at the end of the *Coco* tour, on February 24, 1971. In the years after Spencer's death, Kate had assembled around her a new community of women. They were a varied group: some younger, some older. Some were friends of long standing. Others, like Louella West, had only recently come around.

But having lived through what the world was now celebrating as a great American love story, the sixty-four-year-old Kate felt no desire to ally herself with another man. Though she'd always be flirtatious with men she found attractive, she made plain that from this point forward, her emotional nurturance would come from women. To James Prideaux, a gay man, she declared, "You like men. I like women." That would be the way of her life for the next thirty years.

Unlike many stars, Kate preferred to socialize almost exclusively with her private inner circle rather than with other famous folks. "I don't know very many people," she'd say. "In fact, I know very, very few people." She meant *famous* people, and while she did, in fact, know many of them, few (if any) were intimates. Her close friends remained what her niece Katharine Houghton called "her group, her people"—nearly all of them independent, rule-defying, difficult-to-categorize women like Kate herself.

For the next decade or so, this core group included old faithfuls like Laura Harding, Eve March, and Fran Rich, as well as newer friends like Sue Seton and Laura Dubman Fratti. After Katharine Cornell died in 1974, Nancy Hamilton also moved back into Hepburn's inner circle. Sharing a love for chocolate, the two women could consume several pans of Kate's famous brownies in one sitting. When Nancy died in 1985, her will specified that Kate be given five hundred dollars' worth of the best dark chocolate.

Younger blood was also continually being brought in, often through Kathy Houghton, who lived with her aunt for a time. The gatherings on Forty-ninth Street were lively. Among the new faces were the journalist Katharine Mac-Donald (daughter of Eve March) and the actress-director Valentina Fratti (daughter of Laura Dubman Fratti), both of whom called Hepburn godmother. A close bond was also shared with Emily King, Laura Harding's grandniece.

Many felt Kate's most significant enchantment in these years, however, was with the twenty-two-year-old Sally Lapiduss, whom she'd met in 1979 at the Pittsburgh Public Theater when Kathy Houghton was performing there in *The Seagull*. Taking Sally under her wing as an assistant, Kate encouraged the talented young woman's ambition to work in television; eventually Lapiduss became a successful writer and producer. Toward the end of this period, there was also a close friendship with the hairstylist Michal Bigger, who would work on several Hepburn films and on whom some friends thought Kate developed a lighthearted, "older woman, younger woman" crush.

Just as Em Perkins had done forty years earlier, Kate's cook, the strong-willed Norah Considine Moore, now played den mother to Kate and her friends. Again like Em, Norah would become much more than simply hired staff, proving a devoted companion and fierce protector. And of course, last but hardly least, there was Phyllis, never far from Kate's side.

Kate's intimates were quite a diverse lot. Some had been married with children (Eve March, Laura Fratti, Norah Moore) while others were lifelong singles (Nancy Hamilton, Fran Rich, and most of the women Kate and Nancy socialized with on Martha's Vineyard). Of them, only Sally Lapiduss would ever publicly identify as lesbian, though Hamilton's relationship with Katharine Cornell was well-known in theatrical circles.

It's doubtful that sex played a large role in any of these relationships, however; it's significant to remember that Kate often said "lust was scarce" as she got older. But she was now free to resume the largely female associations she'd known in the 1950s. Since the public presumed Kate had already had the great love of her life, she was no longer expected to be seen in the company of men, and that suited Hepburn just fine. "At a certain age," she told one reporter, "you decorate yourself to attract the opposite sex, and at a certain age, I did that. But I'm past that age."

Yet in Louella West's statement to the West Hartford police, there's evidence of at least some physicality among Kate's crowd. West had been brought into the circle by Phyllis, who'd met the fifty-two-year-old light-skinned black woman outside Kate's house on Forty-ninth Street. At the time, Louella was living across the way at the New York Theological Seminary. Long known as a bulwark of conservative evangelical Christianity, the seminary had recently been transformed under the Reverend George Webber into a liberal, inner-city ministry. Just what position West held there is not clear; Kate thought she'd been a nurse. Small but solid, West had extraordinary strength, and she'd later tell police that Kate often called on her to give massages to her and her friends. One acquaintance recalled seeing West giving a back rub to Eve March "with [her] big strong hands" in Kate's New York town house. "Kate said [West] was a nurse, and all the girls loved her massages," the acquaintance said.

Kate told John Ford that she believed Louella was the daughter of a doctor, when in fact census records show her father had been a butcher. Born in Richmond, Virginia, West had worked her way up out of a working-class background to earn both a bachelor's and a master's degree. She was married, though by the time she crossed paths with Kate there was no husband in sight.

A huge fan of Katharine Hepburn's, West had been thrilled when Phyllis brought her in to meet her idol early in 1970. Equally charmed was Kate, who allowed Louella unusual access. "She'd take [children from the seminary] on tours through my house just to see how a movie queen lived," Kate wrote to John Ford. Her new friend was "very religious and . . . so respectable," Hepburn believed. That November, despite the fact that she felt it was "beneath [Louella's] intellect," Kate asked West to be her driver for the *Coco* tour, which was scheduled to take them through Cleveland, Chicago, Rochester, and Hartford.

Known to her friends as "Lou," West routinely dressed in trousers, boots, and a Cossack-style coat. To the West Hartford police, Kate would call West a "lesbian." Some friends weren't surprised by the description. "I always wondered how such two different women came together," said one. "Kate white and famous, Louella black and poor. But Kate had many lesbians around her, so that seems to explain it."

But when Kate suggested that West give a back rub to orchestra leader Robert Emmett Dolan during the *Coco* company's time in Rochester, Louella reportedly balked. According to her, this precipitated the disagreement that ended on the floor of the Hepburn kitchen. West had wanted to know who would be paying for Dolan's message, and Kate reportedly got angry with her tone, firing Louella on the spot. In a separate statement, Kate told police she'd terminated West only after she'd become fed up with her unpredictable moods. "I feel that Louella West is totally unbalanced," she said, "a Dr. Jekyll and Mr. Hyde."

Clearly, there was more to the story than that, and the police report, long buried in the files of the West Hartford Police Department, tells the rest of it. "Miss Hepburn stated that she believed Louella West was in love with her, and therefore possessive of her," wrote the investigating officer, Robert Moylan. "She feels that Louella is a Lesbian, but adds she never made a pass at her." When Moylan pressed, however, Kate admitted she'd received a back rub from West but had felt so "uncomfortable" that she "vowed . . . no more."

West's firing took place in Rochester. That night, according to the police report, Phyllis was awakened by someone hitting her on the head. Opening her eyes, she saw a figure she believed to be West running out of the room. Nerves on edge, she and Kate drove to Hartford for *Coco*'s opening at the

Bushnell. It was to be a fund-raiser for the Urban League, an inner-city char-
ity, arranged by Kate's sister Marion Grant. After the gala, Kate, Phyllis,
Madeline Hepburn, and a male driver returned to the house on Bloomfield
Avenue.

Earlier that evening, Mrs. Hepburn had reported a possible prowler. Kate
told police she suspected the prowler had been Louella, and when she went
upstairs, she found her former friend and employee hiding in a closet, "looking doped or like a lost dog." West would retort she was not in a closet but
sitting on a chair in the hallway, waiting for Kate. She told police she'd let
herself into the house when she found the door open, and headed upstairs
because she wanted to talk with Kate alone. Her only reason for being there,
she told police, was that she wanted to collect back wages that had never
been paid to her.

Yet West's lurking presence in the dark clearly unnerved Kate. Later,
telling police how she suspected Louella had attacked Phyllis in Rochester,
Hepburn insisted that West's motives in sneaking into the Hepburn house
were equally sinister. West said that was untrue, that she was there only to get
her money.

It does seem peculiar that West would rent a car in Manhattan and drive
to Hartford so late at night simply to collect about thirty dollars. Yet her intent in confronting Kate may not have been violence, but rather reconciliation. After all, Louella admired Kate tremendously, perhaps even excessively,
if Kate's statement about her "possessiveness" is to be believed. Still, Kate was
agitated enough to call downstairs to her stepmother to telephone the police. Accompanying Kate to the kitchen, Louella was stunned when the star
suddenly told Phyllis, "I think we should tie her." As the male driver tried to
get West's hands behind her back, the small, powerful woman resisted. In the
struggle, she fell to the floor.

For reasons that aren't clear, Kate placed her hands over West's face.
Louella responded by biting down hard on three fingers: the left middle and
the right and left index. Hoping to make her let go, Madeline Hepburn began kicking West in the head. Only when Kate shouted that the police had
arrived did West release the fingers from her mouth.

According to Kate's and Phyllis's statements, at some point in the struggle
they noticed that West had a hammer in her coat. Louella, on the other hand,
said it was *Phyllis* who had the hammer, threatening her with it. West tried to
run out the door but was caught by the driver just as the police arrived. Taken
to police headquarters, West made two calls: to her attorney and to Leola Edwards, the wardrobe mistress for *Coco*, asking her not to believe what she

was sure to hear about the incident, "especially the part about the hammer." West was released on a five-thousand-dollar bond.

Kate, according to her sister Peg, was "mad with fear and nerves." The next night, Coco Chanel sang and danced on the Bushnell stage with both hands bandaged. After the show, Detective Robert Moylan of the West Hartford Police Department interviewed the star at her downtown hotel. "She was absolutely explosive," Moylan recalled. "She was so nervous, so worried about [the incident] being talking about . . . the newspapers, all that."

When the phone rang in her room, Kate ordered Moylan to answer it. On the other end of the line was the actress June Havoc, whom Kate barely knew, calling after reading about the incident in the Los Angeles newspapers. Kate was livid that the story had spread so far. She lunged at Moylan, grabbing the phone, knocking him against the window. "It was a good thing it was shut," he said, "because I would've gone right out, and we were several stories up." Slamming the phone down on Havoc, Kate began berating the police for letting Louella go, insisting that she had "to be stopped." Kate was "out of control, shouting and angry," Moylan said. "I felt I had to be on guard at all times."

Yet in truth it wasn't physical violence that Kate feared from Louella West. Her former friend could hurt her far more by talking than by biting. She knew a side of Katharine Hepburn the world had never been allowed to see. Louella was part of a private world that, if it ever became known, would conflict dramatically with Kate's public image. For forty years Hepburn had largely managed to keep the two separate. Now, in 1971, they had collided.

Headlines blared ACTRESS ATTACKED BY IRATE FORMER EMPLOYEE and KATHARINE HEPBURN BITTEN. Short on detail, the newspaper accounts made Kate seem the victim of a surprise attack. But they were still sordid enough to surprise Robert Shaw, who suspected West was "a former lover."

Embarrassed, Kate wrote letters to friends giving her side of the story, embellishing some details. She told John Ford that the attack on Phyllis in Rochester had left blood all over the pillow, and that Louella had used the hammer to come after her in West Hartford. She also claimed that West had tried to steal her diary, a charge she never made to police.

Shortly after the incident, court records show Kate paid West the thirty-two dollars that was owed her. "I always wondered if there wasn't some kind of deal," said Robert Shaw, to keep West from saying anything further. That September, the case was quickly wrapped up when West pleaded guilty. She made no statement. Many were surprised by the light sentence handed down by the judge: a fine of fifty dollars and a six-month suspended jail sentence.

"Attacking Katharine Hepburn in Hartford is like attacking the judge before sentencing," West's attorney told the court. After the hearing, Louella West faded into obscurity, returning to her home in Virginia. She did not respond to requests to comment for this book.

For all her private associations with women, Kate could still enjoy casual flirtations with men. Zoe Caldwell, whose husband, Robert Whitehead, produced Kate's last two plays, *A Matter of Gravity* and *West Side Waltz*, said Hepburn liked "to be with men . . . smart, classy, bright men." Sometimes, when Caldwell wasn't able to accompany Whitehead to Fenwick, she sensed "a slight feeling of relief" on Kate's part. "Kate so enjoyed being with Robert," Caldwell said, "that they had a better time [on their own]."

With William Rose, the handsome, decade-younger screenwriter who'd written *Guess Who's Coming to Dinner*, Kate could often act smitten. When Rose "wanted the moon" for writing a treatment of *Travels with My Aunt*, Kate told Tony Harvey he deserved it. "My God—What a lovely, wild imagination . . . He is, I should think, a genius." So taken with Willie Rose did she appear that she wrote a rambling tale of driving through Italy with him in his sporty little Maserati, hoping to get it made into a movie. Kate thought her tale of "an actress who falls for a young writer" would have great appeal. Producers weren't interested, however, so she included the piece in her memoir, with the two of them holding hands and Rose calling her "sweetie." At her age, she seemed to find it all too delicious.

Rose wasn't her only "beau" in her golden years. David Eichler, her devoted fan from Philadelphia, returned to her life in the 1970s, often accompanying her to the theater and sending her enormous sprays of flowers. In his sixties, never married, Eichler was a real estate broker who recorded the smallest details of his encounters with Kate in his diary. As always, Kate was easily susceptible to such adulation, especially from a man as charming as Eichler, with his gracious, cultured manners and his house in Chestnut Hill. "Something happens to me when you're around that I can't easily explain," he wrote to her. "You know I've been in love with you longer than either of us cares to remember." Kate seems to have been genuinely touched by his devotion. "You make my life very joyful," she wrote to him.

Yet, as ever, the vast majority of the men who flocked around her, sent her flowers, accompanied her to the theater, and balanced supper trays on their laps in her New York living room were homosexual. Both Willie Rose and David Eichler had sexualities at least as ambiguous as hers. Rose, divorced with children, seems to have blossomed around Kate and her unconventional women friends, moving from Hepburn's house to Laura Harding's farm in New Jersey to Nancy Hamilton's cottage at Sneeden's Landing.

Just as they had for nearly five decades, gay men made up most of Kate's male friends. In addition to Michael Benthall and Bobby Helpmann, there were James Prideaux, Tony Harvey, Noel Willman, who'd direct her last two plays, and Bob Borod, *Coco*'s stage manager. And as always, George Cukor and his cronies remained frequent companions. "She'd join us for picnics," re-called Charles Williamson. One time Kate dissolved in fits of laughter be-cause the chicken sandwiches the men had made still had pinfeathers in them. Insisting on driving, she hauled herself up behind the wheel of the big recreational vehicle they were using for the day, her red baseball cap pulled down low over her eyes. Down the sharp turns of the steep Hollywood hills Kate deftly maneuvered the big rig, honking at drivers who went too slow. Stopping for gas, the group encountered a car full of teenagers, who soon spotted the effeminacy of some of the men and began to heckle them. "Kate said not a word," Williamson recalled. "Pretended it never happened." As al-ways, she was adept at seeing only what she wanted to see.

Within her inner circle, with both her male and her female friends, Kate could be herself. Pulling on that baseball cap, she could be Jimmy—instead of a movie star who was expected to be glamorous at all times.

"There was always such a sense of *fun* around Kate," said Noel Taylor. James Prideaux, more than twenty years younger, marveled at Kate's energy and derring-do. Once he was startled when she told her driver to pull the car over—right on the highway—so she could pick wildflowers in the median. "You, too, buster," she said to Prideaux, dragging him along.

Her friends loved all her quirks: the dramatic way she drew out her sylla-bles (*bye* always had at least two when she was ending a phone conversation), the way she had of walking in the middle of the road instead of on the side-walk, her habit of always keeping a fire burning, even in summer, even in Los Angeles. With some of these friends, she even became physically affectionate, a rarity for her; Prideaux recalled her as "huggable."

Her apparently endless optimism cheered them. When Tony Harvey was laboring over a project, he received regular notes of support from Kate. "Don't despair," she wrote. "It's always darkest before the dawn . . . Get enough sleep and get some exercise. It makes a lot of difference. Health! And joy. And don't forget the laughter."

At her house in New York, there was indeed a good deal of laughter in these years. Dinner was rarely served in the dining room anymore but in the living room, on trays balanced on guests' laps. Tony Harvey would be there, or James Prideaux, or maybe Bobby Helpmann from London—all of them in rapt attention, charmed by Kate's eternally youthful demeanor, even if her face and neck bore undeniable signs of age.

"She always seemed so *modern*," said Prideaux—not at all the typical faded, out-of-touch movie star. But Hepburn's modernity was always more aesthetic than anything else. Her political and social conservatism as she got older is evidence of this. Just as she had no empathy for women's lib, she found the militants of gay liberation to be appalling, according to friends. Loudly she lamented the growing tolerance of sexual ambiguity in the culture. "Look at the birds and beasts and the male and female and there are rather definite types," she told Barbara Walters. "We're getting sexually confused." This despite the fact that Hepburn had never been a "rather definite type" herself. But increasingly, she was recasting her history to let the public think she was.

A particular anecdote illustrates this essential tension in Hepburn's life. In the late 1970s, Palache approached Kate about making a documentary film on Carey Thomas of Bryn Mawr. Ringing David Eichler, whose research skills she trusted, Kate asked him if the stories about Thomas being a lesbian were true. Eichler compiled a dossier and mailed it off to Kate in November 1977. "Of course," he wrote, "I'm always suspicious of gossip in these matters so I'm inclined to adopt the 'one swallow doesn't make a summer' theory. But when it comes to two swallows [Thomas's two successive female companions]— well, you'll see what I mean when you read it."

Hepburn's life, of course, was overrun with swallows. Not surprisingly, the documentary on Thomas was never made. Too many awkward issues would have needed to be addressed. This impulse to keep a safe distance from the emerging gay movement likely explains why Garson Kanin had included those transparently disingenuous anecdotes in the *McCall's* piece—which, after all, came out just eight months after the Stonewall riots and during a time when "gay rights" was a common (and sensational) news headline.

Certainly, the same impulse also explains Kate's reaction one day in the mid-1970s when she trudged up the hill from her bungalow into George Cukor's house to find the director poring over his memoirs with a couple of young assistants. "Let me read that," Hepburn demanded, snatching a handful of pages from Cukor's dining room table.

"Now, you must understand how *hard* we had worked with George up until this point," said Michael Childers, one of the assistants who'd been helping Cukor chart his memories. "We told George that he really needed to be honest, and that meant tastefully discussing what it was like to be a gay man in the golden age of Hollywood. He was very nervous, but he finally came around and had written some very good pages." Childers groaned. "Then Hepburn walked in."

"Oh, no, no, no," Kate said, finger shaking, head quivering. "Jo-udge, you have always been discreet until now! What are you thinking? You can't do this! It will ruin you!"

"After that," Childers said, "George scrapped everything he had written."

Childers, with his long hair and mod clothes, represented a new world, one that Cukor was beginning to explore. With the writer Christopher Isherwood he attended avant-garde gay theater. With the Warhol star Joe Dallesandro he sipped champagne at counterculture parties. Cukor adored Childers's lover, the director John Schlesinger, through whom he met a young, disco-partying New Hollywood, many of whom were undisguised about their homosexuality. Expressing envy for the "out in the open" relationship between Schlesinger and Childers, Cukor told them, "You can do what I never could."

Yet his old pal Kate couldn't understand George's embrace of this new way of being in the world. To her, it was simply evidence of a lonely, unfulfilled life. "He was not a happy person," she told Cukor's biographer Patrick McGilligan. "He couldn't possibly be. His life was too complicated. Complicated to such an extent, so many layers, that he did not really know himself."

Very few of Cukor's other friends, however, shared her opinion. "I think what Hepburn was objecting to," mused Gavin Lambert, "was the fact that George had moved with the times and she had not. In some ways, she liked to give off a very modern appearance to the world—certainly much more so than George ever gave off. But in fact he kept his mind open and she closed hers down . . . His life wasn't complicated. I think she would use that word to describe people who had made different decisions about life than she did."

Cukor's close friends all attest to the fact that while the director may have been lonely, he was at heart a happy person. It wasn't Cukor who had too many layers, they said. It wasn't the old man who laughed at Charles Ludlum's drag antics—or expressed amazement over Andy Warhol's art or cried real tears at *Midnight Cowboy*—who didn't know himself. Staring at each other that day across Cukor's dining room table, the unfinished manuscript between them, George and Kate, both of them now in their seventies, no doubt understood that their paths had diverged dramatically over the past ten years. True, Cukor caved in when faced with Hepburn's censure, but his story would still be told. The young men who remembered and loved him made sure of that—even if Kate would be uncomfortable with the truth they imparted. After Cukor's death, she read a draft of Patrick McGilligan's biography of the director and returned it with a brief note: "A bit too much on homosexuality," she said, "and unnecessary to my mind."

To hers maybe. But George seems to have thought differently.

"*Pull*, Phyllis," Kate was commanding. "Pull *hard*!"

Walking into Kate's bungalow on Cukor's estate in the early spring of 1978, Charles Williamson saw the seventy-one-year-old star and her companion ripping the mantelpiece from the wall. They were moving out, and Kate was leaving nothing behind—not even the mantel, which wasn't even hers.

"Dear little house," Kate would recall in her memoir. "I'm deserting you." She was melancholy about leaving, for she knew a chapter in her life was closing. She wasn't going willingly. In fact, she was furious with her old friend George.

"I have never, *ever* owned real estate in California and I'm not about to start now," she'd said, furiously, when Cukor offered to sell her the bungalow in late 1977.

"What she seemed unable to understand was that George was having a very difficult period financially," Williamson said. None of the films Cukor had made in the last ten years had turned much of a profit, and he was finding jobs increasingly difficult to come by. The fabulous Saturday night dinner parties and Sunday brunches were past. His friends recalled being served meat loaf at Cukor's house during this period. Knowing how much George cared about good food, they realized things had truly gotten desperate.

Selling the three bungalows was a last resort. "Hepburn just couldn't grasp how money might be a problem for someone," Williamson said. "She was livid. So she packed up, ripped the mantel from the wall—which George then had to replace before he could sell the place—and left without saying good-bye. George was really very hurt."

With all her money well invested by Hep and later by Palache, Kate never thought twice about cash. She'd bought her New York town house for a song back in the day, only to watch property values skyrocket in the Turtle Bay neighborhood. Fenwick was hers by right of inheritance, even if she still called it "Dick's place" in correspondence. Financial security was something she took for granted. Of Cukor's money woes, she remained a bit distrustful. "Guess what he got for [the bungalow]?" she crowed in disbelief to David Eichler. "Two hundred twenty-three thousand," she told him, stretching out the words. "I wouldn't have paid *eighty* for it!"

But in her memoir the bungalow became priceless, a sacred monument to her time with Spence. No doubt it was difficult leaving, packing up all the mementos of her life in Hollywood—"the stuff one forgets one has," as she wrote to Eichler. She had been happy here—or rather, in the bungalow next door—taking care of Spence, painting with him at their easels, watching Lobo bound across the yard. Before leaving the bungalow, Kate sat down and scribbled some rambling memories in a notebook, sometimes addressing them to Spence: "Corners—lights—shadows. Good days and bad days. Here's where I lived—this was mine. It was yours but it was so many years mine."

Ten years, to be exact. And now she no longer had a Los Angeles address. For the past three decades, Kate's world had been roughly divided in four: Hollywood, New York, Fenwick, London. The last had mostly been spent in hotels, but her long sojourns in London and the English countryside had always invigorated her. Now that, too, was largely in the past. Losing her California home was only further evidence that Kate's life was shrinking. It wasn't just memories of Spence that made her so wistful as she closed the door of the bungalow for the last time, lugging the heavy mantelpiece with Phyllis over to her car. Hepburn was facing her own mortality—and it made her very uncomfortable indeed.

The rift with Cukor was regrettable. He'd recently guided her to her most critically acclaimed performance in years, as Jessica Medlicott in the enchanting television film *Love Among the Ruins*. Her costar was none other than Laurence Olivier.

As in all of her later pictures, Kate was playing a version of herself. In this Edwardian period piece, made in mid-1974, she is a grand lady hidden behind high hats and soft focus. But in her early life, Jessica had been a "boyish and gamine" stage actress named Jessie Jerold, remembered by her adult self in the third person: "What an incorrigible flirt she must have been. I'm glad I remember her so little." But when the film asks us to recall the "wonder of that young girl," we can't help but think of the young Kate. Olivier describes her as "a thousand times more exciting and dynamic" than she has become. "She had more dignity and delicacy and pride than any of you can know."

Kate's exuberant young screen persona, forgotten for many years, was resurrected in the 1970s by a growing Hepburn cult. These fans were drawn not to the safe formula of the Tracy-Hepburn pictures but rather to the edgy, subversive work Kate did in the 1930s. *Sylvia Scarlett, Stage Door, Holiday*, and especially *Bringing Up Baby* were revived in art houses, celebrated for the very iconoclasm that had doomed them decades earlier. "It took a mere thirty-five years before we came into our own," Cukor joked to *Sylvia*'s writer, John Collier, after the film was cheered at a screening in New York. "We were right all the time—it was just 'before its day.'"

In *Love Among the Ruins*, we can sense the impish youngster of Hepburn's RKO days behind Jessica Medlicott's noble bearing, ready to jump out at any time. That's what made Kate's performance so delightful. When the film was broadcast on ABC in March 1975, it received good ratings and mostly critical raves. Kevin Thomas in the *Los Angeles Times* thought Cukor had brought out Hepburn's "enduring radiance." Two months later, the picture made a clean sweep at the Emmys, with awards going to Kate, Olivier, and Cukor.

After this it was back to the stage in Enid Bagnold's *A Matter of Gravity*, which David Eichler had facilitated bringing to Kate's attention. It was a ponderous script, written by the eighty-six-year-old playwright with Kate in mind. As directed by her friend Noel Willman, Hepburn played a cranky old woman fearful of change—again, another shade of her real self. With a young Christopher Reeve essaying the part of her grandson, Kate opened the play in Philadelphia, and for twelve weeks in late 1975 she proved she was still a trouper, touring through Washington, New Haven, Boston, and Toronto. And, just like every play since *Jane Eyre*, she drew standing-room-only crowds, even if the material she was performing was less than inspiring. When the play opened on Broadway at the Broadhurst Theater on February 3, 1976, Clive Barnes wrote in the *Times* that the crowds came to see "Miss Hepburn play, rather than the play Miss Hepburn is in."

Indeed, where once the New York critics had been her greatest nemeses, now they were her staunchest champions. Barnes was no Brooks Atkinson, lying in wait for her, but rather one of those younger critics for whom *Bringing Up Baby* and *Holiday* seemed to grant the septuagenarian Hepburn a free pass with any project she took on. "Even her stylizations have become style in the certainty of their execution," Barnes wrote. Her "way with a cliché [was] unforgettable."

As her contract allowed, Kate left the play after twelve weeks to make a film called *Olly Olly Oxen Free*, a nearly plotless account of an eccentric old woman who tramps around in pants spouting bromides like "You must believe it and do it!" The script was "something that I liked," Kate told David Eichler, probably because she got the chance to play another version of the public's crusty, beloved Kate. Opposite two amateurish child costars, however, her timing is off, and it's impossible not to feel the film's entire raison d'être was the chance to show Katharine Hepburn at the finale dangling from a hot-air balloon. Distributors had little interest in the picture. *Olly*

Olly had a limited release in the summer of 1978 but wasn't seen in New York until June 1981—a full five years after it was made. Still, Vincent Canby of the *Times* thought Kate was just ducky, because she was, well, Kate.

In the fall of 1976, Hepburn returned to the stage in *A Matter of Gravity*. For the next six months, she followed an arduous tour—from Denver to Vancouver to San Francisco to Los Angeles. Not long after the play opened at the Ahmanson Theatre in L.A., Kate fractured her ankle. She had to play her part temporarily in a wheelchair.

The following summer, faced with a lack of job prospects for the first time in four years, Kate headed to London to try to raise money for a film of *Gravity*. The effort proved as futile as her quest to film *The Millionairess* two decades earlier. She had to content herself with some impulsive cosmetic surgery to tighten the skin around her eyes. Thinking she was safe from the press, Kate had the procedure done in Glasgow by Enid Bagnold's doctor, but the aged playwright blabbed to reporters, prompting headlines in the British tabloids: HEPBURN HAS FACE-LIFT. In America, however, St. Katharine would never be so vain. Only the *National Enquirer* carried the story, the rest of the media looking the other way.

After flying to Los Angeles to pack the last of her belongings from Cukor's bungalow, Kate retreated—mantelpiece in hand—to Fran Rich's house in Palm Springs, where she licked her wounds and let her old friend console her. Due to her recent skin surgery, she kept herself covered from "head to toe" in the desert sun, even if it spoiled "the fun of air and walking," as she told David Eichler.

Still, the desert's tranquillity seems to have restored some measure of goodwill toward her former landlord, for Kate showed up as a surprise guest at Cukor's tribute by the Film Society of Lincoln Center in May 1978. Making a dramatic entrance onstage at the very end of the evening, Kate admitted she'd had several sleepless nights about not attending and concluded, "I'd damn well better be here."

Also in the audience were Garson Kanin and Ruth Gordon, though neither Cukor nor Hepburn spoke with them. A few months later, however, a repentant Cukor wrote a long letter to Gar, apologizing for being such "an ungrateful lout," telling his old friend he could "supply the real word." Perhaps Kate's recent harsh treatment of him had convinced Cukor that it was time to make up with Kanin.

Yet no matter Hepburn's volatility, Cukor was eager to work with his favorite leading lady one more time. Heading to Wales in the summer of 1978, they set about filming a television version of Emlyn Williams's play *The Corn*

Is Green, the classic story of a tutor who devotes herself to a bright young pupil in a poor mining town. In 1945, Bette Davis had played the indomitable Miss Moffat in a successful film adaptation. Comparisons between the two versions were inevitable, and for once Kate the Great did not come out on top. Sadly, the last Cukor-Hepburn coupling is far inferior to the eight that preceded it, a creaky old morality tale that can't disguise its inherently sexist story line: when her pupil gets a girl pregnant, Miss Moffat's only concern is for the young man and not for the girl she considers an ordinary tramp. For all that, Kate's standing as a feminist icon was never threatened, because such moments were always countered by dialogue like this: when another woman observes, "Men do know best, I think," the feisty Miss Moffat replies, "Then don't think."

Yet she wasn't as feisty as some thought. Almost seventy-two, Kate was heartbroken when she couldn't ride a bicycle for any great length of time. For long shots of Miss Moffat pedaling through the Welsh countryside, she required a double—something Kate had rarely allowed before.

In the last year, her essential tremor had gotten noticeably worse. When *The Corn Is Green* was aired on CBS on January 29, 1979, reviewers couldn't help but comment. John O'Connor thought Kate was "probably a little too old for the role," though he, like all the rest, felt obliged to add that "the Hepburn magic is still powerful." One critic observed Miss Moffat "epitomizes what Hepburn herself has come to represent: lofty, impertinent resilience."

Yet five months later, Bette Davis made an astounding comeback in a television film of her own, stunning critics by playing *against* type, exchanging her usual mannered volatility for a fine, underplayed turn in *Strangers: The Story of a Mother and Daughter.* When the two films went head to head at the Emmys, Davis deservedly won over Hepburn. Not long afterward, *Life* magazine requested a joint photograph of the two venerable stars. Both were New Englanders; both had endured since the 1930s. Davis was all for it. For years, she had been singing Hepburn's praises, hoping to find a project for the two of them. Kate never returned the compliments. With a terse request to stop bothering her, she turned *Life* down. "She never liked sharing the spotlight unless it was on her terms, like the way Spencer always got top billing," said Max Showalter. "But posing with Bette Davis? Not a chance."

For a brief period in 1979 and 1980, it actually looked as if Katharine Hepburn might finally pull back, retire, close the door. The shaking was the first thing people now noticed about her, and professionally Kate was adrift. Not since *The Lion in Winter* had she enjoyed a real box-office success; but actresses her age weren't expected to make big-budget commercial movies. Instead, if they continued working at all, they were expected to be seen in special "events," like Barbara Stanwyck's appearance in the television mini-series *The Thorn Birds*. But the last time any Hepburn appearance had felt like an event was *Love Among the Ruins*.

Retreating to Fenwick, Kate could have stopped there, rested on her considerable laurels. In the early part of 1980, Kate could have retired with dignity to Fenwick, paddling around in her canoe, playing golf, entertaining her friends. Yet without work, the loneliness would have been overwhelming, even with Phyllis and the entourage. Kate's private circle had been diminishing for the last ten years. In 1974, she'd lost both Michael Benthall and Eve March. The next year her beloved driver Charles Newhill died after forty years of service. The passage of time was felt especially keenly as Kate lost friends who had known her before she was a star: Ali Barbour in 1981, Adele Merrill in 1983, Lib Rhett in 1984. And, perhaps most poignantly, the men with whom she'd shared those sensational headlines in the 1930s were now gone: Leland Hayward had died in 1971, and Howard Hughes drew his last anguished breath five years later.

In early 1972, Kate had spent a week visiting with an ailing John Ford in Palm Desert. Their incredibly moving reminiscences with each other were tape-recorded by Ford's grandson. Kate's beloved "Sean" died in August of the following year.

But there was still one man left. One night during the run of *A Matter of Gravity*, a note was brought to Kate that "Ogden Ludlow" was in the audience. Delighted, Kate had Luddy come backstage after the show. Throwing her arms around the gaunt seventy-seven-year-old, Kate found her former husband as dapper as ever in his tweed jacket and striped tie. Now a widower, Luddy lived in New Canaan, Connecticut, about an hour and a half from Fenwick. Kate sensed Luddy wasn't well; indeed, he had begun chemotherapy for the cancer that would eventually kill him.

Within days, Kate and Phyllis were loading a Buick with baskets of food and making the drive out to New Canaan. Barging into Luddy's house and firing up his oven, the two women started baking crumpets, which were then served piping hot with lots of butter, jam, and Philadelphia cream cheese. In her autobiographical screenplay, Kate gives us a window on this latter-day relationship with Luddy. He gazes over at her fondly, calling her "baby," while she pooh-poohs any talk of death, insisting he'd get well now that she was there.

Looking around his house, Kate could see Luddy had done well for himself, finally achieving the life his father had wanted for him. During the

1950s, Luddy had invented the "Ludlow System," an accounting procedure credited within the banking industry as a precursor to electronic computers. As president of Ogden Ludlow, Inc., he had become recognized as a world authority on savings bank systems. With his wife, Betty, Luddy had two children, a son, Lewis, and a daughter, Ramsay, who'd made him a grandfather.

But what Luddy needed now—according to Kate—was a change of scenery. Every time she visited, she rearranged his furniture. Rugs were dragged in from different rooms, couches angled against different walls, quilts hung over various chairs. "He would literally just sit there while she was moving the furniture around," said his daughter, Ramsay, who didn't much appreciate Kate's interior design efforts. Visiting the next day, Ramsay routinely returned the furniture to the way her mother had always kept it. Still, without fail, the next time Kate showed up, she'd move it all back again. Finally, Ramsay asked her father to tell Kate to stop. "Oh, it's such a small thing," he replied. "It seems to make her happy."

One day, in Luddy's kitchen, Kate came face-to-face with Luddy's children, a young man and woman who could have been hers. She was tender to them, inviting them to accompany their father to Fenwick sometime. Lewis took her up on the offer and spent a pleasant day at the beach.

Between the two former spouses, Luddy's daughter observed a real bond. "Despite the divorce," Ramsay said, "I think either of them would have done anything for the other, because there was this history and understanding." When Luddy finally died in July 1979, Kate asked for two things: his oven and all the letters she had written to him. The oven was used at Fenwick for another decade. The fate of the letters is unknown.

As poignant as Kate's caregiving efforts for Luddy were her regular visits to an ailing Laura Harding by the end of the decade. Never as athletic as her movie-star friend, Laura, approaching eighty, was slowing down, finding mobility increasingly difficult. Standing over her old friend, arms akimbo, Kate would tell her, "Suck it up and get out of bed." Laura would try. Together, the two elderly women picked apples in a nearby orchard and baked them in pies.

For such a vital woman, whose charm and style had dazzled people well into her seventies, Laura's enforced inactivity often left her depressed. George Cukor helped out by inviting her to the premiere of what would be his last film, *Rich and Famous*, in 1981. As Laura and Cukor headed into the gala afterward, photographers crowded around, snapping pictures.

A few years later, Laura's memory began to fail. Social excursions like the premiere became increasingly rare. Still, whenever Kate was in New York, she made the drive out to Laura's farm, sitting beside her old friend at least once a week and talking a blue streak.

But the most significant break with the past was Cukor's death in January 1983. Kate didn't see her old friend before he died. Neither did she attend his funeral. She did phone Tucker Fleming to ask him about a certain photograph of herself by Cecil Beaton that Cukor had always kept hanging on his wall. She wanted it, but Cukor had left it to Fleming. "Well," she huffed, "I hope it doesn't end up on Hollywood Boulevard"—a reference to the street's nostalgia shops.

But there could be no doubt Cukor's death had affected her. "He'd been her champion," said Max Showalter. As recently as *The Corn Is Green*, George had still been there, keeping her name above the title. "They had fifty years of history," said Showalter. "No one knew her better, and now he was gone."

Yet Kate was planning on sticking around. The moment when she might have retired had come and gone. Instead of discouraging her, the loss of her friends and the decline of her professional prospects seem to have had the opposite effect, galvanizing her to charge ahead. "When I go too long [between jobs], I get anxious," she told David Eichler. "[Work] is like air for me." For fifty years she had lived in the public eye. Without public acclaim, some part of her seemed to think she might simply cease to exist.

One more dance with her public was what Kate wanted. And not just in yet another television movie or even a Broadway play. The last act of Katharine Hepburn's life would take her back to the big screen, setting into motion her final, most glorious transfiguration. Pundits said it was impossible for a seventy-four-year-old actress to star in a successful major motion picture, but Kate proved them wrong. The film was called *On Golden Pond*.

ON THE TOP OF THE WORLD

In the fall of 1982, Kate was causing a commotion at Macy's. Just by trying on a scarf she'd drawn a crowd. "How does this look?" she asked a friend, wrapping the pink scarf around her head, ignoring the onlookers who craned their necks to catch a glimpse of her.

Her friend, feeling protective, tried to block their view: "I was afraid they might lunge for her. After all, she was a little old lady by then."

Yet the little old lady knew exactly what she was doing. Replacing the pink scarf, she tried a striped one. More people had gathered by now, whispering that the star of *On Golden Pond* was just a few feet away. Kate's friend even heard one of them doing an imitation of the star: "Norman, do you hear the loons?" She seemed in no hurry to leave, just "letting them have a look at her," her friend said. A great show was made of trying on at least thirty scarves; then suddenly she announced she didn't like any of them. Grandly she made her way through the assembled crowd, aware of all the eyes on her and loving every second of it.

But then she paused in front of one woman. Leaning in, her head trembling unmistakably, Kate said: "I'm not the person you think I am. You can all go home now."

By the 1980s, the public's attention to and affection for Katharine Hepburn had never been greater. David Eichler remembered attending the play *Children of a Lesser God* with her. As they filed up the aisle after the show, Kate couldn't disguise her pleasure when one woman started to applaud. Another gushed, "Oh, Miss Hepburn, I've just read *Tracy and Hepburn* and enjoyed it so much."

Two weeks earlier she'd been to see Mickey Rooney in *Sugar Babies* at the Mark Hellinger Theatre, the site of her triumph in *Coco*. As far as the audience was concerned, Kate was still the star of the show. "Hundreds of people trooping down the aisle," she described the scene for Eichler. "I must have shaken two hundred hands!" It's why she always wore gloves, she explained. With her was her *Summertime* director, David Lean, who went unrecognized when nearly the entire audience applauded for Kate during the intermission, filling the Hellinger once again with cheers for Hepburn.

And if she wasn't recognized immediately, she made sure to change that. James Prideaux recalled a visit to a movie theater where they slipped into seats near the front. Before the film began, Kate insisted on standing up so she could count the number of seats in the theater. "I couldn't imagine why she cared," said Prideaux, "until I realized she was turning around so the people could see her. Part of her craved being recognized even if she pretended she didn't want to be."

Richard Stanley, a longtime friend of George Cukor's, remembered standing with Hepburn outside her house in New York one day in the 1980s. "At that moment a Greyhound bus pulled down the street," Stanley recalled, "and I thought she was going to flee. But instead she just looked up at the bus and gave it a big wave. She was standing there at the gate, her hands up high, in this beautiful, white, almost *Philadelphia Story* robe, and I thought, 'My God, she looks like a little angel come down to perch on East Forty-ninth Street.'"

After winning an unprecedented fourth Best Actress Oscar in March 1982 for *On Golden Pond*—the much celebrated, surprise box-office hit that paired her with Henry Fonda—Kate reigned supreme among the stars of Hollywood's golden age. No one else could touch her. Her performance as the supportive wife Ethel Thayer—telling Fonda's infirm Norman that he is her "knight in shining armor"—embodied everything the public loved about her. She was tough; she was resilient; she was eccentric; she was a survivor. When she jumps into the pond, there's a moment of stunned disbelief in the audience. Is this really a seventy-four-year-old woman? Even with the tremors—her director, Mark Rydell, believed they'd give authenticity to the part of Ethel—Kate seems ageless, an unstoppable life force.

There had been talk of Barbara Stanwyck playing the part, but that's all it was: talk. From the start, everyone wanted Hepburn. *On Golden Pond* was intended as Fonda's swan song, his one chance to act with his daughter, Jane, then at the height of her own box-office appeal. Several representatives, including Fonda himself, were sent to woo Kate in late 1979. It seems likely that she had already snared the part when it was announced in January 1980 that she'd appear in *West Side Waltz,* a Broadway play penned by Ernest Thompson, who was also the author of *On Golden Pond.*

Kate had never met Hank Fonda before, but she liked him immediately. "Fonda's not one to make new friends, and neither am I," she said, "but we got along okay . . . He likes to sit and fish, I like to walk through the woods alone. We are quite similar. He doesn't waste time. No small talk. And I hate to have idiotic conversations."

Much was made of Kate's symbolic presentation to Fonda of a fishing hat that had belonged to Spencer Tracy. More than one reviewer, in fact, commented that *On Golden Pond* seemed like one more Tracy-Hepburn outing, with Hank standing in for Spence. Echoes of *Guess Who's Coming to Dinner* are everywhere, with the conflict between the father and daughter (the two Fondas) and the mediation of the mother (Kate). Like Tracy fifteen years earlier, Fonda was frail during the making of the picture; it was expected to be his last. (In fact, he made the television film *Summer Solstice,* with Myrna Loy, shortly afterward.) In the end, Fonda's luck proved better than Tracy's. He was still alive when the film came out and, unlike Spence, nabbed an Oscar. He died six months later.

Yet despite all the shaking she does, the film demonstrated Kate's continued vitality, and she was soon in demand for other parts. *West Side Waltz* had opened in tryouts in late 1980, appearing in San Diego and Denver, and at the Spreckels Theatre in Los Angeles. The official premiere was on January 21, 1981, at the Ahmanson Theater in L.A. Once again directed by her friend Noel Willman, Kate played a combative, eccentric, upper-class widow and former concert pianist who takes in a coarse, lower-class violinist as a boarder. Together the two women find that, despite their differences, they make beautiful music together. As costar, Kate approved Dorothy Loudon, whose track record in *Annie, Ballroom,* and *Sweeney Todd* allowed her to hold her own next to Hepburn. Long practice sessions with Laura Fratti ensured that Kate's playing of the piano onstage would look authentic.

In some ways, that was the most challenging aspect of the part. The chief distinction between Margaret Mary Elderdice and Katharine Hepburn was that one lived on New York's West Side and the other on the East. "We all know what a delight I am," Margaret Mary croaked at one point, raising cheers from the audience—not for Margaret Mary but for Kate. Once again, she was playing herself. Critics loved her and—true to form—hated the play. "It shows off Hepburn's fight and brains most attractively," Dan Sullivan wrote in his review after the Los Angeles premiere. "What deeper purpose Thompson had in mind for his play is not made clear."

By the time *West Side Waltz* opened on Broadway in November, *On Golden Pond* had been released, and the media couldn't get enough of Kate. The play's three-month engagement at the Ethel Barrymore Theatre was sold out nearly every night. "I'm not sure that author Ernest Thompson realizes . . . what multiple small miracles Katharine Hepburn is bestowing upon his play," Walter Kerr wrote in the *New York Times*. When the play went on tour during the summer of 1982, rapturous audiences followed. Margaret Mary Elderdice might go from a cane to a walker to a wheelchair in the course of the play, but there seemed no limit to Kate's vim and vigor.

Convinced of her box-office draw and overall health, Cannon Films agreed to finance a project Hepburn had long dreamed of making, a black comedy about euthanasia called *The Ultimate Solution of Grace Quigley*. Her pal Tony Harvey was set to direct.

"She's on the top of the world," Kate told one friend at this time, referring to her public image in the third person. It's how she always saw her public self, the part of her that was forever on exhibition—"for sale" to the public, she said. In her screenplay, "Me and Phyllis," she wrote she often felt as if she were dressing up and hawking an old doll.

Nearly every month, there was a new interview with Katharine Hepburn—many billed as "a rare visit" with the reclusive star. In November 1984, *Good Morning America* trumpeted its segment on Kate as the "interview of a lifetime." In April 1985, in another "rare" television appearance, Kate said she wished she'd pursued "a more private profession"—a claim friends laughed off.

Indeed, as the decade went on, Hepburn seemed ready and willing to talk to whoever knocked at her door—sometimes literally. When the journalist Gregory Speck came calling unannounced in the summer of 1985, he was stunned when she let him in, eager to talk. "Are you sure you're not a terrorist?" she asked as she brought him upstairs, proceeding to launch into a detailed rundown of her career, far more than Speck had hoped for.

After so long holding the reins in her own hands, Hepburn seemed determined not to forfeit control to outside chroniclers. Letters to Tony Harvey show that by the summer of 1985, she was hard at work on "Me and Phyllis," her first attempt to tell her personal story. Completed in 1988, the screenplay was a slice of Hepburn's daily life, taking her on road trips with Phyllis and a visit to Luddy. It's a testament to Hepburn's great sense of herself that she really believed the public would be interested in such mundane details of her life as a visit to an eye doctor. But given the clamor for all things Kate by the 1980s, she may well have been proven correct.

The producer Joseph Levine was interested in "Me and Phyllis," but ultimately the powers-that-be saw the script for what it was—a vanity affair—and passed. Kate was furious with Levine, Prideaux said. So she turned her focus to something else, something she guessed would have more widespread appeal: her memoir about *The African Queen*.

Published by Knopf in 1987, the book wisely retained Kate's signature style of dashes, sentence fragments, and exclamation points, giving readers a sense that she was speaking directly to them. She made sure to wax poetic about those two big strong men whose names she placed in the subtitle—Bogart and Huston—so much so that Pauline Kael commented in her review, "I don't know that I would read this sort of gush by anyone else." But this was Katharine Hepburn, Kael wrote, "an icon showing herself in a new light."

In truth, what was new was Kate's willingness to meld all the philosophizing and pontificating she'd been doing ever since the Cavett interview with tales culled directly from her own life. Never before had she telescoped for us such revealing detail, such as the moment when Huston gave her that surprisingly intimate massage when she took ill. The public's appetite was whetted for more. But it wasn't Huston or Bogart they wanted to hear about.

"Kate knew that to keep her legend alive she needed to talk about Spence," said Max Showalter. "Other people were doing it. Now it was her turn."

With an eye on an eventual memoir, she had in fact been writing passages for years; a chunk of what would eventually turn up in *Me* had been published in the *Hartford Times* in 1968. But by the mid-1980s, with more downtime between acting gigs, Kate focused her attention on the task—and appears to have found an unexpected partner.

In August 1985, Ruth Gordon died. Kate paid her respects to Garson in a personal visit. The ice was broken. By the end of the year, Kanin and his new companion, Marian Seldes, were having dinner "practically every Monday night" with Kate. Their conversation, Seldes said, usually focused on Spencer Tracy. "By then Kate was having dinner upstairs on trays," Seldes said, "because she used downstairs for writing her book. The dining table was covered with papers. It had been turned into the book room."

In the "book room," Kate sometimes showed Gar what she had written.

Sometimes, according to one friend, he scribbled a few notes himself, handing them to Kate with a plea that she finally read his book. There was "no need," he said, "for her to reinvent the wheel."

There's a certain logic to all this. If she was going to talk about Tracy, who better than Kanin to help her along? The timing of his return to Kate's life is significant. Within months, she'd made the decision to pay tribute not only to Spencer's talent, which she'd been doing for years, but also to the deep, mythic love they'd had for each other.

Sitting in the audience at New York's Majestic Theatre on March 3, 1986, Irene Selznick had her misgivings about the evening. It was a testimonial to Spencer Tracy, a benefit to fund scholarships in his name at the American Academy of Dramatic Arts. All that was well and good. But what made Irene leery, according to several who knew her, was how much the event had been orchestrated by Kate. For months now, Hepburn had been making phone calls, securing the participation of Stanley Kramer, Sidney Poitier, Frank Sinatra, and Robert Wagner. There was also the matter of the eighty-seven-minute documentary to be shown that evening, audaciously titled *The Spencer Tracy Legacy: A Tribute by Katharine Hepburn*. For Irene, it seemed out of character for her old friend to be so obvious and explicit about her relationship with Spence.

One by one, the distinguished speakers told tales of Tracy's craft. But just as often they relayed anecdotes about his life with Kate, sounding as if they were reading pages out of Kanin's book. Poitier told of Kate sitting at Spencer's feet, "looking up at him like a smitten seventeen-year old." Around Tracy, Poitier assured the crowd, "she was a little pussycat."

When the pussycat herself walked out onto the stage, the audience rose to its feet. Friends thought they'd never seen Kate quite so beaming. Taking the podium, she read Spencer's ratings from his first audition for the academy in 1921. "Proportions, good. Physical condition, very good. Personality, sensitive but masculine . . . Pantomime, crude but manly. Temperament, masculine." To each description she gave her inimitable twinkle, emphasizing each utterance of the words *masculine* or *manly*. This was the Spence of her exalted memory. Every word described how she remembered him, and how she wanted the world to remember him.

Louise Tracy had died in November 1983. If she'd still been alive, friends were certain, this night would never have taken place—at least not in this way. But Kate had befriended Spencer's daughter, Susie, who was there to accept the award on her father's behalf.

The friendship of Kate and Susie was an odd, unexpected coupling. According to Kate, they'd run into each other one day at the Beverly Hills Hotel. Susie had recognized Spencer's dog, Lobo, and approached Hepburn to say hello. Since that time, they had cooperated in making the documentary. When the lights dimmed and the film flashed on the screen, there was Susie, poring over Spencer's scrapbooks with Kate.

Settling back in her seat to watch, Irene Selznick could not believe what she was seeing. In the documentary, Kate is giddy and giggly as she recounts her first meeting with Spencer—exactly what we'd expect from a "smitten seventeen-year-old." She twitters, "I hope he likes me," as she looks directly into the camera. In the audience, aghast, Irene whispered, "What has happened to Sister Kate?"

A few days later, the film was broadcast on PBS, bringing Hepburn's new vision of her life with Tracy to a national audience. The *Washington Post*, unnerved by Kate's girlish prattle, called the documentary "squirmily mortifying," but the film nonetheless got its point across. It ends with Kate's misty-eyed letter to Spence, the one that had left Noel Taylor speechless. When she'd read the letter to Taylor, she'd wanted to know how it sounded, how it made him feel. Now, all she had to do was look around the audience. People were in tears.

"Are you happy finally?" Kate asked, her tremulous face filling the screen. "Living wasn't easy for you, was it? But why the escape hatch? . . . What? What did you say? I can't hear you . . ." Fade out on Kate, chin up, eyes misty.

It was a peculiar way to end a tribute to a man whose life, craft, and honor had just been lauded not two hours before. Robert Shaw, who saw the documentary on PBS, asked himself, "What is Kate *thinking*?" On the one hand, Shaw said, "she was painting this romantic vision [of her life with Tracy] that wasn't the way it happened," and on the other, "she was implying [he'd been] a tormented, pathetic drunk."

But Kate knew what she was doing. She was giving the impression that her time with Tracy had been twenty-six years of steady, unbroken togetherness. She was giving the deliberate impression of a marriage in everything but name, of a relationship that had been romantic and, presumably, sexual. Yet fifteen years earlier, she'd been more honest in her descriptions, openly dismissing "erotic exaltation" while celebrating a relationship that had defied easy definition. Then, she had described what she had with Tracy as "more than ordinary." Such a description recalled the end of *Pat and Mike*, when Tracy's character says he's not exactly sure what it is they have together, but whatever it is, it's special, to which Kate's character replies, "You bet."

But such a sophisticated, intricate, nuanced story would never be taken to heart by the public. They needed tales of smitten seventeen-year-olds and pussycats. They needed old bromides affirmed, traditional values and expectations upheld. So instead of the far more fascinating reality, Kate provided the basis for what would become a cherished American folktale.

The truth was, few were left alive who could directly challenge her version of life with Spencer. Louise was gone. Cukor was gone. So were Ruth Gordon and Lawrence Weingarten. Chester Erskine would be dead within the month. But the handful of survivors—Irene Selznick among them—were appalled. "It was typical of the way Mother felt about Kate toward the end," Daniel Selznick said, "that she was inflating the legend, so to speak."

On the West Coast, Dorothy Gopadze shared her outrage with the publicist Emily Torchia over what she saw as Kate's unfair depiction of Spencer's drinking and torment. Fran Rich, too, was surprised by the romance of it all but kept silent. Joe Mankiewicz, shaking his head over Kate's new spin, gave his warning to one potential Tracy biographer not to let Hepburn take the ball in telling Spencer's story.

But back on Forty-ninth Street, Kate and Garson Kanin were clinking glasses over a successful tribute. Soon Kate was back to giving interviews every couple of months—with the added benefit that Spencer was no longer off-limits. Reporters often led off with questions about Tracy, and Kate was glad to answer them. When the writer Philip Hoare visited her, Kate made sure to pause in front of a photograph of Spence and shed a few tears.

"He and his interests and his demands came first," she told Christopher Andersen when he began his series of talks with her around this time. "It must be complete or it isn't love"—the new central tenet of the Hepburn legend. A year later, Barbara Lovenheim could write in the *New York Times* that Hepburn had "attained the mystique of a culture hero" in part because of "her fierce determination to . . . protect the privacy of her 27-year liaison with Spencer Tracy." The testimonial and the PBS broadcast had had the desired effect.

By finally embracing the romantic stories of her affair with Tracy, Kate had ensured her legend would be raised to an even higher, more transcendent level. In 1988, *Harper's Bazaar* named her one of its "Ten Most Beautiful Women." At eighty-one—the public still thought she was seventy-nine—Kate was ranked up there with the decades-younger Cindy Crawford and Farrah Fawcett. Her beauty stemmed, according to one scribe, from having known "true love."

A few years later, the reporter Caryn James wrote that Hepburn "drops [Tracy's] name casually these days." That was, no doubt, because she had a book to promote. Her long-awaited autobiography, *Me* (for which Kate was reportedly paid $4 million), was published by Knopf in 1991. Nearly every major magazine and newspaper featured spreads on Kate and her book. She was on television with Barbara Walters and Phil Donohue. Much of the focus was on the relationship with Spence, which Kate was happy to talk about in glowing, romantic terms. No more beating around the bush for her.

In actuality, Tracy doesn't appear until near the end of Kate's memoir. But then he gets a whole chapter, titled "Love." Another chapter tells the reader all about "their" house. Hepburn recounts, in effect, the same basic story that Garson Kanin had told in 1971—the same story about which she had once been so angry.

As ever, Kate is cautious about flagrant exaggerations of the truth, spinning her tales mostly through implication. But many of the facts in *Me* are just plain *wrong*. Indeed, the only bit of authentic, previously unknown truth is Kate coming clean about her real birth date. On many other points, she was—consciously or unconsciously—rewriting large parts of her history, particularly her history with Tracy. For example, she implies they were together that whole summer in Venice when she was making *Summertime*. In fact, Spence was there only briefly, and when she calls it a "perfect" holiday, she seems to have forgotten the misery others recall, and contemporary letters confirm.

But by now, whole chunks of her life with Spencer were being conflated one on top of the other. Timelines were blurred. Separations were forgotten. Important relationships—Irene, Fran Rich, Bobby Helpmann—were left out almost altogether from *Me*. But the biggest omission was the fact that Kate had left Spencer in 1952, not to mention all that had led up to it. Though she seemed only too happy to report that "living wasn't easy" for Tracy (she ended the memoir with her letter to Spence, asking him why he was so tortured) she blotted out all the telling details of her own unhappiness.

The outstanding success of *Me* led to a television "sequel" of sorts, *All About Me,* which aired on the TNT cable channel in January 1993. Afterward, it was made available on home video. In *All About Me*, Kate was even more explicit about her love affair with Spence than she'd been in her book. To those who had expressed surprise that she'd given up her vaunted independence for a man, she explained she'd done it because it made her happy. Only with Tracy, she said, did she "truly understand what it meant to be in love."

All of the women's magazines celebrated the Tracy-Hepburn love story. The only journalist who inquired a bit deeper, who challenged the romantic image even in a respectful, courteous way, was Liz Smith, who was by then also a personal acquaintance of Hepburn's. "You don't really tell us much about the beginning and middle of those thirty-odd [sic] years you spent together," Smith prodded. "Are you aware that you left all that out? Did you do it on purpose? The meeting? The real meeting, the romance part, the sex, the living together?"

Sitting in her New York town house in front of the crackling fire—ablaze even in summer—Kate didn't hesitate in her reply. "I suppose I remembered what impressed me the most," she said. She was being completely honest.

But how had it happened that this woman—who once wrote a piece for a law magazine about the right of privacy for public figures and who told John Ford she was too "secretive" to ever tell the story of her life—seemed, by the 1990s, to never stop talking? And why was she telling this particular, romanticized version of her story?

The first clue to that mystery takes us back to the cold, brisk morning of Monday, December 13, 1982. Temperatures were below freezing, but the weather in Connecticut was sunny and clear. Kate and Phyllis were driving back to Manhattan after spending the weekend at Fenwick, heading down Route 154. Shortly before eleven o'clock, Kate ran the car directly into a utility pole. Phyllis was thrown to the floor. Kate went smashing into the steering wheel. Blood poured forth from her nose, and her right foot was in terrible pain.

The newspapers reported that Katharine Hepburn had broken her ankle in a minor car accident. But few were aware of just how badly it was broken, and how that accident affected her life. That night, she underwent surgery at Hartford Hospital. A year later, she was back at New York University Hospital to have the ankle reset and fused. It meant a major delay in shooting *The Ultimate Solution of Grace Quigley*, which annoyed Kate to no end.

Scott Berg said she lived with "pain far worse than she ever let on." Her pain severely curtailed her physical activity. Tennis was now a thing of the past. Even golf could be difficult. Only a few years ago, David Eichler had arrived at Kate's town house to find her on the roof, overseeing a repair; another time, he found her in a tree, cutting off branches. Now just climbing the steep flight of stairs to her bedroom was an enormous effort.

It wasn't just the ankle, either. Only a few months before the accident, she'd had surgery on her shoulder; it was the second time she'd needed to have her rotator cuff repaired after "lousing it up" during the filming of *On Golden Pond*. For the rest of Kate's life, lifting her arms over her head could be terribly painful. This was in addition to always needing to favor her arti-ficial right hip. And of course there were also the tremors, getting more pro-nounced with every passing year. "It could all leave her very frustrated and angry," said James Prideaux.

Her physical pain helps us to understand why, sometime in the mid-1980s, Kate began to drink. Though she'd always enjoyed a cocktail or a glass of wine, now alcohol became an increasingly important part of her daily rou-tine. "Do you drink?" was one of the first questions she asked people, includ-ing Liz Smith, for whom she poured a "whopper" the first time she met her. When Smith brought her a gift of several bottles of Vermont gin and vodka, Kate was offended that they were only 60 proof. "What is this?" she asked. "It's not liquor!" In her kitchen she kept a list of important telephone numbers. The local liquor store came just after her doctor and the laundry.

At one point, Norah Moore confided to Scott Berg that Kate was drink-ing two glasses of scotch before dinner every night and then two afterward, which left her foggy and befuddled. Concerned, Norah took to diluting the bottles of scotch with water. Given Kate's long history with alcoholics, all this seems surprising, but Berg thought Kate was using the alcohol as an an-odyne to her physical pain and the emotional depression it brought on.

She may have also been using her Famous Grouse scotch to calm her tremors. According to experts, alcohol is the most widely used treatment for essential tremor. If the doctors at Columbia University Medical Center had suggested Kate take a drink to calm her shakes, they likely weren't aware that she was multiplying their advice by four every night.

Kate's tremors raise another consideration as well. The usual medication for essential tremor is Mysoline. It seems almost certain she would have at least tried it. One of the main side effects of the drug is depression—the very condition Scott Berg thought Kate was using alcohol to counteract. By the time she turned eighty in 1987, Kate may have been caught in a confus-ing cycle of pain, alcohol, and drug dependence—allowing for a more com-passionate view of the irritability and imperiousness that so colored her later years.

For a woman long used to changing her own tires and swimming thirty laps before breakfast, Kate's reduced physical activity was devastating. The high energy and good spirits that had prevailed through much of the 1970s dissipated, and she was often once again the angry shrew of *Coco*. Of course, Kate was always known for her temper. During the run of *A Matter of Gravity*, Kate had barged out after the final curtain on one performance to scold a man for taking a photograph while the second act was in progress. "It's my school principal blood," Kate wrote to Lillian Gish, who'd been in the audience that night and witnessed Kate's spectacle. "I just plain lose my temper."

But ten years later, even the affection of her fans could seem to irritate her. One Washington audience for *West Side Waltz* gave her a standing ovation at her first entrance onstage. Kate snarled at them to sit down. "You don't know if I deserve this until I do my job," she said. "Now let's start over." She went backstage and returned to utter silence.

Mostly, the press treated these amusing little "Hepburnisms" as evidence of the eccentricity the public so loved. But a few critics didn't find her all that lovable. In April 1982, the editorial cartoonist Bill Gallo took Kate to task after she chastised a man for putting his feet up on the stage. "After you told him how rude he was, what a complete bore he was, you would not let up . . . you wanted the death penalty back," Gallo wrote in a series of panels. "Katie, you grand lady you. You know how to get off the stage, but you sure don't know how to get off the dime!"

In person she could be brutal. Kate's first words upon meeting Jane Fonda were "I don't like you!" Fonda never quite knew why she said it, even after they became friendly making *On Golden Pond*. When Kate was introduced to Brooke Hayward by a mutual friend—"Kate, I'd like you to meet Leland and Maggie's daughter"—she looked the young woman up and down, ignored her outstretched hand, and made a guttural sound in her throat as reply. Possibly any reminder of Margaret Sullavan was enough to put Kate in a bad mood.

As the 1980s progressed and Kate's physical health continued to decline, she became "legendarily cantankerous," according to one of her friends. When the columnist Liz Smith arrived for a dinner party wearing red cowboy boots, Kate had no qualms about announcing the boots were "the ugliest things" she'd ever seen. Sometimes Kate could be vituperative without warning. Once, after a warm good-bye the night before, James Prideaux phoned Kate the next morning to suddenly discover she was no longer speaking to him. He said she had the ability to reduce him to tears.

A part of Kate seemed aware of how irascible she was becoming. When David Eichler described for her Enid Bagnold's physical and emotional difficulties, Kate replied: "She's really frightening, so selfish . . . that terrible will . . . It's like a big wheel moving fearfully, connected to nothing." She paused. "God—am I like that?"

Yes, she could be, especially after the pain started, and she turned to alcohol. No wonder she was cross, after a night spent tossing and turning. It's likely she'd spent just such a night when the *Time* magazine journalist Margaret Carlson arrived ten minutes late for a morning interview in June 1992.

"How dare you keep me waiting?" Hepburn bellowed. "Are you that stupid?" Carlson was stunned. She knew Kate could be cranky, but she'd heard she was being "adorable" and "charming" now that she was promoting her memoir. But Kate's charm was not evident that morning. Carlson's piece would be one of the few truly scathing accounts written about Hepburn in the post–*African Queen* era.

Yet Carlson's portrait of a self-absorbed woman, too impatient for introspection, was just as true as the panegyrics of *McCall's* and *Ladies' Home Journal.* Only by reading them together does the full picture of Katharine Hepburn emerge. Yes, she could be adorable and charming. She was, as she said in "Me and Phyllis," a piece of delicious chocolate for the public's consumption. But tellingly, at that moment in the screenplay, Kate wrote a line for Phyllis, who observes that the chocolate is bitter.

Her sister Peg believed it was more than just the pain that made Kate so irritable in her old age. "She was lonely," Perry said.

It was a sentiment echoed by several of her friends. "She just hated the fact that she was alone," said James Prideaux. Robert Shaw thought Kate's loneliness "drove her to talk so much about Spencer . . . She was thinking back to a time when she was happy, even if in looking back she made it all seem more romantic and traditional than it was."

For all her enduring close friendships, Hepburn in her midseventies began to lament growing old alone. Writing her memoir had prompted some uncharacteristic moments of soul-searching, according to her brother-in-law Ellsworth Grant. Once, looking over at him, she wondered why some people strove so hard for things, then felt so "restlessly unhappy" when they got them. "I suggested it was the pursuit," Grant said, "not the achievement, that was exciting and compelling." He reported that Kate found the idea "fascinating."

"Toward the end of her life," Grant went on, "she had run out of pursuits. She had done it all. She was fond of saying that she lived by that motto that hung over the family's fireplace on Hawthorn Street: LISTEN TO THE SONG OF LIFE. But, tragically, though she listened, her upbringing and her temperament prevented her from enjoying the song."

She had done it all—except find someone to love who would love her back in a fulfilling, lasting, equal relationship. Never had she found that, despite all the passion she'd directed at her various lovers. That's why she remembered those last five years with Tracy with such a rosy glow, why she gave them such power and allowed them to define the whole of their relationship. Those years were the closest Kate ever came to domestic happiness.

"At the end," said her sister Peg, "the loneliness took over." It's what made her lash out at times, friends believed. It's what made her bitter. And it's what made her "so determined," said one old friend, "to tell the stories about her great love affair with Spencer. If she could convince the world she'd had it, maybe she could convince herself."

But she did have Phyllis. Always, there was Phyllis.

"Phyllis was the closest Kate came" to a real, solid union with another person, Prideaux said. "Phyllis and I are one," she told him. "Joined at the hip."

She painted a portrait of the two of them as seagulls, one bird standing, head proudly cocked, the other resting behind, its head turned away. Kate's screenplay, "Me and Phyllis," is a loving, if quirky, portrait of a marriage. The two old women bicker over what to have for dinner. They irritate and amuse each other. When Kate is perturbed by something Phyllis says, she tells her to watch out, that she divorced Luddy for less than that.

Indeed, "old married couple" is exactly the way many people—Prideaux, Scott Berg, Noel Taylor, Bob Hepburn among them—would describe Kate and Phyllis. Phyllis was always there, eating dinner with Kate, playing Parcheesi with Kate and Dick, taking naps on the set of Kate's television films. A comparison with Luddy isn't off the mark. Neither relationship was about sex. Instead, it was all about devotion—which existed on both sides, even if outside observers rarely saw Kate's share of it.

Even as Phyllis turned eighty, Kate continued to treat her like a slave. "It was always, 'Phyllis do this, Phyllis do that,'" said John Dayton, who served as producer on several of Kate's television films in the 1980s. To the end, Palache thought Kate's treatment of Phyllis was "just awful." Yet Palache understood, down deep, that Kate adored Phyllis. "She'll tell you she's the most marvelous person—'and how she can stand me I don't know,'" Palache said, quoting Kate. "But from Phyllis's point of view, I'm sure she wouldn't do anything else in the world. It's her life. It's just absolute total devotion."

"I don't know what she would have done without Phyllis," said Noel Taylor. "By this time, you must understand, Phyllis didn't do any work. She just sat with Kate, talked with her, rode in the car with her up to Fenwick on weekends. Kate was lonely in her old age, that's true, but she would have been completely godforsaken without Phyllis."

"Me and Phyllis" is, in fact, Kate's valentine to the woman who put up with so much from her. It is the story of two women and their walk through life, shoulder to shoulder, even if one is carrying most of the bags. The screenplay ends with the two of them in the ambulance after their auto accident. Kate reaches over and takes Phyllis's hand. On that image, the camera fades to black.

Five years older than Hepburn, Phyllis was aging right along with her. The worst part was Phyllis's battle with dementia, which began around 1990, when she was eighty-seven. Kate could be very impatient with her ("She'd forget her nose if it wasn't already on her face!"), but she could also be kind. "She would yell at Phyllis, but she loved her," John Dayton said. One time, eating their dinner on trays as usual, Phyllis became disoriented and fell, knocking her tray over. "It was the first time I ever saw Kate lunge out of her chair," Dayton said. "She gently put Phyllis back in the chair, telling her, 'It's going to be all right. Don't worry. I'll take care of it.'" The caretaking roles had been reversed.

At times, it felt as if Phyllis was the last link to an increasingly distant past. In 1950, Kate had boasted to one reporter that while her friends teased her for being "an exercise nut," she expected "to bury them all." She pretty much did. Bobby Helpmann died in 1986, as did Kate's sister Marion, a real blow given how much younger Marion was. In June 1989, word came from upstate New York that Palache had passed away—the last of the Three Musketeers and D'Artagnan, the last friend who remembered Kate pre-stardom.

But the most wrenching loss, certainly, was the death of Laura Harding in August 1994. Laura was ninety-two years old. For some years she hadn't recognized anyone who came to see her. Her family liked to believe she brightened, however, when she saw Kate, who still regularly came to sit beside her bed.

Back in 1935, Kate had, in effect, exiled Laura from Hollywood, putting her career before friendship. But the two women had never completely severed their bond. At Laura's funeral, her grandniece Robin Chotzinoff remembered "a flurry" as Kate made her entrance: "Everyone knew it was Hepburn arriving." But, predictably, Kate was stoic. No overt expressions of grief for her. What she wanted, she told Laura's family, was Laura's pile of seasoned firewood. Could she have it? When the family agreed, Kate had her driver load it into the trunk of the car.

With Irene Selznick, there had been distance for much of the 1970s and 1980s. Part of it, her son Daniel felt, dated back to "Martha," with both Kate and Irene blaming the other for the fact that the project never got off the ground. Yet more significant, Daniel said, was the 1972 publication of *On Cukor*, Gavin Lambert's collection of interviews with George Cukor. "Mother thought George was rewriting history, making himself out to be this great auteur and leaving out the collaboration of my father [David O. Selznick] on several of his films." Relations between George and his old pal Irene had, in fact, been strained since 1954, when she'd fired him as director of *The Chalk Garden*. So Irene phoned Kate to complain, and expected her to call Cukor "on the carpet." Kate refused, and for several years there was iciness between Kate and Irene as well.

But there was a deeper issue, too. According to several friends of both women, Irene had pulled back because she sometimes felt Kate's embrace of a younger crowd of companions teetered on the brink of gaucherie. Such an impression was perhaps inevitable when stories of Hepburn hosting the singer Michael Jackson for a bizarre little powwow made the news in the summer of 1984. "Mother definitely disapproved of all that," Daniel Selznick said.

Still, when Irene was diagnosed with cancer and was hospitalized in 1985, it was loyal Kate who visited her every day. Refusing to see most people—even her sons—while she recovered from surgery to remove cancerous cells from her nose, Irene did allow regular visits from Kate; it was Hepburn from whom Daniel Selznick received updates on his mother's condition. "I told her she didn't need to go to see her *every day*," Daniel recalled, "but Kate just said, 'Of *course* I need to see her every day!' "

Yet Irene would grow increasingly uncomfortable with Kate's sentimental musings about her life with Tracy. "She thought Kate had gone over the edge," said one friend, "and so she withdrew." Kate never understood the distance between them. When Irene died in 1990, Kate attended her memorial service, but refused to speak when asked.

Though Irene could never understand it, Kate's eagerness to embrace some unlikely companions was her way of alleviating the loneliness. Among her new friends was the tennis champion Martina Navratilova, who at the time was going through a widely publicized split with her female lover. To visitors, Kate often proudly showed off a tennis racquet that Martina had given her. This was also the period in which her friendship began with Scott Berg. In his early thirties, Berg had approached Hepburn for a piece in *Esquire*. The article never happened, but they formed a close bond.

There were still some old friends, too: James Prideaux, David Eichler, and Tony Harvey remained in her life. For Harvey, Kate had finally gotten around to starring in *The Ultimate Solution of Grace Quigley*, shot in late 1983, playing the part of an old woman who hires a hit man (Nick Nolte) to kill off all her ailing friends. Watching friends like Laura and Luddy suffer with declining health, not to mention her own struggles, had left Kate sympathetic to the subject. Euthanasia—even in a form gentler than what was portrayed in the movie—was a political hot potato in the conservative 1980s. The practice was strongly opposed by many religious and political groups. With *Grace Quigley*, Kate was taking an equally vehement stand for the other side. Remembering how long and difficult her father's death had been, she told reporters that shooting him would have been an act of mercy.

As the country lurched rightward under Ronald Reagan, Kate was returning to her leftist roots, once again proving her essential contrariness. Of course, her dislike of Reagan dated back to the late 1940s and HUAC, and despite Spencer's friendship with Nancy Reagan's parents, Kate had little use for the first lady either. In March 1988, David Eichler found it amusing that Kate would turn down the Kennedy Center Lifetime Achievement Award because she did not want to be seen alongside her "friends the Reagans"— *friends* used here sarcastically by Eichler.

Kate was especially leery of Reagan's appointees to the Supreme Court. "If they toss out *Roe* versus *Wade* . . . it will be the biggest setback for women," she told the press. "Anyone with half a brain can see that. I cannot believe it is happening . . . It's all going backwards. They're tearing down everything my mother fought for." In April 1989, she allowed Planned Parenthood to send out a fund-raising letter in her name—the first time she'd publicly signed onto a "cause" since walking out at Gilmore Stadium in that red dress.

Meanwhile, she didn't expect to win any minds and hearts with *The Ultimate Solution of Grace Quigley*. "The Moral Majority," she said, "they won't come. And the Right to Life people and the Catholics. They'll hate it. I just hope the kids will find it funny."

They didn't. In fact, it was hard to find anyone who did. The problem with the film is the script, which loses any logic it may have had about halfway through. Harvey elicits a playful performance from Kate, but the slapstick—a ridiculous hearse chase through Manhattan—just never gels with what's meant to be more sophisticated satire. At the Cannes Film Festival in May 1984, the selection committee was so appalled by the film that it was suggested it be shown out of competition.

With a new ending (completely upsetting the original black comedy intent) and a shorter title (just *Grace Quigley*), the picture was finally released in New York a year later. Reviews were predictably abysmal. Kate, as ever, got off lightly, with Vincent Canby remarking that her characterization of Grace was informed by her own "indomitability [and] personal courage." Yet there were limits. When she asks Nolte to call her "Mom," the line rings hollow. "In the person of Miss Hepburn," Canby astutely observed, "Grace Quigley is not someone who needs anyone to call her 'Mom.' "

Harvey's friendship with Kate withstood the disaster. He remained one of her most frequent companions—and in May 1990 he was witness to one of her most famous outbursts of temper. Waiting for Harvey in a car parked illegally on Forty-ninth Street, Kate spotted the police officer Angie Hopkins about to write her ticket. Rolling down the car window, she asked that Hopkins refrain from doing so; after all, she'd been parking here for years, and the cops of the Seventeenth Precinct affectionately called her their "queen." When Hopkins ignored her request and proceeded to write the ticket anyway, Kate called her a pig. The policewoman later claimed Hepburn spit at her as well, though the star denied it. The fracas was only heightened when Harvey followed Hopkins to her cruiser and slammed the door on her hand as she was getting inside. Both Harvey and Hepburn were hauled down to the police station, where Harvey was charged with harassment. "She's a good actress, a strong forceful character," Officer Hopkins told reporters in a story that made headlines in the tabloids. "But she doesn't have to be that way off of the screen."

Friends say Kate's temper was never roused so much as it was during the period of time in the late 1980s and early 1990s when Howard Hildebrand was her driver. Since the death of Charles Newhill, Kate had gone through many drivers, but Hildebrand was the most memorable. He and Kate would fight like cats and dogs, with Kate constantly firing, then rehiring him. "Let's get something clear," she once barked at him. "When I say nine o'clock, I really mean eight forty-five."

An offbeat, fortyish man everyone called "Hilly," Kate's driver was a "Jekyll-Hyde" character, said James Prideaux. Hilly could be perfectly charming one moment, whipping up a fabulous meal for everyone, then turn moody and sullen a short time later. Paired with Hepburn, the combination was easily combustible. But when Hilly was hospitalized with AIDS in late 1993, Kate was deeply saddened. "She went to visit him, made sure he was comfortable," recalled Prideaux. "She had no worries about the disease or anything like that." Kate was often on the phone with Hilly in the months before his death in April 1994.

Despite the failure of *Grace Quigley*—or perhaps because of it—Kate was eager to get cooking with a new film. Prideaux persuaded her to star in a television script he'd written. It was the beginning of a new phase in her career, and the last.

Kate's inner circle during her final years would consist largely of people from these television movies—three with Prideaux and two others after that. Of the bunch, her closest friend was Noel Taylor, whom Kate initially didn't want to design her costumes because she wasn't familiar with his work. So the acclaimed Broadway designer (*Dial M for Murder, The Night of the Iguana, One Flew Over the Cuckoo's Nest*) swallowed his pride, packed a suitcase of samples, and flew from L.A. to New York.

"What the hell have you got in there?" Kate asked when she saw Taylor's enormous suitcase. "Let me show you," he offered. "Well, give it to me," she replied. "Only *I* know how to get up these damn stairs." Weak ankle or not, she took the heavy suitcase from him and hobbled up the stairs, Taylor following behind. Pulling a sweater from the suitcase, she asked Phyllis, "What do you think?" When Phyllis called it beautiful, Taylor had the job.

"We were best of friends after that," he said. "Whenever George [Schaefer, the director of her first three television movies] would find himself in trouble with Kate, he'd say, 'Well, I *did* introduce you to Noel Taylor,' and she'd forgive him." Kate told Prideaux that Taylor was the best designer she'd ever had—and she'd had the best.

All three of Kate's television films with Prideaux were shot in Vancouver. Each also had a part for the octogenarian Brenda Forbes, Nancy Hamilton's former lover and longtime friend. The first, *Mrs. Delafield Wants to Marry*, is the best of the lot. Airing on CBS on March 30, 1986, it's the story of an old woman who wants to marry a man (Harold Gould) against the wishes of her children. Despite the obvious sentiment, the script manages to get in some pointed commentary on anti-Semitism and how the culture treats older people. Kate proves quite engaging, especially in her Auntie Mame–like turn at the end, when she shows up in a colorful sari for her wedding. She told Prideaux she'd had so much fun that she wanted him to write another picture for her. The film's executive producer, Merrill Karpf, was likewise pleased with the final product, immediately signing the whole team for another go-round.

Prideaux wasn't as happy with his second effort, *Laura Lansing Slept Here* (named as his insider's tribute to Laura Harding, who was then very ill). "This was really a device for Kate," Prideaux admitted, "and her character was shamefully based on what I knew of the real person." The same could be said of her next outing. In *The Man Upstairs* (airing December 6, 1992), Kate again plays Kate, this time in the form of a formidable dowager whose house is invaded by an escaped convict (Ryan O'Neal). She manages to win him over (surprise!) with her wise and wondrous ways.

Kate was eighty-five when she made *The Man Upstairs*. By now, she was showing signs of the same forgetfulness that plagued poor Phyllis. John Dayton, one of the film's producers, recalled her distress when she realized she couldn't remember her lines. Taking him aside, she said, "I think I'm having a stroke." Dayton immediately took her to the hospital and checked her in under his mother's maiden name. She wasn't having a stroke, of course; she was facing the first onslaught of dementia. When the hospital released her, she took refuge with Dayton, horrified that this should be happening to her. "Spencer always said acting is hitting your marks and knowing your lines," she said, bereft. When Dayton suggested she start using cue cards, she characteristically thought it a sign of weakness and refused. Only when Dayton told her Angela Lansbury, eighteen years Kate's junior, used cue cards on her series, *Murder She Wrote,* did Kate agree to give them a try.

Hepburn's final television films are mostly fluff. Some have called them unworthy of her. "Why did she do them?" asked one of her friends. "Why not end with *On Golden Pond* and go out on top?"

Perhaps because work kept the loneliness at bay. Dayton recalled taking Kate on a leisurely drive through the country. During their drive, Kate suddenly announced that she loved him. Dayton returned the sentiment, surprised at how vulnerable she seemed.

Yet the loneliness that pervaded Hepburn's last years was assuaged somewhat by a young woman she'd met some time before. In 1983, Kate had looked up at the beach at Fenwick to see a blond young woman striding across the sand. Just a few years later, this woman would be the most important person in her life. Her name was Cynthia McFadden.

When Cindy McFadden was a girl growing up in Auburn, Maine, she liked to imagine that Katharine Hepburn was her "secret biology." From the time she was very young in the early 1960s, Cindy had always known she was adopted. Her parents, Warren and Arlene McFadden, were wise, loving people who explained how special she was: "The queen of England could be your mother," her father said. "You can be anyone."

For Cindy, his words resonated. The imaginative little girl grew up in a very working-class world: Warren McFadden toiled for the telephone company, and his father had run a grocery store. Arlene McFadden's father had owned a laundry. Yet far beyond Auburn did little Cindy's imagination roam. When she was seven, she pulled on a turkey wishbone with her mother and won. Her wish, she confided, was to "meet everyone in the world."

In 1968, twelve-year-old Cindy sat in the Empire Theatre in nearby

Lewiston staring up at Katharine Hepburn in *The Lion in Winter*. Then and there she decided that Hepburn was her secret mother. Her own high cheekbones seemed to confirm the fact.

Early on, her parents recognized Cindy's ambition. Whenever she read her father a school essay, his standard line of response was "It'll win the Pulitzer Prize." But finding a way into the big, wide world would be quite the task for a telephone repairman's daughter from a small town in Maine.

"When I was growing up," McFadden recalled, "I used to watch Walter Cronkite and he was always talking about L.A. Well, I thought he meant Lewiston-Auburn. For a long time I didn't realize there was another L.A. I was that provincial, I guess."

That changed when she attended Bowdoin College in nearby Brunswick. An important mentor for her was Barbara Kaster, one of Bowdoin's first tenured women faculty. In 1980, Kaster oversaw a study of sexual harassment in the workplace that was reported to Congress. She was the first of several older women to take Cindy under their wings, who helped her see the world of possibilities that awaited her. Upon graduation from Bowdoin in 1978, Cindy enrolled at Columbia University School of Law.

By now, she had a new mentor, Marion Hepburn Grant, introduced to her through a Bowdoin connection. "Marion took Cindy on as a kind of project," Bob Hepburn recalled. Marion admired the ambitious student's "go-getter attitude," he said. With Marion, Cindy admitted spending a great deal of time "crying into a telephone, whether [over] a failed exam, a broken heart, no ride to the Thanksgiving feast, or no more money for tuition." To Cindy, Marion was her "ally, co-conspirator, and salvation." By 1981, Cindy was working as Marion's assistant, traveling to Cleveland with her for the annual meeting of the United Church of Christ, for which Marion was a Hartford board member.

Cindy also spent time at Fenwick, where the Grants had a house at the other end of the beach from Kate. It was during one of those times that Cindy took her serendipitous stroll across the sand that led her to Marion's famous sister. One glance at the lithe twenty-five-year-old and Kate declared, "You look like me." With those words, she came close to fulfilling Cindy's childhood dream.

It wasn't long before Irene Selznick was telling Scott Berg about a young woman who had "taken over" his room on Forty-ninth Street. Cindy was soon seen everywhere with Kate. Liz Smith said the aging star acted as a kind of "fairy godmother" for the young woman. She took her to the theater; she introduced her to famous people. In Boca Grande, where Kate sometimes retreated in the winter to play tennis, she and Cynthia socialized with Brooke Astor. But for all the glamour and glitz Kate offered the starry-eyed girl from Maine, Cindy also had what Berg called "an obviously tonic effect" on Hepburn. Kate eagerly anticipated Cindy's visits and began referring to her guest room as "Cindy's room."

"Let's be honest here," said another friend. "Kate fell in love with Cindy. She wasn't expecting a relationship with her, but there's no question she was enchanted by how young Cindy was, how energetic, how she had her whole life ahead of her. She reminded Kate of herself at that age. It was plain to see. Kate was *dazzled*."

Certainly, Cindy could be dazzling. "She's *beautiful*," said Noel Taylor. "Clean cut, like a diamond."

In a group of people, Cindy could command attention from those around her to the exclusion of anyone else—just like the young Kate Hepburn. "She's like a balloon that fills up the room and takes all the available air and space," said one person close to her. "She walks in and puts on a huge smile and instantly becomes positively incandescent. All the moths begin to flutter around."

For a time, Cindy was great friends with Kathy Houghton. But some family members eventually came to resent just how close Cindy was to Kate. "I always liked Cindy," said Bob Hepburn, "but there were some in the family who felt Cindy used Marion to get to Kate." Eventually, some accused Cindy of displacing Kathy Houghton in Kate's life; one observer said Houghton was "around a great deal in the beginning, but not by the early nineties, when Cindy had sort of taken over." Some of Kate's old friends were also wary of the young woman. Irene Selznick was reportedly suspicious of Cindy's motives.

Others, however, found nothing suspicious about Cindy at all. "Let me tell you about Cindy McFadden," said John Dayton. "She was one of those people who loved Kate and who were not out to get something *from* Kate. And I can't say that about everyone."

By 1984, Cindy was the executive producer of Columbia University's "Media and Society" seminars, working for former CBS news president Fred Friendly. She got the job on her own, with no assistance from Kate. If Hepburn offered McFadden help in her career, it was advice on how to dress, how to talk, how to charm, how to set her goals. "I used to marvel at how much Cindy seemed to copy Kate," said one of Kate's friends. "The way she said certain words, the way she walked."

But never does it appear that Cindy exploited Hepburn for personal career advantage. "I think she just genuinely liked being with her," said James Prideaux. "Cindy was the perfect foil for Kate, teasing and joking without a trace of the awed fan that would have bored Kate to death. They thoroughly enjoyed one another."

Noel Taylor recalled several dinners at his house to which Kate brought Cindy. His lover, the artist Adnan Karabay, was the same age as Cindy, and the four of them spent many happy hours together. One dinner was catered by a Chinese restaurant. When the deliveryman arrived with the telltale white boxes, Kate said in mock outrage, "You're serving take-out Chinese to Katharine Hepburn?" Cindy told her, "Kate, you love it!"

The two women, five decades apart in age, could be uncannily alike. "Cindy loves to be the life of the party," said one person close to her. "She lives to be the center of attention"—rather like another high-cheekboned New England girl.

Indeed, when considering Hepburn and McFadden together, they seem almost the same person, even if they were separated by half a century. No wonder that after Cindy became well known on her own, rumors started that she really *was* Kate's daughter, that she might in fact be the secret love child of Kate and Spence. It's also not surprising that—as Cindy became more successful, becoming one of the founding reporters of Court TV in 1991—she insisted on being known as Cynthia. It was not so very different from the way Kath had become Kate.

APOTHEOSIS

Like the bride, Kate was dressed in white. White slacks above white sneakers. Though she didn't approve of Cynthia's wedding to the *Hartford Courant* publisher Michael Davies, she seemed to be having a grand enough time anyway. On the morning of September 9, 1989, Kate opened up the grounds of Fenwick to more than two hundred people. Indeed, when friends of Cynthia and Mike had received their invitations to the wedding, very few sent back their regrets—less out of any desire to wish the couple well, some admitted, than to catch a glimpse of the inside of Hepburn's famed estate, over which Howard Hughes was reported to have once dipped his wings.

After the ceremony in the small chapel nearby, guests walked back to the house along a short path. Kate rode beside them in a car that was driven very, very slowly. Through the window she looked small but regal, like a dowager queen.

"What surprised me the most," said one guest, "was how much the house was in disrepair. I mean, it was the pits. There were clothes hanging over furniture, books lying about, cracks in the plaster, soot from the fireplace all over the floor." One man used the bathroom and was alarmed to see water dripping steadily from a hole in the ceiling.

Outside, however, where the tables were set up under a large tent, the view of the sea and the marshes was spectacular. Kate didn't mingle much with the guests, and seemed never to sit, but when she was spotted, she was always laughing. Once she even danced a few steps with the bridegroom. But it was only when Cynthia rose to cut the cake that she seemed to show any real interest in the proceedings. Pausing off to the side, she watched carefully. Cynthia sliced a piece of cake and placed it on a napkin. Stepping around her new husband, she carried it over to the woman she was heard addressing as "Aunt Kate."

"What happened next, I will never forget," said one guest. "Everyone was talking when Cynthia walked up to Hepburn. She had the cake in her right hand and put her left arm around Hepburn's shoulders. Suddenly the whole wedding fell dead silent, because Cynthia had hit Hepburn right in the face with the cake. Everyone was stunned. Then Hepburn laughed, so everyone else felt it was okay to laugh too."

Off to the side, however, Michael Davies looked distinctly uncomfortable. A tall, handsome man, born in England, he was only a couple of years divorced, and getting married again had not been his idea. He and Cynthia, after meeting at one of Fred Friendly's seminars, had bought a house together in nearby Essex. Davies had been content to just go on living together, but Cynthia wanted a big wedding. And she wanted it held at Fenwick.

Kate liked Davies—even if once, when she ordered him to fill the trunk of his new car with firewood, he refused. "What do you mean, *no?*" bellowed this tiny woman. (She had shrunk three to four inches in her old age.) Observers recall Davies refused to give in.

Yet as much as she liked him, Kate took Davies aside a few days before the wedding. She told him what she was telling everyone else: that the marriage was a mistake. "Cynthia's too much like I was," she said. "She will be focused solely on herself and her own progression." It didn't deter Davies. According to friends, Cynthia had told him she'd be with him forever.

Certainly, Kate knew about personal progression. By the time of Cynthia's wedding, she'd reached the pinnacle. As she waved good-bye to the newlyweds as they headed off on their honeymoon, Kate occupied a unique place in American life. No other star of the golden age had achieved the kind of exaltation she had. Kate reigned supreme.

"I can think of few actresses who served, as Hepburn has, as inspirational 'role model' for so many of us," wrote the critic Judith Crist. "[P]art tomboy, part romantic, part poet, her beauty is so ingrained that it has always gone against the fashion, her spirit so valiant that it has always implied defiance of convention, her courage so much the moral effort of a sensitive and vulnerable personality, her independence an inspiration for us all."

These were years of accolades. Though she'd been unwilling to accept the Kennedy Center award while Reagan was in office, Hepburn consented to attend the ceremony in late 1990 with his successor, George Bush. Phyllis attended with her. Reportedly, Kate lectured Bush on abortion rights.

That same year Kate was named a "Contemporary Hero" in a line of children's textbooks, the only actress so honored. Her qualifications? "Throughout her long and successful career, Hepburn has fought against the stereotyping of women in our culture," the text read. "Reportedly a tomboy in her youth, she was discouraged from a career in medicine by the social restrictions placed on women at that time [and] instead studied drama at Bryn Mawr College." The facts were already being picked and chosen (and ignored) to suit the purpose at hand.

Of course, much of Kate's public veneration arose out of what we now knew about her love for Tracy. Indeed, "Tracy and Hepburn" had become an archetype used as shorthand by journalists. When in 1993 the *New York Times* called the commentators James Carville and Mary Matalin "the Tracy and Hepburn of American politics," the public understood exactly what was meant by the comparison.

At university film schools, essays were being penned about why the romance between Spence and Kate continued to resonate for the public. He was working class; she was upper class—always an irresistible combination. He was earth; she was air—both elemental life forces. Meanwhile, the film critic and screenwriter Penelope Gilliatt assured us that despite Kate's famous independence, she was "certainly never mannish." Quite an evolution since 1934.

"I've been around so long," Kate said in *All About Me*, "that people treat me as some sort of oracle. They want to know what I think of the important things in life." So we got the absurdity of *Katharine Hepburn Once Said*, as if Kate were Confucius or the Dalai Lama. We also got running battles in the staid *New York Times* over whether Hepburn's official brownie recipe called for cocoa or "real, unadulterated chocolate."

She had become immortal.

Yet in "Me and Phyllis," Kate had asked how long the top could keep spinning. Several of her associates thought it was kept in motion for a few years past the point when it should have come to rest.

"Those last few movies . . ." A friend's voice trailed off as he suppressed a shudder. "She was really in no shape to make them. But she couldn't admit to the world that the great Kate Hepburn had slowed down, that she was failing. She just couldn't give up the spotlight."

Without work, the emptiness would have suffocated her. With Cynthia married and busy in her career, Kate once again felt the sting of loneliness. At Fenwick, Dick seemed a ghost, wandering in and out of rooms talking to himself. Hepburn's New York house, after more than sixty years of fascinating people rushing up and down the stairs, was equally quiet. Phyllis was gone, committed to the Mary Manning Walsh Home in New York, a nursing home maintained by the Catholic Church. By 1992, poor old Phyllis recognized very few people. Without her devoted companion, Kate seemed lost, unsure of every step she took. "She'd still try to lord over everyone, but the difference was, no one was afraid of her anymore," said her friend. "And the saddest part of it was—she knew it."

By agreeing to make *This Can't Be Love* in late 1993, not only was Kate keeping up the pretense of her indomitable energy and stardom; she was also escaping the aching void she knew at home, replacing it with the embrace of her television-movie family. For several months, the duration of the shoot, she'd be enveloped by close friends. Tony Harvey was on board as director, John Dayton returned as producer, and Noel Taylor once again did the costumes. Anthony Quinn was brought in as Kate's costar after she nixed Kirk Douglas—no reason given, but maybe she recalled Douglas's intimacy with Gene Tierney.

By now, there was no longer any pretense of acting. Kate was simply called on to play the creature of the public imagination. "I had Duane [Poole, the film's writer] sit with Kate for long stretches of time," said Dayton. "Then I had him go out and read everything he could biographically of Kate. He read *Me* cover to cover. Everything Duane wrote was directly applicable to Kate, something she would have said or done."

Indeed, the whole film is constructed around the moment when Kate can impart life's true meaning to her younger costars. On the set, she quarreled with Quinn, neither of the two old stars proving very accommodating to the other's infirmities. Yet no matter the film's mediocrity. Kate enjoyed making it, and ultimately that was the most important thing for those around her. "If I can't have fun," she told Dayton, "I don't want to work."

But Cynthia, who had a house with Davies not far from Fenwick, was reportedly telling Kate it was time to withdraw from the grind of moviemaking. The savvy McFadden now moved in high-powered media circles and had heard the talk that these films—and their filmmakers—were "exploiting" Kate. According to a couple of Kate's friends, one time Cynthia even showed up at the airport to try to talk Kate out of flying to Vancouver.

But the star wasn't listening. By the time *This Can't Be Love* aired on March 13, 1994, Dayton was already negotiating with none other than Garson Kanin, now eighty-one, about writing Kate's next picture. Any hope that Kanin may have had about trying his hand at the mythology one more time was dashed when Dayton read his treatment and found it lacking. He paid Gar a kill fee.

Meanwhile, Dayton had gotten an inquiry from Warren Beatty about Kate's possibly doing a cameo in his upcoming picture. Scott Berg had also received similar entreaties. If Kate agreed, the role would be a departure for her; she had never been anything less than the star in every film she'd ever made. Even in her first picture, *A Bill of Divorcement*, where she'd technically played supporting actress to John Barrymore and Billie Burke, the story had ultimately turned around her. And no matter the predictable plotlines of her recent television vehicles, they had preserved her central starring position. No other actor of her generation could claim such a lifetime achievement.

Beatty was determined, however, to appear in a film with Katharine Hepburn, and so promised her the full star treatment. She'd be billed above the title—right after himself and his costar (and real-life wife) Annette Bening. The film was to be a remake of *An Affair to Remember*, retitled *Love Affair*. Beatty wanted Kate to play his wise old aunt. Her part might be small, but it would be Aunt Ginny—no surprise—who imparts the necessary life lessons for Beatty and Bening to fall in love.

Kate hesitated—not least because the script called on her to say the word *fuck*. She'd sworn on film before—even said *shit* on stage—but this was a "nasty word," she told her friends, "the worst." She was also worried about forgetting her lines, which had been a nearly constant occurrence on *This Can't Be Love*.

Both Norah Moore and John Dayton accompanied her for the shoot. "Kate asked me to stand right next to the camera for all her scenes," Dayton said, "because she wanted to be able to see me out of the corner of her eye at all times."

Norah told friends Kate was impressed by how solicitous Beatty was of her. The house he rented for her was not far from his own. Yet he failed to heed Dayton's advice on the best way to work with the eighty-eight-year-old star. "I told Warren that Kate's first take was always her best take," Dayton said. "Unless something happened, there was no reason to do it beyond the second take. Warren was used to doing thirty-nine or forty takes." In a scene where Kate had to sit on a very low couch, she was to stand up and say her line, then cross off camera left. "Remember she was using a cane, too," said Dayton. "So Warren rehearsed her; she got up; it was perfect. He shot it, printed it—and then he asked her to do it again."

Dead silence fell over the set. "Kate looked at me and gave me this evil eye," Dayton remembered. "So she did it again. She had done the rehearsal, then the first take, now the second take. She had gotten up off that couch *three times.*"

That wasn't the end of it. Beatty called for still another take. Kate glared at him, then hobbled over to Dayton and said, "You take me home right now." Dayton said panic ensued as they began walking off the set. "Warren was chasing us," he said. "By the time we got out to my car, the heads of Warners were yelling at us back on the set, and I told them, 'It's not going to happen.'"

Better times were to be had off the set. She had a happy reunion with her longtime friend Jack Larson. She also wanted, since she was in Los Angeles, to see some of her old haunts. Dayton toured her through what was left of MGM. Pulling up in Dayton's rented white Ford, Kate was thrilled that the gateman recognized her. Nearby she spied an enormous poster of herself and Peter O'Toole from *The Lion in Winter.* "She couldn't believe that her picture was still up there," Dayton said.

Afterward, they drove to Trancas Beach, Kate pointing out where she and Cukor had shot *Sylvia Scarlett.* Heading back into Los Angeles, Dayton took her by Jimmy Stewart's house. Stewart was one of the last of Kate's costars still alive. Pulling into Stewart's driveway, Dayton saw that the venerable old actor was home. "But Kate just didn't have the heart [to see him]." They were both many years past *The Philadelphia Story.*

Kate had, in fact, for the first time in her life, gotten a bit plump, her famous hollow cheeks filling out, her eyes narrowing as her face became fleshier. The weight was due to her inability to swim and play tennis the way she once did, and was exacerbated by her medications, which reportedly included several antidepressants, known for adding pounds. But the main cause of weight gain was her alcohol consumption, which had by now increased to sometimes six or seven drinks a day.

Love Affair was not a success. "She deserved better for her final picture," said James Prideaux. For all his promises of star treatment, Beatty didn't even allow Kate a star entrance. Her first appearance comes in a quick cut to the kitchen, where she's half glimpsed with her head in the refrigerator. Yet when the time came to speak the infamous line "Fuck a duck," Kate proved quite canny. The offending word is rather hard to hear, uttered almost under her breath. Still, critics hoped it wouldn't be the last line Katharine Hepburn ever spoke on film.

It wasn't. Despite her precarious health, in the summer of 1994 Kate agreed to do another picture: *One Christmas*, based on a short story by Truman Capote. This time, Cynthia spent a couple of days with Kate on the set just to make sure she was all right. In fact, she wasn't. Easily tired, Kate was also frequently disoriented, the dementia getting progressively worse, causing some embarrassing moments. When the columnist Army Archerd interviewed her and asked her what she remembered about working with Cary Grant, Kate replied by asking how Grant was doing these days. When Archerd awkwardly told her that Grant had been dead for some years, Kate said she was sorry to hear of it.

It got far worse than that. At one point, surrounded by a group of people, Kate was trying, with great difficulty, to tell a story about one of her earlier films. "And she suddenly forgot the name of one of her costars," Noel Taylor said—not an unusual occurrence, so he moved in to try to help. "Charles Boyer?" he asked. "Paul Henreid? Rossano Brazzi?"

"No, no, the one I made all those pictures with," Kate said.

"Cary Grant?"

"No, no, *no!*" Kate was getting agitated. "All those pictures! They were so popular!"

Taylor felt his heart sink. "Kate . . . You don't mean *Spencer Tracy*, do you?"

"Yes!" she crowed. "*Spensuh!*"

It seems almost impossible to believe, but Taylor insisted the story was true. Sometimes Kate would get so confused on the set she could barely speak. Though once again she had only a couple of glorified cameos, Kate had many worrying that she'd never make it through to the end of production. She seemed to have little concept of the rest of the picture outside her own scenes.

Dayton, again serving as producer, knew this was finally it, Hepburn's last film. He remembered her last day of filming, with temperatures near one hundred degrees Fahrenheit. "She was ready for her scene," Dayton said, "but the set wasn't. I could see that she was turning red, so I went to [the writer] Duane Poole and had him rewrite the scene. We did it in the hallway, so we could get it done and I could take her home. I knew it would be her last scene in front of the cameras. Duane just wrote it off the cuff. I cried, because we wrote it as Kate, not the character."

In Hepburn's last appearance on the screen, here is what she says: "I have always lived my life exactly as I wanted. I've tried to please no one but me, me, me." (Here she made her familiar little gesture of pointing toward her heart.) "Very likely I've displeased a number of other people. But I'm entirely content. I can sit back in my old age and not regret a single moment or change a single thing."

While the speech wasn't entirely true for Hepburn the woman—she was far from being content in her old age, no matter how much those who loved her wished it were so—it was a fitting epitaph for Kate the icon, the public creature.

After that, she finally shut the door.

Sitting up in bed, Kate looked like a chubby little doll. When Scott Berg heard she'd been checked into the Manhattan Eye, Ear and Throat Hospital, he went immediately to see her. He found a doctor standing over her addressing her in a "peculiarly hostile tone."

This most recent hospitalization followed one a short time before at Hartford Hospital. Then, the stated cause was *exhaustion*, but it was really a code word for *disorientation,* friends said, which itself was code for *drinking too much.* Increasingly worried once Kate had returned to New York, Norah Moore was on the phone with Cynthia, who—as Kate had predicted—had divorced Davies and was now moving up in the news department at ABC as a legal correspondent. Yet as busy as she was, Cynthia never lost sight of "Aunt Kate"'s welfare. According to several friends of Kate's who shared Norah's concerns, Cynthia had agreed that Kate should be checked into the Eye, Ear and Throat Hospital. There, her doctors—including the one Berg recalled as hostile—tried to drill into Hepburn a stark fact: that she was slowly killing herself.

"Do you think I'm a drunk?" Kate asked, looking up at Berg.

He told her he did not. He blamed the interaction of her prescription medications with the alcohol as the cause of "her general funk." In his memoir, Berg left the impression that his "common sense" talk with Kate that day in the hospital persuaded her to stop drinking. But other friends thought differently.

"Right to the very last, when she simply could not take a drink without the help of others, Kate continued imbibing her scotch," said one person close to her. "I think it was the only way she could face what had happened to her. She had never prepared herself to be alone, to be idle, not making movies. The public's acclaim had kept her going for seventy years. Without it, she seemed just to wither away."

Certain routines were still kept up. Every weekend, Kate was driven to Fenwick, then back to New York on Monday—even if she had no schedule to keep anymore. It was simply what she had done for years, and she couldn't stop now. At Fenwick, she and Dick would shuffle past each other, sniping at each other to get out of the way. On good days, they played a game of Parcheesi.

She saw few others. John Dayton admitted he didn't see her again after *One Christmas*. Scott Berg came less and less. Cynthia, whom Kate had made executor of her estate, came whenever she could, but she was increasingly busy at ABC, named coanchor of the network's newsmagazine *20/20* in 1996. Cynthia was also now close to the columnist Liz Smith, and they had a house not far from Fenwick. They often spent time with Kate and sometimes brought her to their home.

Still, the legend continued to spin without her, with a series of books purporting to reveal "new secrets" of Kate and Spence. In 2000, CNN's *Larry King Live* devoted an entire show to Kathy Houghton, who talked about the fabled love affair. "Was it really secret?" King asked. "It *had* to be, Larry," Houghton replied earnestly, "because of his being married. And they had to work *hard* at it, never staying at the same hotels, going in back doors. My aunt went up lots of fire escapes, climbed in and out of windows, across roofs."

Of course, the fire-escape story is actually an echo of Kate's stunt at the Ambassador Hotel in Chicago, when she was trying to elude reporters during her affair with Howard Hughes. And the hotel-back-door story likely refers to Kate's feud with Claridge's in London, where the proprietors made her use the back entrance because they didn't want her walking through the lobby wearing slacks. Neither story had anything to do with Tracy.

But Houghton, like so many around Kate, was probably unaware just how much of the so-called history they spouted instinctively was simply legend on top of myth on top of romance. They had only Kate's stories on which to base their versions of truth—and Kate had been telling stories now for a very long time.

As Kate declined, different camps became apparent in the circles around her. Cynthia shared executorship of the Hepburn estate with Erik Hanson, Kate's accountant, who'd become a good friend after serving in a similar capacity for Nancy Hamilton. Hanson and McFadden also held power of attorney for Phyllis, who was now completely senile. Cynthia and Erik made most of the important decisions concerning Kate, which sometimes reportedly alienated Kathy Houghton, who'd once been her aunt's chief advocate.

Conflicts with the Hepburn clan were perhaps unavoidable. A decade before, Palache had rued how Kate spoiled her family "rotten." She told an interviewer, "They depend terribly on her for money." She cited Dick and his children—"not Bob, he's on his own"—and Peg, "the youngest sister, just a great gal but who's had terrible luck in her life." Peg was struggling to support a granddaughter with cystic fibrosis. In addition, there was Kathy Houghton, Palache said, whom Kate supported "practically entirely" as well.

Even among Kate's family of choice, there were divisions. In his memoir, Scott Berg seemed to take great pains to imply that he and Cynthia weren't rivals, but other friends told a different story. "Of course there was competition, and it wasn't just between Scott and Cynthia," said one observer, who had a close-up view of the circles around Hepburn. "Every one of Kate's friends believed that they and they alone were her true confidant, that she told them things that she told no one else. Who knows? Maybe, even in her confusion, she did that deliberately to keep them all off guard."

Or maybe she simply forgot what she had said to one person by the time she spoke to the next. Scott Berg said that Kate agreed that he should write about her after she died; John Dayton said that she told him emphatically that she did *not* want Berg writing about her. Friends were sometimes hurt when they discovered her double-talk, calling it "backstabbing." But among sufferers of dementia, it's a common trait.

No matter any rivalries, however, each and every one of Kate's friends and family shared her heartbreak on the morning of May 11, 1995. Two weeks earlier, on April 28, Phyllis had died, and her ashes were sent up to Hartford for burial in the Hepburn family plot. It would have been Phyllis's ninety-second birthday.

In a driving rain, the entire Hepburn clan, as well as Scott Berg and Tony Harvey, gathered around the gravesite. The minister had just finished speaking and was about to lower Phyllis's ashes into the ground when Kate stood up. "I want to do it myself," she told her brother Bob, hobbling over to the minister and taking the box containing the remains of her devoted companion of nearly forty years—longer and more constant than any other relationship in her life. With great effort Kate got down onto her hands and knees, in the rain and mud, and lowered the ashes into the grave. When she lifted her face, onlookers were moved to see she was crying.

Leaving the gravesite, Bob gestured to the marble slabs bearing their parents' names. "The place next to them is yours," Bob told Kate. "You're the oldest."

"No," Kate replied. "I want to be put next to Tom."

"It touched me," Bob said, "that she still remembered him."

Phyllis's estate (worth about $700,000) was divided between Peg's family and Norah Moore. What Kate may have written in her own will, no one—except Cynthia and Erik Hanson—was absolutely sure.

If the newspaper headlines could be believed, however, it wouldn't be long before they found out. In March 1996, the tabloids placed Hepburn at death's door after she was admitted to Lenox Hill Hospital in New York for intestinal flu. The *Daily News* quoted "hospital insiders" as saying Kate's family had been told to be prepared for her death.

She rallied. But now, those around her bowed to the inevitable. Shortly after Kate's release from the hospital, she was moved from her New York house and ensconced permanently at Fenwick, where the stairs weren't so steep and where the view outside her window always seemed to bring her comfort. According to Emily King, Laura Harding's niece who still visited from time to time, Kate had also wandered onto Forty-ninth Street a couple of times by herself and become disoriented. Norah had had to run after her and bring her back into the house. Everyone concerned agreed Kate would be safer in the exclusive confines of Fenwick.

That Easter she spent with Cynthia and Liz Smith. "She was quite perky, all dressed up in a tan cashmere turtleneck sweater, tan trousers and white running shoes," Smith—now Kate's unofficial spokesperson—reported in her column. "Her white hair was neatly caught back in a barrette. She was the picture of style, copied by everyone from Calvin Klein to the Gap."

Smith knew exactly the kinds of anecdotes the public wanted to hear. In her column, we were treated to the Kate of old, walking into a room "in her usual brisk fashion" and ordering another log be put on the fire. When a bouquet of lilies arrived, Smith reported that Kate quipped, "That looks like something Howard Hughes would have sent."

A year later, when the *National Enquirer* reported Kate was "battling for her life" on the occasion of her ninetieth birthday, Smith once again charged to the rescue. Taking the tabloid to task, she reported how she'd just had lunch with Miss Hepburn, and that Kate "ate heartily" from a tray set on a pillow in front of her. "It is true that this great star no longer resembles the goddess she was in her movie days," Smith told her readers, "but she needn't be turned into an object of pity."

According to Smith, Kate was still being taken for drives and occasionally she still sketched with a charcoal pencil, even if her painting days were behind her. "She doesn't chat much," Smith said, "but when I came in, she gave me a strong handshake and a clear greeting in her unmistakable voice."

For Christmas 2000, Cynthia and Liz threw a party for about a hundred people at their Saybrook home. Among them was the writer Dominick

Dunne, who lived in nearby Hadlyme. He was surprised to see the ninety-three-year-old Kate seated at a table. People were mingling, talking, laughing, but Kate sat there quite alone, just staring straight ahead.

"Please," Cynthia said to Dunne, "go talk to Kate."

He obliged. "There was this stool that someone had placed beside her, for people to sit on while they spoke to her," Dunne recalled. "It was like being at the confessional. When she did speak, it was just an unintelligible whisper. All the things she had once liked to talk about—none of that seemed to interest her. I don't know if she was out of it, or if she had finally just run out of things to say."

By now, there was a little two-year-old boy running around the place, occasionally drawing a curious, uncomprehending eye from Kate. This was Cynthia's son, born in July 1998; his father was James Hoge, the editor of *Foreign Policy* magazine. What seemed to draw Kate's attention to the boy was the name he was being called: *Spencer*. Cynthia told the press the name was Kate's idea.

In truth, Kate had only the barest awareness of the child. There were days when she didn't even know who Cynthia was. Around this time, Emily King also brought her son to meet Hepburn. "When I told her who I was, she just looked at me strangely," King said. "Of course, if she remembered the name, she was remembering a face ten years younger. It must have been very confusing for her."

A lift was installed on the stairway to take Kate up and down the stairs. Most of the time, her only company was her staff of devoted nurses. Norah Moore came when she could, and the longtime caretaker would report back to Hepburn's friends with updates on her health. Cynthia wasn't often there, Bob Hepburn recalled. "She had her job," he said by way of explanation. Still, Cynthia oversaw all of Kate's care and, with Hanson, handled the financial end of the estate.

It was Kate's family who saw her most. Peg Hepburn Perry made weekly visits, and Kathy Houghton came as often as possible.

For several years, Bob Hepburn remembered, Kate had made a great show of always keeping a stack of scripts beside her chair. When Bob would visit, she'd tell him she was reading them, considering which movie she was going to make next. Bob would just smile, going along with her. "And then the point came when she made no pretense of reading anymore," Bob said. The stack of scripts remained at her side for a while, but Kate just sat there by the window with her eyes closed. The end of Kate's life, her nephew Mundy said, was "a gentle fade to gray."

All along, Dick had been in his own slow decline, but somehow, even if they never spoke to each other, Kate knew he was in the house. When Dick died in his sleep in October 2000 at the age of eighty-seven, Kate refused to believe the news. She had to be wheeled into his room to see his body. Even then she wouldn't allow the reality to penetrate her mind. At Dick's memorial gathering held at Fenwick, Kate remained adamant in her denial, demanding to know why all these people were in the house. Scott Berg, who'd flown in for the service, told her it was because Dick had died. "You have misinformation," Kate said.

Some sixty years before, she had squelched Dick's dream of theatrical success. Forever afterward, Kate had felt—rightly or wrongly—responsible for her brother. In her will it would be revealed she had made elaborate provisions for him if she died before he did, allowing him to remain at Fenwick for as long as he lived. Some thought dreamy old Dick had never amounted to anything. But the number of people who showed up at his memorial service—people who recalled his friendly hello, who laughed at his antics, who had read some of his poetry or maybe one of his plays—seemed to give the lie to that idea. Dick had lived his life according to his own rules, sometimes irresponsibly, sometimes self-indulgently, but in the end no one had defined Dick Hepburn but himself.

The public would think the same of his sister Katharine. Though she wrapped herself in so much legend, part of that impression is true. She had refused, as Scott Berg wrote of her, "to live as a 'woman' in what was very much a man's world." No studio had ever dictated to Katharine Hepburn. She had chosen her films, her plays, her directors, her publicity all on her own. Partly because she had the financial means to be independent. Partly because she would have had it no other way.

But in the end, something other than Katharine Hepburn defined who she was. Or at least who the world believed she was. Call it ambition. Call it the expectations of the public. But consider: What if, in 1934, she hadn't come back on the *Paris*? What if she had refused to play the publicity game with Leland? What if she'd never sent Laura away?

What if, instead of *The Philadelphia Story*, she'd come back to the stage in 1939 in a different vehicle, one that didn't seem to renounce her subversive heroines? What if she'd had Phil Barry, or someone else, write her a *different* kind of play, one that told all those people who'd been made uncomfortable by Susan Vance's rebellion (*Bringing Up Baby*) and Linda Seton's unconventionality (*Holiday*) that the times were changing and they'd better get used to women like her?

What if she'd insisted on top billing over Spence once in a while, or at the fade-out of a picture, she'd taught *him* a lesson for a change? What if after Spence died, she hadn't been so obsessed with convincing the world she'd been more than just a rumor? What if she'd been less concerned about fulfilling the idealized romantic vision of a man and a woman—of becoming a version of her father and her mother?

What if she had stood up at that testimonial at the Majestic Theatre and told the truth—the *real* truth—about her relationship with Tracy? How wonderful it had been, how unconventional, how "more than ordinary"? What if she'd nudged the public along in its thinking? What if she'd pushed them to see the beauty of relationships that don't fit proscribed patterns— that, instead, upend expectations and defy easy categorization?

What if she had let Jimmy Hepburn—instead of Kate—take the lead in her life? Would she have been happier? Even more of an artist? Would she have found a fulfilling, enduring, equal relationship with another human being? Would that have enabled her, at the end, to enjoy the song of life?

One thing seems likely: if she'd done all that, she probably would never have become the heroine that the world remembers. She would never have been named the Greatest Movie Star of All Time by the American Film Institute in 1999. She had done what it takes for public acclaim, not personal fulfillment.

As a little girl, Kathy Hepburn had wanted to be noticed and admired. She spent her entire life making sure she was. Yet fame wasn't what was on her mind at the end. The last time she saw Scott Berg, she asked him if he was loved. When he told her yes, she said, "I've been loved, too." He presumed she was talking about Tracy—a romantic presumption, and a lovely note on which to end his book about her.

But while Spencer may well have been in her thoughts, might she have been thinking of others, too? Phelpie and Luddy and Laura and Cukor and Irene and Cynthia? And—just maybe—the fans who threw kisses to her in the street? It would be nice to believe that, in those last years, Hepburn knew—and took comfort in knowing—just how much she had made people love her. She might never have found exactly the one, but she had the world.

She always said she didn't fear death. She was simply "looking forward to a nice, long rest in the ground." Yet certainly she held on to life tenaciously enough at the end. Though she was taken to Hartford Hospital for a respiratory infection in July 2001, she once again rallied and was released. "She's not ready to go," Cynthia told friends.

For Kate's ninety-fifth birthday the following May, Kathy Houghton decorated the house with blown-up stills from *Woman of the Year, Adam's Rib,* and *The African Queen.* Hepburn seemed to enjoy herself tremendously. Ready to go she certainly was not.

When her father lay dying, he'd told her, "I'm getting ready to go somewhere, and I think I should get interested in it, but I just can't." Kate shared his disinterest in the next life. This one had preoccupied all her thoughts for almost a century. "I don't believe in God," she said many times. "I think that anything good that you're going to do, you should do for other people here, and not do anything to make yourself have a happy time in the next world."

Yet for all her disdain for religion—one more inheritance from Hep and Kit—she was not altogether lacking in spirituality. Her friends noted, even when she was healthy, a certain longing as she sat at the beach at Fenwick, looking out over the water. "Do you think there's something more?" she asked Robert Shaw after she lost her mother. She insisted she didn't—death was just "a long sleep"—but Shaw thought maybe she wanted him "to convince her otherwise." Of course, heaven and hell could never be more than fairy tales to a woman like her; but maybe, as she hinted to Shaw, there was "something." In "Me and Phyllis," she wrote of setting photographs of her departed loved ones on a table and talking to them through the new moon.

In late 2002, a call came from the actress Cate Blanchett, who had been cast to play Katharine Hepburn in Martin Scorsese's upcoming film about Howard Hughes, called *The Aviator.* Blanchett hoped to meet Hepburn, but by this time Kate was confined to her bed, and no introduction was possible. The few who saw Kate said she had shrunk to just a tiny shell of her former self. An aggressive tumor had been discovered in her neck. Doctors advised against surgery, given her age. Her only treatment now would be palliative.

In early June, she stopped eating. Gradually, her intake of fluids fell off as well. At 2:50 p.m. on June 29, 2003, Katharine Hepburn died. She was ninety-six. Her ashes, as she wished, were buried next to her brother Tom's.

Her will directed that $100,000 be given to Norah, $50,000 to Erik Hanson, and various smaller monetary gifts to her goddaughter Valentina Fratti, her agent Freya Manston, and her faithful caretakers. Cynthia was bequeathed $10,000 and some furniture. Real estate, however, was Kate's most valuable asset, and she'd directed that both Fenwick and the New York town house be sold and the proceeds divided among her family.

SPIRITED ACTRESS is how the *New York Times* bannered her front-page obituary the next day. CLASSY FILM FEMINIST read the *Los Angeles Times.* But equally prominent in her death notices was Spencer Tracy. The obituary writer Caryn James observed that Kate's "life and career were dominated by her love affair with Spencer Tracy." She reported they had lived together for twenty-seven years—right there on the front page of the *New York Times*, so it must be true. "The greatest love story never told," CNN trumpeted about the lovers' legendary union.

"Here's what's most important about Katharine Hepburn," Michael Moriarty, Kate's costar in *The Glass Menagerie*, told *Premiere* magazine soon after her death. "Not her career and not her brilliance and not her talent—it was her profound, unconditional love for Spencer Tracy. That was her greatest achievement."

Respectfully, it was not. For all the wonderful celluloid memories Kate and Spence gave us, Hepburn's career, her brilliance, her talent—those things Moriarty dismisses—any might ultimately serve as Kate's more important legacy. What makes Hepburn transcendent is how, at a young age, she set her sights on immortality and sacrificed all to achieve it. How she created her public image out of the raw clay of her personality and made us all want to be just like her. How she never wavered in finding herself, cold sober, endlessly fascinating—and how she convinced us to do the same.

What makes Hepburn immortal is not any one of the many legends that are told about her—including the one about her star-crossed love with Tracy—but rather the culmination of all of them. Without the spunky rabble-rouser of the 1930s we would not have the red-dressed subversive of the 1940s or the noble spinster of the 1950s or the indefatigable survivor of her old age. The prank-playing tomboy is just the flip side of the wise old grandmother of the world. The brilliance and singular devotion she gave to the creation and maintenance of her public image should inspire awe—especially when one sees all that went on behind it. That there was sometimes a human cost to her determination is undeniable. But the Creature was unlike anything else that came before. Or likely ever to come again.

What makes Hepburn so endlessly fascinating is not how she conforms to our expectations but how she defies them. Not how she comforts us, but how she surprises us. Even now, as her mythmaking inevitably falls to the realm of history, she catches us off guard, making us see her in a new but equally compelling light. That much of her legend is indeed that—*legend*—should not detract from our esteem, but rather enhance it. How many people single-handedly turn themselves into paragons? The contradictions of her life only make Kate more fascinating. They will, in fact, ensure her true immortality.

Cynthia McFadden once recalled a professor's words: "It ain't that simple." Those four words, she said, have offered a guiding principle in her career. "When you work in journalism," McFadden explained, "you have to resist the temptation to paint the world in black and white."

No one deserves full color more than Katharine Hepburn. That she chose to give the public only one small part of her story was a concession to her times and culture. She knew what would work, what would catch hold, what would give her the attention she had craved ever since she was a little girl.

But a part of her loved that dance she played with the press and public. Catch her if we can. One is left to wonder if, despite all of Kate's presumed fear of the truth, her attitude might have been more like her friend Noël Coward's, who speculated in his journal what they would say about him after his death: "There will be books proving conclusively that I was homosexual and books proving equally conclusively that I was not. There will be detailed and inaccurate analyses of my motives for writing this or that and of my character. There will be lists of apocryphal jokes I never made and gleeful misquotations of words I never said. *What* a pity I shan't be here to enjoy them!"

Since Kate's death, at least three books have been published about her. Fashion shows have been held in her name. Cate Blanchett won an Oscar for her portrayal of Hepburn in *The Aviator*—a film that brilliantly spun a whole new set of myths about the star.

And on television, in retrospectives and film festivals, the movies go on. Kate still comes dancing down that staircase in *A Bill of Divorcement*. Jo March still yells "Heeey!" in *Little Women*. Alice Adams and Jane Hudson still break our hearts. Amanda and Adam Bonner still battle outrageously in the courtroom in *Adam's Rib*. Rose Sayer still croons "Chaaarlie" in *The African Queen*. And Susan Vance will still be knocking over that brontosaurus skeleton for as long as people watch movies.

In many ways, the legend has only begun.

ABBREVIATIONS

AAM: All About Me, 1993 documentary

AHC: Anthony Harvey Collection, Lilly

AMPAS: Margaret Herrick Library, Academy of Motion Picture Arts and Sciences

Beinecke: Beinecke Rare Book and Manuscript Library, Yale University

Berg: A. Scott Berg, *Kate Remembered* (Putnam, 2003)

BU: Boston University

Cavett: Television interview with Dick Cavett, ABC TV, October 2–3, 1973

DEC: David Eichler Collection, Lilly

Edwards: Anne Edwards, *Katharine Hepburn: A Remarkable Woman* (St. Martin's, 2000)

FBC: Frederick Brisson Collection, NYPL

FMP: F. O. Matthiessen Papers, Beinecke

GCC: George Cukor Collection, AMPAS

GCF: George Cukor, letters held by Tucker Fleming

Higham: Charles Higham, *Kate: The Life of Katharine Hepburn* (W. W. Norton, 1975)

HTC: Hedgerow Theatre Collection, Boston University

IMSC: Irene Mayer Selznick Collection, Boston University

JFC: John Ford Collection, Lilly

Kanin: Garson Kanin, *Tracy and Hepburn* (Viking, 1971)

KH: Katharine Hepburn

LAT: Los Angeles Times.

Leaming: Barbara Leaming, *Katharine Hepburn* (Crown, 1995)

Lilly: Lilly Library, Indiana University

Me: Katharine Hepburn, *Me: Stories of My Life* (Knopf, 1991)

NYPL: Billy Rose Theatre Collection, New York Public Library for the Performing Arts

NYT: New York Times

PFP: Palache Family Papers, Radcliffe College

PPP: Phelps Putnam Papers, Beinecke

RDP: Russell Davenport Papers, Library of Congress

ROSS: "Reflections on the Silver Screen," television interview by Richard Brown, American Movie Classics, August 3, 1994

SEP: Saturday Evening Post, five-part series by Lupton Wilkinson and J. Bryan III, 1941–42

SFP: Smith-Houston-Morris-Ogden Family Papers, American Philosophical Society, Philadelphia

TCMK: They Called Me Kathy, 1988 documentary

TGC: Theatre Guild Collection, Beinecke

WP: Washington Post

All references to weather conditions throughout were confirmed through contemporary newspaper weather reports. All dialogue was taken from contemporary reports or anecdotes from those who were involved or intimately familiar with the scene in question. In quotations from telegrams, punctuation has been inserted if necessary to make the meaning intelligible.

Where not indicated, quotes and other information come from personal interviews.

1. A SEA CHANGE

3 **Debarkation on the *Paris***: My description is taken from contemporary newspaper accounts: *NYT, New York Sun, LAT, Chicago Daily Tribune*, others from collections at NYPL and AMPAS.

3 **Maria Riva**: Riva, *Marlene Dietrich* (Ballantine, 1994).

5 **"Don't expect"**: GCF.

5 **"totally demoralized"**: Higham.

5 **Atkinson**: *NYT*, December 27, 1933.

5 **Parker**: Edwards sourced this famous quote to the *New York Journal-American*, December 27, 1933. However, the *Journal-American* didn't yet exist; it was called the *Evening Journal* at that point, and a search through relevant issues did not reveal Parker's quote. The *Evening Journal* reviewer for *The Lake* was, in fact, John Anderson, not Parker. It appears that the famous quote was not from a review of the play but was instead one of those dinner-party bon mots repeated endlessly in newspaper and magazine columns—which actually made it worse for Hepburn. The earliest version of the quote in print that I could discover was in the February 19, 1934, issue of *Time*, which reported it this way: "During an intermission of 'The Lake,' Dorothy Parker remarked to others in her party: 'Well, let's go back and see Katharine Hepburn run the gamut of human emotion from A to B.'" Clearly the quip had been making the rounds for a while.

6 **"I thought"**: *New York Sun,* March 8, 1935.

7 **"Miss Hepburn's husband"**: Hepburn told this story herself in *Me*. It was also recalled by several members of Harding's family, among whom it had long been part of Laura's "lore."

8 **"What kind of"**: Unsourced clip, NYPL.

8 **Suzanne Steell**: *NYT,* April 2, 1898; *Theatre Magazine*, February 1908; *NYT*, December 19, 1920; *New York Sun,* November 1, 1922; *NYT*, January 15, 1922; January 17, 1923; *Evening State Journal* (Lincoln, Nebraska), January 24, 1923 (which includes a photograph of her); *LAT*, March 11, 1926; *NYT*, February 2, September 19, October 5, November 9, December 11, December 14, 1930; March 17, 1931; *Daily Northwestern*, March 16, 1931; *NYT*, March 18, 1932; *Detroit Free Press*, January 17, 1933; *NYT*, March 18, 1933; April 13, 1933; April 17, 1933; *New York Herald Tribune*, April 17, 1933; *New York Sun*, April 17, 1933; *LAT*, May 20, 1934; *NYT*, December 15, 1934; July 29, 1937; December 14, 1940; February 1, 1941; December 2, 1953; *Playbill*, "Auntie Mame," November 18, 1957; *NYT*, September 7, 1958; *New York Post*, August 29, 1958; *NYT*, September 7, 1958; November 14, 1959; *WP*, November 12, November 26, 1959. See also U.S. Census, 1920, New York; probate file, Susan Steell Allen, November 1959, Surrogate Court, New York City.

According to Steell's longtime friend Henry Lewis, Steell moved in with Hepburn during the run of *The Lake* and "cooked all the time for her, since Hepburn was too embarrassed to be seen outside." Whether the friendship between Hepburn and Steell was sexual is unknown. I don't believe it was, given that Steell was physically very different from all the other (slim and boyish) women who were romantic attachments of Hepburn's. In *Me*, Hepburn remembered Steell as "very tall" and "very fat." Although we know from photographs and from friends' recollections that Steell was not yet "very fat" in 1934, she was still a big woman. In one photograph of Kath on the pier, a heavyset woman with her was identified as her mother, and there is some resemblance. But a notice in the *Hartford Times* on March 16, 1934, indicates Kit was in Hartford at the time.

8 **Maria Jeritza**: *NYT*, November 8, December 30, 1930; *Chicago Tribune*, December 30, 1930. See also Maria Jeritza, *Sunlight and Song: A Singer's Life* (Appleton, 1924, reprinted by Arno Press, 1977); Roderick Mueller-Guttenbrunn, *Riffraff Around a Singer* (Fiba, 1930); and Ernst Decsey, *Maria Jeritza* (J. Fischer-Verlag, 1931).

10 **Fan-magazine spy**: *Movie Mirror*, June 1934.

10 **Jeanne Aubert**: *NYT*, February 14, March 17, 1934; *Chicago Daily Tribune*, July 18, 1934; various clippings, NYPL.

11 **KH's return on the *Paris***: *NYT*, April 3, April 4, 1934; *LAT*, April 4, 1934; *Chicago Daily Tribune,* April 4, 1934. Hemingway's presence on the ship is confirmed by the newspaper reports. In many accounts, Hemingway's return to the United States was placed on the *Ile de France*, where the

actress he met on board was not Katharine Hepburn but Marlene Dietrich. But the *Ile de France* had not yet left Le Havre when newspapers confirm Hemingway's arrival in New York on the *Paris*. James R. Mellow, in *Hemingway: A Life Without Consequences* (Houghton Mifflin, 1992), corrects this error, stating that Hemingway did indeed sail on the *Paris,* and he places the writer's meeting with Dietrich on board that ship (though he does not mention a meeting with Hepburn). Although there is no definitive evidence that Dietrich was actually on the *Paris,* she may well have been, as we know she did return from Europe about this time, and Maria Riva remembered the meeting with Hemingway; she apparently just incorrectly recalled the name of the ship. If so, Dietrich seems to have managed better than Hepburn in slipping in under the radar of the press—bolstering my belief that Hepburn deliberately turned the spotlight toward her at this moment. Had she really wanted to sneak back home incognito, she could have done it, just as Dietrich did. And although it's possible that the two stars met on board, there's no record of it.

12 **"I was a star"**: *Times* (London), November 24, 1973.

14 **"sudden, radiant"**: Kanin.

2. SUCH A GOOD FAIRY-TALE TELLER

15 **Hartford Club**: Notes to the script of *TCMK,* written by KH and Ellsworth Grant.

16 **"Fairy tales"**: Christopher Andersen, *Young Kate* (Henry Holt, 1988).

16 **"I am totally"**: *AAM.*

17 **"Every conceivable"**: Notes to script of *TCMK.*

17 **"Mother's Mandarin," "completely crazy"**: These quotes come from *Young Kate,* presumably from interviews Hepburn gave to Andersen. However, there is a very similar quote about Shaw in Kanin: "He was mad about Bernard Shaw—most people in Hartford hadn't even heard of Shaw." I tend not to quote directly from Kanin because of his screenwriter's propensity for re-creating dialogue. If, however, Hepburn told Kanin a very similar anecdote to the one she told Andersen, perhaps Kanin was accurate in this case. Or, perhaps, Hepburn was using Kanin, yet again, as a blueprint for her own memory. Or, alternatively, it may have been Andersen who was paraphrasing Kanin. Such is the difficulty of untangling the threads of the Hepburn legend.

17 ***Damaged Goods***: This play was printed in 1911 and translated by John Pollock. *NYT,* July 29, 1911.

17 **American Social Hygiene Association**: *NYT,* January 27, 1913; *LAT,* January 28, 1913; *Chicago Tribune,* January 27, 1913; *Atlanta Constitution,* January 27, 1913.

18 **Hemlock tree**: In some versions of this story, it's Kit, not Hep, who tells the caller that Kathy doesn't know sitting up that high is dangerous.

18 **Hep and Kit**: In this work, I have chosen to refer to Katharine Hepburn's parents in this way, although her father was also called Tom and her mother occasionally called Kate. But with another Tom and Kate Hepburn figuring in the story, it is less confusing to stick with the single nicknames.

19 **A. Barton Hepburn**: The full account of Hepburn's false early origin has never been revealed before and is taken from various accounts: *LAT, Los Angeles Herald, Chicago Daily Tribune,* other newspapers, AMPAS, and NYPL. Biographical information on this alternate Hepburn family is drawn from accounts in the *NYT* and the *WP* as well as U.S. census records.

19 HOLLYWOOD'S SIXTEEN: *Screen Book,* December 1932.

19 **Early images of Hep and Kit in the Hepburn legend**: Various clippings, including *LAT,* February 26, 1933. See also Henry F. Pringle, "A Mind of Her Own," *Collier's,* October 28, 1933.

20 **First telling of KH's "origin"**: Adela Rogers St. Johns, "The Private Life of Katharine Hepburn," *Liberty,* January 6, 1934.

21 **Suppression of true work of Hep and Kit**: Grace Mack, "Private Life of Katharine Hepburn," *Movie Mirror,* [n.d., 1934], NYPL; Martha Kerr, "The Truth About Katharine Hepburn's Marriage," *Modern Screen,* February 1933. Kit's work was finally acknowledged in Beatrice MacDonald, "The Career of an Ugly Duckling," *Modern Screen,* March 1934, April 1934. Yet even here it was downplayed, adhering to RKO's preferred view of the Hepburns. "Katharine grew up in the wholesome,

everyday atmosphere of the average middle-class American household," MacDonald wrote. In all of these articles, Dr. Hepburn's work was avoided, other than to acknowledge his eminence as a surgeon; venereal disease was clearly even more of a hot potato than birth control.

21 **"Mother and Dad"**: *TCMK*.

21 **"This is to introduce"**: KH to Theresa Helburn, January 19, 1941, Beinecke. A concurrent letter from Lupton Wilkinson affirms Hepburn's active involvement in constructing the piece. Scrawled across the top is a note from Joseph Heidt, press agent for the Guild, indicating he'd checked and found Wilkinson "OK." Presumably, he'd checked with Hepburn.

3. NOBODY LIKES CRYBABIES

23 **Dr. and Mrs. Hepburn's relationships with their children**: I drew most of my account from conversations with Bob Hepburn, Peg Hepburn Perry, and several close friends of Hepburn's, as well as from reconsidering critically what Hepburn had to say about her parents over the years. The two anecdotes set in Keney Park were described to me from family lore by Bob Hepburn. "Kathy on the bike" is also portrayed (with the script written by Hepburn herself) in *They Called Me Kathy*. The phony spanking scene was described by Hepburn in *Young Kate*. Leaming provides additional details on the complex relationships between Thomas and Kit Hepburn and their children. Indeed, this is where Leaming shines, creating a fully realized world for the young married couple.

26 **"the child is entitled"**: *SEP*, November 29, 1941.

27 **Tom Hepburn's background**: Most accounts have implied that Tom Hepburn came from poverty. While it is true that his father, Reverend Sewell Hepburn, made very little money as an itinerant minister, he did come from an established family of some means. Sewell's father, also named Sewell, was a farmer and blacksmith in Kent County, Maryland, whose real estate in 1860 was valued at $8,240; in addition, he declared a personal estate worth $6,500. (Part of this came from his wife, Martha Maslin, whom Sewell remembered as "somewhat of an heiress.") While the Hepburn money pales beside the estate of Katharine's other great-grandfather—Amory Houghton's 1860 estate was valued at $175,000 (real) and $50,000 (personal)—it was still a considerable sum for the period. When Sewell began living a life of religious nomadism, he seems to have given up any connection to the family money; in 1870, living as a boarder in Falls Church, Virginia, he had no estate, real or personal, to declare. Source: U.S. Census, 1850–70. See also "Memoirs of the Rev. Sewell S. Hepburn," *Old Kent, The Historical Society of Kent County, Maryland*, vol. 17, no. 2, Summer 2000, and vol. 18, no. 3, Fall 2001.

28 **James Hepburn, earl of Bothwell**: Family tradition held that the first of the line to immigrate to America, James Hepburn (died 1709 in Maryland), was a grandson of Bothwell. If so, it was through an illegitimate son, as Bothwell had no children from his two marriages, first to Jean Gordon and then to Mary Stuart. Still, the family legend was strong enough for Sewell Hepburn to change their last name, until then spelled *Hepbron*, to the more familiar and historically referential version.

28 **"lifelong chip"**: *Hartford Magazine*, December 2003.

28 **Ida Wood**: U.S. Census, 1910.

28 **Lizzie Byles, Bertha Bitner, Fanny Ciarrier**: U.S. Census, 1920.

28 **"In this machine age"**: "Memoirs of the Rev. Sewell S. Hepburn."

29 **"inclined to be proud"**: *NYT*, May 8, 1912.

29 **Kit's activism**: *Daily News* (Frederick, Maryland), January 21, 1911; *WP*, November 29, 1913; *Atlanta Constitution*, January 4, 1914; *NYT*, October 18, 1915; *Evening Times* (Warren, Pennsylvania), November 19, 1917; *Bridgeport Telegram*, April 1, 1919. Kit's entry into activism was not, as has been written, a response to hearing the British suffragist Emmeline Pankhurst speak at Hartford's Parsons Theatre. That event did not occur until October 1909, and by that time Kit was already serving as vice president of the Connecticut Woman Suffrage Association.

29 **"a torpid"**: From Katharine Houghton Hepburn's introduction of Emmeline Pankhurst at Parsons Theatre, November 13, 1913. Pamphlet printed by Connecticut Woman Suffrage Association (Connecticut Historical Society).

29 **"I've got"**: Cavett.

29 **"It was Sunday"**: May 15, 1914, journals of Florence Ledyard Cross Kitchelt, Smith College.

31 **"would continue"**: *Atlanta Constitution*, January 4, 1914.

31 **"It was not"**: Speech given by Katharine Houghton Hepburn to the National Association of College Alumnae (Connecticut Historical Society).

31 **Fusco and Hartford white slave traffic**: *Hartford Courant*, November 23, December 23, 1911; *NYT*, November 23, November 25, December 24, 1911; U.S. Census, 1910; Hartford city directories.

32 **Bertha Rembaugh**: *Lincoln* [Nebraska] *Evening News*, April 8, 1910.

32 **"divide into"**: *NYT*, October 1, 1910.

33 **Bessie Wakefield**: *Hartford Courant*, November 4–8, November 13, December 9, December 10, 1913; March 3, March 4, July 30, July 31, 1914; *NYT*, November 5, November 11, November 13, December 10, 1913; March 4, July 31, 1914; *Atlanta Constitution*, November 7, 1913; *WP*, December 10, 1913. Bessie Wakefield was eventually pardoned and released from prison in 1933, at the age of forty-four. *NYT*, November 7, 1933.

4. JIMMY WAS HER NAME

36 **KH versus tree**: An extraordinary clip of a private home movie is included in the little-seen 1988 documentary *They Called Me Kathy*.

36 **Jimmy**: Reconsidering what Katharine Hepburn had to say about her childhood alter ego allowed for a fresh look on the subject. She spoke about being "Jimmy" as early as the 1941 article in the *Saturday Evening Post*. Jimmy became a more fully fleshed figure in Hepburn's memoir, *Me*, and the 1993 documentary *All About Me*.

37 **Inghams**: U.S. Census, 1900–1930. Various records, History and Genealogy Department, Connecticut State Library.

38 **"Now it's summer"**: *Me*.

38 **Kathy and Tommy**: Their athletic exploits, and Hep's reactions to them, were described to me by their brother Bob. There is also documentation in the yearbooks of the Kingswood School. Various close friends of Hepburn also echoed Bob's stories of Kathy's determination to stand out from her brother's shadow and please her father.

39 **"A pompous egotist"**: Richard Hepburn to Robert Hanley, March 4, 1936, HTC.

39 **"I expect"**: Katharine Houghton Grant, ed., *Marion Hepburn Grant* (Fenwick Productions, 1989).

40 **"I could"**: TCMK.

41 **"self-dramatizing"**: Grant, *Marion Hepburn Grant*.

41 **Cathy Watson**: *Kingswood-Oxford Today*, commemorative edition, 1984. Catherine D. Watson, born in 1898 in New Jersey, left the Oxford School in 1921 to teach girls' gymnastics at Arnold College in New Haven. She was still unmarried in 1930, living with Minerva Haust, dean of women. Source: U.S. Census, 1930; Hartford and New Haven city directories.

42 **Ali Barbour's appearance**: A large portrait accompanies her wedding notice in the *Hartford Times*, October 8, 1927.

42 **"no longer"**: *Me*.

43 **"Whatever it was"**: Berg.

44 **The move to Laurel Street**: Various accounts have said the family left Hawthorn Street because it was set to be demolished—the only justification the legend could offer for leaving such an enchanted house for such an ordinary dwelling. But in fact they left at Hep's insistence. His daughter Marion wrote that he was "determined to move his growing family into a house that he owned." The house at 133 Hawthorn wasn't demolished until 1951, when the family, carrying Kit's ashes past the address as a final tribute, was stunned to witness a wrecking crew tearing down their beloved old home. (Houghton, *Marion Hepburn Grant*)

5. SOME PEOPLE ARE NEW YORK

47 **"Some people"**: Andersen, *Young Kate.*

48 **"One should"**: *NYT*, March 27, 1921.

48 **Mary Towle and Bertha Rembaugh**: *NYT,* November 30, 1913; June 9, 1918; October 5, October 10, October 14, October 20, October 22, October 26, October 28, November 5, 1919; June 9, June 16, June 26, 1921; June 25, 1927; February 1, 1950. Rembaugh's report to the nation's governors about the legal status of American women was reported in the *Syracuse Herald*, September 8, 1911. See also U.S. Census, 1870–1930; New York City directories, 1911–24. The City Register's office in New York confirmed property owned by Towle and Rembaugh. They formed the 30 Charlton Street Corporation with Towle's sister Sarah Towle Moller and purchased the property on April 8, 1920. I am also grateful for Bob Hepburn's recollections of these two extraordinary women. The children called Mary Towle "Auntie Towle" or just "Auntie"; Bertha Rembaugh was "Aunt Bertha."

50 **Mencken quote**: *Chicago Tribune*, April 5, 1925.

50 **"grave intellectual ladies"**: *Modern Screen*, May 1933.

50 **Heterodoxy**: See the various papers of Elizabeth Gurley Flynn and Inez Haynes Irwin. Also see Judith Schwarz, *Radical Feminists of Heterodoxy: Greenwich Village, 1912–1940* (New Victoria, 1986). See also Margaret Anderson, *My Thirty Years' War* (Horizon Press, 1969); Lillian Faderman, *Odd Girls and Twilight Lovers* (Columbia University Press, 1991); and Mabel Dodge Luhan, *Intimate Memories* (Harcourt, Brace, 1933–37).

51 **Heterodoxy and Kit's radicalism**: The association with Heterodoxy nudged Kit farther and farther to the left. By 1914, her name was being linked in the press with some of the more radical members of the group, including La Follette and founder Marie Jenney Howe, as being part of a feminist "insurgency." The Antis set out on a press campaign to "indict" these women for trying to inaugurate a "futurist age of extremes," releasing their names (Kit's included) as if they were wanted criminals. See *NYT*, January 19, 1914; *Daily Northwestern* (Oshkosh), January 23, May 18, 1914.

51 **Mary Towle at Rector's**: The fracas at Rector's was documented in *NYT*, April 7–8, 1917. Towle was at first reported to be a part of the name-calling, chair-throwing melee, during which the socialist writer Frederick Boyd was beaten when he refused to stand during the playing of the national anthem. Later Towle would insist to the press that she hadn't been there for the fight, that she'd arrived only later as legal counsel for Boyd's companion, the well-known birth control activist Jessie Ashley. With war fever gripping the nation, Towle felt obliged to declare quickly and publicly that she was no pacifist and had, in fact, "rejoiced" when the United States joined the war against Germany.

53 **Towle, Rembaugh, and Heterodoxy**: While not official members, Kathy's two aunts clearly knew many of the women of Heterodoxy through overlapping interests and social worlds. A few were literally neighbors. Just down the block on Grove Street lived the anarchists Stella Commins Ballantine and Eleanor Fitzgerald, as well as the writer and socialist agitator Rose Pastor Stokes.

53 **"marriage customs"**: Florence Woolston Seabury, "Marriage Customs and Taboos Among the Early Heterodites," included among the papers of Inez Haynes Irwin.

53 **"I've always"**: *Ladies' Home Journal*, August 1975.

53 **"Oh, then"**: *Life*, December 1939.

54 **"bobbed-haired"**: *NYT*, March 27, 1921.

54 **"romantic friendships"**: There is considerable literature on the nineteenth-century tradition of women's romantic friendships. For my purposes, I consulted Faderman, *Odd Girls and Twilight Lovers*, as well as two books by Helen Lefkowitz Horowitz: *The Power and Passion of M. Carey Thomas* (Knopf, 1994) and *Alma Mater: Design and Experience in the Women's Colleges from Their Nineteenth-Century Beginnings to the 1930s* (Knopf, 1984).

55 **Kate's statement to Kanin**: *McCall's*, February 1970.

6. TAKING WHAT LIFE HAS TO OFFER

58 **Tom misses school**: This absence was reported in the aftermath of Tom's death by the *New York Herald*, April 4, 1921, apparently based on the reporter's questioning of Dr. Hepburn. The article called Tom a "nervous, high-strung boy."

58 **"maybe a girl"**: Berg. Of the girl to whom Hep referred, there is no record, but the boy might have been Tommy's inseparable chum, James Thrall Soby, who would go on to become the chairman of the department of painting at the Museum of Modern Art. See Soby's papers at the Getty Research Institute in Los Angeles, as well as Nicholas Fox Weber, *Patron Saints: Five Rebels Who Opened America to a New Art, 1928–1943* (Knopf, 1992). Of interest as well are the references to Soby's unpublished boyhood memoir in Leaming, in which Soby revealed himself every bit as sensitive and high-strung as Tom Hepburn.

58 **Greenwich Village**: A remarkable snapshot of the Village on the very week of Tom and Kathy's fateful visit can be found in Eleanor Hayden's "The Friendliest Place in New York," *NYT*, March 27, 1921. (As Eleanor Kittredge, Hayden went on to become a longtime book reviewer for the *Times*.) Another important contemporary portrait of the Village is found in *NYT*, December 23, 1917. See also Andrea Barnet, *All Night Party: The Women of Bohemian Greenwich Village and Harlem, 1913–1930* (Algonquin Books, 2004); George Chauncey, *Gay New York* (Basic Books, 1994); Allen Churchill, *The Improper Bohemians* (Dutton, 1959); Bernadine Kielty, *Girl from Fitchburg* (Random House, 1964); and Caroline Ware, *Greenwich Village, 1920–1930: A Comment on American Civilization in the Post-War Years* (Houghton Mifflin, 1935).

58 **Tom Hepburn's last days in New York**: I synthesized what Katharine Hepburn had said (and implied) with the memories and family lore shared by Bob Hepburn and Peg Perry. Then I attempted to reconcile all of this information with primary sources. The most immediate and informative record comes from the office of the chief medical examiner, cited here for the first time. This is where I found Dr. Thomas Hepburn's assertion that his son had been trying to "break off " an affair with a girl. Also of vital importance is the police report, Fourteenth Precinct, case number 1612. See also: *NYT*, April 4, April 5, 1921; *New York Herald*, April 4, 1921; *Hartford Courant*, April 4, April 5, 1921; *Hartford Times*, April 4, April 5, 1921.

Also useful for color were various issues of the *NYT* and other New York papers for the current amusements in the city. The siblings did *not* see Pavlova dance, as asserted in Edwards and in *Young Kate*. The Russian ballerina gave her final performance in New York on March 19 and sailed with her company on the SS *Finland* on the twenty-sixth, three days before Kath and Tom even arrived.

59 **Robbery on Bleecker Street**: *NYT*, April 2, 1921.

59 *A Connecticut Yankee in King Arthur's Court*: The only print available to researchers exists at the Museum of Modern Art in New York, where I viewed it on May 13, 2005. At least three reels, including the last one, are missing from the originally eight-reel film. Although Twain's book contains several scenes set at the gallows, there are no references to hangings in descriptions of the missing scenes of this film. A film critic who saw a slightly more complete print in a private collection some years ago recalled no hanging scene in the film, and certainly not in the climactic rescue of the king from the gallows that occurs in Twain's novel.

61 **Immediate aftermath of Tom's death**: Bob Hepburn recalled that his parents received the news of Tom's death via a telephone call. However, contemporary newspaper accounts in Hartford all concur that it was a telegram, delivered at 11:00 a.m. on Sunday, that relayed the tragic news. Perhaps both means of communication were used. Newspaper reports also inform us that Kit and Hep departed for New York immediately after getting word of Tom's death. The exact time of their arrival is unknown but would probably be close to 1:30 p.m. given the time it took to drive from Hartford. The *Hartford Courant* reported they arrived in the "afternoon."

Barbara Leaming wrote that Tom's body had been removed from Mary Towle's house by the time his parents arrived. This is not so. When the medical examiner's report (which includes input from Dr. Hepburn) was written, Tom's body was still "lying dead at 26 Charlton Street."

61 **Doctor from St. Vincent's**: This doctor was identified in newspaper reports and in the police record as either "Dr. Condy" or "Dr. Candy." From a check of city directories and census records, no doctor of either name appears to have lived in New York at the time, suggesting the name is a corruption of something else.

62 **Dr. Thomas Gonzales**: Various articles, *NYT*, including obituary, May 15, 1956. Gonzales would go on to become chief medical examiner for the city of New York.

62 **Accident or suicide**: A careful reading of the records suggests another way to consider Tom's death. It's true that the facts of Tom's death indicate a fierce determination to choke himself, but the conclusion previously drawn was that the intent of that choking was to *die*. Yet the description of his death—so drawn out, so difficult—does not in fact read like a manual for suicide. It's possible the teenager was instead practicing autoerotic asphyxiation. Also known as sexual hanging, this is the practice of inducing heightened sexual pleasure by means of self-applied ligatures or suffocating devices while bringing oneself to orgasm. Until recently, deaths resulting from autoerotic asphyxia were often misidentified as suicides by hanging. And, significantly, the most common practitioners of the technique are adolescent and young adult males from strict homes where censure is common and praise is rationed.

As a theory for Tom's death, autoerotic asphyxia actually fits better than any of the others. If Tom had wanted to kill himself, why choose a process in which he wasn't assured of success? He was a bright boy, after all; he would have clearly seen that the beam was too low for him to hang, at least not with that extralong length of muslin sheet he'd fashioned. As described in the reports, his determined efforts to cut off his breath are identical to the mechanics used during autoerotic asphyxia. And the fact that he was doing all of this at three o'clock in the morning (as estimated by Gonzales) has always been a jarring detail in the "accidental" theory. Why would a boy get up at that hour to practice a stunt?

Yet even if the theory of autoerotic asphyxia is true, it does not entirely remove the stain of suicide. Today experts classify it as "subintentional suicide," along with such other high-risk pursuits as "chicken" games and bridge-walking—activities in character for what we know of Tom Hepburn.

It's not surprising Gonzales didn't consider it as a theory. Autoerotic asphyxia was not commonly understood by the medical profession in the 1920s. G. A. Auden's 1927 article, "An Unusual Form of Suicide," in the *Journal of Mental Science,* has been cited as the first documentation of the practice in the English medical literature.

63 **"I can remember"**: *Me.*

63 **"left me"**: *Hartford Times*, April 5, 1921.

65 **The Hepburns' return to Hartford**: Dr. Hepburn did *not* leave New York on Sunday night, as previous accounts have asserted. The *Hartford Times* and *Hartford Courant* both report that he and Kit returned together on Monday afternoon.

66 **Katharine Houghton**: Her letter, dated May 12, 1995, was kept in the medical examiner's files.

67 **"Negro who"**: Wilkinson, *SEP*, November 29, 1941.

67 **Christopher Andersen**: There are errors too numerous to itemize in his *Young Kate,* from the "holding the body off the ground" story to having Dr. and Mrs. Hepburn arrive in New York by train at Grand Central Station. Grieving parents would hardly have waited for train schedules. Andersen also wrote that "the sight of Kathy, tears streaming down her face as she held up her brother, would stay with Dr. Condy for years." It's unclear how he knew this, since the actual name of the doctor isn't even known.

67 **"When my brother"**: *TV Times, LAT,* December 6–12, 1992.

7. NEVER A MEMBER OF THE CLUB

69 **Kath at Bryn Mawr**: My account of Kath's early college experiences was gleaned from reading dozens of issues of the campus *College News* during her time there, as well as from other resources (pamphlets, oral histories, clippings) in the Bryn Mawr Archives. In addition, the letters of Alice Palache, held at Radcliffe College, provided tremendous detail and insight. The March 1934 issue of *Modern Screen* also contained an account of Kath's college days.

70 **"I was stupid"**: ROSS.

70 **Physics entrance exam**: Cavett.

70 **M. Carey Thomas**: I disagree with Leaming's contention that Thomas would have seemed like a "relic" to students; in fact, Thomas was held in awe, even by a generation rapidly moving beyond the values she had stood for. On Thomas and her lasting influence, I am grateful for the insightful

assistance of Helen Lefkowitz Horowitz, the biographer of Thomas and an expert on women's colleges of the era. See Horowitz, *The Power and Passion of M. Carey Thomas* and *Alma Mater*.

71 **Kath's untidiness**: Recollections of Bryn Mawr faculty, *Modern Screen*, September 1934.

71 **Kath's appendicitis**: Cavett, Bob Hepburn.

71 **"I knew something"**: *Me*.

71 **"I was like"**: Cavett.

72 **Jack Strait**: He was a local golf champ who had quite the name in Connecticut in the early 1920s. See, for example, *Bridgeport Telegram*, September 26, 1923.

72 **Kit's renewed activism**: For the rest of 1921 and throughout 1922, Kit kept a low profile. But she was definitely back in public life by March 22, 1923, when she spoke to the Stratford League of Women Voters on the right of women to serve on juries now that they could vote, as reported in the *Bridgeport Telegram*.

72 **Kath assumes Tom's birth date**: Hepburn herself acknowledged doing this. In 1990, her nephew Mundy Hepburn told me that she'd once explained to him that she celebrated her birthday in November because she "liked getting flowers in the fall."

72 **The younger siblings**: Later, they too would receive individualized at-home schooling, with Marion and Peg at least also coming under Wow's tutelage.

73 **William O. Williams**: Previous accounts have implied Wow was Kath's tutor for the entire three-year period of 1921–24, when in fact he did not arrive in the United States until 1923. He died in 1942, his ashes interred with Kingswood's founder and headmaster G. R. H. Nicholson, his longtime friend and former student. Sources: U.S. Census, 1930; Melanchthon W. Jacobus, *Kingswood: Fifty Years, 1916–1966*, Kingswood School, 1966; various issues, *Hartford Courant*, *Hartford Times*.

74 **Kath's courses and major**: Bryn Mawr does not keep records on students' announcements of majors. However, a study of Hepburn's transcripts gives some indication of where she was going. Most of her first year was filled with requirements: the biology course (which tradition holds she failed) as well as Latin and First-Year Composition, Literature, and Diction. As a sophomore, she took First-Year Economics, Second-Year Literature and Diction, Greek Mythology, and two psychology courses. Only by her junior year does her major become apparent, when she was enrolled in two philosophy courses as well as a European history course. At this stage, the college required another biology course and a trigonometry course. In her last two years, Kath also began the study of languages—French, German, and Italian—although she never became fluent in any of them. In her senior year, she took two advanced philosophy courses, including a semester-long study of Kant. College policy does not allow grades to be released on students' transcripts, so we cannot know how well (or poorly) Kath did in any of these courses. Christopher Andersen wrote that she flunked Latin, based evidently on her own testimony.

75 **"Conscious beauty"**: *SEP*, December 6, 1941.

75 **"New York sophisticate"**: Speech given by Katharine Hepburn at the Bryn Mawr Convocation, May 18, 1985, Bryn Mawr Archives.

76 **Kath's appearance**: Taken from her first passport, dated June 15, 1927, reproduced in the Sotheby's auction catalog.

76 **"Katharine was"**: *Modern Screen*, March 1934.

76 **"I was never"**: Wilkinson, *SEP*, November 29, 1941.

76 **"Megs" Merrill, Verona Layng, Hope Yandell, Alita Davis**: U.S. Census, 1920, 1930; *NYT*, November 21, 1924; February 8, 1925; November 10, 1925; September 23, 1926; September 18, 1932; *WP*, July 9, 1926; August 14, 1935.

77 **"Everybody is so nice"**: Alice Palache (AP) to Charles Palache, [nd, 1924], PFP.

77 **"desolate"**: AP to Helen Palache, [nd, 1924], PFP.

77 **"Ali Barbour has"**: AP to Helen Palache, [nd, 1924?], PFP.

77 **"She was somewhat"**: AP to Helen Palache, [nd, 1925], PFP.

77 **Marriages of Layng, Merrill**: Verona Layng married John O. Chiles on October 7, 1926

(*NYT*, September 23, 1926); Megs Merrill married Armitage Watkins on June 16, 1928 (*NYT*, October 21, 1927, June 17, 1928).

78 **"If I had"**: *SEP*, December 6, 1941.

8. GETTING HER BALANCE

79 **"Bryn Mawr was"**: Speech given by Katharine Hepburn, with her handwritten additions, at the Bryn Mawr Convocation, May 18, 1985, Bryn Mawr Archives.

80 **Tuition and costs**: This is what Charles Palache paid for Alice, invoices, PFP.

80 **Palache and Barbour**: After Ali's departure from college, Palache wrote to her mother [n.d., circa 1925–26], "I can't at present quite get over Ali's absence, but time may heal that." It seems Kath Hepburn did the healing instead, for soon Palache's letters home are filled with the kind of devoted passages about Kath that Palache had previously penned about Ali. (PFP)

80 **"[Kath] really"**: AP to Helen Palache, [nd, fall 1926], PFP.

80 **Lack of beaux**: Although the Wilkinson *Saturday Evening Post* article would make mention of Hepburn's "beaux," and Edwards would extrapolate a "beau" from a story Kate told about a Roman Catholic boy who ran afoul of Hep's unacknowledged prejudice, there is no evidence of any romantic connections prior to Kate's senior year in college.

80 **Palache family and genealogy**: From a Web site memorializing Charles Palache, "renowned Professor of Mineralogy at Harvard University, and one of the greatest morphological crystallographers of all time," found at http://franklin-sterlinghill.com/cp. See also U.S. Census, 1930, and Helen and Charles Palache's obituaries: *NYT*, October 29, 1949; December 6, 1954. That Alice Palache wasn't as affluent as Ali Barbour and some of her other friends is reflected in a letter she wrote to her mother, circa 1925, after Ali had asked her to go into New York with her: "C'est tout à fait impossible je crois, as they will no doubt stay at the Ritz."

80 **"I never in"**: AP oral history, interviewed by Jessica Holland, 1985, Bryn Mawr Archives. In a letter to her mother obviously in anticipation of this first visit, Palache wrote that Kate promised to take her to see her father operate at the hospital. "I must say I am intrigued with the prospect of visiting Kate," Palache wrote. "It promises to be quite a unique experience." How unique she couldn't have guessed. (PFP)

81 **"I could hear"**: Andersen, *Young Kate*.

81 **"the new fad"**: AP to Helen Palache, [nd, 1927?], PFP.

81 **"I really get"**: AP to Helen Palache, [nd, 1926?], PFP.

82 **Kay**: *Modern Screen*, March 1934. The new nickname makes sense, as Ali Barbour knew her as Kathy or Kath from Hartford; once Ali and her friends had left campus, a new name (and persona) could more easily emerge.

82 **Muggle**: AP oral history; conversations with relatives of KH's college friends.

82 **Lib Rhett, Adele Merrill**: *Me*; AP oral history; *NYT*, May 28, 1931; January 7, 1935; U.S. Census, 1880–1930.

82 **"charming beyond belief"**: AP to Mary Palache, [nd, April? 1926], PFP.

82 **Musketeers**: Another name for their clique was "the Tenement," the meaning of which is unclear.

82 **Kath's new status on campus**: This is confirmed by the rebalanced friendships she enjoyed with such former eidolons as Alita Davis and Hope Yandell. With her roommate Hope, Kath often took excursions into Connecticut, as evidenced by Palache's letters.

83 **"It was Kate"**: Critical insight into Kath's last two years at Bryn Mawr was provided by a relative of one of her close college friends. This source spoke freely and enthusiastically, but then contacted me later to report that other family members had felt such discussions had been "indiscreet," making their relative, Kath's friend, seem too "out there." Consequently, I was asked to use anonymously any quotes I'd previously been given.

83 **"Before you can"**: AP oral history.

84 **"We really"**: AP oral history.

84 **The new college girl**: In addition to Horowitz's studies of the women's college experience, I drew from a fascinating piece by the writer Mary Lee, published during Kath's senior year, titled "The College Girl Starts a Revolution" (*NYT*, May 13, 1928). For other contemporary examples particular to Bryn Mawr, see *NYT*, June 3, 1925; May 9, 1926.

84 **"Young people today"**: *Bridgeport Telegram*, November 10, 1923.

84 **Smoking**: See Horowitz, *Alma Mater*. Horowitz called smoking "the outward sign of acknowledged female sexuality."

84 **"part of "**: The North Carolina teacher-activist A. T. Allen in general approved of the right of women to smoke. *NYT*, November 29, 1925.

85 **"The cigarette"**: *NYT*, November 25, 1926.

85 **Alonzo B. See**: *NYT*, May 12, 1926. See was also on record as saying he believed children of women college graduates should be taken away from their mothers as soon as they had been weaned, and placed in an institution where they "would be properly cared for."

85 **"Woman purloined"**: *LAT*, January 4, 1926.

85 **Park's letter and Hep's response**: *Me*.

86 **Girls in *Captive* audience**: "The Empire Theater has been full of them since news of the play first got around the boarding schools," the critic George Jean Nathan wrote in *American Mercury*, March 1927.

86 **"unescorted girls"**: *NYT*, March 9, 1927.

86 **"Lesbian love"**: *New York Telegraph*, September 30, 1926.

86 **"If all the ladies"**: Quoted in Kaier Curtain, *We Can Always Call Them Bulgarians: The Emergence of Lesbians and Gay Men on the American Stage* (Alyson, 1987).

87 **"She sits"**: AP to Mary Palache, [nd, fall? 1924], PFP.

87 **Bette Whiting**: AP to Jeannette and Mary Palache, [nd, fall? 1924], PFP.

87 **"Yes, I did"**: AP to Mary Palache, [nd, fall? 1924], PFP. Emily Glessner was the sister of John Jacob Glessner II, who, along with his lover, James McLane, was close with both Jeannette and Mary Palache, as part of a circle that also included F. O. Matthiessen and Russell Cheney.

87 **Crushes**: Horowitz writes in *Alma Mater* that the "crush" was immortalized in college fiction and poetry, "unwittingly [exposing] the play of sexual attraction among women students in the setting of college dances."

87 **Palache's orientation**: That Palache's letters do not reveal more intimate details of her friendships is not surprising; even the letters written to her sisters, in which she might be expected to be more forthcoming, were often sent to the girls' mother to read after the sisters were through. Besides, as the historian Lillian Faderman has written, "There were few women before our era who would have committed confessions regarding erotic exchanges to writing." This is a guide for understanding the entire body of Hepburn's correspondence and that of her friends. See Faderman's *Odd Girls and Twilight Lovers* as well as her *To Believe in Women: What Lesbians Have Done for America* (Houghton Mifflin, 1999).

87 **"orange and lace"**: AP to Helen Palache, [nd, 1926?], PFP.

87 **"to no end"**: AP to Helen Palache, [nd, 1926?], PFP.

87 **"no time"**: AP to Mary Palache, [nd, 1927?], PFP.

88 **College study**: See Edward Westermarck, *The Future of Marriage in Western Civilization* (Macmillan, 1936). His findings were based on studies taken circa 1930 and reported in *Time*, August 17, 1936, *NYT*, August 11, 1936, among others.

88 **Rhett's marriage**: She married Walter Murphy, her badminton partner, in 1935. See *NYT*, April 5, 1931; March 17, 1933; July 16, 1935.

88 **Davis's marriage**: In 1930, she was living temporarily with Pearl Traft of San Francisco on West Seventh Street in Los Angeles (*LAT*, December 25, 1930). She married William B. Weaver in 1935. See also *NYT*, July 26, 1928; *WP*, February 23, February 24, 1930; *NYT*, February 24, 1930; *WP*, August 14, 1935.

88 **Carey Thomas's influence**: Palache became something of a Thomas scholar. In the 1980s,

she asked Hepburn to consider making a film about Thomas for public television, and together they conducted considerable research into the school founder's papers. Through Thomas's letters—which Palache no doubt read and shared with Hepburn—we gain insight on other women who thought and lived like her. "If only it were possible for women to select women as well as men for a 'life's love,'" Thomas wrote in 1880. "It is possible but if families would only regard it in that light!" (M. Carey Thomas to Mary Thomas, November 21, 1880, Bryn Mawr archives) The Thomas letters are filled with documentation of her intimate relationships with Mamie Gwinn and Mary Garrett, as well as thoughts and feelings—sometimes positive, sometimes conflicted—on same-sex desire and affection. She predicted that someday women "will choose to live with each other and go off and make homes." Lest it seem she was avoiding the physical, a letter about her reaction to seeing Sarah Bernhardt makes plain her sexual feelings: "I think I told you of my desire, granted once that I were a man," she wrote to Mary Garrett, "to have her once as my mistress."

88 *The Making of Americans*: Stein originally wrote about the triangle of Carey Thomas, Mamie Gwinn, and Alfred Hodder in 1904, in an unpublished novella titled "Fernhurst." Some accounts of Thomas's life have implied "Fernhurst" was published during Thomas's tenure at Bryn Mawr, when in fact it did not appear as originally written until 1971, in a collection called *Fernhurst, Q.E.D., and Other Early Writings by Gertrude Stein* (ed. Leon Katz; Liveright). However, Stein had incorporated much of the central story within *The Making of Americans*. Although the first popular American edition of this novel did not come out until 1934, it was published in 1925 as a limited edition by A. & C. Boni in Paris. Newspaper accounts prove *The Making of Americans* was being read by a sophisticated American readership at least by 1926, and anecdotal evidence indicates it was well known on the Bryn Mawr campus at exactly the time Kath was there. See *Chicago Tribune*, July 24, 1926; *NYT*, February 8, 1934. See also James R. Mellow, *Charmed Circle: Gertrude Stein and Company* (Houghton Mifflin, 1974.)

89 **"a bit too conscious"**: *College News*, April 20, 1927. In *Me*, Hepburn wrote she used the wig to cover her long hair, but Palache remembered her cutting her hair, and her passport photo, taken a few weeks later, shows her with short hair, although grown in some from the severe shearing.

89 **"silly business"**: AP oral history.

90 **"They want"**: *News, Bryn Mawr-Haverford College*, March 23, 1973.

90 **Barbara Leaming**: Her avoidance of any discussion of same-sex desire or association is both perplexing and frustrating. Clearly, she did the research that would raise the topic—she studied Carey Thomas's letters, she read the analysis of campus life by Thomas's biographer Helen Lefkowitz Horowitz, she spoke to Bob Hepburn—but she chose to exclude any mention of bisexual or lesbian experience from her work. In fact, Leaming avoided any discussion that might contradict her presentation of Hepburn as a conventional heterosexual woman—and the one thing Katharine Hepburn was *not* was conventional.

90 **"She wasn't"**: AP oral history.

91 **Kath waving the check**: AP oral history. Penelope Gilliatt got it wrong in the November 1981 issue of *Vogue*, where she has Palache arriving on the train *into* Cambridge rather than *from* Cambridge (where Palache lived). Christopher Andersen compounded the error by assuming Gilliatt meant Cambridge, *England,* and so placed the scene with Kath waving the check after they'd arrived in Europe, which makes no sense at all.

91 **"It will be"**: AP to Mary Palache, [nd, spring? 1927], PFP. Earlier, writing to her mother, she'd used a similar phrase: "Kate wants me very much to go abroad with her this summer. Just us two."

91 **Departing for Europe**: In her memoirs, Hepburn wrote she went to Europe during the summer of her freshman year, 1925; Palache's letters prove it was the summer of her junior year, 1927. Kath was far too depressed to have made the trip in 1925.

91 **The *Sierra Ventana* and *Paris***: Using Palache's letters as a guide, we can zero in on these two ships as the only ones to have left New York and docked at Plymouth within the dates that are possible. For conditions at the piers during late June 1927, see *NYT*, June 25–28, 1927.

91 **"the eternal talking," "generally full"**: AP to Helen Palache, July 3, 1927, PFP.

91 **Eugene O'Dunne**: Eugene O'Dunne Sr. made a groundbreaking ruling in 1935 demanding the admission of a black student into the University of Maryland (*Murray v. Maryland*, July 25, 1935). The physical description of Eugene O'Dunne Jr. comes from his daughter, Christina Griffin. He was never known as "Jim" by his friends or family; it was apparently an affection bestowed by Kath and Palache on that crossing in 1927.

91 **Louis Rawlins**: He went on to become a commercial aviator. He died in 1942 in a stateside accident while serving as an army captain in World War II.

91 **The crossing**: Kath and Palache also spent time with a "Mr. Bleecker," a piano teacher and music theorist. "Beyond this," Palache wrote to her mother, "the crowd is what one might call extremely mixed" (AP to Helen Palache, July 3, 1927, PFP).

92 **"the handsomest creature"**: Kanin.

92 **"She is"**: AP to Helen Palache, [nd, August? 1927], PFP.

92 **"and she didn't"**: AP to Helen Palache, July 26, 1927, PFP.

93 **Cayre's Hotel**: Palache wrote to her mother on stationery from this hotel; the receipt from their stay, totaling 598 francs, including room and meals, was sold at auction by Sotheby's.

93 **"two lovely days"**: AP to Helen Palache, August 12, 1927, PFP.

93 **"an appalling spectacle"**: AP to Helen Palache, August 26, 1927, PFP.

93 **Cigarette girls, vaccination, "all the way up"**: AP oral history.

93 **Armed guards**: *NYT*, August 29, 1927.

93 **O'Dunne's later life**: Periodic communication continued between O'Dunne and Hepburn. In 1940 he made an attempt to see her when he was in New York, but Hepburn was away; in a letter to "Jim," she suggested he contact Palache at her office on Wall Street. "[She] has done well," Hepburn wrote, adding in that arrogant yet endearing way of hers, "So have I" (KH to Eugene O'Dunne, postmarked December 27, 1940, courtesy Christina Griffin). By this time, O'Dunne had become a successful lawyer, moving to Washington, D.C., and representing several prominent clients including the U.S. Navy. Late in life (1942), he married the daughter of the Swedish minister to the United States. They had one daughter. He died in 1959 at the age of fifty-two.

94 **Ali's wedding**: *Hartford Times*, October 9, 1927.

94 **Kissing Robert McKnight**: The story originates in the 1941 *Saturday Evening Post* piece by Lupton Wilkinson, in which McKnight, with Hepburn's permission, recalled their friendship. McKnight said the kiss occurred during Easter break 1927, but Palache's letters do not mention him at the Hepburn house at that time, and she was there. More likely it was during his stay in October for Ali's wedding. Another reason to place the connection with McKnight later than the spring is McKnight's memory of Kath telling him she wanted to be an actress; Easter 1927 seems too early for such a declaration on her part, but she may well have started thinking about it by the fall.

94 **McKnight's background**: *NYT*, May 4, May 8, June 22, 1932; May 9, 1935; *Chicago Tribune*, May 22, 1932. He would tell his children that he and Hepburn "talked about getting married until they decided mutually that they were both too interested in their careers" (interview with Peggy McKnight). In the early 1930s, McKnight once again became friendly with Hepburn, spending time with her and Laura Harding and Frances Rich.

94 **"Katherine"**: *College News*, December 20, 1927.

9. FLYING UP ONTO A PINK CLOUD

96 **"conscious pride"**: Wilson wrote the introduction for Charles R. Walker, ed., *The Collected Poems of H. Phelps Putnam* (Farrar, Straus and Giroux, 1971.)

96 **"It is"**: Russell Davenport (RD) to Witter Bynner, quoted in an unpublished essay, "In Defense of Putnam," sent by Bynner to Phelps Putnam (PP), [nd], PPP.

96 **"I took"**: *Me*.

97 **H. Phelps Putnam's appearance**: World War I registration card, May 28, 1917.

97 **"[A] rising flame"**: "Marjory," *Trinc* (George H. Doran, 1927), reprinted in Walker, *The Collected Poems*.

97 **Leaming on Putnam:** Her use of Putnam's poetry (without identifying it as such) for the purposes of re-creating conversations with friends or describing his feelings for Hepburn is misleading. At one point, Leaming has Kath singing a song that Putnam used for a character in one of his poems. She also places Edmund Wilson's observation about the gashes on Putnam's back within the context of his time with Hepburn, even insinuating Kath made the marks herself, when there is no evidence whatsoever for such a presumption.

98 **a poet who:** *Saturday Review of Literature*, December 3, 1927.

98 **"Marjory" was based on Kath:** PP to RD, June 10, 1930, RDP.

99 **Kath returns Put's infatuation:** This happened either off-campus—in New York, Hartford, or Boston—or else during a brief visit to Bryn Mawr sometime in late October or early November, although there is no hard evidence that Putnam went to Bryn Mawr at this time. All I could confirm was a stop in Philadelphia (PP to F. O. Matthiessen, December 7, 1927, PPP), but since he was so close and was such a frequent guest of the Mannings, it's very possible Putnam was at Bryn Mawr for a few days. He was also in Hartford in late November, when Kath was home for Thanksgiving.

99 **"I flew":** *Me.*

99 **Pregnant girl:** PP to RD, January 28, 1928, RDP.

99 **"I allowed":** PP to Russell Cheney (RC), January 23, 1928, PPP.

100 **May Day descriptions:** May Day Committee files, PFP; *NYT*, April 29, May 5, 1928; *WP*, April 29, 1928.

100 **"the girl with the tight bun":** *NYT*, May 21, 1939.

101 **"I was just thinking":** Andersen, *Young Kate.*

101 *Strange Interlude*: AP to Helen Palache, February 20, 1928, PFP.

101 **"I think it":** ROSS.

101 **"Being snubbed":** *Ladies' Home Journal*, August 1975.

101 **Jack Clarke and Luddy Smith's retreat in the woods:** In *Me*, Hepburn called it Luddy's "hut." It was owned not by Luddy (a search of land records for Chester, Delaware, and Montgomery counties did not turn up his name) but by Jack, as part of his family's property in Easttown, Chester County. It was sold in 1945. Land records, Chester County.

101 **Nude photos:** *Me.*

102 **Autocar:** *NYT*, September 8, 1901; January 10, 1909; August 27, 1917 (advertisement); *WP*, November 13, 1927; January 8, 1957; Clifton Swenk Hunsicker, *Montgomery County, Pennsylvania: A History* (Lewis Historical Publishing, 1923); David Schmidt, "Autocar in Lower Merion," originally published in *Main Line Life*, collected on the Web site lowermerionhistory.org. Louis Clarke was also the inventor of the first U.S. spark plug.

102 **John S. Clarke Sr.:** His wife, Caroline, was living at the Pennsylvania State Hospital for the Insane. They were eventually divorced. Around the time of Kath's graduation, Mr. Clarke remarried; with his new wife, Marion, he continued hosting a new generation of Bryn Mawr students.

102 **"Today we had":** AP to Jeannette Palache, January 10, 1927, PFP.

102 **Louise and Agnes Clarke:** U.S. Census, 1900–1930. Louise owned a house in the Berkshires at this time, where she hosted the golf star Marie R. Jenney (*NYT*, June 28, 1925). According to Virginia Soule, Louise died young. By 1932, Agnes lived with a woman, Ruth Medlyn, at 127 East Thirty-fourth Street, New York.

103 **Richard Aldrich and Francis R. Hart:** In 1927, Jack Clarke was one of the guests at Aldrich's farewell bachelor dinner at the Harvard Club (*NYT*, November 4, 1927; *WP*, November 4, 1927) and was one of the ushers at Aldrich's wedding to his first wife, Helen Beals (*NYT*, November 6, 1927). Francis Hart was also in the wedding party. After divorcing Beals, Aldrich married Gertrude Lawrence in 1940; Lawrence's lesbian affairs have been discussed in several studies. Some on Cape Cod, where Aldrich operated the Cape Playhouse for many years, recalled Hart and Aldrich as lovers; Hart served as president of the Playhouse for a time.

103 **McKnight pays train fare:** In *Me*, Hepburn wrote that he drove her to the audition. Not so, said his daughter Peggy. "He loaned her the money for the train because her father objected to her

trying out and would not pay her way." McKnight did not cash the check she sent him as repayment "as good luck for her career."

104 **"There is no easy way"**: *NYT*, June 4, 1928.

104 **"When I come"**: PP to RC, February 28, 1928, PPP.

105 **"I have always"**: PP to RC, March 6, 1928, PPP.

105 **"liquid nightingale"**: Unpublished poem, "Dirge for Hart Crane," PPP. Putnam's sense of affinity with Hart Crane is significant for the fact that Crane, even then, was considered homosexual, and his drinking attributed (at least in part) to internal conflicts about it. See *Time*, May 17, 1937, which called homosexuality "the open secret" of the poet's life.

105 **"bleak friend," "Les Enfants"**: *Trinc.*

106 **"This is"**: PP to F. O. Matthiessen, [n.d., written after Cheney's death], PPP.

106 **"I've seen so many people"**: PP to RC, December 8, 1916, PPP.

106 **"Your letter"**: RC to PP, December 14, 1916, PPP.

106 **"One thing"**: PP to RC, [nd, 1917], PPP.

106 **"The female adventures"**: Notes by PP for a eulogy for RC, 1944, PPP.

106 **Putnam's sexuality in his poetry**: Putnam's frequent allusions to Whitman only reinforce the idea of homoerotic bonding in his work. Such bonding was what Whitman called "adhesiveness," which women, through their demands upon men, were constantly destroying. Consider in this light Putnam's poem "About Women": "Well, give them kisses, scatter flowers, / And whisper that you cannot stay, / We shall have insolence and hours / Which women shall not take away" (PPP).

106 **"Fucking Is Fun"**: Unpublished poem, PPP.

106 **"Sonnets"**: Walker, *The Collected Poems*.

106 **"That nifty little piece"**: PP to RD, January 28, 1928, RDP.

107 **"As Put says"**: RC to F. O. Matthiessen, February 5, 1925, FMP. See also Louis Hyde, ed., *Rat and the Devil: Journal Letters of F.O. Matthiessen and Russell Cheney* (Archon Books, 1978).

107 **"The . . . 'Third Sex' school"**: PP to F. O. Matthiessen, July 12, 1928, FMP.

107 **Knapp's personal life**: In letters to Putnam, he wrote of feeling "deprived" of his life, forced to socialize at a stuffy men's club where all the talk was of "sports and drunken parties, neither of which I partake of." He slept apart from his wife. She and their two children made a "great burden" for him, and Knapp saw no way out. He had only two choices, he believed: married life or "solitude, and I can't face that." (Farwell Knapp to PP, [nd, circa 1933], PPP)

107 **Davenport's homosexual experiences**: In his journals, he writes of love for women, particularly his first fiancée, in an idealized way. Since love for women was so sacred, Davenport wrote, he "suppressed" his "animal desires" for them—which, he then rationalized, came out "highly unnaturally," that is, through sex with men. In college, he had a sexual relationship with his classmate Bob Bates, later a professor of French literature at Yale. Bates seems to have wanted the relationship to continue, writing love sonnets to Davenport. He asked him at one point, after clearly being rebuffed, "Ah, Mitch—are you still seeking 'experience'? Are you still looking for material for novels—are you still that same strange self of yours, forever just not happy?" (Bob Bates to RD, October 25, 1924, RDP)

108 **Walker's arrest**: In a letter dated December 1916, Cheney included a newspaper clipping reporting that Charles Walker had paid a fine of five dollars and costs in police court "for violating the light ordinance." In a handwritten note, Cheney added, "It's Walker's first offense evidently from the tactful wording of the discharge in his case."

108 **Gerald Murphy**: See Amanda Vaill, *Everybody Was So Young* (Houghton Mifflin, 1998).

108 **Witter Bynner and Edna St. Vincent Millay**: See Nancy Milford, *Savage Beauty: The Life of Edna St. Vincent Millay* (Random House, 2001).

108 **"little boys"**: RC to F. O. Matthiessen, December 26, 1929, FMP.

108 **Pre-Stonewall identity**: "Most gay history lies buried in bachelor graves," wrote Douglass Shand-Tucci in *The Crimson Letter: Harvard, Homosexuality, and the Shaping of American Culture* (St. Martin's, 2003). A review of the book by Walter Wadas in *Bay Windows* (August 5, 2004) added

to that idea: "There is some buried in the graves of heterosexually married men, too." But Wadas agreed with Shand-Tucci's point that much of gay history is about "acknowledging the homosexuality that's unadmitted, despite being present."

Putnam's homosexual friends would not have challenged his assertion that he was not homosexual: if he said he was not one of them, he wasn't. Yet he seems to have known that at least some didn't buy the show he put on so extravagantly. At the time of Cheney's death in 1944, he prepared a eulogy, planning at one point to say, "I have said that I was his friend and that is fine. Cheney had a great love of me although he knew I was so heterosexual." But he crossed it all out and never spoke the words. Too many people might have thought he was protesting too much.

108 **Knapp's suicide**: *NYT*, September 20, 1942.

108 **Lloyd-Smith's suicide**: *NYT*, September 17, 1931; also various letters, papers, RDP.

108 **Matthiessen's suicide**: *NYT*, April 1, April 8, 1950; *Chicago Tribune*, April 7, 1950; see also Hyde, *Rat and the Devil.*

109 **"[D]earest"**: F. O. Matthiessen to RC, February 27, 1928, FMP.

109 **"My trouble"**: PP to RC, March 6, 1928, PPP.

109 **"The doc"**: PP to RC, May 2, 1928, PPP.

109 **Reviews for *Trinc***: Unsourced Chicago review, November 21, 1927, PPP; *NYT*, January 15, 1928; *San Francisco Chronicle*, December 4, 1927.

109 **"I am proud"**: John Farrar to PP, January 11, 1928, PPP.

109 **"I always liked"**: *Ladies' Home Journal*, August 1975.

109 **Others' awareness of Putnam's relationship with Kath**: From various letters and other sources, it does not appear that many people knew as yet how serious her friendship with Putnam had become. The fact that Robert McKnight would recall wanting to ask her to marry him shortly before her graduation suggests the relationship was not common knowledge.

10. ECSTASY

111 **Confrontation between Kath and parents**: My account is based on reconsidering carefully what Hepburn had to say about the experience as well as, critically, the eyewitness testimony of Bob Hepburn and Peg Hepburn Perry. Marion Hepburn Grant's recollections are found in Houghton, *Marion Hepburn Grant.*

112 **Bloomfield Avenue**: Hep might have viewed it as "his" house, but the deed for 201 Bloomfield Avenue was, in fact, in Kit's name only. The Hepburns purchased the land from Robert Huntington, president of Connecticut General Life Insurance, on September 28, 1925; a building restriction was not resolved until November 9, 1927, which cleared the way for the house to be built. (West Hartford land records, vol. 70, p. 2; vol. 81, p. 220) The architect was Milton Hayman, the builder Robert Swain. See also Marion Hepburn Grant, *In and About Hartford: Tours and Tales* (Connecticut Historical Society, 1978).

113 **"I think Mother"**: Cavett.

113 **"horrified"**: *TV Times, LAT,* December 6–12, 1992. Curiously, she also said that her father had *liked* her career choice. She probably meant he came to appreciate it more than her mother did, as Hep enjoyed the movies and had taken the children "every Saturday."

113 **Kath doesn't stay with Edith Hooker**: In *Me*, Kath notes that the Hookers had gone to Maine for the summer. Why they couldn't have opened their house for her or left a key is not explained.

114 **"all awed"**: *SEP*, December 6, 1941.

114 ***The Czarina* and Auditorium Players**: *Baltimore Sun*, May 27, June 10, June 17, June 19, June 24, June 26, July 1, July 8–10, 1928; *NYT*, July 10, 1928. In another example of the legend spinning triumph out of tragedy, Lupton Wilkinson would write in the myth-building *Saturday Evening Post* article that Knopf 's trip to Europe was a holiday because he'd "cleared so much money in Baltimore." Patently untrue.

114 **"all sorts"**: *Me*.

115 **"She was the"**: H. Phelps Putnam, "The Daughters of the Sun" (Walker, *The Collected Poems*).

116 **"Up in your room"**: PP to RC, June 18, 1928, PPP. The poem was "suggested" by Cheney, possibly as a way for Putnam to deal with the feelings of inadequacy and guilt he was sharing with his friend in letter after letter.

116 **"deeper in hell"**: Farwell Knapp to PP, January 25, 1929, PPP.

116 **"more noble"**: PP to Farwell Knapp, October 11, 1928, PPP.

116 **"high spirits"**: Farwell Knapp to PP, August 17, 1928, PPP.

117 **Davenport's departure**: In his journals, he wrote of crossing on the same ship with Katharine Cornell; Cornell was documented as leaving New York on August 3, 1928, on the SS *France*.

118 **"Dear Frances"**: Reproduced in *Me*.

118 **Frances Robinson-Duff**: *Night Life*, April 1939; various papers in her file at NYPL, including "Miss Robinson's Breathing Exercises."

119 ***The Big Pond***: *NYT*, July 22, July 30, August 11, August 19, August 22, 1928.

119 **"Kate is really"**: AP to Helen Palache, August 11, 1928, PFP.

120 **"a tool for the play"**: *LAT*, July 7, 1929.

120 **"all prepared"**: AP to Helen Palache, August 12, 1928, PFP. Later, Hepburn would say she did take the train up to see her parents in Hartford, and they all had a big "ha-ha" about her firing. If that happened, it was *much* later. Like *years* later. No one, least of all Kath, was laughing in August 1928.

120 **Graeme Smith**: He would work as a stockbroker in Hartford and later as a partner in the Hartford law firm of Alcorn, Bakewell and Smith. His wife was the dean of Miss Porter's School in Farmington.

121 **"Like a kid"**: PP to RC, March 6, 1928, PPP.

121 **"cranky"**: Farwell Knapp to PP, August 17, 1928, PPP.

121 **Putnam and Taft**: As fond as he was of the former president, Putnam likely kept his socialist politics to himself, as Taft was deeply suspicious of the "Bolshevist" movements in the United States.

122 **Luddy's background**: U.S. Census, 1880–1930; Pennsylvania vital records; obituary of Lewis Lawrence Smith, *NYT*, June 26, 1931; alumni catalogs, University of Pennsylvania; various records of the Chester County Historical Society. See also David R. Contosta, *A Philadelphia Family: The Houstons and Woodwards of Chestnut Hill* (University of Pennsylvania Press, 1988).

122 **Luddy's railroad**: Ludlow Ogden Smith (LOS) to Gertrude Smith, May 7, 1919, SFP.

123 **"I gave him"**: "The Lost Child," essay dated November 25, 1912, SFP.

123 **"for he is not"**: Robert Rossow, Culver Summer Schools, to Lewis L. Smith, August 24, 1916, SFP.

123 **Luddy at Penn**: According to university records, he attended the college of arts and sciences during the 1916–17 and 1917–18 school years. The second year, he was not on campus, however, at least not during the first semester, as he was undergoing basic training in Charleston and Pensacola in the Students' Army Training Corps. This was the wartime successor of the Reserve Officers Training Corps, of which all three Smith sons were members. Although Luddy may have returned for the spring semester in 1918, university records indicate he dropped out soon thereafter and never received a degree. During his brief time at Penn, he lived at the Phi Kappa Sigma house at 3539 Locust Street.

124 **"I have"**: LOS to Gertrude Smith, September 21, 1918, SFP.

124 **Burglar**: Luddy's account of this incident is in the file "Clippings and Writings," SFP.

124 **"It is hard"**: LOS to Gertrude Smith, August 6, 1918, SFP.

124 **"We are"**: LOS to Gertrude Smith, July 28, 1918, SFP.

124 **"Underneath"**: LOS to Gertrude Smith, September 12, 1918, SFP.

124 **"I was up"**: LOS to Gertrude Smith, September 29, 1918, SFP.

125 **Death of Lewis Smith**: *NYT*, February 19, 1919; *Daily Local News* (Chester County), January 17, 1919; various documents, SFP.

125 **Luddy on merchant ship**: This information comes from his children, Lewis and Ramsay Ludlow, who still have their father's battered bugle from the experience.

125 **Luddy and Ouija board**: Luddy wrote about his consultations with the Ouija board, including the time it supposedly predicted his altercation with the burglar at Sherraden (SFP). One message from his brother said: "Mother must stop grieving for me. I am very happy. Life is short anyway."

125 **Luddy at Grenoble**: Various papers, SFP. Luddy received a certificate from Grenoble, but this was not the equivalent of a university degree, which he appears never to have obtained. He did not attend the Sorbonne, as Hepburn asserted, although he did consider taking classes there while at Grenoble. Back in the United States, he'd reject his father's demand that he return to Penn by railing against the "lack of efficiency and fair play" at American colleges, adding for good measure (and revealing the ingrained anti-Semitism characteristic of the period): "The number of fine men who choose the University of Pennsylvania to finish their education is rapidly approaching the zero mark and the number of Jews and men of like type is correspondingly increasing" (LOS to Lewis L. Smith, August 22 1920, SFP).

126 **"Not for me"**: LOS to Lewis L. Smith, August 22, 1920, SFP.

126 **"As a matter of fact"**: LOS to Lewis L. Smith, June 27, 1920, SFP. He often justified his lack of interest in marriage by citing the precarious postwar economy. "I think anybody is just a plain ordinary damned fool to get married these days," he told his father. "Anyone that gets married now must have either a grand fortune or an indefinable nerve" (LOS to Lewis L. Smith, August 25, 1920, SFP).

126 **"Goodness"**: LOS to Gertrude Smith, December 22, 1920, SFP.

127 **"I should like"**: LOS to Gertrude Smith, March 28, 1929, SFP.

127 **Luddy's breakdown**: Many letters in the SFP attest to Luddy's emotional and physical collapse during this time, among them: LOS to Lewis L. Smith, February 28, 1923; March 5, 1923; March 11, 1923; LOS to Gertrude Smith, March 1, 1923; March 7, 1923.

11. THE END OF HER VIRTUE

129 **Herbert Hoover**: Despite charges that the Democrat Alfred Smith had socialist leanings, it was the Republican Hoover who was the choice of many progressive activists, including Kit Hepburn, who signed her name to a well-publicized document of support (*NYT*, November 4, 1928). Leaming's presumption that Kit was anti-Hoover is wrong.

130 **"prolonged talks"**: Marion Hepburn's diary, February 28, 1930, quoted in Houghton, *Marion Hepburn Grant*.

130 **"People will admire"**: LOS to Gertrude Smith, March 6, 1920, SFP.

130 *Night Hostess*: *NYT*, August 24, September 9, September 13, 1928; various clippings, NYPL.

130 **"Why would I"**: *Playbill*, October 30, 1995.

130 **Katherine Burns**: U.S. Census, 1930; Internet Broadway database; NYPL.

131 **Barbara Willison**: *National Enquirer*, October 12, 1974; also various clippings, NYPL.

133 **"Not only"**: *Hartford Times*, October 24, 1928.

133 **"natural nervousness"**: *Hartford Times*, October 26, 1928. See also *New Haven Register*, October 30, 1928.

133 **"bleary-eyed"**: F. O. Matthiessen to RC, October 31, 1928, FMP. Leaming referenced a letter that Putnam left for Matthiessen after despairing of reaching Kath; despite several searches, I did not locate such a letter in the correspondence of Putnam, Matthiessen, or Cheney.

134 **"I'm going to beat it"**: PP to RC, November 14, 1928, PPP.

134 **"If you lay hands"**: *Me*.

136 *Holiday*: Leaming wrote that the day after *These Days* closed, Hopkins sent Hepburn to New Haven to start understudying Hope Williams in *Holiday* tryouts at the Shubert. This is not possible, as *Holiday* had completed its tryout in New Haven by the time *These Days* closed. Hepburn remembered she was back to pounding the pavement between producers' offices after the closing of the play. That leaves only a few days before the opening of *Holiday* on Broadway for Kath to get hired as understudy.

136 **"casually retired"**: *NYT*, February 3, 1929.

136 **"I was acting"**: *Me*.

136 **"I have descended"**: PP to RC, November 29, 1928, PPP.

137 **"Kate Hepburn Senior"**: PP to RD, [nd, 1928], RDP. Curiously, when Putnam called Luddy a bastard, he added, "I use the word 'bastard' not in anger, as I can show you." His meaning is unclear.

138 **"ghastly"**: PP to RD, "Sat. p.m.," [nd, 1928], RDP.

138 **Marriage to Luddy**: Edwards claims no marriage announcement was printed in Hartford, New York, or Philadelphia; but indeed there was one in the *Hartford Times*, December 15, 1928, which gave full particulars.

138 **Kath and Luddy's honeymoon**: *NYT*, December 3, December 15–16, December 18, 1928. Their return was most likely on the *Fort Victoria*, since, like the ship they arrived on, it was part of the Furness Withy line.

Some accounts, trying to paint Hepburn with broad strokes as a lesbian, have stated that Kath took Laura Harding with her on her honeymoon, implying the marriage with Luddy was a deliberate sham. Anne Edwards, reticent about making the claim in her book, went on record after Hepburn's death insisting it was so. It was not. Although Kath first met Laura briefly at Frances Robinson-Duff's studio sometime in 1928, they were not yet close friends at the time of Kath's marriage. In any event, Laura sailed with her brother William B. Harding on December 14, 1928, on board the *Berengaria* to spend the Christmas holidays with their mother in Paris. This was the day *before* Kath and Luddy set off, in an entirely different direction, for Bermuda (*NYT*, December 14, 1928). A notice in the society pages of the *Times* the following March confirms that Laura had spent the winter in Europe (*NYT*, March 10, 1929). She missed her father's funeral, in fact, because she was abroad.

139 **"one of her phases"**: Notes prepared by George Cukor for an article he wrote about Hepburn in March 1947 for a later issue of *Photoplay*. An editor suggested he delete the remark. GCC.

139 **"I sometimes"**: LOS to Gertrude Smith, May 7, 1919, SFP.

139 **"I am so"**: LOS to Gertrude Smith, March 28, 1929, SFP.

139 **"It was a comfortable relationship"**: *Scotsman*, August 16, 2003.

139 **Putnam's pining**: A little more than a week after Kath's marriage, Putnam wrote to Cheney, "What would be nicer than to sit before your fire with a cup of tea in one's gin-struck hands and talk over the old days—the broken noses and blackened eyes, the adventures in the park" (PP to RC, December 22, 1928, PPP).

139 **"The Kid"**: PP to RD, January 22, 1929, RDP.

12. ALL THE SORT OF HIGHBROW CUSTOMS

141 **"dissipation and gaiety"**: *Pittsfield Sun*, quoted at www.berkshiretheatre.org.

141 **Description of life at Stockbridge**: Laura Harding scrapbooks, courtesy Emily King; Higham; U.S. Census, 1930; various clippings, *NYT* and other newspapers, NYPL.

143 **Luddy in Stockbridge**: Some accounts have said that Luddy and Jack Clarke stayed at the historic Red Lion Inn in Stockbridge during this time, but a check of the Red Lion's registers for June–August 1930 did not reveal their names.

143 **Kath's departure from Berkshire Players**: The *Hartford Courant* reported on July 20, 1930, that Hepburn had already appeared in three productions in Stockbridge and that she might appear in *The Torchbearers*, the Berkshire Players' fourth show, which opened on July 21. If so, she left before the end of the show's run.

143 **Luddy burns himself**: LOS to Gertrude Smith, March 28, 1929, SFP.

144 **Kath's frustration in understudying Williams**: Not once during the original run of the play did Hepburn have a chance to go on in place of Williams. After Hepburn and Williams became social friends, the truth of Kath's frustration during *Holiday* was obscured. In biographical notes to the program for Hepburn's play *Without Love* (1942), the absurd claim was made that Williams had offered Hepburn "the chance to play the role any performance she wished, a generous and unselfish gesture which Miss Hepburn has never forgotten." Quite possibly, this may have been Hepburn's way of subtly needling Williams.

144 **"the chief source"**: F. O. Matthiessen to RD, [nd], RDP.

144 **Putnam's politics**: Draft of an unpublished poem, "Fellow Traveler," PPP. In this poem, Putnam wrote he "knew Marx had something," as well as Lenin and Engels, and called himself "a friend of these."

145 **Luddy and Stanley Haggart**: Harry Hay, the gay-rights pioneer and an actor in Los Angeles in the 1930s, told me in 1998 that he knew men with whom Ludlow Ogden Smith had had sexual affairs, though he did not name any names. In Darwin Porter's book on Hepburn, *Katharine the Great* (Blood Moon Press, 2004), the claim is made that Luddy was sexually involved with the Hollywood publicist Stanley Haggart, who, as it turns out, was Hay's lover and intimate friend. However, given the lack of attribution in Porter's book, I cannot reliably document this story.

145 *Young Alexander*: The play opened on March 11, 1929, at the Biltmore Theater, with Henry Hull as Alexander. Jack Clarke formed the Nevin-Clarke Corporation to produce the play; his sister Agnes designed the costumes. (Various clips, especially *Chicago Tribune*, March 24, 1929)

145 **Filling in for Hope Williams**: Edwards says this performance occurred in July. However, the run at the Riviera did not begin until October 14.

146 **"fiasco"**: LOS to Lewis L. Smith, November 5, 1929, SFP.

146 **Bronson Cutting**: The senator's homosexuality, whispered about during his career among his political foes, is evidenced in his letters, especially those to and from Clifford McCarthy. Cutting's biographer, Richard Lowitt, seemed reluctant to "out" New Mexico's progressive hero, who died in a plane crash in 1935. Still, Lowitt documents the "effusive" correspondence between the never-married Cutting and McCarthy. Reading the correspondence leaves the unmistakable impression that the missives are, in fact, love letters. See Richard Lowitt, *Bronson M. Cutting: Progressive Politician* (University of New Mexico Press, 1992).

146 **Putnam's later circle**: Although Putnam would meet his second wife, Una Fairweather, through this New Mexico group, after 1930 he seemed to establish himself within a largely gay world. Bynner, especially, was famous for being overtly gay: Mabel Dodge Luhan claimed he'd "single-handedly" introduced homosexuality into New Mexico. On visits with Putnam back East, Bynner got to know Hepburn, who brought him home with her at least once to Fenwick. She also visited Bynner out West at some point; years later he'd send her a sculpture of two burros that she would cherish for reminding her of the trip. See KH to Witter Bynner, January 22, 1943; January 10, 1945; Witter Bynner Papers, Houghton Library, Harvard College Library, Cambridge.

147 **"They're absolutely right"**: *NYT*, June 18, 1967. In *Me*, Hepburn would go to pains to revise this negative anecdote about her father, presenting him as saying he'd liked her characterization and it was the *play* that was "bunk." Bob Hepburn said the earlier story was more the way he remembered it.

147 **"petal-like"**: *NYT*, December 27, 1929.

147 *A Month in the Country*: According to Gavin Lambert, Nazimova's biographer, stories of Nazimova harboring a dislike for Hepburn seem to have no basis in fact. Such tales seem to have been used by the legend to exaggerate Hepburn's difficulties in the already difficult season of 1929–30. Leaming implied that Kath was fired from the play; this was not so. She did, however, emerge from the experience with a grudge against the Theatre Guild for its parsimony, which would take years to overcome.

148 **Group Theatre**: The tale of Hepburn announcing all she wanted was to be a star has long been part of the Group's lore. See Wendy Smith, *Real Life Drama: The Group Theatre and America, 1931–1940* (Grove Weidenfeld, 1990), and Harold Clurman, *The Fervent Years: The Group Theatre and the Thirties* (Harcourt Brace, 1975).

148 **Laura Harding's background**: Laura Harding scrapbooks, courtesy Emily King; U.S. Census, 1900–1930; *Bridgeport Telegram*, February 11, 1922; *NYT*, March 25, July 2, 1920; December 21, 1923; February 3, April 13, April 16, May 10, October 17, 1924; August 16, 1925; May 9, 1926; February 11, July 4, 1927; *San Mateo Times*, August 13, 1926.

150 **Top two hundred**: *Chicago Tribune*, January 19, 1921.

150 **"She knew all"**: *Me.*

150 **"socially OK"**: *Vogue*, September 1991.

151 **Laura's coming out**: *NYT*, October 2, October 24, November 27, November 30, 1920.

152 **"I do not"**: *Daily Northwestern*, November 5, 1929. See also *NYT*, October 18, 1929; *LAT*, October 18, 1929.

153 **Kath stays in Laura's room**: Details of this scenario were gleaned from conversations both Hepburn and Harding had with family and friends. To the author Charles Higham, Laura acknowledged that Kath left her room in Bradley's to share hers, ostensibly because Laura had the better room. Still, Bradley's house was quite crowded, and it's significant that Kath traded privacy, usually her holy grail, for shared quarters.

153 **Louisa Carpenter**: Born in 1907, she was a frequent guest at Hollywood parties and later became a close friend of Tallulah Bankhead's. She married but dropped her husband's name (Jenney). Her brother was Ruly Carpenter, owner of the Philadelphia Phillies baseball team. She died in February 1976 when a plane she was piloting crashed in Maryland.

153 **Meaning of *lesbian***: Lillian Faderman writes in *Odd Girls and Twilight Lovers*: "[A]n erotic interest in another female, and even sex with another female, was not necessarily sufficient to make a woman a lesbian. She might consider her experiences simply bisexual experimentation, which was even encouraged in certain milieus. One had to *see* oneself as a lesbian to be a lesbian."

Indeed, Laura's rejection of the term was shared by other class-sensitive women of the era. Despite living openly with her female partner, the film director Dorothy Arzner also recoiled at the word, calling it "ridiculous—tag put onto friendship." This comes from comments Arzner scrawled on Deborah Derow's senior thesis for Barnard College, Columbia University, "What Is This We Hear—A Broad Is Going to Direct," May 1976, in the Dorothy Arzner Collection, UCLA. For more on this discussion, see my *Behind the Screen: How Gays and Lesbians Shaped Hollywood* (Viking, 2001).

154 **Lesbians in literature**: *The Well of Loneliness* had been published in 1928 but was only the latest in a string of popular novels to deal with the subject: Virginia Woolf's *Mrs. Dalloway* (1925), *Dusty Answer* by Rosamund Lehmann (1927), and *Extraordinary Women* by Compton MacKenzie (1928). In *Dusty Answer*, widely acclaimed, a lesbian undergraduate student was an object of both desire and fear for the novel's protagonist. Given such lesbian visibility in the culture, it's difficult to believe Hepburn's assertions that she was unaware of the impression she made by living with Laura Harding.

155 **"pastime"**: *McCall's*, November 1984.

155 **"have the same need"**: Tape-recorded interview with John Ford and KH by Dan Ford, JFC.

155 **"[R]omantic magic"**: Transcript, GCC, folder 620.

155 **"I think men"**: *Ladies' Home Journal*, August 1975.

155 **"not female"**: *Vogue*, September 1991.

155 **"I put on pants"**: KH on *The Barbara Walters Special*, ABC, June 2, 1981, quoted in *NYT*, May 21, 1981.

155 **Gender identity**: For more on this subject and the insights it offers into Hepburn's psyche, see Kate Bornstein, *Gender Outlaw: On Men, Women and the Rest of Us* (Routledge, 1994); Jennifer Finney Boylan, *She's Not There: A Life in Two Genders* (Broadway Books, 2003); Leslie Feinberg, *Transgender Warriors* (Beacon Press, 1997); Joan Nestle, ed., *Genderqueer: Voices from Beyond the Sexual Binary* (Alyson, 2002); Susan Stryker and Stephen Whittle, eds., *The Transgender Reader* (Routledge, 2003); Riki Wilchins, *Read My Lips: Sexual Subversion and the End of Gender* (Firebrand, 1997).

156 **World of theatrical lesbians**: See Mercedes de Acosta, *Here Lies the Heart* (William Morrow, 1960); Gavin Lambert, *Nazimova: A Biography* (Knopf, 1997); Robert Schanke, *That Furious Lesbian: The Story of Mercedes de Acosta* (Southern Illinois University Press, 2003) and *Shattered Applause: The Lives of Eva Le Gallienne* (Southern University Press, 1992); Robert Schanke and Kim

Marra, eds., *Passing Performances: Queer Readings of Leading Players in American Theater History* (University of Michigan Press, 1998); and Helen Sheehy, *Eva Le Gallienne: A Biography* (Knopf, 1996). For further discussion of the construct of the "open secret," see Eve Kosofsky Sedgwick, *Epistemology of the Closet* (University of California Press, 1990).

156 **"It was"**: *Me.*

156 **"queer"**: Sheehy, *Eva Le Gallienne.*

157 **"Ridiculous"**: *Vogue*, September 1991.

158 **Wilmarth Lewis**: Lewis was independently wealthy and set up a Walpole museum in his home in Farmington, Connecticut. With his close friend John DeKoven Alsop, the bachelor son of the prominent Connecticut family, Lewis was part of Gerald Murphy's social (and somewhat sexually ambiguous) circle. After Alsop's death, Lewis married Laura's friend Annie Burr Auchincloss. They never had children. Annie became her husband's partner in collecting Walpoliana. Lewis's two memoirs do have the unmistakable ring of a repressed gay narrative. He was also a friend of Justice Felix Frankfurter. (See discussion on p. 572 regarding Frankfurter's association with Garson Kanin.) See Wilmarth Sheldon Lewis, *Collector's Progress* (Knopf, 1951) and *One Man's Education* (Knopf, 1967).

158 **Carleton Burke**: Not until he was fifty did Burke marry, to Mrs. Myrtle Wood Hook. Burke and Mrs. Wood had no children. Various members of George Cukor's circle recalled Burke as gay. He was also friendly with Tim Durant, Spencer Tracy's close friend.

158 **Alan Campbell**: Several accounts have said that Campbell was in the cast of *The Warrior's Husband.* This is not so. He was rehearsing for *The Danger Line* when *Warrior's Husband* opened on March 12, although he either quit or was fired; in any event, he was soon in the cast of *Border-Land*, which ran concurrently with *The Warrior's Husband.* It's possible that after *Border-Land* closed in April, Campbell may have taken a small part in *Warrior,* but he was also busy rehearsing for *Show Boat* at the time, which opened in May. A more likely genesis for the friendship between Campbell and Hepburn was *Echo*, the play by Leila Manning Taylor for which both were announced in February 1930. Although *Echo* was not produced, the two seem to have stayed in contact and likely moved in similar social circles.

158 **Kath in New York theatrical world**: I attempted to re-create this world and Hepburn's place in it after reading letters and memoirs written by Philip Barry, Billie Burke, George Cukor, Russell Davenport, Nancy Hamilton, Laura Harding, Beatrice Lillie, Donald Ogden Stewart, Clifton Webb, and Hope Williams. In addition, the recollections of Eunice Stoddard, who remembered Hepburn as part of a very cosmopolitan set, added a great deal. The correspondence between Hope Williams and Mercedes de Acosta, held at the Rosenbach Museum and Library in Philadelphia, was also important in documenting this world. Laura Harding's family recalled stories of their aunt mingling in this mix of high society and Broadway; both Robert Shaw and Michael Pearman reported that Clifton Webb told them he'd met Hepburn and Harding at this time.

158 **Lillie Messenger**: 1930 Census. Later Messenger would marry "Prince" Alexis Thurn-Taxis, who claimed to be a member of the Austrian royal family. He was born Cliff Wheeler, the son of a Massachusetts dentist, and was remembered by many within the Hollywood gay subculture as a rather pretentious, not-so-circumspect homosexual. Lillie would go on to be a reader at MGM; with her "Prince" she often entertained Los Angeles society at their elegant Beverly Hills home. They had no children.

159 **Social Register**: *LAT*, January 31, 1930.

159 **"I was impressed"**: De Acosta, *Here Lies the Heart.*

13. THE BEAUTIFUL SCENT OF ORANGE BLOSSOMS

161 **The *Chief***: Many accounts, including Edwards, Leaming, and Hepburn's own memoir, have her arriving in Los Angeles on the *Super Chief.* However, that legendary locomotive didn't start its run until 1937. Hepburn came in on its predecessor, the more simply named *Chief.*

161 **"As long as"**: Adela Rogers St. Johns, *The Honeycomb* (Doubleday, 1969).

163 **KH professional inactivity in 1930**: Among the "might-have-beens" during this period

were *Echo* by Leila Manning Taylor, announced in February 1930 with Hepburn in the cast but apparently not produced until 1932 in London, and the Professional Players' *Michael and Mary* by A. A. Milne, which was scrapped in place of another play.

163 ***Art and Mrs. Bottle***: The Internet Broadway Database incorrectly states that the show closed in December 1930; its final curtain was January 24, 1931.

164 **"that child," "Could I"**: *SEP*, December 13, 1941.

164 **"decisive ability"**: *NYT*, November 19, 1930.

164 **"uncommonly refreshing"**: *New York World*, November 20, 1930.

164 **Ivoryton**: *The Cat and the Canary* ran August 11–15; *Let Us Be Gay* August 18–22; *The Man Who Came Back* August 24–29; and *Young Sinners* September 1–5. *Middletown Press,* July–September 1931.

164 **"I learned"**: *Me.*

164 **"This is the first time"**: *SEP*, December 13, 1941.

165 **"a real daughter"**: Florence Kitson to LOS, July 26, 1931, SFP.

165 **"a rich girl"**: Kanin.

165 **Kath and Laura at Fenwick**: These descriptions and memories come from Bob Hepburn.

166 ***The Animal Kingdom***: Leaming seems to have taken Hepburn's comment in *Me* ("Phil had really written it for me") as fact. Not only should one never take Hepburn's statements literally; it seems this time she actually didn't intend her remark to be taken that way. The comment was made during a gushing moment of excitement about the part and the play. She was saying, in effect, that she was "born to play the part." Leaming's contention that Barry had based the entire play on Kath's relationship with Phelps Putnam also has no basis in fact. Although Barry and Putnam did know each other through Yale connections, Barry was not, as Leaming contends, one of Putnam's "closest friends." In fact, the plot of *The Animal Kingdom* bears very little resemblance to the Kath-Putnam-Ruth triangle.

166 **Jack Clarke in Brazil**: Jack left with a party of several experienced explorers on the *Western World* on December 26, 1930. The expedition was financed by E. R. Fenimore Johnson of the Victor Talking Machine Company. The plan was to chart 2,500 miles of the Paraguay River, where the British explorer G. H. Fawcett had disappeared several years earlier. Newspapers followed the perilous journey with regular updates. In late September, Jack was accidentally shot in the shoulder by one of his own men just moments after he'd killed a jaguar, prompting his early departure from the expedition. He remained involved with the film, however, which was titled *Matto Grosso* and released in January 1933, produced by Sol Lesser (who'd go on to produce *Peck's Bad Boy*, the film of *Our Town*, and Johnny Weissmuller's later *Tarzan* adventures). The *New York Times* called *Matto Grosso* "definitely superior" to most travel films. *NYT*, December 26, 1930; March 7, July 24, August 4, September 22, September 23, December 11, 1931; January 10, January 14–15, 1933; *WP*, January 31, 1933; *Time*, October 5, 1931.

166 **"I don't feel"**: LOS to Gertrude Smith, February 10, 1932, SFP.

167 ***Animal Kingdom*** **contract**: This contract was signed on November 6, 1931, between KH and Charles Frohman. It was sold at auction and reproduced in the Sotheby's catalog.

167 **Kath's firing**: Here the legends tell an almost identical story to the time Kath was fired from *These Days*. She doesn't know she's fired, but the rest of the cast does. She's driven home by a fellow player who assures her that "no part is that important." Here we also get the usual prophetic warning that accompanied most stories of Kath being fired: Miller's wife calls him "stupid" for getting rid of Hepburn, as she was certain she was "going to be a big star someday." To Dick Cavett, Hepburn would repeat the nonsense about being "an inch taller" than Howard.

167 **"Don't worry"**: ROSS.

167 ***The Warrior's Husband***: Her contract was signed on February 9, 1932, between KH and Harry Moses. It was sold at auction and reproduced in the Sotheby's catalog.

168 **"It was very controversial"**: Higham.

168 **Atkinson's review**: *NYT*, March 12, 1932.

168 **Mantle's review**: *Chicago Tribune*, March 20, 1932.

168 **"I was just full"**: *Me*.

170 **Leland Hayward's background**: In addition to my conversation with Brooke Hayward, I drew considerable color from her family memoir *Haywire* (Knopf, 1977), as well as from Sonia Berman, *The Crossing—Adano to Catonsville: Leland Hayward's Producing Career* (Scarecrow Press, 1995). Also, *LAT*, October 22, 1927; *NYT*, October 31, 1926; February 12, 1928; February 16, 1930; March 10, 1931; December 2, 1932.

171 **Leland goes off on his own**: According to the contract he signed with Hepburn on June 17, 1932, sold at auction and reproduced in the Sotheby's catalog, he was already working with Myron Selznick but remained affiliated with the American Play Company. By July 13, however, he had already begun the process of setting up his own company. A letter on this date from John Rumsey of the APC expressed dismay at Leland's departure: "I feel you have used me and the company as a stepping stone, for you never had any business until you joined up with me." This letter is among Leland's papers held at NYPL.

171 **Kath's screen tests**: According to letters in George Cukor's files, the RKO test—the one directed by Messenger—was filmed sometime during the first two weeks of June. This suggests it was done *after* the Paramount test, which, if Ford directed it, likely was filmed in late April or early May. Preserved at the Film and Television Library at UCLA, the Paramount test runs four minutes. The only source that claims Ford was the director of this bit of film is the credit given him in the UCLA catalog; where this information came from, no one could be quite sure. According to Hollywood historians Anthony Slide and Robert Gitt, it would seem more likely that Fox would designate the shooting of a New York screen test to its newsreel crew, since it was based in the city. This scenario is far more credible than Ford flying East, especially given what we know about his schedule. Despite all this, Leaming described the encounter very specifically, with Ford marveling at Kate through the haze of his pipe smoke.

172 ***Electra***: This play was performed on May 26 at the Academy of Music in Philadelphia. Others in the cast were Dorothy Gish and Lawrence Tibbett.

172 **Ossining**: Kath opened at the Croton River Playhouse in *The Bride the Sun Shines On* on June 27. The play ran until Saturday, July 2. The next morning, Kath left for Hollywood from nearby Croton Station, Luddy having brought up a suitcase from the city. The station was convenient, but it also allowed her to avoid any New York tabloid reporters.

172 **"excessive," "I agree"**: Katherine Brown to George Cukor, May 26, 1932, GCC. Much has been made about how Hepburn demanded $1,500 right from the start, but this letter clearly refutes that.

172 **Cukor and Hepburn's first meeting**: This comes from an extraordinary tape-recorded conversation between the two old friends, made in the summer of 1969. Cukor had it transcribed and was using it to help write his own unfinished memoirs. The story of Cukor smacking Laura's shoulder also comes from this source. Folder 620, GCC.

173 **Cukor's background and character**: Cukor's papers at AMPAS, including his unfinished memoirs, offer an invaluable window onto his world. I am also indebted to two biographies on the director: Emanuel Levy, *George Cukor: Master of Elegance* (William Morrow, 1994), and Patrick McGilligan, *A Double Life: George Cukor* (St. Martin's, 1991), as well as to the enormously helpful insights, anecdotes, and observations offered by Cukor's good friends, listed in the acknowledgments.

174 **"the most photogenic"**: Cecil Beaton diary, September 26, 1969, from Hugo Vickers, ed., *Beaton in the Sixties: The Cecil Beaton Diaries as He Wrote Them, 1965–1969* (Knopf, 2003).

175 **"At times," "Kate was quite"**: Higham.

175 **"his skin"**: *Movie Mirror*, March 1933.

175 **John Barrymore**: Late in life, as so often happened, Hepburn succumbed to the myths that had been written about her, and repeated to Scott Berg the tales of a supposedly lecherous costar. She apparently told him the legendary exchange of her saying "I'll never play another scene with you" and Barrymore's pithy reply, "But my dear you never have." This seems like classic Hollywood

hokum. Barrymore's admiration of Hepburn's performance comes through quite genuinely in numerous contemporary accounts, making such latter-day tales ring false. It's a testament to the stamina of the Hepburn legend that even Berg, so punctilious in his other biographies, felt obliged to repeat such stories in *Kate Remembered*.

176 **"due to be"**: Merian C. Cooper to George Cukor, August 17, 1932, GCC.

176 **"half Botticelli"**: *New Yorker*, quoted in Edwards.

176 **"geometrically fascinating face"**: *LAT*, October 23, 1932.

176 **"far from being a stencil"**: *LAT*, October 9, 1932.

177 **"all over the Fifth Avenue buses"**: AP to Helen Palache, February 4, 1933, PFP.

14. LIKING EVERYTHING ABOUT THE MOVIES

178 **Kath's physical appearance**: Her driver's license, granted on December 20, 1932, gives us her height and weight; various newspaper accounts describe her appearance.

179 **"any of that nonsense"**: Transcript, GCC, folder 620.

179 **"I liked"**: ROSS.

180 **Kath's contracts**: These are kept in the RKO Studio collection, NYPL.

180 **"everyone was"**: Higham.

180 **Kath's trip to Europe**: Various accounts have said she cut her trip short when the glowing reviews from *Divorcement* started coming in. Yet she had already been abroad eight weeks when she returned on October 17; it's unlikely she planned to be away much longer than that. (*NYT*, October 18, 1933)

181 **Luddy's rental on East Forty-ninth Street**: The *New York Times* carried a notice of Luddy's rental from Mrs. Maud Knowlton Smith (no relation) on January 13 and 17, 1933. Other notices of the rental were printed on June 20 and again on July 14, possibly indicating the first lease had been for six months.

181 **"Lud's house"**: AP to Helen Palache, February 4, 1933, PFP.

181 **Kath's Los Angeles hospitalization**: Various clippings, AMPAS microfilm biographical file, January 27–28, 1933.

181 **Kath's Hartford hospitalization**: *Chicago Tribune*, February 26, 1933; *LAT*, February 26, 1933.

181 **"live or die"**: LOS to Lawrence Smith, March 10, 1933, SFP. For ninety minutes, Luddy was terrified that she might die; the operation in fact went on even longer than this, which also supports the idea of a hysterectomy. If indeed this was the case, it's likely that not all the ovaries were removed, as this would have induced menopause, and there is no evidence in Hepburn's appearance or behavior at this time to support this.

181 **"which is"**: AP to Helen Palache, March 23, 1933, PFP. The fact that Hepburn's hospitalizations took place four months after her European trip with Luddy has led to some speculation that she may have been pregnant, and that she may have had an abortion or a miscarriage. When the reporter Myrna Blyth asked her in 1991 if she'd ever had an abortion, Hepburn said, "I wouldn't answer that . . . but I would have an abortion if I wanted to" (*Ladies' Home Journal*, October 1991). A child certainly would have interfered with her screen career, which was just set to take off with the release of *A Bill of Divorcement*. However, we must remember that this was the daughter of Kit Hepburn, then in the midst of her national birth control campaign. Even if Kath did allow Luddy to have sex with her in Europe, she knew how to protect herself. There is also no suggestion of pregnancy in the letters of Luddy or Palache; Luddy, especially, with his great desire for children, would have come across more grieving than simply frightened. Finally, an abortion (or any procedures following a miscarriage) would not have been as likely to leave a scar on the lower anatomy.

182 **Dorothy Arzner**: Her papers, at the Film and Television Library at UCLA, document her relationship with Morgan. The possible affair with Billie Burke was speculated on by the director Andrew Stone, who was at the studio during that period, to the historian Anthony Slide for an article in *Film Quarterly*, Summer 1999. For more discussion on both Arzner and Akins, see my *Behind the Screen*.

184 **Kath's pranks**: These are detailed in various accounts and interviews given over the years. According to Laura Harding's family, they are all true.

184 **"subcollegiate idiotic"**: *SEP*, December 14, 1941.

184 **"The Marx Brothers' long-disputed title"**: RKO publicity, AMPAS.

185 **John Farrow**: *LAT*, December 29, 1932. Hepburn would later tell Scott Berg that she considered Farrow "depraved," making us ache for a story clearly left untold.

186 **Cukor and the ham**: Transcript, folder 620, GCC.

186 **"No, I'm not"**: *WP*, January 29, 1933.

186 **Claudette Colbert's marriage**: Various articles, Colbert files, AMPAS, NYPL; see especially *LAT*, August 17, 1930; *Silver Screen*, June 1931; *WP*, May 5, 1932; *Motion Picture*, August 1932; and my *Behind the Screen*.

187 **Name change to Ludlow**: In the SFP, there is the announcement: "Please be advised that my name has been legally changed to Ogden Ludlow. Kindly revise your records accordingly. Ludlow O. Smith, 244 East 49th Street, New York. November 6, 1933."

188 **Hollywood in the early 1930s**: Various studies have documented this remarkably vibrant and tolerant culture. See especially McGilligan, *A Double Life*; William McBrian, *Cole Porter: A Biography* (Knopf, 1998); Steven Bach, *Marlene Dietrich: Life and Legend* (William Morrow, 1992). See also my *Behind the Screen*.

188 **William Haines**: See my *Wisecracker: The Life and Times of William Haines* (Viking, 1998).

189 **Goulding's parties**: See Frederica Sagor Maas, *The Shocking Miss Pilgrim* (University Press of Kentucky, 1999); Matthew Kennedy, *Edmund Goulding's Dark Victory: Hollywood's Genius Bad Boy* (University of Wisconsin Press, 2004).

190 **"seventy-five percent"**: *Catholic Transcript*, February 8, 1934.

191 *Grounds for Divorce*: *LAT*, February 2, February 14, 1933.

191 **Hollywood Barn**: *LAT*, March 9, 1933.

191 **"continue the party"**: *Hollywood Reporter*, [nd], Anderson Lawler scrapbook, NYPL.

191 **"Give my love"**: William Haines to George Cukor, [nd, 1933], GCF.

192 **Bankhead and Hepburn**: Hepburn and Cukor recalled this anecdote in their tape-recorded reminiscences, folder 620, GCC.

192 **Cukor and James Whale**: Lambert thought that Cukor made an exception in this regard to William Haines and Jimmie Shields because he felt directors had a more "important, serious reputation to safeguard" than actors. Cukor would eventually fall out with Haines anyway, thinking him too indiscreet, though the two would reconcile in later years.

193 **Kath and the ice cream**: Lambert, *On Cukor* (Putnam's, 1972).

193 **"The best of"**: Transcript, folder 620, GCC.

193 **"There's a complete absence," "We've the same taste"**: *NYT*, January 28, 1979.

193 **"here was"**: McGilligan, *A Double Life*.

193 **"It was as if"**: *Me*.

194 **Cukor's French**: Lambert, *On Cukor*.

194 **"We're not all"**: George Cukor to Laura Harding, November 14, 1962, GCF.

195 **"We always"**: McGilligan, *A Double Life*.

195 **"It rather suited"**: Transcript, folder 620, GCC.

195 **"I could say"**: Berg.

195 NEW HEPBURN FILM: *NYT*, November 26, 1933.

196 **"A triumph"**: *LAT*, November 1, 1933.

196 **"Miss Hepburn's performance"**: *NYT*, November 26, 1933.

15. NO SECRETS FROM THE WORLD

197 **"Not a breadline"**: *WP*, September 13, 1933.

198 **Production Code enforcement**: For a detailed discussion of this tumultuous period, see Gregory D. Black, *Hollywood Censored: Morality Codes, Catholics and the Movies* (Cambridge Uni-

versity Press, 1994); Thomas Doherty, *Pre-Code Hollywood: Sex, Immorality, and Insurrection in American Cinema, 1930–1934* (Columbia University Press, 1999); Leonard J. Leff and Jerold L. Simmons, *The Dame in the Kimono: Hollywood, Censorship and the Production Code* (University Press of Kentucky, 2001).

198 **"It will be"**: *NYT*, September 13, 1933.

198 **"vigorous campaign"**: *LAT*, October 8, 1933. What's telling is that, as ever, the objections of the church centered more on sex than violence. In *The Picture Snatcher*, even with its "good" rating, Cagney knocks back a sexually aggressive moll and throws her roughly into the backseat of a car.

198 **"A pall"**: NYT, July 22, 1934.

199 SEX-APPEAL ERA: *LAT*, December 3, 1933.

199 **"The young actress"**: Unsourced clipping, September 6, 1932, Hepburn microfilm biography file, AMPAS.

199 **"A new sartorial thrill"**: *LAT*, September 11, 1932.

199 **"Not only does La Hepburn"**: Unsourced clipping, April 27, 1933, NYPL.

199 **George Shafer on Kath's overalls**: *Chicago Tribune*, March 4, 1933.

199 **"twenty impertinent questions"**: *Movie Classic*, March 1933.

199 **"queer duck"**: *New York Daily Mirror*, March 8, 1933.

199 **"miscast"**: *LAT*, September 7, 1932.

200 **"Katy's closest"**: *New York Daily Mirror*, October 25, 1933.

200 **"shared a secret hideaway"**: Unsourced clipping, September 12, 1933, NYPL.

200 **"inseparable companion"**: *Los Angeles Examiner*, January 12, 1933.

200 **"two ruffians"**: Various clippings, October 17, October 18, 1933, AMPAS, NYPL.

200 **"husbands, wives"**: *LAT*, December 10, 1933.

201 THE TRUTH: Although the article, written by Martha Kerr for the November 1933 issue of *Modern Screen*, is a good example of the new stridency of the Hollywood press, it seems to have had at least some inside cooperation. Someone slipped the magazine photos of Kath as a young girl at Fenwick—photos later identified as part of Hepburn's estate. Might the perpetrator have been Luddy himself, whom Kerr identifies as being friendly to her and who surely had access to the pictures among Kath's belongings? Was he hoping to put some pressure on her to live openly as his wife?

202 **"latent sadism"**: Alexander Walker, *The Shattered Silents* (William Morrow, 1979).

202 **"The history"**: The journalist John Moffitt wrote this piece in the *Kansas City Star*, and it was reprinted for wider dissemination in the trade journal *Cinema Digest*, January 9, 1933.

203 **Kath's official studio biography**: A copy is preserved in the Hepburn biography collection, on microfilm, at AMPAS.

203 KATHARINE HEPBURN'S STYLE SECRETS: *Modern Screen*, August 1933.

203 **"I used to have"**: ROSS.

204 **Elissa Landi**: The Venice-born actress, of Austrian noble blood, had made her first big splash on the London stage playing a free-loving girl in *Lavender Ladies*. In Hollywood, she was looked at with even more suspicion than Hepburn. Like Kath, she didn't often play the usual studio publicity game, and as a result was called "cold" and "aloof." Also like Kath, she had a nontraditional marriage; in fact, when she and her husband divorced, it was learned that they'd been allowed to see other people. A blind item dated April 3, 1933, in Landi's microfilm clipping file at AMPAS is clearly about her (the subject is identified as living with her mother, which Landi did): "Lack of interest in the opposite sex displayed by a femme player who is being groomed for stardom on a major lot has gone so far that it is worrying execs. . . . Execs admit they have hinted to her that she ought to make a date once in a while, but the actress, who is in her 20s, doesn't take heed." Landi remarried late in life and had one daughter, who said she'd heard the stories of an affair with Hepburn, but since her mother died when she was very young, had no way of knowing if they were true. The two women likely met through David Manners, who had acted with both of them and was a regular at Cukor's.

204 **Laura's abrupt departure**: She may have left early for health reasons; in an article in the *Los Angeles Times* on October 29, Kath mentioned that Laura had been ill.

205 **Kath and Luddy are dropped from Social Register**: *NYT*, December 21, 1933.

205 **"I think"**: AP to Helen Palache, December 5, 1933, PFP.

205 **Luddy moves across the street**: This was mentioned in a couple of later articles by reporters who tracked him down there. The 1930 Census reveals that a twelve-room guesthouse was located at 245 East Forty-ninth Street, run by Louise Toben, a German-born immigrant.

205 **"You are"**: LOS to Gertrude Smith, December 20, 1933, SFP.

205 **"He asked me"**: Marion Hepburn's diary, January 1, 1934, quoted in Houghton, *Marion Hepburn Grant*.

205 **Linsley Dodge**: U.S. Census, 1930; various *NYT*.

206 **"Set back"**: *Independent*, July 1, 2003.

206 **Lillian Russell on Forty-ninth Street**: *NYT*, June 8, 1930.

206 **Jed Harris**: My descriptions of the man and the experience of *The Lake* are gleaned from several sources, including *Me*; Martin Gottfried's biography, *Jed Harris: The Curse of Genius* (Little, Brown, 1984); and two memoirs by Harris himself: *Watchman, What of the Night?* (Doubleday, 1963) and *A Dance on the High Wire* (Crown, 1979). In addition, various letters between Harris and Thornton Wilder in the Wilder Collection at the Beinecke Library were valuable windows on Harris's mercurial personality.

207 **"I could see"**: Higham.

207 **"thought he was accomplishing"**: *Me*.

209 **"The first thing"**: *Times* (London), November 24, 1973.

209 **New York opening**: That Kath was well aware of a scheduled New York opening is also documented by a letter from Luddy to his brother Lawrence "Sam" Smith, dated November 22, 1933, that says the play would be opening on the day after Christmas and that the Martin Beck was already sold out (SFP). If Kath really wanted to tour with it before the New York opening, it would have meant canceling that engagement and refunding all those tickets.

209 **Parker's book and the play based on it**: The *WP* book review by Theodore Hall ran on March 1, 1934. For *After Such Pleasures*, see *Time*, February 19, 1934.

210 *The Lake* **on tour**: *LAT*, January 30, 1934; *Chicago Tribune*, February 4, 1934.

210 **"vital and persuasive"**: *NYT*, March 9, 1934.

210 *tedious*: Various clips, NYPL.

210 **"queer"**: *Time*, March 12, 1934.

210 **Chicago premiere of *Spitfire***: *Chicago Tribune*, March 18, 1934.

210 *Little Women*, *Spitfire* **receipts**: By the middle of 1934, *Little Women* had gross rentals of $2,250,000, a record shared with, among others, *Grand Hotel* and *I'm No Angel* (*NYT*, July 22, 1934). Although records have not been preserved for costs of RKO films, we know that *Spitfire* went over budget due to delays, such as the time that a canary escaped from a cage in one scene and hours were spent idly waiting for another to be brought up to the location in the San Jacinto Mountains (*LAT*, February 17, 1934). Although exact box-office receipts are hard to come by for the 1930s, with such dismal business after its release, *Spitfire* was likely one of RKO's biggest financial losses that year.

210 **"Hepburn does"**: *Movie Mirror*, March 1933.

210 **"Anything for publicity"**: *Collier's*, October 18, 1933.

210 **"constantly sticking out"**: *Vanity Fair*, January 1934.

210 **"If I cannot be interviewed"**: *Movie Classic*, March 1933.

211 **"Well, come here"**: *LAT*, September 2, 1933.

211 **"Her whole attitude"**: *LAT*, November 26, 1933.

211 **"topnotcher"**: *LAT*, November 19, 1933.

211 **"Haughty Hepburn"**: *New York Dramatic Mirror*, March 30, 1934.

212 **"young boy"**: *Modern Screen*, March 1934.

212 **"feminine to a glamorous degree"**: *Pictorial Review*, April 1934.

213 **"on a chicken farm"**: *Time*, January 8, 1934.

213 **Code campaign against deviance**: *Variety*, February 28, 1933; see also my *Behind the Screen*.

213 **Kit's testimony**: *Hollywood Citizen-News*, January 18, 1934; *Los Angeles Examiner*, January 19, 1934; *NYT*, January 19, 1934; other articles, Hepburn AMPAS biographical file.

16. A TERRIBLE PRICE FOR FAME

215 **Kate in Mexico**: The description and timeline are derived from the widest possible selection of contemporary newspaper reports. The actual Mexican divorce papers are apparently no longer extant, according to William Asunción Ramírez Lara of the Yucatán Civil Registry at Mérida. However, they were obtained by journalists in 1934 and were quoted in several reports. A copy may well exist among Hepburn's papers at AMPAS. See also *Chicago Tribune*, May 9, 1934; *Illustrated Daily News* (Los Angeles), May 1, May 3, 1934; *Los Angeles Examiner*, May 1, May 4, May 6, 1934; *LAT*, May 1–3, 1934; *NYT*, May 1, May 9, 1934; *WP*, May 1, May 3, 1934.

216 **"I do not expect"**: Associated Press report, *Daily Northwestern* (Oshkosh), May 1, 1934.

216 **"I can't believe"**: *LAT*, May 1–2, 1934.

216 **"favorably impressed"**: *Hollywood Citizen-News*, May 1, 1934.

217 **"deep disagreements"**: *Illustrated Daily News* (Los Angeles), May 3, 1934.

217 **"assist Miss Hepburn"**: *Chicago Tribune*, May 3, 1934.

217 **"Did you accomplish"**: *WP*, May 3, 1934.

217 **"Would *you*"**: *LAT*, May 3, 1934.

217 **"Who is"**: *Los Angeles Herald*, May 4, 1934.

217 **Kate's letter to Gertrude**: This was revealed by Luddy's niece Eleanor Smith Morris, in the *Scotsman*, August 16, 2003.

218 **"very close to"**: LOS to Lawrence Smith, [n.d., 1934], SFP.

218 **Kate's 1934 contract**: In addition, Hepburn received 5 percent of the gross receipts on each picture; if the receipts totalled more than $750,000, she would receive 7½ percent; over a million, 11 percent. It's not likely she saw anything near those figures for *The Little Minister* or *Break of Hearts*, but very likely made a nice sum off *Alice Adams*.

219 **"unlimited"**: *Photoplay*, July 1934.

219 **Persian kitten**: *Los Angeles Examiner*, May 5, 1934 and other newspaper articles. Was the kitten a prop? Hepburn was never partial to animals; except for adopting Spencer Tracy's dog after Tracy's death, she never had pets. (The dogs she mentioned in *Me* were actually Laura's.) Just whose kitten this was is unknown—possibly just a stray—but in any event Kate didn't seem that attached to it. Once the interview was concluded, she gave it to the newsman to keep.

220 **"He loved you"**: *Me*. This may have been Hepburn's way of having the last word about whom Leland really preferred—even though Margaret Sullavan had been dead at that point for thirty-one years. The remark was then picked up and made into official history by Sally Bedell Smith, who included it in her biography of Pamela Churchill Harriman, *Reflected Glory* (Simon and Schuster, 1996). These are the small ways in which the Hepburn legend has become codified as fact in the public consciousness.

220 **Leland with Hepburn, Sullavan**: Contemporary newspaper accounts, *NYT, LAT, Chicago Tribune*, others from collections at NYPL and AMPAS.

221 **Leland and aviation**: Berman, *The Crossing*. I am also grateful to Berman for sharing material from Leland's personal papers, now closed to researchers. Brooke Hayward also painted a colorful picture of her father's aviation.

223 **George Cukor's party**: This took place on board the SS *Majestic*, docked in New York harbor, on May 4, 1934, two days after Kate had returned from obtaining her divorce. However, Leaming would place the party before Kate left for Mexico, in mid-April, and depicted her as callously talking about marrying Leland even before she'd untied the knot with Luddy. This is not only uncharacteristic of Hepburn, but just plain wrong. The *New York Times*'s list of ocean travelers for May 4, 1934, includes George Cukor and David O. Selznick, who were sailing for England that night to begin research for Cukor's upcoming film *David Copperfield*.

223 **"free advertising"**: *LAT*, August 2, 1936.

223 **"Maybe those two"**: Unsourced, May 15, 1935, NYPL.

223 **Flops of *The Little Minister* and *Break of Hearts***: Exact box-office receipts are very hard to come by for films of the 1930s, as records were not often preserved. *The Little Minister* did better business than *Break of Hearts*; it was, in fact, among the top ten box-office champions for the first half of 1935, according to the monthly survey of key cities by the *Motion Picture Herald*. But this was still so far below *Little Women* that the film was generally written off as a failure. Both *Minister* and *Break of Hearts* were in the nation's theaters for just under five months, faring better than *Spitfire*, which was around for only three. Comparatively, *Little Women* was still showing in selected theaters in May 1934 after being released seven months earlier in November 1933.

224 **"I feel very much"**: Laura Harding to RD, June 18, 1935, RDP.

224 **"I think"**: Laura Harding to RD, June 19, 1935. From this letter also comes the information on working with Schiaparelli.

224 **Laura and Lubitsch**: Syndicated, *Mansfield* [Ohio] *News*, September 4, 1934.

224 **Pickup truck**: *LAT*, October 14, 1934.

224 **"gal pals"**: Syndicated, *Edwardsville* [Illinois] *Intelligencer*, May 1, 1935.

225 **"It had"**: Higham.

225 **"Well, it bothered *her*"**: *Vogue*, September 1991.

225 **"stop living"**: Higham.

225 **"So many moods"**: Laura Harding to RD, September 20, 1935, RDP.

225 **"[A]ll of us"**: Laura Harding to RD, June 19, 1935, RDP.

226 **Laura's return to the States**: She arrived into New York on board the *Bremen* on December 6, 1935.

226 **"I hear"**: Laura Harding to RD, September 20, 1935, RDP.

226 **Suicide of Parker Lloyd-Smith**: *NYT*, September 17, 1931. Davenport's letters have numerous mentions of Lloyd-Smith's suicide, from which Davenport took years to finally recover (RDP).

226 **"I really loved him"**: David Thomson, *Showman: The Life of David O. Selznick* (Knopf, 1992). Laura and Selznick may have first become friendly while she was still in Hollywood, but Thomson told me that their courtship didn't really begin until she was back East, where on his visits to New York Selznick would often head out to Laura's farm in New Jersey for "restful" breaks from an otherwise hectic schedule.

228 **Upton Sinclair's campaign**: For background and analysis, see Greg Mitchell, *The Campaign of the Century: Upton Sinclair's Race for Governor of California and the Birth of Media Politics* (Random House, 1992). See also *LAT*, November 2–3, November 7, 1934; *NYT*, November 2, November 4, November 7, 1934; *WP*, November 1, 1934; *Literary Digest*, October 13, 1934.

228 **"admirer"**: *LAT*, November 4, 1934.

228 **"an example"**: *Chicago Tribune*, November 1, 1934; *NYT*, November 1, 1934.

229 **"Nonsense"**: *NYT*, November 1, 1934.

229 **"No sale"**: *Photoplay*, April 1935.

229 **"Is Hepburn"**: *Photoplay*, September 1935.

230 **"Katharine had," "She didn't know"**: Interview with George Stevens by Robert Hughes, 1967, George Stevens Collection, AMPAS; also reprinted in Paul Cronin, ed., *George Stevens Interviews* (University Press of Mississippi, 2004).

230 **"Which side"**: Interview with George Stevens by James Silke, *Cinema*, December–January, 1964–65, reprinted in Cronin, *George Stevens Interviews*.

230 **Window scene**: Through careful consideration and comparison of the various versions of this story, told first in Lupton Wilkinson's *Saturday Evening Post* piece and carried on from there, I attempted to get at the underlying truth and significance of the anecdote.

231 **"Above all"**: Higham.

232 **"Our chance"**: Pandro Berman to KH, George Stevens, Mortimer Offner, Dorothy Yost, June 3, 1935, George Stevens Collection, AMPAS.

232 **"there was"**: AP to Helen Palache, July 18, 1935, PFP.

232 **"I am left speechless"**: Laura Harding to RD, September 20, 1935, RDP.

232 **"It just goes to show"**: *WP*, October 2, 1935.

232 TOPS AGAIN: *Modern Screen*, December 1935.

17. A YOUNG MAN WEARING LIPSTICK

234 *Sylvia Scarlett*: Various newspaper accounts, NYPL, AMPAS; transcript of conversation between Cukor and Hepburn, folder 620, GCC.

235 **"Every day"**: Lambert, *On Cukor*.

235 **"I despised"**: Higham.

235 **"sex confusion"**: Joseph Breen to B. B. Kahane, August 5, 1935, Production Code Administration (PCA) files, AMPAS.

235 **"We suggest"**: Joseph Breen to B. B. Kahane, August 12, 1935, PCA files, AMPAS.

236 **"I think"**: Interview with Larry King, CNN transcripts.

236 **"It was terribly embarrassing"**: *LAT*, August 4, 1935.

236 **"close-cropped goat"**: *WP*, September 29, 1935.

237 **"the whole joke"**: Higham.

237 **Palache in Hollywood**: AP to Charles Palache, June 13, 1935; AP to Palache family, July 18, July 20, July 21, 1935, PFP.

238 **Trudy Wellman**: Born in 1906, she was married to the cameraman Harold E. Wellman and appeared in *What Price Hollywood?* (1932) as well as other films. She died in 1995 in Simi Valley, California. See various newspaper accounts, NYPL; *Modern Screen*, February 1938.

238 **The Doyle sisters**: They were the daughters of William P. Doyle, a lawyer who practiced in Los Angeles for thirty-seven years. Patsy, born in 1913, stood in for Hepburn on *Spitfire, The Little Minister, Break of Hearts, Alice Adams, Mary of Scotland*, and *Quality Street*. She later married the noted director Robert Wise (*West Side Story, The Sound of Music*), who served as president of the Academy of Motion Picture Arts and Sciences. She died in 1975. Mimi, Patsy's twin, was a stand-in on *Quality Street* and possibly others. She married the drama critic and screenwriter Wells Root and died in 1979. (See more about Mimi, page 565 below.) There was another acting Doyle sister as well, Katherine, who was a stand-in for Barbara Stanwyck. See *Chicago Tribune*, July 4, 1936; February 15, 1937; *LAT*, October 14, 1933; *NYT*, November 21, 1937.

238 **Adalyn Doyle/Eve March**: Adalyn Doyle, born in 1910, bore a resemblance to Hepburn that was much commented upon. For her early career, see *LAT*, October 14, 1933; January 29, 1934; July 4, 1936; *NYT*, June 10, 1936; December 18, 1938; program for *Here Come the Clowns*, December 7, 1938, NYPL.

238 **Emily Perkins**: Hedda Hopper's column, *LAT*, July 17, 1943; U.S. Census, 1920, 1930; U.K. Census, 1901; probate file, September 3, 1974, York County, Maine. Various members of her family also shared information.

239 **Jane Loring**: No Jane Loring can be found in the U.S. Census for 1900, 1910, or 1920; even searches on the single name Jane, born circa 1890 in Colorado, do not reveal her identity. Her mother, according to her death certificate, was named Clara Logan; no information was given about her father. According to one report, Jane was related to the scenarist Hope Loring, but no family connection could be determined. She married Hanshaw after 1920, when the census listed him as single. She divorced him in 1924, according to her probate file. Hanshaw later married the actresses Ethlyne Clair and Miriam Christina Wills, the latter of whom he committed suicide with in 1938. Loring remained with Pan Berman after he moved over to MGM, but didn't remain long; Michael Berman said Louis B. Mayer didn't like Loring, not surprising, given how undisguised in her sexual orientation she was.

Jane spent her later years with Anna Graf, sister of the movie producer William Graf (*Lawrence of Arabia, A Man for All Seasons*), to whom she left all her papers. Graf, "a very private person," according to her attorney, left boxes of old papers in storage at the time of her death in 1993. These were destroyed, leaving unanswered the question of whether they contained Hepburn's letters to

Loring. The lawyer who handled Loring's estate, Noel Hatch, was also Dorothy Arzner's lawyer. Sources on Loring: *Chicago Tribune*, June 28, 1934; *Coshocton* [Ohio] *Tribune*, May 22, 1938; *LAT*, August 25, 1929; September 25, 1932; October 15, 1934; September 21, 1935; July 19, 1941; *WP*, February 7, 1932; probate file, Jane Loring, March 15, 1983, Los Angeles Probate Court; probate file, Anna Graf, July 29, 1993, Los Angeles Probate Court.

240 **"could live"**: Faderman, *Odd Girls and Twilight Lovers*.

241 **"flirting"**: Transcript of "George Stevens: A Filmmaker's Journey," interview with KH by George Stevens, Jr., George Stevens Collection, AMPAS.

241 **Hepburn and Boyer**: Although the press was silent about any romance between them, *Picture Play* magazine did report that she'd had some interest "in a former brunet leading man." *Picture Play*, [nd, 1936], Hepburn file, NYPL.

242 **"she found him"**: Higham. The supposed Hepburn-Stevens affair hasn't required much evidence for writers to presume it as fact. Stevens's biographer Marilyn Ann Moss, in *Giant: George Stevens, a Life on Film* (University of Wisconsin Press, 2004), wrote, "[M]ost of the cast and crew knew that despite an occasional creative dispute Hepburn and Stevens were having an affair off the set." How they knew this (and how she knew they knew this) Moss does not say.

242 **"sort of very male members"**: Transcript, "George Stevens: A Filmmaker's Journey."

242 **"In private life"**: *A Woman of Substance: Katharine Hepburn Remembered* (documentary on DVD of *On Golden Pond*).

242 **"Previewed our little love child"**: George Cukor to KH, December 9, 1935, GCC.

243 **"a queer sort of picture"**: *Chicago Tribune*, December 31, 1935.

243 **Flop of *Sylvia Scarlett***: Again, since box-office figures are almost nonexistent, I searched for how long the film was in theaters compared to others, which had averaged about five months for previous Hepburn films. *Sylvia Scarlett*, placed into wide release in January, was gone by March.

243 **"Shutters shudder"**: *Los Angeles Daily News*, October 24, 1936.

243 **"She looks like"**: *Modern Screen*, June 1936.

243 **Leland "husband" remark**: *Chicago Tribune*, November 7, 1935; *Los Angeles Examiner*, November 7, 1935; *LAT*, November 7, 1935.

244 **Kate and the propellers**: *Brooklyn Daily Eagle*, November 7, 1935; *Chicago Tribune*, November 10, 1935; *Los Angeles Examiner*, November 7, 1935; *Hollywood Citizen-News*, November 8, 1935.

244 **Furniture shopping**: *Los Angeles Herald*, November 20, 1935; *Hollywood Citizen-News*, November 20, 1935.

244 **"I'm so dreadfully afraid"**: *LAT*, August 4, 1935.

245 **"She is possessed"**: *Modern Screen*, January 1936.

245 **"Why sit"**: Unsourced clip, circa 1970, NYPL.

246 **"I can't think"**: *Modern Screen*, February 1936.

246 **"I had cause"**: PP to RD, January 20, 1936, RDP.

18. THINKING A THOUSAND THINGS

247 **Frank Scully visits set of *Mary of Scotland***: *Screen Book*, date missing, 1936, NYPL. Leaming relates part of this encounter without sourcing it, and presumes the writer (despite his byline being prominently featured on the page) was a woman. Various columns in the 1930s list Scully in the company of Ford, Nichols, and the writer Liam O'Flaherty, on whose story Ford based *The Informer*. The widely quoted Ford command to Hepburn—"You'll give your best performance or I'll break you across my knee"—is from this piece and seems just the sort of quip fan-magazine writers frequently made up with studio publicists' approval.

248 **Photo of KH on the *Araner***: This photo is reproduced in Dan Ford's biography of his grandfather, *Pappy: The Life of John Ford* (Prentice Hall, 1979).

248 **"Oh, Sean"**: KH to John Ford, April 10, 1937, JFC.

248 **John Ford, background and description**: Reading through the letters and other papers in the John Ford Collection—not only those that have to do with Hepburn but a wide selection of

other material as well—offered a fascinating glimpse into this conflicted man. Listening to his free-ranging tape-recorded conversations with Hepburn was perhaps even more illuminating. I also consulted Dan Ford's memoir, as well as several other books on the director: Lindsay Anderson, *About John Ford* (McGraw-Hill, 1981); Peter Bogdanovich, *John Ford* (University of California Press, 1978); Ronald L. Davis, *John Ford: Hollywood's Old Master* (University of Oklahoma Press, 1995); Scott Eyman, *Print the Legend: The Life and Times of John Ford* (Simon and Schuster, 1999); and Joseph McBride, *Searching for John Ford: A Life* (St. Martin's, 2001).

249 **Dorris Bowden**: Eyman, *Print the Legend.*

250 **KH looking through camera**: *LAT*, March 28, 1936.

250 **"Direct it"**: Tape-recorded interview with John Ford and KH by Dan Ford, JFC (hereafter DF interview), quoted in McBride, *Searching for John Ford.*

251 **"unsnobbish"**: DF interview.

251 **Loring's work on *Mary of Scotland***: *NYT*, June 28, 1936.

251 **"like a carpenter"**: DF interview.

252 **Photos in dressing room**: "Hepburn's Four Loves," *Picture Play*, month missing, 1936, NYPL.

252 **"so depraved"**: The attack on Kit ran in the March 7, 1935, issue of the *Catholic Transcript*, the publication of the Diocese of Hartford. Kit's response and the Diocese's apology (tempered though it was) ran on March 14.

252 **Ford with Hepburns, "You are," "secretive New Englanders"**: DF interview.

253 **"You know"**: KH to John Ford, June 27, 1936, JFC.

253 **"gingery miss"**: *LAT*, April 1, 1943.

254 **"My darling"**: Mimi Doyle to John Ford, December 5, 1938, JFC. Mimi had recently played a small part in Ford's film *Four Men and a Prayer*. In his biography of the director, Joseph McBride raised the possibility that this letter might not have been written to Ford. While it's possible it was written to someone else and then found its way into Ford's possession later, it seems to me Ford is the most likely target of Mimi's orchestrations. While she'd go on to play bit parts in several of Ford's later pictures, including *The Long Gray Line, Mister Roberts*, and *The Quiet Man*, no other letters were found from Mimi in Ford's files.

254 **KH tries to buy off Mary Ford**: Cecile de Prida, Ford's niece, told the same story in McBride's book. (De Prida died in 1991.) As McBride points out, there is no other documentation for this story. Dan Ford told me that de Prida did not have the kind of inside knowledge of his grandfather's life to be able to speak with certainty about such matters. McBride, however, found her to be "a generally reliable chronicler of family history."

254 **Maureen O'Hara**: See Maureen O'Hara, with John Nicoletti, *Tis Herself: A Memoir* (Simon and Schuster, 2004). When I questioned Dan Ford about O'Hara's claims, he dismissed them out of hand. In one other relevant story, O'Hara refuted speculation that the director had named her character in *The Quiet Man* after the two women he loved most: his wife and Hepburn. Instead, O'Hara insisted, "Mary Kate" came from the name she was almost given as a child, an amusing tale Ford had enjoyed.

254 **Ford as possibly repressed homosexual**: There is also this fact to consider: in September 1934, Ford was diagnosed with, among other conditions, an infected prostate (McBride, *Searching for John Ford*). While his enlarged liver may have been a result of his drinking, the prostatitis was likely caused either by a bacterial infection or by physical injury. Whether bacterial or injury-induced, medical experts say anal sex is a very likely agent.

255 **Comparison to Cukor**: DF interview.

255 **Ford and homosexuality**: Just as Phelps Putnam often did, Ford made a clear distinction between himself and homosexuals. In 1951, at the behest of Republic studios, he took over the director Budd Boetticher's film *The Bullfighter and the Lady*, starring his good buddy John Wayne. Looking at one scene, Ford complained to Boetticher, "You've got these two guys acting like they love each other. People will think they're a couple of queers." Boetticher argued, "Two men can love each other without being homosexual." Ford replied, "Not in my picture they can't," and snipped out the

scene. (David Chute, "Man of the West," *LA Weekly*, July 28–August 3, 2000) The picture has since been restored to Boetticher's original vision.

257 **Boston curtain calls**: *NYT*, January 3, 1937.

257 **Ivoryton**: After rehearsing the part, Kate clashed with her costar, the English actor Stanley Ridges, who eventually withdrew. At that point, Kate balked about starting over, leaving Ivoryton high and dry for its summer season. Several of Hepburn's friends suggested to me that the real problem was Kate's severe stagefright about being seen in live theater again.

257 **"drop dead"**: Cavett.

258 **Theatre Guild**: The voluminous papers in the Theatre Guild Collection (TGC) at Beinecke offer a rich, detailed window onto the lives of its three extraordinary leaders, Theresa Helburn, Lawrence Langner, and Armina Marshall. Also consulted were Langner's papers at NYPL. See also Theresa Helburn, *A Wayward Quest* (Little, Brown, 1960), and Lawrence Langner, *The Magic Curtain* (Dutton, 1951).

258 **RKO contract**: Hepburn's final contract with RKO was signed on July 1, 1936, and ran through November 15, 1937. She was making $240,000 per film, and the studio was prohibited from impersonating her easily imitated voice for any radio broadcast without her consent. RKO Collection, NYPL.

259 **KH's conflict with Franchot Tone**: This conflict is implied in a column by Eleanor Barnes in the *Los Angeles Illustrated News*, October 24, 1936.

259 **"Phoebe"**: *NYT*, April 9, 1937.

259 ***Quality Street* loses $248,000**: Moss, *Giant*.

260 **"seemed never to be still"**: *NYT*, August 21, 1959.

261 **"Will your illusive highness"**: Theresa Helburn (TH) to KH, August 2, 1939, TGC.

261 **"What are"**: TH to KH, August 9, [1943?], TGC.

262 **"her not too exacting role"**: *Boston Globe*, January 12, 1937.

262 **"Word from Chicago"**: *NYT*, January 14, 1937.

262 **"tinkling piquancy"**: *New Haven Journal-Courier*, December 28, 1936.

262 **"simple ingenuousness"**: *WP*, March 23, 1937.

262 **"ladylike deportment"**: *NYT*, January 3, 1937.

262 ***Peter Pan***: There were several mentions in the Broadway columns of this possibility in early 1936, with Max Gordon producing. See *NYT*, May 27, 1936.

262 **"We forgive"**: *New Haven Register*, December 27, 1936.

263 **Howard Hughes**: Hughes has generated as much, or even more, legend as Hepburn. Every one of the myriad biographies of Hughes takes a radically different perspective on his life. I consulted several of them in trying to draw the most accurate portrait of the man. I also read various depositions that were included in the multiple court cases dealing with the administration of his estate, notably those of Hepburn herself, her maid Johanna Madsen, Hedda Hopper, Cary Grant, Howard Hawks, and several others (Los Angeles Superior Court and Harris County, Texas, Probate Court). Significantly, I reread with a critical eye what Hepburn herself wrote and said about Hughes and their time together, trying to reconcile it with other accounts and with the actual record, as documented by their telegrams, film production records, and newspaper reports. For background see: Richard Hack, *Hughes: The Private Diaries, Memos and Letters* (New Millennium Press, 2001); Donald L. Bartlett and James B. Steele, *Howard Hughes: His Life and Madness* (Norton, 2004); Charles Higham, *Howard Hughes: The Secret Life* (Putnam, 1993); Peter Harry Brown and Pat H. Broeske, *Howard Hughes: The Untold Story* (Da Capo Press, 2004); and Richard Mathison, *His Weird and Wanton Ways: The Secret Life of Howard Hughes* (William Morrow, 1977).

263 **Start of KH's affair with Hughes**: Leaming insisted that Hepburn did not begin seeing Hughes until January 1938, and wrote it was only "out of boredom" that Kate agreed to meet Hughes for dinner in Boston. Her implication was that the star had not yet begun to think of Hughes romantically by that point. Of course, to acknowledge that the affair between them had begun several months earlier would be to encroach upon the time Leaming had allotted for the affair with Ford,

which was the raison d'être for her book. But, in fact, from the telegrams Hepburn and Hughes sent back and forth to each other, it's clear the two of them were involved by December 1937 at the very latest (it was probably earlier), just as Kate was starting off on her tour with *Jane Eyre*. Their golf-club meeting has been dated as October, though without any hard evidence.

264 **"He was sort of the top"**: *Me*.

19. PEOPLE WHO WANT TO BE FAMOUS

265 **KH pilots plane**: This account comes from *Me*, as well as from several friends who recalled Hepburn often telling the story.

267 **"the face of a poet"**: *NYT*, July 16, 1938.

267 **"People who want to be famous"**: *Me*.

267 **"Darling," "Dan"**: This telegram is just one of many that Hughes sent to Hepburn. These were long held in Hepburn's private papers, auctioned off at Sotheby's after her death. Since then, the telegrams have been posted on several auction sites online. Many of the cables are addressed to Emily Perkins in an attempt to keep the press from tracking the lovers' plans. Yet several are quite openly addressed to Katharine Hepburn at whatever hotel she happened to be staying.

268 **Hughes in late 1936**: *LAT*, September 25, November 11, November 16, December 29, 1936; January 1, 1937; *NYT*, November 16, 1936; *WP*, September 18, 1936.

268 **Hughes's cross-country record**: *Chicago Tribune*, January 20, 1937; *LAT*, January 20, 1937.

268 **"Howard Hughes has done it!"**: *LAT*, January 21, 1937.

268 **KH and Hughes in Chicago**: Various accounts have stated that Hughes was in the audience for Kate's opening night on January 11, then flew back to Los Angeles to make his record-breaking flight. This was reported as a rumor in the Chicago press during the frenzy over a possible marriage between the two, but there is no confirmation of it. The account of that frenzy comes from the *Chicago Tribune*, January 22–25, 1937; *LAT*, January 22, 1937;*WP*, January 22, 1937.

269 **"The Katharine Hepburn–Howard Hughes romantic drama"**: International News Service report datelined January 23, 1937, Hepburn file, NYPL.

270 **"the lustiest relationship"**: Berg.

270 **Hughes homosexual rumors**: Charles Higham based many of his stories of Hughes's homosexual affairs on testimony from Lawrence Quirk, who was repeating what he'd been told by his uncle, James Quirk, the editor of *Photoplay*. While the Quirks are important sources, Higham's information is nonetheless third (or even fourth) hand, which is simply not strong enough for inclusion here. The Hughes biographer Richard Hack took a more nuanced approach, believing that Hughes was not essentially homosexual but that he clearly preferred the company of men to women, feeling more natural and at ease among men—a mirror image of Kate's preference for the company of women.

271 **"too damned much"**: Telegram, Howard Hughes (HH) to Emily Perkins, February 3, 1937.

271 **"an impudent"**: Telegram, HH to Emily Perkins, [nd, February 1937].

271 **"[F]orgive me"**: Telegram, HH to Emily Perkins, February 16, 1937.

271 **"one large . . . magnolia"**: Telegram, HH to Emily Perkins, March 12, 1937.

271 **"Would you"**: Telegram, HH to KH, February 16, 1937.

271 **"Certainly I felt"**: *Me*.

271 **"My dear"**: John Ford to KH, January 16, 1937, JFC.

271 **"one-hundred percent wool"**: KH to John Ford, January 16, 1937, JFC.

272 **"I wish"**: *Chicago Tribune*, January 24, 1937.

272 **"girl in every port"**: John Ford to "William Kilbourne," January 25, 1937, JFC.

272 **"I know"**: Emily Perkins to John Ford, January 28, 1937, JFC.

272 **"Wee Willie Winkie"**: KH to John Ford, February 19, 1937, JFC.

272 **"the best letter," "I can only say"**: KH to John Ford, March 1, 1937, JFC.

273 **"came right down"**: *Me*.

274 **"to risk"**: *LAT*, February 19, 1937.

275 **"[W]here human relations"**: KH to John Ford, April 10, 1937, JFC.

275 **Hughes and the Hepburns**: *Me*. Hughes clearly wanted to ingratiate himself with Kate's parents. When Kit was visiting with Kate during the run of *Jane Eyre* in Washington, Hughes wired that he was on his way to see her as well. "Darling, do not send your mother away, or at least let her take late train, as would like to say hello," Hughes cabled. HH to Emily Perkins, March 27, 1937.

276 **Hughes and Grace Bradley**: *LAT*, May 14, 16, 1937.

277 **"bottled"**: Telegrams, HH to Emily Perkins, March 8, 9, 1938. A headline in the *LAT* on March 9 read, RESIDENTS WARNED TO BOIL ALL CITY DRINKING WATER.

277 **KH buys New York house**: Manhattan deeds, block 32, serial C1997, grantor Maud Knowlton Smith of Marion, Massachusetts, grantee Katharine Hepburn of 244 East Forty-ninth Street. When Smith bought the property in 1919, her mortgage was for eighteen thousand dollars, giving a truer picture of the worth of Hepburn's house and the amount she paid for it.

277 **KH leaves Muirfield**: Much has been made of the fact that she left her staff behind to work for Hughes, trying to make it seem as if she'd left in a huff. In fact, she already had a maid and a driver in New York, and the most important member of her entourage, Emily Perkins, went with her.

277 **"until his nibs"**: KH to John Ford, [nd, Spring 1938], JFC.

277 **Hughes calls Fenwick**: Grant, *Marion Hepburn Grant*.

277 **"Seven million New Yorkers"**: *NYT*, July 15, 1938.

278 **KH and Rogers on the lot**: *Modern Screen*, November 1937.

278 **mink**: For Rogers's take on the tale, see *Ginger: My Story* (HarperCollins, 1991).

279 **Broadway version of *Stage Door***: Leaming wrote that Hepburn lost the chance to star in the Broadway production when Leland Hayward, jealous over her relationship with John Ford, had refused to push her for the part. There is no evidence of this that I could find. In truth, Hayward was already deeply involved with Margaret Sullavan when he got her the part in the play.

279 **"What the hell"**: ROSS.

279 **"To win her"**: *Movie Mirror*, [nd, 1937], NYPL.

280 **"The calla lilies"**: Contrary to reports, the line was not lifted from *The Lake*. It does not appear in any of the original scripts for the play. Rather, it is the *atmosphere* of the scene that *Stage Door* lifts from *The Lake*, the morose woman grieving the death of her husband. If audiences wanted to connect the play-within-the-film with Hepburn's notorious flop, however, so much the better.

280 ***Mother Carey's Chickens***: The project was on RKO's agenda at least as early as March 1936, when it was mentioned in the *WP* on March 24. Rogers was announced as the star on June 17, 1936, in the *NYT*. By April of the following year, preproduction planning had begun, with John Beal replacing James Stewart as Rogers's proposed costar. At this time, it was announced as Rogers's next vehicle after *Stage Door* (*LAT*, April 15, 1937). After Rogers apparently withdrew, Joan Bennett was announced as the star on March 28, 1938 (*NYT*). She was still in the part on April 5 (*LAT*). Bennett appears to have withdrawn sometime in the next week or so. If Hepburn had a dispute with the studio about appearing in the film, it would have had to have occurred between that point and April 22 (when her contract was terminated), a stretch of maybe ten days to two weeks. That's hardly enough time to warrant severing a six-year relationship. Clearly, poor *Mother Carey* was scapegoated for all the mutual dissatisfaction between Hepburn and the studio over the last four years. The film was finally made with Anne Shirley, Ruby Keeler, and Fay Bainter. Released in July 1938, it garnered excellent reviews. That Hepburn likely turned down a part in the film because of its ensemble nature is suggested by this review of the eventual film by *Time* on August 1, 1938: "RKO had originally planned *Mother Carey's Chickens* for Actress Katharine Hepburn. Fortunately, Actress Hepburn refused the part. Result: Instead of pointing at the star, the camera manages to keep all the cast in focus."

281 **Surrealist quote**: Dan Callahan, "The Passion of Katharine Hepburn, or The Yankee Ambiguity of Being Sadly Happy" (*Film International* online, www.filmint.nu).

281 **KH's opinion of Cary Grant**: Her letters to him are friendly but clearly do not contain the intimacy or warmth that comes through in letters to Cukor or other friends. Off the set, they rarely socialized. Cukor felt Grant was a bit of a "phony," likely because Grant aggressively assumed a het-

erosexual image, marrying several times. Cukor knew him from an earlier, pre-Code period, when Grant did not try to obfuscate his relationships with homosexual men.

281 **"If you've"**: *NYT*, March 4, 1938.

281 **"Maybe I'm just a crank"**: *Chicago Tribune*, March 13, 1938.

282 **Ed Sullivan**: *Chicago Tribune*, February 27, 1938.

282 **"goofy comedy"**: *LAT*, March 21, 1938.

282 **reviews for *Bringing Up Baby***: Not all were bad. *Time* thought it proved Hepburn could be "as amusingly skittery a comedienne as the best of them" (March 7, 1938).

282 **KH buys back her contract**: RKO Collection, NYPL; Wilkinson, *SEP,* January 3, 1942.

283 **"Box office poison"**: *Hollywood Reporter*, May 3, 1938; *Chicago Tribune*, May 5–6, 1938; *LAT*, May 4–6, May 12, 1938; *NYT*, May 5–6, May 22, 1938; *Time*, May 16, 1938. The box-office poison charges overshadowed the real source of the exhibitors' frustration. By demanding a reduction in overblown star salaries, what they hoped to end was the "double-feature" policy enforced by most producers. Too many films were being made with out-of-fashion stars, forcing independent exhibitors (those not aligned with a studio-owned chain) to play them alongside popular pictures. This meant increased admission fees and therefore a declining audience. At a luncheon at New York's Hotel Astor on May 11, a week after their box-office poison bombshell had gotten Hollywood's attention, the exhibitors laid out their real demand, to "put the industry back on an artistic basis with single features or face the wrath of the men who buy the pictures" (*LAT*, May 12, 1938). Double-booking would remain a staple, however, for as long as the studios controlled large chunks of exhibition, that is, for another decade.

20. THEY SAY SHE'S A HAS-BEEN

285 **"grace, jauntiness"**: *NYT*, March 29, 1939.

285 **"They say"**: *Time*, May 16, 1938.

286 **Hepburn-Hughes rumors revived**: *Los Angeles Herald*, May 27, 1938, and other newspaper articles.

286 **"New Hepburn"**: *Los Angeles Daily News*, March 30, 1938, and many other newspaper articles.

286 IS IT TRUE: *Hollywood Citizen-News*, May 11, 12, 1938.

287 **"quite stunning"**: *LAT*, May 25, 1938.

287 **Frank Nugent's review**: *NYT*, June 24, 1938.

287 **"She is almost masculine"**: *Modern Screen*, February 1938.

287 **Delight Evans's open letter**: *Screenland,* [nd, 1937], NYPL.

287 **"I'd lose ground"**: *WP*, October 3, 1937.

288 **Helen Hope Montgomery**: *NYT*, November 17, 1980.

288 **"Make her"**: Bob Hepburn.

288 **"getting sunburned"**: KH to John Ford, August 15, 1938, JFC.

289 **"which is somewhat frequently"**: *WP*, August 21, 1938.

289 **"Someone dropped," "Conservative Hartford Insurance"**: KH to John Ford, [nd, July 1938], JFC.

289 **"conservative people"**: *WP*, August 21, 1938.

289 **"First I landed"**: KH to John Ford, August 15, 1938, JFC.

290 **Dick Hepburn**: Much insight into Dick's character and ambition was gleaned from the Hedgerow Theatre Collection (HTC) at Boston University. Dick wrote to the director Jasper Deeter frequently through the years, stretching from his first association with Hedgerow in 1935 through the 1950s.

290 **"in order to bring out"**: Richard Hepburn to Robert Hanley, March 4, 1936, HTC.

290 **"His family"**: Material for *Behold Your God,* HTC.

290 **"We are"**: Richard Hepburn to Jasper Deeter, [nd], HTC.

291 **"Ineffective satire"**: *Philadelphia Inquirer*, April 21, 1936.

291 **"Even the name"**: *Variety*, quoted in Leaming.

291 **"inevitable"**: *Photoplay*, August 1938.

291 **"looked pretty"**: *NYT*, October 29, 1938.

291 *"Gone With the Wind"*: KH to John Ford, August 15, 1938, JFC.

291 **Selznick and *Gone With the Wind***: See Thomson, *Showman*. Typically, in later years, Kate made it seem as if she hadn't really wanted the part. "I was too strong for it," she told Thomson. "George [Cukor] said I was too noble." For all her latter-day indifference, however, the fact remains she'd arranged to delay the premiere of the play *The Philadelphia Story* in the event she was offered the part of Scarlett.

292 **"Everything for me"**: KH to John Ford, August 15, 1938, JFC.

292 **hurricane**: *Me*, various contemporary reports in *NYT, Hartford Courant, Hartford Times, Middletown Press*.

293 **"I think we"**: *Times* (London), November 24, 1973.

293 **KH signs contract with Guild**: A separate contract with Barry was signed on January 16, 1939. Philip Barry Papers, Georgetown University.

293 **"personal triumph"**: *WP*, March 7, 1939.

294 **"Your girls"**: KH to George Cukor, [nd, 1939], GCC.

294 **"For once"**: KH to John Ford, April 1939, JFC.

294 **Hughes buys rights to *The Philadelphia Story***: An agreement between KH and the Hughes Tool Company, dated April 11, 1939, gave Kate the movie rights to the play.

295 **"Love had turned"**: *Me*.

295 **"I can't"**: Mimi Doyle to John Ford, December 5, 1938, JFC.

295 **"terrific"**: Telegram, HH to Emily Perkins, March 21, 1939.

296 **"Missing"**: Draft of telegram, KH to HH, [nd].

296 **"remedy"**: Telegram, HH to Emily Perkins, March 23, 1939.

296 **Romantic depiction of Hughes and Kate in *The Aviator***: Hughes certainly did not buy up copies of indiscreet photos of Kate and Spencer Tracy, either. It's hard to imagine those two in any kind of situation that would appear indiscreet.

296 **"I feel better"**: *WP*, December 23, 1939.

296 **"either a fool"**: Richard Hepburn to Jasper Deeter, October 13, 1939, HTC.

296 **"another Jed Harris"**: Richard Hepburn to Jasper Deeter, [nd, October, 1939], HTC.

297 **"It seems"**: Kanin.

297 **"I am faced"**: Richard Hepburn to Jasper Deeter, October 13, 1939, HTC.

297 **"I never"**: Richard Hepburn to Jasper Deeter, [nd, 1939], HTC.

297 **"There is"**: Lawrence Langner to Richard Hepburn, February 26, 1940, TGC.

298 **Dick and Cukor**: Richard Hepburn to George Cukor, January 16, 1940, GCP.

298 *Love Like Wildfire*: Whereas Hedgerow Theatre may have been willing to produce "Sea-Air," Jasper Deeter wrote to Dick in late 1940 that it was not interested in this new play. *Love Like Wildfire* was staged instead at the Stony Creek Theatre in Stony Creek, Connecticut, in August 1941, with O. Z. Whitehead in the lead role. *NYT*, June 8, July 21, July 29, 1941.

298 **Dick and Langner**: In a letter dated January 13, 1941, Langner tells Dick that maybe he ought to take a playwriting class from Hatcher Hughes. "Eugene O'Neill told me that he learned a tremendous amount from taking such a course. . . . You should get the technique behind you so that you do not have to bother about it." (TGC)

299 **David Thomson**: In addition to my interview and correspondence with him, I quoted from his essay on Hepburn in *A Biographical Dictionary of Film* (William Morrow, 1981).

299 **KH's 1930s films**: For a detailed examination of Hepburn's film, especially comparing her pre- and post-1940 work, see Andrew Britton, *Katharine Hepburn: Star as Feminist* (Columbia University Press, 2003). See also Andrew Sarris's groundbreaking essay, "The Premature Feminism of Katharine Hepburn," *Village Voice*, August 26–September 1, 1981.

300 **"She had to do"**: *LAT*, July 1, 2003.

301 **"as if they'd both"**: Callahan, "The Passion of Katharine Hepburn."

21. SIMPLY AHEAD OF THE TIMES

303 **"That *can't* be her"**: Unsourced clip, January 12, 1942, Hepburn file, NYPL.

303 **Frank Nugent's review**: *NYT*, March 13, 1938.

305 **"Sweetness and light"**: *NYT*, May 21, 1939.

305 **"They're quite a family"**: *LAT*, December 6, 1941.

305 **"right down"**: *Silver Screen*, November 1940.

305 **"every girl"**: *Modern Screen*, December 1940.

305 **"Hepburn came"**: *Screenland*, November 1940.

307 **"The picture ought"**: *Washington Star*, November 2, 1941.

307 **Harmonizing with sexual politics**: For more on this topic, see Sarris, "The Premature Feminism of Katharine Hepburn."

307 **KH's arrest**: *LAT*, March 6, 1939; *Los Angeles Herald*, March 6, March 20, 1939.

308 **KH's refusal to cross picket line**: *NYT*, March 12, 1939.

308 **AAAA**: *NYT*, August 6, 1939.

308 **"I often wonder"**: *WP*, December 17, 1940.

308 *democracy*: An example of this buzzword being used to deflect Hepburn's politics is in "Hepburn's Four Loves," *Picture Play*, [nd, 1936], NYPL. There are many other examples.

309 **"Nobody tells"**: *Modern Screen*, July 1938.

309 **"For several weeks"**: *WP*, August 21, 1938. Maureen O'Hara in *Tis Herself* wrote that Ford had been emotionally attached to Murph in a way that was similar to his attachments to O'Hara and Hepburn. Given Murph's sister Mimi's apparent attachment to Ford, I wonder if O'Hara wasn't confusing the two sisters.

310 **Nancy Hamilton**: Various correspondence collections offered insight into Hamilton's life, particularly the Billie Burke Collection at BU, which revealed the intense, devoted companionship between Hamilton and Cornell. It's clear that Burke herself was smitten with the charismatic Nancy. Hepburn wasn't completely outside the circle, for in the late 1950s, Burke inquired of Hamilton, "How is dear Lady Kate?" The John Gielgud Collection, NYPL, also offered insights. See also "By Starlight," unsourced clipping, [nd, 1934], NYPL; *NYT*, February 27, March 16, 1934; *WP*, January 13, October 6, 1935; *New York Herald Tribune*, December 22, 1935; Harris Theatre publicity, "One for the Money," 1939, NYPL; *WP*, February 12, 1939; *Brooklyn Daily Eagle*, February 19, 1939; *NYT*, May 20, 1939. Other sources: U.S. Census, 1910–30; Nancy Hamilton probate file, New York Surrogate Court; Richard Mangan, ed., *Gielgud's Letters* (Weidenfeld and Nicolson, 2004), as well as the Katharine Cornell Collection, NYPL; Bea Lillie Collection, NYPL; Tad Mosel with Gertrude Macy, *Leading Lady: The World and Theatre of Katharine Cornell* (Little, Brown, 1978); and Schanke and Marra, *Passing Performances*.

310 **Frances Rich**: Her original name was Deffenbaugh, being the daughter of her mother's first husband, Elvo Deffenbaugh. Irene Rich's second husband, Major Charles Rich, later gave his name to the young Frances. As with Hamilton, various collections offered a window on Frances Rich's life. The John Ford Collection contains several letters from her, from the 1930s through the 1960s. For their entire lives, Ford and Rich shared a deep friendship. It would be Rich who persuaded Ford to move to the desert near Palm Springs later in his life. The Noel Sullivan Papers at the Bancroft Library at the University of California, Berkeley, also were illuminating. See: *LAT*, November 8, 1938; *WP*, November 9, 1938; *NYT*, January 17, 1943; *LAT*, April 29, 1943; *WP*, July 29, 1944; *LAT*, March 22, 1946; *Payson Roundup*, April 7, 2001. Other sources: Smith College archives; U.S. Census, 1910–30.

311 **Garson Kanin's background**: *NYT*, March 15, 1933; *WP*, April 16, June 13, 1937; *Chicago Tribune*, January 22, 1940; *LAT*, April 16, 1972; *NYT*, December 8, 1975; *Los Angeles Herald-Examiner*, November 29, 1979; *LAT*, June 21, 1988.

312 **"We are"**: *Pageant*, October 1946.

312 **"They are"**: *Movie Mirror*, December 1940.

313 **"guide and mentor"**: Ruth Gordon to Thornton Wilder, January 20, 1942, Thornton Wilder Collection, Beinecke.

313 **Kanin's homosexuality**: Thornton Wilder's sexuality offers a possible window on Kanin's. As preliminaries, see Gilbert A. Harrison, *The Enthusiast: A Life of Thornton Wilder* (Fromm, 1986), and Edward M. Burns et al., *The Letters of Gertrude Stein and Thornton Wilder* (Yale University Press, 1996). Also see the correspondence between Kanin, Ruth Gordon, and Wilder in the Thornton Wilder Collection, Beinecke.

Kanin's closeness to Wilder might not seem so informative if so many of his other important friendships didn't contain similar underlying dynamics. Kanin enjoyed an intense friendship with Somerset Maugham, about whom he wrote an affectionate memoir, *Remembering Mr. Maugham* (Atheneum, 1966). Maugham had been, like Kanin, rather famously married. That didn't stop Maugham from having a longtime relationship with a male partner, Alan Searle. Even Kanin's long friendship with the Supreme Court Justice Felix Frankfurter may carry similar resonance. One Frankfurter scholar with whom I spoke admitted he considered the possibility, after reading the justice's voluminous letters, that he had been a deeply repressed homosexual. Frankfurter endured a troubled, often distant relationship with his wife, taking refuge with male friends like Kanin and Wilder. Rarely had Frankfurter met anyone who had "so quickly enlisted" his devotion as Kanin (Frankfurter to Ruth Gordon, April 13, 1943, Felix Frankfurter Papers, Library of Congress). His correspondence with Kanin and Gordon gives some insight into their relationships. See also Frankfurter's letters to Alexander Woollcott and Kanin's tribute to Frankfurter in the *Atlantic*, March 1964, as well as H. N. Hirsch, *The Enigma of Felix Frankfurter* (Basic Books, 1981).

Further insight into Kanin's mind might be found in the words of his first mentor, George Abbott, who wrote in his memoir that the average reader would be surprised at how many heroes of stage and screen were "gay boys." See George Abbott, *Mister Abbott* (Random House, 1963).

313 **"After all"**: *New York Daily News*, March 18, 1972.

314 **"How can"**: *Me*.

314 **Spencer Tracy's background**: Selden West, who worked on a biography of Tracy for years, shared with me her take on his early life. I also consulted the two Tracy biographies: Larry Swindell, *Spencer Tracy* (New American Library, 1969), and Bill Davidson, *Spencer Tracy: Tragic Idol* (Dutton, 1987). Also, biographical materials from the Wisconsin Historical Society; U.S. Census, 1880–1920; Milwaukee city directories; *NYT*, January 19, 1898; World War I draft registration cards. In his tape-recorded reminiscences with Hepburn, John Ford recalled drinking with Tracy (JFC).

315 **"You know"**: Kanin.

317 **Tracy's 1933 arrest**: *Chicago Tribune*, September 27, 1933; *Los Angeles Evening Herald Express*, September 21, 1933; *LAT*, September 22, 1933; *WP*, September 22, 1933.

317 **Mankiewicz's take on Tracy's drinking**: From an interview conducted by Selden West, courtesy West.

317 **Separation from Louise**: *Los Angeles Herald Express*, August 29, 1933.

317 **Sightings of Tracy with Loretta Young**: *LAT*, December 16, 1933; April 15, May 22, May 28, June 14, August 14, December 2, 1934. Significantly, Tracy parted from Loretta Young and returned to his wife just as the political climate was shifting in Hollywood, when happily married, domesticated stars were suddenly in demand.

317 BECAUSE SHE LOVED HIM: *Modern Screen*, August 1938.

318 **Kidnapping/extortion threat**: This threat is detailed in the records of the Federal Bureau of Investigation, Spencer Tracy, file 7–749. The first letter was received on February 23, 1934; a follow-up threat was received on March 3. Both were written in pencil, in longhand, on green-lined paper and mailed to Tracy's home. The money was to be dropped off on Western Avenue and was ordered to consist of four thousand dollars in one-thousand-dollar notes and another four thousand dollars in fifties, twenties, and tens. For the next six months, various former employees and acquaintances were hauled before FBI investigators. They were questioned and fingerprinted and had their handwriting analyzed. No one was ever charged, and the FBI closed its books on the case late in 1934. Another threat was received in March 1936; investigators concluded it was not related to the first case. The identity of "Rattlesnake Pete," the author of the threat, remains unknown.

318 **"various bootlegging"**: Federal Bureau of Investigation, Spencer Tracy, file 7–749, August 10, 1934.

318 **Tully and racehorses**: U.S. Census, 1930; *LAT*, October 23, 1935; August 1, 1938; *WP*, March 27, 1938.

318 **Tracy's 1935 arrest**: *LAT*, March 12, 1935; *Reno* [Nevada] *Evening Gazette*, March 11, 1935; Associated Press reports, various newspapers; Tracy biographical files, NYPL and AMPAS.

319 **"I'd like to know"**: *Modern Screen*, December 1935.

319 **Tracy as most popular star**: *Boxoffice*, November 4, 1939.

319 **London riot**: *Daily Mail*, April 27, 1939; *Evening Standard*, April 26, 1939.

319 **"Spencer's face"**: *Me*.

320 **"A bull neck"**: James Bacon, *Hollywood Is a Four-Letter Town* (Henry Regnery, 1976).

22. WHAT WAS IT, SPENCE?

321 **Kaspar Monahan**: *Pittsburgh Press*, May 12, 1942.

322 **KH returns to New York**: Letters from Alice Palache document that Kate was back in New York by October 1941. She returned to Los Angeles briefly in December, probably for previews of *Woman of the Year*, as a notice in the *NYT* reports she was "due back from the Coast" late the previous week (December 21, 1941).

322 **Tracy on *Without Love* tour**: Most accounts have presumed the Hepburn-Tracy relationship, from the very beginning was exactly what the legend insisted it was later on. Even in these first few months, Kate is depicted as worrying about Spencer's drinking, already playing the caretaker. Edwards says Tracy went along on tour with Kate, but that was impossible, since he was making the film *Tortilla Flat*. As the encounter in Pittsburgh proves, he did meet up with her at least by the spring, once the film had wrapped. There is no evidence, however, as some have claimed, that the Theatre Guild ever seriously considered Tracy as Kate's costar in *Without Love* or that Kate had demanded his casting.

322 **David Eichler**: David Eichler (DE) to KH, June 25, 1939; KH to DE, June 30, 1939; DE to KH, July 8, July 17, July 20, 1939; February 3, 1940; May 25, 1941; March 9, 1942; KH to DE, April 11, 1942; DE to KH, April 24, May 25, November 21, 1942, DEC.

323 **Shaw's review of *Without Love***: In a memo sent to Langner and Helburn, Shaw called the plot "implausible" and thought Hepburn performed, at least in the first half, "in her best 'The Lake' manner." He concluded, "I don't like the play and I don't think Broadway will either." ([nd, late 1941], TGC)

323 **KH leaves Guild meeting**: TH to KH, September 10, 1942, TGC.

323 **"incommunicado"**: Elliott Nugent to TH, September 9, 1942, TGC.

323 **KH would be responsible for salaries**: TH to KH, September 13, 1942, TGC. Leaming describes an emotional scene with Helburn laying all this out in person. My reading of the Guild letters is that Helburn spelled out her grievances in writing.

323 **"a mechanical performance"**: *NYT*, November 11, 1942.

323 **"which is"**: KH to George Cukor, [nd, early 1943], GCC.

323 **John R. Hall's suicide**: *NYT*, July 30, 1936. Just what motivated Hall to jump to his death is unknown; Luddy refused comment when approached by the press. Police paraphrased Hall's suicide note as saying he was "tired of living" and seeking the "easiest way out." It was the height of the Depression, and Hall may have had financial problems. One of his associates, Harry Acton, to whom he addressed his suicide notes, had once been charged with a $5 million stock fraud. (*NYT*, May 28, 29, December 22, 1926)

323 **KH and Luddy's 1942 divorce**: *Ogden Ludlow v. Katharine H. Ludlow*, September 18, 1942, Hartford Superior Court, docket 67612; Ogden Ludlow to KH, April 30, 1942, SFP; *Hartford Times*, September 18, 1942; *Hartford Courant*, September 19, 1942.

324 **Luddy's remarriage**: *WP*, September 23, 1942. Luddy would have two children with his second wife: a son, Lewis, named for his father, and a daughter, Katharine Ramsay. Several writers have speculated romantically that Luddy named his daughter after Kate, his true love, but in fact she

was named for Elisabeth Albers's mother. Katharine was also Elisabeth's middle name. It was just a coincidence that the name was spelled in both cases with an *a*.

324 **Judy Garland and Joe Mankiewicz**: See Gerald Clarke, *Get Happy: The Life of Judy Garland* (Random House, 2000). The anecdote was further detailed by Charles Williamson, who was a good friend of Judy's.

324 **"Hit over the head"**: Berg.

325 **"curious"**: This remark comes from an unpublished interview with Hepburn conducted by Selden West during her research for her biography on Tracy; I am grateful that she shared the account with me.

326 **"In my relationships"**: *Ladies' Home Journal*, August 1975.

326 **Negulesco's view of the Tracy-Hepburn relationship**: Jean Negulesco, *Things I Did . . . and Things I Think I Did* (Simon and Schuster, 1984).

326 **"highly civilized people"**: Kanin.

327 **Hedda Hopper's review of *Keeper***: *LAT*, April 2, 1943.

327 **Republican legislators complain about *Keeper***: *NYT*, October 10, 1943.

327 **Tracy's politics**: Some accounts inexplicably paint Tracy as a conservative; Bill Davidson in his biography of the actor quotes Gene Kelly as implying Spencer was anti-Roosevelt. Nothing could have been further from the truth. Spencer admired Roosevelt greatly and was definitely liberal in his political outlook.

327 **Edith and Loyal Davis**: Bob Colacello, in his book *Ronnie and Nancy: Their Path to the White House* (Warner Books, 2004), quoted Nancy's brother Richard as saying Spencer "went bananas" in his anger over voting restrictions for blacks in the South.

327 **"The more high-minded"**: *NYT*, February 21, 1943.

331 **"twisting his hat around"**: Interview with Larry King, CNN transcripts.

332 **Cukor's mid-1940s dinner party**: GCC.

332 **Entente Cordiale**: Cukor's unfinished memoir, GCC.

332 **"I think"**: *NYT*, October 5, 1969.

332 **"whole hog"**: Cecil Beaton, *Photobiography* (Oldhams Press, 1951).

333 **Tracy strikes KH**: Although Scott Berg's book got the most publicity for telling this story, Christopher Andersen's *An Affair to Remember* (William Morrow, 1997) reported the same anecdote in very similar terms six years earlier; in each case, the source was apparently Kate herself.

333 **"It was like leaning"**: *TV Guide*, September 17, 1977.

334 **"I never said"**: Patrick McGilligan told me that when he was writing his biography of Cukor, he asked Kanin how much truth there was in *Tracy and Hepburn*.

334 **Laura Harding on KH and Tracy**: This anecdote was shared by Emily King.

335 **"Why don't"**: Hume Cronyn, *A Terrible Liar* (William Morrow, 1991).

335 **"a wreck"**: KH to Philip Barry, September 7, 1942, Philip Barry Papers, Georgetown University.

336 **"a voluntary thing"**: *Me*.

336 **"an oversensitivity to life"**: DF interview, JFC.

336 **Jekyll and Hyde**: Kate wrote about this in *Me*, but I get the sense that, yet again, she was being influenced by something Kanin had already written. Kanin documented Tracy's fascination with the story in *Remembering Mr. Maugham*. "That damned part was something that had haunted me for years," he quoted Tracy as saying. "The idea of two personalities was fascinating to me."

337 **Scotty**: I interviewed Scotty once in 2004 and again in 2005. It wasn't easy reaching him; we met only after two other sources had interceded on my behalf, and then not at Scotty's house but at a third-party location. After being told by several sources that he would never reveal the details of what happened with Kate and Spencer, I was surprised, even flabbergasted, when he opened up. After my first interview with him, I returned several months later to talk to him again, and his story was exactly the same. I found him forthright and honest and not interested in personal fame

or gain. He turned down my offer to profile him for a magazine article or to hook him up with an agent to write his own memoirs, which would certainly, as they say, blow the lid off Hollywood. Several people whose reputations I respect vouched for Scotty's essential trustworthiness and reliability as a source. In addition to Gavin Lambert, these included Dominick Dunne, John Schlesinger, Noel Taylor, Michael Childers, Kevin Thomas, Tucker Fleming, Charles Williamson, and Robert Wheaton.

338 **"cast of just four"**: Arthur Laurents, *Original Story By* (Knopf, 2000).

339 **John Tracy Clinic**: To Daniel Selznick, Kate would also use Louise's work at the clinic to explain why she and Tracy never married. "She needs to remain Mrs. Spencer Tracy," she told Selznick. "That's how she's able to do such good works."

339 **"to find"**: This quote comes from Louise's own letter to the editor, *LAT*, March 21, 1947. See also *LAT*, February 19, 1943; May 19, 1945.

339 **"if Louise"**: *LAT*, October 22, 1949.

340 **"I don't think"**: *Vanity Fair*, April 2001.

340 **"everybody everywhere"**: *LAT*, May 7, 1958. Gully was often mentioned in the gossip columns from the 1940s through the 1960s as an escort for various women, including Constance Collier and the Countess di Frasso.

340 **Tim Durant**: See *Chicago Tribune*, January 22, 1940; *Los Angeles Herald*, April 2, 1945; *LAT*, July 26, August 20, December 13, 1936; December 16, December 22, 1938; January 6, February 10, February 13, March 3, April 10, June 4, June 6, 1939; February 18, March 23, May 1, June 2, September 12, 1940; April 2, November 4, 1941; June 22, 1942; March 7, 1958; April 18, 1961; December 16, 1984; *NYT*, December 11, 1938; August 7, 1950; January 11, 1954; February 4, 1966; April 23, 1967; *WP*, March 23, 1940; April 2, 1941.

340 **"rare quality"**: *LAT*, August 6, 1936.

341 **"one of our better bachelors"**: *LAT*, January 4, 1939.

341 **"peas in a pod"**: *Chronicle Telegram* (Elyria, Ohio), February 28, 1940.

341 **"Spencer and I"**: Tim Durant to Theresa Helburn, May 29, 1939, TGC. In later life, Durant worked with John Huston as an adviser and horse trainer. In 1950, he married again on Huston's estate in Ireland, where he spent a good deal of time racing horses in the Irish Sweepstakes. In 1966, he was called the "Galloping Grandfather" (his daughter from his first wife by now had children) when he rode in the Grand National Steeplechase in Aintree, England. In 1968, he entered again, finishing fifteenth out of a field of forty-five, the oldest man ever (at age sixty-nine) to finish horseracing's most difficult event. Tim Durant died in 1984. See also his letters in the John Huston Collection, AMPAS.

342 ***The Rugged Path***: Spencer's telegrams and Sherwood's letters offer a backdrop to the production. See also Sherwood Papers, Houghton Library, and John F. Wharton, *Among the Playwrights* (New York Times Book Company, 1974). Also David Hanna's report in the *Los Angeles Daily News*, February 16, 1946, and various news reports, *NYT, Boston Globe*, other clippings, NYPL.

343 **Don Taylor sees Spencer in hospital**: Taylor told this story to Bill Davidson for his biography of Tracy.

343 **Tracy's hospitalization in Chicago**: Colacello, *Ronnie and Nancy*.

343 **Esmé Chandlee quote**: Davidson.

23. SILENCING THE MOST ARTICULATE VOICE

344 **"I wonder"**: *Los Angeles Examiner*, May 18, 1947.

345 **KH's Wallace speech**: A tape of the speech is kept in the register of the Hollywood Democratic Committee Papers at the Wisconsin Historical Society, Madison. Only by listening to Kate's speech, so well spoken and articulate, can one truly get a sense of the passion she felt for the issue. See also *LAT,* May 20, 1947; *NYT*, May 25, 1947; *Daily Worker*, May 27, 1947.

345 **"like an angel"**: Harry Hay, an early Communist Party member in Los Angeles, recalled for me in 1997 the political beliefs of various Hollywood stars.

346 **Great inquisition**: For background and context, see the classic text by Larry Ceplair and

Steven Englund, *The Inquisition in Hollywood: Politics in the Film Community, 1930–1960* (revised edition, University of Illinois, 2003).

346 **"We were"**: Will Geer oral history, interviewed by Ronald L. Davis, Southern Methodist University Oral History Project.

346 **"The House committee"**: Walter Bernstein, *Inside Out: A Memoir of the Blacklist* (Da Capo Press, 2001).

347 **"At your age"**: Leonard Lyons's column, *WP*, July 28, 1947.

348 **Box office for *Dragon Seed*, *Without Love*, and *Undercurrent***: *Motion Picture Herald* monthly tabulation; the Eddie Mannix Ledgers, AMPAS.

348 **"They play"**: *NYT*, March 25, 1945.

348 ***Undercurrent***: See also Vincente Minnelli, *I Remember It Well* (Berkeley, 1974).

349 **"When I've had a director"**: *Times* (London), November 24, 1973.

349 **"not on my side"**: *Me*.

350 **"To him"**: Irene Mayer Selznick, *A Private View* (Knopf, 1983).

350 **KH remains in Hollywood**: On August 30, 1946, Kate wrote to Armina Marshall that her only time in the East for the foreseeable future would be during the month of September, and then mostly at Fenwick (TGC).

351 **"I wish," "sog-brained"**: KH to Lawrence Langner, March 10, 1944, TGC.

351 **Guild's cajoling of KH**: Lawrence Langner to KH, March 20, 1944; January 2, 1945; May 18, 1946, TGC.

351 **Spencer's logbooks**: Information courtesy of Selden West.

351 **"quite dumb"**: KH to Lawrence Langner, March 10, 1944, TGC.

351 **Repertory company**: Lawrence Langner to Spencer Tracy, June 6, 1946, TGC.

355 **"She really"**: AP oral history.

355 **Leaming's baby theory**: This theory apparently came from Palache's oral history, though I could not find where this was actually stated. What makes the story highly unlikely is that if it were true, Kate would have been asking Palache to get pregnant when she was in her mid-forties.

355 **Signe Hasso**: She told this story to both Noel Taylor and Charles Williamson, who relayed it to me separately and unbeknownst to the other, without much difference in the telling.

356 **Bey's letters**: According to Nancy Perkins, the letters remained in Emily's possession for many years. Nancy read them and was "absolutely certain that the letters from Bey to Hepburn were love letters." What she could not recall was whether the letters implied the relationship was in any way reciprocal. The letters were eventually destroyed.

356 **Orchids**: *WP*, October 21, 1943. Hedda Hopper was only too pleased to discredit her rival's story on November 8. Bey later said the orchids were all part of a studio-generated publicity romance. Possibly—but that doesn't explain the letters in Em Perkins's possession. In many ways, Bey fit Hepburn's profile for nonromantic male friends. Charming and cultured, he never married. "I was not a great lover," he admitted late in life. "Many of the ladies I dated found out I was a great listener. They told me about the troubles they had with their husbands or their boyfriends." (*Hollywood Drama-Logue*, July 22–28, 1993) Bey was brought back to Hollywood for a party in 1988 by David Gest, who later married Liza Minnelli.

356 ***Sea of Grass***: See Elia Kazan, *A Life* (Knopf, 1988).

357 **Leo McCarey doesn't hire KH**: *Variety*, June 11, 1947.

357 **"a word-for-word copy"**: Colacello, *Ronnie and Nancy*.

357 **"plea for the Communists"**: *Hollywood Citizen-News*, May 26, 1947.

357 **"flaming"**: *Hollywood Citizen-News*, May 29, 1947.

357 **"It was"**: *Statesville* [North Carolina] *Daily Record*, June 2, 1947.

357 **"Her recent"**: *Joplin* [Missouri] *Globe*, June 22, 1947.

357 **KH to be subpoenaed**: *Waterloo* [Ohio] *Courier*, September 7, 1947.

358 **"Katie for Communism"**: *NYT*, May 25, 1947.

358 **"I thought"**: *Me*.

359 "[She] took it": Marsha Hunt oral history, interviewed by Ronald L. Davis, Southern Methodist University Oral History Project.

359 "We know": *Hollywood Reporter*, May 29, 1947.

360 "You don't think": *Time*, October 27, 1947.

360 KH in newspaper coverage of the hearings: *NYT, LAT, Chicago Tribune, Syracuse Post Standard, Zanesville* [Ohio] *Times-Recorder*, October 21, 1947.

360 "she of the tiptoeing voice": *Mexia* [Texas] *Weekly Herald*, October 30, 1947.

360 KH's FBI file: Katharine Hepburn file, Federal Bureau of Investigation. The letter from an agent in Paris to Secretary of State George Marshall was dated November 19, 1947. The agent's name has been blacked out by the FBI.

360 Stoning of Chapel Hill theater: Eric Johnston reported this incident at a meeting of the Motion Picture Association of America at the Waldorf-Astoria in New York. His report can be found in notes taken by Robert Kenny, now in the Robert W. Kenny/Robert S. Morris Papers, Wisconsin Historical Society. The police department at Chapel Hill did not begin to keep any records until the 1960s, and only those since 1982 are still extant. A careful read through the *Chapel Hill News* weekly newspaper also did not turn up any evidence of a stoning at a theater. Although the incident most likely occurred during the showing of *Song of Love* the week of October 24, which would have made Eric Johnston's announcement of it timely a month later, it might also have happened during the showing of *Undercurrent* at the Pick Theatre that previous June 12, which would have been just three weeks after Kate's speech for Wallace. In both cases, nothing was reported in the press. Since Chapel Hill was and is a fairly liberal town, it's quite possible that the patrons who threw the stones were out-of-towners there for a college football game. During the week of *Song of Love*, in fact, a crowd of more than thirty thousand had amassed in Chapel Hill for a game.

361 "Lady in Red": Unsourced clipping, November 5, 1947, NYPL.

361 *State of the Union* casting: Bob Thomas syndicated column, April 4, 1947; *LAT*, October 11, 1947; *NYT*, October 11, 1947.

362 Fidler on KH and Menjou: *Joplin* [Missouri] *Globe*, November 16, 1947.

362 Fulton Lewis Jr.'s announcement about KH and her response: This is documented in Hepburn's FBI file in a memorandum stamped "Confidential" with the identifying code "LA 100–15732."

362 "Hepburn wanted": FBI file. The inclusion of Frank Capra's name in the effort to protect Kate from HUAC is not surprising. In his memoir, *The Name Above the Title* (Macmillan, 1971), Capra proved himself as adept as Kanin in mythologizing Tracy and Hepburn. Planning *State of the Union*, Capra asked Tracy if he had "any girlfriends—I mean actresses" who were available to play the part of the wife. "Waaal," Spence replied, completely in character, "come to think of it, Katie isn't hamming it up at the moment." But on the air in ROSS, Hepburn would deny Capra's version of how she came to appear in *State of the Union*. In fact, she'd been the original choice for the film and was brought back when all concerned thought the part would help her.

362 KH avoids HUAC: Christopher Anderson made the claim in *An Affair to Remember* that Richard Nixon, fearful of a public backlash, convinced HUAC to leave Hepburn alone. There is no evidence of this that I could find. When I asked Andersen where he had gotten this information, he responded it had been many years since he'd written the book and he had forgotten. He promised to check and get back to me. I did not hear from him further. From his book, there seems to be some suggestion that the information came from Joseph Mankiewicz, but if so, Mankiewicz could only have been speaking speculatively.

363 "policy to never attend": Mrs. A. J. Noble to Hedda Hopper, October 14, 1947, Hedda Hopper Collection, AMPAS.

363 "Although I dislike": *LAT*, March 25, 1948.

364 "Katy may look": *LAT*, October 25, 1947.

364 "take the stump": *LAT*, March 18, 1948.

364 "whether films": *NYT*, November 2, 1947.

364 *Szabed Nep* defends KH: *LAT*, January 18, 1948.

24. FANCY HER, A HEROINE

366 **Tenney committee:** *NYT*, June 9, 1949; *LAT*, June 9, 10, 1949.

367 **Myron C. Fagan:** *Red Treason in Hollywood* (1949); *Documentation of the Red Stars in Hollywood* (1950). Both booklets, printed on newsprint paper, were published by a group called the Cinema Educational Guild and have been preserved by AMPAS. *Red Treason* went through at least five printings by December 1950. In *Documentation,* Fagan reprinted the sensational speech he delivered at the opening of his anti-Communist play at the El Patio Theatre on April 12, 1948. Earlier, the play had been shut down by the illness of its leading man, which Fagan blamed on threats "from Communist quarters" (*NYT*, February 6, 1948).

368 **"charged with betraying":** *Hollywood Nite Life*, April 23, 1948.

369 *Adam's Rib* **receipts:** Rental earnings as reported annually by *Variety*.

369 **Garland's suicide attempt:** See Clarke, *Get Happy*. The anecdote was also told to me by Charles Williamson, who was a good friend of Judy's.

370 **Sam Spiegel calls:** Katharine Hepburn, *The Making of the African Queen* (Knopf, 1987).

371 *As You Like It*: The correspondence in the TGC was invaluable in offering background and context on this production. See also *New Haven Register*, December 9, 1949; *LAT*, January 25, 1950; *Los Angeles Herald Express*, January 27, 1950; *Chicago Tribune*, January 28, 1950.

372 **"romantic and disarming graces":** *NYT*, January 27, 1950.

372 **KH's arrest and singed mink:** *Daily Oklahoman*, November 25, 1950; *Los Angeles Daily News*, November 24, 1950; *LAT*, November 25, 1950.

372 **"That policeman":** George Cukor's unpublished, unfinished memoir, GCC.

373 **Tracy meets pope:** *Chicago Tribune*, May 19, 1951.

374 **"Did he leave":** Hepburn, *The Making of the African Queen.*

374 **Tracy in the Alps:** *LAT*, June 13, 1951.

374 **Louise's honorary degree:** *LAT*, June 11, 1951.

374 **"The natives":** Lauren Bacall, *By Myself* (Knopf, 1979).

374 **Production on** *The African Queen*: See Hepburn's *The Making of the African Queen*; Bacall, *By Myself*; John Huston, *An Open Book* (Ballantine, 1981).

375 **"the deftest thing":** *Chicago Tribune*, February 27, 1952.

375 *African Queen* **receipts:** *Variety* year-end review.

376 **"An unapproachable person?":** *Sight and Sound*, August 1956.

377 **"Hepburn's birthdays":** *Hartford Courant Magazine*, November 9, 1952.

377 **Problems faced by the Kanins:** In *Documentation of the Red Stars in Hollywood*, Fagan wrote that Garson Kanin was "active on behalf of the ten branded men" (the Hollywood Ten) but that he "keeps off Fronts" (organizations considered to be fronts for Communist activity). The *Hollywood Reporter* wrote on April 18, 1952, that Kanin had been a member of the Communist Party, prompting Kanin's lawsuit. Even after the *Reporter* apologized, Kanin initially refused to drop the suit. In a letter published on April 15, he wrote that he was not a Communist, never had been, never had any sympathy for Communists, and never refused to cooperate with any investigation. Given his deep belief in socialism and his sympathy for Russia, it was a capitulation far greater than anything Kate ever made.

Ruth Gordon's name was one of those read from the stage by Myron Fagan at the El Patio Theatre. After Ruth acted in the Guild's radio play *Over Twenty One* on May 18, 1952, letters criticized the Guild for working with her. It was a clearly organized campaign against her, as many of the letters had very similar wording. Rather than defend free speech, the Guild, like everyone else cowed by the temper of the times, wrote letters in response insisting that Ruth was opposed to communism and that any political activity on her part had been "ill-advised." See Gordon's file in TGC.

378 **"I can't":** KH to John Ford, June 27, 1936, JFC.

378 **KH at mother's funeral:** My insights into her feelings at this time come from Bob Hepburn and Kate's friend Max Showalter, who both felt Kit's death caused her to reevaluate her life. Robert

Shaw added that it was his opinion that she was saddened that she could never have the kind of relationship with Tracy that her parents had had with each other.

380 **"It is hard to believe"**: Lawrence Langner to KH, October 11, 1948, TGC.

380 **Shaw asks about KH's athleticism**: Lawrence Langner to KH, June 27, 1950, TGC.

380 **"go down the hill"**: KH to George Cukor, January 9, 1953, GCC.

380 **"three wholesome meals"**: George Cukor to KH, January 11, 1953, GCC.

383 **"Who is"**: Unsourced clipping, June 25, 1952, NYPL.

383 **"She's been madly in love"**: *Movieland*, March 1948.

383 UNTOLD STORY: *Inside Story*, October 1956.

384 **"Fear"**: Edwards.

384 **"Mr. Cukor"**: McGilligan, *A Double Life*.

384 **"I always forget"**: Laurents, *Original Story By*.

385 **"seriously considering"**: Andersen, *An Affair to Remember*.

25. SOMEHOW VERY RIGHT ABOUT THINGS

386 **Coward's puppies**: Cole Lesley, *Remembered Laughter: The Life of Noel Coward* (Knopf, 1976).

386 **Irene Selznick**: The Irene Mayer Selznick Collection (IMSC) at Boston University offered considerable insight into this remarkable woman's character and her friendships with many people, including Kate. Many of the letters between the two women, however, have been withheld from the collection.

386 **"escape thinking"**: Irene Mayer Selznick (IMS) to Hugh Beaumont, February 18, 1953, IMSC.

387 **"she was having misgivings"**: Cukor memoir, GCC.

387 **"a complete separation"**: KH to John Huston, April 3, 1952, John Huston Collection, AMPAS.

388 **"an awful, impossible woman"**: *Saturday Review*, November 1, 1952.

388 **"a human hurricane"**: *Daily Express*, June 27, 1952.

388 **"force of nature"**: *Times* (London), June 27, 1952.

388 **"The worse"**: Cavett.

388 **Tracy and Tierney**: The writer Selden West, after many years of researching a family-authorized biography of Tracy, told me that the only latter-day affair she believed was real and not rumor was the one with Gene Tierney. See also Gene Tierney, *Self-Portrait* (Wyden Books, 1979), and Kirk Douglas, *The Ragman's Son* (Pocket Books, 1988).

389 **June Dally-Watkins**: Much of this information comes from my conversation with her. See also Watkins, *The Secret Behind My Smile* (Viking Australia, 2002).

389 **"Drive on!"**: *Daily Express*, September 25, 1952.

390 **"My elusive tenant"**: George Cukor to KH, February 26, 1954, GCC.

391 **KH parts with Theatre Guild**: Long-simmering frustrations had finally come to a head. Months before the *The Millionairess*, Terry Helburn wrote to Kate that she and Lawrence Langner were tired of hearing only criticism from her, "never any appreciation for anything we have done with or for you." When the cast of *As You Like It* celebrated its fiftieth performance, for example, Kate had pointedly not invited the Guild directors, though she expected them to supply the champagne. Helburn called Kate their favorite daughter, and she understood "that children, especially modern ones, can't ever be expected to say a good word to their parents." Whether Kate ever replied is unknown. In fact, it's not clear if Helburn ever sent this letter; it remains only in draft form. Still, her words expose the fault line in their relationship, offering insight into why, after *The Millionairess*, the Guild and Hepburn went their separate ways. (TGC)

391 **KH in hospital**: In *Me*, Kate implied her time at Columbia-Presbyterian Hospital was working with "a theatrical doctor" on her voice. One undated clipping from the NYPL biographical file says "Miss Hepburn has checked herself into a clinic for exhaustion now that she's finished Shaw's 'Millionairess.'" Leaming's contention that she was suicidal seems to come from one line in *Me*, where Kate wrote, facetiously, that her struggles with her voice left her "contemplating jumping out the window—anything."

391 **"There is"**: Noël Coward to IMS, Feb 17, 1953, IMSC.

391 **"the Royal National Jamaican Theatre"**: Hugh Beaumont to IMS, March 13, 1953, IMSC.

392 **"so well in years"**: Constance Collier to Theresa Helburn, April 14, 1951, TGC.

392 **"George had"**: IMS, *A Private View* (Knopf, 1983).

393 **"She is not"**: IMS to Hugh Beaumont, November 8, 1957, IMSC.

393 **"With your head"**: *NYT*, November 10, 1990.

394 **Em Perkins's poor health and retirement**: "How frightfully badly Em looks," Kate wrote to Lawrence Langner in August 1944. "It is pathetic. She seems to have just wilted." Hepburn was "deeply shocked" to see Em in such a weakened condition when she returned to New York after making *Dragon Seed*. Kate was after Em to see a doctor, preferably her father, but Em was resistant. (TGC) In letters to John Ford dating back into the 1930s, there was similar concern over Em's health. Her well-being was not helped when her son Blynn took ill and died unexpectedly. In Maine, Em joined the Christian Science Society in Sanford and ran a teahouse at 29 Stearns Road in Ogunquit. Her clientele was largely "leisurely ladies" who came to partake in the English tradition of afternoon high tea. She died in 1978. Ogunquit Village Directory, 1951; *York County Coast Star*, November 2, 1978; Emily Perkins probate file, December 12, 1978, York County, Maine.

394 **Constance Collier**: For biographical detail, see Constance Collier, *Harlequinade: The Story of My Life* (Boadley Head, 1929); *Screen and Radio Weekly*, circa 1930, NYPL; *Photoplay*, May 1935; *Harper's Bazaar*, July 1954; *NYT*, April 26, 1955; *Times* (London), April 27, 1955; biographical files, AMPAS and NYPL. Letters to and from Collier in the TGC, IMSC, and the Zoe Akins Collection, Huntington Library, also added to my portrait.

395 **"the essence"**: *New York Herald Tribune*, January 17, 1932.

396 **"Ah, poor dear Max"**: *Saturday Review of Literature*, July 3, 1947.

396 **Julian L'Estrange**: World War I draft registration card; Cambridge University alumni records; *LAT*, May 30, 1911; *New York Globe*, January 25, 1912; *New York Herald*, December 31, 1908; *New York Telegraph*, November 9, 1910; *NYT*, January 6, March 15, 1912; October 23–24, 1918; February 9, February 27, 1941; *Rochester Evening Times*, September 29, 1911; various biographical files, NYPL. Albert Morris Bagby later gained fame as the originator of the annual Bagby Morning Musicals, a prestigious society event held in the grand ballroom of the Waldorf-Astoria.

397 **"I spent"**: *LAT*, April 28, 1955.

397 **Collier and Le Gallienne**: Perhaps using Constance and Phyllis as a model, Eva Le Gallienne retained a former lover, Marion Gunnar Evensen, as her companion-secretary-housekeeper after the romance was gone between them and Le Gallienne had moved on to a new lover. See Schanke, *That Furious Lesbian*; Sheehy, *Eva Le Gallienne*.

397 **"[Constance] had"**: KH interview with Ward Morehouse, transcript, Ward Morehouse Collection, NYPL.

397 **"They are"**: KH to George Cukor, [nd], GCC.

398 **"Human beings cannot flourish"**: Constance Collier to IMS, April 29, 1954, IMSC.

398 **"particular warmth"**: IMS to Hugh Beaumont, February 2, 1954, IMSC.

398 **Scotty introduces KH to young woman**: I discovered the woman's identity through independent sources; Scotty did not provide her name. When contacted about this book, the woman confirmed she had known Hepburn but refused to say anything other than the comment quoted. When I tried asking further questions, she ended the conversation.

399 **"She's extraordinary"**: AP oral history.

399 **KH helps Ethel Barrymore**: Letters in the GCC show Hepburn was one of the primary contributors to a fund to keep Barrymore solvent in her old age.

399 **KH helps Lionel Pape**: Letters in the JFC show how solicitous she was of Pape, promising Ford to look for parts for the older actor. One of Pape's last roles was in *The Philadelphia Story*.

399 **"treat"**: ROSS.

400 **Tracy in Venice**: *Hollywood Reporter*, [nd, August?], 1954, NYPL. Tracy was back in Los An-

geles by September 29, when Dorothy Kilgallen's column reported he was seen with Leo Durocher and Laraine Day. Kate was still working on *Summertime* at that point.

400 **"Very lonely"**: Hugh Beaumont to IMS, September 28, 1954, IMSC.

400 **Maggie Shipway**: Later she married the cinematographer Geoffrey Unsworth, best known for his blue-screen work on *Superman* (1978), the year he died.

401 **Robert Helpmann**: Elisabeth Salter, *Helpmann: The Authorised Biography* (Angus and Robertson, 1978), and Julie Kavanagh, *Secret Muses: The Life of Frederick Ashton* (Pantheon, 1996). See also the *Queen*, October 30, 1946; *Theater World*, February 1957; *Stage*, July 24, 1958; *NYT*, January 26, 1971; the *Times*, September 29, 1986; *NYT*, September 29, 1986; various biographical files, NYPL.

402 **KH and *Chalk Garden***: In May 1954, Irene Selznick was working with George Cukor to direct the play, but found him less than inspiring at the task, and eventually they parted company. Kate may have been more willing to consider the part had Cukor been on board, but she resisted whenever Irene suggested it. Letters between Irene and the play's author, Enid Bagnold, show they were still somewhat hopeful of getting Hepburn for the part (which Irene called "the Miserable Madrigal") in late 1954. But by early the next year, the talk had shifted to others: Wendy Hiller, Ida Lupino ("Ugh," Irene said), Katharine Cornell, Judith Anderson, and Helen Hayes. Kate suggested either Celia Johnson or Siobhan McKenna, the latter of whom eventually got the part. (IMSC)

402 **"They're the toughest race"**: Ward Morehouse Collection.

403 **Collier's death**: *NYT*, April 26, 27, 1955; *Times* (London), April 27, May 3, 1955.

403 **Phyllis takes ashes**: *LAT*, May 5, 1955.

403 **KH's Australian press conference**: The press conference was reported by several newspapers, including the *Sydney Morning Herald*, [nd, May 1955]; the *Times* (London), May 26, 1955; various clippings, NYPL.

404 **Maie Casey**: See Diane Langmore, *Glittering Surfaces: A Life of Maie Casey* (Allen and Unwin, 1997), as well as Langmore's profile, "The Other Lady Casey," *Australian Magazine*, June 21–22, 1997. Casey's papers at the National Library of Australia were also valuable.

404 **Pat Jarrett**: See Audrey Tate, *Fair Comment: The Life of Pat Jarrett* (Melbourne University Press, 1996). Tate's book is not forthcoming about Jarrett's sexuality, although it is certainly there between the lines. Langmore's book takes a far more direct approach to the relationship between the two women. Jarrett's papers at the National Library of Australia offered considerable insight into her life and to her friendship with KH.

404 **"I hope"**: KH to Pat Jarrett, [nd, September–October 1955], Patricia Jarrett Papers.

405 **"so *there*"**: KH to Pat Jarrett, October 14, 1955, Patricia Jarrett Papers.

405 **"I just lie"**: KH to Pat Jarrett, [nd, November, 1955], Patricia Jarrett Papers.

405 **lyrebird**: Higham. Kate also frequently mentioned her fascination with the lyrebird in articles and various correspondence.

26. QUALITY COMES FIRST

407 **Shooting *Long Day's Journey into Night***: *NYT*, October 22, 1961, various clips, NYPL.

408 **"Do you have any worms?"**: *Newsweek*, May 1957, quoted in Edwards.

408 **"Our friend"**: IMS to Hugh Beaumont, August 28, 1957, IMSC.

408 **"beautiful, debonair"**: *NYT*, August 8, 1957.

408 **"that stardom"**: John Houseman, *Final Dress* (Simon and Schuster, 1983).

408 **"lack of self confidence"**: Interview with Larry King, CNN transcripts.

408 **"steadily worse"**: Ward Morehouse Collection.

409 **"Hers is"**: *NYT*, August 1, 1960.

409 **"Miss Hepburn"**: *New York Herald Tribune*, June 4, 1960.

409 **"dramatic poem"**: Tennessee Williams to KH, January 5, 1961, Tennessee Williams Collection, University of Delaware. It appears that this letter was never sent.

409 ***Suddenly Last Summer***: For Mankiewicz's take, see Kenneth L. Geist, *Pictures Will Talk:*

The Life and Films of Joseph L. Mankiewicz (Da Capo Press, 1978). See also Patricia Bosworth, *Montgomery Clift: A Biography* (Harcourt Brace Jovanovich, 1978).

410 **KH spits at Mankiewicz**: Kate loved telling people, including Scott Berg, that she spit in the director's face. But Mankiewicz said it was at his feet, and Irene Selznick, "a stickler for accuracy," also insisted to Berg that it was on the floor. A letter in the Tennessee Williams Collection from the playwright to Kate also references that she "spit on the soundstage."

410 **"a playwright's dream"**: This is from an interview Williams gave to the press, quoted in Edwards and sourced to the *NYT*, though I could not confirm its actual date. It is also quoted in Kanin, perhaps where Edwards got it.

410 **"cool, strong ladies"**: Tennessee Williams to KH, January 5, 1961, Tennessee Williams Collection. Although the letter was likely not sent, it references a telephone call between Williams and Kate; other letters also reference calls. This was clearly Williams's line of argument with Kate, and he likely used it speaking to her as well as writing to her.

410 ***Night of the Iguana***: Kanin wrote that after seeing Davis play Maxine, Kate told Williams, "You're lucky. I would've ruined it." Could it be possible that all along she thought Williams wanted her to play *Maxine*? Was that what she thought she was agreeing to play? If, in fact, those letters in the Williams Collection were not sent, she may have been going on telephone conversations with the playwright. It seems inconceivable that she would imagine he wanted her for Maxine, which was also a smaller part than that of Hannah. But this was the impression that Kanin seems to have had, and it was echoed by Noel Taylor.

411 **"From being"**: Kael's review originally ran in the *New Yorker* and was collected in *Kiss Kiss Bang Bang* (Little, Brown, 1968).

411 **"Marvelous and miraculous"**: *LAT*, December 19, 1962.

411 **"Her transformations"**: *Saturday Review*, May 1962.

412 **"The thing is"**: *Ladies' Home Journal*, August 1975.

412 **"strange aberrations"**: *WP*, November 12, 1961.

412 **"Quality in material"**: *LAT*, January 2, 1963.

412 **"Where the old time"**: *Time*, May 13, 1957.

413 **"I don't know why"**: Hedda Hopper to KH, December 2, 1964, Hedda Hopper Collection, AMPAS.

413 **"You and I"**: KH to Hedda Hopper, December 12, 1964, Hedda Hopper Collection.

414 **Bellevue Hotel owner**: Interview on ABC Television (Australia), October 17, 2004.

414 **"Calling old Kath"**: The photos were included among Hepburn's private papers donated to AMPAS. The envelope was postmarked May 16, 1955.

415 **"To this day," "Kid, I want you"**: Davidson, *Spencer Tracy*.

415 **Tracy throws snifter**: Frank Westmore, *The Westmores of Hollywood* (Lippincott, 1976). See also Davidson, *Spencer Tracy*.

416 **"rich, fat actor"**: Swindell, *Spencer Tracy*.

417 **"Spence and Dick"**: KH to Maie Casey, June 21, 1967, Maie Casey Collection. The date of their gathering at Kate's house, September 24, 1957, comes from Richard Casey's diary, in which he wrote they had "an interesting and entertaining evening" (Richard G. Casey Collection, National Library of Australia).

417 **KH with Frances Rich in Hawaii**: KH to John Ford, October 10, 1960, JFC.

417 **"When people's paths"**: DF interview.

417 SPENCER TRACY'S DEAF SON: *LAT*, August 29, 1957; various other articles, Spencer Tracy biographical files, NYPL; Final Judgment of Divorce, Los Angeles County Superior Court, September 25, 1958.

417 **Spence somehow got lost**: Houseman, *Final Dress*.

418 **Louise as Citizen of the Year**: *LAT*, September 24, 1957.

418 **KH at Tracy's motel room**: This story has long circulated in the underground tales of Kate and Spencer. It apparently happened sometime in the late 1950s or in the early 1960s. Since Tracy wasn't drinking as much in the later part of that period, it seems likely to have occurred around the time of his son's divorce. It also appears to have happened in California. Charles Williamson, by then close with

George Cukor, recalled specifically Phyllis's part in it, making sandwiches at Tracy's bungalow and bringing them over to the motel, which Williamson remembered as "seedy." Leaming's description of Kate sleeping in the hallway outside Spencer's room at the Beverly Hills Hotel years earlier may actually find its genesis in these anecdotes, which were repeated by many of Hepburn's associates. I'm skeptical of the stories set at the Beverly Hills Hotel. As concerned about privacy as Kate was—and if nothing else to keep gossips from talking about Spence—Kate wasn't likely to do such a thing as sleep in the hallway of a prestigious hotel. After all, she surely had a *key*.

418 **"best you can expect"**: Constance Collier to Hedda Hopper, November 17, 1941, Hedda Hopper Collection.

418 *The Last Hurrah*: DF interview.

419 **"But, gosh"**: KH to John Huston, March 27, 1952, John Huston Collection. *The Deep Blue Sea* was inspired by the suicide of Rattigan's lover, Kenneth Morgan.

420 **"Yesterday Miss Hepburn"**: Phyllis Wilbourn to Irene Burns, January 27, 1958, GCP.

420 **Wilbourn's background**: Phyllis Wilbourn probate file, New York Surrogate Court; England Census, 1881, 1891, 1901; Civil Registration of Births and Deaths; correspondence with Wilbourn family.

420 **"the only one"**: Letter from George Andrew Pocock, September 11, 1995, Wilbourn probate file.

421 **"I have"**: Phyllis Wilbourn to George Cukor, May 2, 1955, GCP.

421 **"now with Katie"**: *WP*, February 18, 1957.

421 **"like a dog"**: AP oral history.

422 **Tracy's return to the United States**: *NYT*, December 19, 1961; *LAT*, December 21, 1961.

423 *Anne Cinquefoil*: Lawrence Langner to TH, December 1, 1954, TGC; *NYT*, January 11, January 13, 1961.

423 **Fran Rich**: Hedda Hopper's column, *LAT*, October 28, 1961; January 10, 1962.

423 **"Seen a lot"**: Frances Rich to John Ford, May 10, 1962, JFC.

423 **"Dad had"**: KH to Leland Hayward, January 4, 1963, Leland Hayward Collection, NYPL.

423 **"I hope"**: KH to John Huston, June 10, 1950, John Huston Collection.

27. DEAR, DEAR FRIEND

426 *Seven Women*: Reminiscing years later, Ford told Hepburn he'd wanted her for the "lead," and Kate, joshing, disagreed, saying it was for some smaller, "lousy" part (DF interview). It seems likely it was for the part eventually played by Margaret Leighton, ironically the same actress Tennessee Williams had gotten for the play *Night of the Iguana* after Kate proved unavailable.

426 *The Lonely Passion*: In March 1962, the Theatre Guild was trying to stage it before Huston made it into a film, apparently eager to work with Kate again. Throughout 1962–63, there were several mentions in the press that Kate would be returning to the screen in the project. Letters in Huston's private files, however, reveal he was being pressured to cast a younger actress, like Anne Bancroft, with more box-office appeal. Elliot Hyman of Seven Arts wrote to Huston on July 23, 1963, "It seems unfair to all of us to almost design this picture toward the goal of an 'artistic success.' " Huston eventually abandoned the project. (John Huston Collection)

427 **Trancas Beach house**: Details of life here come from Fran Rich, Charles Williamson, and others of Cukor's circle.

427 **"house [Tracy] shared"**: Bacon, *Hollywood Is a Four-Letter Town*.

427 **Bill Davidson's article in *Look***: In addition to this article, see Davidson, *Spencer Tracy*.

428 **Tracy's collapse**: *LAT*, July 22–23, August 3, 1963.

429 **Tracy's second hospitalization**: *LAT*, September 1, December 28, 1963.

429 **KH's living arrangements**: Once again, Kate found a way to give a false impression to benefit the legend without directly needing to lie. In *Me*, she said she moved "down to Spencer's tiny house, which we rented from George Cukor." After Spencer's death, she did, in fact, move into his bungalow, which saves her statement from being untrue. But no matter what she implied, they never rented the place from Cukor *together at the same time*. Kate also said that Phyllis lived up at

the old John Barrymore house on Tower Grove Drive. It's true they had been living there before Kate took the second bungalow on Cukor's estate, but both Tucker Fleming and Charles Williamson distinctly remembered Phyllis living with Kate in the bungalow before Spencer died.

429 **Three bungalows:** In the third bungalow lived a "Mrs. Briskin," who was somehow related to the RKO producer Sam Briskin.

429 **"[Spencer] stayed":** *Time*, June 29, 1992.

429 **KH in Dorothy Kilgallen's column:** *WP*, September 13, 1963.

429 **"There was":** AP oral history.

430 **"I gather":** Hugh Beaumont to IMS, August 18, 1964, IMSC.

430 **Spence's prostate surgery:** *LAT*, September 17, 28, 1965.

432 **"Kate is":** IMS to Hugh Beaumont, September 8, 1966, IMSC.

432 **"good wife":** Quoted in Kanin.

433 **"He gave":** KH to Maie Casey, June 21, 1967, Maie Casey Collection.

433 **"I crouched down":** *Me.*

433 **Tracy's death, aftermath, and funeral:** Various newspaper accounts of his death provided many details, as did Kate's account of it in *Me*, along with letters to Maie Casey, Pat Jarrett, and Irene Selznick. A conversation with Selden West also helped elucidate this period.

435 **"You don't think":** Interview with Larry King, CNN transcripts.

435 **"I never":** DF interview.

436 **"I felt":** IMS to Hugh Beaumont, June 23, 1967.

436 **"Miss Harding has bought":** KH to George Cukor, June 1968, GCC.

437 **"I shall love":** KH to George Cukor, [nd, 1967], GCC.

437 **"I feel sure":** [nd, 1968], GCC.

437 **"a remarkable legacy":** *LAT*, June 12, 1967.

437 **"mainly for white people":** Interview with Larry King, CNN transcripts.

438 **"one cool chick":** *New York Daily News*, July 6, 1967.

438 **"the very first Mod":** *NYT*, April 27, 1969.

438 THE COMEBACK: *Life*, January 5, 1968.

438 THE UNSINKABLE KATE: *Look*, August 6, 1968.

438 **"She stands":** *NYT*, April 27, 1969.

28. KISSING HER IN THE STREET

439 **"sisters of a sort":** Kanin.

440 **"An incident":** KH to Rosalind Russell, October 30, 1967, FBC.

440 **"There is something":** *NYT*, October 31, 1968.

441 **"Oh, no":** *NYT*, December 9, 1973.

441 **"an intolerable bitch":** Cecil Beaton diary, November 2, 1969.

441 **"Next time":** Higham.

441 **KH-Selznick partnership:** By September 8, 1967, Irene was writing to Binkie Beaumont of her "little film" and that "it is no less than our friend Kate who is mad about the material" (IMSC).

442 **"all up for Tracy":** Notes taken by Frederick Brisson (FB) at a November 1967 meeting with KH. Also present were Alan Jay Lerner (AJL) and Phyllis Wilbourn. FBC.

442 *Coco* agreement: Signed by FB, February 6, 1968, FBC.

442 **"I was surprised":** AJL to KH, May 18, 1968, FBC.

443 **"cut her hair":** *Time*, November 7, 1969.

443 **"That would be":** Beaton diary, November 1, 1969.

444 **Noelle's "lesbian" hairdo:** Beaton diary, November 8, 1969.

444 **"nauseatingly sycophantic":** Beaton diary, November 7, 1969. The actress playing Noelle, Udana Campbell, was replaced by Gale Dixon during previews.

444 **"also sing quite well"**: Claudette Colbert to Leonard Gershe, [nd, 1970], private collection of Charles Williamson and Tucker Fleming, given to them by Gershe.

444 **Majestic Theatre**: FB notes, June 27, 1969, FBC.

444 **KH's London flight**: Brisson was angry because "it was our understanding that she would not go." FB to AJL, July 11, 1969, FBC.

445 **"defiled [his] London house"**: Cecil Beaton to Enid Bagnold, May 30, 1956, quoted in Hugo Vickers, *Cecil Beaton: A Biography* (Donald I. Fine, 1985). After being unceremoniously cut from the London production of *The Chalk Garden,* Beaton fired off a letter to Irene: "It is sad that so fragrant a blossom as your play should be surrounded by so much stink" (January 16, 1956, IMSC).

445 **"publicity-seeking"**: McGilligan, *A Double Life.*

445 **"complete egomaniac"**: Beaton diary, August 14, 1969.

445 **"Disastrous family news"**: FB notes, July 1969, FBC.

445 **"I don't"**: FB notes, June 20, 1969, FBC.

446 **"There is no way"**: FB to Roger Davis, September 2, 1969, FBC.

446 **"dishonest"**: Beaton diary, September 21, 1969.

446 **"the manners"**: Beaton diary, December 1, 1969.

446 **"When she's rehearsing"**: AP oral history.

446 **"spectacle of Katharine Hepburn"**: *NYT,* October 13, 1969.

447 **"Her skin is revolting"**: Beaton diary, December 1969.

447 **"a fire danger"**: Beaton diary, November 14, 1969.

447 **"Kate would not allow me"**: Higham.

447 **"blinking like a mechanical owl"**: Beaton diary, November 14, 1969.

447 **"greatly relieved"**: Beaton diary, October 29, 1969.

447 **"K.H. can expect"**: Beaton diary, November 14, 1969.

448 **"well-scrubbed"**: *NYT,* December 19, 1969.

448 **"Thank God"**: KH to FB, December 22, 1969, FBC.

448 **"To have made this decision"**: KH to FB and AJL, December 31, 1969, FBC. Brisson drafted a reply that he was "heartsick about what was done to you" and said he told Lerner to put it right. FB to KH, January 2, 1970, FBC.

449 **"fed up"**: FB notes, November 1969, FBC.

449 **"a pig"**: FB notes, January 6, 1970, FBC.

449 **"I am sorry"**: KH to FB, April 3, 1970, FBC.

449 **"would die!"**: FB notes, March 6, 1970, FBC.

449 **"sweet but uncadential"**: FB notes, April 2, 1970, FBC.

450 **"It may"**: Beaton diary, December 1969.

450 **"I don't really"**: KH to FB, April 24, 1970, FBC.

450 **"I don't want it"**: FB notes, April 25, 1970, FBC.

450 **"terrible fight"**: KH to AJL, [nd., 1970], FBC.

450 **"We also told you"**: FB to KH, July 30, 1970, FBC.

450 **"dead and in a morgue"**: FB notes, July 18, 1970, FBC.

450 **"For all her artistry"**: *NYT,* August 7, 1970.

451 **Kanin and Lerner**: References are made to their meeting in Brisson's notes, August 5, 1970, FBC; further details were provided by a Hepburn friend who asked for anonymity.

451 **"emotional strain"**: FB notes, August 7, 1970, FBC.

451 **"Bellevue"**: FB notes, February 7, 1971, FBC.

452 **"If I could describe"**: *Me.*

452 **"to discuss"**: Laura Harding to George Cukor, January 20, 1970, GCP.

452 **"People kiss me"**: KH to Anthony Harvey, [nd, 1970], AHC.

453 **"across the footlights"**: *Me.*

453 **"You cannot imagine"**: Previous reports of Kate's final curtain speech for *Coco* have given a slightly different version. This is taken from a contemporary transcription found in the FBC.

453 **"old-fashioned"**: Beaton diary, December 5, 1969.

454 **"tore up"**: Phyllis Wilbourn to Irene Burns, April 19, 1970, GCP.

455 **Ramo kidnapping**: Kanin mentioned the story in *Tracy and Hepburn*. But by locating the actual coverage, I was able to see the truth of the anecdote. The story was followed in *NYT*, September 14, 1969; *LAT*, September 14–15, 1969; and other newspapers. There is no mention of Katharine Hepburn in any of these accounts. Her "involvement" in the case was reported only later in various syndicated columns, including Leonard Lyons's on September 27, 1969; also in the "Personalities" column, *WP*, October 7, 1969.

455 **"doesn't act"**: John Gielgud to Hugh Wheeler, March 25, 1969, John Gielgud Collection, NYPL.

455 **"People have"**: *Time*, November 7, 1969.

456 **"nothing allegorical"**: TH to KH, January 1941, TGC.

29. PROVING SHE'S THE BEST GUY

457 **KH at Cukor's**: This anecdote was described to me by Lon McCallister.

457 **"You must"**: Kate recalled talking with Irene in the DF interview.

458 *Tracy and Hepburn* **best-seller status**: It made its debut on the *New York Times* best-seller list on December 12, 1971, in the tenth spot. A week later it was at number six, and Christmas sales pushed it to number three by January 9, 1972. It peaked on the *Times* list at number two in mid-January and held on to that slot into March. It never overcame *Eleanor and Franklin* on the *Times* list to make number one, although it did reach that level in other lists. In all, *Tracy and Hepburn* was on the *Times* best-seller list for more than four months.

458 **"Keeping Kate"**: Garson Kanin biographical file, NYPL.

458 **"one of those enviable creatures"**: *McCall's*, February 1970.

459 **"Now then"**: DF interview.

459 **"Gar Kanin"**: KH to Anthony Harvey, November 27, 1971, AHC.

459 **Kanin's promotion of his book**: As part of his efforts, he asked Thornton Wilder for a quote. "If you can find it within yourself to say a sentence or phrase or a word in its support," Kanin wrote, "it would mean more than I have the power to express." He promised to explain more when they met in person—if, in fact, Wilder hadn't already guessed the reason for Kanin's need for help. Aware that the book would arouse hostility among those loyal to Kate, Kanin was appealing for support from those, like Wilder, who were not fond of her. "I *know* how you feel about KH," he wrote, "but that is not what the book is about, as you will see if you grant the favor" (Garson Kanin to Thornton Wilder, July 31, 1971, Thornton Wilder Collection, Beinecke).

460 **"Once in a while"**: *Pageant*, October 1946.

460 **"There I was"**: DF interview.

461 **Cukor on Kanin's book**: This was told to me by Gavin Lambert.

461 **"As a hopeless Tracy-Hepburn buff"**: *Chicago Tribune*, October 25, 1971.

461 **"closer to their privacy"**: *LAT*, November 28, 1971.

461 **KH dodging photographer**: DE notes, [nd, circa 1973–74], DEC.

462 **"He *did* get a picture"**: *Daily Express*, November 20, 1967.

462 **"Reports tell me"**: George Cukor to KH, November 28, 1972, GCC.

462 **"Before we permit"**: Garson Kanin to George Cukor, December 22, 1971, GCC.

462 **"They are"**: DF interview.

462 **"how Garson"**: DE diary, April 17, 1980.

462 **"Why should she?"**: *LAT*, May 16, 1978.

463 **"a few things"**: *LAT*, April 16, 1972.

463 **"A lady cannot wear," "I don't believe it"**: *McCall's*, February 1970. What had prompted the conversation was a discussion about the influence of homosexuals in the theater—in particular, Bebe Berard's production of *Les Fourberies de Scapin* by Molière. One of Berard's patrons was James Soby, the close companion of Kate's brother Tom.

464 **"kind of naïve"**: KH to John Huston, March 27, 1952, John Huston Collection, AMPAS.

464 **"didn't know"**: Salter, *Helpmann.*

464 **"totally engrossed"**: KH to Maie Casey, June 21, 1967, Maie Casey Collection.

464 **"I have"**: *Modern Screen*, March 1972.

465 **"It was common knowledge"**: *WP*, November 16, 1971.

465 **Champlin's piece**: November 28, 1971.

466 **"Although Miss Hepburn"**: *Hartford Times*, February 22, 1971.

466 **"We have gotten"**: DF interview.

467 **"Now they make movies"**: *Hartford Times*, February 22, 1971.

467 **"The state of human affairs"**: *WP*, December 26, 1971.

467 **KH politics**: In 1968 and again in 1970, the FBI ran routine security checks on Hepburn, finding nothing objectionable. For Nixon, Kate always harbored a deep dislike. When John Ford told her he'd voted for Nixon, whom he considered "a close personal friend," she called it "insane." Momentarily at a loss for words, Kate finally spit out, "This shows you have no political philosophy." She then promptly ended the conversation (DF interview).

467 **Rene Auberjonois**: Higham.

469 **Kate's bulbs**: DE diary, April 16, 1980, DEC.

469 **"treatment to her face"**: Chester Erskine to George Cukor, December 1971, GCC.

469 **"I'm putting the potion"**: KH to Anthony Harvey, November 27, 1971, AHC.

470 **Jody Jacobs on KH's "Parkinson's"**: Memo to FB, January 7, 1970, FBC.

470 **"I'm a very private person"**: *NYT*, December 9, 1973.

471 **"occasionally"**: *NYT*, December 14, 1973.

472 **"for talking's sake"**: Beaton diary, September 22, 1969.

472 HEPBURN ON LIFE AND DEATH: *WP*, October 3, 1973.

474 **"The character"**: Chester Erskine to George Cukor, December 7, 1971, GCC.

474 **"And Sister Kate too"**: *Time*, November 18, 1974.

30. ALWAYS DISCREET UNTIL NOW

475 **Louella West**: Case report and follow-up reports, February 24–March 23, 1971, West Hartford Police Department.

476 **"I don't know"**: *Ladies' Home Journal*, August 1975.

476 **"her group"**: Interview with Larry King, CNN transcripts.

476 **Hamilton leaves KH chocolate**: Probate file, Nancy Hamilton, Surrogate Court, New York.

476 **Sally Lapiduss**: She was identified as a lesbian in the *Advocate*, September 30, 1997, and June 11, 2002. Among her credits have been *The Nanny* and *Mad About You.*

477 **"At a certain age"**: *Time*, November 7, 1969.

478 **"She'd take"**: KH to John Ford, [nd, 1971], JFC.

478 **KH's encounter with Louella West**: All descriptions and quotes are taken from the lengthy case report in the West Hartford Police Department files, including separate statements given by KH, West, Phyllis Wilbourn, and Madeline Hepburn. Detective Robert Moylan also shared information in a personal interview.

480 ACTRESS ATTACKED: There were many reports of the incident, including the *Mansfield* [Ohio] *News Journal*, February 24, 1971, and *WP*, February 25, 1971.

481 **"Attacking Katharine Hepburn"**: *Hartford Courant*, September 10, 1971, and many other newspaper accounts.

481 **"wanted the moon"**: KH to Anthony Harvey, November 27, 1971, AHC.

481 **"Something happens"**: DE to KH, April 5, 1981, DEC.

481 **"You know"**: DE to KH, May 1, 1982, DEC.

481 **"You make"**: KH to DE, June 26, 1988, DEC.

482 **"Don't despair"**: KH to Anthony Harvey, November 27, 1971, AHC.

483 **"Look at"**: ABC Barbara Walters special, June 2, 1981.

483 **"Of course"**: DE to KH, November 20, 1977, GCF.

483 **Cukor's later years**: Various friends described his life. A deeper portrait emerges as well from reading his various correspondence, both at AMPAS and that which is still kept privately. See also McGilligan, *A Double Life*; Levy, *George Cukor*.

484 **"He was not"**: McGilligan, *A Double Life*.

485 **"A bit too much"**: KH to Patrick McGilligan, September 12, 1989, GCF.

485 **"Guess what"**: DE diary, August 26, 1978, DEC.

486 **"Corners"**: *Me*.

486 **"It took"**: George Cukor to John Collier, GCC.

487 **"enduring radiance"**; *LAT*, March 6, 1975.

487 **"Miss Hepburn play"**: *NYT*, February 4, 1976.

487 **"something that I liked"**: KH to DE, [nd, 1976], DEC.

488 **KH's plastic surgery**: *Daily Express*, August 29, 1977, and other newspaper accounts; see also the *National Enquirer*, November 8, 1977.

488 **"head to toe"**: KH to DE, March 25, 1978, DEC.

488 **"I'd damn"**: *NYT*, May 2, 1978.

488 **"an ungrateful lout"**: George Cukor to Garson Kanin, August 25, 1978, GCC.

489 **"probably a little too old"**: *NYT*, January 29, 1979.

489 **"epitomizes"**: *WP*, January 29, 1979.

490 **Luddy's later life**: Interviews with Ramsay and Lewis Ludlow, as well as the *Norwalk Hour*, September 26, 1973; *New Canaan Advertiser*, July 19, 1979; New Canaan directories.

491 **Laura's later life**: Interviews with her grandnephews and grandnieces, including Robert Harding, Emily King, and Christine Tailer.

491 **Laura and Cukor at film premiere**: George Cukor to Laura Harding, October 21, 1981, GCF.

31. ON THE TOP OF THE WORLD

494 **KH at plays**: DE diary, April 17, 1980.

495 **"Fonda's not one"**: Howard Teichman, *Fonda: My Life* (Penguin, 1981).

496 **"It shows"**: *LAT*, January 24, 1981.

496 **"I'm not sure"**: *NYT*, November 29, 1981.

496 **"a more private profession"**: The interview aired on Britain's Channel 4 and was reported in *Newsday*, April 15, 1985.

496 **"Are you sure"**: The anecdote was told by Speck in the *Daily News-Record*, August 25, 2003.

496 **"Me and Phyllis"**: Joseph Levine announced in January 1986 that Kate was "one hell of a writer," and insisted she'd star in the film. Just who would play Phyllis, however, was his concern (*New York Post*, January 27, 1986). The following April, Levine was still trying to get the film mounted, explaining to the press it was the story of the "relationship between a woman and her longtime companion" (*New York Daily News*, April 20, 1986). Levine was off the project by June 1988, when a working draft of the script had been prepared for the producer Merrill H. Karpf. George Schaefer was planned as director, and Noel Taylor had been approached to do the costumes. The same team had made Kate's film *Mrs. Delafield Wants to Marry* in 1985 and were working on *Laura Lansing Slept Here* when "Me and Phyllis" was under consideration.

497 **"I don't know"**: *New Yorker*, September 21, 1987.

497 **Early version of *Me***: *Hartford Times Sunday Magazine*, December 29, 1968.

498 **Description of Tracy tribute**: *NYT*, March 4, 1986; *WP*, March 4, 1986. The evening was described for me by two different persons who were present.

500 **Philip Hoare interviews KH**: *Independent*, July 1, 2003.

500 **"Ten Most Beautiful Women"**: *Harper's Bazaar*, September 1988.

500 **"drops [Tracy's] name"**: *NYT*, September 1, 1991.

502 **"You don't"**: *Vogue*, September 1991.

503 **Treatment of essential tremor**: I am grateful to doctors at Columbia Presbyterian Hospi-

tal for giving me their medical opinions. In fact, one instructional video on essential tremor shown at the hospital features a scene from *Guess Who's Coming to Dinner*, with Hepburn identified as a "classic example of essential tremor." Another scene in the video showed her pouring a glass of scotch as an illustration of "the most widely used treatment for this disorder."

504 **"It's my school principal blood"**: KH to Lillian Gish, March 19, 1976, Lillian Gish Collection, NYPL.

504 **"You don't know"**: *New York Post*, April 5, 1982.

504 **"After you told him"**: *New York Sunday News*, April 25, 1982.

504 **James Prideaux**: For a fascinating account of their friendship, as well as details on the three television movies they made together, see James Prideaux, *Knowing Hepburn and Other Curious Experiences* (Faber and Faber, 1996).

504 **"She's really frightening"**: DE diary, August 26, 1978.

505 **"How dare you"**: *Time*, June 29, 1992.

506 **"just awful"**: AP oral history.

507 **"an exercise nut"**: *Los Angeles Daily News*, September 27, 1950.

507 **Split between KH and IMS**: Some have speculated it was over Hepburn's continued friendship with Laura Harding, whom Irene resented for a time because of her relationship with David O. Selznick. In fact, Irene had extended an olive branch to Laura years before, when she'd hired her as a wardrobe consultant on *The Chalk Garden* (IMSC).

509 **"friends the Reagans"**: DE to KH, March 23, 1988, DEC.

509 **"If they toss out"**: *Ladies' Home Journal*, October 1991.

509 **"The Moral Majority"**: *NYT*, May 12, 1985.

509 *Grace Quigley*: Correspondence between KH and Anthony Harvey, AHC; see also *NYT*, November 27, 1983; *LAT*, May 9, 1984; *NYT*, May 12, May 17, 1985; *Chicago Tribune*, May 19, 1985.

510 **"She's a good actress"**: Various accounts, Hepburn file, NYPL; also NYT, May 26, 1990.

512 **Cynthia McFadden's background**: I am grateful to several people close to McFadden who spoke off the record. U.S. Census, 1920–30; Maine vital records; Lewiston-Auburn city directories; Bowdoin College archives; *Lewiston Sun-Journal*, August 19, 1996; March 29, 1999; *Good Housekeeping*, May 2003. See also Liz Smith, *Natural Blonde* (Hyperion, 2000).

513 **"crying into a telephone"**: Houghton, *Marion Hepburn Grant*.

32. APOTHEOSIS

517 **"I can think"**: Quoted in Elisabeth Weiss, *The National Society of Film Critics on the Movie Star* (Viking Press, 1981).

518 **"Throughout her"**: Ray B. Browne, *Contemporary Heroes and Heroines* (Gale Research, 1990).

518 *Katharine Hepburn Once Said*: Edited by Susan Crimp (HarperEntertainment, 2003).

522 **Army Archerd's interview with KH**: *TV Guide*, December 17, 1994.

523 **"peculiarly hostile tone"**: Berg.

524 **"Was it really secret?"**: CNN transcripts.

524 **"rotten"**: AP oral history.

526 **Phyllis Wilbourn's will**: Probate file, Surrogate Court, New York.

526 **"hospital insiders"**: *New York Daily News*, March 4, 1996.

526 **"She was quite perky"**: *Newsday*, April 15, 1996.

526 **"ate heartily"**: *New York Post*, May 28, 1997.

527 **"a gentle fade"**: CNN transcripts.

A C K N O W L E D G M E N T S

Writing a book of such a carefully constructed and protected life as Katharine Hepburn's required the help of literally hundreds of people, and I could not have accomplished my goal without them. Noel Taylor, one of Hepburn's closest confidants during the last twenty years of her life, was my chief booster, understanding the importance of this project and offering insight and connections. Noel opened many doors that would have otherwise remained closed. The biggest gift of this book has been his friendship.

Likewise, I must thank up front James Prideaux, the screenwriter of several of Hepburn's later films and a frequent companion of the actress (as well as the author of the fascinating memoir *Knowing Hepburn*), for his always witty and extraordinarily telling appraisals; Tucker Fleming and the late Charles Williamson, intimates of George Cukor, whose constant support made all the difference, as did their encyclopedic knowledge of Cukor's (and, by extension, Hepburn's) circle; and especially the late Gavin Lambert, another close friend of Cukor's as well as his biographer, whose sharp intelligence was a source I often turned to for help in understanding the complexities of a long-vanished Hollywood. His support of this project was tremendous. He is deeply missed.

I am extraordinarily grateful to Dominick Dunne for his generosity and encouragement of this project right from the start. I must also acknowledge the insights of Jack Larson, one of the true gentlemen of Hollywood, whose love for Hepburn came through in our conversations, and who allowed me to see her softer, more vulnerable side.

Few of Hepburn's close contemporaries were left living, but I tracked down Frances Rich, her good friend and frequent traveling companion. Although suffering from the early stages of Alzheimer's disease, Rich did her best to answer questions in two telephone interviews, and I am tremendously grateful for her effort. My thanks also to Eunice Stoddard, another traveling companion and an actress for whom Hepburn understudied in 1929, who offered a crystal-clear memory of a time and culture long vanished.

After being so carefully cloaked by decades of mythmaking, Hepburn's truths frequently revealed themselves through the less carefully shielded lives of her closest friends. In this regard, the never-before-used correspondence of her college best friend and lifetime intimate Alice Palache proved invaluable; the heretofore unknown cache of private letters and documents of her husband, Ludlow Ogden Smith, finally shed light on that unconventional union; and the just-released personal correspondence of close Hepburn pals Anthony Harvey and David Eichler filled in many gaps in understanding her inner circle. Eichler kept a diary as well, which documents in detail many outings he took with Hepburn and discussions they had from the 1970s through the 1990s.

But to reach even deeper, I knew I'd have to leave no folder unopened, however seemingly far afield. Sources that appeared, on the surface, to have little connection to Hepburn often proved extremely valuable. Phelps Putnam, Hepburn's first love, has until now been painted the way she cast him in her autobiography, *Me*. But by reading Putnam's letters to his circle of friends, including the scholar F. O. Matthiessen and the painter Russell Cheney, I was able to visualize a far more complex picture of the moody Putnam, and thus Hepburn herself. Other letters, such as those between Billie Burke and Nancy Hamilton, or Robert Helpmann and Maie Casey, wife of the Australian governor-general, or Laura Harding and Russell Davenport, editor of *Fortune* magazine, might at first glance have seemed irrelevant, but they ended up allowing me to re-create with authority the panorama of life around Hepburn. I understood that only by penetrating this inner circle could I really get a grip on this most elusive of biographical subjects.

Fortunately, vital details of Hepburn's world were often forthcoming from the families and friends of her most intimate associates. In this light, thanks go to George Cukor's friends Robert Wheaton, Michael Childers (who assisted Cukor with his unfinished autobiography), Robert Cushman, Daniel Woodruff (who also became an intimate of Hepburn's in her later years), Don Bachardy, Richard Stanley, and Jim Weatherford, in addition to the already mentioned Fleming and Williamson (who also shared stories of their close friend Judy Garland and her various interactions with Hepburn). The late Lon McCallister, another Cukor friend and Hepburn acquaintance, shared some anecdotes with me several years ago but requested that I not use anything he told me until after his death. He died on June 11, 2005.

A round of thanks to the friends and family of Laura Harding: Tim Lovejoy, James Williams, Robin Chotzinoff, Jennifer Rosen, Christine Tailer, Robert Harding, and most especially Emily King, Laura's grandniece, who knew her aunt intimately and offered the kind of open-minded, thoughtful observation that's truly needed for a biography like this.

Irene Mayer Selznick emerges as a key supporting player in this book. For insight and information about her friendship with Hepburn, I thank her son, Daniel Selznick, and her good friend and executor, Robert Gottlieb. Likewise, the sharp, witty observations offered by Brooke Hayward Duchin, the daughter of Leland Hayward, were invaluable, as were the insights of Jones Harris, the son of Ruth Gordon and Jed Harris.

Thanks also to: The family and friends of Phyllis Wilbourn, people I was told could never be found: Elizabeth Pocock Bronn, Stephen Pocock, Janet Jordon, and Marian Toole. The family of Alice Palache: Jude Gregory, Cadigen Wiley, and Probyn Gregory. The family and friends of Emily Perkins: Mary Stanhope, Newell Perkins, Nancy Perkins, and John Phelps. The family and friends of Nancy Hamilton: Oriel Eaton, Nancy Smart, Sally Hamilton, Charles Hamilton, James Hamilton, and Ernest Whitmore. The family and friends of Jack Clarke: Virginia Soule, Theresa Crowley, Cat Adams. The family of Robert McKnight: Peggy McKnight and Jack Massa. The friends of Jane Loring: Teddy Smith, Judith Hall, Noel Hatch, and Billy Graf, the nephew of Loring's longtime companion Anna Graf. The friends of Susan (Suzanne) Steell: Michael Stein and Henry Lewis. Also Michael Berman, the son of Pandro Berman; Christina O'Dunne Griffin, the daughter of Hepburn's first beau, Eugene O'Dunne; Caroline Thomas Benes, the daughter of Elissa Landi; and Dan Ford, the grandson of John Ford.

Last but hardly least, I am deeply thankful for the kind cooperation of Ramsey Ludlow and Lewis Ludlow, the daughter and son of Ludlow Ogden Smith.

Fortunately, previous research had brought me into contact with people who knew Hepburn, worked with her, or (sometimes just as critically) were intimates of people within her inner circle. Although at the time she was not my primary subject, Hepburn was a frequent topic of conversation in these interviews. Many of these people have since passed on, and I am grateful I was able to preserve what stories and insights I did. These include the actor Max Showalter, Hepburn's great friend from Connecticut, whom I first met in 1985; Emily Torchia, the firebrand MGM publicist, who helped shape the

Tracy-Hepburn myth and who was very candid when I spoke to her in 1994; Michael Pearman, one of the true originals, a good friend of Cukor's and a traveling companion of Cole Porter's, who often observed Hepburn in private settings; Miles White, the Tony-winning costume designer, whose offhand remark to me about "Susan Allen and Kate Hepburn running away from Hollywood to Europe together" allowed me to finally solve the mystery of Suzanne Steell; Robert Shaw, the television writer (*Peyton Place, Robert Montgomery Presents*), who often stayed with Hepburn while in New York; Elliott Morgan, the head of research at MGM, who had a privileged view of Hepburn's career; Jean Howard, Hollywood hostess par excellence and a costar of *Break of Hearts*; and the publicist Alan Cahan, who shared insights on how the Tracy-Hepburn legend evolved.

It was through various previous contacts that I finally connected with the legendary Scotty. Anyone who has written about Hollywood's underground history from the 1940s to the 1970s has come across Scotty's name. He's been variously called "Hollywood's male madam" to the "ace procurer for the stars." For someone whose work might be considered a bit indelicate, Scotty continues to be held in high esteem, recalled with real affection by many in Hollywood. A forthright, unpretentious man, Scotty had proven elusive in my previous research, but this time a mutual acquaintance made the introductions. Many well-respected figures in Hollywood and New York vouched for Scotty's reliability as a source (see my notes, beginning on page 574).

Material from my 1990 article, "Hepburn: The Hartford Years," for the now-defunct *Hartford Monthly,* also proved illuminating once I'd dug it out of my files. At the time, I interviewed Jean Poindexter Colby, with whom Hepburn attended the Oxford School; Tom Calhoun, who, as a friend of Hepburn's sister Marion, was a guest at Fenwick during the Howard Hughes period; Mundy Hepburn, the son of her brother Dick; and Ellsworth Grant, her brother-in-law and husband of Marion. I also had access to the original script for the 1988 documentary *They Called Me Kathy*, as well as portions of Marion Hepburn's diary not included in Katharine Houghton's biography of her mother.

I spoke with Ellsworth Grant again early on in the course of this book. He was reluctant to embrace yet another Hepburn biography but came around when I explained the different approach I was taking. He proved charming and candid. Meeting the members of the Hepburn clan offered some memorable moments. When Hepburn's sister Peg Perry left me a voice mail to come see her, she sounded spookily like my subject. Over heavily sugared coffee at her farmhouse in Connecticut, Peg was forthright. Chain smoking, she leveled a cigarette at me and said, "It's all been said before. Say something different this time." Peg died in early 2006.

Dr. Robert Hepburn, Katharine's younger brother, proved to be a kind, thoughtful man who gave considerable time and thought to my questions. After three hours had passed, he came out with what has become a standard Hepburn line: "Use the bathroom. I know you have to. My father was a urologist, and you've been sitting there a long time." No question was off-limits to Bob. Despite his ninety-two years, his probing intelligence and vivid memory proved invaluable to this project. He also shared insights from the unpublished memoir of his mother, Katharine Houghton Hepburn.

I am also grateful to Kuy Hepburn, another son of Katharine's brother Dick, whose interview offered elucidating comments about his father and aunt.

Special thanks to Charles Higham, the only Hepburn biographer to actually interview so many of the key, now-departed players in her life: Jed Harris, Pandro Berman, Laura Harding, Jane Loring, and many others. Higham generously shared his own impressions of these people and, critically, those parts of the interviews he felt inappropriate to use in 1975.

Selden West, who was working on a biography of Spencer Tracy for many years, graciously offered her own opinions on the Tracy-Hepburn legend, insights from interviews she conducted, and important information from Tracy's daily logbooks.

My thanks also for the observations and anecdotes shared by these friends, colleagues, and associates of Hepburn's: James Bacon (longtime Hollywood reporter for the Associated Press, interviewed in 1995), A. Scott Berg, Zoe Caldwell (whose husband, Robert Whitehead, produced *A Matter of Gravity* and *West Side Waltz*), June Dally-Watkins (who briefly dated Spencer Tracy in the 1950s), John Dayton (producer of Hepburn's last four films and a mine of fascinating observation), John Gavin (who acted with Hepburn in *The Madwoman of Chaillot*), Lee Gopadze and Tina Gopadze Smith (children of Dorothy Gopadze, Spencer Tracy's longtime assistant), Ruth Hussey (costar of *The Philadelphia Story,* still lively at age ninety-five), Arthur Laurents (interviewed in 1999, he was frank and outspoken about Hepburn's private life as well as her performance in *Summertime,* the film adaptation of his play *The Time of the Cuckoo*), Jayne Meadows (witty and full of anecdotes, she had acted with Hepburn in *Undercurrent*), Dina Merrill (who acted with Hepburn in *Desk Set* and moved in overlapping social circles), the publicist Dale Olson, the writer Lawrence Quirk (who first met Hepburn in 1947 and whose uncle and mentor was James Quirk, the legendary editor of *Photoplay*),

Rex Reed, Jill Robinson (daughter of Dore Schary, who as a girl was rowed around in a canoe by Hepburn), Marian Seldes (as the widow of Garson Kanin, she was able to set the record straight about the Kanin-Hepburn feud), Gloria Stuart, the late Gwen Verdon, Gore Vidal, and Robert Wagner.

Surprisingly, some of the more obvious sources have never been thoroughly utilized until now. For all that's been written about her brother Tom's suicide, the medical examiner's report, with its telling details, has never been cited. George Cukor's vast correspondence (some of which is still held privately and is utilized here for the first time) as well as his unfinished memoir yielded much more than has been previously reported. Much has been made of the supposed scandalous contents of the FBI files of both Hepburn and Tracy, but until now, apparently no one has consulted them under the Freedom of Information Act. Meanwhile, far juicier source material has been overlooked: the 1950s scandal magazines, and what they had to say about Hepburn. And inevitably I made my way out to Indiana University to read the letters between Hepburn and director John Ford to determine the truth, once and for all, of their reported love affair.

The West Hartford Police Department provided a copy of the full report and investigation of the bizarre 1971 episode in which Hepburn was attacked by a former employee. I am most grateful for the sharp memories of the officer investigating the case, retired police detective Robert Moylan.

In most projects of this sort, there are sources who consent to talk only on the condition of anonymity. Despite so many opening up publicly here for the first time, some sources remained leery, agreeing to speak only if I never revealed their names. Among these were intimates from long ago as well as some surprisingly up-close players of Hepburn's later years. Their assistance was invaluable. Through them, I obtained copies of Kate's autobiographical screenplay, "Me and Phyllis," and Dick Hepburn's unproduced play about his sister, "Sea-Air"—neither of which has ever been made available to the public before. The stories these people told fundamentally shaped this narrative. All of these sources are extremely reliable in their information.

In some cases, persons being interviewed on the record would ask that certain other details not be attributed to them; in 90 percent of these cases, the topic being excepted was sexuality. Therefore, while a source may be identified by name at one point in this book, later on, as part of a different discussion, that same source may be anonymous.

New technology also allowed my research to be more comprehensive than any historian might have dreamed of in the past. Online searching is now available by any word or phrase for every issue of the *New York Times,* the *Los Angeles Times,* the *Washington Post,* the *Chicago Tribune,* and many other newspapers, from the nineteenth century to the present day. That means I have been able to pinpoint Hepburn's movements, associations, and activities—not to mention every time she ever appeared in any gossip column—with a thoroughness never before achieved.

The Katharine Hepburn Web site (www.katethegreat.net) is a truly re- markable resource, a classy, comprehensive labor of love. Here I was able to find original trailers of several Hepburn films, a couple of her radio broad- casts, clips from documentaries and Oscar telecasts, and a complete tran- script of the important 1973 interview with Dick Cavett. Fan postings allowed me to understand the devotion so many continue to have for Hep- burn. In particular, Judy Samelson and Kerrie Tickner provided articles, in- sights, and facts only true Hepburn fans would have at their fingertips.

The fundamental structure of this book is held together by the numerous collections of private papers and personal correspondence I consulted. All were vital in re-creating Hepburn's life and times. These included: The Zoe Akins Collection, Huntington Library, San Marino, California. The Dorothy Arzner Collection, the University of California at Los Angeles. The Philip Barry Papers, Georgetown University, Washington, D.C. The Michael Benthall Collection, Theatre Museum, London. The Frederick Brisson Collection, Billy Rose Theater Collection, the New York Public Library for the Performing Arts (hereafter abbreviated as NYPL). The Bryn Mawr Archives at the Mariam Cof- fin Canaday Library, Bryn Mawr College. The Billie Burke Collection, Boston University. The Witter Bynner Collection, University of New Mexico, Albu- querque, and Houghton Library, Harvard College Library, Cambridge.

The Papers of Maie Casey, the National Library of Australia. The Katharine Cornell Collections, NYPL. The Cheryl Crawford Collection, NYPL. The George Cukor Collection, the Academy of Motion Picture Arts and Sciences (hereafter abbreviated as AMPAS). The George Cukor Collec- tion, University of Southern California. (In addition, I was able to read many letters to Cukor still held privately, courtesy of Tucker Fleming and Charles Williamson.) The Senator Bronson Cutting Collection, Manuscripts Divi- sion, Library of Congress.

The Papers of Russell Wheeler Davenport, Manuscripts Division, Library of Congress. The Mercedes de Acosta Collection, Rosenbach Museum and Li- brary, Philadelphia. The David Eichler Papers, Lilly Library, Indiana Univer- sity, Bloomington, Indiana. The Elizabeth Gurley Flynn Papers, Immigration History Research Center, University of Minnesota, and the Elizabeth Gurley

Flynn Collection, Tamiment Library. Robert F. Wagner Labor Archives, New York University. The John Ford Collection, Lilly Library, Indiana University. The John Gielgud Collection, NYPL. The Cary Grant Collection, AMPAS.

The Gladys Hall Collection, AMPAS. The Anthony Harvey Papers, Lilly Library, Indiana University. The Hedgerow Theatre Collection, Boston University. The Papers of Sir Robert Helpmann, the National Library of Australia, Canberra. The Hedda Hopper Collection, AMPAS. The John Huston Collection, AMPAS. The Inez Haynes Irwin Papers, Schlesinger Library, Radcliffe Institute for Advanced Study, Cambridge. The Papers of Patricia Jarrett, the National Library of Australia. The Journals of Florence Ledyard Cross Kitchelt, Smith College, Northampton, Massachusetts. The Robert W. Kenny and Robert S. Morris Papers, Wisconsin Historical Society Archives. The Lawrence Langner Collection, NYPL. The Beatrice Lillie Collection, NYPL.

The Archibald MacLeish Papers, Manuscript Division, Library of Congress. The F. O. Matthiessen Collection, Houghton Library, Harvard College Library, as well as the Beinecke Library, Yale University. The Mielziner Family Papers, NYPL. The Archives of the Motion Picture Producers Association, AMPAS. The Palache Family Papers Collection, Schlesinger Library, Radcliffe Institute. The Production Code Administration files, AMPAS. The H. Phelps Putnam Collection, Beinecke Library, Yale University. RKO Studio Correspondence, NYPL.

The Irene Mayer Selznick Collection, Boston University. The Robert E. Sherwood Papers, Houghton Library. The Sidney Skolsky Collection, AMPAS. The Smith Family Papers, American Philosophical Society, Philadelphia. The James Thrall Soby Papers, Getty Research Institute, Los Angeles. The George Stevens Collection, AMPAS. The Noel Sullivan Papers, Bancroft Library, University of California, Berkeley. The Theater Guild Collection, Beinecke Library, Yale University. The Hal Wallis Collection, AMPAS. The Tennessee Williams Collection, University of Delaware Library. Also: various collections at the British Film Institute, London; the Museum of Modern Art, Film Studies Center, New York; and the University of Southern California, Los Angeles.

A few archivists and librarians provided assistance that singles them out for special acknowledgment: Barbara Hall and Robert Cushman at the Margaret Herrick Library of the Academy of Motion Picture Arts and Sciences; Charles Silver of the Museum of Modern Art Film Studies Center (who screened for me a very rare print of *A Connecticut Yankee in King Arthur's Court*); Debbie DeJonker-Berry, head librarian in Provincetown, Massachusetts, where I wrote much of this book, who arranged for many obscure microfilms to be sent out to the very tip of Cape Cod; J. C. Johnson of the Howard Gotlieb Archival Research Center, Boston University; Becky Cape of the Lilly Library at Indiana University; Lorett Treese at the Mariam Coffin Canaday Library, Bryn Mawr College; Charles Greifenstein and Earle Spamer of the American Philosophical Society; Ned Comstock of the Cinema-Television Library, University of Southern California; Nancy Finlay of the Connecticut Historical Society; Dee Anna Grimsrud of the Wisconsin Historical Society; Tim Richardson of the Chapel Hill Library; Flora Parrish, records supervisor at the Chapel Hill Police Department; Sherill Redmon of the Neilson Library, Smith College; Helene Sepulveda, recorder of deeds, Montgomery County, Pennsylvania; Deborah Edel of the Lesbian Herstory Archives in New York; Miles Krueger of the Institute of the American Musical in Los Angeles; Greg Giuliano of the Rosenbach Museum and Library in Philadelphia; Jane Edgecomb and the staff of the Welles-Ogunquit Historical Society; Rob Kyff of the Oxford School archive; Nancy Miller and J. M. Duffin of the University Archives and Record Center at the University of Pennsylvania; Donna Lewis of the West Hartford Police Department; and Ed Minshall of the Friends of Autocar Society (who helped me in locating the family of Jack Clarke).

To colleagues who offered insights, encouraged me to consider new ideas, challenged me on key points, or provided contacts or information, I offer deep gratitude: Dr. Carl Bazil of Columbia University Medical Center, who helped me understand Hepburn's various medical conditions; David Bergman; Sonia Berman, who shared her research into the Leland Hayward papers, currently closed to historians; Gary Carey; Lillian Faderman; Richard Hack, who shared material concerning Hepburn from the Howard Hughes papers at the courthouse archives in Austin, Texas; Val Holley; Helen Lefkowitz Horowitz, whose insight into the world of women's colleges in the 1920s, and particularly Bryn Mawr, was enlightening; Jack Kimberling; William Kizer; Emanuel Levy; Kim Marra; Jocelyn McClurg; Patrick McGilligan; James Robert Parish; Robert Schanke; Richard Schneider; Henry Scott; Ed Sikov; Anthony Slide; Kevin Thomas; David Thomson; and Stuart Timmons.

A special thank you to my assistants, Matthew Capaldo, Dan Curd, Joan Garvan in Australia, Shirl Roccapriore, and especially Dan Callahan, whose knowledge of Hepburn's life and work was encyclopedic. As ever, my agent, Malaga Baldi, proved resourceful and supportive, always a steady hand to guide the ship.

George Hodgman comes as close as I've ever found to the description of a writer's dream editor. From the beginning, he believed in this project, possessing an uncanny ability to give shape and substance to my ideas. Without his support and vision, this book would not exist. Likewise, I am deeply grateful for the sharp, intuitive guidance of my British editor, Walter Donohue. And I'd be remiss not to acknowledge the stunning artistic contributions of the book's jacket designer, Lisa Fyfe.

Finally, for everything else, my gratitude and love to my partner, Dr. Timothy Huber.

WILLIAM J. MANN is the author of *Edge of Midnight: The Life of John Schlesinger*; *Behind the Screen: How Gays and Lesbians Shaped Hollywood*; and *Wisecracker: The Life and Times of William Haines*. He divides his time between Provincetown, Massachusetts, and Palm Springs, California.